CONTEMPORARY MUSICIANS

*Explore your options!
Gale databases offered in
a variety of formats*

DISKETTE/MAGNETIC TAPE

Many Gale databases are available on diskette or magnetic tape, allowing systemwide access to your most-used information sources through existing computer systems. Data can be delivered on a variety of mediums (DOS formatted diskette, 9-track tape, 8mm data tape) and in industry-standard formats (comma-delimited, tagged, fixed-field). Retrieval software is also available with many of Gale's databases that allows you to search, display, print and download the data

ONLINE

For your convenience, many Gale databases are available through popular online services, including DIALOG, NEXIS (Mead Data Central), Data-Star, Orbit, Questel, OCLC, I/Plus and HRIN.

CD-ROM

A variety of Gale titles is available on CD-ROM, offering maximum flexibility and powerful search software.

The information in this Gale publication is also available in some or all of the formats described here. Your Customer Service Representative will be happy to fill you in.

For information, call

GALE

Gale Research Inc.
1-800-877-GALE

ISSN 1044-2197

CONTEMPORARY MUSICIANS

PROFILES OF THE PEOPLE IN MUSIC

SUZANNE M. BOURGOIN,
Editor

VOLUME 12
Includes Cumulative Indexes

080868

STAFF

Suzanne M. Bourgoin, *Editor*

Geri J. Speace, *Associate Editor*

Marilyn Allen, *Editorial Associate*

Robin Armstrong, Susan Windisch Brown, Marjorie Burgess, John Cohassey, John Cortez, Ed Decker, Robert Dupuis, Mary Scott Dye, Ben Edmonds, Stewart Francke, Alan Glenn, Simon Glickman, Joan Goldsworthy, Joyce Harrison, Gina Hausknecht, Kevin Hillstrom, Carol Hopkins, Anne Janette Johnson, Charlie Katagiri, Mary P. LaBlanc, Michael L. LaBlanc, Ondine E. Le Blanc, James M. Manheim, Emily McMurray, Sarah Messer, Diane Moroff, John Morrow, Rob Nagel, Debra Power, Susan Reicha, Joseph M. Reiner, Joanna Rubiner, Julia M. Rubiner, Mary K. Ruby, Pamela Shelton, Sonya Shelton, Iva Sipal, Jeffrey Taylor, Mary Katherine Wainwright, Elizabeth Wenning, Megan Rubiner Zinn,
Contributing Editors

Peter M. Gareffa, *Senior Editor, Contemporary Biographies*

Margaret A. Chamberlain, *Permissions Supervisor (Pictures)*
Pamela A. Hayes, Arlene M. Johnson, Keith Reed, Barbara A. Wallace, *Permissions Associates*
Susan Brohman, *Permissions Assistant*

Mary Beth Trimper, *Production Director*
Shanna Philpott Heilveil, *Production Assistant*
Cynthia Baldwin, *Production Design Manager*
Barbara J. Yarrow, *Graphic Services Supervisor*

Cover illustration by John Kleber

While every effort has been made to ensure the reliability of the information presented in this publication, Gale Research Inc. does not guarantee the accuracy of the data contained herein. Gale accepts no payment for listing; and inclusion in the publication of any organization, agency, institution, publication, service, or individual does not imply endorsement of the editors or publisher. Errors brought to the attention of the publisher and verified to the satisfaction of the publisher will be corrected in future editions.

∞™ This book is printed on acid-free paper that meets the minimum requirements of American National Standard for Information Sciences—Permanence Paper for Printed Library Materials, ANSI Z39.48-1984.

♻ This book is printed on recycled paper that meets Environmental Protection Agency Standards.

This publication is a creative work fully protected by all applicable copyright laws, as well as by misappropriation, trade secret, unfair competition, and other applicable laws. The authors and editors of this work have added value to the underlying factual material herein through one or more of the following: unique and original selection, coordination, expression, arrangement, and classification of the information.

All rights to this publication will be vigorously defended.

Copyright © 1994 by Gale Research Inc.
835 Penobscot Bldg.
Detroit, MI 48226-4094

All rights reserved including the right of reproduction in whole or in part in any form.

Printed in the United States of America
Published simultaneously in the United Kingdom by
Gale Research International Limited (An affiliated company of Gale Research Inc.)

No part of this book may be reproduced in any form without permission in writing from the publisher, except by a reviewer who wishes to quote brief passages or entries in connection with a review written for inclusion in a magazine or newspaper.

ISBN 0-8103-8553-8
ISSN 1044-2197
10 9 8 7 6 5 4 3 2 1

I(T)P™

The trademark **ITP** is used under license.

Contents

Introduction ix

Cumulative Subject Index 289

Cumulative Musicians Index 307

Abba 1
Swedish pop/disco superstars

Tori Amos 5
Strong-voiced poetic chanteuse

Gene Autry 8
Widely respected "Singing Cowboy"

Cecilia Bartoli 12
Breathtaking mezzo-soprano

Black Uhuru 16
Reggae legends

Bobby "Blue" Bland 20
Smooth and sexy blues vocalist

Anthony Braxton 23
Prolific "free jazz" virtuoso

Brooks & Dunn 27
Hot country hitmakers

Cheap Trick 30
International 1970s arena rock act

The Cocteau Twins 33
Dark, ethereal dance pop trio

Elvis Costello 37
Thoughtful new wave pioneer

Cracker 43
Alternative rock's former "Campers"

Steve Cropper 46
Funky guitar great of Booker T. and the MG's

Crowded House 50
Melodic rockers spawned from Split Enz

The Dave Clark Five 54
Clean-cut 1960s Brit-pop megagroup

Al Di Meola 58
Acclaimed jazz guitarist

Céline Dion 61
Octave-spanning, bilingual belter

Champion Jack Dupree 64
Southern blues master

Earth, Wind and Fire 66
Pop/soul supergroup

Kenneth "Babyface" Edmonds 69
Architect of early 1990s black pop

The Fall 73
British working-class post-punkers

Eddie Fisher 77
1950s teen idol pop singer

Five Blind Boys of Alabama 80
Long-standing gospel harmonizers

Stan Getz 83
Sax sensation from bossa nova to ballads

Lee Greenwood 86
Patriotic country vocalist

Charlie Haden 89
Improvisational jazz bassist

Thomas Hampson 92
Admired, attractive opera singer

Juliana Hatfield 95
Bird-voiced solo star and guest Lemonhead

Woody Herman 99
Big band "Herder" and horn blower

Natalie Hinderas 102
Race barrier-breaking classical pianist

Earl "Fatha" Hines 106
Swinging jazz pianist and bandleader

Burl Ives 110
"Just folks" entertainer

James 113
Flamboyant dance pop darlings

Billy Joel 117
Pop/rock's mega-successful "Piano Man"

L7 123
Gender gap-closing women of hard rock

Chris LeDoux 127
American cowboy songster

The Lemonheads 130
Pop trio fronted by "alternahunk"

The Louvin Brothers 134
Rootsy gospel/country duo

Kirsty MacColl 138
Thinking woman's pop singer

Sarah McLachlan 142
Relationship-exploring music maker

John McLaughlin 145
Fusion guitar innovator

Jim and Jesse McReynolds 149
Timeless bluegrass institution

Meat Loaf 153
Hulking, operatic rocker

Melanie 156
Illuminated 1970s folk sensation

Moby Grape 159
Conceptual, psychedelic 1960s rockers

Yves Montand 163
French screen star and singer

Bill Morrissey 166
Literary-influenced folk performer

Nana Mouskouri 170
Continent-hopping Greek songstress

Alison Moyet 173
Soulful synth-pop singer

Red Norvo 176
Jazz music's champion of the vibraphone

NRBQ 180
Eclectic, enduring cult act

Laura Nyro 184
Seminal folk and pop songwriter

Alan Parsons 188
Creative producer and "Project" founder

Pearl Jam 192
Runaway grunge success story

Sam Phillips 197
Unconventional, articulate pop stylist

Chris Rea 201
"The British Bruce Springsteen"

Joshua Redman 203
Jazz sax skyrocketer

Restless Heart 206
Soft country-rock crossovers

Jonathan Richman 209
Whimsical, charismatic tunesmith

Max Roach 213
Godfather of modern jazz drumming

Otis Rush 217
Fiery bluesman

Boz Scaggs 220
Versatile singer-songwriter

The Scorpions 223
Teutonic monsters of rock

Sepultura 228
Grinding death metal thrashers

Terrance Simien 231
Colorful zydeco front man

Donna Summer 234
Disco Queen turned pop/country diva

Sweethearts of the Rodeo 237
Singing sisters of country

Tangerine Dream 240
Avant-garde keyboard collaborators

Aaron Tippin 244
Proud, twangy country songsmith

Tony! Toni! Toné! 247
Soulful hip-hoppers and balladeers

Sophie Tucker 250
Vaudeville's "Red Hot Mama"

U2 253
Ireland's sociopolitical rock bigwigs

Dave Van Ronk 258
Finger pickin' good folk singer

Bobby Vinton 261
Love song crooner and "Polish Prince"

Violent Femmes 263
Catchy, minimalist "teen angst" alt-rockers

Tom Waits 267
Scruffy, poetic, gravel-voiced hipster

Jimmy Webb 270
Pop standards penner and performer

Kurt Weill 274
Multifaceted composer

Kelly Willis 278
Photogenic country crowd-pleaser

Cassandra Wilson 281
Sultry style-fusing vocalist

The Winans 284
"All in the family" gospel group

Introduction

Fills the Information Gap on Today's Musicians

Contemporary Musicians profiles the colorful personalities in the music industry who create or influence the music we hear today. Prior to *Contemporary Musicians,* no quality reference series provided comprehensive information on such a wide range of artists despite keen and ongoing public interest. To find biographical and critical coverage, an information seeker had little choice but to wade through the offerings of the popular press, scan television "infotainment" programs, and search for the occasional published biography or exposé. *Contemporary Musicians* is designed to serve that information seeker, providing in one ongoing source in-depth coverage of the important names on the modern music scene in a format that is both informative and entertaining. Students, researchers, and casual browsers alike can use *Contemporary Musicians* to meet their needs for personal information about music figures; find a selected discography of a musician's recordings; and uncover an insightful essay offering biographical and critical information.

Provides Broad Coverage

Single-volume biographical sources on musicians are limited in scope, often focusing on a handful of performers from a specific musical genre or era. In contrast, *Contemporary Musicians* offers researchers and music devotees a comprehensive, informative, and entertaining alternative. *Contemporary Musicians* is published twice yearly, with each volume providing information on more than 80 musical artists and record-industry luminaries from all the genres that form the broad spectrum of contemporary music—pop, rock, jazz, blues, country, New Age, folk, rhythm and blues, gospel, bluegrass, rap, and reggae, to name a few—as well as selected classical artists who have achieved "crossover" success with the general public. *Contemporary Musicians* will also occasionally include profiles of influential nonperforming members of the music community, including producers, promoters, and record company executives. Additionally, beginning with *Contemporary Musicians 11,* each volume features new profiles of a selection of previous *Contemporary Musicians* listees who remain of interest to today's readers and who have been active enough to require completely revised entries.

Includes Popular Features

In *Contemporary Musicians* you'll find popular features that users value:

- **Easy-to-locate data sections:** Vital personal statistics, chronological career summaries, listings of major awards, and mailing addresses, when available, are prominently displayed in a clearly marked box on the second page of each entry.

- **Biographical/critical essays:** Colorful and informative essays trace each subject's personal and professional life, offer representative examples of critical response to the artist's work, and provide entertaining personal sidelights.

- **Selected discographies:** Each entry provides a comprehensive listing of the artist's major recorded works.

- **Photographs:** Most entries include portraits of the subject profiled.

- **Sources for additional information:** This invaluable feature directs the user to selected books, magazines, and newspapers where more information can be obtained.

Helpful Indexes Make It Easy to Find the Information You Need

Each volume of *Contemporary Musicians* features a cumulative Musicians Index, listing names of individual performers and musical groups, and a cumulative Subject Index, which provides the user with a breakdown by primary musical instruments played and by musical genre.

Available in Electronic Formats

Diskette/Magnetic Tape. *Contemporary Musicians* is available for licensing on magnetic tape or diskette in a fielded format. Either the complete database or a custom selection of entries may be ordered. The database is available for internal data processing and nonpublishing purposes only. For more information, call (800) 877-GALE.

Online. *Contemporary Musicians* is available online through Mead Data Central's NEXIS Service in the NEXIS, PEOPLE and SPORTS Libraries in the GALBIO file.

We Welcome Your Suggestions

The editors welcome your comments and suggestions for enhancing and improving *Contemporary Musicians*. If you would like to suggest subjects for inclusion, please submit these names to the editors. Mail comments or suggestions to:

The Editor
Contemporary Musicians
Gale Research Inc.
835 Penobscot Bldg.
Detroit, MI 48226-4094
Phone: (800) 347-4253
Fax: (313) 961-6599

CONTEMPORARY MUSICIANS

Abba

Pop group

Reviled by rock purists but admired by observers as diverse as Nelson Mandela and the late Kurt Cobain, Abba was a 1970s Swedish pop group that achieved unprecedented worldwide success. The group specialized in light love songs with instantly memorable musical "hooks" and cultivated a cheery pop style that rarely permitted the exploration of serious themes. Some of Abba's music was aimed at dancers, and when popular taste shifted toward the pulsing dance music called disco at the end of the decade, it was easy for the group to exploit the trend. To an observer around 1980, Abba's recordings might have seemed dubious candidates for any listing of 1970s music likely to endure. The group broke up in 1983.

Yet by the early 1990s a full-scale Abba revival was underway. *Village Voice* critic Barry Walters pointed out that "[like] the Doors, ABBA has nearly as many greatest hits packages as it has regular albums"; each repackaging of the group's output attracted new fans. Abba's success proved to be more than temporary,

Archive Photos/Fotos International

> **For the Record...**
>
> Members include **Benny Andersson** (born December 16, 1946, in Stockholm, Sweden); **Agnetha Fältskog** (born April 5, 1950, in Jankoping, Sweden); **Anni-Frid Lyngstad** (born November 15, 1945, in Narvik, Norway); **Björn Ulvaeus** (born April 15, 1945, in Gothenburg, Sweden). Ulvaeus and Fältskog married, 1972-78; had three children. Andersson and Lyngstad married, 1978 (divorced).
>
> Group formed in Stockholm, 1972; released internationally successful series of pop-rock recordings, 1974-83; recorded multiplatinum LP *Arrival,* 1976; group dissolved, 1983; Andersson and Ulvaeus co-authored musical *Chess,* 1986; revival of public interest in group, including release of retrospective reissues and cover recordings by other artists, early 1990s.
>
> **Awards:** Winner, Eurovision song contest, 1974; named Sweden's fastest-growing corporation by Swedish publication *Business World,* 1978.
>
> **Addresses:** *Record company*—Polygram, 825 8th Ave., New York, NY 10019.

and, in retrospect, the group's multiple talents came more clearly into view. Their song lyrics, always economical and ideally suited to the requirements of the three-minute radio single, ascended to the level of incisive little dramas about romance. Their tunes, easily memorable after one hearing, turned out to contain subtleties that made them memorable after twenty years. And, in addition to participating in the disco trend, Abba helped make it possible through its pioneering use of dense, multitrack arrangements and sophisticated musical electronics.

Members Successful in Sweden

The group's name (which was sometimes spelled with all capital letters) was an acronym formed from the initial letters of the first names of each of its members. Agnetha Fältskog, Benny Andersson, Björn Ulvaeus, and Anni-Frid ("Frida") Lyngstad were all active in the Swedish pop music business while they were still teenagers. In the 1960s Fältskog and Lyngstad gained some renown as solo vocalists, while Andersson and Ulvaeus fronted a succession of bands with widely varying musical styles, and also worked steadily as session musicians. By the time Abba took shape as a group in 1972, all four of its members were veterans of the Swedish pop music scene.

Abba's first hit came with the singsong "Ring Ring" in 1973, but the group's success was cemented the following year when the song "Waterloo" was named the winner of the Eurovision Song Contest, an annual program televised in 32 countries and watched by hundreds of millions of people. "Waterloo" was released as a single and rocketed to top chart levels in many countries, reaching number six in the United States. Versions in several different languages were released, but Andersson and Ulvaeus wrote "Waterloo" and all of the group's other songs in English. From the start, the group aimed toward the global success they eventually achieved.

Although some critics have made light of the group's use of English ("they had a way of making English sound like Esperanto," maintained *Time*'s Richard Lacayo), few native-born American songwriters would have been capable of controlling and developing the central device of the "Waterloo" lyric: Napoleon's final defeat becomes a metaphor for a woman's total surrender to romantic attraction.

Throughout the 1970s, Abba was a consistent generator of worldwide chart successes, and while Andersson and Ulvaeus aimed more at entertainment than at rock "authenticity" in their writing, their compositions were always original and sharp, drawing on a large variety of pop music traditions. "Money, Money, Money" had the dark cynicism of German composer Kurt Weill's satiric cabaret songs. "The Name of the Game" expertly manipulated major and minor harmonies to depict a romance in its breathless opening stages. And "Dancing Queen," though it treated a subject no more profound than a 17-year-old girl on a dance floor, vividly captured the moment when a dancer becomes the center of attention to everyone around her. "Dancing Queen" brought Abba its only American Number One early in 1977.

Pioneered Lush Multitrack Sound

"Dancing Queen" was also the first of a group of Abba songs that took dancing and nightclubs for their themes, a trend that intensified with the worldwide popularity of disco in the late 1970s. Abba had major hits with pulsing seduction anthems like "Voulez-vous" and "Gimme! Gimme! Gimme! (A Man After Midnight)," both in 1979. But the synthesized-sound wizardry associated with disco had always been one of the group's hallmarks, with even early hits like "SOS" (1975) featuring a dense rhythm track and a parade of unexpected sonic effects. "Abba eclipsed the bland top 40 of their day by insisting on a big beat," noted Walters. "In doing so, they virtually invented Eurodisco."

Abba's multitrack recording equipment was state-of-the-art in its time, and producer Stig Anderson, like the Beatles' producer George Martin, was sometimes referred to as a fifth member of the group. An Abba tour was a major undertaking, for it was difficult to recreate the band's sound in live performance. Abba's lush production values, blending, strings, keyboards, and synthesized sounds with the electronically modified voices of the group's two female vocalists have been likened to those of pioneering American pop producer Phil Spector and his "wall of sound."

Abba entered the 1980s with another string of hits, including "The Winner Takes It All" and "Super Trouper." But the latter song, which deals with the rigors of touring, might have taken root in tensions that divided the group at the time: the six-year marriage of Ulvaeus and Fältskog had dissolved in 1978, and a long relationship between Andersson and Lyngstad also broke up. And, most importantly, Andersson's and Ulvaeus's musical interests seemed to shift away from the short, hook-oriented single.

Several of Abba's pieces in the early 1980s were complicated structures that seemed as if they could come to life as part of a live stage musical. The title track of the 1981 LP *The Visitors* was a long, free-form depiction of a woman's mental breakdown; "The Day Before You Came" (1983), one of the group's last single releases, completely lacked a chorus melody and more closely resembled a dramatic speech set to music than a simple piece of dance pop. Andersson and Ulvaeus pursued this dramatic bent after Abba's breakup in 1983, collaborating with *Jesus Christ Superstar* lyricist Tim Rice on the successful stage musical *Chess*, which premiered in 1986 and included the hit single "One Night in Bangkok."

Revival

Village Voice critic Robert Christgau expressed a common attitude in the rock-music community when he evaluated Abba this way in 1979: "We have met the enemy and they are them." Yet the group's public covered the globe. Australia and Germany were particularly devoted, while the United States was one of the few places where Abba's success was sporadic rather than continuous. Bootlegged Abba tapes proliferated in Southeast Asia; even its legal sales alone allowed the group to surpass Volvo as Sweden's most profitable producer of goods for export. In 1982 the *Christian Science Monitor* estimated the total income from Abba's large entertainment-industrial empire at over $200,000,000.

Abba's deep reservoir of public support made them a natural for revival when popular taste shifted back to sonically inventive dance pop in the early 1990s. A greatest hits package, *Gold,* stayed at Number One on many of *Billboard*'s European charts for months on end, and in late 1993 *Time* reported that the Abba revival was "surfacing fast in America" as well. This revival was spearheaded partly by urban homosexuals, whose affection for Abba's music Walters ventured to explain this way: "ABBA was *so* mainstream, you had to be slightly on the outside to actually take them to heart."

Two new releases seemed to point to the depth of Abba's influence. The British technopop duo Erasure released a four-song CD of Abba covers that itself topped the charts in the United Kingdom, while a disc of Abba instrumentals by the Munich Philharmonic Orchestra showed off Andersson and Ulvaeus as the skilled musical craftsmen they were. Although Andersson and Ulvaeus joined the Irish supergroup U2 on stage for a performance of "Dancing Queen" early in 1992, the individual members of the quartet rarely showed up in the public spotlight during the early 1990s. Their place in the worldwide history of popular music, however, was steadily growing in importance.

Selected discography

Waterloo, Atlantic, 1974.
Abba, Atlantic, 1975.
Arrival, Atlantic, 1976.
The Album, Atlantic, 1978.
Voulez-vous, Atlantic, 1979.
Super Trouper, Atlantic, 1980.
The Visitors, Atlantic, 1981.
The Singles—The First Ten Years, Atlantic, 1982.
I Love Abba, Atlantic, 1984.
Gold (greatest hits, contains all pieces discussed in text), Polygram, 1994.

Sources

Books

Gammond, Peter, *The Oxford Companion to Popular Music,* Oxford University Press, 1991.
Larkin, Colin, *The Guinness Encyclopedia of Popular Music,* New England Publishing Associates, 1992.
The New York Times Great Songs of Abba, Cherry Lane Books, 1980.
Pareles, Jon, and Patricia Romanowski, editors, *The Rolling Stone Encyclopedia of Rock & Roll,* Rolling Stone Press, 1983.

Stambler, Irwin, *Encyclopedia of Pop, Rock & Soul,* revised edition, St. Martin's Press, 1989.

Periodicals

Billboard, June 27, 1992.
Christian Science Monitor, September 1, 1982.
Circus, March 30, 1978.
Details, May 1994.
Rolling Stone, February 3, 1983.
Time, October 11, 1993.
Variety, October 7, 1981.
Village Voice, September 1, 1982.

—James M. Manheim

Tori Amos

Singer, songwriter, pianist

Photograph by Loren Haynes, courtesy of Atlantic Records

After spending years in classical piano training, then experimenting with the Los Angeles rock scene, Tori Amos attracted a popular music audience with her pure talent and honest expression of emotion. Though Amos's debut album, *Little Earthquakes,* received only a smattering of college radio airplay, press coverage, and video exposure—MTV could never quite decide whether she belonged on Alternative Nation or VH1—it quietly insinuated itself into 600,000 American homes and earned a gold record. Her sophomore effort, *Under the Pink,* repeated this trajectory in the spring of 1994, vaulting into the Top Ten and going gold.

Amos was born Myra Ellen Amos on August 22, 1963, in Newton, North Carolina, the youngest of the three children of the Reverend Edison Amos and his wife, Mary Ellen. Amos grew up in Baltimore, Maryland, where her father had transplanted his Methodist ministry from its orginial base in Washington, D.C. Her older brother and sister were taking piano lessons, but Amos didn't seem to need them. From the time she could reach the keys, she could play. When she was two, she could reproduce pieces of music she'd only heard once, and by age three she was composing her own songs.

At five she became the youngest student ever admitted to Baltimore's prestigious Peabody Conservatory, where for the next six years she did her best to be the dutiful child prodigy. Amos and the conservatory had a mutual parting of the ways when she was 11. "They know nothing about any other world than their own," she told an interviewer years later. "How can you teach musicians to be all they can be when all they're getting is guys that have been eaten by the worms? Hey, Bartok is amazing stuff; learning that has given me a foundation. But so did Jimmy Page. So did John Lennon. So did Joni Mitchell. So did Patti Smith. To really be a musician is to keep expanding."

Tried Los Angeles Rock Scene

With her father's encouragement, Amos began playing clubs in the Georgetwon section of Washington, D.C. It must have been an odd sight, the 13-year-old girl and the Methodist minister showing up at mostly gay bars. But the audiences were tolerant, and as long as she played enough of what they wanted to hear, they were receptive to occasionally being serenaded by her personal song experiments as well.

By the time Amos was 17 she'd amassed a stock of homemade demo tapes that her father would send to record companies, producers, and anybody else who might be able to help his daughter. Producer Narada

For the Record...

Born Myra Ellen Amos, August 22, 1963, in Newton, North Carolina; daughter of Edison (a Methodist minister) and Mary Ellen Amos. Education: Studied classical piano at the Peabody Conservatory in Baltimore, 1968-74.

Played clubs in and around Baltimore and Washington, DC; signed by Atlantic Records; formed hard rock band Y Kant Tori Read and released self-titled album, 1988; embarked on solo career; moved to London, early 1990s; released debut solo album, *Little Earthquakes,* Atlantic, 1992.

Awards: "Silent All These Years" nominated for four 1992 MTV Music Video awards; won Best New International Artist and Best International Solo Artist at the 1993 BRIT awards; recipient of numerous reader poll awards from publications including *Rolling Stone, Q,* and *Keyboard;* gold records for *Little Earthquakes* and *Under the Pink.*

Addresses: *Record company*—Atlantic Records, 75 Rockefeller Plaza, New York, NY 10019.

Michael Walden responded favorably, and they actually cut some tracks together, but none were released. Eventually Atlantic Records responded to one of the tapes, and when A&R man Jason Flom flew to Baltimore to audition her in person, the label was convinced: Amos was signed to Atlantic.

Then, in a move *Creem* magazine would later characterize as "a creative running away from home of sorts," Amos decided to reinvent herself as a Los Angeles "rock chick," as she deemed her persona of that time. She formed a band called Y Kant Tori Read that included future Cult and Guns n' Roses drummer Matt Sorum. When the group's self-titled album sank without a trace in 1988, Amos was crushed and withdrew from the music business and even her own songwriting. While visiting a friend some months later, however, Amos sat down at the piano and watched in amazement as unconscious music poured out of her for the next five hours. What she reconnected with that night was a sense of musical self and an inner voice that she could not deny.

Atlantic executive John Carter teamed her with producer Davitt Sigerson (The Bangles, David & David) in 1990, and the six tracks they cut in Los Angeles became the basis for her debut solo album. The emotional power of this new material was undeniable, the intensity of its confessional tone occasionally even discomforting. But Atlantic, not seeing a natural slot for this material in the fragmented American radio market, suggested that Amos move to England.

Gained European Cult Following

Amos's cross-Atlantic move was the turning point for her success. European audiences in the past had been willing to give eccentric American originals—from Joesphine Baker to Jimi Hendrix—a sympathetic ear. They were no less receptive to the offbeat charms of Amos. Her solo piano performances gained her a cult following that had spread so organically that when *Little Earthquakes* was released in January of 1992 it entered the British charts at Number 15.

The album's most celebrated song was "Me and a Gun," Amos's unvarnished account of the kidnapping and rape she had endured in Los Angeles a few years before. The writing of the song was not only a brave act, but an essential one. "Yes, it was painful to go through," she told Paul Zollo of *Musician*. "But it's about passing through to the other side. Sometimes writing songs is the only sense I can make out of anything.... This particular issue was something I had buried for six years. While writing it, I was caught up in the trauma and the euphoria. I was finally able to cry about it. When you're walking around tripping over your intestines you've got to do something, and writing songs is it for me."

Little Earthquakes was released in America in February of 1992 and slowly but steadily began to attract listeners. It was helped along by a breathtaking video for the single "Silent All These Years," though the power of her words and music was such that it created its own visuals. Brook Hersey, writing in *Glamour,* pinpointed the appeal of Amos's music: "People don't just discover Tori Amos, they become obsessed.... Listeners who've felt unimportant or powerless, who've gone through the emotional struggle for self-worth, seem to feel she is telling their long-overdue story." Amos had created her own audience, with *Little Earthquakes* selling a million and a half copies worldwide.

Another Gold Record

Under the Pink, Amos's follow-up album, released early in 1994, was also well received and enjoyed quick commercial success as well, with the first single, "God," selling over a million copies within months of hitting the shelves. Amos told Bill DeMain in *Performing Songwrit-*

er, "When I wrote ['God'] I was having a complete conversation with the concept of what God is.... To me, it's the root of all problems, that song right there. For me, [it is] one of the most important things I've ever done. You can call it my prayer if you want." Greg Sandow of *Entertainment Weekly* wrote, "Measured simply by her raw ability, Tori Amos is a phenomenal talent. Few pop artists ever offer such variety of such richness of musical detail." Marie Elsie St. Leger of *Rolling Stone* noted: "The album is focused, the lyrics quirky and personable, the melodies eccentric enough to entice and simple enough to be catchy. Those qualities—and her emotional fearlessness—make Tori Amos a musical find to treasure."

Amos cherishes her audience as much as they do her. "Some of the most interesting, growing conversations I've had," she told an interviewer, "and some of the most incredible wisdom I've gotten, has been backstage from the people who come to see me play. They all have a story to tell. And most of them are really working on consciousness; there is a commitment to the idea that the earth is going to the next stage of development. I just try to strip myself, peel myself like an onion. At different layers I discover stuff. I do it publicly, and if it helps to inspire somebody else, which inspires somebody else, which inspires somebody else ... then we're talking about a really exciting world here."

Selected discography

On Atlantic Records

(With Y Kant Tori Read) *Y Kant Tori Read,* 1988.
Little Earthquakes, 1992.
Under The Pink, 1994.

Sources

BAM, March 11, 1994.
Billboard, March 28, 1992; February 20, 1993; December 4, 1993.
Creem, March 1994.
Details, November 1992.
Entertainment Weekly, February 4, 1994.
Glamour, August 1992.
Keyboard, September 1992.
Metro Times (Detroit), October 28, 1992.
Musician, May 1992.
Performing Songwriter, March 1994.
Rolling Stone, April 2, 1992; April 30, 1992; February 24, 1994; June 30, 1994.
Spin, March 1994.

Additional information for this profile was obtained from Atlantic Records publicity material, 1992 and 1994, and from interviews with Amos, December 1993 and January 1994.

—Ben Edmonds

Gene Autry

Singer, guitarist, actor

The life of Gene Autry reads like a chapter from the American Dream. Rising from classically obscure roots on a Texas ranch, Autry became the personification of "The Singing Cowboy" as well as one of the most financially successful entertainers of this century. In addition to being the Number One country music star of the 1930s, Autry numbered among the Top Ten popular actors from 1940 to 1942, eclipsing film legends Tyrone Power, James Cagney, Judy Garland, and Bette Davis in box-office appeal.

During his career, Autry sold more than 50 million recordings—1949's "Rudolph the Red-Nosed Reindeer" sold 25 million copies alone. In addition, Autry authored over 250 songs, including "Tears on My Pillow," the 1939 classic that he co-wrote with Ray Whitley, "Back in the Saddle," "Buttons and Bows," and the Christmas classic "Here Comes Santa Claus." While remaining relatively unknown in larger cities, Autry gained phenomenal popularity in hundreds of small towns throughout the West and Southwest.

His good looks, singing ability, and charisma helped to popularize the Western elements in country music, lending romance and dignity to a musical genre that had once only identified with Appalachian "hillbillies." As a star, Autry took seriously his influence upon the legions of young boys who formed Gene Autry clubs and strove to live according to Gene's "Cowboy's Code" of the Western hero.

Autry was born on a ranch outside of Tioga, Texas, but moved to Ravia, Oklahoma, where he spent the greater part of his childhood. In addition to the hard work of ranch life, music played a significant role in his upbringing: Autry was taught to sing at age five so he could join the choir of his grandfather's Baptist church. His mother supplemented her son's vocal ability with guitar lessons.

The Right Man at the Right Time

Although Autry dreamed of becoming a baseball player, he discovered that his singing could earn him money. As a teenager, he toured for three months as a ballad singer with the Fields Brothers Marvelous Medicine Show. But at 15, the hardworking and pragmatic Autry put his musical talent aside to work at the railroad telegraph station in nearby Chelsea, Oklahoma, to help support his family.

Autry passed long hours working the graveyard shift at the small telegraph office by singing and playing guitar. He strummed familiar cowboy tunes and worked at emulating the sounds of his musical hero, Jimmie Rodgers. Known popularly as "The Singing Brake-

> **For the Record . . .**
>
> Born Orvon Gene Autry, September 29, 1907, in Tioga, TX; son of Delbert (a livestock dealer) and Elnora (Ozment) Autry; married Ina Mae Spivey, 1932 (died, 1980); married Jacqueline Ellam, 1981.
>
> Worked as a freight handler and roustabout, St. Louis & San Francisco Railroad, Chelsea, OK, 1922, and became telegrapher, 1925; sang on local radio show, beginning in 1928; signed with Victor Records, 1929; signed with American Record Corp. and performed on WLS Barndance, beginning in 1931; first film appearance, 1934; signed with Republic Studios, 1935; signed with Columbia Pictures, 1947; formed Gene Autry Productions, 1947; formed Flying A Productions (television production company), 1950; began as organizer and became co-owner, California Angels (formerly Los Angeles Angels) baseball team, 1960—; opened Gene Autry Heritage Museum, Los Angeles, CA, 1988. Film appearances include *In Ole Santa Fe*, 1934; *The Phantom Empire, Melody Trail, Sagebrush Troubadour,* and *Singing Vagabond,* all 1935; *Boots and Saddles,* 1937; *Shooting High, Back in the Saddle,* and *Melody Ranch,* all 1941; *The Last Roundup,* 1947; and *Last of the Pony Riders,* 1953. *Military service:* U.S. Air Force, 1942-45.
>
> **Awards:** Inducted into Country Music Hall of Fame, Country Music Association, 1969; inducted into the Broadcasting Hall of Fame, National Association of Broadcasters, 1977; D. W. Griffith Career Award, 1991; Lifetime Achievement Award, Songwriter's Hall Of Fame, 1991; inducted into Broadcast and Cable Hall of Fame, 1993; Horatio Alger Award, Horatio Alger Association of Distinguished Americans.
>
> **Addresses:** *Office*—Golden West Broadcasters, 5858 West Sunset Boulevard, Hollywood, CA 90028; P.O. Box 710, Los Angeles, CA 90078.

man," Rodgers's famous yodeling style was itself the result of long hours spent in a railroad telegraph office imitating the plaintive moan of a train whistle.

As it so often happens in music legend, chance sends an influential stranger in the direction of an unknown but talented young person. One night in 1926, a traveler stopped in Chelsea to send a wire. The man who walked into the St. Louis & Frisco telegraph office was the famous American folk humorist Will Rogers. Rogers sat down and listened to the telegraph operator, who, unaware of a customer, was immersed in a song. After Autry strummed his final chord, Rogers stepped forward and complimented the young man, encouraging him to go and try his luck in New York City.

Rogers's praise didn't convince Autry to jump aboard the first train headed East. Leaving a secure job during hard economic times would be foolish. But encouragement from a man of Rogers's stature made Autry seriously consider a musical career. About a year after Rogers paid his visit, Autry used a free rail pass to board a train for New York.

In the city, Autry was fortunate to link up with Johnny and Frankie Marvin, two fellow Oklahomans who had met with success in radio and recordings. After listening to the young singer, they offered encouragement but recommended that he get more performing experience. Autry returned to Oklahoma full of confidence that he could be a success. He got a job as "Oklahoma's Yodeling Cowboy" on a Tulsa radio station and wrote several songs with his boss, train-dispatcher Jimmie Long. One of these, "That Silver-Haired Daddy of Mine," gained Autry a write-up in the local paper and a good amount of regional exposure. A 1935 recording of the tune would eventually become Autry's first gold record.

Hollywood: The Phantom Empire

With six months of experience on Oklahoma radio behind him, Autry returned to New York where the Marvin boys landed him a recording contract with Victor in the fall of 1929. His ability to imitate the popular Jimmie Rodgers style sparked the interest of several other record companies: Autry would record with such labels as Grey Gull, Gennett, and Velvet Tone during his time in New York.

After two years of mimicking Rodgers, Autry was eager to branch out into his own singing style. He signed on with the American Record Corporation in 1931 and joined WLS Radio's *National Barn Dance,* at that time inarguably the most popular country radio show in the nation. Mail-order giant Sears, Roebuck & Company, the owner of WLS (the call-letters stood for "World's Largest Store"), wasted no time in marketing Autry's popularity. Gene Autry Special Round-Up guitars were featured in the pages of the Sears catalog along with Gene Autry songbooks. An entire section was devoted to Gene Autry recordings.

WLS even gave Autry his own radio show, *Conqueror Record Time,* to promote Autry's recordings on the

Sears-owned Conqueror record label. Despite the Depression, by 1934, "Oklahoma's Singing Cowboy" was one of the most well-known recording artists in America.

During the Depression, Hollywood's film industry became a shield against the economic worries of many Americans. Fred Astaire and Ginger Rogers danced amid opulent settings in lighthearted romantic comedies, Tarzan swung across many a hometown movie screen, and stars such as Errol Flynn and the beautiful Olivia de Havilland drew willing audiences into the past in escapist costume dramas.

> "It occurs to me that music, with the possible exception of riding a bull, is the most uncertain way to make a living I know."

Likewise, Western films provided a means of escape. As Hollywood looked for new ways to promote its steady crop of willing cowboy actors, the "horse opera" was born. The first Western with musical highlights was a 1930 film starring Ken Maynard. Autry was persuaded to try his hand at acting four years later when his appearance beside Maynard in Republic Studios' In Ole Santa Fe engaged film audiences. The Singing Cowboy was suddenly more than just a pleasant voice—now he had a face.

Autry's popularity prompted Republic to cast him in a 13-chapter Western/sci-fi serial called The Phantom Empire. This quirky cliffhanger was such a success with audiences that by 1935 Autry was hard at work on Tumblin' Tumbleweeds, the first of many two-reelers that would make his name a household word. Less than a month later, Autry's name appeared at theaters around the country in association with another film, Melody Trail, in which his horse, Champion, was introduced to eager film audiences.

Following a tried-and-true formula, Autry's films were set on a Western landscape replete with automobiles, airplanes, and avaricious businessmen, the modern-day version of cattle-rustlers. Each hour-long film would allow its star the opportunity to break into song an average of six times. As the Number One western box-office star from 1937 into the 1940s, Autry helped define the B Western. Helped only by his humorous sidekick and trusty horse, Autry would save the oppressed from the evil menace while always following the Cowboy's Code: Never shoot first, never hit a man smaller than yourself, and never go back on your word.

Altogether, Autry would star in over 90 films, as well as in Melody Ranch, a radio series whose theme song, "Back in the Saddle," would be heard by American families for over 17 years. While Roy Rogers would finally rise to become America's favorite Western star in 1947, Autry would remain a close second in popularity until his semi-retirement from show business in 1957 at the age of 50.

The Singing Cowboy and His Music

Musically, Autry's style began as a derivative of that of Jimmie Rodgers. Indeed, Rodgers was a great influence on many of the country artists of the 1920s and 1930s—Jimmie Davis, Ernest Tubb, Hank Snow, and Merle Haggard were only some of the musicians inspired by Rodgers's "blue yodels" and sentimental balladry. The sparse backup of Autry's early works— "The Yellow Rose of Texas," with harmony by Jimmie Long, and "Tumblin' Tumbleweeds," with vocal back-up by Long and movie sidekick Smiley Burnette—gave way to more Western swing-based arrangements when Gene hired Indiana jazz violinist Carl Cotner in 1937.

Cotner was responsible for much of the "Autry sound" from the late 1930s into the 1940s with arrangements using violins, steel guitar, and an occasional horn. In his 1979 autobiography, Back in the Saddle Again, Autry described a typical working session. "I would stop in the middle of a song and say, 'Right there, that's the place. We need ... Carl, you know what it is. We ought to put it in right there.' And Carl wouldn't know. He would fiddle around until he stumbled onto what I wanted ... until my ear told me it was right. In time," noted Autry, "after years of working closely, and Carl having to read my mind, he developed an instinct for it."

As Bill C. Malone commented in Singing Cowboys and Musical Mountaineers, "Autry had a repertory, like most country entertainers of the era, that lacked clear definition." His interest in pop music motivated him to record a number of popular songs originally recorded by top bandleaders of the day. Amid hits such as "Hillbilly Wedding in June" and "Empty Cot in the Bunk House" appeared a rendition of Kay Kyser's "Jingle, Jangle, Jingle"; "Blueberry Hill," first recorded by Glen Miller, became a Gene Autry hit in 1940.

The pop approach of the Autry-Cotner team made Autry one of the first "crossover" country stars and invited country music in the front door of middle-class homes from Boisie to Boston. His popularization of country music provided a leg-up for the many talented musicians who would perform with him over the years.

Unlike Cotner, many of these, including Burnette, Johnny Bond, Merle Travis, Whitey Ford, Jimmy Wakely, Pat Buttram, and the Cass County Boys, came from so-called hillbilly backgrounds.

Even with Autry's astounding popularity, as Douglas Green noted in *Journal of Country Music,* Autry's career has been a paradoxical one. The star's desire to look ahead has been accompanied by a lack of desire to reflect upon his early years. "Gene Autry's career is surely one of the half dozen most important in country music," wrote Green, "yet we really know little about it.... We know nothing of the inspiration that first fired his interest in music, the music which directed his talent ... or the forces which shaped his music." In public perception, Autry the legend has obscured Autry the man.

The Sunset of the B Western

After a musical career spanning over 40 years, Autry went on to become involved in other areas of the entertainment industry. A savvy investor since purchasing his first radio station prior to joining the Air Force during World War II, Autry had the foresight to see potential in the new medium of television. At one point, Autry was the owner of over ten radio and television stations, as well as president of Flying A Productions, a company that produced such television series as *Range Rider* and *The Adventures of Champion*. In sports circles, much of Autry's fame as a singing cowboy has been overshadowed by his high profile as co-organizer and owner of the California Angels baseball team.

"It occurs to me that music, with the possible exception of riding a bull, is the most uncertain way to make a living I know," Autry stated in his autobiography. "In either case, you can get bucked off, thrown, stepped on, trampled—if you get on at all. At best, it is a short and bumpy ride. It isn't easy to explain why you keep coming back, but you do." Autry's willingness to work hard and take risks brought him much farther than that "short and bumpy ride." And the personality he projected on both screen and radio—the openness and honesty he epitomized—made Autry the embodiment of "The Singing Cowboy," a cultural icon that sustained Americans, young and old alike, through the lean years of the Depression and beyond.

Selected discography

Greatest Hits (contains "You Are My Sunshine," "Lonely River," and "Blues Stay Away from Me"), Columbia, 1961.
Golden Hits, RCA Victor, 1962.
Great Hits, Harmony, 1965.
The Essential Gene Autry (contains "The Yellow Rose of Texas" and "Back in the Saddle Again"), Columbia, 1992.

Sources

Books

Autry, Gene, with Mickey Herskowitz, *Back in the Saddle Again,* Doubleday, 1978.
Biracree, Tom, *The Country Music Almanac,* Prentice Hall, 1993.
Malone, Bill C., *Singing Cowboys and Musical Mountaineers: Southern Culture and the Roots of Country Music,* University of Georgia Press, 1993.
Miller, Lee O., *Great Cowboy Stars of Movies and Television,* Arlington House, 1979.

Periodicals

Country America, March 1994.
Country Song Roundup, February 1994.
Journal of Country Music, vol. 7, no. 2; vol. 7, no. 3.

Additional information for this profile was obtained from Charles Wolfe's liner notes to the Columbia reissue *The Essential Gene Autry, 1933-1946,* February 1992.

—*Pamela Shelton*

Cecilia Bartoli

Opera singer

Photograph by J. Henry Fair, courtesy of Vincent & Farrell Associates

The young, beautiful, and exceptionally talented mezzo-soprano Cecilia Bartoli has critics raving and opera fans flocking to her concerts. She is the rarest of creatures, press reports say, a coloratura mezzo. Opera lovers call Bartoli's voice a gift, something that comes along only once a generation. *Newsweek*'s Katrine Ames raved: "She has a voice that bubbles up through three and a half octaves, and runs down like rich, warm brandy, the range matched by breakneck agility and breathtaking *fioriture*." Linda Blandford of the *New York Times* noted: "[Her voice] is all of one piece, seamless, as vibrant at the top as it is on the bottom."

Bartoli was born in Rome on June 4, 1966, the daughter of professional singers, a lyric soprano and a dramatic tenor. To support the family (there are three children—a son and two daughters), Pietro Bartoli abandoned his solo career and joined the Rome Opera chorus. By all reports, he was a temperamental man and not easy to please. Bartoli told Blandford in the *New York Times:* "When I was young, I was always afraid of my father." The Bartoli household was far from wealthy. Shoes were passed from brother to sisters.

Bartoli's interest in music began when she was a child. She would go about the house imitating her mother's voice. Bartoli's mother trained her daughter to sing and today remains her only vocal teacher. Bartoli has said that her mother hated voices edged with rigidity and tension, and she credits her mother with helping her develop her agile singing style.

First Performance at Age Nine

Bartoli's first public performance occurred at age nine when she sang the shepherd's song offstage at the Rome Opera during Puccini's *Tosca*. As a teenager, she grew disinterested in voice and considered becoming a flamenco dancer and then a trombone player. Eventually she returned to voice. As she observed to *Newsweek*'s Ames: "Slowly, I got very passionate about it. When my voice started developing, it was such a strange feeling." At 17 she enrolled at the Academy of Saint Cecilia in Rome for further training.

Two years later talent scouts selected Bartoli to appear on *Fantastico,* a Rome television show starring two opera singers, Leo Nucci and Katia Ricciarelli. On the program, Bartoli sang the "Barcarolle" duet from Offenbach's *Les Contes d'Hoffman* and a duet from Rossini's *The Barber of Seville*. While she has acknowledged she was frightened at the time, Bartoli told Innaurato of *Vanity Fair:* "I had the good fortune to be seen by a big audience."

For the Record...

Born June 4, 1966, in Rome, Italy; name pronounced "Cheh-*cheel*-ya Bar-*toe*-lee"; daughter of Pietro Angelo and Silvana (Bazzoni) Bartoli. *Education:* Attended Academy of Santa Cecilia in Rome, Italy.

First sang professionally on television in Rome, mid-1980s; made American debut at the Mostly Mozart Festival, 1990; made Paris stage debut as Cherubino in *The Marriage of Figaro;* made La Scala (Milan, Italy) debut in Rossini's *Le Comte Ory*, 1990; sang roles of Cherubino in Mozart's *The Marriage of Figaro* and Dorabella in Mozart's *Cosi fan tutte* with the Chicago Symphony Orchestra, 1992; made American operatic stage debut with the Houston Grand Opera singing Rosina in Rossini's *The Barber of Seville,* 1993.

Addresses: *Management*—Vincent & Farrell Associates, 157 W. 57th Street, New York, NY 10019.

The exposure was just the career boost she needed. Bartoli soon debuted in *The Barber of Seville* in Rome. She was then given an audition before record producer Christopher Raeburn. He secured a deal for her to record *The Barber of Seville* and several Rossini arias. Raeburn later played Bartoli's tapes for agent Jack Mastroianni, a highly regarded agent with Columbia Artists Management. Mastroianni was so impressed he made arrangements to listen to Bartoli in person. Her mother accompanied the young singer to the audition. Mastroianni remembered the day to Blandford in the *New York Times:* "The intensity between the two women was so strong that it was as though musically they were a union, as though every breath the one took, the other took with her." Mastroianni liked what he heard and agreed to manage the unknown singer. As Blandford reported, "[He] became passionate on her behalf: he leaned on friends and longtime colleagues to hire her on his word."

Mastroianni also decided he would steer Bartoli's career away from operatic productions and concentrate instead on recitals. As Blandford noted: "Instead of a four-minute aria or two in which to make an opera debut, he gave her two hours in which to seduce."

Sacrificed Volume for Quality

It was not easy at first finding places that would book Bartoli. As Mastroianni told *Vanity Fair's* Albert Innaurato: "They all said, 'When she's at the Met, come back.' They thought her voice was too small. They'd say, 'It has to be a big voice or it's no voice.'"

Some critics continue to argue that Bartoli's voice lacked the power to reach the back seats in an auditorium. Bartoli responded to the charge to *Newsweek's* Ames: "If you have agility, you don't have much volume. The most important thing isn't size, but projection. Some people have both, but they're gods." As Bartoli told Innaurato, "I am a singer of quality, not quantity. I am not worried about volume. I want to control the timbre, the nuance. In Italy there is a big obsession with a big voice. I prefer control. When the voice is big, it is not possible to play with it. Mine is a voice for those who know how to listen."

She made her American debut at Lincoln Center's Mostly Mozart concert in 1990. There she sang selections from Mozart's *La clemenza di Tito* and from Rossini's *La Donna del Lago*. Reviews were generally favorable for the new mezzo, and word began circulating about her. Bartoli soon made her Paris debut singing for the role of Cherubino in Mozart's *The Marriage of Figaro*.

Made Operatic Stage Debut

Because her voice is so well suited to the flourishes and scale runs of Rossini and Mozart, the two composers have become her favorites to sing and record. Bartoli discussed her opinions of them with Matthew Gurewitsch of the *New York Times:* "Rossini is more spicy, more of the earth. Mozart is sweeter, more spiritual, an angel from paradise. Rossini is pure virtuosity. Mozart is more legato; his music needs more support, more control. It's harder for me." Gurewitsch commented: "The effort does not show." After Bartoli performed at an all-Rossini recital in New York in the spring of 1992, critic Allan Kozinn observed in the *New York Times:* "Her technical assets are considerable. Her scale passages, runs, roulades and trills are cleanly and precisely articulated. She uses her vibrato selectively and thoughtfully, rather than just lavishing it uniformly on everything she sings. The sound she produces is smooth and strong throughout her range, particularly at the top, and her coloristic sense is impeccable."

Critics and fans began clamoring for Bartoli to sing a major operatic role. She had performed with the Chicago Symphony Orchestra in three Mozart operas in 1992, but, as reviews noted, this was an orchestra, not a opera company. In April of 1993 Bartoli made her operatic stage debut as Rosina in the Houston Grand Opera's production of Rossini's *The Barber of Seville*.

The hype surrounding her helped the Houston company sell out all seven shows, one month before opening night. William Spiegelman of the *Wall Street Journal* commented on her Houston performance: "Displaying the instincts of a born actress, [Bartoli] expresses Rosina's mercurial temperament with her whole body: Eyes, hands, feet (she studied flamenco as a teenager) work together to create a character who can be alternately docile or dangerous, a kitten or a lynx, depending on her mood."

Interviewers who have met Bartoli in person comment on her playfulness and her down-to-earth personality. "She is a natural comedian," Innaurato wrote, adding that "her features are so mobile that her eyes manage nuances within nuances. Her mouth footnotes, italicizes, and sometimes contradicts her words. Bartoli the singer can manage impressive staccati—rapid notes sung detached up and down the scale. Cecilia the person also has a staccato; she can touch rapidly on a dozen moods in half a second, leaving her interlocutor charmed but a little behind and slightly off-balance."

The public's appetite for Bartoli's music appears to be unsated. Concerts continue to sell out, and her performances are described in detail in major publications. Admirers can purchase her 100-minute video, *A Portrait*. Most reviews referred anxiously to Bartoli's debut with New York's Metropolitan Opera, where she would play Despina in Mozart's *Cosi fan tutte* during the 1994-95 season.

Hit the Top of *Billboard's* Classical Chart

Bartoli's recordings continue to sell well, and shrewd marketing hasn't hurt. Her first solo recording, *Rossini Arias*, released in 1989, featured her posed provocatively in a black lace dress and red gloves. The public responded. One of her later recordings, *If You Love Me*, hit the top of Billboard's classical chart in 1993 and stayed there for months.

The *Stereo Review* commentary about this recording of 17th- and 18th-century Italian songs reflects the general reaction to the work: "Immerse yourself in Bartoli's recital and savor her singing. This captivating young artist never allows monotony to set in: Her light, dusky mezzo-soprano enfolds these lovely songs in caressingly warm and purely focused tones free of excessive vibrato. They flow with an unforced naturalness, and the decorative passages (Lotti's *Pur Dicesti* is a good example) are delivered with unostentatious ease. Bartoli's art combines simplicity and sophistication. The passion in her singing is conveyed with a Baroque sensibility, with unfailing taste, and, whenever the texts call for it (as in the Paisiello operas), with an enlivening spark of humor."

In reviewing Bartoli's various recitals and opera recordings, Matthew Gurewitsch observed in the *New York Times:* "As total performances, the opera sets cannot be recommended, but that is no fault of her [own]: against the rest of the unimpressive cast in The Barber [of Seville], her Rosina sparkles; in [Daniel] Barenboim's leaden treatments, she is the bright spot; her rhetorical fire even sets Mr. [Nikolaus] Harnoncourt's grim, Prussian performance momentarily ablaze. The recitals, though, are altogether bewitching."

Talent Enhanced by Beauty

Bartoli's formidable talent is enhanced by her striking appearance. Martha Duffy described the singer in *Time:* "Her dark good looks project grandly across the footlights: a mane of lustrous hair, huge brown eyes, a generous mouth and milky shoulders that enhance a decolletage." Reports often refer to her melodious, easy laugh, her stable temperament and her "Italian-ness." She is considered unique in the opera world for her admiration of motorcycles, rock stars like Led Zeppelin, and jazz great Ella Fitzgerald. Unmarried, Bartoli lives with her mother and sister. Her parents separated in 1989, and her father now lives in Rimini, Italy.

When asked why she sings, Bartoli told *Vanity Fair's* Innaurato: "My parents, my character, and God. I sing because I sing, not to earn money. I love music, not the business." As for her future, Bartoli seems to be biding her time about taking on the big-money roles like Carmen, the lead in the opera of the same name by Bizet. "I don't feel a soprano color in my voice," she told *Newsweek's* Katrine Ames. She has said she knows how she must proceed with her career because she has lived with singers all of her life. "I've been in the front row."

If doubt remains about the depth of Bartoli's talent, the undecided may wish to consider music critic Peter G. Davis's comments, as quoted in *Vanity Fair:* "Every time I've heard her, she has been even better. She has sumptuous tone, dazzling coloratura, and is a wonderful musician. She's been hyped like everybody else, but she actually is the real thing."

Selected discography

Rossini Arias, London/Decca, 1989.
Mozart Opera and Concert Arias, London/Decca, 1989.

Rossini Heroines (with Orchestra and Chorus of Venice's Teatro la Fenice), London/Decca, 1992.
If You Love Me, London/Decca, 1993.
Cenerentola, London/Decca, 1993.

Sources

Newsweek, May 3, 1993.
New York Times, February 23, 1992.
New York Times Magazine, March 14, 1993.
Stereo Review, April 1993.
Time, December 14, 1992.
Vanity Fair, April 1993.
Wall Street Journal, April 30, 1993.

—Carol Hopkins

Black Uhuru

Reggae band

In 1982 *Rolling Stone* reviewer Ken Emerson wrote that "When Bob Marley died last year, one consoling ray of hope illuminated reggae's future: the release of Black Uhuru's *Red.*" In a 1984 concert review for the same magazine, Chris Morris referred to the vocal trio as "Jamaica's premier post-Bob Marley reggae outfit." In the world of reggae music, no compliment could be higher than a comparison to Bob Marley, the leading legend of Jamaican music. In the mid-1980s Black Uhuru laid the foundation for its own legend and pioneer status in reggae music—one that would provide the band with remarkable longevity despite several changes in the line-up. By 1989, more than ten years after the band's inception, *Red* would be logged as one of the top 100 albums of the decade by *Rolling Stone*.

By the late 1970s Black Uhuru referred to three vocalists who constituted the "golden age" of Black Uhuru's popularity: Michael Rose, Derrick "Duckie" Simpson, and Sandra "Puma" Jones. The singers gathered instrumental backup from a variety of musicians and had a long-standing collaboration with two of the finest

Photograph by Nathaniel Welch, courtesy of Mesa/Bluemoon Recordings, Ltd.

> **For the Record . . .**
>
> Members include **Don Carlos** (born c. 1950s in Jamaica; left group, c. 1977), vocals; **Garth Dennis** (born c. 1950s in Jamaica; left group, c. 1977), vocals; **Errol Nelson,** vocals; and **Derrick "Duckie" Simpson** (born June 24, 1950, in Kingston, Jamaica), vocals. Later members include **Sandra "Puma" Jones** (born c. 1950s in Columbia, SC; died of cancer, 1990; joined group, 1978; left group, 1987), vocals; **Delroy "Junior" Reid** (joined group, 1985), vocals; **Janet Reid;** and **Michael Rose** (born July 11, 1957, in Kingston, Jamaica; left group, 1985), vocals.
>
> Group formed in Kingston, Jamaica, 1974; recorded several singles with Top Cat, an independent Kingston label. Simpson and Rose worked together briefly as duo before bringing in Jones, 1978; began working frequently with Sly Dunbar and Robbie Shakespeare and recording under Taxi label; made first U.S. appearance at Hunter College and signed recording contract with Island records, 1979; original members reunited at *Reggae Times* awards ceremony, 1987; embarked on European tour, late 1980s; recorded comeback album *Now*, Mesa, 1990.
>
> **Awards:** Grammy Award for best reggae album, 1985, for *Anthem*; *Reggae Times* award for best group, 1987.
>
> **Addresses:** *Record company*—Mesa/Bluemoon Recordings, 209 E. Alameda Ave., Burbank, CA, 91502.

musicians in the industry, drummer Sly Dunbar and bassist Robbie Shakespeare. The accompaniment of Sly and Robbie, as they are known familiarly in reggae circles, contributed to the group's breakthrough in the 1980s.

Black Uhuru's roots, however, reach back well before that breakthrough to 1974, when Simpson decided to form a group. The name he chose, the second part of which means "freedom" in Swahili, reflected reggae music's origins in the slums of Kingston, Jamaica, where Simpson was born in 1950. Then, as today, young black men in Kingston had little opportunity to break away from the poverty of the city's slums. Reggae offered one of the few escape routes, but it was already packed with talented hopefuls; the chances of actually succeeding were slim. Nonetheless, Simpson, Garth Dennis, and Don Carlos—the original bandmates—began playing local club engagements in Kingston. They even had the opportunity to produce a few singles—"Folk Songs," "Time Is on Our Side," and "Slow Coach"—with a small reggae production outfit called Top Cat; unfortunately, nothing ever came of it.

Within a few years Dennis and Carlos separated from Uhuru—Carlos for a solo career and Dennis for an eight-year stint with the Wailing Souls. Simpson quickly reformed the band in 1977, bringing in two more Kingston men: Michael Rose and Errol Nelson. This time, the group's singles, "Natural Mystic" and "King Selassie," caught the attention of a London distributor named Count Shelley. Consequently, Black Uhuru's debut album, *Love Crisis*, which they had recorded on a small label called Prince Jammy's, was released in England in 1977.

Nelson departed soon after the release, leaving Simpson and Rose to work as a duo for a while. During this period they began to collaborate on recordings with Sly Dunbar and Robbie Shakespeare, the rhythm section that would become the most famous and influential in reggae music. At this time, Sly and Robbie were just putting together their Taxi label, and Black Uhuru's "Observe Life" was issued as that company's first release.

Puma Jones Completed Chemistry

Simpson found a replacement for Nelson in 1978. Sandra "Puma" Jones had an unusual background for a reggae musician; in 1986 she described that background for Constance C. R. White of *Ms.* magazine, who referred to Jones as "a woman whose artistic expression comes from a blending of the various cultures to which she's been attracted over the years." She had been born in Columbia, South Carolina, and raised in New York City before settling in Jamaica in the late 1970s. Jones began to investigate her African heritage in college, where she studied African culture and, particularly, African dance.

She went to graduate school at Columbia University and earned a master's degree in social work while continuing her other interests, including work in local television. But it was travel that would change her course in life; after a period of employment in Ghana, Africa, Jones took a position working with homeless families in Jamaica. She took side jobs as a backup singer in reggae bands and eventually encountered Simpson, who was hoping to change his band's sound by replacing Nelson with a female vocalist. Jones became the third term in the equation that critics would embrace as *the* Black Uhuru.

The new Black Uhuru combination went back into Sly and Robbie's studio to record a series of singles including future hits, "General Penitentiary," "Guess Who's Coming to Dinner?," "Plastic Smile," and "Shine Eye Gal." Their productivity and success as a singles band gave them the impetus for their second album, *Showcase,* which appeared in 1979, also on the Taxi label. That in turn brought an invitation from a New York City radio station, WLIB, that was ready to sponsor a concert at Hunter College. It was Black Uhuru's first performance outside of Jamaica—an opportunity most reggae bands never had.

> "All kinds of things go on, good things and bad things. But things just have to change. Time for people to wake up!"
> —Garth Dennis

Showcase went on to win the favor of Chris Blackwell, president of Island Records, and Black Uhuru's first major-label contract soon followed. The band made their U.S. album debut in 1980 with *Sensimilla,* named for a type of seedless marijuana used in the rituals of Jamaica's Rastafarian religion. Subsequent albums solidified Black Uhuru's reputation with U.S. audiences, who were at that time greatly expanding the reggae market. The most significant of these releases was 1981's *Red,* the album that prompted comparisons between Black Uhuru and Bob Marley, reggae's unofficial king.

Red Completed Rise to Fame

Red put the band into the Top 30 on British music charts and yielded several popular cuts, with "Youth of Eglinton" becoming a reggae classic. In the 1989 write-up for *Rolling Stone*'s Top 100 of the 1980s, the critic recaptured the excitement of the album's release, asserting, "At a moment when the music was in critical need of a strong new voice, Black Uhuru's finest album, *Red,* shone with all the musical intensity and political fervor of the Rastafarian movement." He further summarized the album as "a plea for cultural revolution and religious faith." *Anthem,* the band's 1983 release, won the first Grammy that was ever awarded for best reggae album.

Ken Emerson summed up the attitude of that early reception in a September 1982 *Rolling Stone* article, declaring, "The exuberance of their Rastafarian faith was uplifting; their songs evoked not only Kingston but the equally mean streets of Brooklyn and Brixton; their firm stand against sexism was refreshing." Three months earlier, Fred Shruers called Black Uhuru "the most exciting reggae band around" in his *Rolling Stone* review of *Tear It Up.* The particular strength of their music was, Emerson claimed, "the improvisatory interplay of three singers." Their live performances were similarly received; one in 1984 prompted Chris Morris to announce that "Black Uhuru have the finesse and firepower to galvanize a crowd, and by set's end, the aisles were jammed with skanking, spliff-smoking devotees."

Changes Weakened Popularity

For Emerson, the weak link in the chain of successes was the 1982 release *Chill Out,* which he claimed "put a damper on Black Uhuru's flame." Emerson objected to the album's shift away from the simple sound of traditional reggae to a more synthetic sound called "dub". Even critics called the release "overdubbed and doctored to death with synthesized whooshes and whistles and Vocodorized vocals." Emerson's dislike aside, the new sound was becoming the height of reggae fashion in the mid-1980s.

In 1985, after the band's rise to success began to slow, Michael Rose decided to try his hand at a solo career. Delroy "Junior" Reid came in to replace him, appearing first on *Brutal* in 1986. Sandra Jones was compelled to leave for health reasons just before the recording of *Positive* in 1987: the singer was battling cancer and would pass away in 1990. It was only a year before her departure from the band that she spoke with *Ms.* and talked about her dual commitment to her music and her family, which consisted of a husband and six children. She described her musical career as a part of her dedication to social change, prompting the magazine to comment that Jones "sees her singing as a logical extension of her social work since Black Uhuru's lyrics are usually social and political commentary."

When Jones left, Janet Reid came in as the third vocalist for the *Positive* recording sessions. This particular combination lasted only briefly, however, since Simpson was uncannily reunited with his two original collaborators. The *Reggae Times* Awards in 1987, honoring Don Carlos as Best Vocalist and Black Uhuru as Best Group, arranged for Simpson, Carlos, and Dennis to play together. A European tour followed, and by 1990 the threesome was recording as Black Uhuru once again, releasing *Now* under a new contract with Mesa records.

The album ultimately produced more than a reunion of the original members. It garnered praise from the critics and made headway in the music charts, winning the Number Two position on *Billboard*'s world music charts. David Hiltbrand of *People* described the album as a return to "a much simpler, more traditional reggae sound" and reserved special praise for Carlos's "balmy, sonorous voice." *Now* also brought the group back to the attention of the Grammys, with a nomination for best reggae recording.

In 1992, the band released *Iron Storm,* an album that emphasized Black Uhuru's continuing involvement with social and political issues. An award-winning video was made of the single "Tip of the Iceberg," which featured controversial rap star Ice-T. The video was filmed on the burned-out streets of South Central Los Angeles in the wake of the Rodney King police brutality trial verdict.

Black Uhuru's next offering, 1993's *Mystical Truth,* made it to the top of the New World Music chart and was called "an exceptional project" by critics. The 12 tracks are an eclectic mix of rasta-rock and soul, including reggae renditions of War's "Slippin' Into Darkness" and Peter Gabriel's "Mercy Street." *New Music Report* noted, "Black Uhuru ... implores social action in its smooth, always loquacious manner and strives to expand the boundaries of reggae in the process" and hailed *Mystical Truth* as "an all-time classic."

The trio planned a 30-plus city tour of North America in 1994 to coincide with the release of *Strongg,* their seventh album on the Mesa label. The 11 selections feature the musical contributions of Sly Dunbar, Ranguten Smith, and Sydney Wolf, and though the album highlights Black Uhuru's commitment to the eradication of oppression, it also offers hope amid the injustice. As Garth Dennis observed in a Mesa Records publication release: "All kinds of things go on, good things and bad things. But things just have to change. Time [for] people to wake up!"

Selected discography

Love Crisis, Prince Jammy's, 1977.
Showcase, Taxi, 1980.
Sensimilla, Island, 1981.
Red (includes "Youth of Eglinton"), Island, 1981.
Tear It Up, Island, 1982.
Chill Out, Island, 1982.
The Dub Factor, Mango, 1983.
Anthem, Mango/Island, 1984.
Brutal, RAS, 1986.
Guess Who's Coming to Dinner (includes "Shine Eye Gal," "General Penitentiary," "Guess Who's Coming to Dinner," and "Plastic Smile"), Heartbeat/Rounder, 1987.
Positive, RAS, 1987.
Black Sounds of Freedom (includes "I Love King Selassie" and "Natural Mystic"), Shanachie Records, 1990.
Now, Mesa, 1990.
Now Dub, Mesa, 1990.
Mystical Truth, Mesa, 1992.
Iron Storm, Mesa, 1992.
Mystical Truth Dub, Mesa, 1993.
Liberation: The Island Anthology, Chronicles/Mango, 1993.
Strongg, Mesa, 1994.

Sources

Books

Rolling Stone Encyclopedia of Rock & Roll, edited by Jon Pareles and Patricia Romanowski, Rolling Stone/ Fireside Books, 1983.

Periodicals

Billboard, April 24, 1993; October 9, 1993.
Boom, February 1994.
Down Beat, June 1991.
High Fidelity, February 1989.
Inroads, April 2, 1993.
L.A. Weekly, April 15, 1993.
Los Angeles Times, April 21, 1993.
Ms., March 1986.
New Music Report, March 26, 1993.
People, March 19, 1990.
Reggae Roots, May/June 1993.
Rolling Stone, June 10, 1982; September 16, 1982; October 11, 1984; November 16, 1989.
Urban Network, February 2, 1993.

Additional information for this profile was obtained from Mesa/Bluemoon Recordings.

—Ondine Le Blanc

Bobby "Blue" Bland

Singer

As a singer, Bobby "Blue" Bland is regarded as the definitive blues stylist, the "black [Frank] Sinatra," as Dave Marsh described him in the *Rolling Stone Record Guide*. Often backed by a simple rhythm section and deftly arranged horn lines, Bland became known for his sexy, liquid-smooth approach. He rarely sang hard blues; his style was one of distilled fervor.

Although Bland never really crossed over to white audiences, as has his friend B. B. King, he has been enduringly popular. According to Joel Whitburn's *Top R&B Singles: 1942-88*, Bland is the Number 11 rhythm and blues chart artist of all time; in the blues genre he trails only King. In a listing of top artists of the 1960s, Bland is at Number Four, ahead of a slew of household names. Bland has never been highly visible; his core audience remains the black blues crowd. Another explanation offered for his neglected mainstream status is that he is mainly a singer and not an instrumentalist. Still, saying Bobby "Blue" Bland is *just* a singer is akin to calling Picasso just a painter.

Bland was born January 27, 1930, in Rosemark, Tennessee, and had a rural boyhood. He listened primarily to gospel and white country singers while growing up. At the age of 17, Bland moved with his mother to Memphis, where the youngster continued to sing in church and in secular street groups. His first group, the Miniatures, was short lived.

By 1949 Bland was working as B. B. King's chauffeur and at times as Roscoe Gordon's valet—anything to stay close to blues music. He was soon a part of the Beale Streeters, a vocal group that also included Johnny Ace, Gordon, and King. Based on a love of spirituals and the urban blues that filled the street for which they were named, the Beale Streeters continued on for a year.

By 1951 Bland had signed with D.J. James Mattis's Duke Recordings. Prior to that the singer had cut three singles that were released on three different, although prominent, R&B labels: Chess, Modern, and Duke. Though he had yet to find his own style, Bland was in the thick of the R&B scene—the Chess sides were produced by Sam Phillips, the Modern single by Ike Turner.

In 1952 Bland was drafted into the U.S. Army; by the end of his tour he was performing in Special Services, covering Nat King Cole and Charles Brown songs. When he returned in 1955, Bland began touring as Junior Parker's valet and opening act. In the meantime, rock and roll had arrived in the person of Elvis Presley; crossover possibilities for black acts were subsequently opened. Duke had been purchased by Don Robey,

Courtesy of Malaco Records

> **For the Record . . .**
>
> Born Robert Calvin Bland, January 27, 1930, in Rosemark, TN.
>
> Briefly joined group the Miniatures, 1949; worked as B. B. King's chauffeur, 1950; with Johnny Ace and Roscoe Gordon, formed the Beale Streeters, 1951; signed with Duke label, 1951; began playing 300 one-nighters per year with Junior Parker, 1958; arranger Joe Scott and guitarist Wayne Bennett left Bland, 1968; signed with Malaco label, 1984; boxed set of the Duke recordings, *I Pity the Fool: The Duke Recordings,* released by MCA, 1992. *Military service:* U.S. Army, early 1950s.
>
> **Awards:** Nominated for a Grammy Award, 1989, for "Get Your Money Where You Spend Your Time"; inducted into the Rock & Roll Hall of Fame, 1991.
>
> **Addresses:** *Record company*—Malaco Records, P.O. Box 9287, 3023 Northside Drive, Jackson, MS 39206.

a shadowy Houston businessman. Robey admired Bland and quickly teamed him with the Bill Harvey Orchestra, a Memphis group; the result was the song "It's My Life Baby."

When "Farther on up the Road" hit Number One on the R&B charts in 1957, it was the beginning of a tremendous run for Bland at Duke. The song's success is difficult to pinpoint—it is typical blues in both arrangement and sensibility. The difference may have been that Bland was now telling a convincing story, making brief lyrical vignettes highly believable with his conversational style. All of his songs were written for him; even when a song was written by a member of Bland's band, Robey would credit it to the anonymous pseudonym of "Deadric Malone," thus pocketing songwriting royalties himself.

In 1958 Robey hooked Bland up with Joe Scott, a gifted arranger, writer, and trumpeter. Hits like "Little Boy Blue" and "Bobby's Blues" kept coming, often increasing in orchestral sophistication and emotional facility. Bland was greatly influenced by the Reverend C. F. Franklin, soul sensation Aretha Franklin's father, who cried out biblical passages in what Bland referred to as a "squall." As he lost his high falsetto, Bland began combining the squall with a rapid vibrato—a style that would be a cornerstone of modern soul singing. With Scott, Bland continued to work on his diction and phrasing, making each song an entity unto itself. And the touring was nonstop; between 1958 and 1968, Bland played 300 one-nighters a year for several years in a row. In addition to collecting gold records and critical accolades while continually working on the road, Bland also picked up a pernicious problem with alcohol. An alcoholic for 18 years, drinking up to three fifths a day, Bland would not confront his problem until the early 1970s.

Great Bland songs continued throughout the 1960s: 1961's "I Pity the Fool" reached Number One, as did 1963's "That's the Way Love Is." Other songs, including "Stormy Monday" and "Turn On Your Lovelight," went on to earn the distinction of R&B standards. The body of work Bland created while with Duke—collected in 1992 in a CD boxed set—lifted him to the status of sole patriarch of soft soul singing; only B. B. King's influence has been more enduring overall.

In 1968 Scott and guitarist Wayne Bennett left Bland. Between 1968 and 1971 the singer fought depression while touring with the Ernie Fields Orchestra, a Tulsa band that by many critics' accounts inappropriately translated Bland's distinct style. In 1973, after Robey's death, Duke was purchased by ABC/Dunhill, a label that soon attempted to make Bland a mainstream artist, pairing him with Four Seasons producer Steve Barri for both *His California Album* and *Dreamer*. Both releases successfully crossed over to white audiences, though many blues fans felt the music to be compromised. In 1979, after experimenting with the disco sound, Bland moved to MCA Records. Although he was floundering artistically, Bland did record the monumental "Ain't No Heart in the City," later a hit for the rock band Whitesnake.

In 1985 Bland signed with Malaco, the fiercely independent R&B label based in Jackson, Mississippi. It has been a positive pairing for both artist and label. Unlike many blues and soul acts that were preeminent in the 1960s, Bland has matured well. His first album for Malaco, *Members Only,* was a triumphant return to form. He was nominated for a Grammy Award in 1989 for the song "Get Your Money Where You Spend Your Time" and followed the achievement with the acclaimed *Midnight Run,* an album that spent nearly a year and a half on the R&B charts.

In 1991 Bland was inducted into the Rock & Roll Hall of Fame, an honor evidencing the quality of his work and his influence on subsequent generations. It could be argued that more than any other figure, Bland moved the blues away from its arcane and primitive origins while still keeping its spirit intact. He was, as one of his greatest albums noted, "two steps from the blues"; yet he was also just a step from starting rock and roll.

Selected discography

Two Steps From the Blues, Duke, 1961.
Call on Me, Duke, 1963.
Touch of the Blues, Duke, 1968.
His California Album, ABC Dunhill, 1973.
Try Me, I'm Real, MCA, 1981.
First Class Blues, Malaco, 1987.
Midnight Run, Malaco, 1989.
I Pity the Fool: The Duke Recordings, MCA, 1992.

Sources

Guralnick, Peter, *Lost Highway,* Vintage, 1982.
Heilbut, Anthony, *The Gospel Sound,* fourth edition, Limelight, 1992.
Rees, Dafydd, and Luke Crampton, *Rock Movers and Shakers,* Billboard Books, 1991.
Rolling Stone Album Guide, edited by Anthony DeCurtis, James Henke, and Holly George-Warren, Straight Arrow, 1992.
Rolling Stone Encyclopedia of Rock & Roll, edited by Jon Pareles and Patricia Romanowski, Rolling Stone Press, 1983.
Rolling Stone Record Guide, edited by Dave Marsh, Rolling Stone Press, 1979.
Scott, Frank, *The Down Home Guide to the Blues,* A Capella Books, 1991.
Whitburn, Joel, *Top R&B Singles, 1942-88,* Billboard Books, 1990.

Additional information for this profile was obtained from Don Snowden's liner notes to *I Pity the Fool: The Duke Recordings,* MCA, 1992.

—Stewart Francke

Anthony Braxton

Composer, instrumentalist, writer, educator

Courtesy of Worldwide Jazz

"My motto since I was 11 years old was, 'Play or Die,'" multi-instrumentalist and jazz soloist, leader, and composer Anthony Braxton divulged to Peter Rothbart in *Down Beat*. A virtuoso who has won *Down Beat* magazine's critics poll number one player award numerous times for various instruments, Braxton performs alto saxophone, contrabass clarinet, sopranino, flute, piano, percussion, and virtually every reed. He has written nearly 400 compositions, recorded more than 70 albums, and appeared on at least 50 others. The writer, lecturer, and educator cites John Coltrane, Paul Desmond, and Warne Marsh as major influences, but has also disclosed his love for the music of Frank Sinatra and Barbra Streisand.

Acknowledged as a gifted artist and composer of "free jazz," Braxton dislikes the name given his genre. "That gives the impression that there's no preparation," he stated in *Newsweek*. Braxton even considers "jazz" too limiting a term to describe the evolution of his music over the years. "The music that pushed my button was more than a word 'jazz,'" he asserted in *Down Beat*. "It was individuals who were approaching the music in a certain way, with a certain set of value systems and intentions, a certain honesty and humility."

Titling his compositions with numerical configurations, linear designs, and idiosyncratic arrangements of letters, Braxton developed his own geometrically based notational system as well as philosophical stance about jazz in a cultural context. Though financial reward has proved elusive to Braxton, he disclosed to Rothbart, "If I wasn't able to achieve what I wanted in my life as far as my creativity and my life's growth is concerned, I would feel bad, but not too bad. But I would find it hard to forgive not trying and not giving everything to the struggle."

Alienated From His Surroundings

Born in Chicago, Illinois, on June 4, 1945, Braxton grew up amid the violence and squalor of the city's toughest neighborhoods. His musical and philosophical temperament set him apart from family and friends at an early age. "I came from a poor family—not really impoverished—we had enough food to eat," Braxton related to Michael Ullman in *Jazz Lives*. "But my reality was the reality of the south side and I couldn't understand what was happening there." He discovered that literature, chess, and music were antidotes to his feelings of alienation.

Initially, Braxton's parents and his brothers were pleased when he began to play an alto saxophone, but their feelings changed as Braxton delved into avant-garde

For the Record...

Born June 4, 1945 in Chicago, IL; married; wife's name, Nickie; children: two. *Education:* Attended Chicago School of Music, Wilson Junior College, Roosevelt University, and Chicago Musical College.

Jazz alto saxophonist and avant-garde composer. Multi-instrumentalist, including bass, contrabass clarinet, sopranino (Eb soprano saxophone), Eb clarinet, flute, piano, and percussion; played with U.S. Army bands, beginning in 1963; joined Association for the Advancement of Creative Musicians (AACM) as a performer and instructor, 1966; formed trio Creative Construction Company, 1967; released debut album, *Three Compositions of New Jazz,* 1968; recorded first solo saxophone album ever made, *For Alto,* 1968, released, 1971; member of Chick Corea's quartet Circle, 1970-71; led his own quartets, 1971-76; made concert debut at Town Hall, New York City, 1972; Carnegie Hall performance, 1973; performed with Derek Bailey and Company, London, 1974-77; Mills College, Oakland, CA, professor of music, 1985-88; Wesleyan College, Middletown, CT, chair of music department; published three-volume *Tri-Axium Writings,* 1985, and five-volume *Composition Notes, Books A-E,* 1988; has performed numerous concerts, solo and with others, in the United States and Europe.

Awards: Named number-one player on various instruments in *Down Beat* magazine's critics' polls; best LP, *Down Beat* magazine's critics' poll, 1977, for *Creative Music Orchestra*; readers' and critics' poll awards from various periodicals.

Addresses: *Office*—Music Department, Wesleyan University, Middletown, CT 06459.

---

jazz. Braxton dated his separation from his family from the moment he brought home a Cecil Taylor recording in his early teens. Since peers did not share his interest in mathematics, music, and logic, Braxton spent most of his time alone. "You see," he told Ray Townley in *Down Beat,* "I had a lot of problems as a teenager. I could never venture out to where there were a lot of people in a crowd situation. I used to stay in the house most of the time, and practice ... play music, stuff like that."

Braxton refined his craft in his adolescent years studying with Jack Gell of the Chicago School of Music beginning in the mid-1950s. In the early 1960s Braxton met jazz legend John Coltrane in Chicago, but was too in awe of Coltrane to join him—upon Coltrane's invitation—in a set. When Braxton enrolled briefly at Chicago's Wilson Junior College, he became friends with two budding jazz artists who helped him later in his career, Roscoe Mitchell and Jack DeJohnette.

In 1966 Mitchell urged Braxton to join the renowned Association for the Advancement of Creative Musicians (AACM) after Braxton's Army stint, which began in 1963. Founded in the late sixties in Chicago, the AACM promoted experiments with sound and improvisation that were pivotal to Braxton's career. No longer confined to notes to make music, Braxton and AACM members investigated whistles, shrieks, and percussion made from hubcaps, among other devices, to develop sonic textures. Braxton thrived in the AACM's creative atmosphere; however, he was unable to support himself financially.

Hustled to Maintain Profession

One of the AACM's most accomplished instrumentalists, Braxton hustled, playing chess to pay the bills. When he contemplated marriage and family life on his income, he pondered relegating music to a hobby. Studying to become a philosophy teacher at Chicago's Roosevelt University, Braxton reached a career crisis in 1969. "I left Chicago because I was desperate," Braxton confessed to Townley in *Down Beat.* "I really wanted to play or else I wanted to see what it was like to really make the commitment. I split to Paris with $50.00 in my pocket."

In Paris, Braxton performed with the Creative Construction Company, a group he formed with AACM members violinist Leroy Jenkins and trumpeter Leo Smith in 1967. Braxton released his first recording with the Creative Construction Company, *Three Compositions of New Jazz,* in 1968. That same year he recorded *For Alto,* the first album ever made of unaccompanied saxophone, but the release date for the record was not until 1971.

Braxton was not successful in Paris, where his music was labeled "cold." He returned to New York to play with the Italian improvisational group Musica Elettronica Viva in 1970. Reduced to hustling chess games in the park at Washington Square to make ends meet, Braxton was introduced to keyboardist Chick Corea through Jack DeJohnette at the Village Vanguard in 1970. He joined Corea, bassist Dave Holland, and percussionist Barry Altschul to form the short-lived but highly influential quartet Circle from 1970 to 1971.

Introduced Saxophone Solos

Of Braxton's milestone album *For Alto*, *Down Beat*'s Townley wrote, "The closest thing to it in recent centuries happened back in 1720 when Bach wrote six sonatas for unaccompanied violin and six suites for unaccompanied cello." A delayed success in 1972, the recording prompted invitations for Braxton to perform numerous solo concerts. From 1971 to 1976, he led his own groups, which included Circle alumni Holland and Altschul as well as trumpeter Kenny Wheeler and trombonist George Lewis. Braxton performed in London with avant-garde guitarist Derek Bailey from 1974 to 1977 and received *Down Beat* magazine's critics' poll best LP for the album *Creative Music Orchestra* in 1977.

His symphonies for large orchestras, parade marches, and a series of twelve operas called *Trillium* occupied Braxton in the eighties, but most of his monumental output rarely got published. In 1985, he took a teaching position as professor of music at Mills College in Oakland, California, then later moved to Wesleyan College in Middletown, Connecticut, to head the music department there. Though Braxton drafted 350 compositions and eight volumes of writings that codify his world view—*Tri-Axium Writings*, 1985, and *Composition Notes, Books A-E*, 1988—his success in mass marketing has been minimal.

Unyielding in his methodological approach to composition, Braxton confessed to Ullman that his analytical style "turns jazz critics off." In 1976 *Down Beat* labeled Braxton "overrated and overpublicized," describing the musician in concert as "a studied player" and "great technician" who "is loathe to reveal—and therefore include—his deepest emotions in his playing." The following year *Newsweek* paid him homage, lauding, "Anthony Braxton *is* original. His music is unique, and he is the most innovative force in the world of jazz." However, more critics responded to Braxton's play like Gene Santoro in *Nation* in 1989, who wrote, "His music isn't easy to pick up on: It has neither the glib melodic hooks of 'jazz' radio stars ... nor an easy reliance on canonized traditions like bebop. It can be knotty and passionate, Cageian and Coltranesque, highly structured and deliberately destabliized—and usually tries to be all those things at once."

Critical Studies Published

By the late 1980s, Braxton's work began receiving more critical attention. Full-length studies on his work were published, such as *Forces in Motion*, by Graham Lock, and *New Musical Figurations*, by Ronald Rada-

no. John Corbett in *Down Beat* suggested, "What's refreshing, if not surprising, is the fact that there's so little redundancy in these studies—a clear testament to the breadth, depth, and richness of Braxton's sound world."

Reviews of Braxton's releases were becoming more laudatory as well. Corbett insisted that Braxton's *Willisau (Quartet) 1991*, recorded with Marilyn Crispell on piano, Mark Dresser on bass, and Gerry Hemingway on drums, was "a miraculous four-disc set that should become a contemporary jazz landmark." Of *Victorville 1992*, a *Pulse!* writer commented, "No one in jazz organizes sets that flow more compellingly; this is one of [Braxton's] classic quartet's best." The writer also widely praised *Wesleyan (12 Altosolos) 1992*.

> "I left Chicago because I was desperate. I really wanted to play or else I wanted to see what it was like to really make the commitment."

In addition, *Down Beat*'s Corbett was impressed with *Duo (London) 1993*, claiming, "Indeed, though he's expressed waning interest in completely open playing of late ... Braxton proves himself to be one of its most skilled practitioners—sensitive, reactive, relaxed, and full of ideas."

Braxton is a purveyor of provocative, more so than melodic, jazz. His writings document the complexity of a man who regrets none of the hardships brought on by his singular genius. He told Bill Shoemaker in *Down Beat*, "I was fortunate to discover something that I really love. Not many people are fortunate enough to find something that they can dedicate their lives to. The discipline of music is so wonderful, there's always something new to learn.

Selected discography

Three Compositions of New Jazz, Delmark, 1968.
For Alto, Delmark, 1968.
Donna Lee, American, 1972.
In the Tradition, Inner City, 1974.
Creative Music Orchestra, Arista, 1976.
Performance (Quartet) 1979, hat ART, 1979.
Anthony Braxton With the Robert Schumann String Quartet, Sound Aspects, 1979.
One in Two, Two in One, 1979.

Six Compositions: Quartet, Antilles, 1981.
Four Compositions (Quartet) 1983, Black Saint, 1983.
Composition 113, Sound Aspects, 1984.
Four Compositions (Quartet) 1984, Black Saint, 1984.
Eugene (1989), Black Saint, 1992.
2 Compositions (Ensemble) 1989/91, hat ART, 1992.
(With Peter Niklas Wilson) *Duets: Hamburg 1991,* Music & Arts, 1992.
Willisau (Quartet) 1991, hat ART, 1992.
Composition No. 165, New Albion, 1992.
4 Compositions 1992, Black Saint, 1993.
Composition 95 tor Two Pianos, Arista.
Composition 98, hat ART.
Open Aspects '82, hat ART.
Seven Standards 1985, Volume 1 & Volume 2, Magenta.
Five Compositions (Quartet) 1986, Black Saint.
London, November 1986, Leo.
Six Monk's Compositions (1987), Black Saint.
19 (Solo) Compositions, 1988, New Albion.
Ensemble (Victoriaville) 1988, Victo.
Eight (+3) Tristano Compositions 1989, hat ART.
Seven Compositions (Trio) 1989, hat ART.
Compositions 99, 101, 107 & 139, hat ART.
Duets Vancouver 1989, Music & Arts.
The Aggregate, Sound Aspects.
Kol Nidre, Sound Aspects.
Victorville 1992, Victo.
Wesleyan (12 Altosolos) 1992, hat ART.
Duo (London) 1993.

Sources

Books

Ullman, Michael, *Jazz Lives,* New Republic, 1980.

Periodicals

Down Beat, March 1974; March 25, 1976; August 12, 1976; February 22, 1979; October 1981; February 1982; May 1983; April 1987; March 1989; February 1990; May 1990; November 1990; February 1993; March 1994; April 1994; May 1994.
Guitar Player, February 1988.
High Fidelity, October 1988.
Nation, May 8, 1989.
Newsweek, August 8, 1977.
New Yorker, April 4, 1977.
Pulse!, holiday issue 1993; December 1993; March 1994.

—Marjorie Burgess

Brooks & Dunn

Country duo

Fine dance musicians and expert wordsmiths as well, Brooks & Dunn meld the guitar-driven kick of early 1990s country dance music with the elegance of lyric that has long been country music's backbone. The duo's first single release, 1991's "Brand New Man," shot to the top of the charts, and Brooks & Dunn have proved to be consistent hitmakers with almost every subsequent release. In a typical country-oriented nightclub in 1993 and 1994, little time could pass before the band or disc jockey selected one of Brooks & Dunn's compositions.

Brooks & Dunn's success is testimony to how important collaboration can be in propelling popular musical artists to prominence. Before the two joined forces in 1990, Kix Brooks was a minor Nashville songwriter a few paychecks away from poverty, and Ronnie Dunn was a Tulsa-area dance band leader of purely regional repute. It was their teamwork that forged the tricks learned over long years of apprenticeship into the catchy, irresistible sound that took Brooks & Dunn to the top. Bob Guerra, an influential Los Angeles-area country radio executive, came closer than most music critics when he was asked by a *Los Angeles Times* writer to account for Brooks & Dunn's success. "It's their songs," he answered. "It's as simple as that. They're just good songwriters, writing the kind of songs people like to hear."

Raised in Country Music's Heartland

Both Brooks (who acquired the nickname "Kix" as an energetic unborn baby) and Dunn were born into the Texas-Louisiana oil industry setting that in the early 1940s gave birth to honky-tonk dance music itself. Leon Eric Brooks was born in Shreveport, Louisiana, in 1955; he grew up in a house on the same block as the boyhood home of country legend Johnny Horton. Ronnie Gene Dunn was born in the central Texas town of Coleman and grew up in Eldorado, Arkansas, just north of Shreveport. Both men were entertaining beer-hall audiences before they reached the age of 20. Brooks financed studies at Louisiana Tech University with his musical activities; the venues he played were so rowdy, he told a *People* magazine interviewer, that he sometimes had to quiet the crowd by shooting blanks from a pistol on stage.

Dunn, meanwhile, was ejected from a small Christian college for the sin of playing bass in a bar band on weekends. He moved to Tulsa, Oklahoma, and there joined forces with a group of musicians that had once backed rock music giant Eric Clapton (and that also included Garth Brooks's sister Betsy on bass). The band enjoyed some local success, but Dunn was still

> **For the Record . . .**
>
> **L**eon Eric "Kix" Brooks (born May 12, 1955, in Shreveport, LA; married; wife's name, Barbara; children: Molly, Eric). **Ronnie Dunn** (born June 1, 1953, in Coleman, TX; married; wife's name, Janine; children [from a previous marriage]: Whitney, Jesse). *Education:* Brooks graduated from Louisiana Tech University.
>
> Country vocal duo; partnership suggested by Arista executive Tim DuBois; formed in Nashville and signed to Arista Records, 1990; recorded *Brand New Man,* 1991, and *Hard Workin' Man,* 1993; six Number One country singles, 1991-94.
>
> **Selected awards:** Top vocal duet, Academy of Country Music, 1991 and 1992; album of the year, Academy of Country Music, 1992; single of the year, Academy of Country Music, 1992, for "Boot Scootin' Boogie"; vocal duo of the year, Country Music Association, 1992 and 1993; Grammy Award, best country vocal duo or group, 1993; triple-platinum record for *Brand New Man,* 1994.
>
> **Addresses:** *Management*—Robert R. Titley & Associates, 706 18th Avenue South, Nashville, TN 37203. *Record company*—Arista Records, 1 Music Circle North, Nashville, TN 37203. *Fan Club*—Brooks & Dunn Fan Club, P.O. Box 120669, Nashville, TN 37202.

forced to take a series of day jobs, including a stint as a liquor-store clerk, to support his wife and two children.

Brooks eventually moved to Nashville and began working his way up in the city's hierarchy of songwriters. Though he wrote hit tunes for Highway 101 and the Nitty Gritty Dirt Band, among others, and eventually attained the position of staff songwriter with the giant Sony/Tree publishing concern, he too faced lean years. "I worked Manpower jobs," he recalled in *Country America* magazine. "I'd go downtown with forty or fifty other guys and line up for work. It really opened my eyes to America, that's for sure."

Dunn's fortunes turned upward in 1989 with a surprise first-place finish in the Marlboro National Talent Search contest—he didn't even know that one of his bandmates had submitted his tape for consideration. He moved to Nashville in 1990 when Arista Records executive Tim DuBois selected his composition "Boot Scootin' Boogie" for inclusion on a work by the western swing band Asleep at the Wheel. Brooks and Dunn were aiming toward individual stardom at this point, but a 1990 solo release from Brooks was a commercial failure. The two performers reacted coolly when DuBois, impressed by the strength of a group of songs they had composed together at his behest, suggested that they join together as performers too. "They both wanted solo careers very badly," DuBois recalled in an interview with *USA Today*'s David Zimmerman. "I think there was that element of letting go of that dream." But let go they did. Brooks & Dunn's *Brand New Man* album was released in August of 1991.

Teamwork Quickly Led to Stardom

Among the songs Brooks and Dunn wrote together were "Brand New Man" and "My Next Broken Heart," which became the duo's first two single releases late in 1991. Both rose to Number One on *Billboard* magazine's country singles chart, as did the next Brooks & Dunn release, a reflective barroom lament called "Neon Moon." The duo's ascent to stardom was complete when the fourth single from *Brand New Man,* a bass-heavy, eminently danceable version of "Boot Scootin' Boogie," also climbed to the top spot. The recording crossed over to non-country dance clubs, and this resulted in the release of a dance remix of the song. Although they initially resisted the remix idea, Brooks & Dunn were responsible for inaugurating the genre of the country dance mix, or "club mix," which attained considerable popularity in the following years.

Sales of the *Brand New Man* album mounted steadily, eventually reaching a total of more than three million copies. As Brooks & Dunn worked toward the release of their second album in early 1993, they were reluctant to tamper with a successful formula. "We thought it was kind of funny that a lot of the critics of the second album seemed to be real surprised that we continued with the same kind of music," Brooks told a *Music City News* writer.

Critical reviews of Brooks & Dunn's music are mixed, despite the duo's success; some critics take them to task for what is seen as a lack of seriousness in their music. "Taken one at a time on country radio, these songs make for satisfying morsels. But when they're over, you may want to devour something a little meatier," wrote David Browne in *Entertainment Weekly*. But the public vindicated the pair's decision to style the *Hard Workin' Man* album after its predecessor. The assortment of up-tempo country dance-party songs was approaching double-platinum status in mid-1994. The "Hard Workin' Man" single, driven by Dunn's intense lead vocals, was a sort of rock updating of

Merle Haggard's 1960s hit "Workin' Man Blues," and "Rock My World (Little Country Girl)" carried forward the club-mix technique.

High-Level Lyric Craft

Brooks & Dunn may have encouraged the impression that they rarely strive toward great depth in their lyrics. "We leave the profundity to Billy Ray Cyrus," Brooks once explained in *Newsweek,* with a characteristic modesty that often borders on self-deprecation. In fact, "Hard Workin' Man" is a good example of how skillfully Brooks & Dunn have mined long traditions of country songwriting and reconciled them with the high energy of contemporary country. Especially noteworthy in this regard is the fusion of religious and romantic imagery in "Brand New Man," all unfolding against a backdrop of electric guitars and charged vocal harmonies: "I saw the light, I've been baptized/By the fire in your touch and the flame in your eyes/I'm born to love again—I'm a brand new man."

Brooks & Dunn's long-term prospects seem to depend on whether they can maintain the consistently high level of songwriting that characterized their first two album releases. By mid-1994 the duo were a well-established concert draw, with Brooks's manic on-stage presence effectively complementing Dunn's more restrained demeanor. Their image was enhanced by the release of a line of western wear bearing their names; a shirt with a red and black flame pattern sold particularly well.

In the first few years of their career, Brooks & Dunn backed up their image with songwriting substance, and if they continue to do so, they seem well on their way to admission into the longstanding pantheon of great duet acts in country music.

Selected discography

Brand New Man (includes "Brand New Man," "My Next Broken Heart," "Neon Moon," and "Boot Scootin' Boogie"), Arista, 1991.
Hard Workin' Man (includes "Hard Workin' Man" and "Rock My World [Little Country Girl]"), Arista, 1993.

Sources

Billboard, May 22, 1993.
Country America, September 1993.
Country Music, May/June 1993; July/August 1993; May/June 1994.
Country Weekly, May 17, 1994.
Entertainment Weekly, September 18, 1992; February 26, 1993.
Los Angeles Times, January 3, 1993.
Music City News, August 1993.
Newsweek, October 19, 1992.
People, March 29, 1993.
Rolling Stone, May 13, 1993.
USA Today, March 10, 1993.

—James M. Manheim

Cheap Trick

Rock band

Contrary to the claim in a free comic book promoting Cheap Trick's 1990 album *Busted,* (the comic carried a warning label: "Another Cheap Promotional Trick!!"), the band did *not* form in Sweden during bassist Tom Petersson's stint in a sardine factory. The event actually took place in Rockford, Illinois, during the mid-1960s, when guitarist Rick Nielsen started a band originally called the Boyz. By the late 1960s, when Petersson joined the group, the name had been changed to Fuse—the name the band used on their unsuccessful debut album in 1969. Drumming for Fuse was Brad Carlson, who used the stage name Bun E. Carlos. The band moved to Philadelphia and adopted the name "Sick Man of Europe." Following a 1973 European tour, they returned to Illinois, added folk singer Robin Zander, and became known as Cheap Trick.

The foursome created a sound that was an appealing blend of hard-edged rock and hummable pop melodies; their music was often compared to that of the Beatles. Cheap Trick played clubs and bars throughout the Midwest, gathering a legion of loyal fans and

Photograph by Mark Seliger, © 1994 Warner Bros. Records/Reprise Records

> **For the Record...**
>
> Members include **Bun E. Carlos** (born Brad Carlson, June 12, 1951, in Rockford, IL), drums; **Rick Nielsen** (born December 22, 1946, in Rockford, IL), guitar; **Tom Petersson** (born May 9, 1950, in Rockford, IL), bass; and **Robin Zander** (born January 23, 1952, in Loves Park, IL; joined group, 1973), vocals.
>
> Group formed by Zander as the Boyz in Rockford, IL, mid-1960s; name changed to Fuse, late 1960s; released debut album (as Fuse), 1969; band relocated to Philadelphia, PA, and changed name to Sick Man of Europe, early 1970s; returned to Rockford, added vocalist Zander, and adopted name Cheap Trick, 1973; released self-titled debut album on Epic, 1977.
>
> **Addresses:** *Record company*—Warner Bros., 3300 Warner Boulevard, Burbank, CA 91505.

establishing themselves as one of the hardest-working and dedicated groups on the local circuit. At the urging of their manager, Ken Adamany (who'd been a member of rocker Steve Miller's high school group), the band began to focus on their stage show. Nielsen made use of his vast guitar collection, often switching between dozens of differently designed models during performances.

The band's members also displayed a diversity in style and demeanor. Zander and Petersson, *Stereo Review* noted, "looked like air-brushed teen dreams." Carlos's appearance suggested seedy, smoke-filled jazz halls, while Nielsen exuded an air of fun-loving geekiness. Cheap Trick went on the road in the early 1970s, opening for megastars Kiss, Santana, Boston, and the Kinks, among others, and averaged an astonishing 250 shows a year.

Despite a core of devoted fans, *Cheap Trick,* the band's first album, wasn't released until 1977. Critics praised its wit and mainstream, Beatle-esque melodies, and though it did well in Europe and especially well in Japan, audience response was slower in the United States, where the record sold only 150,000 copies. In Japan, where Western music was enjoying unprecedented popularity, *Cheap Trick* went gold.

The following year the band's second release, *In Color,* also achieved gold status in Japan, but U.S. sales were again disappointing. During their 1978 tour of Japan, Cheap Trick was besieged by mobs of screaming, adoring fans. The hysterical response became known as "Trickmania."

The band squeezed out another album in 1978, *Heaven Tonight,* which did somewhat better in the United States than their past albums, climbing to Number 48 on the U.S. charts and earning platinum status in Japan. In February of 1979 the group's crowning achievement, *Live at Budokan,* settled in for a year-long stay on the American charts, peaking at Number Four. The album's single, "I Want You to Want Me," also made it to the Top Ten. Later that year, when Cheap Trick's next release, *Dream Police,* soared to an impressive Number Six in the United States, the group took a break during which all of the band members, except Petersson, contributed to John Lennon's 1980 *Double Fantasy* sessions in New York.

Petersson left Cheap Trick in August of 1980. He and his wife formed a group called Dagmar and recorded a 1982 album that Epic refused to release. The company had used the same tactic with a 1981 Cheap Trick album, precipitating lawsuits. Replacing Petersson on bass was Pete Comita and, later, Jon Brant. Cheap Trick releases during the 1980s included *All Shook Up,* 1980, *One On One,* 1981, *Next Position Please,* 1983, and *Standing on the Edge,* 1985. Though the critics lauded the band's musical artistry, none of the albums came anywhere near the Top Ten.

During the late 1980s, many bands that had been popular in the 1970s were planning comeback albums. Cheap Trick took advantage of the revival and hired Don Grierson, the vice-president at Epic Records who had resuscitated the floundering popularity of Heart. He persuaded Cheap Trick to use outside writers for their material and hired a number of top tunesmiths, including Mike Chapman (who had worked with Pat Benatar) and Janna Allen (Daryl Hall's writing partner). A total of 13 writers received credit for the ten songs on the band's 1983 release, *Lap of Luxury.*

The album went platinum and produced a Number One hit, "The Flame"—a ballad that Nielsen so disliked on first hearing that he yanked it from the tape player and ground the cassette beneath his boot heel. One track cut from the album, "Don't Be Cruel," was the first Elvis Presley cover to hit the U.S. Top Ten since Presley's death. Some credit for the band's revival was attributed to Petersson, who had returned to the group in time to record the album. At the time Cheap Trick had been opening for Robert Plant, but with the overwhelming success of *Lap of Luxury,* they began a headline tour of their own.

Cheap Trick began a grueling schedule of concert tours that took them to all 50 states and to 22 countries. Their 1990 album, *Busted,* made it to Number 48 on the U.S. charts and the band's music found its way onto movie soundtracks including *Top Gun, Spring Break, Heavy Metal, The Roadie, Tequila Sunrise, Over the Top, Encino Man,* and *Gladiator.* Zander cut a solo album, *Robin Zander,* which featured "Surrender To Me," a duet with Heart's Ann Wilson. For this solo effort, *Spin* magazine noted that the singer had "dug through his collection of classic rock to appropriate a wide variety of styles" and went on to add that he'd made "a damn fine job of it." Zander rejoined Cheap Trick in time for the band's tour of Japan, their former stronghold, where they recorded *Live At Budokan II.*

In 1994, Cheap Trick released *Woke up With a Monster,* their first studio recording since 1990's *Busted.* The album contains 12 original songs and features Cheap Trick's distinctive blend of foot-tapping pop and searing rock. "In a way it's a return to the basic energy of our first albums," bassist Petersson explained in a Warner Bros. promotional release. "It's also the first one in a while where our own songwriting is front and center. This time around we wanted it to be all us."

Selected discography

Cheap Trick, Epic, 1977.
In Color, Epic, 1978.
Heaven Tonight, Epic, 1978.
Live at Budokan, Epic, 1979.
Dream Police, Epic, 1979.
All Shook Up, Epic, 1980.
Found All the Parts, 1980 (10-inch release).
One on One, Epic, 1981.
Next Position Please, Epic, 1983.
Standing on the Edge, Epic, 1985.
Lap of Luxury, Epic, 1988.
Busted, Epic, 1990.
Live at Budokan II, Epic, 1993.
Woke up With a Monster, Warner Bros., 1994.
The Doctor.

Robin Zander recorded self-titled solo album, Interscope, 1993.

Sources

Books

Pareles, Jon, and Patricia Romanowski, *The Rolling Stone Encyclopedia of Rock & Roll,* Rolling Stone Press/Summit Books, 1983.
Rees, Dafydd, and Luke Crampton, *Rock Movers & Shakers,* Billboard Books, 1991.
Salicrup, Jim, *Cheap Trick Busted,* Marvel Comics, 1990.

Periodicals

Billboard, December 18, 1993.
Boston Herald, February 2, 1989.
New York Tribune, August 4, 1988.
RIP, June 1994.
Spin, August 1993.
Stereo Review, August 1988.

—Joseph M. Reiner

The Cocteau Twins

Pop band

It's apparent that a band occupies an odd place in the terrain of pop music, even alternative rock, when reviewers can make claims such as Timothy White's remark in *Billboard* that cuts from Cocteau Twins 1993 release "actually boast whole sentences of accessible verse, plus springy tempo turns that could qualify as grooves." Reviewing the same album in Detroit's *Metro Times,* Ralph Valdez noted that lead singer "Liz Fraser's cryptically indistinct vocals have gradually become decipherable like an angel or an alien who, after floating to Earth, has finally begun to speak the language." After a decade making music whose sounds are so unconventional that they prompt these comments, Scotland-grown Cocteau Twins have not only "become decipherable," they are also being recognized as an influence behind the growing spate of musicians who conduct similar experiments in ethereal sound, such as Enya and Mouth Music.

The three original members of the band, Elizabeth Fraser, Robin Guthrie, and Will Heggie, share a background in stark contrast to the celestial musings of their music. Interviewed by White, Fraser and Guthrie described their birthplace of Grangemouth as a town whose main industries, oil refinery and textile production, offered its working-class citizens little escape from a life of dead-end labor. Guthrie referred to Grangemouth as "a great chemical-refining works that's not at all picturesque," adding that he had spent some youthful years working for British Petroleum. Fraser worked temporarily for a whiskey distillery. She stressed to White, "You have to understand how few the choices were. Most of the women worked where my mother did, in a sewing factory called Rackes. And most of the men worked for B.P. [British Petroleum], but my father was a tool grinder in a wood yard."

Music Provided Escape

A long tradition of folk music deeply ingrained in Scotch culture offered Grangemouth youth some of the only relief from their labor lives. Fraser described for White the significance of music in her home: "My mother had been a drummer in a pipe band, and my father played accordion. There were hundreds of British pop records at home—the Beatles, Petula Clark, Lulu—and I got shanghaied into singing hymns at Beancross Primary School when I was six. It was wonderful growing up with music in the house, because there was so much tension just outside the door, like our Protestant segregation from Catholics." Guthrie told White, "Our music has always been a reflection of our desperate desire to get as much distance from where we came from as possible."

> **For the Record . . .**
>
> Members include **Elizabeth Fraser** (born c. 1962 in Grangemouth, Scotland; children: [with Guthrie] Lucy Bell), vocals; **Robin Guthrie** (born c. 1960 in Grangemouth, Scotland) guitar; **Simon Raymonde** (children: Stanley), bass, keyboards, drums. Original band included **Will Heggie** on bass and keyboards.
>
> Group formed in Grangemouth, Scotland, 1979; embarked on tour, early 1980s; relocated to London and signed a recording contract with 4AD, 1981; released debut album *Garlands,* 1982; first U.S. release, *The Pink Opaque,* 1986; opened recording studio in London, 1989; left 4AD, 1992.
>
> **Addresses:** *Record company*—Capitol Records, 1750 North Vine St., Hollywood, CA 90028-5274.

Dissatisfied with their options, Guthrie and Heggie began putting their free time and energy into making music. Guthrie recollected the atmosphere of the late 1970s pop music scene, telling White, "It was a post-punk sort of time when Will and I bought our first drum machine." In search of a vocalist, Guthrie and Heggie met Fraser at a pub in 1979. Soon after, the three began writing and performing music together, finding most of their experience playing in Scotland pubs. At the time, Fraser and Guthrie also moved in together, having begun a romance that would prove to be long-lasting. With very little money coming in, the embryonic Cocteau Twins actually went on the road first just to make a living. As Guthrie explained to White, "Liz and I had to leave our apartment in Falkirk because we couldnt afford it, and we went on tour just to feed ourselves." Their struggling artist phase didn't last for too long, however, since their live performances and first album, *Garlands,* soon attracted what White called "international cult status."

Garlands Took Independent Charts

Fraser, Guthrie, and Heggie left Scotland for London in 1981, two demo tapes in hand. The first went to John Peel, an important London radio deejay, who arranged two radio recording sessions. The second, and more profitable, went into the hands of Simon Raymonde, who was only a shop assistant at 4AD at the time, but who nonetheless brought the tape to the attention of manager Ivo Watts-Russell. The band signed on with 4AD in 1981, and *Garlands* was released in the spring of 1982. Despite the expenses that were spared on its production, it quickly jumped to the Number Two spot on the U.K. independent charts.

Alec Foege, in his 1993 *Spin* review of *Four-Calender Café,* commented briefly on that beginning: "The Cocteaus signing to the now-influential 4AD label in 1982 set a distinct aesthetic for the label and sparked a cult following which interpreted the group's muddled ethe-realness as profound self-contemplation." Foege's dislike notwithstanding, the band was soon fending off offers from influential managers and major labels; they chose to reject all of these for the continued autonomy they would have with 4AD. As Valdez noted, they had quickly become "the darlings of the underground." They finished 1982 with a 12-inch release called *Lullabies,* consolidating their success with the "indies" charts. They started 1983 with a European tour, opening for the then well-established alternative music band, Orchestral Maneuvers in the Dark (OMD).

Maintained a Productive Pace

A series of successful releases followed, despite Heggie's departure in 1983. Fraser and Guthrie spent a year performing and recording as a duo, turning out a second album, *Head Over Heels,* in 1983. Their *Sunburst and Snowblind* 12-inch single took the Number One spot on the independent charts, setting the precedent for most of their subsequent releases. Simon Raymonde took over on bass and drums just in time for the recording of the 1984 single "Pearly-Dewdrops Drop," which brought Cocteau Twins their first break in the pop market, hitting the Top 30 on the mainstream charts. Valdez dubbed their 1984 album, *Treasure,* "their stylistic breakthrough." Like the work that preceded it, the album entered the mainstream Top 30 and grabbed the Number One position on independent charts.

Over the next few years the band maintained a pace of impressive productivity that kept them in the public eye and favor. They turned out three extended play releases in 1985, followed by two albums and a well-received single, "Loves Easy Tears," in 1986. *The Pink Opaque* marked their first U.S. release, available on CD only, and their British release for the year, *Victorialand,* took the Number Ten position on the charts. The success of *Victorialand* insured the success of their 1986 U.K. tour, which they played to capacity houses.

The Cocteau Twins' somewhat odd position in pop music was marked in many ways, not the least of which was the incompatibility of their music with the clubs and auditoriums usually used by pop bands; instead, as

Guthrie explained to *Spin* in 1991, "People are used to us playing places like the Royal Festival Hall and Sadlers Wells," both known in England as spaces for classical music performance. But the music also didn't hold to the conventions of classical, New Age, or easy listening music, as White's general description of their sound betrayed: "Most of the beautiful elegies in the group's repertory resist either identifiable time signatures or lyrical dissection, so ineffably fluid is the uninflected celeste of Fraser's singing voice."

Describing *Heaven or Las Vegas* in *Stereo Review,* Parke Puterbaugh had a similar response: "The songs of Cocteau Twins are so much more about sensation than sense that they do not easily yield to interpretation or comparison with familiar things." Writing for *Spin* in 1991, Frank Owen called it "rock more akin to geography than music, an otherworldly no-place outside of language and meaning." Most critics credited this particular quality of the music to Fraser, as Hannaham did when he remarked that she "sounds like she's inventing her own language as she goes along." Guthrie confirmed this in an interview with *Guitar Player*'s Steph Paynes, when he confessed that he also finds his partner's work mysterious: "I don't know what she's singing!... I've seen the lyrics written down, and they're brilliant—it's all English, you see—but she twists everything around, putting accents on different syllables than you would in normal speech. Once we were in Japan, and the whole audience thought Liz was singing in Japanese."

Had U.S. Breakthrough

For two years after the success of *Victorialand* and "Loves Easy Tears," the Cocteau Twins stepped back from the rapid production schedule that had produced those hits. They didn't reappear until 1988, when *Blue Bell Knoll* climbed to Number 15 on British charts and broke the Top 200 on U.S. charts, almost cracking the Top 100 as well. Their growing fan base in the United States paved the way for their first U.S. tour in 1990, after the release of *Heaven or Las Vegas,* an album that enjoyed a great deal of popularity in the United States as well as the United Kingdom. It simultaneously served as what Hannaham called their "U.S. breakthrough" and surfaced in the Top Ten on English charts.

The general American response to *Heaven* epitomized the kind of lyrical hyperbole Cocteau Twins music prompted from critics, although it was the first such indulgence in the U.S. press. Puterbaugh decided that "Cocteau Twins makes music that seems to emanate from the far edge of consciousness." He found the album "beautiful, flowing, and fragile, like a rainbow on the surface of a bubble." Paynes tried to pin it down in *Guitar Player:* "Youre assaulted by a barrage of beautiful, shimmering, swirling ... *stuff.* There are guitars there somewhere, but they're textural, oblivious, environmental.... Meanwhile, the rich, emotive voice of Liz Fraser flies merrily around the mix." Much of the praise was reserved specifically for Fraser's voice, as in the *People* review, which claimed that she "injects a feeling of ecstasy into even slow, quiet songs. She swoops with amazing ease from angelic soprano notes down to a rich alto." Puterbaugh waxed poetic as well: "No less an instrument ... is the sensually sibilant voice of Elizabeth Fraser, which is as delicate as fine crystal."

> "Our music has always been a reflection of our desperate desire to get as much distance from where we came from as possible."
> —Robin Guthrie

Even as the band continued to take more time between releases, they also saw considerable professional and personal growth in the early 1990s. After an official break with 4AD in 1992, they began recording in their own September Studio and releasing under the auspices of Capitol Records. Guthrie tackled the problems he encountered writing his music, confessing to White that he has depended on alcohol and other drugs to carry him through the task of composition; he claimed that "I've cleaned myself up, but creating these things can hurt so much." Guthrie and Fraser began their family in 1989, with the birth of daughter Lucy Bell; Raymonde and his wife had their first child, Stanley, in 1991, and were expecting their second in September of 1993.

Four-Calender Café, the band's 1993 release, received mixed reviews, prompted by the turn toward a slightly more traditional use of music and lyric; some found the accessibility refreshing, while others expressed disappointment. Valdez captured the second response, saying that "it would have been nice if by this ... they had gotten progressively stranger rather than more normal sounding and familiar." He feared that, instead, "they seemed to be allowing themselves to assimilate into the tireless mega-machine that is pop music." James Hannaham, on the other hand, argued that they "drop some of their willful obscurity without deserting their singular path." He declared, "Rather than acknowledge their legions of imitators or accommodate the pop-song format, Cocteau Twins have become much more accessible simply by refining their time-tested methods."

Selected discography

Garlands, 4AD, 1982.
Lullabies (EP), 4AD, 1982.
Head Over Heels, 4AD, 1983.
Sunburst and Snowblind (EP), 4AD, 1983.
Aikea Guinea (EP), 4AD, 1985.
Tiny Dynamine (EP), 4AD, 1985.
Echoes in a Shallow Bay (EP), 4AD, 1985.
The Pink Opaque, 1986.
Victorialand, 4AD, 1986.
Blue Bell Knoll, 4AD, Capitol, 1988.
Heaven or Las Vegas, Capitol, 1990.
Four-Calender Café, Capitol, 1993.

Sources

Books

Rees, Dafydd, and Luke Crampton, *Rock Movers & Shakers*, Billboard Books, 1991.

Periodicals

Billboard, September 11, 1993.
Details, November 1993.
Guitar Player, February 1991; January 1994.
Metro Times (Detroit), September 15, 1993.
People, February 11, 1991.
Request, December 1993.
Rolling Stone, January 10, 1991; March 10, 1994; April 21, 1994.
Spin, March 1991; December 1993.
Stereo Review, January 1991.
Strobe, January/February 1994.
Variety, November 19, 1990.

Additional information for this profile was obtained from Capitol Records.

—*Ondine Le Blanc*

Elvis Costello

Singer, songwriter

"Since his arrival on the postpunk scene 17 years ago," wrote *Time* magazine critic Guy Garcia in 1994, "Elvis Costello has shown himself to be one of the most prolific and protean songwriters of his generation." Combining piercing, literate lyrics and an uncompromising attitude with the melodicism and stylistic breadth of classic pop groups like the Beatles, Costello forged a much-imitated style that led the way for a great deal of the "alternative" music that followed.

With his band the Attractions, Costello led the "New-Wave" pack into the early 1980s, producing a catalogue of songs to rival almost any other in popular music. His own artistic restlessness, however, would never permit him to settle in one mode for long; reasoning that the Attractions limited his vision, he left the group abruptly in the middle of the decade. He then experimented with country music, soul and avant-garde textures; wrote film scores; produced and wrote for other acts; and even recorded an album with a string quartet before he reunited with the Attractions for 1994's *Brutal Youth*. And despite the passage of time, Costello's articulate fury burned just as brightly. "Costello's lyrics have always been stuffed with cleverness, frequently overstuffed," opined Jeffrey Stock of *Pulse!* "But his genius for melody, evident even in his fast and furious numbers, is what truly sets him apart. Besides Paul McCartney, there is quite simply no one that comes close."

Name Poked Fun at Stardom

Costello wasn't born an Elvis. Declan Patrick McManus was born in the mid-1950s in London, England; his father, Ross McManus, worked as a jazz bandleader. Young Declan first heard pop music on the radio and on demonstration records his father received, falling in love with rock and soul at an early age. "I had quite a pleasant childhood, actually," he recalled in *Pulse!* Ross left his wife and children, however, and Declan moved to Liverpool with his mother before finishing school. Immediately upon graduating, he went in search of a job and ended up working with computers by day and playing his own songs in local clubs at night. Though McManus later disparaged his early work for its derivative qualities—he was strongly influenced by eclectic American songwriters like John Prine and Lowell George, as well as the great tunesmiths of the jazz era—his earliest demo recordings, from 1974 to 1975, show signs of the lyrical sophistication and melodic invention that brought him acclaim. The recordings surfaced on bootlegs years later before being officially released on the 1993 Rykodisc boxed set *2 1/2 Years*.

Photograph by Amelia Stein, © 1994 Warner Bros. Records

For the Record...

Born Declan Patrick McManus, August 25, 1955, in London, England; son of Ross McManus (a bandleader) and Mary (Costello) McManus; married first wife, Mary, 1974 (divorced, c. 1985); married Caitlin O'Riordan (musician and actress), 1986; children: (first marriage) one son.

Worked as computer operator, Elizabeth Arden, London, early 1970s; performed on English club scene, both solo and with group Flip City, early 1970s; signed to Stiff Records, 1976; released debut album *My Aim Is True* (released in United States on Columbia), 1977; performed with group the Attractions, 1977-86, and intermittently thereafter; produced other artists, 1979—; appeared on various benefit albums and as guest artist on others' recordings, 1979—; cameo role in film *No Surrender,* 1986; wrote score for film *The Courier,* 1988; signed with Warner Bros. and released album *Spike,* 1989.

Awards: Album of the year, *Rolling Stone* critics' poll, 1977, for *My Aim Is True;* songwriter of the year, *Rolling Stone* critics' poll, 1989; best male video, MTV video awards, 1989, for *Veronica.*

Addresses: *Home*—London, England, and Dublin, Ireland. *Record company*—Warner Bros., 3300 Warner Blvd., Burbank, CA 91505; 75 Rockefeller Plaza, New York, NY 10019.

After suffering repeated rejections, McManus brought his tape to Stiff Records, one of England's stalwart supporters of the burgeoning underground scene. It was there that he met songwriter-producer Nick Lowe, who would become a steadfast friend and collaborator; he also met Jake Riviera, who became his manager and gave him his professional name: the "Elvis" poked fun at rock star pretensions, while Costello was the maiden name of the young performer's mother. Though McManus felt skeptical at first, he followed Riviera's suggestion; over time the name would strike many listeners as a perfect fit for his musical synthesis.

Early Efforts Showed Deadly "Aim"

The newly-christened Elvis Costello went into the studio with American bar-band survivors Clover and—with two thousand English pounds and in twenty-four hours of recording time—completed an album called *My Aim Is True.* The title came from a line in the anguished ballad "Alison," which would become one of Costello's most popular songs. The album also contains the edgy, reggae-inflected rock of "Watching the Detectives," buoyant, sardonic pop songs like "(The Angels Wanna Wear My) Red Shoes," and "Mystery Dance," a concise rockabilly lament about sexual confusion.

The album cover of *My Aim Is True* sports a photograph that would cement Costello in rock iconography: with spiky hair, horn-rimmed glasses, suit, and gawky stance, he represented a brazen challenge to the ultrasmooth rock superstars of the day. Indeed his "faux nerd" looks, as a *Time* writer would later call them, gave rise to the witticism—credited to various sources, including rock writer Dave Marsh—that Costello was popular with the critics because he looked like one of them. Released in America on Columbia Records, the album and its creator were hailed on both sides of the Atlantic as major arrivals. *My Aim Is True* was named album of the year in a *Rolling Stone* critics' poll.

Costello then proceeded to assemble the Attractions, which consisted of keyboardist Steve Nieve, bassist Bruce Thomas, and drummer Pete Thomas (no relation); the group joined the "Stiffs Live" tour with labelmates Ian Dury, Wreckless Eric, and others. The group's barnstorming tour of the United States included a stop at the television program *Saturday Night Live,* where Costello committed his first Stateside outrage: at the last minute, over the frenzied objections of the staff, he substituted his new song "Radio, Radio"—a scabrous broadside at mainstream programmers—for the scheduled "Less Than Zero."

Costello's musical output with the Attractions during this period was astoundingly prolific. The group went into the studio in late 1977 and the following year released *This Year's Model,* a collection of ferocious, streamlined songs that departed from the eclecticism and intermittent whimsy of Costello's debut. The American edition includes "Radio, Radio," not to mention virulent rockers like "Lipstick Vogue" and "Pump It Up."

Already certain signature themes were emerging in his songs: sexual misadventures, power struggles in interpersonal relationships, and the tyranny of fashion. And often these conflicts occurred in the vexed realm of speech: "little triggers," as he sang in the song of the same name, "that you pull with your tongue." In the words of *Creem* writer Richard Gehr, Costello's "earliest records seemed like nothing more than knotty, nerve-jangled expulsions on the mouth and the damage it can do."

"Pop Expressionism" and Road Fatigue

Eager to avoid the pitfalls of repeating a formula, Costello and the Attractions recorded their next album in 1978; the singer told the compilers of the Rykodisc boxed set that "the sessions took what we regarded as a very extravagant six weeks." Originally titled *Emotional Fascism,* the album signalled the beginning of what a *Rolling Stone* writer would later call his "pop expressionism." Released as *Armed Forces,* it demonstrated Costello's increasingly ambitious songwriting approach and his band's seemingly unlimited dexterity. The album begins with the symphonic "Accidents Will Happen," which Costello aficionados generally number among his best songs, and concludes—in the United States version—with Lowe's sincere, upbeat "(What's So Funny 'Bout) Peace, Love and Understanding." In between fall a panoply of meditations on fascism both emotional and political, from "Green Shirt" and "Oliver's Army" to the menacing "Goon Squad" and the deceptively bouncy "Two Little Hitlers." Unfortunately, while on tour in the United States in 1979, Costello gained a reputation as something of a fascist himself, thanks to racist comments he made in an Ohio bar brawl with American rockers Stephen Stills and Bonnie Bramlett. Though he regretted his words and said so publicly on numerous occasions, the fallout of this incident lasted for many years.

It was a time of excess: alcohol and drugs fueled the band's touring and, to some degree, Costello's writing. But when the group hit a wall trying to find a sound for the next album, it was downing a few beers in a local pub that gave them their approach. Thus was born the sound of 1980's *Get Happy!!,* which bore the stylistic imprint of American soul groups like Stax Records house band Booker T. and the MGs. The good-time feel of the arrangements provided a unique tension with Costello's typically pun-riddled, multi-layered, and conflict-filled lyrics. *Get Happy!!* features the galloping "Love for Tender," the melancholy, Beatlesque "New Amsterdam," and a cover version of "I Can't Stand Up for Falling Down"—originally recorded by Stax soul legends Sam and Dave—which was a fair-sized hit in England.

Increasingly Ambitious Songwriting

Next came *Trust,* which displayed an even greater compositional reach: "Clubland" is a moody, noirish piece with an R&B-influenced refrain, while the stark piano ballad "Shot With His Own Gun" shows the influence of modern composers like Kurt Weill. By this time Costello's songwriting had captured the fancy of his more commercially successful peers, including singer Linda Ronstadt, who recorded several of his songs; Costello disparaged Ronstadt's versions, but they indicated that the musical mainstream now saw him as a major songwriter. He, in turn, had begun to refine his talents as producer, working with the English ska band the Specials, among others. He also recorded an album of country standards, *Almost Blue.*

Costello's next album, *Imperial Bedroom,* was a hit with critics; many hailed it as his first masterpiece. Suggesting the sonic grandeur of pop's greatest moments, its best songs have been compared to the Beatles' and Beach Boys' finest work. 1983's *Punch the Clock,* meanwhile, opted for a more radio-friendly sound at the expense of its predecessor's baroque explorations; it yielded the small-scale hit "Everyday I Write the Book," but also included one of Costello's most highly regarded compositions, the elegiac "Shipbuilding," which he co-wrote with Clive Langer and which features a trumpet solo by jazz idol Chet Baker. With their 1984 album *Goodbye Cruel World,* however, despite the airplay granted the single "The Only Flame in Town"—a duet with blue-eyed soul star Daryl Hall—Costello and the Attractions appeared to be running out of steam.

End of Road for Attractions

Costello worked with the Attractions for part of his next album, *King of America,* the first recording that identified him as Declan McManus (he added an imaginary second middle name, "Aloysius," on the sleeve) and his musical enterprise as "The Costello Show." Mixing roots-based forms like country, rockabilly and folk and including numerous guest artists, the album suggested a new direction for Costello. His personal life took a new direction as well: having left a previous marriage of some thirteen years, he married Cait O'Riordan, former bassist for the band the Pogues, with whom Costello had worked as producer. The two have periodically collaborated as songwriters.

After a return to garage-pop for the album *Blood and Chocolate,* Costello peremptorily left the Attractions and began to work as a solo artist. "To be honest, I didn't handle the situation with much grace," he confessed years later in an *Entertainment Weekly* interview. "I just sort of announced that I was going, and it wasn't negotiable. That must have been pretty hurtful after what we'd put in. I guess I got a little arrogant, you know, as I got more confident." This confidence was no doubt bolstered by the fact that he was invited to collaborate with Paul McCartney, first on a B-side to a single and then on some songs for the former Beatle's album *Flowers in the Dirt.* The two also co-wrote some songs that ended up on the first Costello solo album,

Spike, which was also his first release on his new label, Warner Bros. Among these is the single "Veronica," which enjoyed some rotation on MTV; the album also includes Costello's cabaret-like "God's Comic." *Spike* features guest appearances by Roger McGuinn of the seminal folk-rock band the Byrds, Chrissie Hynde of the Pretenders, and McCartney himself. In the *Rolling Stone* Critics' Awards for 1989, Costello was voted best songwriter.

> "Rock & Roll is a ludicrous response to most things. Most of what goes on is pretty puny, including what I do myself. I fall very short of really great work. Nobody's that smart."

By the time of his next album, 1991's *Mighty Like a Rose,* Costello was adamant that there would be no reunion with his old band. "The divorce is final," he maintained in *Creem.* "Costello and the Attractions are history." As though to embody his break from the past, he sported a new look: long hair, full beard and wire-rim glasses. *Mighty* includes the McCartney co-composition "So Like Candy"; a *Rolling Stone* reviewer, despite some reservations, called the album "Costello's most ambitious and adventurous music in ages." Bruce Thomas wrote a dishy book about the Attractions' touring days that never mentioned Costello by name and was generally trashed by critics. "The boring member of the band always writes the book," Costello himself scoffed in *Creem.*

Costello appeared on a number of anthologies and tribute albums; he also elected to take a rare—and, to some, commercially misguided—step: recording an album of songs with a string quartet. Based on the letters written over the centuries to the heroine of Shakespeare's *Romeo and Juliet,* the suite of songs were the result of mutual admiration between Costello and the Brodsky Quartet. The resulting album was *The Juliet Letters.* "We wanted to explore the under-used combination of voice and string quartet, but were anxious to avoid that junkyard named 'crossover,'" Costello explained in a Warner Bros. publicity release. "This is no more my stab at 'classical music' than it is the Brodsky Quartet's first rock and roll album." Reviews were mixed; *Request* magazine's write-up was typical in its assertion that the album was "neither the transcendent triumph one might have hoped for, nor the embarrassing fiasco one might have feared."

Costello's next project resulted after he was contacted by former Transvision Vamp singer Wendy James about writing a song for her solo album; he eventually decided to write an entire album's worth. Working alone and with O'Riordan, he composed all the songs in a weekend. It was while recording the song demos for her—with Thomas on drums—at Pathway, the tiny London studio where he'd recorded some of his earliest work, that Costello rediscovered the unadorned, scruffy pop sound he'd long since abandoned. James's album fared poorly, but the project sowed the seeds for the long-forestalled reunion with the Attractions.

Costello contacted Lowe and Nieve, as well as producer Mitchell Froom, and brought in Pete Thomas in play drums. Soon, through Lowe, he met with Bruce Thomas; the two hadn't spoken in several years, but Bruce played bass on about half the album. Lowe and Costello played bass in the other songs, and soon the vaunted return of the Attractions—and the messy sonic grandeur of the early days—was a reality. The recording, which Costello first wanted to call *Idiophone,* was released in 1994 as *Brutal Youth.* "I deliberately made the music crude," reads a quote from Costello in a Warner Bros. press release. "I know it's going to offend some people, while others will dig it because it's very throwaway. Other people are going to be slightly ill at ease with it because it isn't crafted or something. But it's a sort of template of how to play like this."

Accused of "Raiding His Own Catalogue"

He was right; a *Rolling Stone* writer accused Costello of "raiding his own catalogue," particularly the 1979 to 1981 material, "reprising both that period's trademarks and shortcomings," and tending toward overly busy arrangements. A *Spin* reviewer called the album's songs "15 fresh slices of warmed-over genius," and an *Entertainment Weekly* writer found the latest tunes "frustrating, metaphor-ridden jigsaw puzzles."

Chris Willman of the *Los Angeles Times,* however, declared, "You don't have to have underrated Costello's recent work to agree this is his finest album since his last with the Attractions," and Timothy White called the recording a "magnificent return to form" in his *Billboard* article. Costello obviously had little concern about reviews. "I got accused by the *New York Times* of not having a coherent world view," he told a *Pulse!* interviewer. "I thought, 'What do you mean, like [Adolf] Hitler? Or [former U.S. President] George Bush?'"

And just as clearly, Costello would continue to follow his own muse, despite the desires and expectations of his listeners. "I find it amazing that I've managed to be making records for 17 years!" he exclaimed to *Billboard*'s White. He has continued to oppose the hype of the pop world; as he insisted in *Creem,* "Rock & Roll is a ludicrous response to most things. Most of what goes on is pretty puny, including what I do myself. I fall very short of really great work. Nobody's that smart." Yet the trajectory of his own development as an artist caused him to declare—in an *Option* magazine dialogue with fellow musical maverick Tom Waits—"I don't believe anybody hasn't got a voice," but that "they haven't found it yet. I believe everybody can write songs in the same way."

Selected discography

On Columbia

My Aim Is True (includes "Alison," "Watching the Detectives," "Red Shoes," "Mystery Dance," and "Less Than Zero"), 1977.
This Year's Model (includes "Radio Radio," "Lipstick Vogue," "Pump it Up," and "Little Triggers"), 1978.
Armed Forces (includes "Accidents Will Happen," "[What's So Funny 'Bout] Peace, Love and Understanding," "Green Shirt," "Oliver's Army," "Goon Squad," and "Two Little Hitlers"), 1978.
Get Happy!! (includes "Love for Tender," "New Amsterdam," "Man Called Uncle," and "I Can't Stand Up for Falling Down"), 1980.
Taking Liberties, 1980.
Trust (includes "Clubland" and "Shot With His Own Gun"), 1981.
Almost Blue, 1981.
Imperial Bedroom, 1982.
Punch the Clock (includes "Everyday I Write the Book" and "Shipbuilding"), 1983.
Goodbye Cruel World (includes "The Only Flame in Town"), 1984.
The Best of Elvis Costello and the Attractions, 1985.
King of America, 1986.
Blood and Chocolate, 1986.
Girls, Girls, Girls (compilation), 1989.

On Warner Bros.

Spike (includes "Veronica" and "God's Comic"), 1988.
Mighty Like a Rose (includes "So Like Candy"), 1991.
The Juliet Letters, 1993.
Brutal Youth, 1994.

On various labels

Out of Our Idiot (B-sides and unreleased material), Demon, 1987.
The Courier (film score), Virgin, 1988.
2½ Years (four CD boxed set comprising remastered versions of first three albums, unreleased and import material, and concert disc *Live at El Mocambo*), Rykodisc, 1993.

With other artists

Various, *Live Stiffs,* Stiff, 1978.
Various, *Concert for the People of Kampuchea,* Columbia, 1980.
The Coward Brothers (pseudonymous recording with T-Bone Burnett), "The People's Limousine," Imp, 1985.
John Hiatt, *Warming up to the Ice Age* (appears on "Living a Little, Laughing a Little"), Geffen, 1985.
Various, *Deadicated* (appears on "Ship of Fools"), Arista, 1991.
Various, *Weird Nightmare: Meditations on Mingus* (appears on "Weird Nightmare"), Columbia, 1992.
Rob Wasserman, *Trios* (appears on "Put Your Big Toe in the Milk of Human Kindness"), MCA, 1994.

As songwriter

'Til Tuesday, *Everything's Different Now* (co-wrote "The Other End [of the Telescope]" with Aimee Mann), 1988.
Ruben Blades, *Nothing But the Truth,* Elektra, 1988.
Paul McCartney, "Back On My Feet" (co-wrote with McCartney), Columbia, 1988.
McCartney, *Flowers in the Dirt* (co-wrote "My Brave Face," "You Want Her Too," "Don't Be Careless Love" and "That Day Is Done"), Columbia, 1989.
Wendy James, *Now Ain't the Time for Your Tears,* Geffen, 1993.

As producer

The Specials, *The Specials,* 1979.
Squeeze, *East Side Story,* 1981.
The Special AKA, "Free Nelson Mandela," 1981.
The Pogues, *Rum, Sodomy and the Lash,* 1985.

Sources

Books

Contemporary Musicians, Volume 2, Gale, 1989.
Costello, Elvis, *A Singing Dictionary* (lyrics and sheet music), Plangent Visions, 1980.
Costello, *Everyday I Write the Song (Grumbling Appendix to the Singing Dictionary)* (lyrics and sheet music), Plangent Visions, 1983.
Gouldstone, David, *Elvis Costello: God's Comic,* St. Martin's, 1989.
Rees, Dafydd, and Luke Crampton, *Rock Movers & Shakers,* Billboard, 1991.

Stambler, Irwin, *Encyclopedia of Pop, Rock & Soul,* St. Martin's, 1989.

Periodicals

Billboard, February 5, 1994; March 12, 1994.
Creem, June 1991.
Details, April 1993.
Entertainment Weekly, March 11, 1994; March 18, 1994.
Los Angeles Times, March 6, 1994; April 15, 1994.
Musician, May 1990; March 1991.
Option, July 1989.
Pulse!, May 1993; April 1994.
Raygun, April 1994.
Request, March 1993.
Rolling Stone, May 16, 1991; March 24, 1994.
Spin, April 1994.
Time, April 11, 1994.
Village Voice, April 5, 1994.

Additional information for this profile was obtained from Warner Bros. publicity materials, 1991-94, and from the liner notes to the 1993 Rykodisc boxed set *2 1/2 Years.*

—*Simon Glickman*

Cracker

Rock band

Photograph by Dennis Keeley, courtesy of Virgin Records

With a few simple, twisted lines like "Here comes ol' Kerosene Hat / With his earflaps waxed / A'courtin' his girl," Cracker frontman David Lowery can conjure up more images in one song than many of rock's current young songwriters can paint on entire albums. The laid-back alternative band reaped much success after it arose in 1992 from the ashes of college radio favorite Camper Van Beethoven. In that time, Cracker released its self-titled debut on Virgin Records and the smash follow-up *Kerosene Hat* a year later and has moved ploddingly but steadily through the alternative rock consciousness teetering on the mainstream.

But Lowery's bands have always defied labels as well as convention. He calls Cracker "weirder than alternative" and fails to see how a band like Cracker, which can sandwich a straight-ahead country ballad in between a couple of semi-thrash numbers and look good while doing it, can be lumped in with alternative bands ranging from Afghan Whigs to XTC. Cracker has used the alternative outlet as a springboard to methodically achieve mainstream success, with *Kerosene Hat* going platinum in early 1994. There are those who have called his former group, Camper Van Beethoven, the prototypical alternative band; for Lowery, the term is quite nebulous and ultimately meaningless. "I remember first seeing that word applied to us," he told *Rolling Stone*. "The nearest I could figure is that we seemed like a punk band, but we were playing pop music, so they made up this word *alternative* for those of us who do that."

Earlier Band a College Rock Fave

It's that kind of small-town California straight talk that infuses Lowery's music with refreshing observational wit and endears it to fans both white and blue collar, both alterna-hip and backwoods wise. Lowery was born in Texas, the son of a U.S. enlisted man and his English postwar bride. He was raised in Europe, but ended up spending his formative teenage years in Redlands, California. He began his musical journey like many others—by making experimental guitar noises as a teenager. Lowery went to college in Santa Cruz, where he formed Camper Van Beethoven and recorded their music on his own label, Pitch-a-Tent. His bandmates included drummer Chris Pederson, violinist Jonathan Segel, bassist Victor Krummenacher and guitarist Greg Lisher.

The Campers followed the classic route to alternative stardom: putting out their own independent tapes, gaining a cult underground following, and riding the mid-1980s college radio explosion. They followed on the heels of contemporaries R.E.M., 10,000 Maniacs,

> **For the Record...**
>
> Members include guitarist **David Lowery** (formerly of Camper Van Beethoven), guitar; **Johnny Hickman** (formerly of the Unforgiven), lead guitar; **David Lovering** (formerly of the Pixies), drums; and **Bruce Hughes** (formerly of Poi Dog Pondering), bass.
>
> Group formed in 1992; self-titled debut album released by Virgin, 1992.
>
> **Awards:** Album *Kerosene Hat* went platinum, 1994.
>
> **Addresses:** *Record company*—Virgin Records America, 338 North Foothill Rd., Beverly Hills, CA 90210.

Hüsker Dü, and the Replacements, winning scores of fans with their eclectically quirky blend of everything from European folk to ska to hardcore punk to reggae. "Take the Skinheads Bowling," from 1985's *Telephone Free Landslide Victory*, became a college radio staple. Though the group sold over 100,000 copies of their first three indie records, and moved on to record two major-label albums on Virgin, it was the Campers' unpredictable live shows that made the music world stand up and take notice.

Camper Van Beethoven disintegrated on tour in 1989 and Lowery was left to his own devices. He moved to Virginia and eventually contacted an old California jam partner, Johnny Hickman, who had played in several bluegrass and country bands and had a disillusioning stint in the pop music business with a band called the Unforgiven. Having turned down offers to join the Campers because of previous commitments, Hickman was now ready to collaborate with his old Redlands pal Lowery. The two holed up in a Richmond apartment and turned out a 20-song demo that interested Virgin Records.

"Crackpot Humor and Lowbrow Wisdom"

The two formed Cracker and set out on tour with an album that was more straight than Camper's music, but still laced with "crackpot humor and lowbrow wisdom," according to *Rolling Stone*. The album generated hits like "Teen Angst (What the World Needs Now)" and "Happy Birthday to Me." It also kept the alternative label affixed to Lowery's work. "Johnny and I ... feel a little more crude, a little more crass, a little more redneck ... than our alternative brethren," Lowery told *Rolling Stone*. "I was sort of the 'cracker' of Camper Van Beethoven. That's where the name Cracker came from. It was a way of expressing how I feel in alternative land. I ain't got the right credentials. I like that."

Cracker wasted no time producing the follow-up. *Kerosene Hat* was recorded in five weeks on a deserted movie soundstage in Pioneertown, a tiny hamlet in the California high desert 150 miles east of Los Angeles. It bowed in August 1993 and built momentum throughout the year with grass-roots support and word-of-mouth. It was the album that wouldn't go away, forcing radio and MTV to eventually cave in and allow it some airtime, which gave it enough second wind to propel it to platinum. Although the slow process was a sharp contrast to the sudden success faced by Cracker's 1993 to 1994 tourmates, Counting Crows, the band was undaunted. "I like the way our career is going," Hickman told *Rolling Stone*. "It's not going through the roof; it's sneaking through the kitchen."

Creative Zaniness Continued

Kerosene Hat mined the same vein as Cracker's debut, though it was perhaps a little more tightly produced. The first single, the swirling "Low," started its climb up the charts once MTV began regularly airing the video clip, a black-and-white film noir piece that featured Lowery climbing in a boxing ring and sparring with comedienne Sandra Bernhard. The second track, "Get Off This," followed strongly and even received airplay on album-oriented rock stations, once off-limits to alternative bands. The album, said *Rolling Stone*, finds musical moods that "run the gamut from neorockabilly whoop-it-ups such as 'Lonesome Johnny Blues' to the desert-induced paranoia of 'Low' and the band's cover of the Grateful Dead's 'Loser.'"

And just to show fans that the zaniness of the Camper days still remained, the CD listed tracks 13 and 14 as "No Songs," while track 15, titled "Hi-Desert Biker Meth Lab," was a 40-second sound collage. Then they fooled with the indexing to make the disc contain 99 tracks, most of them three seconds long and silent. The reward for the shenanigans comes with three vintage Cracker tracks buried at tracks number 69, 88, and 99. And how does Lowery pull such a stunt for a major label? "You just have to tell them it's genius," he told *Rolling Stone*. "And generally they'll take your word for it."

The only thing that hasn't been steady for Cracker is its rhythm section. The band has been through four drummers and three bassists, including drummer David Lovering, formerly of the Pixies, and Bruce Hughes, formerly of Poi Dog Pondering, who joined the group in 1994. Whomever he's playing with, Lowery maintains his ability to deftly hit the mark on offbeat subjects like former Soviet leader Joseph Stalin's Cadillac, winning the lottery, Russian cosmonauts, and Eurotrash girls without ever reverting to writing pop song cliches in the mode of "I love you, baby. Why don't you love me?" A writer for *Request* noted, "At his peak moments as a songwriter ... Lowery transcends his wry mannered persona, speaking (without intending to) for the suburban youth that make up modern California mall culture."

Through all the overanalysis and labeling, Lowery remains seemingly unaffected. "The longer I've been in the business," he told *Request,* "the less I understand about what I do, except for one thing: You can only play music for yourself. If you do music you like and you get really popular, that's great. But if you do music that you like and nobody gives a shit about you, that's great, too."

Selected discography

Cracker, Virgin, 1992.
Tucson (EP), Virgin, 1992.
Kerosene Hat, Virgin, 1993.

Sources

Billboard, August 28, 1993; February 12, 1994; April 9, 1994.
High Fidelity, December 1988.
Musician, September 1993.
Request, October 1993.
Rolling Stone, March 26, 1987; April 7, 1988; May 19, 1988; August 11, 1988; December 14, 1989; September 16, 1993; April 7, 1994.
Stereo Review, September, 1988; May, 1992.

Additional information for this profile was obtained from Virgin Records publicity materials, 1994.

—*John Cortez*

Steve Cropper

Guitarist, songwriter, producer

Photograph by Dennis Keeley, © 1994 Sony Music, courtesy of Columbia Records

The incisive guitar lines of Steve Cropper helped define the contours of soul and funk in the 1960s, when he worked unflaggingly as the house guitarist—and often as composer, arranger, producer, and engineer—for Stax Records in Memphis, Tennessee. As part of the instrumental quartet Booker T. & the MG's, Cropper not only wrote material for and backed up some of the most famous names in soul but also helped popularize the minimalist funk style that would later engulf rhythm and blues.

Cropper worked as a solo artist and journeyman session player and producer during the 1970s before joining the Blues Brothers group, which introduced Memphis soul to a new generation of listeners. When Booker T. & the MG's regrouped in the early 1990s, they found themselves hipper than ever: they were inducted into the Rock and Roll Hall of Fame and toured as rock survivor Neil Young's backup group. By this time, as Walt Hetfield of *Guitar Player* wrote, Cropper was widely acknowledged to be "the most imitated guitarist of the soul genre."

Cropper was born in Willow Springs, Missouri, in 1941. His family moved to Memphis when he was still a child, and Cropper began playing guitar in his teens; his primary influences were blues players and such early rock and rollers as Bo Diddley and Chuck Berry. While still in high school, Cropper and his friend Donald "Duck" Dunn, who played bass, formed a band called the Mar-Keys. Cropper was just 20 years old when the Mar-Keys' single, an instrumental called "Last Night," surged up the charts. The following year, Cropper was hired by Stax to play in the house band.

At a 1962 session backing up rocker Billy Lee Riley, Cropper ended up playing on an instrumental jam composed by keyboardist Booker T. Jones. The result so enthralled Stax head Jim Stewart—who happened to be engineering the session—that Stewart decided to release "Behave Yourself" as a single on his label's subsidiary Volt. Jones had another little idea for the B-side: a slice of Hammond organ-driven funky blues called "Green Onions." Mixing the sensual, murky proto-rock of Howlin' Wolf with the ultracool jazz grooves of organists like Jimmy Smith and "Big John" Patton, the song became one of the most enduring instrumental tracks of its time.

Cropper, Jones, drummer Al Jackson, Jr., and bassist Lewis Steinberger, all of whom had been playing with the Mark-Keys, became the first incarnation of Booker T. & the MG's—"MG" standing for "Memphis Group"—and Stax had a monster hit single on its hands, even if it was originally supposed to be the B-side. The song sold over a million copies, reached the

For the Record . . .

Born October 21, 1941, in Willow Springs, MO; married and has children.

Recording and performing artist, c. 1957—; producer, session musician, and songwriter, 1962—. Member of Mar-Keys; house guitarist at Stax/Volt label and member of group Booker T. & the MG's, 1962-71; reunited with Booker T. & the MG's in 1977, 1980s, and 1990s, and recorded reunion albums on Asylum, 1977, and Columbia, 1994; founded TMI (Trans Maximus) studio and label, 1971; member of Blues Brothers band, 1978—; appeared in film *The Blues Brothers,* 1980; toured with Dave Edmunds's Rock & Roll Revue, 1990; performed with Booker T. & the MG's at presidential inauguration festivities, 1993.

Awards: Booker T. & the MG's inducted into Rock and Roll Hall of Fame, 1992.

Addresses: *Record company*—Columbia Records, 550 Madison Ave., New York, NY 10022-3211.

top of the R&B charts, cruised to the Number Three position on the pop charts, and supported an album of the same name, which reached the Top 40. Other singles, including "Chinese Checkers" and "Mo' Onions," followed to less success.

Influential Rough Edges

Steinberger was fired in 1964 and was replaced by Dunn, who subsequently anchored the MG's rhythm section. Cropper and company spent the next few years accompanying soul artists like Otis Redding, Wilson Pickett, and many others, establishing the Stax sound as one of the most influential in all of pop. In fact, the generation of rock musicians in the United States and England who came of age in this period frequently cite Stax and its Detroit competitor Motown as titanic influences. But whereas Motown's silky, refined artists helped make black music more acceptable to white audiences, the Memphis sound refused to hone its rough edges and was thus arguably more important to the development of both the funk and the rock that followed.

Much of the credit for the Memphis sound goes to Cropper, who not only lent a raw urgency and honest emotionalism to his playing but helped nurse many of the classic Stax recordings from inception to mixdown. "I spent all my time—15 hours a day, on average—in the studio," Cropper recalled to Hetfield of *Guitar Player*. "My wife hated it, my kids hated it, and my friends hated it. I would go to bed at 2:00 or 3:00 in the morning, get an hour or two of sleep, be on the golf course at 6:30 or 7:00, and be in the studio by 10:30 or 11:00. I would work until midnight or after, go to bed, and do it again."

Indeed, as Cropper testified in a *Rolling Stone* interview, the classic Sam and Dave single "Soul Man"—though credited on the label to Isaac Hayes and David Porter—bore the imprint of Cropper's style before it had lyrics. Cropper's description of the song's evolution evokes the spontaneous, loose, creative environment at Stax: "Well, when it first started Ike [Hayes] just had some changes on the piano and then it built into that [song]. I worked with him a while and came up with a guitar line; he worked with Duck a while and came up with a bass line. David and Isaac put words to it, Al put the drum beat to it. The horns were worked up on the session. Sam and Dave were taught the song as soon as they got into the session."

Cropper had similar collaborations with Otis Redding and Wilson Pickett. "Otis did more to change my sound than anybody," Cropper told Hetfield of *Guitar Player*. "He made me think and play a lot simpler, so that different notes would really count dramatically." Cropper co-wrote Redding's monster hit "(Sittin' on) The Dock of the Bay." Pickett, a New York sensation in need of a national hit, came to Memphis "with [Atlantic Records executive and soul music visionary] Jerry Wexler. It was kind of an experience for everybody really to work with somebody like [Wexler]." Wexler picked up the story in his memoir *Rhythm and the Blues:* "Instead of trying to provide material, I urged [Pickett]—with local genius Steve Cropper—to create his own. I put the two of them in a hotel room with a bottle of Jack Daniels and the simple exhortation—'Write!'—which they did." The result was "The Midnight Hour," which was one of Pickett's greatest hits.

"Play It, Steve"

As the 1960s progressed, Booker T. & the MG's scored several more hits, notably "Hip Hug-Her," "Soul Limbo," and versions of movie themes, including "Hang 'Em High" and *The Graduate*'s "Mrs. Robinson." The MG's backed Redding at the Monterey International Pop Festival in 1967, one of the most important such festivals of the decade. Yet the group showed signs of creative fatigue by 1970, when they released *McLem-*

ore Avenue, an album featuring instrumental versions of all the songs on Abbey Road, the unofficial swan song of British pop revolutionaries the Beatles.

Jones quit the group soon thereafter, and in 1971 Cropper left Stax to found his own label and studio, TMI, in Memphis. He worked as session guitarist and songwriter and acted as producer for a number of disparate artists, including the California funk collective Tower of Power, rockers Poco, folk singer-songwriter John Prine and guitar wizard Jeff Beck. Cropper also released a solo album that featured guest appearances from the MG's and a plethora of other talented players, among them Leon Russell and Buddy Miles.

> "The main idea is not what you play; it's what you don't play. The less you play, the more it means."

Later in the 1970s Cropper collaborated with a number of high-profile artists in Los Angeles. Sadly, original MG's drummer Jackson was murdered in 1975, but the surviving members reunited with various drummers; with Stax skinsman Willie Hall they recorded Universal Language in 1977, and nine years later they shared a stage for a couple of songs at the Memphis Music Festival.

When comedians John Belushi and Dan Ackroyd developed the personae of the Blues Brothers and performed a mixture of Memphis soul and Chicago blues, they assembled a large band that included Cropper and Dunn. First appearing on television's Saturday Night Live, the popular sketch led first to an album, Briefcase Full of Blues, then to a movie—in which Cropper and Dunn played themselves—and later a tour and more records. The Blues Brothers version of "Soul Man" allowed Belushi to echo the vocal cue that preceded Cropper's guitar break on the original recording: "Play it, Steve."

Though Belushi died in 1982, Cropper collaborated with Ackroyd on several other Blues Brothers projects in the ensuing years. In his interview with Hetfield, the guitarist characterized the Blues Brothers' repopularization of the Stax sound as "the greatest thing there ever was." Another MG's reunion was scheduled for Atlantic's 1988 40th Anniversary celebration at New York's Madison Square Garden, but Booker T. was too ill and Late Night keyboardist Paul Shaffer, who had helped Belushi and Ackroyd assemble the Blues Brothers band, stepped in.

By 1990, despite periodic reunions, Cropper had become sufficiently obscure to warrant a "what happened to" query in Guitar Player. Cropper reported at the time that he was "having fun getting out there and seeing the world" on tour with other Blues Brothers alumni.

A Revue and More Reunions

In 1990 Cropper joined British rockers Dave Edmunds and Graham Parker and 1950s rock singer Dion, among others, in a touring "Rock & Roll Revue." Parker expressed to Musician writer Scott Isler his hope that young audiences would appreciate the music bypassed by so-called "classic-rock" radio. "If there is something classic it's Steve Cropper's guitar style," Parker insisted. Indeed, Isler reported, everyone on the tour "is in awe of Steve Cropper." Cropper, who initially resisted going on the tour, recalled, "I said, 'I don't know if I'm your guy. I'm not really a rock 'n' roll guitar player.'" Once on the road, however, he felt grateful to the tour organizers "for talking me into it, 'cause I was really trying to slip out of it." Cropper also did some writing with younger bluesman Robert Cray, who described Cropper to Guitar Player's Hetfield as "a great working partner" who "has these great titles, great potential stories. He leaves you with that, and it just opens you up."

In the early 1990s the MG's reassembled at the Montreaux Jazz Festival and at the Lone Star Roadhouse in New York. In 1991 a boxed set of Stax singles spanning nearly ten years and featuring not only the group's greatest hits but best-known performances by Pickett, Redding, Eddie Floyd, Rufus and Carla Thomas, and many others, won a Grammy Award. At a March 1992 Lone Star show, Shaffer's drummer, Anton Fig, filled in for Jackson. Rolling Stone's Steve Futterman observed, "It was obvious that whatever bond united Jones, Cropper and Dunn in the Sixties still coursed through their veins and that Fig had received a transfusion." The show Futterman reviewed took place one day after the group's induction into the Rock and Roll Hall of Fame. "One day we got a phone call saying, 'You guys are definitely going into the Hall of Fame.' We said, 'What?!' We had been nominated once or twice before and didn't get in, so we figured that we wouldn't get in again," Cropper told Hetfield. "At that point things changed."

Renewed Fame Led to Album

The revitalized Booker T. & the MG's played at U.S. President Bill Clinton's 1993 inaugural ball and were the "house band" at the all-star tribute to trailblazing rock songwriter Bob Dylan at Madison Square Garden. The group went on tour with Neil Young—with drummer Jim Keltner attempting to fill Al Jackson's shoes—and soon found themselves with a new record deal, this time with Columbia. The result was the 1994 album *That's the Way It Should Be*. Versatile sidemen Steve Jordan and James Gadson handled drum duties, and the group tackled such varied material as Irish rock group U2's "I Still Haven't Found What I'm Looking For" and the soul nugget "I Can't Stand the Rain," as well as several originals.

"I wouldn't refer to [*That's the Way It Should Be*] as a comeback until we have a hit," Cropper said in an interview with *Billboard*'s Carlo Wolff. "I'd like to follow in the footsteps of [R&B and rock diva] Tina Turner. Wouldn't that be nice? A 30-year overnight success." A quote from the guitarist in a Columbia press release read, "The biggest challenge was to sound like Booker T. & the MG's. It might seem easy but how do you sound like you sounded thirty years ago and still have it fresh, up to date and technically together? I'd lay a rhythm pattern and Booker would put a melody on top of the pattern and then Duck would come in and put an incredible bass on it. Somehow we did it. We believed in it and it happened."

Whatever might happen with the MG's reunion, Cropper had already left an indelible mark on popular music. Long before the profusion of flamboyant, ultra-fast lead guitarists, Cropper had provided an example of economical, generous grooving that would stand the test of time. "I can't play guitar if I'm not playing it from the heart," he insisted to Hetfield. The musician elaborated on his philosophy: "The main idea is not what you play; it's what you *don't* play. The less you play, the more it means."

Selected discography

With Booker T. & the MG's; on Stax/Volt, except where noted

Green Onions (includes title track and "Behave Yourself"), 1962.
"Boot-Leg," 1965.
"My Sweet Potato," 1966.
Hip Hug-Her (includes title track), 1967.
Back To Back, 1967.
Doin' Our Thing, 1968.
Soul Limbo, 1968.
Up Tight (soundtrack; includes "Time is Tight"), 1969.
The Booker T. Set, 1969.
McLemore Avenue, 1970.
Booker T. & the MG's Greatest Hits, 1970.
Melting Pot, 1971.
Union Extended (U.K. only), 1976.
Universal Language, Asylum, 1977.
That's the Way It Should Be, Columbia, 1994.

Solo albums

With a Little Help From My Friends, TMI, 1970.

With the Blues Brothers; on Atlantic

Briefcase Full of Blues (includes "Soul Man"), 1978.
The Blues Brothers (soundtrack), 1980.
Made in America, 1980.

With other artists

The Complete Stax/Volt Singles, Vol. I: 1959-1968, Atlantic, 1991.
The Complete Stax/Volt Singles, Vol. 2: 1968-1971, Stax, 1993.

Also contributed to and/or produced albums by Poco, John Prine, Tower of Power, Jose Feliciano, Paul Shaffer, Jeff Healey, Sammy Hagar, and others.

Sources

Books

Rees, Dafydd, and Luke Crampton, *Rock Movers & Shakers*, Billboard, 1991.
Wexler, Jerry, and David Ritz, *Rhythm and the Blues: A Life in American Music*, Knopf, 1993.

Periodicals

Billboard, February 26, 1994.
Entertainment Weekly, June 17, 1994.
Guitar Player, July 1990; December 1993.
Musician, August 1990.
Rolling Stone, August 24, 1968; March 5, 1992.
Vibe, June/July 1994.

Additional information for this profile was obtained from Columbia publicity materials, 1994.

—*Simon Glickman*

Crowded House

Rock band

Photograph © 1993 by Youri Lenquette, courtesy of Capitol Records

"America's been a bit tricky for us," Crowded House's lead man Neil Finn told *Pulse!* "We tend to fall between the cracks." It's true that this New Zealand-bred and Melbourne, Australia-based combo has, since their first single, just missed American superstardom. As Finn put it, "Radio formats [in the United States] are very restrictive, and if you're a band like us who are quite happy to flit between being raucous and noisy and doing a slow melodic ballad, people here can get a bit confused." Fans, however, have flocked to Crowded House's door from the beginning, liking whatever it is they *are* hearing, whether it's easily categorized or not.

Crowded House is the offspring of New Zealand's Split Enz, the eccentric pop group that made it big in the late 1970s and 1980s, and that remains a cult favorite in the United States and abroad. Neil Finn's older brother formed Split Enz in 1972 and welcomed 19-year-old (some sources say 18-year-old) Neil into the fold in 1977. The band had been looking to change their androgynous art-rock sound, and Neil's tastes blended well with the band's new melodic approach.

Their successes grew with Neil's singing and songwriting talents added to the mix, culminating in several international hits. In the United States, the band had most of its success with the song "I Got You." By 1983 Tim was ready for a solo career, and the band, frustrated by that elusive final breakthrough in the United States, began to splinter. Neil decided to disband the group in 1984 after a last album and a farewell tour.

First Single Finally Took Off

Neil asked new Split Enz drummer Paul Hester to join the smaller, more guitar-oriented band that he had in mind. At Split Enz's breaking up party, Australian bassist and film art director Neil Seymour struck up a conversation with Neil Finn, and after a later audition, the new, nameless band was complete. In 1985 they sent a demo around and were signed by EMI Worldwide and Capitol Records in the United States. It was not until the cover art (designed by Seymour on all the group's albums) was nearly ready that the band settled on a name. The crowded house after which the group is named is the small Hollywood, California, bungalow where the band lived, recorded, and entertained a constant flow of family and friends.

The debut album, *Crowded House,* was released in July of 1986. No songs were hits in the United States immediately, although within five months the album was certified gold in Australia. Since Split Enz had been monumental in Australia, a gold record was no sur-

For the Record . . .

Members include **Neil Finn** (born c. 1958 in Te Awamutu, New Zealand), lead vocals, guitar; **Paul Hester** (born c. 1959 in Australia), drums; **Neil Seymour** (born c. 1959 in Australia), bass; **Tim Finn** (born in New Zealand; joined and left group in 1991), guitar, vocals; and **Mark Hart** (born in California; joined group in 1993), guitar, keyboards.

Band formed in Australia, 1984, from former members of the New Zealand-based group Split Enz; signed by EMI Worldwide and Capitol Records in the United States, 1985; toured Australia under the name the Mullanes before moving to Los Angeles to record first album, 1985; released *Crowded House* and single, "Don't Dream It's Over," 1986.

Addresses: *Record company*—Capitol Records, Inc., 1750 North Vine St., Hollywood, CA, 90028.

---

prise, but Crowded House was fixated on the American market. The band knew their music was good and so did Capitol Records, who never stopped the earnest support and never-say-die promotion. Intensive touring and sheer willpower finally began to pay off after eight months. Almost suddenly, as if it had just been released, the first single, "Don't Dream It's Over," soared to Number Two. In April of 1987, the Number Seven hit "Something So Strong" cinched *Crowded House* as one of 1987's sleeper hits; the LP found its place at the top of music critics' year-end Best Album lists and later on *Rolling Stone*'s "Top 100 Albums of the Decade" list.

The songs on *Crowded House* typified a certain style already equated with Neil Finn. Mark Peel of *Stereo Review* described the songs as "still energetic and tuneful, but there's a twist: beneath that cheery surface lurks an angst-ridden, somewhat sinister mind." Similarly, Chris Willman in *Rolling Stone* commented, "Rarely has any modern music sounded so cheerful *and* so creepy as some of the off-center love songs that pop out of the red head of Neil Finn."

Some reviewers likened the band's sound to the Beatles: "From nice, *Rubber Soul* pop to edgy, *White Album* hysterics," noted Peel; "*Revolver*-era Beatles," wrote David Handelman in *Rolling Stone*. Willman summarized: "It's great, nervous pop. Part of that fetching paradox lies in Finn's distinctive melodies—filled with irresistible borderline-bubble gum chord progressions that often descend just at the point in the chorus where you'd figure they ought to be ascending—and part of it is tied to the mixed messages his love songs send out. For Finn is the worst kind of romantic: the honest kind."

Accusations of Sophomore Slump

"The moodier [second album] *Temple of Low Men* boasted more emotional and musical variety, but subtly effective tunes like 'Better Be Home Soon,' 'I Feel Possessed' and 'Into Temptation' attracted shortsighted accusations of a sophomore slump," wrote Scott Schinder in *Pulse!*. *Temple of Low Men* is a darker, less commercial album, with songs no less beautiful or melodic than those of the first. The title came from a bit of graffiti Finn spotted on a Los Angeles church on his way home, where he found the TV broadcasting the noisy atonement of philandering Reverend Jimmy Swaggart. "It's sort of about slimeballs inhabiting sacred places," Finn told *People*. "Reviewers," wrote Steve Pond in *Rolling Stone*, "found the record darker and moodier than its predecessor and pointed out that while it takes longer to appreciate, in the long run it's probably a deeper, more rewarding record." As another *Rolling Stone* reviewer observed, "One hopes that each successive phase of the Crowded House journey will prove so rich a tale."

Although long-simmering tensions in the band—amplified by *Temple*'s poor showing—caused a brief breakup, Crowded House emerged from it seemingly unscathed. *Woodface,* the next leg of their journey, did prove to be as rich a tale and brought the band back into wider public notice. Perhaps part of the reason for the increased publicity was the re-pairing of the Finn brothers. Neil and Tim had been writing songs together and asked Hester to join them on some tracks. They soon realized that instead of creating a brothers Finn project, they appeared to be writing another Crowded House album. They went with it, and Tim Finn moved into the more crowded house.

Rolling Stone's Kristine McKenna called *Woodface* "a swinging record that finds the band gliding through its material with ease-crisp harmonies and memorable hooks abound." *Interview* commanded, "Go buy *Woodface*.... This album is sure to hit you in the groove spot." The gleeful review found *Woodface* to be "an album with cleverness, passion, and allure that speaks to the head, heart, and loins with equal fluency."

Almost without fail, reviewers praised *Woodface*, perhaps because they felt Crowded House had found the fine balance between their cheery debut and their more moody—"underrated," according to *People*—second album. A few criticisms came through in McKenna's otherwise positive review: "One could fault Finn's writing for the fact that the content of his songs is sometimes more original then their form.... Such provocative ideas, alas, come in standard pop packaging." Meanwhile, the Crowded House population of fans grew as the single "Chocolate Cake" took *Woodface* to the Top 20 in eight countries. Another of the singles, "Weather With You," hit the Top Five in such diverse countries as Singapore, Greece, Holland, and South Africa.

> *No Crowded House show is the same, and nothing is out of the question—including inviting audience members on stage to perform with the band.*

Crowded House is known for being hilarious in concert; the witty banter flies in lethal doses—usually between Hester and Neil Finn—and when Hester's in the lead, it is often extremely bawdy. This warm stage presence, however, actually had a great deal to do with Tim Finn's leaving the band after touring for *Woodface*. Although they all seemed to get along well, the bandmembers "agreed that it wasn't feeling right," according to the younger Finn in *Pulse!* The chemistry of the original three had been so powerful, that it was hard for Tim to find a place. The strong Finn personalities kept talking over each other on stage and caused general disorder. After *Woodface,* Tim decided to continue with his solo career. Considering their fondness for brotherly collaboration, and the success it always brings, they felt sure they would team up again in the future.

In addition to the usually perfect rapport, Crowded House's live sound quality is brilliant. From the first note, each instrument is clean and distinct, each lyric enunciated and harmonious. Although their songs are often extremely lush, the band is surprisingly able to recreate that sound live. It's no wonder that they have earned such honors as Great Britain-based *O Magazine's* Best Live Act award. No Crowded House show is the same, and nothing is out of the question—including inviting audience members on stage to perform with the band.

One addition to the stage mix who did fit—perhaps because he rarely spoke—was Mark Hart, who had been touring with Crowded House as auxiliary guitarist/keyboardist and was promoted to full membership in time for the new album. This amendment to the lineup only furthered the band's desire for something new. For a change of scenery and a change of sound, Crowded House headed home to the bush, this time recording on a beach called Kare Kare on the remote rugged west coast of Auckland, New Zealand. There, between the bush-clad hills of the Waitaker Ranges and the roar of the Tasman Sea—Kare Kare literally means "rippling surf"—Crowded House recorded *Together Alone.*

Producer Mitchell Froom (Richard Thompson, Elvis Costello, Los Lobos, among others) had been the hand that helped mold the Crowded House sound on the band's first three albums. "Mitchell's the most musical person I've ever met," Finn explained in *Pulse!,* "and he was instrumental in helping us create a sound, but we felt like we needed a change." The band turned to onetime Killing Joke member turned techno-hippie guru Youth.

Neil Seymour insisted in *Billboard* that they "picked him for his sense of humor and his use of adjectives." Mostly, they picked him for the anarchy inherent in his producing style, which was something totally new to the Crowded House method. "*Together Alone,*" wrote Schinder in *Pulse!,* "maintains its predecessors' impassioned lyricism, understated humor and elegant tunefulness. However, a new found sense of sonic adventurism amplifies the more disquieting undercurrents that have always been implied in the band's prior work."

Sought the Elusive "Number One"

Some reviewers, including Geoffrey Welchman for *People,* were unnerved. "Despite Finn's usual gift for melody ... the first half of the album is filled with tunes that meander along with no apparent destination. When the album does produce some real excitement (like the catchy rocker 'Locked Out') or a memorable melody ('Walking on the Spot'), the band's potential becomes as obvious as its short fall this time around." *Rolling Stone's* Christian Wright wrote that "such exotic flourishes may seem bizarre coming from the nice boys who make up Crowded House, but at moments, those touches sound ethereally beautiful."

With each step of the way, and with each record, these "nice boys" of Crowded House keep plugging away towards that elusive Number One position in the United States. Their first single off of *Together Alone,* "Locked Out," was featured in the popular film *Reality Bites.* Though perched just on the edge of "big name" stature in the United States, the status of the band's members is in question. In April of 1994 Paul Hester left Crowded House citing the pressures of touring and a lack of motivation. It is unclear whether Hester's departure is another short-lived breakup, perhaps due to his preference to be with his newborn baby, or if maybe he has moved out for good. Regardless, it is doubtful that Neil Finn will ever stop making music. Whether it is with a redecorated Crowded House, or under a different moniker altogether, he is sure to keep chasing that American Number One.

Selected discography

On Capitol Records

Crowded House (includes "Don't Dream It's Over" and "Something So Strong"), 1986.
Temple of Low Men (includes "Better Be Home Soon," "I Feel Possessed," and "Into Temptation"), 1988.
Woodface (includes "Chocolate Cake" and "Weather With You"), 1991.
Together Alone (includes "Locked Out" and "Walking on the Spot"), 1994.
Contributors to *Reality Bites* (soundtrack), BMG, 1994.

Sources

Billboard, July 17, 1993; January 15, 1994; April 30, 1994.
Consumers' Research, December 1992.
Entertainment Weekly, January 14, 1994.
Guitar Player, March 1992; June 1994.
Interview, August 1991.
Mademoiselle, September 1991.
People, September 19, 1988; August 12, 1991; July 17, 1994.
Playboy, September 1991.
Pulse!, February 1994.
Rolling Stone, February 12, 1987; February 26, 1987; May 7, 1987; November 17, 1988; November 16, 1989; July 11, 1991; November 11, 1993; April 7, 1994; June 16, 1994.
Seventeen, July 1987.
Stereo Review, December 1984; July 1987.
'Teen, August 1987.

Additional information for this profile was obtained from Capitol Records press materials, 1994.

—Joanna Rubiner

The Dave Clark Five

Pop band

The accessible pop sound of the Dave Clark Five, with its driving percussion and chanting vocals, made it one of the most popular "British invasion" bands of the mid-1960s. A savvy publicity campaign promoting their rivalry with the Beatles stimulated sales and generated a string of hits for the band from 1964 to 1966 that was second only to the Fab Four. During their career, the Dave Clark Five sold an estimated 50 million records and had 30 hit singles worldwide.

While guitar riffs were the focus of most British pop bands of the time, drums drove the Dave Clark Five. Their strong percussion section was characteristic of the so-called "Tottenham Sound" that differed from popular Merseyside, London, groups like the Beatles and Gerry and the Pacemakers. The band's strong identification with this sound would cause their popularity to wane when psychedelic rock and other new trends began drawing listeners in the late 1960s. The Dave Clark Five's extremely clean-cut image also hurt their career during the rise of "bad boy" groups like the Rolling Stones, the Who, and the Kinks, which had more raw appeal.

MICHAEL OCHS ARCHIVES / Venice, CA

For the Record...

Original members include **Dave Clark** (born December 15, 1942, in Tottenham, London, England), drums; **Rick Huxley** (born August 5, 1942, in Dartford, England), rhythm guitar, then bass guitar; **Mick Ryan** (left group c. 1960), lead guitar; **Stan Saxon** (left group 1961), lead vocals, saxophone; and **Chris Walls** (left group c. 1960), bass. Later members include **Lenny Davidson** (born May 30, 1944, in Enfield, London), guitar; **Denis Payton** (born August 1, 1943, in Walthamstow, London), saxophone; **Mike Smith** (born December 12, 1943, in Edmonton, London), vocals, organ; and **Jim Spencer** (joined and left group c. 1961), saxophone.

Group formed in 1958, in Tottenham, London; originally named the Dave Clark Five Featuring Stan Saxon; signed long-term contract with Mecca ballroom chain, London, 1961; signed with Picadilly Records (Congress Records in U.S.), London, 1962; sold first instrumental song, "Chaquita," to Ember Records, 1962; signed with Columbia (Epic in U.S.), 1963; appeared in film *Catch Us If You Can* (*Having a Wild Weekend* in U.S.), 1965; formed Big Five Films (production company), London, 1965; Clark produced music video for "Nineteen Days," 1966; filmed television documentary *Hold On—It's the Dave Clark Five,* 1967; stopped large-scale touring, 1969; group disbanded, 1970.

Awards: Mecca Gold Cup award for best band, 1963.

The Dave Clark Five was created in 1958, an attempt by a young Tottenham football player named Dave Clark to help fund his team's traveling expenses. He and soon-to-be bassist Chris Walls ran an ad in *Melody Maker* to locate other musicians. After the ad brought in rhythm guitarist Rick Huxley, Stan Saxon as singer and saxophonist, and Mike Ryan on lead guitar, the "Dave Clark Five featuring Stan Saxon" was born.

By 1961, Walls and Ryan had left the group and Huxley had moved to cover bass guitar. Denis Payton joined the band as a saxophonist. And Lenny Davidson, former lead guitarist for the Impalas, also came on board, bringing with him lead vocalist/keyboardist Mike Smith. Backed by ten years of classical piano lessons, Smith was the only member of the group with formal musical training.

Built Reputation as Live Act

By 1962, the Dave Clark Five had developed some renown as a live band. The group landed a contract to play regularly on England's popular Mecca ballroom chain. The rigors of three-hour, nightly performances on the circuit honed the group's skills during the next few years; they would win the Mecca circuit's Gold Cup for the best live band in the United Kingdom in 1963.

However, 1963 would be a mixed year. The award from Mecca came on the heel of a bitter disappointment over their cover recording of the Contours' "Do You Love Me?" After its release, the song would only make it to the Number 30 spot on the British charts after a version of the same song by Brian Poole and the Tremeloes released around the same time hit Number One and upstaged them. The turning point for the group came in December with the release of "Glad All Over."

Soaring to Number One in the United Kingdom early the following year and selling over two and a half million records, the song was also a smash in the United States, leading Epic Records to plan an American tour for the band. Two consecutive appearances on *The Ed Sullivan Show* and several coast-to-coast tours sealed the group's popularity in the American market, which would turn out to be a far more lucrative one for them than Europe. The Dave Clark Five would log up 18 appearances on *Ed Sullivan,* the most ever by any British act.

As in "Glad All Over," Clark's pounding drum sticks were the hallmark of "Bits and Pieces," the group's follow-up hit. At this point, the group finally decided to turn professional. The Dave Clark Five would have a succession of 12 more American Top Twenty hits, reaching their popularity peak in the United States with their Number One hit "Over and Over" in 1965. Due to a tremendous demand for their music in the United States, the group released 14 American albums; only four would reach British audiences from 1964 to 1967. Many of the group's songs distributed in the United States never even received airplay in Britain.

Total Control Exercised by Clark

In addition to composing most of the group's songs with co-writer Smith, Clark wielded extensive control over the group's recording activities and promotion. "I knew the sort of sound we wanted," he explained in his liner notes for 1993's *The History of the Dave Clark Five.* "It was like being a conductor: build it up here, slow it down there, change it before they get bored. This is where the experience we gained earlier as a live band became invaluable." More skilled as a businessman than as a musician, Clark maneuvered business deals far more sophisticated than those usually made by pop groups of his day. He established and ran a company to publish the Dave Clark Five's compositions, and secured a deal giving the group higher royalties than those earned by the Beatles. In his contract, Clark shrewdly inserted a clause granting him ownership of the group's recordings after the licensing period, a highly unusual practice for the time.

Clark kept his band in the public eye by touring relentlessly around the world, and the group was in continual demand as stage performers even after they had stopped generating new hit songs. He jumped onto the movie bandwagon in 1965, and the result was the critically acclaimed *Catch Us If You Can*. Released as *Having a Wild Weekend* in the United States, the film is a bittersweet comedy that deals with the stress that follows a rock group's sudden fame. Bosley Crowther of the *New York Times* called it the best young generation film of its era, and it was one Great Britain's Top Twenty box-office attractions of the year.

Ahead of his time, Clark foresaw the music video, producing and directing a promotional film for the song "Nineteen Days," which was showcased on *Ed Sullivan* in 1966. He later produced and directed the short film *Hits in Action*, which highlighted a series of Dave Clark Five hits and was shown in theaters around the globe. Clark wrote, produced, and directed *Hold On—It's The Dave Clark Five*, an award-winning special for British television that featured the group performing various songs.

Failure to Adapt Hurt Popularity

Despite the continual momentum of touring, recording, and television appearances organized by Clark, the Dave Clark Five began to lose its popularity around 1966. As the group held its musical ground, it was left behind by groups eager to follow the trend towards more mystical sounds. They made a brief comeback in 1967 when their cover of Marv Johnson's 1959 hit, "You Got What It Takes," made it to Number Seven on the U.S. charts. Later that year, "Everybody Knows (I Still Love You)," featuring a rare lead vocal by Davidson, climbed to the Number Two spot in the United Kingdom.

A solitary attempt at psychedelia by the group was "Inside and Out," a song originally written for the 1968 film *Romeo and Juliet* but that didn't make it into the film's soundtrack. "Inside and Out" was a mix of bold string arrangements and a dominant fuzz guitar that sounded like the Beatles's "I Am the Walrus." But ultimately, they were unwilling to adapt to new tastes and new technology, and until their breakup in 1970, the group met with only sporadic success.

After the demise of the Dave Clark Five, Clark and Smith continued to release singles as Dave Clark & Friends until 1973. Smith also collaborated with Mike D'Abo, onetime vocalist for Manfred Mann. Payton entered the real estate business, Huxley got into electronics, and Davidson became an antiques dealer. Clark continued with production work and had a major success with 1978's *25 Thumping Great Hits*, a collection of the group's songs that went platinum.

In the 1980s Clark co-wrote and produced the British musical *Time*, starring Cliff Richard and Sir Laurence Olivier. The show broke box-office records for London's West End, and Clark produced the soundtrack that featured Olivier, Richard, Freddie Mercury, Julian Lennon, Dionne Warwick, Burt Bacharach, Ashford & Simpson, and Stevie Wonder. In 1992, Clark co-wrote and produced two songs for Mercury that would have triple-platinum sales worldwide.

Although many rock critics considered the Dave Clark Five lightweight, their music has been claimed as inspiration by guitarist Eddie Van Halen and drummer Max Weinberg of Bruce Springsteen's E Street Band. The group will be remembered for their highly polished stage performances and for the relentless urgency with which they delivered their material. According to the liner notes for 1993's *The History of The Dave Clark Five*, the group displayed "a mastery of the elusive art of compressing the sheer power, excitement, and emotion of the best rock 'n' roll into a two-to-three minute single."

Selected discography

On Epic, except where noted

Glad All Over, 1963.
The Dave Clark Five Return!, 1964.
American Tour, 1964.
Coast to Coast, 1965.
Having a Wild Weekend (soundtrack), 1965.
I Like It Like That, 1965.
Greatest Hits, 1966.
Try Too Hard, 1966.
More Greatest Hits, 1966.
You Got What It Takes, 1967.
Everybody Knows, 1968.
Best of The Dave Clark Five, Starline, 1970.
25 Thumping Great Hits, Polydor, 1978.

Sources

Books

The Guinness Encyclopedia of Popular Music, volume 1, edited by Colin Larkin, Guinness, 1992.

The Harmony Illustrated Encyclopedia of Rock, sixth edition, Harmony Books, 1988.

The Illustrated Encyclopedia of Rock, compiled by Nick Logan and Bob Woffinden, Harmony, 1977.

Pareles, John, and Patricia Romanowski, *The Rolling Stone Encyclopedia of Rock & Roll,* Rolling Stone Press/Summitt Books, 1983.

The Penguin Encyclopedia of Popular Music, edited by Donald Clarke, Viking, 1989.

Shannon, Bob, and John Javna, *Behind the Hits,* Warner Books, 1986.

Stambler, Irwin, *Encyclopedia of Pop & Soul,* St. Martin's Press, 1977.

Periodicals

Billboard, December 12, 1987.
Entertainment Weekly, August 6, 1993.
Rolling Stone, May 27, 1993.

Additional information for this profile was obtained from liner notes to *The History of The Dave Clark Five,* 1993, and Hollywood Records publicity materials.

—*Ed Decker*

Al Di Meola

Guitarist

Photograph by Nathaniel Welch, courtesy of Mesa Records, a division of Mesa

"If you don't advance creatively," Al Di Meola once told *Guitar Player*'s Jim Ferguson, "then all you have left is playing Vegas." From his stunning arrival on the scene as the fiery virtuoso in Chick Corea's jazz fusion group Return to Forever to his international acclaim as the member of an acoustic guitar trio, to his championing of the musical legacy of tango master Astor Piazzolla, guitarist Di Meola has held firm to this credo. Passionate, opinionated, and immensely gifted, he has covered more musical terrain in his 20-year career than many artists have in a lifetime.

Di Meola's accomplishments are made all the more remarkable by the fact that he has achieved them on both electric and acoustic instruments. Outwardly the electric guitar might seem similar to its acoustic counterpart, but as Di Meola explained to Herb Nolan of *Down Beat,* "There are certain things you can do on electric guitar you can't do on acoustic. You can bend strings differently on electric than on acoustic so your ideas will flow differently." Yet, though he enjoys the versatility of the electric guitar, Di Meola admitted to *Down Beat*'s Josef Woodard that "the acoustic guitar is more demanding. It separates the men from the boys." Talented performers on the two instruments have emerged from time to time, but few other artists have shown such a mastery of both or have been able to use them in such a wide variety of musical contexts.

As a youngster in the New Jersey town of Bergenfield, some 20 minutes away from New York City, Di Meola's first musical experience was on drums. However, when he was eight he began taking lessons from a local guitarist named Robert Aslanian who introduced him to a wide variety of music. As Di Meola related to Bill Milkowski of *Down Beat,* "The Ventures and Elvis were big at the time, and the Beatles were just coming in, so naturally I wanted to be a rock & roll guitar player. And Bob would teach me that stuff, but he also made sure that I learned jazz and bossa nova and even a little classical as well." Di Meola's exposure to many different musical repertories would continue to inform his development as a guitar soloist.

In the early 1970s Di Meola studied instrumental performance at Boston's Berklee School of Music and performed with keyboardist Barry Miles. It was a call from keyboardist Chick Corea in 1974, though, that truly set his career in motion. Corea, who a year earlier had founded a second version of his influential fusion group Return to Forever, heard tapes of Di Meola performing with Miles's group and found him a worthy replacement for Bill Connors, who had recently left the band. After only a few days of rehearsal, Di Meola made his Carnegie Hall debut with Corea's group, and the following night Return to Forever played for a crowd of 40,000 in Atlanta.

For the Record...

Born July 22, 1954, in Jersey City, NJ; son of immigrants from Naples, Italy. *Education:* Studied privately with guitarist Robert Aslanian; attended Berklee School of Music, Boston, 1971 and 1974.

Played drums until age eight, when he began taking private guitar lessons; played in keyboardist Barry Miles's Quartet, 1973-74; member of Chick Corea's group, Return to Forever, 1974-76; launched solo career; began touring and recording with Paco De Lucia and John McLaughlin, 1980; founded Al Di Meola Project, 1985; toured with Larry Coryell and Berelli Lagrene as Super Guitar Trio, 1987; maintained dual career as electric guitarist and acoustic guitarist, 1991—; formed group World Sinfonia, featuring bandoneon player Dino Saluzzi, percussionist Arto Tuncboyaci, and guitarist Christopher Carrington, 1991.

Awards: Grammy Award, with group Return to Forever, for *No Mystery,* 1975; Thomas A. Edison Award (Holland), with guitarists John McLaughlin and Paco De Lucia, for *Friday Night in San Francisco,* 1981; Award for Outstanding Merit, City of Atlanta, 1982; inducted into *Guitar Player* magazine's Gallery of Greats, 1982; Best Jazz Guitar LP for *Kiss My Axe, Guitar Player,* 1992.

Addresses: *Management*—Don't Worry, Inc., 111 West 57th St., New York, NY 10019. *Record company*—Mesa Records, 209 East Alameda Ave., #101, Burbank, CA 91502.

Over the next two years, Return to Forever continued to tour successfully and released three albums. When the group suddenly dissolved in 1976, Di Meola, who had just released his first solo album, *Land of the Midnight Sun,* was momentarily disoriented by the group's disbandment but decided to use the opportunity to pursue a solo career. *Elegant Gypsy* followed in 1977, and the album became Di Meola's first major commercial success, ultimately selling nearly a million copies.

With Di Meola's developing popularity as a soloist came a certain amount of negative press. Though most writers agreed that Di Meola was a phenomenal technician on his instrument, a few felt that his pyrotechnics masked a lack of emotional content. The controversy reached a head when Di Meola first teamed with acoustic virtuosos John McLaughlin and Paco de Lucia for a world tour and a live album, recorded in 1981. Though the album, *Saturday Night in San Francisco,* was hugely successful and won several awards, *Stereo Review* critic Joel Vance commented that the trio was so intent on displaying their virtuosity that "not one moment of real emotion is allowed; with all the dazzling zip, the result is sterility."

During his first decade in the music business, Di Meola was quick to defend his dazzling guitar technique. As he pointed out, virtuosity and precision provide the basis of Spanish flamenco music, a long and rich tradition that the guitarist frequently mined in his own improvisations. "In Spain people don't even think something like 'he's just trying to show off,'" Di Meola commented to Herb Nolan in 1978. "That's the style and you can't criticize it. It's what propels the feeling and makes it happen."

After his second recording with Lucia and Mclaughlin in 1983, however, Di Meola seemed to reevaluate his approach to his instrument. The following year, exhausted by nearly nonstop touring and recording, he took a hiatus from the music business to gain some perspective on his career. He emerged in 1985 with the music for two new albums, *Cielo e Terra* and *Soaring Through A Dream,* both of which showed a new maturity and subtlety of approach. Zan Stewart of *Down Beat* noted that Di Meola's solo improvisations on the two projects were "essays in economy and relaxation" rather than "here's-everything-I-can-think-of-right-now demonstrations," and the guitarist himself admitted that his musical ideas had fundamentally changed. "I'm doing a different kind of music now, and playing fast all of the time is completely out of place," he told Jim Ferguson. "Just because you have phenomenal technique doesn't mean you have to prove it on every song."

Di Meola began another important new phase of his career in 1991, when he founded the acoustic ensemble World Sinfonia. The guitarist's inspiration for the group could be traced back to a meeting in 1985 with Astor Piazzolla, the father of the modern tango. Piazzolla, Argentinian by birth, had brought a fascination with jazz and a solid grounding in classical composition to bear on the music of his native country, performing for many years with the influential group Quinteto Nuevo Tango. Di Meola was immediately drawn to this music, impressed by, as he described to Charlie Hunt of the *Detroit Free Press,* "the depth of passion and romance and the intricacies and harmonies and rhythm."

World Sinfonia included Dino Saluzzi on Piazzolla's own instrument, the bandoneon—a type of accordion—and sought to capture the intense emotion of

Piazzolla's music in a fresh new setting. During the early 1990s the group toured extensively and recorded two critically acclaimed albums, the first featuring what *Down Beat*'s Jon Andrews called Di Meola's "strongest acoustic work and most imaginative arrangements to date." World Sinfonia proved another intriguing chapter in a rich and varied career, and it seemed likely the future would find Al Di Meola following other musical paths with similar passion and vigor.

Selected discography

As leader

Land of the Midnight Sun, Columbia, 1976.
Elegant Gypsy, Columbia, 1977.
Casino, Columbia, 1978.
Electric Rendezvous, Columbia, 1981.
Splendido Hotel, Columbia, 1982.
Tour de Force "Live," Columbia, 1982.
Scenario, Columbia, 1983.
Cielo e Terra, EMI, 1985.
Soaring Through a Dream, EMI, 1985.
Tirami Su, EMI, 1987.
Kiss My Axe, Tomato, 1991.
World Sinfonia, Tomato, 1991.
The Best of Al Di Meola: The Manhattan Years, Manhattan, 1992.
Heart of the Immigrants, 1993.

With John McLaughlin and Paco de Lucia

Friday Night in San Francisco, Columbia, 1981.
Passion, Grace and Fire, Columbia, 1983.

With Return to Forever

Where Have I Known You Before, Polydor, 1974.
No Mystery, Polydor, 1975.
Romantic Warrior, Columbia, 1976.

Sources

Detroit Free Press, January 1, 1991.
Down Beat, February 23, 1978; September 1983; February 1986; November 1991; January 1992.
Guitar Player, February 1986; February 1992; December 1993.
Musician, July 1992.
Stereo Review, September 1981.

Additional information for this profile was provided by Don't Worry, Inc., 1994.

—*Jeffrey Taylor*

Céline Dion

Singer, songwriter

Photograph by Phillip Dixon, © 1993 Sony Music, courtesy of Epic Records

Céline Dion, with her five-octave range and passionate style, has sung her way to the top of the pop-music scene in Canada, Britain, France, and the United States. She first cultivated French-speaking fans in Canada with a series of albums, four of which went platinum there. In the early 1990s, Dion made the difficult transition from her native French to English, in which she repeated her success, making both gold and platinum albums.

The youngest of 14 children, Dion grew up in Charlemagne, Quebec, surrounded by music. Her mother played the violin, and her father, the accordion; the family spent much of its time together singing and playing various instruments. Dion's parents owned a piano bar and restaurant, and the children took turns singing and waiting on tables. Céline got her start in the family enterprise quite early—she first stood atop a table to belt out the songs of Ginette Reno at age five. Soon local residents were calling ahead to be sure they would catch her performances.

La Petite Québecoise

When Dion was 12, her mother sent a demonstration tape to Rene Angelil, a well-known Montreal agent, with the note, "This is a 12-year-old with a fantastic voice. Please listen to her. We want her to be like Ginette Reno." Angelil, who had steered Reno to fame, tossed the tape aside. He later explained in *Macleans*, "Every kid of 12 in Quebec wanted to be either Ginette or Rene." When he finally listened to it weeks later at the urging of one of Dion's brothers, Angelil wanted to see Dion immediately.

Angelil took complete control of Dion's career, arranging the contracts and choosing the material for her early French albums. His belief in her was so strong that he mortgaged his house to finance her first album. He did not have to wait long for his opinion to be confirmed by the Canadian public. They flocked to her performances and affectionately dubbed her *la petite Québecoise* (the little Quebecker) as they watched her grow up. Dion quit school at the age of 14 to devote herself to her music. By the time she was 18, she had recorded a string of best-selling French-language albums. In 1983 her single "L'amour ou d'amite" went gold in France, the first from a Canadian artist to do so.

At 18, Dion was ready to conquer new territory: adulthood and the English pop market. Balking at her little-girl image, she followed Angelil's recommendation that she disappear from the public eye for a year. She took that time to exchange her childish clothes for sexier and more sophisticated outfits and to begin to study En-

For the Record . . .

Born c. 1970 in Charlemagne, Quebec, Canada; engaged to René Angelil, 1994.

Singer, c. 1984—. Released seven French-language albums in Canada by age 18; first English-language album, *Unison,* released by Epic, 1990.

Awards: Juno awards for female vocalist of the year, 1990, 1991, and 1992, and for album of the year, 1990, for *Unison;* best dance recording, 1992, for "Love Can Move Mountains"; Juno awards for best-selling Francophone album for *Dion chante Plamondon* and for single of the year for "Beauty and the Beast," both 1992; Grammy Award for best pop performance by a duo or group with vocal, 1992, for "Beauty and the Beast"; Academy Award, 1992, for "Beauty and the Beast"; multi-platinum record for *The Colour of My Love,* 1994.

Addresses: *Home*—Quebec, Canada. *Record company*—550 Music/Epic, 550 Madison Ave., New York, NY 10022.

glish. Command of the English music scene would take only slightly longer than her image change.

From French to English

Dion's first album in English, *Unison,* was recorded before her command of the language was firm, and she ended by singing much of it phonetically. As a result, although her sound was praised, the material was accused of being banal and overproduced. E. Kaye Fulton contended in *Maclean's* that "in her native language, Dion is known for her passion, wit, and rollicking sense of humor. Her French material tends to be more substantial, with fewer songs about love and loss." By her second English album, however, Dion had taken more control of the recording process. She told *Maclean's,* "On the second album I said, 'Well, I have the choice to afraid one more time and not be 100 percent happy, or not be afraid and be part of this album.' This is my album." However, *Céline Dion,* released by Epic in 1992, was still accused of lacking the emotional intensity Dion displays in French. These criticisms, however, belie the strong sales these albums generated; *Unison* went gold, and *Céline Dion* went platinum in the United States.

Dion's fame in the United States grew when she won a Grammy in 1993 for singing the theme from the movie *Beauty and the Beast,* a duet with Peabo Bryson. Dion created another movie-theme hit with "When I Fall in Love," a collaboration with Clive Griffin for *Sleepless in Seattle.* Around that time, her next English album, *The Colour of My Love,* was released as the flagship album of Epic's new imprint, 550 Music. Several prominent American producers worked with Dion on the album, including Ric Wake, Walter Afanasieff, and David Foster. Foster's contribution, the song "The Power of Love," quickly reached Number One on the Billboard Hot 100 chart. Charles Alexander praised the hit in *Time:* "The power behind the song ... is her bring-the-house-down voice, which turns an old, schmaltzy ballad into a soaring pop aria. That voice glides effortlessly from deep whispers to dead-on high notes, a sweet siren that combines force with grace."

Success in Both Languages

Dion feared her success in English would cost her her French-speaking fans. However, her French-language release, *Dion chante Plamondon,* became the best-selling French album in Canada in 1992. "The Power of Love" went to Number One in Canada, and her rising fame in the United States was a source of pride back home. The Montreal daily *La Presse* proclaimed: "It's a first in the history of popular music in Quebec. All indications are that [*The Colour of My Love*] will consecrate, once and for all, the chanteuse Montrealaise with our neighbors to the south."

Not only did Dion manage to hold her Canadian fans, but the popularity of her English music has encouraged wider interest in her French albums. Her 1991 release, *Des mots qui sonnent,* became a best-seller in France in 1994 and a single from the album reached Number One there.

Dion was known in Canada for the passion and humor she displayed in her French concerts, but according to Fulton, her "English concerts, by comparison, are frequently stilted by a rehearsed patter." After the release of *The Colour of My Love,* John Doelp, vice-president of marketing for Epic, told *Billboard,* "This time around, we want to fully establish the fact that Céline is a strong live performer. It's actually her strong suit." Dion's first U.S. tour as a headliner took her to ten cities, from San Francisco to New York, in early 1994. A review of her final performance of the tour in New York, by Elisabeth Vincentelli for *New York Newsday* indicated that Dion had grown more comfortable with English: "Ad-libbing between songs, Dion managed to seem down-to-earth and accessible. Whether this was consummate manipulation or spontaneous joy, she pulled it off with gusto and humor."

To achieve widespread fame, critics have suggested that Dion must expand her audience beyond the adult-contemporary market, which she has firmly conquered with her soft rock ballads and G-movie duets. Her Top-Ten singles give some evidence that she is doing so; because adults tend to buy albums, hot singles sales indicate teenagers are listening. Dion explained her goal, however, to *Time* in 1994: "I don't want to sell 5 million records and be rich, and then that's it. I'm afraid of that. I want a career. I want to sing all my life."

Selected discography

Incognito, Sony Canada, 1987.
Unison, Epic, 1990.
Dion chante Plamondon, Sony Canada, 1991.
Des mots qui sonnent, 1991.
Céline Dion, Epic, 1992.
The Colour of My Love, 550 Music/Epic, 1993.

Sources

Billboard, November 13, 1993; November 27, 1993.
Entertainment Weekly, June 24/July 1, 1994.
Maclean's, June 1, 1992.
New York Newsday, March 3, 1994.
People, June 13, 1994.
Time, February 28, 1994; March 7, 1994.
Us, December 1993.

Additional information for this profile was provided by publicity material from Epic and Sony Canada.

—*Susan Windisch Brown*

Champion Jack Dupree

Singer, songwriter

"When people appreciate what you do, it's medicine to your soul" was one of the credos of blues great Champion Jack Dupree, who overcame an early life of hardship and deprivation to become an accomplished musician. Dupree learned his craft as a teenager living on the streets of New Orleans, Louisiana, before being taken in by the Gardner family. The Gardners adopted Jack upon hearing of his parents' tragic death in a house fire when he was only one year old. It was a rare act of charity towards the young man, who, despite having older—but estranged—brothers and sisters, was the only child in the New Orleans Colored Waifs' Home for Boys never to get a gift of money or toys. "One of the warders there said to me 'How come you don't have any presents or money to buy candy?,'" Dupree once recalled. "I told him nobody left me none. And after that he always left me a little money ... for me to buy peppermint candy."

Like his contemporary Joe Pleasant, Dupree sang as a child in the bars of the former Storyville district of New Orleans. There he came into contact with a rough generation of barroom singers and pianists whose work was never recorded and survives only in anecdote and the aural memory of players like Pleasant and Dupree. Champion Jack, who acquired his nickname after training as a boxer and carving a second career as a prizefighter, knew such early New Orleans bluesmen as Little Butch and Ruby Gales. Not yet famous as a pianist, Dupree became known in his hometown as a singer at open-air concerts with the bands of legendary jazz pioneers Kid Rena and Chris Kelly.

In the late 1920s, as work grew scarce, Dupree took to the road and made his way to Chicago, where he claimed to have witnessed the murder of blues pianist Pinetop Smith. All through the 1930s he traveled the length and breadth of the United States, generally riding freight trains, panhandling, and scratching out a living as a singer or boxer. One town he visited from time to time and where he got to know the local musicians was Indianapolis. Finding himself there again in 1940, he looked up blues pioneers Scrapper Blackwell and Little Bill Gaither, through whose contacts he ended up landing a pianist job at C. Ferguson's Cotton Club. In a double act with comedienne Ophelia Hoy, Dupree became a local celebrity, and this led to his first recordings, made later that year in Chicago.

Apart from a stint of service in World War II, Dupree lived as a musician thereafter. His recording career resumed in 1945 with sides for New York City entrepreneur Joe Davis, and he went on to record prolifically through most of the next 40 years. He made many sides with Brownie McGhee and Sonny Terry and, for Atlantic in 1958, one of the first "theme" albums, *Blues From*

For the Record...

Born William Thomas Dupree, July 4, 1910, in New Orleans, LA; died of cancer, January 21, 1992, in Hanover, Germany; pseudonyms include Champion Jack, Brother Blues, Big Tom Collins, Blind Boy Johnson, Meathead Johnson, Willie Jordan, and Lightnin' Jr.; adopted at age 14 by Olivia Gardner; married first wife, Ruth, 1930 (divorced, 1944); married Lucille Dalton, 1948 (divorced, 1959); married third wife, Shirley, 1960 (divorced c. 1975); children: William Jack, Kelvin, Ann Lucille, Julie Ann, Rose Mary, Georgiana, Jackie.

Sang for tips on street corners and became self-taught pianist, New Orleans, LA; sang with New Orleans jazz bands led by Kid Rena and Chris Kelly, mid-1920s; semi-professional boxer at Kid Green's Boxing School, New Orleans; traveled Illinois Central Railroad, working as a singer and prizefighter; left boxing, became house pianist at C. Ferguson's Cotton Club, and signed with Okeh Records, 1940; moved to New York City and made records for Joe Davis and other labels, beginning in 1945; toured England, 1959; moved to Europe, 1960, and recorded and toured widely, playing concerts, clubs, and festivals; appeared in film *If You Got the Feelin'*, 1973. *Military service:* U.S. Navy, 1943-45; served as cook in the Pacific.

the Gutter, which focused on narcotic addiction and low life.

The British agency Harold Davison brought Dupree to Europe in the late 1950s, and he decided to stay, becoming a celebrity on the club, concert, and festival circuit. As a blues pioneer, he was welcomed by jazz musicians such as Chris Barber and Keith Smith, both of whom recorded and toured with him, as well as the rhythm and blues enthusiasts that were led in England by John Mayall's Bluesbreakers and guitarist Eric Clapton. After settling in Switzerland, Dupree eventually found his way to a small house in Halifax in the north of England, where he settled with his third wife, Shirley, and pronounced that he had never been happy until he arrived in Europe.

Dupree's repertoire consisted of traditional blues, southern songs—such as "Cabbage Greens" and "Chain Gang Blues"—and topical lyrics of his own, including those featured on *Warehouse Man Blues*. An album of recordings that didn't make it on 1992's *Forever and Ever* was released posthumously in 1993 on Bullseye Records. *One Last Time* was termed by James Lien in *CMJ* "quintessentially Champion Jack ... fitting in seamlessly beside his classic albums like *Blues From the Gutter* from three decades previous."

Critic John Cowley has praised the "underlying richness" of Dupree's voice, relating how it "adds a cutting edge to [his] understatement." There was an earthy soul to Dupree's playing, which captured the spirit of a vanished age of New Orleans music that went unrecorded and was preserved only in Dupree's playing and in that of Joe Pleasant. Critics have noted that Dupree became the major influence on rhythm and blues players from the South, including pianist Fats Domino, who found much to marvel at in what Cowley called Dupree's "powerfully percussive" style of playing. Dupree received great adulation and fame in Europe, but his last years in Hanover, Germany, were spent alone; it seemed that at that time the burdens of the blues tinged his ebullient playing. He died of cancer on January 21, 1992.

Selected discography

Junker Blues 1940-41 (includes "Gamblin' Man Blues" and "Cabbage Greens"), Travelin' Man.
(With Sonny Terry and Brownie McGhee) *Slow Boogie*, Folkways, 1942.
Fisherman's Blues, Joe Davis, 1945.
Blues From the Gutter, Atlantic, 1958, reissued, 1992.
(With John Mayall and Eric Clapton) *Shim-Sham-Shimmy*, Decca, 1965.
Anthologie du Blues, Vogue, 1968.
Champion Jack Dupree 1977, Isadora, 1977.
Forever and Ever, Bullseye Blues, 1992.
One Last Time, Bullseye Blues/Rounder, 1993.
I'm Happy to Be Free, GNP/Crescendo.
New Orleans Barrelhouse Boogie, Legacy.

Sources

Books

Harris, Sheldon, *Blues Who's Who,* 1979.
Oliver, Paul, *Blackwell Guide to Blues Records,* 1989.
Oliver, *Blues off the Record,* 1984.

Periodicals

CMJ, August 16, 1993.
Down Beat, May 1994.
Jazz Journal International, May 1992.
Rolling Stone, June 27, 1991.

Earth, Wind and Fire

Pop group

Earth, Wind and Fire took the world of pop music by storm in the mid-1970s with their infectious blend of rhythm and blues, rock, and soul—a sound destined to be imitated by many groups, but never successfully duplicated by any other. From the start, Earth, Wind and Fire appealed to a widely diverse audience; as one of the first black rock/soul groups to cross over to a white audience, they paved the way for the entire rhythm and blues/pop crossover phenomenon of the late 1970s and the 1980s. Built on danceable funk, Latin, and African rhythms, layered with lush horn arrangements, and topped by the sweet falsetto voice of lead singer Phil Bailey, the group's music urged listeners to enjoy life, to love, and to be open to the positive and mystical aspects of the universe.

Over the years Earth, Wind and Fire saw many members come and go from its ranks, but founder and guiding light Maurice White always remained at its heart. Like his brother, Verdine White, Maurice was among those who originally assembled to form the group in 1969. White was born in Chicago, but moved with his family to Memphis when he was still young. There, he began his musical career at the age of six, when he joined a gospel choir. As he grew older, Maurice became fascinated by marching bands and drill teams; this interest led him to take up the drums. He had his first professional gig in high school as part of a band led by Booker T. Jones of the MG's.

After high school, White returned to his home town to study music at the Chicago Conservatory. He furthered his education with club gigs on the side, and eventually got work as a session drummer for Chess Records. Throughout the 1960s, he worked with many top Motown and Chess recording artists and for other Chicago notables, including the Impressions, Billy Stewart, and Muddy Waters. From 1967 until 1969, White was a part of the Ramsey Lewis Trio. He told Melinda Newman of *Billboard* that his time with Lewis proved to be a major influence on his musical philosophy: "I wanted to come from something right in the footsteps of where he was coming from ... something that was musical, yet still entertaining, and something where the subject matter touched your heart." Lewis also introduced White to the kalimba, or African thumb piano, the sound of which would become an enduring Earth, Wind and Fire trademark.

Named for Astrological Elements

As his days with the Lewis trio drew to a close, White began to envision his own group. His dream was to bring together a sizable collection of musicians so that when touring, he would not have to hire local talent. In

For the Record . . .

Original members include **Michael Beale,** guitar; **Leslie Drayton,** horns; **Wade Flemons,** electric piano; **Sherry Scott,** vocals; **Alex Thomas,** horns; **Chester Washington,** horns; **Maurice White** (born December 19, 1941, in Chicago, IL), vocals, drums, kalimba; **Verdine White** (born July 25, 1951), bass; **Donald Whitehead,** keyboards; and **Phillard Williams,** percussion.

Later members include **Phil Bailey** (born May 8, 1951, in Denver, CO; joined band 1972), vocals, percussion; **Roland Bautista,** guitar (left band 1972; rejoined 1981); **Jessica Cleaves** (born 1943, joined and left band 1972), vocals; **Larry Dunn** (born June 19, 1953), keyboards; **Johnny Graham** (born August 3, 1951; joined band 1972), guitar; **Ralph Johnson** (born July 4, 1951), drums; **Roland Laws,** reeds (left band 1972); **Al McKay** (born February 2, 1948; bandmember, 1972-81), guitar, percussion; **Sheldon Reynolds,** vocals, guitar, Tuscanni keyboards; **Freddie White** (born January 13, 1955; joined band 1974), drums; and **Andrew Woolfolk** (born October 11, 1950), sax, flute.

Group formed c. 1969 in Los Angeles as the Salty Peppers; signed with Capitol c. 1969; renamed Earth, Wind and Fire, 1971; signed with Warner Bros., 1971; re-formed and signed with Columbia, 1972; disbanded, 1983; reunited for world tour, 1986; disbanded until 1990; signed with Warner Bros. and released *Millennium,* 1993.

Awards: Grammy Award for best single, 1975, for "Shining Star"; two Grammy awards, 1978; National Association for the Advancement of Colored People (NAACP) Hall of Fame Image Award, 1994.

Addresses: *Office*—Reprise Records, 3300 Warner Blvd., Burbank, CA 91505-4694.

1969, he moved from Chicago to Los Angeles and assembled the precursor to Earth, Wind and Fire. The group, called the Salty Peppers, recorded for Capitol for a couple of years without drawing much notice; in 1971, White signed a new contract with Warner Brothers and renamed the group Earth, Wind and Fire after the elements in his astrological chart.

In less than two years, Earth, Wind and Fire released three albums: *Earth, Wind and Fire, The Need of Love,* and the soundtrack *Sweet Sweetback's Baadasss Song.* They had two chart singles—"Love is Life" in 1971 and "Evil" in 1973—but by the time the latter was released, White had decided that Warner was not the label for him. He signed a new contract with Columbia. At the same time, he disbanded the group that had begun as the Salty Peppers and assembled a new, younger version of Earth, Wind and Fire. In addition to himself and Verdine, the new group featured vocalist Phil Bailey, who had been working with the Stoval Sisters' Band; Johnny Graham, of the Nite-Liters; Jessica Cleaves, from the Friends of Distinction; and Al McKay from the Watts 103rd St. Rhythm Band.

The new group worked well together from the start, and their first Columbia release, *Open Your Eyes,* went to Number 15 on the album charts in 1974. The band's real breakthrough came the following year, however, after their appearance in the film *That's the Way of the World.* The soundtrack album from that movie, which featured their music, climbed into the Top Ten album chart, propelled by the success of Earth, Wind and Fire's Grammy-winning single, "Shining Star." They appeared in another film, Robert Stigwood's 1978 release *Sgt. Pepper's Lonely Hearts Club Band,* and scored another Top Ten hit with their cover of the Beatles' "Got to Get You into My Life." The disco trend made them into true superstars; hit singles, and gold, platinum and double platinum albums became routine. Between 1971 and 1988, they had 38 hits on the rhythm and blues charts, all but six of which crossed over to the pop charts.

Changes in the group's lineup were fairly frequent, but never affected its appeal. Their popularity enabled Earth, Wind and Fire to fill huge stadiums when they toured; they used these cavernous venues to their advantage by creating an innovative stage show featuring magic created by the master of illusion, Doug Henning. Mystical trappings such as giant pyramids wowed the audiences, as did the fireworks, disappearances, and the sight of the band "flying" to their places on stage.

Hiatus After Decade of Hits

In 1983, after ten years of continuous hits, Earth, Wind and Fire officially declared themselves on hiatus. Maurice White formed his own company, Kalimba Productions, and devoted much of his time to producing and composing for other recording artists, including the Emotions (who were featured on Earth, Wind and Fire's 1979 smash single "Boogie Wonderland"), Ramsey Lewis, Deneice Williams, Valerie Carter, Barbra Streisand, Neil Diamond, and Jennifer Holliday. In addition,

White worked on a number of film soundtracks, including *Armed and Dangerous* and *Coming to America*. Phil Bailey also launched a successful solo career, topping the charts with "Easy Lover"—a duet with Phil Collins that was featured on the album *Chinese Wall*—and making his mark in the world of gospel music with offerings such as the Grammy-winning album *Triumph!* In 1986, Earth, Wind and Fire reunited to record *Touch the World,* an album they backed with a nine-month world tour, but members went their separate ways again until 1990, when they recorded *Heritage.*

Earth, Wind and Fire's influence on the sound of popular music was evident in their career retrospective, *The Eternal Dance,* released in 1992. The groundbreaking, 55-track boxed set covered two decades of music, including cuts from long out-of-print recordings from their early years with Warner Brothers, the best of their glory years with Columbia, and a number of previously unreleased tracks. Critic James Hunter remarked in his *Musician* review of the album: "*The Eternal Dance* collects some of the most fluent, centered and elastic pop music ever recorded. Its influence is everywhere."

Released *Millenium*

The release of the retrospective and the group's years of relative inactivity might have seemed to signal the end of an era, but even as the retrospective was being released, Earth, Wind and Fire was working on new music for the nineties. In May of 1992, the core group of Maurice White, Verdine White, and Phil Bailey went into the studio with a revamped horn section to record *Millennium,* an album of all-new music.

Maurice White had grown unhappy with Columbia Records during the last years of his contract with the organization, feeling that executives there were trying to steer his group in a direction that was not in line with his vision of what Earth, Wind and Fire should be. Accordingly, before going to work on *Millennium,* he signed a new contract with his old label, Warner Brothers. The result was a classic Earth, Wind and Fire album, filled with their smooth vocals, trademark horns, and sense of spirituality. Commenting on the album's name to Melinda Newman, White joked: "'Millennium' just felt right to me, I didn't even know the meaning to it. When people ask me, 'What does "Millennium" mean?,' I'm going to have to tell them I had to look it up. Or I can just tell them it took us that long to get another album out."

Selected discography

Earth, Wind and Fire, Warner Bros., 1970.
The Need of Love, Warner Bros., 1972.
Last Days and Time, Columbia, 1972.
Head to the Sky, Columbia, 1973.
Another Time, Warner Bros., 1974.
Open Our Eyes, Columbia, 1974.
That's the Way of the World, Columbia, 1975.
Gratitude, Columbia, 1975.
Spirit, Columbia, 1976.
All 'n' All, Columbia, 1977.
Best of Earth, Wind and Fire, Volume I, Columbia, 1978.
I Am, Columbia, 1979.
Face, Columbia, 1981.
Raise, Columbia, 1981.
Powerlight, Columbia, 1983.
Touch the World, Columbia, 1987.
Heritage, Columbia, 1990.
The Eternal Dance, Columbia, 1992.
Millennium, Warner Bros., 1993.
Electric Universe, Columbia.
The Best of Earth, Wind and Fire, Volume 2, Columbia.
Sweet Sweetback's Baadasss Song (soundtrack).

Sources

Billboard, September 18, 1993; January 15, 1994.
Entertainment Weekly, December 11, 1992.
High Fidelity, March 1988.
Musician, January 1993.
New York Times, December 13, 1992.
Rolling Stone, January 14, 1988; March 22, 1990; December 10, 1992.
Stereo Review, April 1988; June 1990.

—Joan Goldsworthy

Kenneth "Babyface" Edmonds

Producer, singer, songwriter

Photograph by Randee St. Nicholas, © 1993 Sony Music, courtesy of Epic Records

As half of the R&B production team of L.A. and Babyface, Kenneth "Babyface" Edmonds—according to Gordon Chambers of *Vibe*—"is clearly an architect of today's black pop scene." Together with longtime friend and collaborator Antonio "L.A." Reid, Edmonds helped forge the smooth R&B sound that has dominated the charts since the late 1980s, writing and producing hit records for Whitney Houston, Bobby Brown, Paula Abdul, Boyz II Men, TLC, Toni Braxton, and many others. A *Keyboard* magazine writer deemed him "that rarest of creatures, a producer with a Midas touch."

Not content to remain behind the recording console, however, Edmonds has also pursued a successful career as a solo artist. Calling himself a "hesitant artist" in an *Essence* interview with David Ritz, Edmonds has parlayed his passionate vocals, elegant, shy manner, and matinee-idol looks into platinum sales. For his part, he told legendary soul singer Aretha Franklin in a phone conversation transcribed in *Interview*, "I like to think I write romantic songs that affect people strictly in the heart, which is my only concern. I don't look to save the world."

Love and music have always been inextricably combined for Edmonds. He grew up in the Midwest, the second youngest of six boys, and—as he told Ritz—"I fell in love almost every day. I fell in love at the drop of a hat. I can remember falling in love as far back as kindergarten." These episodes of infatuation always had a soundtrack. "When I was falling in love with love, I was also falling in love with melody. [Soul superstar] Stevie Wonder's melodies, the Beatles' melodies—any pretty melody might move me. Melodies spoke to me about the state of my own heart." At a young age he learned guitar. And while he was still an adolescent, Edmonds lost his father, leaving his mother to raise her sons alone. Edmonds became determined to have a career in music.

Learned Production With the Deele

While in the ninth grade, Edmonds used this determination to devise a way to meet some of his musical idols. He confided to Jack Baird of *Musician* that he would phone concert promoters pretending to be his teacher, asking if the musicians would grant his gifted young charge—namely himself—an interview. Civic-minded chart-toppers like the Jackson 5, Stevie Wonder, and funk hitmakers Earth, Wind and Fire agreed, and Edmonds was able to chat with them. Baird theorized that young Babyface made very good mental notes of whatever they divulged and stored them away for later use.

For the Record...

Born Kenneth Edmonds, c. 1958, in Indianapolis, IN; married and divorced, c. 1980s; married Tracey (a model), 1992.

Producer, songwriter, arranger, keyboardist, guitarist, and solo performing and recording artist, late 1970s—. Member of groups ManChild and the Deele; with L.A. Reid, wrote for and produced recordings by the Deele, Shalamar, the Whispers, After 7, Karyn White, Bobby Brown, Johnny Gill, Whitney Houston, Paula Abdul, TLC, Boyz II Men, Toni Braxton, and others; released debut solo album, *Lovers,* on Solar/Epic, 1989; co-founded LaFace Records, 1989; appeared on TV show *Beverly Hills 90210,* 1994.

Awards: (With L.A. Reid) producer of the year, Broadcast Music Inc. (BMI), 1990; platinum awards, 1990, for *Tender Lover,* and 1994, for *For the Cool in You*; (with L.A. Reid) Grammy Award for producer of the year, 1993, for *Boomerang.*

Addresses: *Home*—Beverly Hills, CA, and Lake Tahoe, NV. *Record company*—Epic Records, 2100 Colorado Ave., Santa Monica, CA 90404, and 550 Madison Ave., New York, NY 10022-3297; Arista Records, 6 West 57th St., New York, NY 10019. *Fan club*—Babyface, 14755 Ventura Blvd., 1-710, Sherman Oaks, CA 91403.

In Indianapolis, Edmonds played in Top 40 bands and then in a funk group called ManChild. While in the latter ensemble he realized that, as he explained in a *Keyboard* interview, "the only way I'd really be able to grow in terms of my writing was to pick up keyboards." It was in the Cincinnati group the Deele, however—formed with his friend Reid—that Edmonds first got noticed. After Dick Griffey, the head of Solar Records, noticed the duo's producing skills on their own work, the two were enlisted to write and produce for The Whispers and Shalamar; soon after they were producing big-name acts like the Jacksons, not to mention newcomers Karyn White, After 7 (featuring two of Edmonds's brothers and one of his cousins) and Pebbles (who married Reid). Their work with up-and-coming soul crooner Bobby Brown—particularly his hits "Don't Be Cruel" and "Every Little Step," both of which were written by Edmonds—helped Edmonds and Reid break through to the next level. Soon they were writing for and producing some of the biggest stars in pop, notably Paula Abdul and Whitney Houston. With the exception of R&B stalwarts Jimmy Jam and Terry Lewis, they had little competition among production duos.

Developed Distinctive Sound

"I kind of just stumbled into producing," Edmonds insisted to Franklin in their *Interview* dialogue. "It was more that I was a writer, and the only way you were going to get your songs done was to do them yourself." Yet he and Reid synched more than sounds in the studio: "Our musical souls blended," he declared to Ritz of *Essence.* "We shared a similar drive for success." With Reid programming the drums, Edmonds playing keyboards and guitar and handling most of the backup vocals, their friend Kayo laying down the basslines, and Darryl Simmons providing production assistance, the team developed a distinctive and very influential style.

Musician's Baird wrote that "the core L.A. & Babyface sound has always included spunky electronic textures, explosive percussion and complex, rubbery bass lines, even as it's changed to stay ahead of an army of imitators." Robert L. Oderschuk of *Keyboard* described the duo's trademark sound as "built on crystalline [electric piano] Rhodes-like timbres, light but stinging backbeats flicking through layers of gauzy echo, radical scratch-like gating on the snare in upbeat tunes, sparse synthetic strings, lush backup harmonies, an overall delicacy even on dance tracks."

During this time Edmonds was also tasting his first success as a solo performing artist, as his 1989 album *Tender Lover* went double-platinum, thanks in large part to singles like the smash hit "Whip Appeal." The recording's success, he told a *Billboard* interviewer, "was so gradual, and so quiet, that I didn't realize how well it was doing."

He was equally surprised, he said, by the response of concert audiences when he went on tour with Pebbles before recording the album. "I was blown away by the audience's reaction," he said, though he confided to Ritz of *Essence* that "I wish being a public person came easier to me, but I can't change my character. I can't betray my privacy."

Edmonds's self-effacement in interviews has been almost proportional to his huge success. "I don't call myself a keyboard player," he claimed in his *Keyboard* interview. "I'm a writer who uses keyboards to get the songs done. I'm not even close to being a keyboard player." He evinced similar modesty in *Musician:* "I don't claim to be a great vocalist, but I know how to work my voice with its limitations. My talent is I know how to work what I have. It might not always be a picture-perfect performance, but what we look for is the emotion. Sometimes the emotion comes from it being just a pinch sharp or flat."

Conquered R&B World

Late in 1989 Reid and Edmonds established their own company, LaFace, which would develop and produce talent and make records that its parent company, Arista, would distribute. "With the importance that black music plays in the overall scheme of music," Reid opined in a *Grammy* interview, "to not have more successful black owned and operated record companies is really sad. We obviously have the talent and capable executives who help run so many other labels." The company based itself in Atlanta, and soon attracted an impressive array of talent.

Edmonds and Reid were honored by Broadcast Music Inc. (BMI) as songwriters of the year in 1990. They had emerged as two of the biggest players on the music scene, although this didn't shield them from criticism, some of it delicate (Oderschuk called them "craftsmen" rather than "innovators," citing their commercial savvy at the expense of risk-taking) and some harsh: *Musician* noted that "Critic Nelson George castigated the Reid/Edmonds sound as the epitome of homogenized L.A. pap." The pair fended off claims that such "homogenization" represented an attempt to soften the distinctively African-American traits of the R&B form. "We're Black artists creating out of a Black bag [of styles and influences]," Edmonds insisted in *Essence*.

As the decade progressed, the duo launched a number of successful new acts, most notably Johnny Gill, TLC, and Toni Braxton. "With TLC, it was their personalities," Edmonds told Franklin in *Interview*. "They gave off the vibe that made you feel, O.K., these kids are stars, and you just needed to put the right music with them and let them go. Toni Braxton auditioned with her sisters, and she just shined. And I thought, 'I can write for her.' She can deliver something emotional and get it across. That's really what I look for—someone who can pull off that emotion." In addition, LaFace scooped a number of larger labels in obtaining the opportunity to release the soundtrack album to the movie *Boomerang*, starring Eddie Murphy. The album's single "End of the Road," written by Edmonds and performed by Boyz II Men, won a Grammy.

Split With Reid, Released *Cool*

In 1992, Edmonds, who had been married for a brief period during his twenties, wed again. Tracey Edmonds was a model who auditioned for the "Whip Appeal" video, and when the couple met again at a later date, Edmonds explained in *Jet*, "It was like a 'meant to be' kind of thing." Having begun this new partnership, however, Edmonds elected to end—or at least scale back—his longtime relationship with Reid.

Just after earning a Grammy for producer of the year for the *Boomerang* soundtrack, the two decided to go their separate ways, a move that first reached the press in rumor form before a formal announcement in 1994. "You don't want anyone to have preconceived notions that because you did it as a team that it can't be done separately," Edmonds insisted in *Jet*. "It's still about music. It's not really that different. I'm just bouncing things off myself at this point." Edmonds and Reid vowed to work together on LaFace, but the former told *Entertainment Weekly* that his solo output would now take up more of his time: "It's satisfying to see Boyz II Men or Whitney singing one of my songs. But I've never given my own career as an artist 100 percent. I do wonder if I can turn it into something bigger."

Edmonds's second album, 1993's *For the Cool in You*—co-produced by Reid—turned his career into something bigger when it went platinum in early 1994. "Babyface continues the nearly forgotten tradition of *solo* black R&B lover men," wrote *Rolling Stone*'s Touré, who generally praised the album despite taking issue with its stylistic conservatism. Chambers of *Vibe* noted that "the subtle soul man uses his seductive falsetto, passion-over-precision phrasing, and well-timed growls to woo his listeners," and found the album "a perfect vehicle for his vocal melisma." Edmonds announced in *Jet* his plans to produce an album by R&B veteran El deBarge. Happy with his home life, he appeared poised to conquer more frontiers of the pop world. "I feel settled, comfortable," he remarked, adding "God blessed me. I don't know why. I'm just blessed. There's no particular magic involved."

Selected discography

With the Deele; on Solar/Epic

Street Beat.
Material Thangz.
Eyes of a Stranger.

Solo releases

Lovers, Solar/Epic, 1989.
Tender Lover (includes "Whip Appeal"), Solar/Epic, 1989.
For the Cool in You, Epic, 1993.

With other artists

Boomerang (soundtrack; appears on "Give You My Heart"; album also includes "End of the Road"), LaFace, 1993.

As contributing producer/songwriter

The Whispers, *Just Gets Better with Time,* Solar, 1987.
Shalamar, *Circumstantial Evidence,* Solar, 1987.
The Boys, *Message from the Boys,* Motown, 1988.
Pebbles, *Pebbles,* MCA, 1988.
Karyn White, *Karyn White,* Warner Bros., 1988.
Bobby Brown, *Don't Be Cruel* (wrote and produced title song and "Every Little Step"), MCA, 1988.
Dance... Ya Know It!, MCA, 1989.
Sheena Easton, *The Lover in Me,* MCA, 1989.
Paula Abdul, *Forever Your Girl,* Virgin, 1989.
After 7, *After 7,* Virgin, 1989.
Whitney Houston, *I'm Your Baby Tonight,* Arista, 1990.
The Boys, *The Boys,* Motown, 1990.
Johnny Gill, *Johnny Gill,* Motown, 1990.
Bobby (wrote and produced "Humpin' Around"), MCA, 1992.
TLC, *Ooooooh! On the TLC Tip,* LaFace/Arista, 1992.
Boomerang (soundtrack), LaFace/Arista, 1993.
Toni Braxton, *Toni Braxton,* LaFace/Arista, 1993.

Sources

Billboard, December 1, 1990; June 15, 1991; August 28, 1993; March 26, 1994.
Entertainment Weekly, September 10, 1993.
Essence, September 1990.
Grammy, December 1992.
Interview, March 1994.
Jet, July 16, 1990; March 14, 1994.
Keyboard, November 1990.
Los Angeles Times, July 25, 1993.
Musician, October 1990; March 1994.
Rolling Stone, October 28, 1993.
Upscale, July 1994.
Vibe, September 1993; December 1993.

Additional information was obtained from Epic Records publicity materials, 1993.

—*Simon Glickman*

The Fall

Rock band

The Fall's lead singer, Mark Smith, has at some point or another heaped disapproval on every musical trend that has taken place since his own teenage years in the 1970s, including punk, which is the slot most critics choose for the band. Smith has expressed more comfort with the term "speed metal," which refers to a hybrid of heavy metal and 1970s British punk. He has also called his music "prole," invoking the proletariat, or industrial working-class, roots of his sound and politics. The one constant in an ever-changing line-up of musicians, Smith operates as the band's spokesperson and "boss," as well as its founder. Definition and personnel aside, the Fall has been producing its particular brand of music since 1977, when teenaged Smith, then a dock-worker in Manchester, northern England's industrial capitol, decided to dedicate his free time to forming a band.

Before putting together the Fall, Smith made some effort to become a part of already-working heavy metal bands. David Cavanagh, who wrote the publicity biography for Matador/Atlantic, noted that Smith had "had

Courtesy of Matador / Atlantic Records

> **For the Record...**
>
> Band members include **Dave Bush,** keyboards; **Steve Hanley,** bass; **Craig Scanlon,** guitar; **Mark E. Smith** (married Brix [a musician]) vocals; **Simon Wolstencraft,** drums. Other members include **Martin Bramah,** guitar; **Brix** (bandmember 1983-89), bass; **Karl Burns,** drums; **Tony Friel,** bass.
>
> Group formed in Manchester, England, and recorded demo with New Hormones label, 1977; played locals clubs in Manchester until moving to London, 1978; began recording with Step Forward label; moved to Rough Trade label; recorded with Beggar's Banquet, 1984-89; recorded with Phonogram label, 1989-92; signed contract with Matador/Atlantic, 1993.
>
> **Addresses:** *Record company*—Matador, 676 Broadway, 4th Floor, New York, NY 10012.

a few auditions for local heavy metal bands, all of which he had failed in a spectacular fashion. He was tone-deaf and they all hated him anyway." Always resourceful, Smith simply decided to create a band around himself. He gathered the musicians who would become the first incarnation of the Fall: Martin Bramah on guitar; Tony Friel on bass; Karl Burns on drums. None of them were adept with their instruments, so they had the usual punk sound of the era: loud, harsh, entirely without melody, and generally tuneless. Smith wrote lyrics during his lunch break at the docks; it was, in the long run, the originality, boldness, and social punch of those lyrics that would win the band a following.

Beginning the Fall

An independent label called New Hormones funded the Fall's first demo tape, but the company decided not to produce the album; it turned out that no one else wanted to either. Smith explained to Cavanagh: "Nobody liked it.... Everywhere we went, nobody wanted to know. They wanted to make it New Wave.... It was rough and all that. Out of tune and that. It was good. Stark, sort of." A year after the recording, they finally released the *Bingo Master's Breakout* EP on Step Forward, another independent punk label. Step Forward would work with the Fall for two more releases: *Live at the Witch Trials,* also in 1978, and *Dragnet* in 1979.

As soon as the recording was set in 1978, the band underwent the first in a series of metamorphoses: Smith brought in Una Baines, an organist who also worked as a nurse in a mental hospital. By 1979, however, Baines *and* Friel were gone, replaced by two teenagers: Marc Riley on bass and Yvonne Pawlett on keyboards. The year continued with more acquisitions, including Craig Scanlon on guitar, Steve Hanley on bass, and Mike Leigh on drums. Scanlon and Hanley, unlike anyone else Smith hired, would stay with the band into the 1990s; all three appear on *Dragnet*. Leigh was soon supplemented with a second drummer, Paul Hanley, who was Steve's teenaged brother.

By this time Smith had established a salary system for the band, issuing equal paychecks to all musicians, including himself. When the return on shows and recordings actually exceeded those paychecks, all extra went back into the band itself, rather than into the pockets of the members. Through this method, the band became an investment that would continually employ its members, whoever they may be.

In those early years, however, The Fall was just managing to scrape by on Manchester club dates, as Smith told Cavanagh: "We were doing cabaret circuits at the time, just to earn money.... Workingmen's clubs and all that.... It toughened you up. They'd be throwing glasses—proper glasses, like—and spitting at you." Smith traces devoted cult following from those shows, stressing in particular the working-class element: miners from Wakefield and Newcastle. When the outfit relocated to London in 1978, the band's survival was guaranteed only by Smith's and Baine's jobs, which they used as subsidy.

Brix Entered the Sound

After the first two albums with Step Forward, the band started on a pattern of moving through independent labels, sometimes leaving out of dissatisfaction, sometimes because a label died on them, as small companies were prone to do. They had one of their longer, if still far from perfect, associations with Rough Trade, with whom they first recorded *Totale's Turn (It's Now Or Never) (:Live)* in 1979. During this year the band also produced two singles that would eventually become Fall classics: "How I Wrote Elastic Man" and "Totally Wired." They would stay with Rough Trade for two more albums, *Grotesque (After the Gramme)* in 1980 and *Slates* in 1981.

Despite the productive pace, according to Cavanagh, "Smith was convinced" by 1981 that the band would dissolve soon. With that in mind, he produced what he expected to be "the last Fall album": *Hex Enduction Hour,* released in 1982. Since an hour-long LP was virtually unprecedented, it appeared to be a kind of epic, which contained, in Cavanagh's words, "everything [Smith] felt and thought" and "almost as many words as the Bible." A six-musician lineup appeared on this release, including Karl Burns's return as a second drummer. But *Hex* was not the swan song of the Fall, and they actually released another album in 1982, *Room to Live.* For both of these productions, the band took a break from Rough Trade, "starving away," as Cavanagh wrote, "on the tiny Kamera label, which soon went bust."

Hex coincided with a brief courtship from legendary U.S. label, Motown Records; the interest fizzled when the company that had opened up the record industry for African-American musical talent realized that the Fall's lyrics could sport occasional bursts of troubling racism. The band encountered similar criticisms from Rough Trade; despite its background producing punk outfits, the label was uncomfortable with the coarseness, vulgarity, and violence that permeated Smith's lyrics.

British Media Discovered the Fall

After completing *Perverted By Language* the match proved too difficult, and the Fall moved on. By this time, however, the band had enough of a following to be able to open record company doors fairly quickly. A kind of breakthrough occurred in the same year: the British media actually discovered the Fall, culminating in an appearance on national television.

Their sound had begun to change—becoming more melodic—largely due to the introduction, in 1983, of an American musician named Brix into Smith's life and band. Smith and Brix met at a Fall show in Chicago; they were married soon after. By fall, Brix was playing bass in the band, at first only occasionally and then more and more regularly. She became, as Cavanagh summarized, "The Fall's arranger, key melodic song writer and (undeniably) visual attraction."

Despite growing fame, the band continued to operate on its "prole" work ethic; they put out albums on an at least annual rate, including *The Wonderful and Frightening World of the Fall* in 1984, two albums in 1985, and one a year through 1988.

The 1984 album also led to an unlikely collaboration with ballet-dancer Michael Clark, a Fall fan who wanted to combine their music with his dancing. The product, an operatic ballet entitled *Kurious Oranji,* took Clark and Smith six months to create. After an Amsterdam opening, the performance traveled to Edinburgh and finished with two weeks in London—a respectable run for such an unusual venture. A recording of the work would appear in 1988 as *I Am Kurious Oranji.*

Brix, Clark, and a musician named Simon Rogers all coincided to provide that growth stage that the band was going through. Cavanagh explained, for example, the freshness of Brix's style, which emphasized the former prejudices of Smith's: "It was a bit of new scene for Smith—choruses and structures and middle eights." Simon Rogers, a classically trained musician capable of handling any instrument, furthered those changes in 1985. Rogers first joined the band as a temporary, filling in on bass for Steve Hanley's six-month absence. By the time the Fall released *This Nation's Saving Grace* in 1985, Rogers had moved to keyboard; he stayed with the band until 1986, through the release of *Bend Sinister.*

> *"When I've got nothin' else to say, I'll pack it in."*
> — Mark E. Smith

These various influences appeared to be positive, contributing to their effect on audiences by 1987: "Fall now earn respect of entire music biz," declared Jon Wilde, writing for Matador. They had a further success with the single "Hit the North"; Cavanagh claimed that it "blasted the Fall forward as an unexpectedly menacing dance proposition."

Smith conducted more hirings and firings in the late 1980s, not the least of which was the very emotionally charged departure of Brix in 1989. Rogers and Paul Hanley left, on generally good terms, and were replaced by Marcia Schofield on keyboards and Simon Wolstencroft on drums, both of whom appeared on *The Frenz Experiment* in 1988 and the cover of a Kinks single, "Victoria." After Brix left in 1989, Martin Bramah returned to play guitar. Bramah, however, lasted only through 1990's *Extricate,* after which Smith fired both him and Schofield. The decision seemed odd, since the album received, as Cavanagh noted, "across-the-board rave reviews"; about those changes, Smith told Cavanagh, "I wanted to make the band more sparse.... We were a six-piece, almost a seven-piece."

By this time, Smith had a reputation as a kind of proletarian *enfant terrible*; the press characterized him as an eccentric willing to express an acerbic opinion on everything, particularly the politics, national and international, that he perceived to be keeping the British working class out of work. As Andrew Perry remarked in *Select,* "Mark relishes the opportunity to spout off in interviews." In 1990, Steven Wills declared in *New Musical Express,* "We like Mark because Mark is sharp and because his band have kept the flag flying for white trash music that is impolite and jagged and not ... quite ... *right* ... through all the bitter years of conformist poodlefakery and indie incompetence." More pointedly, Wills commented on the source of that attitude: "Mark has reinvented himself as Mark E. Smith, the working class lad with two chip shops on each shoulder who is convinced of his brilliance, wisdom and uniqueness despite (or because of) his background in an education system that told he was shit and prepared him for the role of under-achieving epsilon."

An association with Phonogram records that began with *Extricate* produced several more critically-acclaimed albums before crumbling in a bitter break-up after *Code: Selfish* in 1992. By this time, however, a resurgence of interest allowed The Fall to strike fast deals with Permanent in England and the Matador/Atlantic combination in the United States. The fresh attention was fostered in part by an evident influence surfacing in young bands, particularly American grunge rock bands, like Nirvana, that catapulted to fame in the early 1990s.

John Harris, writing for *New Musical Express* in 1993, raved over the slew of successful singles that preceded *The Infotainment Scan,* including "Why Are People Grudgeful?," "Lost in Music," and "Glam Racket." "Why Are People Grudgeful?" earned single of the week status from both *NME* and *Select.* In his review for the latter, Andrew Collins claimed that "time cannot tarnish them, age does not lessen their impact, changes of line-up (and, indeed, label) serve only to consolidate Mark E. Smith's unfathomable vision."

Paul Ashby paid similar tribute to their longevity in *Pulse!,* remarking particularly on the band's "dignity": "The Fall has endured (and often presaged) more changes in fashion than any other band, while never compromising its original purpose—to serve as a soapbox for Smith's satiric and mercilessly honest social/political observations." Smith, however, has the last word on that career, as he told *Spin's* Mark Blackwell when he expressed his "deep contempt" for over-the-hill rockers, implying that Elvis Costello, Paul McCartney, and David Bowie were making music without any purpose to it anymore; he set himself apart, saying, "When I've got nothin' else to say, I'll f—in' pack it in."

Selected discography

Live At the Witch Trials, Step Forward, 1978.
Dragnet, Step Forward, 1979.
Totale's Turns (It's Now or Never) (:Live), Rough Trade, 1979.
Grotesque (After the Gramme), Rough Trade, 1980.
Slates, Rough Trade, 1981.
Hex Enduction Hour, Kamera, 1982.
Early Years '77-'79, Step Forward, 1981.
Room to Live, Kamera, 1982.
Perverted by Language, Rough Trade, 1983.
The Wonderful and Frightening World of the Fall, Beggars Banquet, 1984.
Hip Priests and Kamerads, Situation Two, 1985.
This Nation's Saving Grace, Beggars Banquet, 1985.
Bend Sinister, Beggars Banquet, 1986.
Palace of Swords Reversed, Cog Sinister, 1987.
The Frenz Experiment, Beggars Banquet, 1988.
I Am Kurious Oranji, Beggars Banquet, 1988.
Seminal Live, Beggars Banquet, 1989.
Extricate, Cog Sinister/Phonogram, 1990.
Shift-Work, Cog Sinister/Phonogram, 1991.
Code: Selfish, Cog Sinister/Phonogram, 1992.
Kimble (EP), BBC Radio 1/Strange Fruit, 1993.
The Infotainment Scan, Permanent/Matador-Atlantic, 1993.
Middle Class Revolt, Matador, 1994.

Sources

Guitar Player, August 1993.
New Musical Express, August 25, 1990; April 3, 1993.
New York Times, August 20, 1993.
Pulse!, November 1993.
Rolling Stone, September 16, 1993.
Select, May 1993.
Spin, October 1993.
Variety, May 30, 1990.

Additional information for this profile was obtained from Matador/Atlantic press materials.

—Ondine Le Blanc

Eddie Fisher

Singer

Skyrocketing to fame after he was "discovered" by Eddie Cantor in 1949, Eddie Fisher replaced Frank Sinatra as the number-one "bobby-soxer" singing idol in the early 1950s. His innocent good looks, strong and straightforward voice, and choice of material made him one of the most popular recording artists of the first half of the decade. From 1950 to 1956 Fisher recorded 35 Top 40 hits, including 19 in the Top Ten and four that reached Number One on the U.S. Hit Parade.

Although Fisher is Jewish, his style has been compared to those of famous Italian tenors and baritones. Fisher's booming voice hardly needed a microphone to carry to the back rows of big theaters, and his early nickname of "Sonny Boy" reflected his fondness for singing in a style reminiscent of Al Jolson. Fisher has been described as having a freewheeling approach and lack of musical of musical discipline that often tested the patience of his accompanists.

According to George Simon in *The Best of the Music Makers,* "The title of Fisher's biggest hit record, 'Any Time,' reflects rather accurately his unpredictably wandering rhythmic beat that for years musicians tried valiantly to follow as he gaily and unconcernedly created his own time by decimating or elongating musical measures." Although Fisher's rhythm difficulties and his unsubtle singing approach sometimes resulted in unfavorable appraisals by critics, the crooner's deficiencies did not deter millions of fans from buying his records.

Edwin Jack Fisher started singing at a young age while growing up in a poor section of south Philadelphia. Much of his musical development took place while singing in the local synagogue, and by age seven he was performing in local amateur contests. He has said that an early role model for his powerful delivery was his father, who used to yell to customers when selling fruits and vegetables from his truck. At age 13 Fisher won first place in a contest on a local radio show. As a teenager he appeared often on radio stations around Philadelphia, earning as little as 15 cents a week for his efforts. He performed regularly at clubs until the late 1940s, but got little recognition outside the Philadelphia area.

After landing a singing job with Buddy Morrow's band at age 17, he went with the band to New York City and tried out at the famed Copacabana nightclub. Although Fisher was turned down by the club because he hadn't yet turned 18, the club's director, Monte Proser, was impressed and introduced him to Milton Blackstone, an agent who started representing the singer. Blackstone landed Fisher some work, but he performed only sporadically over the next few years.

For the Record...

Born Edwin Jack Fisher, August 10, 1928, in Philadelphia, PA; son of Joe (a vegetable and fruit vendor) and Kate Fisher; married Debbie Reynolds, 1955 (divorced); married Elizabeth Taylor, 1958 (divorced); married Connie Stevens, late 1960s (divorced); married fourth wife; children: actress Carrie Fisher (with Reynolds). *Military service:* U.S. Army, 1951-53.

Pop singer. Performed in local amateur shows and on radio while in high school in Philadelphia, 1940s; won Horn and Hardart Children's Hour radio contest, 1941; began singing between acts at the Broadway Paramount Theatre, New York City, 1946; became singer with Buddy Morrow's band, 1945; sang with Charlie Ventura's band, 1946; won Arthur Godfrey Talent Scout contest, 1948; discovered by Eddie Cantor while performing at Grossinger's in the Catskills, NY, 1949; began singing on Eddie Cantor's radio show, 1949; signed recording contract with RCA Victor, 1949; had first hit, "Thinking of You," 1950; had first million-selling record, "Any Time," 1951; recorded four Top Ten albums, 1952-54; recorded 35 Top 40 hits and appeared frequently on major television shows and in top nightclubs, 1950s; starred in television show "Coke Time and the Chesterfield Supper Club," 1953-57; staged minor comeback with hit "Games That Lovers Play," 1966; performed sporadically during 1970s.

Awards: Named America's most promising new male vocalist in a national poll of disc jockeys, *Billboard*, 1950; five gold records, 1951-56.

Addresses: *Management*—Neal Hollander Agency, 250 Lexington Ave., New York, NY 10016

Fisher's timing was perfect when he sang at Grossinger's in New York state's Catskills on Labor Day of 1949. Singer Eddie Cantor was in the audience for the show, and he found Fisher's style so appealing that he invited him to join his traveling tour. Fisher then signed on with Cantor's radio show, and his continued exposure landed him a recording contract with RCA-Victor in 1949. By 1950 the singer had his first hit, "Thinking of You," and his popularity grew with remarkable speed from that point on. His first million-seller was the 1951 release "Any Time," a song originally performed in the early 1920s.

Fisher's induction into the army in 1951 did not slow the flowering of his fame. In fact, well-publicized photographs of him in uniform helped seal his image as a heartthrob for teenaged girls. Fisher was soon put to work on the recruiting effort for the Korean War, and he appeared often on television to promote enlistment. *Variety* said at the time, "His fresh, clean-cut handling of ballads is solid lure to the younger crowd, both male and female, and his wearing of the army khaki adds a glamour touch."

Fisher returned to the recording studio when he had furloughs during his two-year hitch, and while in uniform managed to record ten hits that racked up sales of seven million records. By the time he was released from active duty in 1953, he had become one of the most popular recording artists in the United States. Among his blockbuster songs of that time were "Lady of Spain," "Outside of Heaven," and "Wish You Were Here" in 1952, followed by "I'm Walking Behind You" and "Oh, My Papa" in 1953.

During the first five years after Cantor helped bring him into the big time, Fisher's recording sold over ten million records. From 1952 to 1954, he made four albums that soared into the Top Ten. A frequent headliner at major nightclub and a featured guest on highly rated television programs, Fisher began starring on his own television show, "Coke Time and the Chesterfield Supper Club," with comedian George Gobel in 1953. Gobel and Fisher starred in alternate weeks on the show, which stayed on the air for four years. He later appeared in films, including *Bundle of Joy* in 1956 and *Butterfield 8* in 1960.

Fisher was particularly successful with recordings of songs from Broadway shows. His rendition of "Heart" from *Damn Yankees* reached Number Six on the Hit Parade in 1955. But by 1956 his fame began to fade. Although his records sold enough to keep him in the recording studio, the rise of rock and roll left him behind as a teen idol. At this point his name appeared less on the marquis than in newspaper gossip columns reporting on his various marriages. Fisher married actress Debbie Reynolds in 1955, then abruptly left Reynolds to marry actress Elizabeth Taylor in 1958 after Taylor's husband, film producer Mike Todd, was killed in an airplane crash.

Legal and financial problems besieged Fisher in the early 1960s, and his performances dwindled. He managed to reach the Hit Parade again in 1966 with "The Games Lovers Play," but that was his last song to make the charts. He continued trying to make a comeback but had become a has-been before turning 40 years of age. In his autobiography, Fisher claimed that he was not cut out for superstardom. He blamed the relentless attention and other trappings of celebrity for his downfall, even claiming that the press had forced him to marry Debbie Reynolds. After his marriage to Taylor ended, Fisher married, then divorced, singer Connie Stevens in the late 1960s.

After he stopped recording, Fisher remained in action as a concert performer. In early 1994 he filed a $10 million lawsuit against companies that he said had illegally taped and sold a recording of one of his live concerts. A phenomenon who enjoyed spectacular fame but became old musical news while still a young man, Eddie Fisher still ranks high among singers in terms of record sales, and he bridged the gap between Frank Sinatra and Elvis Presley as the top teen singing idol of the 1950s.

Selected discography

Singles

"Wish You Were Here," 1952.
"I'm Walking Behind You," RCA-Victor, 1953.
"Oh, My Papa," RCA-Victor, 1953.
"I Need You Now," RCA-Victor, 1954.
"Dungaree Doll," RCA-Victor, 1955.
"Heart," RCA-Victor, 1955.
"Games That Lovers Play," RCA-Victor, 1966.

Albums

I Love You, RCA-Victor, 1955.
I'm in the Mood for Love, RCA-Victor, 1955.
As Long as There's Music, RCA-Victor, 1958.
Eddie Fisher at the Winter Garden, Ramrod, 1963.
Eddie Fisher Today!, Dot, 1965.
Games That Lovers Play, RCA-Victor, 1966.
People Like You, RCA-Victor, 1967.

Sources

Books

Fisher, Eddie, *My Life, My Loves,* Harper & Row, 1981.
Green, Myrna, *The Eddie Fisher Story,* P. S. Eriksson, 1978.
Simon, George, T., with others, *The Best of the Music Makers,* Doubleday, 1979.

Periodicals

Billboard, April 2, 1994.
Look, March 23, 1954.
People, September 25, 1992.
Time, September 4, 1950.
Variety, May 20, 1953; March 31, 1954.

—Ed Decker

Five Blind Boys of Alabama

Gospel group

According to Jonathan Eig of the *Dallas Morning News*, singing gospel music in church might have become too easy for Clarence Fountain and the Five Blind Boys of Alabama. Instead of preaching to the choir, this group takes its act to nightclubs, where they still have the power and style to win over mainstream audiences. As Fountain, the leader of the group, related in the *San Jose Mercury News*, "It's simple. The people in the church, they know already. We play to those who don't know. Jesus mingled with the sinners and the wine drinkers. My concept is that gospel must go into every phase of life. If God is in you, no matter where you are, you'll feel it. *I'm sure.*"

However, the musical message delivered in secular venues is not quite the same as the impassioned testimonials and songs of joyful redemption that make up a typical Five Blind Boys performance. As Fountain explained in the *San Diego Union*, "When you're in a church, doing a gospel concert, you have an all-black audience. In a club, you have to manipulate your product to the best of your ability and mix it up, so it's not all gospel." They perform songs like "Steal Away," by Dobie Gray, and try to stick to gospel more than anything else, but they also try to sing tunes rearranged in their own style that are familiar to white audiences.

That style reminded Philip Elwood of the *San Francisco Examiner* of the opening of Jon Hendrick's "The Evolution of the Blues"—"It all began in the house of the Lord"—because the Five Blind Boys and their listeners are first and foremost moved by their religious faith. This is reflected in their music despite the popular elements, a tradition that can be traced back to the roots of gospel. Spirituals had become annotated and formalized by the end of the nineteenth century, and at that time, a new African-American vocal music called jubilee singing revitalized the stuffy sound. Later, gospel music represented the further modification of the spiritual as blues and jazz idioms were appropriated by musicians like the legendary Thomas A. Dorsey, who is often called the father of gospel music.

Group Formed at School

For over 50 years Clarence Fountain and the Five Blind Boys of Alabama have nurtured their music through "about 15 record companies ... and about 35 albums" as they have become known around the world for their pure, traditional sound. But as Fountain told the *San Jose Mercury News*, "Truthfully, I never thought about making a career out of this. We were just kids, and we went into this blind. We thought we could make it and just stuck it out." Fountain's parents were cotton farmers in Selma, Alabama. He was born in Tyler, Alabama,

> **For the Record...**
>
> Members have included **Clarence Fountain** (born November 28, 1929, in Tyler, AL), **George Scott, Olice Thomas, Johnny Fields, Samuel K. Lewis, Paul Exkano, George W. Warren, Percell Perkins,** and **Jimmy Carter.**
>
> Group formed as the Happyland Jubilee Singers at the Talladega Institute for the Deaf and Blind; changed name to the Five Blind Boys of Alabama, 1948; signed with Specialty Records, 1953; Fountain toured as solo artist, 1969; group performed in the oratorio *The Gospel at Colonus,* 1983.
>
> **Addresses:** *Record company*—Specialty/Fantasy Inc., 10th and Parker, Berkeley, CA 94710.

on November 28, 1929, and has been blind since the age of two. When he was seven, he was sent to live at the Talladega Institute for the Deaf and Blind near Birmingham, Alabama. He joined the school's choir, and within three years he and a group of friends had formed the Happyland Jubilee Singers.

According to Fountain, the first time they used the Five Blind Boys of Alabama title was in 1948, a year before their first big hit, "I Can See Everybody's Mother But Mine." The group was booked at a large show in Newark, New Jersey, along with the Five Blind Boys of Mississippi, and their name change reflected a rivalry that was to endure for years to come. The group has had various members over the years, but Fountain, with his commanding presence and roughly sweet voice, and three others—George Scott, Jimmy Carter, and Johnny Fields—date back to the Talladega days. Soon they became so successful that they were forced to leave school, in part because Talladega was reluctant to allow them to accept their many bookings away from campus.

Temptations of Rock and Roll

Like the Dixie Hummingbirds and the Soul Stirrers, who spawned Sam Cooke and Lou Rawls, the Five Blind Boys took the combined elements of European choral singing and harmony, blues and jazz, and a syncopated rhythmic approach—what had become gospel—and connected with the same cultural desires that were to fuel the rise of rock and roll. In 1953, the Five Blind Boys were signed by Specialty Records. There they would do most of their classic work alongside other artists such as the Swan Silvertones, the Pilgrim Travelers, and Little Richard.

In 1991, Fantasy Records distributed the first set of remastered albums from the Specialty gospel archives, which included the Five Blind Boys' albums *Oh Lord—Stand By Me* and *Marching up to Zion.* According to Fountain in the *San Jose Mercury News,* the decision of Sam Cooke to leave the gospel fold for the secular music world "just tore up the entire gospel field. A lot of people began to wonder—including the Blind Boys. My feeling then and now is: If you turn your back on God, he'll turn his back on you. Cooke made a lot of money, but he's not around to enjoy it now, is he?"

Fountain claimed that it takes patience and time to develop as a gospel singer and become established. And, with the exception of a hiatus from the group from 1969 to 1975, when he worked as a solo artist, he has toured almost continuously with the Five Blind Boys. In the *San Jose Mercury News,* he estimated that the group works on the road 40 to 45 weeks each year, and he credits their longevity to discipline and clean living.

Group Split, Re-Formed

In 1983, playwrights Lee Breur and Bob Telson set out to reconfigure the Greek tragedy *Oedipus at Colonus* as an oratorio in which the choir, guest artists, and soloists reinterpret Oedipus's tragic redemption in the terms of Pentecostal Christian theology. Fountain stated in the *San Jose Mercury News,* "Originally they just wanted me, but I brought the Blind Boys and argued for the chorus concept (in which the entire group sings Oedipus' role)." The show became a surprise hit, *The Gospel at Colonus,* and enjoyed a Broadway run and a long touring life. This Obie-winning musical became one of the Five Blind Boys' most heralded projects, and Fountain considers it one of the high points of his career. In the *Seattle Times* he remarked, "I'd been away from the group a while then, but got it back together again for that. It really put us in the right perspective as far as the public notice, really got us the attention we deserve."

Although the opera exposed the group to new listeners and led to an appearance on PBS's *Great Performances,* it also brought on a brief split. Johnny Fields and George Scott sang throughout the Southeast using the original name, the Five Blind Boys of Alabama, while some of the group elected to tour with the show as Clarence Fountain and the Five Blind Boys of Alabama. By 1989, the original group members reunited and began to take advantage of their newfound popularity. Their 1992 recording for Elektra, *Deep River,* was released as a part of the acclaimed American Explorer Series, and in 1993 Specialty Records released *The Sermon,* which featured remastered tracks recorded from 1952 to 1957.

In 1994 the Five Blind Boys of Alabama took part in a Richard Thompson tribute album, *Beat the Retreat,* on Capitol, singing with Bonnie Raitt. Their involvement with popular music might seem inevitable; Fountain's voice has been compared to that of the great Temptations vocalist David Ruffin by Jeff Pike in the *Seattle Times.* Pike admired both singers' ability "to deliver a quality of gruff, earthbound grit, which is nonetheless lifted to the heights by sheer, masterful poise.

But Fountain remains apart from rock and roll, even though he has sometimes said that the only difference between it and gospel is that he sings 'Lord' while others sing 'babe.'" Fountain clearly stated the group's policy in *The Oregonian:* "Our goal is to show people the reality in serving God. Everybody got a part of God in them whether they like it or not. God breathed the breath of life and created the living soul. That's the part we're trying to reach." And the Five Blind Boys, like many contemporary gospel singers, are willing to work with other musicians from other musical genres to reach that goal. As Fountain has said: "Sometimes jazz or rock musicians are not oriented to the gospel side. It's a different feel. We know when it's right and when it's wrong." And they usually get it right.

Selected discography

I'm a Changed Man, Wajji, 1989.
Brand New, Wajji, 1990.
I'm Not That Way Anymore, Atlanta International, 1991.
Deep River, Elektra/Warner, 1992.
Bridge Over Troubled Waters, HOB, 1992.
The Soul of Clarence Fountain and the Five Blind Boys of Alabama, HOB, 1993.
The Sermon (re-released tracks from 1952-57), Specialty, 1993.
Oh Lord Stand by Me, Specialty.
Original Blind Boys of Alabama, Savgos.

Contributors, with Bonnie Raitt, to *Beat the Retreat,* Capitol, 1994.

Sources

Books

Heilbut, Anthony, *The Gospel Sound: Good News and Bad Times,* Limelight Editions, 1985.

Periodicals

Daily News (Los Angeles), February 15, 1993.
Dallas Morning News, February 20, 1993.
Oregonian, February 5, 1993.
Rejoice!, April 1992.
San Diego Union, November 2, 1988.
San Francisco Examiner, January 18, 1989.
San Jose Mercury News, June 21, 1991.
Seattle Times, January 29, 1993.

—John Morrow

Stan Getz

Saxophonist

AP/Wide World Photos

Best known for his relaxed, melodic improvisations, Stan Getz was one of the most celebrated jazz musicians of his time. He first broke into the public consciousness as "The Sound" during his tenure with the big bands in the 1940s; he became an important figure in the "cool" movement of the 1950s; and, in the 1960s, was the primary disseminator of bossa nova, a mixture of jazz and Brazilian samba rhythms. He remained a primary force in modern jazz throughout his life. As Joseph Hooper said of Getz in the *New York Times Magazine,* "Inarguably he is one of that ever-diminishing handful of geniuses who have shaped jazz since the 1940s, about half the music's natural life."

Getz practiced tenor sax and bassoon as a child, although he had only six months of lessons and never studied music theory or harmony. In order to contribute to the family finances, he quit school in the ninth grade to get work as a musician. Two years later, in 1942, he was given the chance to play with Jack Teagarden, the best jazz trombonist of his day. He then joined Stan Kenton's big band, contributing to the hits "Eager Beaver" and "Tampico." After stints with Jimmy Dorsey and Benny Goodman, in 1947, Getz found a spot in Woody Herman's band as one of the original Four Brothers, the sax section that gave the band its unique sound. He established himself as a lyricist with his improvisational solo "Early Autumn," which he recorded with Herman.

With his reputation established, Getz left Herman's band in 1949 to front a quartet. Once the guitarist Jimmy Raney joined the group, the quintet solidified their following among be-bop fans. Jack Sohmer of *Down Beat* describes Getz's versatility in a review of *The Complete Recordings of the Stan Getz Quintet with Jimmy Raney:* "Such tracks as 'The Song Is You'... and 'Budo' will immediately belie the notion that Getz was only comfortable with ballads and, somewhat later, lilting Latin melodies. On these selections, as well as many more throughout, Getz proves himself an early master of cookery, 52nd St.-style." Getz collaborated with a number of jazz greats in this period, including Oscar Peterson, Coleman Hawkins, Dizzy Gillespie, and Bob Brookmeyer. His 1957 concert with J. J. Johnson resulted in one of his most highly acclaimed recordings, *At the Opera House.*

The Cool School

Getz's cool style and his self-destructive desire to live on the edge made him a hero of the beat generation. As Hooper explained, "It was no accident that Getz rose to stardom in the '50s, the decade of Dean and Brando, of cool surfaces and passionate, roiled interiors."

For the Record...

Born Stanley Getz, February 2, 1927, in Philadelphia, PA; died of liver cancer, June 6, 1991; son of Alexander and Goldie Getz; married Monica Silfveskiold, 1956 (divorced, 1987); children: Steven, David, Beverly, Pamela, Nicholas.

Played with the big bands of Jack Teagarden, Stan Kenton, and Benny Goodman, 1942-47; played with Woody Herman's original Four Brothers sax section, 1947-49; leader of various quartets, beginning in 1949; toured Europe and lived in Copenhagen, 1958-61; recorded *Jazz Samba,* 1962; signed with Columbia, c. 1970; returned to leading traditional jazz quartets, 1980s.

Awards: Grammy Award for best recording, 1962, for "Desafinado," and 1964, for "The Girl from Ipanema"; National Academy of Recording Artists' best record of the year for "The Girl from Ipanema," 1964; ranked at the top of *Metronome* and *Down Beat* readers' polls every year throughout the 1950s.

However, alcohol and drugs played an important part in the lives of jazz musicians at the time, and Getz's life was no exception. His increasingly expensive addiction to heroin led to his attempt to steal narcotics from a Seattle drugstore in 1954. After his arrest and a six-month prison term, he jumped back into his musical career, resuming his pattern of frequent appearances and record dates, with his fame undiminished. He headlined for Norman Grantz's Jazz at the Philharmonic in 1958 and toured with them in Europe. The same year he moved to Copenhagen, where he stayed until 1961.

When Getz returned to the United States, the "cool school" of jazz was out and John Coltrane's aggressive tenor sax style was in. However, rather than cater to popular opinion, Getz continued to play in his own relaxed style. His self-knowledge paid off: His improvisations over Eddie Sauter's compositions for strings on the album *Focus* received widespread praise from critics. It has been considered one of the only successful with-strings jazz albums ever produced.

Bossa Nova

In 1962, guitarist Charlie Byrd suggested to Getz that they collaborate on an album that would incorporate a new sound he had heard in Brazil. This sound, a combination of traditional folk samba rhythms with jazz improvisation, was called bossa nova, or new wave, by the Brazilians. Getz's and Byrd's collaboration, released in 1962 as *Jazz Samba,* became one of the most popular jazz albums ever recorded. It included the hits "Desafinado" ("Slightly Out of Tune") and "Samba de Una Nota So" ("One Note Samba"), which were composed by the Brazilian pianist Antonio Carlos Jobim.

Jazz Samba initiated a bossa nova craze in the United States, and many jazz and pop artists attempted to cash in on the enthusiasm with their own bossa nova recordings. Most were considered far inferior to *Jazz Samba* and Getz's subsequent releases, *Big Band Bossa Nova* and *Jazz Samba Encore,* which were both artistic and commercial successes. By 1964, bossa nova had been overplayed and was falling out of favor with the public. However, Getz revived the form's popularity with *Getz/Gilberto,* a collaboration with the Brazilian innovators of bossa nova, singer-guitarist João Gilberto and pianist Antonio Carlos Jobim.

Because Gilberto sang only in Portuguese, his wife, Astrud Gilberto, sang a few of the pieces in English. Although she had never before sung professionally, her seductive rendition of "The Girl from Ipanema" combined perfectly with Getz's wafting, lyrical sax playing, making this song phenomenally successful. It won the 1964 Grammy for best record, and the National Academy of Recording Artists voted *Getz/Gilberto* the best jazz album of the year.

Back to the Traditional Quartet

After concentrating on bossa novas in the mid-'60s, Getz returned to playing more traditional modern jazz. Many talented musicians emerged from Getz's groups, including Jack De Johnette, Steve Swallow, Tony Williams, and Chick Corea, whose famous "La Fiesta" first appeared on Getz's *Captain Marvel* album. Getz also encouraged young composers. He was one of the first to recognize and use the talents of Eddie Sauter and Lalo Schifrin.

Although Getz made approximately 130 records throughout his career, he never applied that expertise in playing to composing. As he explained to *Down Beat*'s Josef Woodard, "I'm a sad-ass writer, a lazy writer. Everytime I did try to write something over the years, I'd get up the next morning and change it and the next morning change it again and the next ... until I'd finally rip it up. It's because I'm a player, and players play something different every time."

Getz signed with Columbia in the 1970, and, according to *Down Beat*'s John McDonough, "felt subtle company pressures to 'broaden his audience' in the manner of Miles Davis." Getz complied by experimenting with electronics and rock rhythms, particularly in his album *Another World,* but returned eventually to his traditional acoustic rhythm section. As he told Woodard, "For my taste, there's really nothing in the whole world better than an acoustic rhythm section when it's popping. It seems to vibrate inside your body. You seldom get it, but when you get it, that can be felt....A lot of times, listening to electric music just feels like I'm taking shock treatments."

The Mature Getz

Getz released several critically acclaimed jazz quartet albums in the 1980s, particularly *Anniversary* and *The Stockholm Concert.* Of *Anniversary, Down Beat* reporter Kevin Whitehead said, "His tone had deepened a little bit, but at 60 he was playing as elegantly as ever. If anything, his ballads ... may be even richer and more beautiful." *The Stockholm Concert* is considered equally resonant and Getz's playing perhaps even more emotionally complex.

The last album Getz released before his death from liver cancer in 1991 was *Apasionado,* which included aspects of most of the major styles of Getz's career: the melodic balladry, the Latin rhythms of his bossa nova days, even hints of the big band sound. He departed from the acoustic quartet format he had been using for the last several years in order to improvise over the synthesizer compositions of Eddie de Barrio. The album was received enthusiastically by jazz fans, reaching the top of the jazz charts. Although critics claimed that the album as a whole did not compete with his best, his improvised solos achieve the lyrical beauty, emotional depth, and spontaneity one would expect from a musician whose work has been enjoyed and admired for half a century.

Selected discography

The Soft Swing, Verve, 1957.
(With J. J. Johnson) *At the Opera House,* Verve, 1957.
(With Bob Brookmeyer) *Stan Getz and Bob Brookmeyer,* Verve, 1961.
Focus, Verve, 1962.
Jazz Samba (includes "Desafinado" and "Samba de Una Nota So"), Verve, 1962.
Big Band Bossa Nova, Verve, 1962.
Jazz Samba Encore, Verve, 1963.
Getz/Gilberto (includes "The Girl from Ipanema") Verve, 1964.
Au Go Go, Verve, 1964.
Getz/Gilberto No. 2, Verve, 1966.
Sweet Rain, Verve, 1967.
What the World Needs Now, Verve, 1968.
Didn't We, Verve, 1969.
Dynasty, Verve, 1971.
Newport in New York '72, Cobble, 1972.
Captain Marvel, Columbia, 1975.
Another World, Columbia.
Pure Getz, Concord Jazz.
Classics: Stan Getz, Prestige.
The Stockholm Concert, Gazell, 1983.
Anniversary, EmArcy, 1987, reissued, Verve, 1993.
Apasionado, A & M, 1989.
The Complete Recordings of The Stan Getz Quintet with Jimmy Raney, Mosaic, 1991.
Stan Getz and Zoot Sims, LRC, 1992.
Spring Is Here, Concord Jazz, 1992.
(With Kenny Barron) *People Time,* Verve, 1992.
Essential, Polygram, 1992.
Best of the Verve Years, Vol. III, Verve, 1993.
Opus De Bop, Savoy, reissued, 1993.
The Artistry of Stan Getz Vol. II, Verve, 1993.
Jazz Masters 8, Verve, 1994.

Sources

Books

Feather, Leonard, *The Encyclopedia of Jazz in the Sixties,* Horizon Press, 1966.
Feather, Leonard, and Ira Gitler, *The Encyclopedia of Jazz in the Seventies,* Horizon Press, 1976.
Lyons, Len, and Don Perlo, *Jazz Portraits: The Lives and Music of the Jazz Masters,* Morrow, 1989.

Periodicals

Down Beat, June 1990; July 1990; January 1991; September 1991.
New York Times Magazine, June 9, 1991.
Rolling Stone, August 8, 1991.

—Susan Windisch Brown

Lee Greenwood

Singer, songwriter

Photograph by Peter Nash/Michael Ochs Archives/Venice, CA

Although possessing a strong love of pop music, songwriter and vocalist Lee Greenwood had to pay his musical dues for many years before his rise to stardom in the mid-1980s. Early in his musical career, he worked small venues in Las Vegas, where he grew frustrated watching the headlines go to other performers. Greenwood's break came when he found an outlet for his talent in the field of country music. Like Kenny Rogers, to whom he is often compared, he mixes his smoky, bluesy vocal style with a fondness for elaborate musical arrangements and soft romantic material.

Despite a long string of hit records, Greenwood is most often identified with "God Bless the U.S.A," a song he recorded in 1984. While country music tends to shy away from direct involvement in politics, national events sometimes bring strong patriotic sentiment to the surface. Greenwood's song, self-composed like most of his material, was adopted by the conservative movement that was sweeping the political landscape at the time of its release. This was so even though Greenwood himself disavowed any overtly political intentions. The song has tended to overshadow Greenwood's career since its release.

Greenwood, who claims Cherokee descent, was born in Sacramento, California, in 1942, and was raised on a chicken farm by his grandparents. Interested in music from an early age, he taught himself to play guitar, saxophone, bass, banjo, and keyboards. Greenwood joined a band in high school and made his first television appearance at age 15 as a bandmember of country singer Chester Smith. On the day of his high school graduation, he left for Las Vegas to pursue his musical fortunes.

Though Greenwood didn't find his musical roots in country music's traditions, he was also largely untouched by the more urban development of rock and roll. As he confessed to *People,* in his youth he was "naive, unhip, even a little square." The type of music he performed was mostly middle-of-the-road pop.

For two decades, Greenwood endured the career ups and downs of a workaday Las Vegas musician, where his instrumental expertise landed him a spot in the band of country singer Del Reeves. From there, he went on to form his own band, The Lee Greenwood Affair, which signed a recording contract with Los Angeles's Paramount label in 1965.

Unfortunately for him, the label was soon swallowed up by a corporate merger, leaving Greenwood with no job to support his wife and two children. Working as a fried-chicken cook and as a blackjack dealer in Las Vegas's famed casinos, Greenwood continued to perform in

> **For the Record...**
>
> Born Melvin Lee Greenwood in 1942 in Sacramento, CA; married third wife, Melanie (a choreographer; divorced); married Kimberly Payne, 1992; four children.
>
> Country and pop vocalist, 1965—; formed band, the Lee Greenwood Affair, and signed with Paramount, 1965; entertainer, Las Vegas, NV, 1965-81; signed with MCA Records, 1981; released single "God Bless the U.S.A.," 1984; appeared at televised Republican Party victory celebration, 1984; released *American Patriot,* 1992.
>
> **Awards:** Named Country Music Association male vocalist of the year, 1983 and 1984.
>
> **Addresses:** *Management*—Lee Greenwood, Inc., 1311 Elm Hill Pike, Nashville, TN 37210. *Record company*—Liberty, 3322 West End Ave., Nashville, TN 37206.

small clubs and restaurants. Describing this phase of his life, he told the *Los Angeles Times* he was "a nobody." The instability took its toll on his personal life: two marriages would dissolve.

Greenwood's break came in 1978, when a bandleader for country star Mel Tillis heard one of Greenwood's performances. The man was impressed by both his vocal ability and the talent that showed in Greenwood's original compositions. With encouragement from such a music-industry professional, Greenwood began to concentrate on country-oriented songwriting, and shipped demo recordings of some of his compositions to various Nashville labels. But he stuck to his goal of being recognized as a recording artist as well. As he recalled to the *Chicago Tribune's* Jack Hurst, "I told [my managers in Nashville] that if a record deal didn't happen, I was going back to Las Vegas." When MCA Records decided to take a chance on the 39-year-old singer in 1981, Greenwood moved to Music City.

His voice—raspy, yet smoothly controlled—fit well into the country-pop arrangements that made up the "Nashville Sound" characteristic of the early 1980s. Greenwood's first album release, 1981's *Inside and Out,* generated four singles that scaled up to the Top Twenty on the country charts. He threw himself wholeheartedly into his new career. "I worked the business," he told Hurst. "It *is* a business, and you have to divide the ethereal part from the business part."

Composing the jingle for the "McDonald's and You" advertising campaign brought additional financial rewards for the now-country songwriter. Soon thereafter, Greenwood achieved star-recognition with the release of 1983's *Somebody's Gonna Love You,* which, in addition to its Number One title track, included "I.O.U.," a romantic declaration which became a popular choice for wedding music. He received back-to-back Country Music Association Male Vocalist of the Year honors in 1983 and 1984, a rare feat.

Greenwood continued to turn out hit singles, paired in some cases with MCA's popular female country star, Barbara Mandrell. His greatest success of all came with "God Bless the U.S.A.," a memorial for America's war-dead that inspired prolonged ovations from the time it was first introduced into the singer's act. The song became a hit in the summer of 1984, and was noticed at the White House where then-President Reagan's handlers were preparing his re-election campaign. Greenwood granted permission for the song to be used in a Reagan campaign film, and ended up appearing on television on election night, amidst the triumphant pageantry of Reagan's victory. The song seemed a perfect anthem for twelve years of Republican control of the presidency.

Greenwood later said he had misgivings about becoming involved with partisan politics, claiming no personal party affiliation. "I really wasn't going as a Republican," he told the *Chicago Tribune's* Tom Popson concerning his appearance with Reagan at a Texas Republican rally. "I was just going to Texas as a guest of the President and I thought that was the best way to get my song out to as many people as possible." Despite Greenwood's personal political beliefs, many listeners inevitably identified the singer with the sentiment.

Although his career never attained the high profile it had in 1984, Greenwood has since scored several more Top Ten recordings. In 1992, his duet with singer Suzy Bogguss, "Hopelessly Yours," climbed into country's Top 20.

Meanwhile, "God Bless the U.S.A." took on a life of its own. It received extensive airplay during the 1991 Persian Gulf War. The following year, its composer attempted to capitalize on the image with which the song had branded him. He released *American Patriot,* an album of patriotic songs old and new, including "God Bless the U.S.A."; the album failed to make a commercial impact. *People* assessed it this way: "He has never been one to suppress his flag-waving impulses, but Old Lee really outjingoes even himself on this album..... Other than as background for a Fourth of July celebration, though, it's hard to see where such a unidimensional album would fit into anyone's listening schedule."

Greenwood's success as a country performer has guaranteed that he will never deal cards for a living again. He now presides over a group of business enterprises under the name of Lee Greenwood, Inc., and has received an honorary doctor of humanities degree from Tennessee's Cumberland University. Prompted, no doubt, by his long years working as a performer in Las Vegas, he has been active in regard to labor-union issues in the performing arts. Married and divorced three times—his third wife, Melanie Greenwood, is the Nashville choreographer who devised Billy Ray Cyrus's famed "Achy Breaky" line dance—Greenwood wed Kimberly Payne, a former Miss Tennessee, in the summer of 1992.

Selected discography

Inside Out, MCA, 1982.
Somebody's Gonna Love You (includes "I.O.U."), MCA, 1983.
Greatest Hits (includes "God Bless the U.S.A."), MCA, 1985.
Christmas to Christmas, MCA, 1985.
(With Barbara Mandrell) *Meant for Each Other,* MCA, 1985.
Greatest Hits, Volume 2, MCA, 1988.
If Only For One Night, MCA, 1989.
A Perfect 10, Liberty, 1991.
Best of Lee Greenwood, Curb, 1992.
American Patriot, Liberty, 1992.

Sources

Books

The Harmony Illustrated Encyclopedia of Country Music, edited by Fred Deller, Harmony Books, 1985.
Lomax, John, III, *Nashville: Music City U.S.A.,* Abrams, 1985.

Periodicals

Chicago Tribune, April 8, 1984; November 30, 1984.
Country Music, September/October 1992; November/December 1992.
Los Angeles Times, September 12, 1984.
People, October 31, 1983; August 24, 1992.
Spin, August 1992.

—*James M. Manheim*

Charlie Haden

Bassist

Photograph by Dennis Keel, courtesy of Verve Records

When he was 15 years old, Charlie Haden traveled to Omaha with his father to hear a performance by jazz saxophone greats Lester Young and Charlie Parker. The experience was a revelation; after the event, as Haden recalled to Jay Cocks of *Time,* "it was pretty much decided inside my soul that jazz was what I was going to do. It was like having the music born inside you." Over four decades later, Haden remained one of the most sensitive and innovative masters of the string bass, whose impact on both his chosen instrument, and jazz in general, continued to be felt. On saxophonist Joshua Redman's 1993 recording, *Wish,* for example, the veteran Haden teamed up with one of jazz's fastest-rising young stars. Redman's youthful ebullience blended effortlessly with Haden's seasoned musicianship, bringing jazz to a generation of new listeners at the same time it paid homage to an illustrious lifelong career.

Haden's playing of the 1990s, though firmly rooted in tradition, seemed far distant from the early history of the jazz bass. In the first two decades of the twentieth century, the bass filled mainly an accompanimental role in the jazz ensemble, providing the fundamental notes of the harmonic structure and adding rhythmic momentum. During the swing era of the 1930s and 1940s, however, especially in the work of the great Duke Ellington bassist Jimmy Blanton, the instrument began to play a more prominent part in the ensemble texture, interacting with the improvising soloists and occasionally employed in solos.

Haden built on the contributions of players such as Blanton and developed something of a musical "sixth sense" by which he could follow the complex lines of many of the avant-garde players of the 1950s and 1960s—especially saxophonist Ornette Coleman—and continually align his playing to what he heard. This unusual perceptiveness, combined with a richness of tone and an economy of means—in which one senses each individual note is significant—made his style instantly recognizable.

Began as Country-Western Performer

Strangely enough, Haden's early roots were not in jazz but in another uniquely American art form—country and western music. His parents were regulars at Nashville's Grand Ole Opry and became close associates with some of the venue's most prominent names, including Hank Williams, the Carter Family, and the Delmore Brothers. When he was only two, Haden joined his parents on their own radio show, "Uncle Carl Haden and the Haden Family"; as the character Cowboy Charlie he sang harmony and developed a talent for

For the Record...

Born August 6, 1937, in Shenandoah, IA; parents were country-western entertainers; married Ruth Cameron (second wife); four children.

From age two to 15 sang with family's country and western act, "Uncle Carl Haden and the Haden Family"; began playing bass during teen years and in 1957 moved to Los Angeles and worked with saxophonists Art Pepper and Dexter Gordon, trumpeter Chet Baker, and pianists Hampton Hawes and Paul Bley; joined saxophonist Ornette Coleman's quartet, late 1950s; worked with Coleman as well as with saxophonists John Coltrane and Archie Shepp, 1960s; toured with pianist Keith Jarrett, 1966; cofounded Liberation Music Orchestra with composer/arranger Carla Bley, 1969; helped form group Old and New Dreams with trumpeter Don Cherry and several other former Coleman sidemen, 1976; participated in a reunion of the original Ornette Coleman Quartet and formed Quartet West, 1987; performed and recorded with his own groups and with pop artists such as Bruce Hornsby and Rickie Lee Jones, late 1980s and early 1990s.

Awards: Guggenheim Fellowship recipient, 1969; Grand Prix du Disque (Charles Cros) Award, for *Liberation Music Orchestra,* 1969, and *Ballad of the Fallen,* 1983; Grammy nominations for *Liberation Music Orchestra,* 1969, and *Dream Keeper,* 1990; winner of *Down Beat* critics' poll, 1982-92, and *Down Beat* readers' poll, 1985-91, both for acoustic bass category; *Newsday* Jazz Artist of the Year, 1991; four National Endowment for the Arts composition grants.

Addresses: *Management*—The Merlin Company, 17609 Ventura Blvd., Suite 212, Encino, CA, 91316.

yodeling. These early experiences were crucial to Haden's musical development. As he expressed to Bill Forman of *Grammy* magazine, "The way [Mother Maybelle Carter] sang and played guitar had a big influence on me. And the Delmore Brothers were a real influence on my harmonic sense, because they were the first deep harmony in country music."

Haden began to perform on bass during his teen years and in 1957 moved to Los Angeles to establish himself as a professional musician. Anxious to absorb all he could from the vibrant West Coast jazz scene, he aggressively sought out a wide variety of groups and performing venues. As he told Forman, "I used to go up on the bandstand at jam sessions and grab the bass out of the bass player's hands and start playing." Soon he had drawn the attention of some of the greatest names in the Los Angeles area, including saxophonist Dexter Gordon and trumpeter Chet Baker.

Met Ornette Coleman

The direction of Haden's career was changed forever when he was introduced to saxophonist Ornette Coleman in a club in Hollywood. Born and raised in Texas and largely self-taught, Coleman obtained his early musical experience by performing with rhythm and blues groups. However, after moving to the West Coast in 1954, Coleman quickly traveled into uncharted musical terrain. Seeking to move jazz performances beyond the usual technique of improvising over a set harmonic pattern, Coleman began to experiment with more flexible organizing principles in his playing, including tonal centers and melodic motives. Haden sensed an immediate empathy with Coleman's ideas, which became loosely grouped under the heading "free jazz"; as Haden explained to Cocks, "Sometimes I would want to improvise on the inspiration, the feeling rather than the chords. And that's what Ornette was doing."

As a member of Ornette Coleman's quartet, which included trumpeter Don Cherry and drummer Billy Higgins, Haden helped shape the course of jazz history. A four-month stint at New York's Five Spot club in 1959 and influential albums, such as *The Shape of Jazz to Come* in 1960 and *Free Jazz* in 1961, brought the group's revolutionary approaches to jazz improvisation to a wide audience. The instinctive communication between Haden and the other members of the ensemble—what *Jazz Tradition* author Martin Williams has called "responsive inspiration"—assured a sense of structure and balance in these performances, without sacrificing their startling audacity and freedom.

Haden continued to perform with Coleman throughout the 1960s and later, in 1976, helped found Old and New Dreams, a group dedicated to keeping the spirit of Coleman's music alive. Then, in 1969, another important phase of Haden's career began when, with pianist and composer Carla Bley, he founded Liberation Music Orchestra. As Haden explained to *Down Beat*'s Josef Woodard, the formation of the group "was brought about by the Vietnam War, by the turmoil that was going on in the world caused by United States aggression. I felt I had to do something about it in my own way." The group's self-titled first album, a deeply emotional statement about freedom that incorporated themes from the Spanish Civil War, was nominated for a Grammy Award in 1969. With some changes in personnel, the group continued to perform throughout the 1970s and 1980s and in 1993 staged a concert at New York's Lincoln Center.

Founded Quartet West

Haden had always held a special affection for the atmosphere of the 1930s and 1940s so vividly captured in the novels of Raymond Chandler. Therefore, in the late 1980s, when he made his first venture as the leader of a small group, he tried to "pass along the feeling of standing in Philip Marlowe's office looking out at the neon lights blinking off and on in the night," as he expressed to *Time's* Cocks. His Quartet West, which recorded four albums between 1987 and 1993, reflected Haden's fascination with a time when, as he stated to Woodard in *Down Beat*, "popular music had deeper values."

The group's 1993 release, *Always Say Goodbye*, for example, opened with Max Steiner's 1937 fanfare for Warner Brothers, and featured, along with contemporary performances by the group, snippets of movie dialogue and vintage performances such as Jo Stafford's "Alone Together." The use of these musical artifacts contributed both an atmosphere of nostalgia and, as *Musician* writer Tom Moon put it, "guideposts to a world where emotionalism still lives."

In 1991 Haden's affection for classic pop music carried over into another project, Rickie Lee Jones's album *Pop Pop*. On this recording Haden accompanied Jones's performances of such classic standards as "My One and Only Love," lending the tunes his sensitivity, passion, and sense of taste. The album brought Haden's work to a new group of listeners who were perhaps unaware of his long and fruitful career and his unique contribution to American music history.

Selected discography

With Ornette Coleman

The Shape of Jazz to Come, Atlantic, 1960.
Free Jazz, Atlantic, 1961.
Song X, Geffen, 1986.
In All Languages, Caravan of Dreams, 1987.
Beauty Is a Rare Thing: The Complete Atlantic Recordings, Rhino/Atlantic, 1993.

With Liberation Music Orchestra

Liberation Music Orchestra, Impulse, 1969.
The Ballad of the Fallen, ECM, 1983.
Dream Keeper, Blue Note, 1991.

With Old and New Dreams

Old and New Dreams, Black Saint, 1977.
Playing, ECM, 1981.

With Quartet West

Quartet West, Verve, 1987.
In Angel City, Verve, 1988.
Haunted Heart, Verve, 1992.
Always Say Goodbye, Verve, 1993.

Other

(With Hampton Hawes) *As Long as There's Music*, Artists House, 1978.

Contributor

Keith Jarrett, *The Mourning of a Star*, Atlantic, 1971.
Carla Bley, *Musique mecanique*, Watt, 1979.
Michael Brecker, MCA Impulse, 1987.
An Evening With Joe Henderson, Charlie Haden and Al Foster, Red, 1988.
Bruce Hornsby, *Night on the Town*, RCA, 1990.
Rickie Lee Jones, *Pop Pop*, Geffen, 1991.
Abbey Lincoln, *You've Got to Pay the Band*, Verve, 1991.
Joshua Redman, *Wish*, Warner Bros., 1993.

Sources

Books

Porter, Lewis, and Michael Ullman, with Edward Hazell, *Jazz From Its Origins to the Present*, Prentice-Hall, 1993.
Williams, Martin, *The Jazz Tradition*, Oxford University Press, 1993.

Periodicals

Chicago Tribune, September 13, 1993.
Down Beat, August 1992.
Entertainment Weekly, July 17, 1992.
Grammy Magazine, December 1992.
Metro Times (Detroit), September 1, 1993.
Musician, February 1994.
New York Times, June 20, 1987.
People, November 2, 1992.
Pulse!, August 1992; October 1992.
Time, October 12, 1992.
Washington Post, September 27, 1993.

Additional information for this profile was obtained from the Merlin Company, Inc., 1994.

—*Jeffrey Taylor*

Thomas Hampson

Opera singer

Courtesy of Columbia Artists Management Inc.

Thomas Hampson is an enormously gifted, versatile baritone who combines a commanding stage presence with a rich, warm, fluent voice. Although he was originally better-known in Europe than in North America, he is now considered by many to be the premier baritone working today in both the operatic and art song repertory. With his elegant good looks—his fans call him "Thomas Handsome"—he is quickly becoming something of a superstar, a status more commonly reached by tenors than by baritones.

Hampson originally aspired to be a lawyer. He earned a degree in political science from Eastern Washington University, and was not considering a career as a singer even though he had won voice competitions and had performed in his home town of Spokane, Washington. But a prominent Spokane voice teacher, Sister Marietta Coyle, intervened. As Hampson was quoted as saying in an article in *Opera News* in 1989, "She came to me and said 'Young man, God made you a singer, and you have the responsibility to be one. When you're ready to accept that responsibility, call me.'" Hampson took her advice, and the music world is grateful for his decision.

In 1980, Hampson signed a contract with the Deutsche Oper am Rhein in Düsseldorf, Germany—the first European opera company for which he auditioned. He appeared there, first in small parts and then in more prominent roles. In 1984, he went to Zurich, Switzerland, to perform in the Nikolaus Harnoncourt/Jean-Pierre Ponnelle production of the Mozart opera cycle. While in Zurich he caught the attention of Metropolitan Opera conductor James Levine, who invited him to perform at the Met in Mozart's *The Marriage of Figaro* in 1986. Since that time he has appeared there in several productions, most notably in the title role in Mozart's *Don Giovanni,* which won him critical acclaim. He recreated the role for the Teldec recording of the opera in 1990. In 1994 Hampson created the role of Valmont in the San Francisco Opera's world premiere of Conrad Susa's opera *Les Liaisons Dangéreuses*.

In addition to his opera appearances, Hampson spends a large portion of his time giving recitals. He is an outstanding interpreter of the art song repertory—particularly classic German lieder—as well as an inspired performer of less traditional solo songs, such as those by nineteenth- and twentieth-century American composers. He can devote a recital program to a somber song cycle such as *Dichterliebe,* by the nineteenth-century German composer Robert Schumann, and top it off with encores by Cole Porter—enthralling the audience with his ability to slip in and out of the serious and popular repertory while treating each with the same respect.

For the Record . . .

Born Walter Thomas Hampson, June 28, 1955, in Elkhart, IN; son of a nuclear engineer and a medical receptionist; married, 1975 (divorced); engaged to Andrea Herberstein. *Education:* Attended Seventh Day Adventist-affiliated schools in Spokane, WA area; Eastern Washington University, Cheney, WA, B.A. (political science), 1977; studied voice with Sr. Marietta Coyle and received B.F.A. in voice performance, Fort Wright College, Spokane, WA; studied voice with Gwendolyn Koldowsky and Martial Singher at the Music Academy of the West, Santa Barbara, CA; studied voice with Elisabeth Schwarzkopf in Europe, 1980; has studied voice in Europe with Horst Günther since 1981.

Opera singer and concert performer. Sang with Spokane Symphony and other Washington state groups, 1980; signed contract with Deutsche Oper am Rhein, Düsseldorf, Germany, and sang roles of Figaro in Rossini's *The Barber of Seville* and Guglielmo in Mozart's *Cosi fan Tutte;* performed with St. Louis Opera Theatre, 1982; went to Zurich, where he worked on cycle of Mozart operas with Nikolaus Harnoncourt and Jean-Pierre Ponnelle, 1984; Metropolitan Opera debut as Count Almaviva in Mozart's *The Marriage of Figaro,* 1986; appeared at Metropolitan Opera as Figaro in *The Barber of Seville,* Valentin in Gounod's *Faust,* Guglielmo in *Cosi fan Tutte,* and title roles in Mozart's *Don Giovanni* and Britten's *Billy Budd;* recital debut, Wigmore Hall, London, 1984; American recital debut, Town Hall, New York City, 1986; has appeared in numerous solo recitals and performances with orchestras.

Selected awards: Lotte Lehmann Medal, Music Academy of the West, 1979; first prize, Metropolitan Opera auditions, 1981; vocalist of the year, *Musical America,* 1991; honorary doctor of music degree from Whitworth College, Spokane, WA, 1993; five Grammy nominations.

Addresses: *Management*—c/o Ken Benson, Personal Direction, Columbia Artists Management, 165 West 57th St., New York, NY 10019.

Hampson has shown an affinity, rare among performing musicians, for researching the musical, literary, historical, and philosophical aspects of many of the pieces he performs. For example, he has performed the obscure first version of Schumann's *Dichterliebe* song cycle, which contains three additional songs and slightly different forms of some of the songs found in the more frequently performed later version. Hampson also coedited a new critical edition of the songs of Gustav Mahler—an undertaking that is usually left to musicologists. In an article for *Gramophone* magazine in 1992, Edward Seckerson observed that "Singing is not so much a career to [Hampson], more a responsibility—to the repertoire, the poets, the composers."

Hampson believes very strongly that a singer should know a language thoroughly before he or she can perform in that language effectively. "I refuse to interpret [Francis] Poulenc, because my French is very bad," he remarked to an interviewer in the French magazine *Diapason* in 1993. "It's the same as someone who doesn't have good enough German to take on Hugo Wolf. The interpretation of French or German songs is not simply a matter of getting the articulation of the text right—one has to sing." He holds directors to the same high standards: "My blood pressure really rises when I come across, as I did recently, a director who knows neither the music nor the language of the work he's staging," Hampson told Walter Price in a *New York Times* article in 1990.

Hampson has gained a large and appreciative audience through his recordings, several of which have risen high on the classical music charts. Particularly noteworthy are his interpretations of Mahler's *Rückert Lieder, Lieder eines fahrenden Gesellen* [*Songs of a Wayfarer*], and *Kindertotenlieder* [*Songs on the Death of Children*] on the Deutsche Grammaphon label in 1991, with Leonard Bernstein conducting the Vienna Philharmonic.

His albums of Stephen Foster and Cole Porter songs show his adeptness at interpreting music outside the classical canon. Hampson has also been featured in many opera recordings: the *Don Giovanni* recording mentioned above, as well as Mozart's *The Marriage of Figaro, Cosi Fan Tutte,* and *The Magic Flute;* Rossini's *The Barber of Seville,* Puccini's *La Bohème;* and Gounod's *Faust,* among others.

Hampson's inquisitiveness and intelligent approach to music make him an original and refreshing presence in the vocal world, a world that is often content with doing the same things in the same ways, and that sometimes places emphasis on glamour at the expense of musical integrity. "I know what's important to me, and it's not dollars," Hampson stated in the 1989 *Opera News* article. "What's important is what I do—to be taken seriously, to be asked to sing songs, to try to excite someone to literature, poetry, to thoughts—almost like a priest—to be able to convey that to someone, to reach them—that makes it all worthwhile."

Selected discography

Des Knaben Wunderhorn (songs of Gustav Mahler), Teldec, 1989.
Don Giovanni (opera), Teldec, 1990.
Rückert Lieder/Kindertotenlieder/Lieder eines fahrenden Gesellen (songs of Mahler), Deutsche Grammaphon, 1991.
American Dreamer: Songs of Stephen Foster, Angel/EMI, 1992.
An Old Song Resung: American Concert Songs, EMI, 1992.
(With Jerry Hadley) Famous Opera Duets, Teldec, 1993.
Romantic Songs of Berlioz, Liszt, Wagner, EMI, 1994.
Annie Get Your Gun, EMI.
On the Town, Deutsche Grammaphon.
Christmas with Thomas Hampson, Teldec.
Faust (opera), EMI.
Night and Day (songs of Cole Porter), EMI.
The Barber of Seville (opera), Angel/EMI.
Hamlet (opera), Angel/EMI.

Sources

Diapason, October 1993.
Fanfare, November/December 1991.
Gramophone, April 1992.
Newsweek, March 16, 1992.
New York, February 26, 1990.
New York Times, April 15, 1990; May 1, 1991.
Opera News, February 1989.
Vanity Fair, March 1992.

Additional information for this profile was obtained from the program notes for Hampson's recital at Hill Auditorium, Ann Arbor, MI, November 7, 1993.

—Joyce Harrison

Juliana Hatfield

Singer, songwriter, guitarist

Juliana Hatfield has a "gift for making lyrical venom sound like lullabies," according to an *Alternative Press* writer. Such a description aptly conveys the contradictions Hatfield seems to embody. At once confident and vulnerable, possessed of a "wispy voice"—according to Ira Robbins of *Musician*—and given to writing ebullient pop melodies, Hatfield sings sharp-edged, often despairing lyrics. She also poses for magazine fashion supplements and attacks her guitar with great ferocity, playing havoc with preconceived ideas about gender in rock. Moreover, Hatfield has refused to align herself with any particular "school," calling herself an individualist. "That's the only thing I stand by: independence," she proclaimed in *Newsweek,* and in a *Rolling Stone* interview she declared, "I'm not doing this [playing rock music] to advance the cause of women."

Writing songs "about not being able to deal with life," as she described it to Robbins, Hatfield has moved from a stint on the indie scene with Boston's Blake Babies to a burgeoning solo career thanks to the success of her second solo album, *Become What You Are*. She has also seen her personal life—especially her friendship with Lemonheads leader Evan Dando—scrutinized in public, a cause of considerable frustration to her in spite of her declaration to *Spin*'s Rob Sheffield that "I get pleasure in being misrepresented." Yet through it all Hatfield has presented a unique antidote to the frustrations of her growing audience, and this has much to do with the aforementioned contradictions she embraces. As Sheffield observed, "Onstage, Hatfield is a mesmerizing swirl of frumpy glamour. She's half teen-hermit basket case, half guitar-totin', [Free-Will philosopher Friedrich] Nietzsche-quotin', punk-rock dream come true."

Mystical Experience

Hatfield grew up in the affluent town of Duxbury, Massachusetts, where, as she told *Rolling Stone*'s Kim France, "A lot of the activity in town was centered around the yacht club." Her father was a doctor and her mother a style writer for the *Boston Globe*. In a *Creem* interview Hatfield recalled that she first became "self-conscious" in high school, a feeling she dealt with largely through aversion therapy. "My whole life I'd made myself perform in some way. I'd play piano recitals and I was on the gymnastic team so I'd have to get up there in front of the gym and do my routine. I always wanted to do something in front of a crowd."

Although she studied classical music, Hatfield found herself enthralled by rock, discovering the music of the

> **For the Record...**
>
> Born c. 1968, in Duxbury, MA; daughter of a physician and a journalist. *Education:* Attended Berklee School of Music, Boston.
>
> Recording and performing artist, 1987—. Sang and played bass and guitar with Blake Babies, 1987-91; released solo debut, *Hey Babe*, Mammoth Records, 1992; played on Lemonheads albums *It's a Shame About Ray*, 1992, and *Come On Feel the Lemonheads*, 1993.
>
> **Addresses:** *Record company*—Atlantic Records, 75 Rockefeller Plaza, New York, NY 10019; 9229 Sunset Blvd., Los Angeles, CA 90069.

New Wave English pop trio The Police and playing most of their repertoire with a band called the Squids. A bit later, her brother's girlfriend came to live with the family and introduced Hatfield to punk rock—most notably the rootsy songcraft of the Los Angeles band X—and took her to what she would memorialize in the song "My Sister" as "my first all-ages show/It was the Violent Femmes and the Del Fuegos." Punk opened up a new horizon of possibilities. At age sixteen, Hatfield noted in an Atlantic Records publicity interview, she had a "mystical experience," during which "I was in my house in the late afternoon, and there was a lot of sun coming in. I look over to the corner and sort of saw myself singing, and it was the future and I knew that was what I had to do."

After high school, Hatfield attended the prestigious Berklee School of Music; it was there that she met John Strohm and Freda Love Boner, whom she agreed to join in a band that famed poet Allen Ginsberg christened the Blake Babies. Both Strohm and Boner "had an active crush on her," the former related in *Spin*. "We thought we were the only two weird-asses there, but Juliana had braces, and her complexion wasn't so good, she'd just stare at the floor in her leather jacket and floppy ponytail. We thought, 'Hey she's really neurotic. Cool!'"

Hatfield started on guitar with the band but switched to bass. Soon the three were living in a condo they rented from Hatfield's mother Julie, which they also shared with other musicians, including Dando, who joined the band for a time and whom Julie had met on the club scene. "My mom's an indie scene queen," said Hatfield, who referred to the experience of sharing the so-called "condo pad" as "an amazing, spiritual thing. An awakening."

The Blake Babies released their first EP in 1987 and put out three full-length albums before their 1992 breakup. *Spin* writer Nathaniel Wice opined that the band "give expression to the idea that girls are, as a general rule, smarter and cool than boys. If this possibility has never occurred to you, you will probably find the band insufferable." He also felt that "the unpretentious, moodily pretty and talented Hatfield dominates the group." By the time Wice's observations appeared, however, Strohm and Boner had formed a new band, Antenna, and Hatfield had already finished her first solo album; she told *Spin* on another occasion that she had grown "sick of democracy" within the group. "I just started hating being in the Blake Babies," she confessed to France of *Rolling Stone*, "and I knew I had to quit."

Got Noticed With *Hey Babe*

"When Blake Babies was happening," Hatfield reported to *Rolling Stone*, "it was really romantic to sleep on floors and not have any money. But when I look back on it, I can't believe some of the stuff we did." Yet when she ventured out on her own, Hatfield felt deeply depressed and missed having a band. With the help of a variety of guest artists—including alternative rock luminaries like Dando, fIREHOSE bassist Mike Watt, and singer-songwriter John Wesley Harding—Hatfield recorded her solo debut, *Hey Babe*. With songs like "Ugly," she explored female self-doubt with unrelenting honesty, while the song "Nirvana" referred to the hit alternative band's music as an oasis.

Released in 1992 on the Atlantic subsidiary Mammoth, *Hey Babe* made a strong impression. Critic Kurt Loder opined in *Esquire* that Hatfield "manages the difficult trick of using cleverly fashioned pop tunes to deal forthrightly with feelings of personal worthlessness and the dismal romantic behavior they so often engender." *Musician*'s Robbins ventured that "*Hey Babe* offers tart, tuneful pop with flavor that lasts." And an *Entertainment Weekly* reviewer praised the effort as "1992's best alternative album on an independent label," adding that "Hatfield can be cathartic, yet she never forgets the importance of caressing vocal harmonies and good old-fangled melody."

Despite such praise, Hatfield was disappointed with the album—which some regarded as a suite of songs about her conflicted feelings for Dando—on both a musical and thematic level. She complained to *Newsweek* that "I seemed weak on that record, when I envisioned myself as a strong person. When the album was all mixed, I was listening to it and bawling and saying, 'Oh my God, people are going to tear me apart.'" Furthermore, as she told Robbins, *Hey Babe* "was where I learned what *not* to do in a studio."

In addition to her solo work, Hatfield played bass and sang on the Lemonheads' album *It's a Shame About Ray,* and also appeared on the band's 1993 recording *Come on Feel the Lemonheads,* which featured a song about her. Indeed, she and Dando—just friends according to most accounts—became a hot couple in the rock press. Dando's heartthrob status only complicated the public perception of Hatfield, who, to her eternal regret, admitted to being a virgin in an interview and found herself having to discuss the matter. "I didn't realize journalists would be printing it over and over instead of letting it die," she fumed in the *Los Angeles Times.* She left Boston, as she told a *Daily Variety* interviewer, because "I felt like I was becoming a local legend or something." Not having a permanent home, she noted, was liberating.

Formed Trio to *Become* a Star

In any event, Hatfield eventually decided to put together a full-time band and recruited bassist Dean Fisher and former Bullet LaVolta drummer Todd Philips to back her up. "When Jules first met with us," Philips told *Alternative Press,* "she said she wanted to rock." Thus was born the Juliana Hatfield Three, a tighter, harder unit that performed on her breakthrough 1993 album *Become What You Are.* The first single, "My Sister," was an alternative smash, and songs like the ferocious "Supermodel" and "Dame With a Rod" showed that Hatfield had adopted a tougher, less self-blaming stance, even as "Spin the Bottle" offered a bit of giddy romanticism.

"The biggest difference between this new record and *Hey Babe,*" Hatfield told *Request,* "is that as soon as I finished *Hey Babe,* I hated it, and as soon as I finished *Become What You Are,* I loved it." Her instincts were correct; the album helped Hatfield become an important figure on the alternative rock scene. Indeed, she was successful enough to inspire a parody, "The Juliana Hatfield Song," by singer-songwriter Melissa Ferrick, who noted, accurately, that "Juliana Hatfield doesn't even have a sister." Though Hatfield said in a *Spin* interview that she "was not amused" by Ferrick's salvo, the incident showed that she had become part of the pop landscape.

Become What You Are earned generally strong reviews from the music press. A *Rolling Stone* writer called it "a fine album, a remarkable set of songs that subtly calibrates the dynamics of relationships today" and "has a consistency of tone, with most of the songs united by a sense of missed connections and dislocations." Rob O'Connor of *Musician* wrote that "like an unconscious smile, *Become What You Are* has a way of catching you off-guard and making the world seem like a manageable place after all."

Whether Hatfield would feel that way herself remained an open question. "For a long time, music was hope," she told Mike Boehm of the *Los Angeles Times.* "Now it seems music isn't enough to make me happy. It used to be that's all I needed to keep going. Now I need other things to take up the other parts of my life. I want to emphasize that I haven't given up hope. I'm just starting to realize that music might not keep me happy forever. But it's still the main thing in my life, and I love it more than any person, right now." In an interview with *Pulse!,* she elaborated: "Writing songs allows you to deal with so many things that are really hard to deal with normally. It lets you turn something bad or destructive into something good."

Selected discography

With the Blake Babies

Nicely, Nicely, Chewbud, 1987.
Earwig, 1989.
Sunburn, 1990.

Solo releases

Hey Babe (includes "Ugly" and "Nirvana"), Mammoth, 1992.
Become What You Are (includes "My Sister," "Supermodel," "Dame With a Rod," and "Spin the Bottle"), Mammoth, 1993.

With the Lemonheads

It's a Shame About Ray, Atlantic, 1992.
Come on Feel the Lemonheads, Atlantic, 1993.

Sources

Alternative Press, October 1993.
Billboard, July 17, 1993; October 2, 1993.
College Music Journal (*CMJ*), August 1993.
Creem, October 1993.
Daily Variety, July 12, 1993.
Details, September 1993; July 1994.
Entertainment Weekly, December 25, 1992.
Esquire, August 1992.
Guitar Player, October 1993.
L.A. Village View, September 3, 1993.
Los Angeles Times, September 8, 1993.

Musician, October 1992; August 1993.
Newsweek, September 6, 1993.
Pulse!, October 1993.
Raygun, December 1993.
Request, November 1993.
Rolling Stone, September 30, 1993; October 28, 1993.
Spin, January 1992; August 1992; December 1993; March 1994.

Additional information was provided by Atlantic Records promotional materials, 1993.

—Simon Glickman

Woody Herman

Bandleader, saxophonist, clarinetist

MICHAEL OCHS ARCHIVES/Venice, CA

No other bandleader in the history of jazz had the staying power of Woody Herman. From the Band That Plays the Blues, Herman's first ensemble, organized in 1936, through the many "Herds" that came and went from the 1940s to the 1980s, Herman managed to maintain vitality in his big bands as others ran out of steam and dropped out of the race. There were two keys to Herman's success. First, he continuously hired talented young players and arrangers. Second, he refused to lead a nostalgia band that played only hits of the past. The result was an ensemble that was always fresh and exciting, musically sharp, and—especially notable from the 1960s on, as rock music was eclipsing jazz—popular.

Woodrow Charles Thomas Herman was born in Milwaukee, Wisconsin, in 1913. He began performing at the age of eight in a children's group that performed skits before the screening of silent films. He took music and dance lessons, and by age ten was performing year-round in local theaters. Appearing in a Chicago vaudeville house, he was billed as "The Boy Wonder."

By 1925 Herman knew that he wanted to be a jazz musician. He joined Tom Gerun's band, playing saxophones and clarinet, performing later with Harry Sosnick on radio broadcasts, then with Gus Arnheim. He got his big break in 1934 when he joined the Isham Jones Orchestra, in which he added singing to his other duties. In 1936 Herman and some other members of the defunct Jones orchestra formed their own ensemble and called it the Band That Plays the Blues.

The group made several recordings for the Decca label, most notably Joe Bishop's up-tempo blues chart, "Woodchopper's Ball," which was recorded for the first time for Decca in 1939. Herman remarked in his autobiography that when the record was first released, "it was really a sleeper. But Decca kept re-releasing it, and over a period of three or four years it became a hit. Eventually it sold more than five million copies—the biggest hit I ever had."

Herman's bands were always characterized by their rhythmic drive and intensity and by the enthusiasm of the players. In Herman's autobiography, jazz critic Gene Lees is quoted as saying that "Woody had an astonishing capacity to spot talent before it was particularly obvious to anybody else ... the list of careers that he either made or advanced is staggering." Herman's personnel lineup over the years reads like an index to jazz, including such notables as sax players Stan Getz, Zoot Sims, and Flip Phillips; trumpeters Shorty Rogers, Pete and Conte Candoli, and Sonny Berman; trombonists Bill Watrous, Jim Pugh, and Bill Harris; pianists Ralph Burns and Jimmy Rowles; vibraphonists Milt

> **For the Record...**
>
> Born Woodrow Charles Thomas Herman, May 16, 1913, in Milwaukee, WI; died of congestive heart failure, emphysema, and pneumonia, October 29, 1987, in Los Angeles, CA; father was a shoemaker, mother's name, Martha; married Charlotte Neste, September 21, 1936; children: Ingrid.
>
> Performed as a child in dramatic and musical acts in the Great Lakes region; performed with bands led by Tom Gerun and Gus Arnheim, 1920s; joined Isham Jones Orchestra and played saxophone and clarinet, 1934; formed the Band That Plays the Blues, 1936; recorded "Woodchopper's Ball," 1939; band renamed Woody Herman's Herd, mid-1940s; band appeared in motion pictures, including *What's Cookin'?*, 1942, *Wintertime,* 1943, *Earl Carroll Vanities,* 1944, *Sensations of 1945,* and *New Orleans,* 1945; signed with Columbia Records, 1944; premiered Igor Stravinsky's *Ebony Concerto* at Carnegie Hall, New York City, 1946; formed Second Herd, 1947; moved from Columbia Records to Capitol Records, 1948; formed Third Herd, early 1950s; Third Herd replaced by successive "Herd" incarnations throughout 1980s; Herman established nightclub Woody Herman's at the New Orleans Hyatt Regency, 1981; performed in 50th Anniversary Concert at the Paramount Theater in New York City, July 16, 1987.
>
> **Awards:** Grammy awards for the albums *Encore,* 1963, *Giant Steps,* 1973, and *Thundering Herd,* 1974; Woody Herman Music Archives established at the University of Houston School of Music, 1974; honorary doctorate from Berklee College of Music, 1977.

Jackson, Red Norvo, Marjorie Hyams, and Terry Gibbs; bassists Oscar Pettiford and Chubby Jackson; and drummers Dave Tough, Shelley Manne, and Ed Soph.

The Evolution of the Herd

By the early 1940s, recordings and newspaper advertisements were calling the Band That Plays the Blues the Woody Herman Band, and around 1944, it became widely known as Woody Herman's Herd, the name by which *Metronome* jazz critic George T. Simon had been referring to it since the early 1940s. The Herd became tremendously popular during World War II. They appeared on radio broadcasts sponsored by Old Gold cigarettes, and shrewd promotion by Columbia Records—who featured the Herd's recordings in ads along with those of popular singers Frank Sinatra and Dinah Shore—launched it into superstardom. "We became Number One in the country because of that, as much as anything," Herman related in his autobiography. "It pushed us to the very peak of popularity." The Herd made recordings of some of its most successful numbers for Columbia, including "Caldonia," "Happiness is Just a Thing Called Joe," "Goosey Gander," and "Your Father's Moustache."

In October of 1945 the band became the first to sign a contract for a weekly radio show. The program was sponsored by Wildroot, a hair products company. Composer/arranger Neal Hefti wrote a chart based on Lionel Hampton's "Flyin' Home," and called it "Wild Root." "Wild Root" turned into another of the band's most popular arrangements. Classical composer Igor Stravinsky was so taken with Herman and the band that he wrote a piece especially for them that same year—the *Ebony Concerto*. The piece had its premiere at Carnegie Hall in March of 1946.

Kept His Personality in the Background

Herman was different from many other bandleaders of the day—such as Benny Goodman, Harry James, or Artie Shaw—because he never made himself the star attraction of the band. Herman, who played alto saxophone, clarinet, and sang some of the group's numbers, was never as strong a soloist as Goodman, James, or Shaw, and preferred to let the other members of the band have their day in the sun. "I call myself a coach more than a bandleader," he was quoted as saying in an article in *Down Beat* in 1986. "And my teams win."

In 1947, Herman formed the Second Herd. The centerpiece of the band was a three-tenor/one-baritone sax section—a feature that Herman kept in every succeeding band. The band's theme, based on this sax section, was the Jimmy Giuffre chart "Four Brothers." Herman said of the Second Herd in his autobiography: "The bebop evolution had become the core of our music.... Musically, the bebop route [for the Second Herd] was magnificent. But business-wise, it was the dumbest thing I ever did." The Second Herd was dissolved in 1949.

A good part of the various Herds' recognition is due to Herman's composers and arrangers. He made a point of using, whenever possible, his own players to write charts for the band. "I was always intrigued from the earliest days of having guys who were in the band write for the band," said Herman in an article in *Down Beat* in 1986. "I think they'll usually come up with better material than an outsider. And I was always very proud of the fact that we'd have a couple of guys in the sections who also arranged; this was the best situation. In the First Herd we had Ralph Burns and Neal Hefti. I have always tried to utilize people like these. They were closer to the music than I was in many cases. They knew best what guys should take what solos." Other notable composers and arrangers that wrote for Herman were Al Cohn, Shorty Rogers, Dave Matthews, Dizzy Gillespie, and Nat Pierce.

Herman disbanded the Second Herd in 1949, and went on to form a Third Herd. "We stopped numbering the Herds after the third one," Herman says in his autobiography, "but we were still thundering across the country nicely in the seventies." The band came to be called the Thundering Herd, and through the 1980s, captured the attention of young musicians by playing arrangements of tunes by songwriters such as Donald Fagen and Stevie Wonder.

Difficult Times in the 1960s and 1970s

While the Thundering Herd was successful, Herman's own life became progressively more difficult. In the early 1960s he took on a business manager, who was a chronic gambler and so mishandled Herman's finances that a few years later, Herman learned that he owed the Internal Revenue Service 1.6 million dollars. Herman worked the rest of his life to pay off the debt. In 1977, his leg was seriously injured in an automobile accident, and his wife Charlotte died of cancer in 1982. As if all of this were not enough, his house was auctioned off in 1985, with the proceeds going to the government.

Herman's last years did have their up side, however. His band received a Grammy award for their album *Giant Steps* in 1973, and another in 1974 for the *Thundering Herd* album. Also in 1974, the University of Houston established the Woody Herman Music Archives at its School of Music. Recovering from the car accident in 1977, Herman received an honorary doctor of music degree from the Berklee College of Music in Boston—one of the schools from which he drew his players. And in 1987, he celebrated 50 years as a bandleader with a concert at the Paramount Theater in New York City, attended by nearly 3,000 people.

Herman died on October 29, 1987, of congestive heart failure, emphysema, and pneumonia. In September of 1993 alumni from the many Herds gathered in Newport Beach, California, for a performance in his honor.

Selected discography

World Class, Concord Jazz, 1982.
50th Anniversary Tour, Concord Jazz, 1987.
The 40th Anniversary Carnegie Hall Concert, Bluebird, 1988.
The Thundering Herds, 1945-1947, Columbia Jazz Masterpieces, 1988.
The Third Herd: "Early Autumn," Discovery, 1988.
The Best of the Decca Years, MCA, 1988.
Woody Herman, Verve, 1988.
Woody and Friends, Concord Jazz, 1992.
The Early Woody Herman, Pearl, 1992.
Keeper of the Flame, Capitol Jazz, 1992.
The Best of Woody Herman and His Big Band: The Concord Years, Concord Jazz, 1993.

Sources

Books

Herman, Woody, and Stuart Troup, *The Woodchopper's Ball: The Autobiography of Woody Herman,* Dutton, 1990.
Simon, George T., *The Big Bands,* Schirmer Books, 1981.

Periodicals

American Scholar, summer 1989.
Atlantic, April 1986.
Billboard, November 14, 1987.
Down Beat, November 1986; February 1988.

—Joyce Harrison

Natalie Hinderas

Pianist, educator

In the rarefied world of classical music performance, sheer interpretive ability is often the first mark by which an artist is measured. Depth of character and an ability to transmit the artful expression of the composer further delineate the hierarchy of musical performers. Classical pianist Natalie Hinderas, possessed of a profoundly diverse musical expression, from the lyrical to the percussive, was viewed through another spectrum: Her place in the classical music world was reflected not by the tone colors and shadings that infused the notes she played, but by the color of her skin.

At the time of her death in 1987, Hinderas was recognized as "one of the first black artists to establish an important career in classical music," as was reported in her *New York Times* obituary. Although racial description as a means of definition is least expected in the arts, her reputation had to be built—not unwillingly—on advancing the work of the black classical artist, both the composer and the performer. But of equal importance for Hinderas was the indoctrination of young people to the unbiased artistic pleasures and human scope of classical music, the very attributes that guided her into the field.

Natalie Leota Henderson was born on June 15, 1927, in Oberlin, Ohio, into a family with a deep musical heritage. Her great-grandfather had been a bandleader and teacher in South Carolina; her father was a jazz pianist who toured Europe with his own group, her mother a classically trained piano teacher who served on the faculty of the Cleveland Institute of Music. Both parents were graduates of the Oberlin Conservatory. "I grew up with music," Hinderas later understated to Raymond Ericson of the *New York Times*. "I listened to my mother practice. I still remember her playing Rubinstein's D minor Concerto and Franck's Prelude, Choral, and Fugue."

Oberlin Conservatory's Youngest Graduate

This attention to the art of classical music was not lost on the young Hinderas. Indeed, she began playing the piano at age three. Her inherent talents matured under her mother's tutelage, and at the age of eight, she gave her first full recital on the piano. Immediately afterward, she was accepted into Oberlin Conservatory's Special Student's School. Hinderas's orchestral debut, playing Edvard Grieg's Piano Concerto, came with the Cleveland Women's Symphony in 1939. She was 12.

When Hinderas received her degree in music with honors from Oberlin in 1945, she became the conservatory's youngest graduate and one of its most prom-

For the Record . . .

Born Natalie Leota Henderson, June 15, 1927, in Oberlin, OH; died of cancer July 22, 1987, in Philadelphia, PA; daughter of Leota Palmer Henderson (conservatory piano instructor); father was a jazz pianist and bandleader; married Lionel Monagas; children: Michele. *Education:* Oberlin College, B.Mus., 1945; studied with Olga Samaroff at Juilliard School of Music, c. 1945-48; studied with Edward Steuermann at Philadelphia Conservatory, 1948-53; studied with Vincent Persichetti, early 1950s.

Concert pianist and educator. European debut, early 1950s; appeared on NBC-TV network programs and produced shows, early 1950s to 1987; U.S. debut piano recital, Town Hall, New York City, 1954; toured U.S., Europe, and West Indies, mid- to late 1950s; two U.S. State Department tours abroad, 1959 and 1964; produced radio series on classical music, Philadelphia, 1959; Temple University's College of Music, began as associate professor, became professor, 1966-87; toured southern black colleges, giving lectures/recitals, 1968; recording debut, *Natalie Hinderas Plays Music by Black Composers*, 1971; appeared with major U.S. orchestras, including New York Philharmonic, Los Angeles Philharmonic, Philadelphia Orchestra, and Chicago Symphony, 1971-87.

Awards: Fellowships from the Whitney, Rosenwald, and Rockefeller foundations; Leventritt award; Fulbright grant; Governors' Award for the Arts (Pennsylvania); Pro Arte award; honorary doctorate from Swarthmore College.

---

inent—her senior recital had attracted one of the school's largest audiences. She subsequently won an audition for advanced study at the Juilliard School of Music in New York City. There she was guided by the distinguished concert pianist and instructor Olga Samaroff, who brought out from Hinderas's playing a warm, romantic feeling.

Samaroff (who had changed her surname from Hickenlooper, and who convinced her student to change hers to the more exotic Hinderas) recognized Hinderas's potential for greatness but was also realistic in her view of the young pianist's future in the classical world. "She used to say," Hinderas related to Shirley Fleming in *High Fidelity/Musical America*, "'My dear, you're going to have a hard time.'" Previously, Hinderas had been judged—and praised—solely on her talents. Samaroff's forewarning, however, would unfortunately prove prophetic.

After Samaroff's death in 1948, Hinderas continued her studies for the next five years with Edward Steuermann at the Philadelphia Conservatory of Music. Steuermann deepened her ability to handle the arduous technical and intellectual demands of classical music's more exacting compositions. At this time she also studied composition with Vincent Persichetti.

In the early 1950s, Hinderas's career seemed to be blossoming. While continuing her studies with both Steuermann and Persichetti, she made her European debut and signed a contract with NBC-TV to make appearances on network programs, both classical and variety shows. A Cleveland television station broadcast Hinderas in concert in 1953. One year later, she debuted at New York City's Town Hall.

Debut Promised Exceptional Career

With a program featuring Mozart's Sonata in F, Ravel's *Alborado del Gracioso* and *Jeux d'eau,* Berg's Piano Sonata, Hindemith's Sonata No. 1, and Chopin's F minor Ballade, Hinderas demonstrated to a *New York Times* reviewer that she had "honest musical instincts. Very often she shaped a phrase with real authority, leaving no doubt that a strong controlling force was engaged." Although this critic found fault with some of her execution—a certain lack of musical maturity in the Hindemith and Chopin pieces—he nonetheless foresaw Hinderas, after a few more years of experience, taking her place as a world-class pianist accompanied by world-class orchestras.

Hinderas did gain valuable artistic insight in the following years. She traveled around the United States on a recital tour, performed with the National Symphony, and gave concerts in the British West Indies. During 1957 and 1958, she gave televised recitals in Austria, England, Germany, Holland, and Italy. In 1959 she won an award from the Leventritt Foundation, which sponsored subsequent performances with numerous orchestras. None of these, however, were recognized as world-class.

But Hinderas remained tireless in her quest to expose audiences to the classical repertoire, producing two series on classical music for a Philadelphia radio station in 1959. That year she also began a four-month world tour under the auspices of the U.S. State Department, visiting Sweden, Yugoslavia, Iran, Jordan, Taiwan, and the Philippines and giving lecture/recitals on American music and fostering cultural goodwill. In 1961 she appeared on behalf of the American Society for African Society at the opening of a cultural center in

Largos, Nigeria. A second State Department tour took place in 1964. This time she traveled to Sweden, Poland, Yugoslavia, and England, and, in addition to her recitals and seminars, performed with the Dubrovnik and Skopje Symphony Orchestras.

Even after these performances on the world's stages, Hinderas was not given the opportunity to perform with the best orchestras in the United States. "Orchestras simply wouldn't hire a black woman—this was in the days when there weren't even black players in the orchestras," Hinderas told Fleming. "People used to say to me, 'You're the only black musician around.' And I think I was until André Watts—he broke the barrier. Before that I felt like a freak; it was a terrible sense of responsibility."

> "Orchestras simply wouldn't hire a black woman—this was in the days when there weren't even black players in the orchestras. People used to say to me, 'You're the only black musician around.' I felt like a freak."

A more self-centered musician might have been deterred by the lack of exposure with a renowned orchestra, but Hinderas, devoted to the art of classical music, instead sought to reach an audience for the art's sake, not her own. In 1966 she joined the faculty of Temple University's College of Music and began lecturing and performing at various colleges and music festivals around the country. The college lecture/recital became a calling for Hinderas. She explained why to Fleming: "Young people are an untapped source—they can be a good audience because they're less inhibited, less structured than older people, though of course they have their own form of 'structure' and that can be limiting too. But I talk to them about the importance of music, how it is an enunciation of one's life, really the expression of what they're living. I try to set up a dialogue and ferret out their questions and doubts."

Hinderas also sought to reconcile the black community to her art, fighting the idea, as she told *New York Times* contributor Ericson, that "classical music is white man's music." To this end, she began touring southern black colleges in 1968, performing the music of black classical composers and lecturing on the history of black classical musicians in the United States. "I'm trying to change the jazz- and gospel-oriented image," she told Fleming. "People have never associated us with the classics."

To dispel this notion, not only for the black community but for the global community as well, Hinderas recorded *Natalie Hinderas Plays Music by Black Composers* for the Desto label in 1971. The two-record set featured the works of nine composers: R. Nathaniel Dett, Thomas H. Kerr, Jr., William Grant Still, John W. Work, George Walker, Arthur Cunningham, Stephen A. Chambers, Hale Smith, and Olly Wilson.

The significance and necessity of the recording was confirmed by Leslie Gerber in a review for *American Record Guide:* "It is hardly possible to be unaware of the tremendous contributions made by black musicians to American folk, popular, and jazz music; but one may sometimes wonder what blacks have achieved in the more academic forms of the tonal art." This anthology showed Gerber exactly what some of them had achieved, and his highest praise was bestowed on Hinderas. "I would welcome the opportunity to hear her in works from the classical repertoire," he wrote. "Of all the musicians whose acquaintance I have made through these records, she is the one who has made the most thoroughly favorable impression on me."

Recognition at Last

That impression was felt elsewhere as well, and Hinderas's talent was finally fully recognized in the fall of 1971 when conductor Eugene Ormandy invited her to play Alberto Ginastera's Piano Concerto No. 1 with the Philadelphia Orchestra. With this debut, she became the first black woman ever to appear as an instrumental soloist in the regular series of any major symphony. Another first was the selection of music. In this setting, a work by Grieg or Chopin would traditionally have been offered. But Ormandy and Hinderas chose instead to feature the Argentine composer's 1961 work, which would highlight Hinderas's strengths as a pianist. James Felton, reviewing the concert for *High Fidelity/Musical America,* lauded the choice, remarking, "Like some writhing marine animal, the work seemed to ripple over cross rhythms and asymmetrical bars, handled at the keyboard with tensile strength. Miss Hinderas was now leader, now follower, now a full partner in forceful tuttis that reinforced a recurrent percussive wallop."

Immediately afterward, Hinderas was engaged to play with major orchestras across the nation: the New York Philharmonic, the Cleveland Symphony, the Los Angeles Philharmonic, the Atlanta Symphony, the Chicago Symphony, the San Francisco Symphony, the Pittsburgh Symphony. She found her appearance with the Los Angeles Philharmonic at the Hollywood Bowl particularly satisfying; she explained to the *New York*

Times' Ericson that early in her career a manager had told her, "You know, Natalie, a little colored girl like you can't play in the Hollywood Bowl."

Again, an artist of lesser character might have been content to sit and accept the laurels. But Hinderas remained committed to developing the public's recognition and appreciation of classical music. She believed a greater understanding could be achieved through the media, specifically television. "It is time we change the total direction of classical music in this country and got support from the public media," she declared to *High Fidelity/Musical America* contributor Fleming. "Watergate has proved that we are directed by public relations techniques. The major TV networks are molding our minds and they have the responsibility to further the arts. You can lead people into anything if you know how to."

The music Hinderas created was large and physically exuberant, but it took the world almost 20 years to notice it. She fought for and gained recognition and respect not only for herself as a performer, but also for the contributions of black musicians and composers to the world of classical music, a world where color is only a shading of a note. "To begin with, of course, she is a pianist," began Fleming's 1973 profile of Hinderas. In a more color-blind society, this would have been the initial standard by which Hinderas was measured.

Selected discography

Natalie Hinderas Plays Music by Black Composers, Desto, 1971, reissued as *Natalie Hinderas: Piano Music by African American Composers,* CRI, 1993.
Natalie Hinderas Plays Sensuous Piano Music, Orion.
George Walker's Piano Concerto, Columbia.

Sources

Books

Abdul, Raoul, *Blacks in Classical Music,* Dodd, Mead, 1977.

Periodicals

American Music Teacher, January 1975; February 1975.
American Record Guide, April 1971.
Ebony, February 1993.
High Fidelity/Musical America, February 1972; October 1973.
New York Times, November 14, 1954; November 10, 1972; July 23, 1987.
Saturday Review, December 26, 1970; December 16, 1972.

—*Rob Nagel*

Earl "Fatha" Hines

Pianist, bandleader

With his muscled arms and compact, powerful hands, Earl Hines embraced nearly every era of jazz pianism. Credited by many with transforming the idiom with his "trumpet style" keyboard approach, Hines served as a beacon for such followers as Teddy Wilson, Art Tatum, Erroll Garner, Nat Cole, Bud Powell, Stan Kenton, and Oscar Peterson. While he led the band at Chicago's Grand Terrace Cafe his career paralleled that of Duke Ellington in New York's Cotton Club; his swinging ensemble pre-dated Benny Goodman's "King of Swing" orchestra of 1935.

Hines enjoys almost unanimous regard among fellow pianists and critics as one of the geniuses on his instrument. His professionalism and ability to communicate with an audience were unparalleled. His range of expertise as a pianist reached from solo piano to small combos to vocal accompaniment to string-augmented big band. And though Hines always maintained that he considered himself to be a band pianist rather than a soloist, some of the solo work recorded near the end of his 60-year career is astonishing in its impact.

Born near Pittsburgh in Duquesne, Pennsylvania, in 1905, Earl Kenneth Hines heard good music very early. His father, a foreman at the local coal dock, played cornet; his stepmother, who entered his life when he was only three, was an organist; a live-in uncle was master of several brass instruments. After a brief fling with the cornet, Earl took to the piano and applied himself, both with school training and excellent private lessons, toward the goal of becoming a concert pianist. At this time, in addition to great pianistic dexterity, he developed a facility as a reader of music that served him throughout his career.

Developed a Personal Style

When he moved to Pittsburgh to attend high school while living with an aunt who sang light opera, Hines was exposed to a broader world of music and introduced to such luminaries as composers/band leaders Eubie Blake and Noble Sissle. That new, broader world included jazz. The sounds and rhythms of 1919 Pittsburgh's Wylie Street night spots were irresistible to the 14-year-old Earl Hines.

Soon he formed his own trio and continued to soak up the sounds of the more experienced players as he performed at parties and socials. Lois Deppe, a popular baritone and band leader on Wylie Street, took note of Hines's keyboard agility and reading ability and hired him in 1921. His brilliance quickly drew the attention of admiring Leader House club patrons as well as local musicians.

> **For the Record . . .**
>
> Born Earl Kenneth Hines, December 28, 1905, in Duquesne, PA; died April 22, 1983, in Oakland, CA; father, Joseph, was a cornetist; stepmother, Mary, played organ. *Education:* Studied classical music with Von Holz.
>
> Formed a jazz trio at age 14 in Pittsburgh, PA; hired at age 16 by bandleader Lois Deppe and toured Ohio, West Virginia, and New York City; made first records, 1923; moved to Chicago, 1925; played with his own group and with Jimmy Noone and Louis Armstrong, 1928; became leader of band at Grand Terrace nightclub, beginning in 1928; led modern touring group with Dizzy Gillespie, Charlie Parker, and Billy Eckstine, early 1940s; returned to Armstrong's All Stars, 1948-51; "re-discovered" at Little Theatre concerts and resumed world tours and active recording career, 1964-83.
>
> **Awards:** *Esquire* Silver Award, 1944; elected to Jazz Hall of Fame, 1965.

During that two-year stay with Deppe, Hines was rapidly developing a personal style. He gave credit to several local pianists for influencing him, but Hines maintained that his major influence was trumpeter Joe Smith. The pianist's repertoire broadened as his performances ranged from the showy, jazz-oriented tunes in the club to light classics and church recitals, usually accompanying Deppe. Visiting musicians soon made it a point to check out the young phenomenon. With the Deppe band he branched out to Ohio, West Virginia, and New York City. As the band grew in size as well as popularity, Hines developed his famous right hand octave doubling technique—the trumpet style—as a way to cut through the sound of the other instruments with his unamplified piano. In October of 1923, not yet 18, Hines cut his first records, including one original composition, with Deppe at the Gennett studio in Richmond, Indiana.

In 1924 Hines left Deppe to form another band of his own, one that included the multi-talented Benny Carter on saxophone. Then, heeding the admonition of Blake to leave Pittsburgh and showcase his talents elsewhere, Hines moved to Chicago, landing in the midst of such players as King Oliver, Jelly Roll Morton, Benny Goodman, Frank Teschemacher, and, especially, Louis Armstrong.

The handsome, personable pianist quickly developed a following, while continuing his on-the-job training in a variety of settings. Hines and Armstrong formed a musical bond and, with drummer Zutty Singleton, began playing together at the Sunset Cafe, which quickly became the "in" place on Chicago's South Side for musicians as well as for gangsters and other big-spending customers. As Hines told biographer Stanley Dance of his association with Armstrong, "When we were playing together it was like a continuous jam session. I'd steal ideas from him and he'd steal them from me. He'd bend over after a solo and say ... 'Thank you, man.'" The temporary 1927 closing of the club led to a breakup of the Hines/Armstrong/Singleton combo and Hines soon joined clarinetist Jimmie Noone's band at the nearby Apex Club.

Recording Career Burgeoned

In the last eight months of 1928 Hines made records with Noone's Apex Club Orchestra and with Louis Armstrong, some with Armstrong's Hot Five and Hot Seven, that are among the most celebrated in jazz recording. The fully-developed piano style of Hines, not yet 23, shines through on all these sides; amazingly, his playing here still sounds fresh. One gem, "Weather Bird," showcases simply Hines and Armstrong in a remarkable duet on which they stretch the rhythmic and harmonic borders in ways that had not previously been recorded.

In his *The Swing Era,* Gunther Schuller writes that Hines's recordings of this time "reveal a manual ambidexterity and agility of mind that was unprecedented in jazz piano.... Any idea that came into his head was instantly transferable to his obedient fingers." Schuller and other writers point out that Hines often appeared to be staging a challenge, a competition, between his right and left hand as to which one could produce the greater surprises while still sounding integrated. This characteristic remained with Hines throughout his career, as did his penchant for "broken" rhythms in which he avoided a strict four-beats-to-the-bar in favor of multiple variations in meter.

At the end of 1928, on his twenty-third birthday, Hines began a new phase of his career as he took over as bandleader at the Grand Terrace, one of Chicago's most beautiful and popular night clubs. Here, under the protective eye of Al Capone, Hines held forth for eleven years, interrupted by increasingly long annual forays on the road as the band's popularity fanned outward. In his liner notes for *Earl Hines—South Side Swing,* biographer Dance wrote that "from 1934 onwards, the Hines band enjoyed more radio air time than any other in the U.S." This air time helped Hines attract and develop many gifted players and arrangers, both at the

Grand Terrace and later. Among the musicians whose careers he aided were Budd Johnson, Gene Ramey, Trummy Young, Cecil Irwin, Billy Eckstine, Dizzy Gillespie, and Charlie Parker. At one point his band featured perhaps the two finest pure voices ever to sing jazz, Sarah Vaughan and Johnny Hartman.

As a leader Hines expected good performance and appearance from his sidemen and, despite his great personal popularity, he was generous in assigning solos and arranging tasks to others. Though a gifted composer as well ("Rosetta," "Stormy Monday Blues," and "You Can Depend On Me," among others), the leader gave his many arrangers wide berth. Their varying styles precluded the development of a recognizable band sound, save for the driving rhythm propelled by Hines.

> "I'd steal ideas from Louis Armstrong and he'd steal them from me. He'd bend over after a solo and say, 'Thank you, man.'"

It is to this lack of identity that some trace the fact that the Hines band was eclipsed by those of Duke Ellington, Count Basie, Glenn Miller, and Benny Goodman in the polls. And while he recorded some substantial hits—"Piano Man," 1939; "Boogie Woogie on the St. Louis Blues," 1940; "Jelly, Jelly," 1940; "Stormy Monday Blues," 1942, the latter two with Eckstine vocals—true popularity proved elusive. Hines tired of bandleading, with its general postwar decline, and returned to an old friend in 1948.

Hines remained with the Louis Armstrong All Stars—featuring trombonist Jack Teagarden, clarinetist Barney Bigard, bassist Arvell Shaw, and drummer Sid Catlett—until 1951 when, wearying of the same routines night after night, the pianist left and formed a new small group. Touring with this combo until 1955, Hines then settled down at the Club Hangover in San Francisco for five years and bought a home in nearby Oakland. Another extended club date, interlarded with brief trips to other cities, constituted a quiet, part-time musical existence until 1964, when Hines was invited to play three solo concerts at the Little Theatre in New York. These concerts created great excitement and sparked a re-discovery of the keyboard master.

Of these concerts Whitney Balliett wrote in his *American Musicians: 56 Portraits in Jazz*, "Not only was his celebrated style intact, but it had taken on a subtlety and unpredictability that continually pleased and startled the audience.... Between numbers, that smile—one of the renowned lamps of show business—made his face look transparent. It was exemplary showmanship—not wrappings and tinsel but the gift itself, freely offered."

Major Contributions Recognized

What followed were the rebirth of Hines's recording career and a series of world tours in concert, usually with reedman Budd Johnson and drummer Oliver Jackson. In 1966 Hines visited the Soviet Union for the U.S. State Department and in 1969 and 1976 performed at the White House. Between 1970 and 1973 Hines recorded ten LPs for Chiaroscuro, beginning with new interpretations of his arresting eight sides for QRS records in 1928, and including 1973's brilliant live solo concert at New York's New School for Social Research.

This concert displays all of the mighty Hines pianistic elements: startling technique in both hands; inventiveness that permits new approaches to familiar material; unerring time, often broken with displaced accents and implied or real double-time; indefatigable right-hand tremolos; the trumpet style; security; humor; surprise and joy. In *The Great Jazz Pianists,* Len Lyons explains, "Like the circus clown who plays at tripping and falling (but deftly lands on his feet every time), Hines would 'lose' both rhythm and chord changes within a song only to bring them together at the end of the phrase or chorus.

It is these elements that Hines combined while winding down a 60-year playing career. Hines's earliest records reveal an audacity still evident, while those made 40 years later remain models of complete, modern piano work. Despite the encroachment of arthritis and heart problems, he was still in command of these elements while playing until within a week of his death in Oakland on April 22, 1983.

Though Hines never appreciated the "Fatha" nickname hung on him by a radio announcer at the Grand Terrace, he indeed may be considered a father to all jazz pianists who have followed. Schuller considers him "one of the two supreme pianists of our time." Of Hines's playing, writer/arranger/pianist Billy Strayhorn told *Metronome:* "Technically, it is unorthodox; harmonically, it is intriguing; and actually, it is almost impossible to imitate in its entirety. His devotees are legion, his influence tremendous and his artistry incomparable."

Selected discography

Stride Right: Johnny Hodges, Earl "Fatha" Hines, Verve, 1966.
"Fatha": The New Earl Hines Trio, Columbia, 1973.
Earl Hines/Live at the New School, Chiaroscuro Records, 1977.
Giants of Jazz: Earl Hines, Time-Life Records, 1980.
(With others) *The Complete Master Jazz Piano Series,* Mosaic, 1993.
Here Comes Earl "Fatha" Hines/Spontaneous Explorations, (reissue), Red Baron, 1994.
Earl Hines: South Side Swing, 1934-1935.
Jimmie Noone & Earl Hines "At the Apex Club," Vol. 1, 1928, Decca Records.
The Louis Armstrong Story, Vol. 3, Columbia.

Sources

Books

Balliett, Whitney, *American Musicians: 56 Portraits in Jazz,* Oxford University Press, 1986.
Chilton, John, *Who's Who of Jazz,* Time-Life, 1978.
Dance, Stanley, *The World of Earl Hines,* Charles Scribner's Sons, 1977.
Feather, Leonard, *The New Edition of the Encyclopedia of Jazz,* Bonanza Books, 1965.
Lyons, Len, *The Great Jazz Pianists,* Da Capo, 1983.
Lyons, Len, and Perlo, Don, *Jazz Portraits: The Lives and Music of the Jazz Masters,* Quill/William Morrow, 1989.
Schuller, Gunther, *The Swing Era: The Development of Jazz, 1930-1945,* Oxford University Press, 1989.

Periodicals

Detroit Free Press, April 24, 1983.
Down Beat, January 1993.
Metronome, c. 1943.
Pulse!, March 1994.

Additional information for this profile was obtained from the monograph *Giants of Jazz: Earl Hines,* by Stanley Dance, Time-Life Records, 1980, and from the liner notes to *Earl Hines/Live At the New School,* by Hank O'Neal, and *Earl Hines: South Side Swing, 1934-1935,* by Stanley Dance.

—*Robert Dupuis*

Burl Ives

Singer, actor, writer

Throughout his life and career Burl Ives was many things; he was a folk singer, actor, storyteller, writer, and anthologist. His real role, however, was, as Stephen Holden wrote in the *New York Times,* as "an American sentimentalist in the tradition of Carl Sandburg and Norman Rockwell." Ives himself wrote, in his preface to *Burl Ives' Tales of America,* "I was born in America, I grew up in America, and I went to school in America.... I ... tramped the country from one end to the other with my guitar over my shoulder [and] I discovered how dramatic and thrilling the true history of our country really is." In many ways, in whatever he did, in the songs he sang and the stories he told, Ives first and foremost celebrated this love for his country and its history.

Ives was born and raised in what might be looked on as the heart of Americana: a small town in the Midwest. He enjoyed singing with his family and learned to play the banjo as a kid. And it was at the young age of four that Ives started performing in public, singing for change with his brothers and sisters; he also performed in many community productions during his childhood and youth. After playing football in high school, though, Ives entered college intending to become a high school football coach. A sort of musical wanderlust overtook him in his junior year, however, and he left school to travel the country, playing songs for food and shelter when he could, doing day labor when he could, and always collecting songs and stories from the folks he met.

In 1937, Ives moved to New York for formal vocal instruction and to break into show business. The music world did not welcome him immediately, though, for his music was viewed as having too much of a "hillbilly" sound. In the meantime, the stage offered Ives his first successes when he appeared Off-Broadway in *Ah Wilderness!, Pocahontas Preferred,* and *Flight* in 1938. And in the same year he appeared on Broadway in George Abbott's *The Boys from Syracuse.*

In addition to success, Ives' acting also seemed to give him more musical credibility, for by 1940 he had his own radio program, *The Wayfarin' Stranger,* and was considered, at least by the young folk singer Pete Seeger, who appeared with him at the 1940 *Grapes of Wrath* benefit for Californian migrant farm workers, to be one of the country's most distinguished folksingers. After several years of singing in New York City nightclubs, Ives made his recital debut at New York's Town Hall in 1945. That same year, he traded the East Coast for the West Coast and made his Hollywood debut in the film *Smokey* (1945).

In the decades that followed, Ives continued to sing and act, but also added writing to his list of credits. In

For the Record...

Born Burl Icle Ivanhoe Ives, June 14, 1909, in Hunt Township, Jasper County, IL; son of Frank and Cordelia White Ives; married Helen Payne Ehrlich, 1949 (divorced, 1971); married Dorothy Koster, 1971; children: (first marriage) Alexander. *Education:* Attended Eastern Illinois State Teachers College, 1927-30, and New York University, 1937-38.

Itinerant musician 1930-37; stage debut in *Ah, Wilderness!*, Rockridge Theater, Carmel, NY, 1938; hosted radio show *Wayfarin' Stranger,* 1940-42; New York concert debut, New York's Town Hall, 1945. Broadway appearances include *The Boys from Syracuse,* 1938, *Heavenly Express,* 1940, *Sing Out, Sweet Land,* 1944, and *Cat on a Hot Tin Roof,* 1955; film appearances include *Smoky,* 1945, *Green Grass of Wyoming,* 1948, *So Dear to My Heart,* 1948, *Station West,* 1948, *Sierra,* 1950, *East of Eden,* 1955, *The Power and the Prize,* 1956, *Cat on a Hot Tin Roof,* 1958, *Wind Across the Everglades,* 1958, *The Big Country,* 1958, *Desire Under the Elms,* 1958, *Our Man in Havana,* 1960, and *Robin and the Seven Hoods,* 1964; television appearances include *The Bold Ones,* 1970-72; *Rudolf the Red-Nosed Reindeer* (narrator), 1972, and *Roots,* 1977.

Awards: Donaldson Award, 1945; Academy Award, 1958, for *The Big Country.*

Addresses: c/o Beakel and Jennings Agency, 427 N. Canon Dr., Suite 205, Beverly Hills, CA 90210.

1948 he published his autobiography, *The Wayfaring Stranger,* and he also published several collections of short stories throughout his career, including *The Wayfaring Stranger's Notebook* and *Burl Ives' Tales of America.* Ives seemed to see writing these tales of Americana as an extension of his folk singing, with the same origins and the same purposes. And the songs and stories collected during his youthful ramblings were also valuable expressions of the American ethos for Ives.

"My mind is full of the things I have learned," wrote Ives in his preface to *Burl Ives' Tales of America.* "And since I am by nature a collector of all kinds of things—of songs and stories and tidbits of information, and of people who have things to tell me or who can open up new paths for me to explore—I have managed to assemble notes and jottings and clippings and books and documents, and all manner of material which overflow my bookcases and my files. From all these things I have been jotting down my own notes and writing my own stories, and doing this has given me much joy.... All the things I have put down here are living legends for me, and I tell them as I feel and live them. This is the way I sing my songs, too. And just as each song requires a special kind of singing so each of the tales in these pages require a special kind of telling." Ives not only anthologized stories, but also produced several anthologies of folk songs, including *The Burl Ives Songbook* (1953) and *The Burl Ives Book of Irish Songs* (1958). He continued his special kind of telling and singing for decades.

While Ives's motivation for his art was always the celebration of the American people, he was not always viewed as the perfect American. In the 1950s, along with almost every other folk singer and many Hollywood entertainers, he ran into trouble with the House Un-American Activities Committee (HUAC), and the Senate Internal Security Subcommittee. And although Ives was cleared by the committees, his testimony was bitterly criticized by some. Fellow folk singer Pete Seeger, as quoted in *How Can I Keep from Singing,* accused Ives of "fingering, like any common stool pigeon, some of his radical associates."

Ives did testify before the committee, but he volunteered to do so because, according to an interview with the *New York Times,* he was disillusioned with the party when he discovered that they were not, in fact, "professional do-gooders on a political level, as they have long masqueraded." While Seeger claimed that Ives talked to the committee "because he felt it was the only way to preserve his lucrative contracts," Ives stated that he believed that the party was an enemy of the country he loved. Although Seeger remained bitter towards Ives, and Seeger fans avoided Ives' recordings, Ives was not even the one who named Seeger or the Weavers to the committee.

For most Americans, Ives represents the solid, old-fashioned American who tells American stories and sings real American folk songs. In the 1990s, folk music means many different things to many different people, and a "folk music festival" may include such diverse sounds as blues, reggae, electric pop, or jazz. What folk music officially means, though, is a set of traditional songs, sung by ordinary people, for their own pleasure, not in concert, but on the front porch. Ives's music is the real folk music, the traditional songs; Ives brought these songs into the mainstream of American popular music, and has been instrumental in keeping that part of American heritage alive.

Selected discography

Ballads and Folk Songs, Decca, 1949.
Ballads, Folk and Country Songs, Decca, 1949.
Down to the Sea in Ships, Decca, 1956.
It's Just My Funny Way of Laughing, Decca, 1962
Christmas at the White House, Caedmon, 1972.
Greatest Hits, MCA, 1973.
Burl Ives Sings Little White Duck and Other Children's Favorites, Columbia, 1974.
Rudolph the Red-Nosed Reindeer Original Soundtrack, MCA, 1980.
Best of Burl's for Boys and Girls, MCA, 1980.
Santa Clause Is Coming to Town, MCA, 1987.
Have a Holly Jolly Christmas, MCA, 1990.

Selected writings

The Wayfaring Stranger, McGraw-Hill, 1948.
The Burl Ives Song Book, Ballantine, 1953.
Burl Ives' Tales of America, World Publishing Company, 1954.
Sailing on a Very Fine Day, Rand McNally, 1955.
The Burl Ives Book of Irish Songs, Duell, Sloan and Pearce, 1958.
Song in America, Duell, Sloan and Pearce, 1962.
The Wayfaring Stranger's Notebook, Bobbs-Merrill, 1962.

Sources

Books

Drexel, John, editor, *The Facts on File Encyclopedia of the Twentieth Century,* Facts on File, 1991.
Dunaway, David King, *How Can I Keep from Singing: Pete Seeger,* McGraw-Hill, 1981.
Slonimsky, Nicolas, *Baker's Biographical Dictionary of Musicians,* revised 8th edition, Schirmer Books.
Willens, Doris, *Lonesome Traveler: The Life of Lee Hays,* W.W. Norton & Company, 1988.

Periodicals

Billboard, July 3, 1993.
Christian Science Monitor, July 26, 1991.
Detroit Free Press, October 13, 1993.
New York Times, February 25, 1945; December 8, 1945; September 25, 1952; December 3, 1982; December 6, 1982; May 19, 1993.
People, October 15, 1990.

—Robin Armstrong

James

Pop band

The mercurial English band James came out of the fertile early 1980s Manchester postpunk scene, along with such celebrated groups as the Smiths and Joy Division. Though they built a solid fan base in the United Kingdom, they struggled for international recognition, changing labels several times and frustrating journalists with their playful image-shifting. Combining an acerbic wit with honest yearning, the band's vision—which a writer in *Musician* called "eclectic, theatrical and introspective"—kept James relatively underground for many years, though their followers remained enthusiastic.

It wasn't until their 1993 album *Laid,* written and recorded under the aegis of inventive and storied producer Brian Eno, that James broke through to a larger audience in the United States, thanks in large part to the album's title track, which singer Tim Booth described to a *Los Angeles Times* interviewer as "a silly little catchy pop song." At the same time, critics acknowledged the band's increased maturity and depth. The members of James have clearly weathered their shifting fortune by

Courtesy of Fontana/Mercury Records

For the Record...

Members include **David Baynton-Power** (joined band c. 1988), drums; **Tim Booth** (born c. 1964), vocals; **Saul Davies** (joined band c. 1988), violin; **Andy Diagram** (bandmember 1988-92), trumpet; **Jim Glennie,** bass; **Larry Gott,** guitar; **Mark Hunter** (joined band c. 1988), keyboards; **Gavan Whelan** (left band c. 1988), drums.

Group formed in Manchester, England, and signed with Factory Records, releasing singles and EP *Jim One,* 1983; signed with Sire Records, 1986; signed with Rough Trade Records, 1988; signed with Phonogram, 1989; contributed to Velvet Underground tribute album *Heaven and Hell,* 1990; appeared on WOMAD tour, 1993.

Addresses: *Record company*—Mercury Records, 825 Eighth Ave., New York, NY 10019; 11150 Santa Monica Blvd., Suite 1100, Los Angeles, CA 90025.

---

remaining focused on what mattered most. "There were times when we felt like there was no place for us," bassist Jim Glennie recalled to *Musician*'s Paul Zollo. "We'd start feeling down, but then we'd walk into the rehearsal room and songs would appear. Wonderful songs. That's why we kept going. It's why we kept faith. It's the main reason we're still here." As Booth insisted in *Melody Maker,* "We're here to *discover.*"

Bright Colors, Career Blues

The initial band members of James—guitarist Larry Gott, Glennie, and drummer Gavan Whelan—started playing together without a singer. Booth related to Zollo how he was recruited: "The band had only been together about a year since they first stole their instruments and they saw me stuttering in some nightclub and asked me to dance onstage with them. Dancing has always been my main release from life."

The year was 1983; the Manchester scene, populated by a number of uncompromising alternative bands that carried the torch of punk rock, was among the most closely watched on the underground music circuit. The pervasive mood of these groups—particularly the stark Joy Division, which became New Order after the suicide of lead singer Ian Curtis—could be fairly described as gloomy. James, on the other hand—named by Booth after the innovative Irish writer James Joyce—sported bright colors and explored happier themes. "Yeah, everyone was wearing black and being really po-faced," Booth recollected to Paul Lester of *Melody Maker.* "And we were dressed in yellow, red and green. We looked like Smarties [candies], or kids' show hosts! But it was all very tongue-in-cheek and deliberate." The band's popular T-shirts eventually became some of the most visible on the music scene; their independent merchandising empire has received almost as much attention as their music.

It was also in 1983 that James was signed by Factory Records, Joy Division's label, and released the singles "What's the World" and "Hymn from a Village," and the *Jim One* EP. Fellow Manchester popsters The Smiths covered "What's the World"; Smiths vocalist Morrissey was one of James's biggest and earliest fans.

Switched Labels, Personnel

By 1985 the band had moved to Sire Records, which released *James Two* that year. Their disdain for the publicity machinery of the music business created a sense of mystery about them, but it also fed a burgeoning rumor mill. Because Booth practiced abstinence and told journalists he chanted regularly, the U.K. press misidentified the group as Buddhists, and many of their casual, tongue-in-cheek comments were either taken too literally or misconstrued by gullible or sensationalistic music writers. As a result, as Booth related in *Melody Maker,* "We got more serious in interviews [because] we realized it was too risky being flippant." But the larger problem for the group lay in expanding their listenership.

James approached producer Eno when they were preparing to record their debut album, *Stutter.* They'd been impressed by the producer's work with bands like Talking Heads; unfortunately Eno was booked up and couldn't take the project. They ended up instead with guitarist-writer Lenny Kaye, whom they identified as their only other choice. Released in 1986, the album still couldn't take James out of relative cult status. The same was true of its highly praised follow-up, 1988's *Strip Mine.*

Disappointed at their relative lack of career movement, James left Sire in 1988. Whelan departed, and in addition to adding his replacement, David Baynton-Power, the remaining members recruited keyboardist Mark Hunter, violinist Saul Davies, and trumpeter Andy Diagram. "We've found some new musicians that we all agree on at last," Booth explained in *Melody Maker,* "with the right attitude for James. We've got more versatility now, more power. Before, our songs were a bit skeletal." With a fuller sound, the group soon became, in the words of *Musician* writer Zollo, "among the most charismatic live acts in the country. In concert their power derives from an intricate yet rock-solid rhythmic foundation, over which Davies weaves colorful violin lines while Hunter fills in the gaps with keyboards, accordion and melodica. It's also an ideally plush setting for the plaintive, emotional voicings of singer Booth."

After releasing an independent label live album, *One Man Clapping,* James signed with Phonogram. It was with their 1989 album *Gold Mother* that the group saw some real sales, thanks to the hits "Come Home" and "Sit Down"; the latter song reached the number two position on the U.K. charts. Next came 1990's *James;* like its successors it was released in the United States by Mercury.

Increased Popularity

1992 saw the release of *Seven,* another step forward in the band's quest for international popularity. A million-seller, it was the last recording with Diagram, who left the group—"amicably," in the words of a record company press release—that same year. James was poised to break through to mainstream American listeners, particularly as the 1990s began to look like a decade of commercial viability for alternative bands. Joining rock legend Neil Young on an all-acoustic tour, James refined its sound; "we didn't play electric again for three months" after the tour, Booth told a *Billboard* interviewer. "Our ears were sort of tuned to that level of subtlety."

The group then contacted Eno again. "I sent him a demo tape of the stuff we were working on, with a letter saying, 'Come on and play with us'—you know: 'We'll have some fun, we're ready for you now,'" Booth recalled in *Rolling Stone.* "And he rang me up about 10 o'clock one morning, and we had this discussion about cyberpunk and fine wines and culture; and then he said he'd really like to make the album."

The group's admiration for Eno's production had only deepened. "The reason we like Eno is that he doesn't seem to stamp his identity on things," Glennie reasoned in an interview with Glenn Gregory of the *L.A. Village View.* "In the past, on the things he worked with, he has pulled the best out of people and produced great albums, but they're not 'Eno's style.' I think it's the same with this [album]. He makes you work and play to your strengths." Working with Eno for six weeks, the members of James wrote, recorded, and mixed 40 songs. The result was not only their 1993 album *Laid,* but a collection of what Booth described in *Billboard* as "mainly improvised stuff." Eno had listened to the band's jams, Booth averred, and declared, "People would like to hear this." The group, however, decided to wait until *Laid* was sufficiently marketed; Mercury aggressively promoted it and helped push the group to the next commercial level.

The album itself includes a number of soulful, introspective songs, but Eno picked the lighthearted song "Laid" for special attention despite the band's relative disdain for it. "We've been brought up on the kind of maxim that pain is deep you know," Booth admitted to Richard Cromelin of the *Los Angeles Times.* "It's a Western false concept. Very English, very European, I think—suffering for your art. And when something comes as easily and as simply as 'Laid,' you kind of don't take it as seriously as some of the ones that you have to bleed for."

> *"The idea is to move people really, and to move them in different ways. To upset, to agitate, to uplift, to give people happy endings now and again."*
> —Tim Booth

With an infectious melody, bouncy rhythm, and relatively comical lyrics about sexuality, the song began to show up on radio playlists; soon MTV put the video in its "buzz bin," and James was suddenly a player on the commercial rock scene. Critics raved about *Laid:* a *Musician* reviewer called it "what must be one of the best albums of the year. In fact, it sounds like music we'll still be listening to in 10 or 20 years. *Laid* is gentle without being wimpy, smart without being snotty and moody without being morbid." Gregory of the *L.A. Village View* labeled it "probably the band's most mature and creative album to date."

After more than ten years on the music scene, James had truly arrived. After the release of *Laid* the group appeared on Peter Gabriel's international WOMAD tour and enjoyed increased attention from U.S. concert audiences as well, playing "Laid"—with some suggestive lyrics altered—on TV's *Late Show with David Letterman.* Despite the increased visibility, however, James retained its original sense of mission. "The idea is to move people really, and to move them in different ways," Booth remarked to Cromelin of the *Los Angeles*

Times. "To upset, to agitate, to uplift, to give people happy endings now and again, but for the whole trip to be a happy ending." Ultimately, he went on, music is "magic, and we try to keep connecting with that spirit of music rather than get sidetracked into any other cul-de-sac about power or money or fame."

Selected discography

"Hymn From a Village," Factory, 1983.
Jim One (includes "What's the World"), Factory, 1983.
James Two, Factory, 1985.
Stutter, Sire, 1986
Strip Mine, Sire, 1988.
One Man Clapping, Rough Trade, 1988.

On Phonogram and/or Mercury

Gold Mother (includes "Come Home" and "Sit Down"), 1989.
James, 1990.
Seven, 1992.
Laid, 1993.

With others

Heaven and Hell (appear on "Sunday Morning"), Imaginary, 1990.

Sources

Billboard, October 30, 1993; February 19, 1994.
L.A. Village View, October 29, 1993.
Los Angeles Times, March 19, 1994.
Melody Maker, May 5, 1990; December 8, 1990; November 9, 1991.
Musician, February 1993; November 1993.
Rolling Stone, April 21, 1994.

Additional information for this profile was provided by Mercury Records publicity materials, 1993.

—*Simon Glickman*

Billy Joel

Singer, songwriter, pianist

Photograph by Patrick De Marchelier, © 1994 Sony Music, courtesy of Columbia Records

"My music is a synthesis of all the music that I like," said Billy Joel on the occasion of the release of his 15th album, *River of Dreams,* in 1993. "I mix all kinds of things: classical, Broadway, rock 'n roll, blues, jazz, whatever's out there ... I live in a stylistic no man's land. I've always believed that the beauty of American music was its ability to transcend and cross lines." Indeed, with a career spanning more than two decades, Joel has proven his musical range to his loyal audience with a diverse collection of pop and rock hits that have become American standards. Perhaps best known for his soulful ballads, the multiplatinum-selling, Grammy-winning singer/songwriter rose to mega-stardom during the 1970s and 1980s, and continued his successes into the 1990s. His albums have been among those decade's biggest sellers: singles like "Piano Man," "Just the Way You Are," "It's Still Rock and Roll to Me," "An Innocent Man," and "We Didn't Start the Fire" have garnered much commercial and critical acclaim.

Joel's place in American pop history was assured with the 1993 release of *River of Dreams.* "If Bruce Springsteen is the Jersey shore," wrote Richard Corliss in a review of the disc for *Time,* "Billy is Long Island, where the working class that fled Brooklyn stares stilettos at the moneyed folk who summer in the Hamptons." Although Corliss described Joel as "the last, finest heir to the songwriter tradition of soulful '60s pop," the singer's ability to adapt to changing musical tastes while simultaneously maintaining his individuality has contributed to his longevity in the fickle music industry.

Musical Training Began Early

William Martin Joel was born in 1949 and grew up in a comfortable Long Island suburb during the years following World War II. His German-born father, Howard Joel, who was imprisoned by the Nazis at Dachau during the war, moved to America after his release, to begin a new life in New York. That new life included adopting a new faith for his son—although Joel Sr. was Jewish, young Billy was raised in a predominately Catholic neighborhood and frequently attended mass and confession. One of Joel's future hits, "Only the Good Die Young," would feature lyrics about a Catholic girl's reluctance to engage in premarital sex.

Joel's father secured work as an engineer with General Electric while his mother, Rosalind, set to work raising Billy and his sister Judy. Both of Joel's parents provided early musical influences: his father was a classically trained, self-disciplined pianist, and his mother had once sung in the chorus for Gilbert and Sullivan. Billy began piano lessons at age four and continued until he

For the Record . . .

Born William Martin Joel, May 9, 1949, in Hicksville, Long Island, NY; son of Howard (an engineer and classically trained pianist) and Rosalind (a homemaker; maiden name, Hyman) Joel; married Elizabeth Weber (his business manager), 1973 (divorced, 1982); married Christie Brinkley (a model), 1985 (separated, 1994); children: (second marriage) Alexa Ray.

Performed at Hicksville High School with teenage group the Echos (later known as the Lost Souls) c. 1965; worked as housepainter and oyster harvester, late 1960s-early 1970s; joined rock group the Hassles, Long Island, NY, and recorded two albums for United Artists, 1967-68; formed Attila (organ and drum duo) with Jonathan Small, 1970; under alias Bill Martin, played piano in the Executive Lounge, Los Angeles, 1971; signed with Family Productions, 1971; signed with Columbia, 1972.

Selected awards: Best new male vocalist award, *Cash Box,* 1974, for *Piano Man;* record of the year, *Stereo Review,* 1977, for *The Stranger*; Grammy awards for best album and best song, both 1978, for *The Stranger* and "Just the Way You Are"; ASCAP awards for song of the year and artist of the year, both 1978, for "Just the Way You Are," and "She's Always a Woman"; Grand Prix award (Japan), and best male vocalist of the year designation, Radio Pop Disc Awards (Japan), both 1978; Number One pop album, pop album artist, male pop album artist, and male pop artist awards, *Billboard* magazine, all 1979, all for *52nd Street*; Grammy Legend Award, 1990; Humanitarian Award, Cathedral of St. John the Divine, 1990; honorary doctor of humane letters, Fairfield University, 1991; honorary doctor of music, Berklee College of Music, 1993.

Addresses: *Home*—Long Island, NY. *Office*—Columbia Records/Division of Sony Music, 2100 Colorado Ave., Santa Monica, CA 90404.

was 14, though he disliked learning classical music, theory, and the endless hours of practice.

In 1957, Joel's parents divorced; his father returned to Europe, and his mother supported the family by becoming a secretary and bookkeeper. Joel's maternal grandfather, Philip Hyman, became the primary father figure in Joel's life. As a teenager, Joel began to explore his masculinity by skipping school, running with a less-than-tough street gang, and engaging in Bantamweight boxing. Though he scored well on tests, his teachers refused to graduate him from high school due to his many absences. It was also during these years that Joel discovered the power of music.

Soul and Pop Stars Influenced Style

In 1962, Joel saw a live performance for the first time when he went with friends to hear James Brown at Harlem's Apollo Theater. Other early influences included Otis Redding, Sam and Dave, Elvis Presley, and the Beatles. Joel was deeply affected by the British invasion, so much so that he modeled his own budding style after the Beatles' Paul McCartney. Ironically, Joel also admired the hard-rock, psychedelic sound of Jimi Hendrix.

In 1964, Joel joined his first band, the Echos (later known as the Lost Souls), on the organ and vocals and began composing simplistic songs. His fate as a musician was sealed after the band's first paid gig at a Hicksville church. A short-term recording contract with Mercury Records was offered later, but nothing came of the demo versions of two of Joel's songs recorded by the band.

In 1967, Joel and drummer Jonathan Small left the Lost Souls to join the Hassles, another Long Island pop band with more exposure. At age 18, Joel's career was officially launched, though just barely. The group recorded two albums for United Artists that elicited a lukewarm reception from fans, 1967's *The Hassles* and *Hour of the Wolf* released in 1969. Yearning for something better than the "bubble-gum" rock produced by the group, Joel and Small left in 1969 to form the duo Attila. They released one "incredibly loud" self-titled album on the Epic label in 1970 before disbanding.

Discouraged both by the failure of his first attempts as a professional musician and the end of a serious romantic relationship, Joel slid into a depression that included a half-hearted attempt at suicide. A very brief self-imposed stay at a psychiatric hospital convinced him that his problems were minor. As he told Debbie Geller and Tom Hibbert in their 1985 biography, *Billy Joel, An Illustrated Biography,* "I got out and the door closed behind me and I walked down the street and said, 'Oh, I'll never get that low again.' It was one of the best things I ever did, because I've never gotten to feel sorry for myself, no matter what's happened...." Joel's 1985 song, "You're Only Human," would focus on the problem of teen suicide.

Having decided that his future lay in writing songs for others, Joel began composing material for a demo album in 1971. He was soon signed to producer Artie Ripp's Family Productions, a Los Angeles label, and Joel moved to California to record his first solo album. *Cold Spring Harbor,* originally intended simply as a vehicle to showcase his songs, was released in 1972. The album was technically inferior due to problems during the mastering stage of production; Joel's voice was speeded up and sounded, in his words, "like a chipmunk." His association with Ripp would prove to be financially disastrous for the singer, who unfortunately signed away all publishing rights, copyrights, and royalties to his producer/manager for a period of 15 years. This deal reportedly cost millions to break later in Joel's career.

After a six-month tour to promote the ill-fated album, Joel married Elizabeth Weber, ex-wife of fellow Attila member Small. Weber would eventually manage her husband's career and become the model for many of his songs about women.

It was "Captain Jack," one of the songs Joel had performed live while on tour to promote *Cold Spring Harbor,* that indirectly gave him the break he needed. After hearing the song during Joel's set at the Mary Sol Rock Festival near San Juan, Puerto Rico, and later on East Coast FM radio stations, Columbia Records executive Clive Davis tracked Joel down, helped extricate him from his contract with Ripp, and signed him to the Columbia label.

"Piano Man" Hit Top 40

Joel's first Top 40 hit single, "Piano Man," the title track from his second album released in 1973, was based on his experiences in Wilshire Boulevard's Executive Lounge. The album also contained, appropriately, "Captain Jack," Joel's song about a rich young heroin addict. Because of its mellow, narrative style, "Piano Man" was immediately compared to Harry Chapin's "Cat's In the Cradle" and Don McLean's "American Pie." By the end of the year, Joel had been named *Cash Box's* best new male vocalist, and the album had been named record of the year by *Stereo Review. Piano Man* was eventually certified platinum. Indeed, the single would become so synonymous with the singer that Joel would select it as the final song at all of his concerts for the next 20 years.

In an interview for *Entertainment Weekly's* Linda Sanders, Joel reflected on his music. "I was surprised the title song ["Piano Man"] was a hit. In a way, that's the story of any hit record I've had—they're all bizarre, strange, novelty numbers, and not particularly definitive of my work.... My problem is that people tend to define me in terms of my hits and may not know the substantive elements of my composition."

Joel began recording *Streetlife Serenade,* his follow-up to *Piano Man,* in the summer of 1974. With the exception of the single, "The Entertainer," the album was not a success. "Interesting musical ideas, but nothing to say lyrically," was how Joel explained the album's weaknesses in *Entertainment Weekly.* "I was trying to be Debussy in the title track—it didn't work." After three years on the West Coast and the letdown following dismal sales of his third album, Joel and his wife returned to their roots in New York.

With his creative juices flowing once again, Joel began working on what would be his next album, 1976's *Turnstiles.* This was the first album Joel produced himself using musicians of his choosing, rather than those hired by Columbia executives. Joel recruited drummer Liberty DeVitto, bass player Doug Stegmeyer, and tenor saxophonist Richie Cannata, three men who would remain with Joel's backing band for years. Although *Turnstiles,* like its predecessor, was not a spectacular seller, the album contained good material, including "New York State of Mind," a standard that would later be covered by Barbra Streisand.

The Stranger Became a Bestseller

Although Joel began to feel pressure from Columbia Records to record more than one album a year and to replicate his early success with *Piano Man,* he refused to produce formulaic music. Fortunately, he struck much-needed gold with his next album, *The Stranger,* released in 1977. Produced by Phil Ramone, the album was recorded during five weeks of enthusiastic studio sessions full of improvisations by Joel and his band.

In addition to the immense appeal of the title track, *The Stranger* included four U.S. hit singles: "Just the Way You Are," "She's Always a Woman," "Movin' Out (Anthony's Song)," and "Only the Good Die Young." Joel's international reputation was now firmly established, and his national renown was reinforced as *The Stranger* won Grammy Awards for record of the year and song of the year. The album went on to become Columbia/CBS's biggest seller prior to the release of Michael Jackson's *Thriller,* even surpassing Simon & Garfunkel's *Bridge Over Troubled Water.*

With the public—if not the critics—lapping up his work, Joel consolidated his reputation with the 1978 release of *52nd Street.* The music was very well received, and the first single, "My Life," zoomed to Number Three on the *Billboard* charts. The album became Joel's first to reach Number One in the charts and went on to sell millions of copies. Three years later, *Glass Houses,* Joel's second platinum album, heralded a change in the singer's image as a pop stylist. With New Wave replacing disco as the musical fad *du jour,* Joel jumped on the bandwagon and infused the album with more hard-hitting rock songs. His goal, apparently, was to throw figurative stones at his image. The singles "You May Be Right," and "It's Still Rock and Roll to Me" did well with commercial audiences but left the critics cold.

Reviews were relentless, and Joel's attempt to be taken seriously as a modern rock performer failed. Although he supposedly scorned the critics, he had a simultaneous need for their approval and was hurt by their dismissal of *Glass Houses*. "I think there was a perception that I was trying to pose as a New Wave guy, and that wasn't in any way my intention," he told *Entertainment Weekly*. "My intention was to write bigger stuff we could play in arenas."

In 1981, Columbia released the platinum-certified *Songs in the Attic,* a collection of new live recordings of material written in Joel's early days. The album included songs from *Cold Spring Harbor* that had never been properly recorded.

Tragedies Precipitated Soul-Searching

Joel had already begun studio work on his next album when he was involved in a motorcycle accident in the spring of 1982. His left wrist was broken and his hand badly damaged. Following surgery, production of the album was temporarily shut down while Joel recovered. An additional obstacle for the singer was the breakdown of his marriage to Weber, an event partially blamed on the stress created by Weber's management of her husband's career. By the end of 1982, the couple would divorce. When she left, Joel's wife took half of the singer's assets with her.

Even without such personal tragedies, creating the music for the album that would follow *Glass Houses* proved to be difficult, as Joel told Geller and Hibbert in their biography: "You're always in the desert looking for the oasis and all that's out there with you is the piano—this big black beast with 88 teeth ... 50,000 packs of cigarettes later, you start getting it."

Joel's soul-searching paid off with the release of *The Nylon Curtain* in 1982, Joel's first combined commercial and artistic success. It contained several sobering "message" songs about society including "Allentown," the rhythmical tune about the plight of unemployed Pennsylvania steel workers, and "Goodnight Saigon," a slow, mournful look at Vietnam and its veterans. Joel called *The Nylon Curtain* "the album of which I'm most proud." As he told *Entertainment Weekly,* the album was not as fun to make as *Glass Houses* because it was so difficult. "It was an ambitious undertaking—I wanted to create a masterpiece. I remember listening to 'Allentown' and thinking, 'This is good,' and that I had somehow created the feelings I had when I listened to Beatles albums."

Innocent Man Reflected Romantic Life

With "Allentown," Joel made his first transition from vinyl to video to promote his music and gained an even larger following. When his next album, *An Innocent Man,* was released in 1983, the MTV video era was in full swing and the upbeat, platinum-certified *An Innocent Man* featured several studies in romance that lent themselves to an MTV format. Joel's girlfriend, supermodel Christie Brinkley, appeared in the hit video "Uptown Girl," the perfect counterpart to Joel's small-time tough guy. The couple was married in 1985, and later had a daughter, Alexa Ray.

Joel scored big with the title song from his new album. But *An Innocent Man* was significant as more that a collection of catchy tunes. The album was Joel's tribute to and re-creation of some of the sounds of America's favorite pop stylists, including Little Anthony and the Imperials and Frankie Valli and the Four Seasons. It was also the last album on which Joel would use his tenor falsetto. "I knew it was the last time I was going to be able to hit certain notes," he told *Entertainment Weekly*. "I was waving goodbye to the boy voice."

In early 1984, Joel's first concert video, *Billy Joel: Live From Long Island,* was released. The inevitable *Greatest Hits Volume I and II* followed in 1985, a move by Columbia that Joel viewed as a time-stalling technique. *The Bridge,* his first studio album in three years, appeared in 1986 but failed to garner the huge reception from critics and fans Joel had hoped for. "Not a happy album," he told *Entertainment Weekly*. "I wasn't simpatico with the musicians, some of whom I'd been working with a long time. I don't think the material was good; I was pressured by management to put it out too fast. By the end, I sort of gave up caring, which for me was unusual."

In 1987, Joel performed to great acclaim in Leningrad and Moscow in what is now the former Soviet Union. His Leningrad concert was broadcast via some 300 radio outlets. Both concerts were recorded and released later that year as *Kohuept,* the Russian translation of "In Concert."

"We Didn't Start the Fire" Sparked Sales

Two years later, Joel worked with female musicians for the first time on 1989's *Storm Front,* his triple-platinum comeback album with a nautical bent. A seasoned sailor, Joel spends much of his free time aboard a 36-foot fishing boat near his home in Easthampton, New York. *Storm Front*'s cultural critique, "We Didn't Start the Fire," quickly became a Number One *Billboard* hit single along with the album itself. Joel received five Grammy nominations for the album and completed a 15-month world tour to promote it. He was seen by 4.3 million fans during 174 shows in 16 countries, including a performance in Berlin the day after German reunification. He also performed in the United States at Yankee Stadium's first rock concert.

One of the reasons for Joel's frequent touring stints has been to earn money lost over the years as a result of mismanagement of his career. Indeed, Joel has endured his share of legal problems dating back to his contract with Artie Ripp in 1971. In one case, Joel fired Frank Weber, his ex-brother-in-law and manager of nine years, and sued him for $90 million in 1989, citing fraud and misappropriation of funds. Although Joel was awarded $3 million, Weber filed for bankruptcy soon after the ruling. Weber countersued Joel for libel, but the case was dismissed.

To add to his legal woes, a $10 million lawsuit was brought against Joel in 1993 by an aspiring songwriter who claimed Joel stole his material and parlayed it into three hit songs. Joel's statement on the matter was simple: "This is another example of why struggling songwriters can't get anybody, including me, to listen to their songs."

River of Dreams Ran Smoothly

Four years after the *Storm Front* tour de force, Joel released *River of Dreams,* an album that again garnered critical praise. With the cover art for the album provided by Brinkley and a song ("Lullabye [Goodnight My Angel]") dedicated to their daughter, the album appeared to be a family affair. Fans were eager for a new release from Joel and the album hit the charts at Number One in its first week. It was certified multi-platinum by the spring of 1994. The genesis of *River of Dreams* began in 1992 while Joel was in Southhampton with producer Danny Kortchmar recording two Elvis Presley songs for the soundtrack of the movie *Honeymoon in Vegas.* During that time an early version of the album was written and recorded as "The Shelter Island Sessions." Joel later re-recorded the songs in Long Island and New York studios.

"I always thought it was written in stone that you had your era—and that was it," Joel told *People*'s Jim Jerome. "Rock is a cannibalizing business—it eats its own. I was hip for about a second in the '70s. But here we are. I'm 44. It's 20 years since 'Piano Man,' and I have a No. 1 album. That's not supposed to happen."

According to *Time*'s Richard Corliss, *River of Dreams* is "not just a cohesive concept album but also a bunch of damn fine songs with heart and hook." Including such diverse melodies as "No Man's Land," "The Great Wall of China," "Blonde Over Blue," "Lullabye (Goodnight, My Angel)," "Shades of Grey," and "It's All About Soul," the album may be Joel's most significant artistic achievement yet. It represents a move into a more philosophical form of songwriting and a return to his early classical music influences.

> *"I live in a stylistic no man's land. I've always believed that the beauty of American music was its ability to transcend and cross lines."*

As Corliss stated in his review, "To brassily assonant music, [Joel] rages at a social landscape scarred by greed, fame, mongering, obsessive love—all the strategies of self.... On Side 2, the man ponders continuity and eternity.... Joel's gem is the sleepytime title tune. Its consonant-poppin' lyric charts a land where pop merges with gospel, black embraces white, dread is absolved by belief—in God, in dreams, in the rolling sing-along cadence of a doo-wop bass line. 'We all end in the ocean / We all start in the streams / We're all carried along / By the river of dreams.'"

In the fall of 1993, Joel launched what he claimed would be his last marathon world tour to promote the new album. Then, the following spring, he and Brinkley announced their separation. Rumors that the split occurred because of Joel's constant absences while on tour surrounded the breakup.

When country artist Garth Brooks made Joel's "Shameless" a Number One hit on the country charts in 1991, it was just one of many illustrations of the musician's incredible versatility as a songwriter. After a career spanning 25 years in the recording business, Joel has expressed an interest in focusing that versatility on writing for Broadway, although he refuses to limit himself to one musical form.

In an interview with Jancee Dunn in *Rolling Stone,* Joel summarized his long career: "People think I'm this pop meister who just churns out these hit singles.... But I don't view myself as being frozen in cement. And the songs that are the singles do not necessarily represent the sum and substance of my work. People think that I'm 'Just the Way You Are,' and 'Uptown Girl.' OK, I did write those songs, but I wrote many, many more."

Selected discography

(With the Hassles) *The Hassles,* United Artists, 1967.
(With the Hassles) *Hour of the Wolf,* United Artists, 1969.
(With others) *Attila,* Epic, 1970.
Cold Spring Harbor (includes "She's Got a Way"), Family Productions, 1972.
Piano Man (includes "Captain Jack"), Columbia, 1973.
Streetlife Serenade, Columbia, 1974.
Turnstiles (includes "Angry Young Man" and "Say Goodbye to Hollywood"), Columbia, 1976.
The Stranger, Columbia, 1977.
52nd Street (includes "Big Shot," "Honesty," and "Until the Night"), Columbia, 1978.
Glass Houses, Columbia, 1980.
Songs in the Attic, Columbia, 1981.
Nylon Curtain, Columbia, 1982.
An Innocent Man (includes "The Longest Time," "Tell Her About It," "Keeping the Faith," and "Leave a Tender Moment Alone") Columbia, 1983.
Greatest Hits, Volume I and II, Columbia, 1985.
The Bridge (includes "This Is the Time," "A Matter of Trust," and "You're Only Human"), Columbia, 1986.
Kohuept (live concert), Columbia, 1987.
Storm Front (includes "We Didn't Start the Fire," "That's Not Her Style," "I Go to Extremes," "Shameless," and "The Downeaster 'Alexa'"), Columbia, 1989.
River of Dreams, Columbia, 1993.

Sources

Books

Geller, Debbie, and Tom Hibbert, *Billy Joel: An Illustrated Biography,* McGraw-Hill, 1985.
Hardy, Phil, and Dave Laing, *Encyclopedia of Rock,* Macmillan, 1988.
McKenzie, Michael, *Billy Joel*, Ballantine, 1985.
The Penguin Encyclopedia of Popular Music, edited by Donald Clark, Viking, 1989.
Stambler, Irwin, *The Encyclopedia of Rock and Soul,* revised edition, St. Martin's, 1989.

Periodicals

Amusement Business, November 29, 1993.
Billboard, October 7, 1989; December 23, 1989; November 6, 1993; November 13, 1993.
Entertainment Weekly, September 10, 1993.
High Fidelity, August 1987.
Life, September 1987.
Newsweek, January 29, 1990.
New York Times, October 14, 1992; October 4, 1993.
People, December 13, 1993.
Rolling Stone, November 6, 1986; December 23, 1993-January 6, 1994.
Stereo Review, February, 1990; December 1992.
Time, August 30, 1993.
Variety, July 8, 1987.
Washington Post, October 8, 1978.

Additional information for this profile was provided by Columbia Records publicity materials.

—*Mary Scott Dye*

L7

Rock band

"Welcome to the *Sports Illustrated* swimsuit issue rejects," said L7's singer/guitarist Donita Sparks, beginning a show at the Palace in New York in 1992. Part punk, part hard-core, part party band, L7 can be described as raucous, raunchy, and what Kim France of the *Utne Reader* called "triumphantly unladylike." Named for the 1950s term meaning "square" or "unhip," bandmembers Jennifer Finch, Dee Plakas, Suzi Gardner, and Donita Sparks refer to themselves as "humorous hags" and "bra-burning battle-axes," their concert attire consisting of flannel, ripped jeans, motorcycle boots, and shorts belted with duct tape. Bursting onto L.A.'s music scene in 1987, L7 caused ceilings to sweat in small clubs packed with cult followers, encouraged stage-diving, and later took all their thrashing on the road, catching the attention of famous indie rock label Sub-Pop and later Slash Records of Los Angeles.

Jonathan Gold of the *Los Angeles Times* described L7 as "potentially the first female band to rock as if its gender were irrelevant. No T & A, no love songs, no

Photograph by Catalina Leisenring, © 1994 Slash Records

> **For the Record . . .**
>
> Band members include **Jennifer Finch** (raised outside of Los Angeles, CA), bass; **Suzi Gardner** (raised in Sacremento, CA), guitar, vocals; **Dee Plakas** (raised in Chicago, IL), drums; and **Donita Sparks** (raised in Chicago), guitar, vocals. Former drummers include Roy Gurwitz.
>
> Group formed, 1986-87; recorded self-titled debut LP, 1987; Plakas joined as permanent drummer, 1988; toured underground clubs; released *Smell the Magic*, Sub-Pop, 1990; toured Europe with Nirvana; signed with Slash Records and released *Bricks Are Heavy*, 1992; founded "Rock for Choice," a series of benefit concerts to aid bombed abortion clinics; co-sponsored concert for relief for rape victims in Boznia-Herzegovina, Yugoslavia; appeared in the John Waters film *Serial Mom*, 1994.
>
> **Addresses:** *Record company*—Slash Records, 7381 Beverly Blvd., Los Angeles, CA 90036.

flirtation, no come-ons, no wronged woman anthems, no bustiers ... just rock." However, because the bandmembers are females who "rock," L7 is simultaneously exulted and pigeonholed by the media. When simply describing their music, L7 has been compared to great punk and alternative legends the Ramones, Motorhead, and the Buzzcocks, yet because they are an all-female band, they continually get lumped with sister-rockers Babes in Toyland, Hole, and sometimes even their fellow Los Angelites the Go-Go's.

L7, however, actively resists any kind of stereotyping, acting more like rock's bad boys with a self-consciously mocking female flair. For example, they once played a show at a heavy-metal bar—or as Sparks told singer Debbie Harry in *Ray Gun*, "sort of a hair farmer club"—where, as Sparks describes, they "all wore bald caps" and "looked like a band of Sinead O'Connors."

At the 1992 music festival in Reading, England, Sparks extracted and threw her used tampon into the audience as a souvenir for fans, a reversal of the tampon-flinging fad that occasionally happens at hard rock concerts when the band on stage is all male. L7 further betrays their own sexually aggressive attitude and stage antics with songs like "Fast and Frightening."

In true feminist form, L7 defies definition and labelling while still kicking out loud, fast rock that would intimidate the best of all-male bands. As Jennifer Finch told *Request,* "I was really influenced by the whole hard-core thing and the whole punk rock thing. I never thought twice like I can't do this 'cause I'm, you know, a gal."

From "Go-Go's on Draino" to Grunge Goddesses

When they were first looking for bandmembers, Suzi Gardner told *Spin,* "We didn't care what set of sex organs they had. We just wanted to f—ing rock." Guitarist and vocalist Gardner was raised outside of Sacramento, California, and moved to L.A. for the music scene. Bassist Finch was raised outside of L.A., while Donita Sparks and drummer Dee Plakas migrated from Chicago to L.A. for much the same reason as Gardner. "Donita and I met each other in 1985," Gardner told *Spin* in 1993. "We'd been floating around the same town, kind of following each other in jobs and bands, even with dudes, kind of, and we had a lot of people telling us that we had to meet."

According to *Spin,* each bandmember hails from a middle-class background that they rebelled against in variety ways. Finch "forgot" to attend high school for three years, Sparks worked at a White Castle and was a "jock cheerleader who smoked," and Plakas switched prices on drug-store items, a subtle shoplifter.

The members of L7 cite a variety of musical influences: the Ramones, AC/DC, Black Sabbath, the B-52's, the Cramps, Aretha Franklin, and Patsy Cline. Yet each member of L7 felt that she needed to create her "own scene." As Donita Sparks told the *Los Angeles Times,* "We didn't really have role models growing up. The Go-Go's were the only girl group playing their own instruments and they sang about boys." Gardner tells of going to a Quiet Riot show early in her career as a musician and coming away dismayed at the group's ineptitude. She told *Spin,* "I remember getting really drunk and really angry at how lame they were.... If these guys in Spandex could get away with being so lame, I could do it too."

Originally L7 had a male drummer who was later fired for his alcohol problems. "We've been through the ringer in the rhythm section," said Sparks, referring to an exhausting series of problem drummers that finally ended in 1988 with Plakas, who, regardless of her gender, was simply the best drummer they could find. L7 began carving out its own niche in L.A. clubs and were described in an early review as "the Go-Go's on Draino." In 1988 they released a disc called *L7* on the L.A.-based Epitaph label. The album was critically well received, but the distributor folded before the record had been out more than a month. It was at this point that L7 took their show on the road, playing at underground clubs around the country, hauling their own instruments, and sleeping on the floors of friends' homes. Bandmembers assert that those days of shoestring budgets have made them really appreciate everything that they have achieved today.

According to Robert Christgau of the *Village Voice,* "L7 breathed life into what can be inadequately pigeonholed as 'hard pop'; the brief, clear, fast, tough song expanding in ascending order of sweet impurity." L7's cross-country thrash tour of the late 1980s caught the eye of Sub-Pop's alternative guru, producer Jonathan Poneman. L7 played a show in Seattle and was almost immediately signed by the label most singularly responsible for the fashion of "Seattle-Rock" and the grunge sounds of Nirvana and Soundgarden.

Smell the Magic came out in 1990, and L7 took off for a European tour with fellow Sub-Pop heroes Nirvana. "The 'Shove' single was one of the most amazing things," said Poneman. "That singularly blew my top off. I compare L7 with Motorhead or the Ramones, a real primal rock machine." Because of their high-profile U.S. and European tours, L7 finally gained recognition in their home town. In 1992, Slash records (a division of Warner Bros. in Hollywood, California) produced L7's third album, *Bricks Are Heavy,* which sold an estimated 225,000 copies and marked L7's sudden appeal to a mainstream audience.

Against Media Stereotypes

Because *Smell the Magic* was released on the independent Sub-Pop, L7's move to a major label with *Bricks Are Heavy* was seen by some as going against the grain of "indie rock" and the band's former "do-it-yourself" attitude. According to *RIP* magazine, L7's reason for leaving the label and the indie rock scene was painfully simple: it failed them. Apparently L7 would call Epitaph and Sub-Pop and occasionally find the phones disconnected or shut down. The labels also had very poor distribution reputations. "The reason we moved (to Slash)," said Finch, "was that too many kids were coming up to us and saying, 'we can't find your record.'" Finch told *RIP* that the band was never paid for the Epitaph or Sub-Pop albums. "We want to support underground movements. We want to support people who are doing it for themselves. But this is our living and that's very important to us."

Besides casting them as traitors to indie rock, the media, according to L7, pays more attention to the band's gender than to the actual quality of their work. Ironically, because of their no-frills style of music, L7 is a rarity among female musical groups. "The problem with defining L7 as the ultimate in femme-punk," said Renee Christ of *Spin,* "is that femme-punk is not a genre." Groping for some definition that describes their position between "grunge rock" and "girlband," Sonic Youth's Thurston Moore came up with the term "foxcore" to describe the L7-inspired surge of underground female bands. Soon there were foxcore shows and foxcore magazine pictorials; L7 was asked to pose for a foxcore feature in *Spin.* They declined.

> *"I was really influenced by the whole hardcore thing and the whole punk rock thing. I never thought twice like I can't do this 'cause I'm, you know, a gal."*
> —Jennifer Finch

"We had to lay it on the line with our record company, no gender references," Donita Sparks told the *Los Angeles Times.* "It sounds clichéd, but we're not a Russ Meyer fantasy, we're not tough chicks, we're not man-haters and we're not boy-toys—we're just people." Musically, L7 describes themselves as a hard-rock band, in concert style similar to Nirvana: high-energy, slamming, dancing, stage-diving. In their opinion, it shouldn't matter that they are women. But very often L7 does get lumped in with what they term "other chick-bands."

L7 is a difficult group to define, and they actively defy definition, whether that be "foxcore," "girl group," or even "feminist." Although bandmembers describe themselves as feminists, they try to stay away from feminist rhetoric that may draw attention away from, as Sparks told the *Los Angeles Times,* "just doing what we do." Doing "what they do" comes closer in style and character to traditional male rock bands than female ones, and they often parody or adopt big attitudes and raunchy sexual references in songs like "Packin' a Rod" (a cover of the original Fiends tune) and lyrics such as "you and me till the wheels fall off."

During filming of the "Pretend We're Dead" video, a camera crane fell on Gardner, who suffered a fractured cheekbone; the band was involved in an 11-car, three-semi pileup outside of Philadelphia; and they've been asked never to fly United Airlines again because of their apparently unruly pre-flight behavior. This refusal to be "nice girls" reinforces the media tendency to label them "political," even though L7 claims that they are just doing what comes naturally.

Founded "Rock for Choice"

"L7 *are* women, a rare thing among rock musicians, and feminists, a rarer thing. Both categories make them special whether they like it or not," said Christgau of the *Village Voice*. For all L7's grumbling about not wanting to be labelled as feminist or political, they contradict themselves by being one of the most politically active bands on the alternative rock scene. The most obvious manifestation of this is their creation of "Rock for Choice," a series of benefit concerts to aid clinics attacked by anti-abortion activists.

Using their "do-it-yourself" attitude, the band started the organization that is designed to promote awareness-raising concerts and earn money for the Fund for the Feminist Majority, which operates a nationwide clinic defense system. Sparks told the *L.A. Reader* that the Rock for Choice shows were more awareness-raising than fundraising, to get the word out that "hey these bands support pro-choice." L7, in their typical satirical fashion, hosted one Rock for Choice show wearing evening gowns like beauty contestants, sashed with banners of the names of bombed clinics; instead of "Miss Hawaii," or "Miss Illinois," they wore titles saying "Miss Bakersfield Clinic."

Besides being aggressively pro-choice, L7's political beliefs filter into other areas. "In a lot of ways I'm really ashamed of how apathetic my generation's been," Sparks told *RIP*, "and really angry about how many of the gains we made in the 60's have been taken away from us." L7's song "Wargasm" exemplifies the band's disgruntlement with the Bush administration and the Persian Gulf War: "Tie a yellow ribbon round the amputee/ masturbate, watch it on T.V." This song took on a different meaning in 1993 when L7 performed it for a benefit concert to aid rape survivors of Bosnia-Herzegovina. During that performance, Sparks extended her guitar riffs as Finch screamed "Rape!" over and over again until it became an eerie mantra.

In the spring of 1994, L7 had its debut in the John Waters film *Serial Mom* as a femme-punk band called "Camel Lips." In the summer of that year, L7 released *Hungry for Stink* on Slash Records. Though *People* magazine found that "most of the songs aren't particularly memorable," *Entertainment Weekly* gave the album an "A+," stating, *"Hungry for Stink* is ... sophisticated, with a musical surprise on nearly every track."

Because of their consistent political action, L7 is aware of their influence on their fans; they provide for young women an alternative role model to those found in popular magazines, and the movie and record industries. Sparks was quoted as saying in the *Los Angeles Times*, "We get letters from young girls who say we're their inspiration for picking up an instrument, and that makes us really proud."

Selected discography

L7, Epitaph, 1988, reissued, 1990.
Smell the Magic, Sub-Pop, 1990.
Bricks Are Heavy, Slash, 1992.
Hungry for Stink, Slash, 1994.

Sources

Billboard, April 16, 1994.
Creem, April 1992.
Entertainment Weekly, July 15, 1994.
Interview, April 1992.
L.A. Reader, July 3, 1992.
Los Angeles Times, July 28, 1991.
People, July 18, 1994.
Ray Gun, December/January 1993-94.
Request, June 1992.
RIP, August 1993.
Spin, April 1992; July 1993; June 1994.
Utne Reader, September/October 1992.
Vanity Fair, July 1994.

—*Sarah Messer*

Chris LeDoux

Singer, songwriter

Photograph by Butch Adams, courtesy of Liberty Records

A real rodeo cowboy in a musical world saturated with artificial ones, Chris LeDoux has pursued an unusual country music career in at least two respects. Rare indeed are the musicians who succeed in carving out profitable careers independent of the star-making machinery centralized in cities like Los Angeles, New York, and Nashville. Scarce, too, are those who have kept the ancient American art of the cowboy song alive in the last quarter of the twentieth century. But LeDoux laid claim to both of these worthwhile accomplishments.

Identifying rodeo enthusiasts as an underserved musical market played a part in LeDoux's success, as did a noteworthy example of family cooperation and support. But for a long time, his songwriting talents played the most important role. LeDoux is a true musical counterpart to the cowboy poets who sometimes appear at western folk festivals, a chronicler in song of rodeo and range. For many years, he sold his musical creations at the same rodeos where he competed. By the early 1990s, however, he had broken through to a national country music audience.

LeDoux lived the rodeo life and sang about it for many years, but he was not born into it. He was born in Biloxi, Mississippi, in 1948, and his father was a pilot in the Air Force. As a child, he lived in many different places with his parents. When Chris was 14 years old, the family moved to Austin, Texas. There, his grandfather, who had fought in the United States Cavalry against the Mexican outlaw revolutionary Pancho Villa, introduced him to horseback riding and rodeo competition. A poet at heart, LeDoux began to work on ideas for cowboy songs while he was still in high school.

Earned Rodeo Championship

Soon LeDoux was proficient enough to compete on the professional rodeo circuit. His talents won him an unusual athletic scholarship—one for rodeo—to Casper College in Wyoming. It was there that he began to try out his music at parties; soon, he found himself enthusiastically received by rodeo crowds as well. LeDoux's skills in the rodeo ring mounted to a point where, in 1976, he was named world champion in bareback riding by the Professional Rodeo Cowboys Association. Bouncing back from a string of injuries, he trained nonstop for months at the ranch he bought in Wyoming. He lived there with his wife, Peggy, and their five children in a house he built himself out of logs and stone.

In the early 1970s, LeDoux's parents moved to Nashville. They learned the inner workings of the music business there, and in so doing put in place the real cornerstone of LeDoux's musical career. They realized

> **For the Record . . .**
>
> Born October 2, 1948, in Biloxi, MI; son of Al and Bonnie LeDoux; married Peggy, 1972; five children. *Education:* Attended Casper College, Casper, Wyoming, on rodeo scholarship.
>
> Recorded 22 albums of western music on family-owned label, American Cowboy Songs, 1972-90; signed with Liberty Records, 1991.
>
> **Awards:** Professional Rodeo Cowboys' Association bareback bronco world riding championship, 1976; Grammy Award, Academy of Country Music award, and TNN/*Music City News* award nominations, with Garth Brooks, for best vocal duet or collaboration, 1993; gold record for *Whatcha Gonna Do With a Cowboy,* 1993.
>
> **Addresses:** *Record company*—Liberty Records, 3322 West End, 11th Floor, Nashville, TN 37203. *Management*—T.K.O. Artist Management, 4219 Hillsboro Rd., Suite 318, Nashville, TN 37215. *Publicist*—Aristomedia, P.O. Box 22765, Nashville, TN 37215.

his exposure could be maximized through a well-planned series of recordings. So the family formed an independent record label, American Cowboy Songs, and Chris LeDoux's first album was released in 1972. He had just married his wife Peggy, and he was grateful for the extra income: "I didn't mind starvin', but I didn't want my wife to starve with me," LeDoux told *Pollstar.*

American Cowboy Songs was a true family affair, with LeDoux's brother Mike doing the marketing and promotion for the label, his mother Bonnie handling orders, and father Al producing the recordings that Ledoux made during his yearly visits to Nashville. LeDoux sold his records and tapes at rodeo events out of a booth or out of his gear bag. They were also distributed through western wear outlets, and remarkably for a small independent enterprise, at several large retail music chains based in the western United States.

Recorded 22 Albums in 1970s and 1980s

The dimensions of LeDoux's success within his specialized market were nothing less than staggering. Sales for the company's first year in business totaled only $6,000, but they grew steadily. By the end of the 1980s, the catalog of LeDoux's LP recordings had grown to 22 items. In a 1991 interview with *Billboard*, Al LeDoux estimated their total sales at over $4,000,000.

LeDoux wrote much of the music on his 22 albums, and the consistent freshness of his songwriting went a long way toward insuring his success. His style was simple, even naive, but his descriptions of the rodeo could be startlingly vivid ("With his feet on my belly, standing in place/That dirty old bull blew snot in my face," he intoned grimly on 1977's "Bull Rider"). Al LeDoux contributed production values that were in no way amateurish. LeDoux's recordings stood up well when compared to mainstream Nashville productions of their time.

LeDoux's sales totals were not going unnoticed in Nashville. In the fall of 1990, Capitol Records Nashville vice president Joe Mansfield was alerted by western retailers to LeDoux's sales potential. Country megastar-to-be Garth Brooks, a fan of LeDoux's music since his own youth in rural Oklahoma, also helped generate interest in the singer by including a reference to "a worn-out tape of Chris LeDoux" in his 1989 hit, "Much Too Young (To Feel This Damn Old)." In early 1991, LeDoux signed a contract with Capitol Records; his recordings appeared under the company's Liberty label.

Rock Elements Added to Cowboy Style

LeDoux's Liberty recordings, most of them supervised by Capitol president and veteran Nashville producer Jimmy Bowen, for the most part have tried to play to the singer's strengths. He generally stuck to cowboy themes and continued his contributions as a songwriter. "Workin' Man's Dollar," from the first Capitol LP, *Western Underground*, was a LeDoux-penned personification of that always-scarce piece of currency, and the song brought LeDoux some radio airplay. But the second major-label album, 1992's *Whatcha Gonna Do With a Cowboy*, featured some new directions and became LeDoux's commercial breakthrough work.

On the album's title track, LeDoux paired up with his admirer Garth Brooks in a good-natured, western-swing tune with the theme of an upper-class woman's attraction to a cowboy. Brooks' presence propelled the album to a strong start; it debuted at number 13 on *Billboard*'s country albums chart and eventually climbed into the Top Ten.

The album's second single, "Cadillac Ranch," became LeDoux's most successful single release. It borrowed from Brooks in a different way: to LeDoux's plain, untrained vocals was added a backdrop of heavy rock guitar. The song's lyrics cleverly inverted the cowboy theme, describing the transformation of the barn of a bankrupt ranch into a successful country nightclub. Several other selections on the album emulated Brooks' appropriation of 1970s rock styles, with "Hooked on an Eight Second Ride" approaching an arena-rock anthem in its intensity. But, as the song's title indicates, LeDoux's cowboy identity was never submerged. After all, as LeDoux pointed out in a *Pollstar* interview, "Ridin' bulls is rock 'n' roll."

Whatcha Gonna Do With A Cowboy was certified gold (for sales of 500,000 copies) in February of 1993. LeDoux's third album for Liberty, 1993's *Under This Old Hat*, followed the pattern set by its predecessor, combining cowboy themes with Texas swing and rock influences. It included a dance remix of "Cadillac Ranch," strewn with tape loops, that probably represented LeDoux's point of farthest departure from the simple western styles of his early career, but that brought him new fans from the world of so-called "young country."

A greatest-hits package was released in the spring of 1994, and in the summer of that year, LeDoux went to work on his twenty-seventh album—an impressive record of accomplishment for a man who, when he first got married, is said to have listed his assets as "a hundred and fifteen dollars and a good horse in Amarillo" in a conversation with his wife.

Selected discography

Songs of Rodeo Life, American Cowboy Songs, 1971, reissued, Liberty, 1991.
Chris LeDoux Sings His Rodeo Songs, American Cowboy Songs, 1972, reissued, Liberty, 1991.
Rodeo Songs—Old and New, American Cowboy Songs, 1973, reissued, Liberty, 1991.
Songs of Rodeo and Country, American Cowboy Songs, 1974, reissued, Liberty, 1991.
Songs of Rodeo and Living Free, American Cowboy Songs, 1974, reissued, Liberty, 1991.
Life as a Rodeo Man, American Cowboy Songs, 1975, reissued, Liberty, 1991.
Songbook of the American West, American Cowboy Songs, 1976, reissued, Liberty, 1991.
Sing Me a Song, Mr. Rodeo Man, American Cowboy Songs, 1977, reissued, Liberty, 1991.
Songs of Rodeo Life, American Cowboy Songs, 1977 (re-recording of the 1971 album), reissued, Liberty, 1991.
Western Country (Cowboys Ain't Easy to Love), American Cowboy Songs, 1978, reissued, Liberty, 1991.
Paint Me Back Home in Wyoming, American Cowboy Songs, 1979, reissued, Liberty, 1991.
Rodeo's Singing Bronc Rider, American Cowboy Songs, 1979, reissued, Liberty, 1991.
Western Tunesmith, American Cowboy Songs, 1980, reissued, Liberty, 1991.
Sounds of the Western Country, American Cowboy Songs, 1980, reissued, Liberty, 1991.
Old Cowboy Heroes, American Cowboy Songs, 1980, reissued, Liberty 1991.
He Rides the Wild Horses, American Cowboy Songs, 1981, reissued Liberty, 1991.
Used to Want to Be a Cowboy, American Cowboy Songs, 1982, reissued, Liberty, 1991.
Thirty Dollar Cowboy, American Cowboy Songs, 1983, reissued, Liberty, 1991.
Old Cowboy Classics, American Cowboy Songs, 1983, reissued, Liberty, 1991.
Melodies and Memories, American Cowboy Songs, 1984, reissued, Liberty, 1991.
Wild and Wooly, American Cowboy Songs, 1986, reissued, Liberty, 1991.
Powder River, American Cowboy Songs, 1990, reissued, Liberty, 1991.
Western Underground, Liberty, 1991.
Whatcha Gonna Do With a Cowboy, Liberty, 1992.
Under This Old Hat, Liberty, 1993.
Best of Chris LeDoux, Liberty, 1994.

Sources

Books

Brown, David G., *Gold Buckle Dreams: The Rodeo Life of Chris LeDoux,* Wolverine Gallery, 1989.
Larkin, Colin, editor, *Guinness Encyclopedia of Popular Music,* Guinness/New England Publishing, 1992.

Periodicals

American Cowboy, premiere issue, 1994.
Billboard, January 20, 1979; September 7, 1991; August 15, 1992; October 17, 1992.
Country Fever, December 1993.
Country Music, January/February 1993.
Pollstar, April 18, 1994.

Additional information for this profile was obtained from Liberty Records and Aristomedia Publicity and Media Services press material.

—*James M. Manheim*

The Lemonheads

Rock band

Boston-bred alternative popsters the Lemonheads are a band, despite the fact that the lion's share of the media attention awarded them has focused on charismatic singer/songwriter Evan Dando. The group's sound originated in the rough-hewn underground rock scene of the mid-1980s, but it moved toward a more accessible, folk- and country-tinged approach as Dando's compositional abilities matured. Numerous personnel changes ensued, but by the early 1990s the Lemonheads solidified as a trio; even so, they made use of many guest artists.

After attracting recognition for some eclectic cover versions, the band became a big name in alternative rock. Their leader, meanwhile, dealt with the vicissitudes of life as an "alternahunk." *Los Angeles Times* reviewer Richard Cromelin encapsulated the appeal of Dando's songs: "He makes his points with an inviting, tuneful buoyancy rather than withering blasts, offering economical sketches of life that in their best moments resonate with disarming mystery and evocative mood."

Dando's family—his parents were itinerant surfers—moved to Boston when he was nine. His parents split during Evan's adolescence, and the experience left him bitter. Music was always what soothed him; he ranks Motown soul classics like "Heat Wave" by Martha & the Vandellas among his all-time favorites. Dando wrote a lot during high school and described himself as "nerdy" during that time in a *Request* interview. He struck many of his schoolmates, however, as angry and distant. "He was a snappy, angry punk," recalled Jesse Peretz—the first Lemonheads bassist—to *Spin*. "He was really sharp to tell you exactly what was on his mind even if it was kind of cruel, but he always seemed to pinpoint exact truths."

Dando, Peretz, and drummer Ben Deily began playing scrappy punk-pop together under the name the Whelps while still in school. Their influences included Minneapolis punk-pop innovators the Replacements—whose frontman/songwriter Paul Westerberg quietly became one of the most respected tunesmiths in the business—and such underground heroes as Los Angeles punk outfits Black Flag and the Angry Samoans.

Sounded Like Replacements

Indeed, Dando informed *Request* writer Bill Holdship, "The Samoans started our career, because we loved them so much that when they came to Boston in '85, we baked them a cake with icing that had the blonde girl with the axe in the top of her head and blood coming down [a horror-movie image that the Samoans used on an album cover], so the next time they came through,

> **For the Record...**
>
> Members include **Nic Dalton** (joined 1992), bass; **Evan Dando** (born in 1967 in Essex, MA; son of a lawyer and former model), vocals, guitar; **Ben Deily** (left band c. 1989), drums; **Juliana Hatfield** (played on 1992 album, guest thereafter), bass, vocals; **Jesse Peretz** (left c. 1991), bass; **David Ryan** (joined c. 1990), drums.
>
> Group formed as the Whelps in Boston, MA, 1986—; released debut single "Laughing All the Way to the Cleaners" on Taang! Records, 1986; signed with Atlantic and released *Lovey*, 1990; band's rendition of "Mrs. Robinson" appeared on 25th Anniversary videocassette of film *The Graduate*, 1992; Dando contributed to 1993 *Sweet Relief* benefit album and appeared in film *Reality Bites*.
>
> **Addresses:** *Record company*—Atlantic Records, 75 Rockefeller Plaza, New York, NY 10019; 9229 Sunset Blvd., Los Angeles, CA 90069.

we got to open for them." The group gave an early tape to Curtis Casella, of the independent label Taang! Records. "It sounded so familiar at first," Casella related to *Spin's* Mark Blackwell. "Exactly like the Replacements." It wasn't that Dando and friends hadn't found their sound yet, they had just neglected to erase the Replacements songs from one side of their tape. When Casella heard the original tunes, he was suitably impressed with their "intense energy." Taang! subsequently released the single "Laughing All the Way to the Cleaners" in 1986 with the trio re-christened the Lemonheads.

The band's first album, *Hate Your Friends*, appeared in 1987. The group was soon part of the vital Boston alternative-rock scene that also featured such bands as the Pixies. 1988's *Creator* enhanced their underground following. Soon after the release of their next record, *Lick*—which contained an attention-getting cover version of Suzanne Vega's folk-pop hit "Luka" at Casella's insistence and against the band's wishes—the group hit rough seas.

Deily's brother Jonno had become part of the lineup, and the two apparently fought with Dando over control of the band's direction. Dando quit briefly to play bass in the Blake Babies alongside his pal Juliana Hatfield, but returned to the group when *Lick* and "Luka" generated a buzz on MTV and on the college charts. Faced with the prospect of a European tour, Deily balked. David Ryan took his place, but the Lemonheads' new, moderate success was bittersweet: Dando was given to bouts of night terror, and Casella once found him howling incoherently while squatting on a sink.

Hit Cover Unwillingly Included

Despite these nightmares, the Lemonheads signed with a major label, Atlantic, and recorded the album *Lovey* in 1990. Dando found a new place to decompress: Sydney, Australia. The band toured there in 1991 and the singer/songwriter found a community of musical friends—among them Tom Morgan, who would become a frequent collaborator with Dando on Lemonheads songs—far from the maddening crowds of the American record business.

Peretz left the group before the Lemonheads recorded their breakthrough album, 1992's *It's a Shame About Ray*, so Hatfield sat in on bass. Australian bassist Nic Dalton joined the band for its subsequent tour. The album was produced by the three Robb brothers in Los Angeles.

Although *Ray* marked the full-fledged emergence of Dando's more intimate, poppy style, it was a rowdy cover version of "Mrs. Robinson," a Simon and Garfunkel song from the 1967 film *The Graduate*, that helped the band make its biggest waves. Originally recorded after *Ray's* release for the 25th-anniversary videocassette of the film, it was added to later pressings of the album. Once again, the band objected: "See, I try to choose my cover songs very carefully," Dando explained to the *Detroit Free Press*, "and there's no way I'd *choose* that one." Even so, "Mrs. Robinson" and the freewheeling, low-budget video that accompanied it made the Lemonheads alternative-rock stars almost overnight.

Ray itself benefitted from the attention, but reviewers were clearly more smitten with the original songs. "The secret recipe," reasoned Danielle Dowling of *Reflex*, "seems to be Dando's ability to create songs that easily slip in and out of these genres [folk and punk] without abruptly alerting the listener, exemplified by the title track, a catchy piece both in its pleasant acoustic stanzas and bass-driven groove refrain." *People* favored the group's "less alienating, almost folky feel" over the anger and bombast of alternative heavies such as Nirvana and Pearl Jam.

The success of *Ray* also engendered the Cult of Evan; Dando's sleepy good looks graced scores of magazine covers, and interviewers worldwide ignored the group to focus on its leader's spacey charisma. This attention threatened to backfire when Dando's anxiety over recording the follow-up to *Ray* led him to admit to the press that he'd resorted to heroin and crack for a brief spell.

Ultimately, however, the Lemonheads emerged in 1993 with *Come on Feel the Lemonheads,* an expansive album that further explored the country influences that had become part of Dando's sound. With the help of his friend Mac MacCaughan of the band Superchunk, Dando told *Option* that he'd begun to see that country "was valid, viable American music."

> Having solidified as a band and having cleared the hurdle of follow-up to a major label success, the Lemonheads seem to have found their stride.

Songs like "Big Gay Heart"—which employs veteran pedal-steel guitarist "Sneeky" Pete Kleinow—show how country has infiltrated his approach. Hatfield contributed vocals to numerous songs, and vocalists Belinda Carlisle—for whom Dando had originally intended the song "I'll Do It Anyway"—and Rick James also put in appearances. The album was again produced by the Robbs in L.A. "I'd prefer to be just about anywhere else," Dando explained to *Rolling Stone.* "But I wouldn't want to work with anybody but the Robbs, and this is their place. So here I am."

"Melodic Wimp" or "Brilliant Songwriter"?

The Lemonheads, bolstered by extensive touring, were a tighter band in the studio. The album was an immediate smash in the United Kingdom, and the first single, "Into Your Arms" by Australian friend Robyn St. Clare, made a strong showing on MTV. With "The Great Big No," the Lemonheads promised to get some attention for an original song for a change. Even so, reviews of the album were mixed. "With each album, Dando's writing, singing, and guitar playing have grown steadily wimpier," commented *Entertainment Weekly.* "But at least he's a *melodic* wimp."

The *Rocket,* meanwhile, praised *Come on Feel the Lemonheads* as "a charming pop record" that "establishes Dando as a brilliant songwriter." While *Details* felt the album "delivers on the shambling promise" of *Ray,* J. D. Considine of *Musician* poured vitriol on it, reflecting a backlash in some circles against Dando's fashion-model status: "all Dando shows in his songs is smug superiority. So f— him."

The Lemonheads, having solidified at last as a band and having cleared the hurdle of follow-up to a major label success, seemed at last to have found their stride. *Rolling Stone* referred to Dando as "a first-rate songwriter, a worthy heir to the Paul Westerberg estate." The singer—who had been doing some film acting and drumming for the band Godstar with Dalton and Morgan—explained to *Musician,* "It's all about learning to relax, for me. It's really hard for me to relax in the studio and get a good performance.... Someone might even tell you how to do that, but you wouldn't really learn it until you figure it out for yourself. That's what I did, and I'm glad I came through it. You know, that's usually my style. In the last minute, I come through."

Selected discography

On Taang!

"Laughing All the Way to the Cleaners," 1986.
Hate Your Friends, 1987.
Creator, 1988.
Lick (includes "Luka"), 1989.

On Atlantic

Lovey, 1990.
It's a Shame About Ray (includes "Mrs. Robinson"), 1992.
Come on Feel the Lemonheads (includes "Big Gay Heart," "I'll Do It Anyway," "Into Your Arms," and "The Great Big No"), 1993.

With other artists

"Frying Pan" (Dando solo) *Sweet Relief: A Tribute to Victoria Williams,* Thirsty Ear/Chaos, 1993.

Sources

Billboard, November 6, 1993.
Circus, December 31, 1993.
Creem, February 1994.
Details, July 1993; December 1993.
Detroit Free Press, November 13, 1992.
Entertainment Weekly, October 15, 1993; November 19, 1993.
Los Angeles Times, November 7, 1993.
Musician, December 1993.
Option, November 1993.

People, November 30, 1992; May 3, 1993.
Raygun, November 1992.
Reflex, November 10, 1992.
Request, December 1993.
Rocket, October 27, 1993; November 10, 1993.
Rolling Stone, February 1, 1993; April 1, 1993; June 10, 1993; September 30, 1993; February 10, 1994.
Spin, August 1992; December 1992; April 1993; December 1993; February 1994.
Us, November 1993.
Vanity Fair, October 1993.

Additional information for this profile was provided by Atlantic Records publicity materials, 1993.

—Simon Glickman

The Louvin Brothers

Gospel/country duet

The entertainer who did most to expose a new generation of fans to the Louvin Brothers was Emmylou Harris, according to Howard Miller, the author of the biography *The Louvin Brothers: From Beginning to End*. Harris's recordings of "If I Could Only Win Your Love," "When I Stop Dreaming," and "Everytime You Leave" are fan favorites that highlight her clear, expressive voice. Introduced to the Louvins' music by her late musical partner Gram Parsons, she initially thought Ira's voice was that of a woman. Unhesitating in her praise, Harris lauded, "It just amazes me. I think they are the greatest duet as singers, but also their writing is phenomenal. They are really underrated today. They should be played more on the radio, they should have more visibility. Their records should be sort of a staple [of] those classics that are played on air."

The Louvins influenced other popular musicians as well, such as the bluegrass act of brothers Jim and Jesse McReynolds. Jesse first met Charlie Louvin in the U.S. Army in Korea, where they worked together in the Dusty Road Ramblers. The McReynolds brothers later landed a Capitol Records contract in the 1950s with the Louvin Brothers' song "Are You Missing Me" and released a Louvin Brothers tribute album in 1967. The Louvins also had an impact on Johnny Cash, who later helped his boyhood idol Charlie Louvin with a loan that Cash has never allowed Charlie to repay. The Louvins themselves were influenced by the brother duets of the 1930s and the Carter family. But their brand of country gospel can best be traced back to their upbringing on a farm near Henegar, Alabama, where Ira was born on April 21, 1924, and Charlie on July 7, 1927.

Musical Influences

Ira and Charlie Loudermilk were born into a family of seven children. The two brothers were later to abandon their name because people joked about it and found it hard to spell, though their cousin John Loudermilk would have success as a songwriter without any changes. According to Charlie Louvin in *Bluegrass Unlimited*, their lives were always centered around music, no matter what other jobs they held. But when the boys were teenagers, their father thought that they were spending too much time with their music. As Charlie related: "At noon on Fridays, the teachers would let us open the partition separating the two rooms of the school and play for the rest of the day. We sang old songs like 'Kneel At The Cross,' 'Are You Washed in the Blood,' and other songs we had heard all our lives. When daddy found out, he decided that we might as well stay home on Fridays and help with the farming." Their father didn't disapprove of making music: he

For the Record . . .

Ira Louvin (born Ira Loudermilk, April 21, 1924, in Henegar, AL; died June 20, 1965), tenor and mandolin; **Charlie Louvin** (born Charlie Loudermilk, July 7, 1927, in Henegar, AL), vocals and rhythm guitar.

Performed live radio shows and barn dances, 1941-49; signed with MGM Records, 1949; signed with Capitol Records, 1951; hired by the Grand Ole Opry, 1955; disbanded and embarked on solo careers, 1964; Charlie sang duets with Melba Montgomery, 1974; Charlie had hit with "Ten Years, Three Kids and Two Loves Ago," 1980; Charlie opened the Louvin Brothers Music Park and Museum in Henegar, AL.

Awards: Most Programmed Sacred Duet, BMI, 1951-55; duet inducted into the Songwriters Hall of Fame, 1979.

Addresses: *Record company*—Rounder Records, One Camp St., Cambridge, MA 02140.

---

played a five-string banjo in the clawhammer banjo style of Uncle Dave Macon and Grandpa Jones. However, he believed music was for recreation, after the day's work was done, rather than a suitable profession.

The whole Loudermilk family was musical: the boys' mother sometimes played the banjo and all of their sisters sang. According to Howard Miller in *The Louvin Brothers,* their Uncle Verlon played guitar, fiddle, and mandolin well enough to win prizes at regional contests. The brothers were also exposed to music by listening on Saturday nights at the country store to the radio broadcasts of the Grand Ole Opry over WSM from Nashville; they also would listen at home to records of the Carter Family, Jimmie Rodgers, Bill and Charlie Monroe, Roy Acuff and the Blue Sky Boys, The Callahan Brothers, and the Skillet Lickers.

The most important influence on the Louvin Brothers' music was the church. Their mother's family, the Wootens, were well-known Sacred Harp, or shape note, singers, who emphasized the communal singing of complex harmonies with interchangeable parts, and their annual singing gatherings were well attended. As the boys became better singers, their father encouraged them to perform for company, and eventually the boys started buying instruments and learning to play them on their own. When Ira was 19, he got his first mandolin, a Gibson F-12, from a store in Chattanooga.

Charlie was 16 before he started playing the guitar; when he was 17, he bought a half-sized model called the "Black Knight" in a Chattanooga pawn shop. In *The Louvin Brothers* he noted that "I am not a picker, per se. The guitar was something to help me keep the tempo and the pitch. As the years went by I became more proficient, but my guitar playing was adequate."

Making Money Making Music

The Louvins' first professional appearance was at a Fourth of July celebration in 1941 in Flat Rock, Alabama. They sat in the center of a "flying jenny," a mule-powered merry-go-round, and played two songs during each ride. They worked all day for two dollars each. According to Suzy Geno in *Bluegrass Unlimited,* Ira soon married and moved to Chattanooga. Charlie joined him there, and the brothers worked at a cotton mill. After winning a weekly amateur contest at the American Theater on Broad Street three Saturdays in a row, the Louvins received the grand prize, which was a live, fifteen-minute radio show on a 250-watt station starting at 4:30 a.m. For six months, they did the show in the morning, worked all day, and then played music around the area at night.

It was a hectic period, but their success encouraged them to quit their jobs and pursue music full-time. Both men spent a short time in the service. After Charlie had spent a brief stint with Charlie Monroe's group, the brothers started work in the fall of 1946 with Cas Walker in Knoxville. Shortly thereafter they met Hack and Clyde Johnson and landed an early morning show on WNOX radio and later a spot on the Mid-Day Merry-Go-Round and the Tennessee Barn Dance each Saturday night.

In 1947 a few of their songs were published by Acuff-Rose, and they went to work with Smiling Ed Hill's radio show in Memphis. But soon Eddie Hill moved to Nashville to work at a bigger station and times grew difficult for the Louvins. Charlie had married in 1949 and had gotten used to the regular radio paychecks, so they both started work at the Memphis post office, though they continued to play on weekends anywhere they were asked.

From Country to Gospel and Back

The years of radio shows and barn dances finally paid off when the Louvins signed a contract with MGM Records in 1949. Their first album was a mixture of secular and gospel songs that didn't sell well, though it is now considered a classic, according to Shawn Ryan in the *Birmingham News*. In 1951 MGM dropped the group, and the same year they were signed by Capitol Records. According to Charlie Louvin: "[Capitol] said they didn't need us as a country duet, but they would hire us as gospel duet. They had Jim and Jesse and, in the old days, a label wouldn't have more than one country duet. We said, 'OK, we'll take that. Anything.'"

For the next four years the Louvin Brothers recorded nothing but gospel, with such hits as "Weapon of Prayer" and "Satan is Real." Their career continued to rise and they were voted the most programmed sacred duet by BMI from 1951 through 1955. All along they had been trying to get on the Grand Ole Opry, traveling often to Nashville to audition for the show.

> They sat in the center of a "flying jenny," a mule-powered merry-go-round, and played two songs during each ride. They worked all day for two dollars each.

In 1955, they were finally hired by the Opry, where programming considerations would eventually lead them back to secular singing. The tobacco company that sponsored the show limited the number of gospel songs to two per 30-minute program, so the Louvins started singing other songs to get more air time. This led to some of the biggest hits of their career such as "Hopin' That You're Hopin'," "You're Running Wild," "I Don't Believe You Baby," and "When You Stop Dreaming."

The brothers wrote almost all of the songs that appeared on their 24 albums even though neither of them could read music. Charlie remarked in the *Birmingham News* that his brother Ira was the real writer: "I gave ideas and helped on lines. He definitely was the stronger part of the writing team. But he was a drinking man." Their songwriting experiences reveal some of the difficulties Ira was to have throughout his career. "He'd get to drinking and write something and just bring the words over and say, 'Get your guitar. I want to try this song.' I was supposed to know what tune he had in mind just looking at the words. A lot of times the tune was made up as we went. But if I screwed up, he'd wad it up and throw it in the trash can, saying it probably wasn't worth a damn anyway."

Likewise, in the studio, Ira would often force Charlie to sing in higher and higher keys, so that Ira could better show off his seemingly unlimited tenor. The Louvins would break up several times due to Ira's drinking, with the last time being in 1964. After the breakup Charlie started a successful solo career with such hits as "I Don't Love You Anymore," "See the Big Man Cry, Mama," and "Think I'll Go Somewhere and Cry Myself to Sleep." Ira also released a few solo records but only played a few club dates occasionally. Returning from one of those engagements, he and his fourth wife, Florence, who sang under the name of Anne Young, were killed in a car accident on Father's Day, 1965, in Missouri.

Looking back on the Louvin Brothers' career, Charlie recalled in *Bluegrass Unlimited* that even when the group was doing well in the late 1950s they were frustrated: "As we moved toward and into the 1960s, it seemed our records were becoming more modern sounding. On many of our recordings, they added all sorts of studio musicians and Nashville back-up singers. Ira's fantastic mandolin breaks and much of his playing was completely lost. Sometimes, we sounded almost too good to be us."

Others have also commented on the change, as a *Bluegrass Unlimited* writer reviewing *The Best of the Early Louvin Brothers* observed: "Here we have the anachronism of a brother vocal and instrumental duet recording (and selling) while the whole country music industry was reeling under the impact of the new musical sensation that was Elvis Presley." But the reviewer had a more optimistic appraisal of the result, noting that the recordings still featured the group's close and intense harmonies and high degree of conviction, and emphasizing instead the importance of the sidemen, like Ray Edenton, Willie Ackermen, Junior Husky, Paul Yandell, Jimmy Capps, and Chet Atkins, who were to become founders of the emerging Nashville Sound.

The Louvin Brother

Charlie stayed with Capitol Records through 1975 and recorded numerous successful duets with Melba Montgomery. In 1979 Charlie and Ira were inducted into the Songwriters Hall of Fame, and in 1980 Charlie had a hit single with "Ten Years, Three Kids and Two Loves Ago." He continues to play on the Grand Ole Opry and established the Louvin Brothers Music Park and Museum near Henegar, Alabama, which has been the scene of many music festivals.

Charlie Louvin balks at being called a bluegrass artist, insisting instead that he and his brother were always country singers. He suggests that what is now called country is really something else, more akin to rock and roll. Nevertheless, in *Bluegrass Unlimited* he talked about the importance of bluegrass and old-time music festivals in keeping what he calls country music alive: "The bluegrass festivals have proven that audiences and performers can once again feel the closeness, the togetherness, that Ira and I felt when we played and sang on Friday afternoons at Spring Hill School. It's that special feeling that folks had when they gathered on their front porch, propped their feet on the rail after a hard day's work, and sang and played away their heartaches and troubles."

Selected discography

Songs That Tell a Story, Rounder, 1992.
Radio Favorites 51-57, Country Music Foundation, 1993.
Tragic Songs of Life, Rounder.
Louvin Brothers, Rounder.

Sources

Books

Miller, Howard, *The Louvin Brothers: From Beginning to End,* Louvin Brothers Music Park (Henegar, AL), 1986.

Periodicals

Birmingham News (Alabama), May 12, 1989.
Bluegrass Unlimited, March 1983; February 1987; June 1987; January 1993.
The Journal of the Academy of the Preservation of Old Time Country Music, April 1993.
Newsweek, May 18, 1987.

—*John Morrow*

Kirsty MacColl

Singer, songwriter

Photograph by Charles Dickens, courtesy of I.R.S. Records

The virtues of Kirsty MacColl's work—integrity, irony, literateness and independence—are not ones typically associated with success in the world of popular music, especially for a female artist. And indeed, MacColl has not seen great financial success thus far; she has, however, gained the respect of critics and her peers with finely crafted, lyrically complex songs reminiscent of British tunesmiths like Kinks founder Ray Davies and post-punk trailblazer Elvis Costello.

Being likened to a wry pop experimentalist like Costello hasn't particularly helped MacColl "move units," but next to "the Dorothy Parker of pop"—a title bestowed on her by Jim Farber of the New York Daily News—the Costello comparison is pure gold. Parker, whose acid wit made her a journalistic luminary in pre-war America, is as far from the glittery iconography of the MTV generation as one can get. But then, so is MacColl.

From her early days recording singles for the U.K. label Stiff to the release of her 1993 album Titanic Days, the singer-songwriter has purveyed what Amy Linden of Mirabella called "grown-up pop, with layers of luxurious, expansive vocals." MacColl often uses melodic pop as the vehicle for dark subject matter; as Farber noted, she "understates everything, detailing the most violent emotions with the greatest of ease." And despite myriad career disappointments—notably losing money and record deals on three separate occasions—MacColl has stayed focused and optimistic.

Father's "Genetic" Influence

MacColl's father, Ewan MacColl, was an esteemed U.K. folksinger best known for writing "The First Time Ever I Saw Your Face," a 1973 hit for singer Roberta Flack. But Ewan didn't spend much time with his daughter as she grew up. "He lived in a different county and we would see him only on occasional weekends," MacColl recalled for the Los Angeles Daily News, and claimed in an interview with Pulse! that her father's influence on her work was "all genetic," adding that music legend had little to do with her early musical development.

"Everyone assumes that we lived like the Waltons, sitting around a campfire and playing acoustic guitars all day," she related in Pulse!, "But I grew up alone with my mother, and I spent all my time alone in my bedroom listening to records, trying to work out what Donald Fagen [of the eclectic U.S. group Steely Dan] was singing about. And then I realized it was all drug dealers! So I felt like an alien all the time—I was quite scared at school, because it was a rough one and I'd

> **For the Record...**
>
> Born c. 1960, in London, England; daughter of Ewan (a folksinger and writer) and Jean (a choreographer) MacColl; married Steve Lillywhite (a music producer), c. 1980s; children: two sons.
>
> Recording and performing artist, 1979—. Recorded debut single "They Don't Know," Stiff Records, 1979; sang with various artists, including the Rolling Stones, Robert Plant, Talking Heads, the Kinks, Morrissey, and the Pogues, c. 1980s; signed with Polydor and recorded U.K. debut album, c. mid-1980s; signed with Virgin and released U.S. debut album *Kite,* 1989; performed with the Pogues on *Red, Hot + Blue* benefit album, 1990; hosted BBC documentary *Don't Go Near the Water,* 1991; signed with I.R.S. and released *Titanic Days,* 1993.
>
> **Addresses:** *Record company*—I.R.S. Records, 3939 Lankershim Blvd., Universal City, CA 91604.

insisted on going there. I kept thinking, 'Boy, if I can only survive school. If I can only survive 'til I've left home, everything will be all right.' And it was. There you go."

At age 19, MacColl signed with Stiff Records, recording such singles as "They Don't Know," "There's a Guy Works Down in the Chip Shop Swears He's Elvis," and a version of "A New England" by socialist-popster Billy Bragg. She also began working with producer Steve Lillywhite, whom she later married. In 1984 singer-actress Tracey Ullman had a Top Ten hit with "They Don't Know," providing MacColl with much-needed income and a degree of notoriety. "I remember going into a liquor store in San Francisco the first day I got there," she recalled to Wayne Bledsoe of the *Knoxville News-Sentinel.* "They were playing Marvin Gaye's 'How Sweet It Is to Be Loved By You.' And then right after that, 'They Don't Know' came on, and I just started jumping up and down. It was the most exciting thing that had ever happened. I just couldn't believe I was on American radio. Well, it wasn't me, but it was my song."

Unfortunately, Stiff went under—still owing MacColl money. She had even worse luck with her next label, Polydor; she recorded one album there, and it was never released in the United States. That company, too, went bankrupt and MacColl declined to record anything else until the litigation surrounding the album was settled. She worked as a backup singer and guest vocalist on recordings by such artists as the Rolling Stones, Morrissey, Talking Heads, Robert Plant, and The Pogues. The latter group played with her on the Christmas hit "Fairytale of New York" and later on the Cole Porter tribute/AIDS benefit anthology *Red, Hot + Blue.*

Made Impression With Debut

It wasn't until 1989 that MacColl recorded her next album, *Kite,* for the Virgin label; Lillywhite served as producer, while guitarist Johnny Marr—best known for his work with Morrissey's band The Smiths—contributed to several tracks. Consisting mostly of original songs and crystallizing her unique blend of bright melody and dark sophistication, the album was partly intended to prove a point. "I felt I had to prove that I wasn't this bimbo girl-next-door I'd been portrayed as," she confided in a *Melody Maker* interview. "That had been hanging around my neck like a f—ing albatross for so long, and I wanted to make the point that, yes, I can write a f—ing song, pal!"

In addition to such prickly MacColl originals as "No Victims," "The End of a Perfect Day," and "Innocence," the album assays the tender Ray Davies requiem "Days." Steve Hochman, writing in *Rolling Stone,* noted approvingly that "MacColl has created a sparkling, modern folk-rock sound that at turns bounces, forces and eases her scoldings on, with her plain but attractive voice layered throughout." Hochman continued, adding that he regretted only that MacColl hadn't recorded more: "It's unfair for someone with this much to say and this much skill at saying it to be so stingy." Dave Jennings of *Melody Maker* deemed *Kite* "cerebral but instantly likeable; never wild or abandoned but always intriguing. A big surprise, out of the blue."

Though her album was well received, MacColl couldn't seem to get over her crushing fear of live solo performance. "I couldn't imagine doing it," she confessed in *Billboard.* "I'd tried it a few times, and I was just so paralyzed by fear that I couldn't even sing. When the Kinks invited me to get up and sing 'Days' with them, I was in tears at the soundcheck because I was so scared."

These fears, however, are not evident in the subject matter of MacColl's songs. A recurring issue for her is women's strength and independence, something she feels pop music usually fails to address. "There are hundreds of thousands of people out there doing songs where the woman is always a victim and can't really manage without her man," MacColl declared in her *Mirabella* interview with Linden. "I just like sorta seeing it from another angle." Expanding on the theme for Fred Shuster of the *Daily News,* MacColl insisted that the helpless female songs she heard growing up "had nothing to do with how women felt—it was a misrepresentation. The myth of 'If you leave me, I'm nothing,' is a load of garbage and most women know that. We're very strong people and not to be treated as second-class citizens." MacColl displayed the courage of her ecological convictions as well, hosting a BBC documentary on water pollution and purification; she even had a prototype of an organic filtration system built at her house.

MacColl's follow-up to *Kite,* 1991's *Electric Landlady,* displays considerably more musical ambition. Referring wittily in its title to the 1968 sonic watershed *Electric Ladyland* by the Jimi Hendrix Experience, the album saw her exploring everything from funk to samba and injecting considerably more political content into her lyrics. Lillywhite again produced, and MacColl—intent on broadening her rhythmic palette—enlisted rapper Aniff Cousins to lend his cool vocals to the funk-infected "Walking Down Madison," the recording's opening track.

> *"I started in music young and naïve and malleable, and the older I get the more determined I become not to compromise. Getting older is supposed to make you mellower, but I get more militant every day."*

Reviews of the album were mixed, but according to a *Stereo Review* writer, "MacColl moves with ease among jazz, country, samba, salsa and traditional pop rhythm numbers, mindful that her lyrics mean something—about ecological reform, about the hopelessness of New York's street people—instead of just being fodder for the beat. For these reasons—plus her enchanting soft soprano and liberal use of humor—MacColl never fails to hold one's interest."

What MacColl failed to hold onto was her record deal. Even as "Walking Down Madison" moved up the U.K. charts, Virgin reneged on her tour support. Shortly thereafter she heard that she was off the label. "They told the management—they don't bother to deal with you as a person anymore once you're gone. You're just a big nothing," she explained in *Pulse!* Meanwhile, MacColl was rehearsing and recording with a band and preparing to tour; her musicians had to be paid, though no money was being earned.

MacColl was shocked and surprised to find her players willing to work on spec—with the understanding that she'd pay them when she could. "They said, 'It's OK—pay us when you get a deal,'" she recollected to *Pulse!* writer Tom Lanham, "and that gave me a lot of confidence. If all these great people obviously believed in me, why shouldn't I believe in myself?"

MacColl's friend and collaborator Mark E. Nevin—formerly of the band Fairground Attraction—helped her organize a tour. Indeed, she reflected in a *Billboard* interview, Virgin's reversal "was a real kick in the teeth, but it was good in a way, because it made me get off my ass. And I said, 'Well, I'll show you,' and the next thing you know I'm out on the road, and before that I'd been too scared to do it for 10 years."

New Deal, *Titanic* Comeback

A bit later a childhood friend of MacColl's came to see one of her shows and brought her husband Jay Boberg, who happened to be the head of the independent label I.R.S. Records. He was impressed enough to sign MacColl. She had been recording without a deal, but the low budget and lack of label interference had allowed her to stay true to her own goals. "I made it thinking, even if everybody disagrees with me and I never get another deal, this is gonna be a record that I can play for my kids in 20 years and proudly say, 'This is what your mother did.'" The album was *Titanic Days,* released by I.R.S. in 1993. Further refining her formula on the pleasantly wicked "Bad" and the perfect pop of "Soho Square," MacColl surprised even her longtime fans this time around.

"After more than a decade of being the Singer Most Likely To, MacColl finally has—made a great album, that is," declared *Musician*'s J.D. Considine, adding "each of these gems is perfectly set, with clean, carefully colored arrangement and none of the overharmonized excess that marred her previous output. Prepare yourself for a Titanic love affair." A *Billboard* reviewer deemed the album "a brew of pure pop sense and biting wit at least as satisfying as her previous work." Erik Himmelsbach of the *Los Angeles Reader* found the singer "better than ever" and the album "far more lyrically realized" than *Electric Landlady,* if "not as musically challenging."

And though she still hasn't sold enough records to be a hot property in the industry, MacColl has only doubled her resolve. "My attitude to the music business now is that I've got to make what I've got to make, regardless," she stated in *Pulse!* "I will try and sell it, try to promote it, but I'm not gonna go to a gym and get anorexia and a blonde wig just so the company can sell a few more copies to people who are so stupid they only want to buy things by air-brushed photographs." Rather, MacColl has created an intelligent adult woman's pop persona and stuck to it. "I started in music young and naïve and malleable," MacColl insisted in a *Request* interview, "and the older I get the more determined I become not to compromise. Getting older is supposed to make you mellower, but I get more militant every day."

Selected discography

"They Don't Know," Stiff, 1979.
Kite (includes "No Victims," "The End of a Perfect Day," "Innocence," and "Days"), Virgin, 1989.
Electric Landlady (includes "Walking Down Madison"), Virgin, 1991.
Titanic Days (includes "Bad" and "Soho Square"), I.R.S., 1993.
"There's a Guy Down the Chip Shop Swears He's Elvis," Stiff.
"A New England," Stiff.
"Fairytale of New York," Stiff.

With others

Talking Heads, *Naked* (appears on "Nothing But Flowers"), Sire, 1988.
Red, Hot + Blue (appears with the Pogues on "Mrs. Otis Regrets"), 1990.

Sources

Billboard, October 9, 1993; December 11, 1993.
Daily News (Los Angeles), October 15, 1993.
Knoxville News-Sentinel, October 10, 1993.
Los Angeles Reader, October 15, 1993.
Melody Maker, May 13, 1989; June 22, 1991.
Mirabella, November 1993.
Musician, November 1993.
New York Daily News, October 10, 1993.
Pulse!, Holiday Issue 1993.
Request, November 1993.
Rolling Stone, May 31, 1990.
Stereo Review, October 1991.

Additional information for this profile was provided by I.R.S. publicity materials, 1993.

—*Simon Glickman*

Sarah McLachlan

Singer, songwriter, guitarist

Photograph by Kharen Hill, courtesy of Arista/Nettwerk

Sarah McLachlan knows where the best music comes from: "Sonically," she told *Cover* magazine's KK Kozik, "moving water is perhaps my all-time favorite sound." Water has both its aural and thematic relevance for McLachlan. "Being around any kind of water is one of the most important things in my life," she averred. "I find it soothing and it's a very female thing, too. The ocean is like the womb and I'm fascinated, drawn in." Indeed, McLachlan herself has a fluid quality; her voice is noted for its liquidity, and her lyrics and production values, for their tempest and storm.

McLachlan comes by her turbulent personality honestly. Born in Halifax, Nova Scotia, McLachlan led a relatively sequestered life while growing up. David Thigpen of *Time* reported that McLachlan was "a shy, awkward child who never fell in with the crowd." He described her as a teenager who "would kill time on long, frozen winter nights writing songs." *Billboard*'s Timothy White provided a more complex portrayal of McLachlan's youthful existence. Her mother, Dorice, sacrificed her "own academic aspirations" in order to support her husband, Jack, an American marine biologist, and then acquainted "her little girl with the isolation that regret places in the path of personal fulfillment." But for White, the results were worth celebrating. "McLachlan was able to fuse her mother's depth of pathos and her father's detached analysis into a calm grasp of our culture's callous objectification of women," he concluded.

From the start of her career at age 19, McLachlan was compared to other female song-writers such as Joni Mitchell, Kate Bush, Sinead O'Connor, and Tori Amos, comparisons one might ascribe to what Elysa Gardner of *Rolling Stone* called a voice of "astonishing strength and clarity [that] may drift at any given time from a sirenlike middle range to a ghostly soprano." She has remarkable range and tends toward lyrics which explore relationships between women and men.

During her childhood, McLachlan sought out the serenading voices and sentiments of folk-rock singers Joan Baez, Cat Stevens, and Simon and Garfunkel. She had twelve years of training on guitar, six on piano, and five years of voice lessons, all of which surely contributed to what *Billboard*'s Timothy White referred to as "the wit, literate grace, and unfussy intricacy of her material." As a teenager, McLachlan worked at restaurant counters and as a dishwasher in Halifax, riding out the calm before her musical storm.

Critics generally agree that with McLachlan's third album, *Fumbling Towards Ecstasy,* released in 1994, she revealed a new maturity as singer, songwriter, and woman. Her first album, *Touch,* released in 1988,

> **For the Record . . .**
>
> Born January 28, 1968, in Halifax, Nova Scotia, Canada; daughter of Jack (a marine biologist) and Dorice (a student) McLachlan.
>
> Trained in classical guitar, piano, and voice; worked as dishwasher and counter person in Halifax; discovered by Nettwerk Records while performing with a new wave band in Halifax; signed a contract with Nettwerk at age 19; moved to Vancouver; released debut album, *Touch,* Nettwerk, 1988; contributed "Hold On" to *No Alternative* compilation, Arista, 1993; featured on American Public Radio's "E-Town," February 27, 1994.
>
> **Addresses:** *Home*—Montreal, Canada. *Record company*—Arista Records, 6 West 57th St., New York, NY 10019.

suggested a waif-like quality to Elysa Gardner. But her second album, *Solace,* in 1991, revealed a sturdier woman, one less "ethereal," one "trying to come down to earth a bit." McLachlan said of *Solace,* "There's a lot more of myself in my writing [there]—more the way I think, more the way I talk." *Fumbling Towards Ecstasy* reveals a woman with a more broad sensibility; her self-awareness and her melancholy meet a political consciousness.

McLachlan has referred to the relevance here of her increased self-respect and gender appreciation. She told *Billboard,* "It took me six years to learn how not to edit myself, to remain open in my music so that I touched greater levels of darkness as well as some positive areas of escape." When KK Kozik noted the "femininity" of *Fumbling,* McLachlan succinctly replied, "I love women. I'm fascinated by them.... I'm definitely starting to realize more of my responsibility as a woman."

While the bulk of critical response to McLachlan's music has been admiring, some criticism contained a disparaging tone. Dave Jennings of *Melody Maker* was dismayed by the excess of "vulnerability" he found in *Solace,* which while couched in nature imagery did not add up to "New Age consciousness, but really ... just old-school singer-songwriter preciousness." Similarly, *Spin's* Joy Press found the lyrics of *Fumbling* "mature with a capital M, to the point of sophomoric pseudo-profundity." Press's criticism ventured into the realm of gender. Sardonically, she concluded that McLachlan "obviously places herself in the category of the self-defined, strong, female song-writer," and that ultimately *Fumbling* provided only "an easy-listening portrait of a woman—a perfectly graceful, confident, and smart woman—but it's not the portrait of an artist."

Other critics, however, found in that album both an artist and a portrait of that artist. *Time's* Thigpen attempted to remove the debate from the gender-biased charge of confessionalism: "Far from indulging in simple emotional bloodletting," he wrote, "McLachlan creates exquisitely poised songs that resist anger or pathos."

In *Fumbling,* KK Kozik appreciated McLachlan's newfound "desire and capacity to understand more than just herself," a departure from the concerns of *Touch* and *Solace.* McLachlan agreed. A trip to Southeast Asia in 1993, for which she represented her Canadian peer group, afforded her both disillusionment and wisdom. She admitted that she sang less about victimization and self-pity as a result of that mission whose focus was AIDS, prostitution, and poverty, and where McLachlan saw rooms full of photographs of "thousands and thousands ... of victims, men, women, and children looking at the camera and they all died immediately thereafter.... There are all these souls trapped in this building ... such intense oppression.... I all of a sudden got so horrified with humanity and so disillusioned. How can people be so cruel.... Do we learn nothing from history? But the aftermath of that is, 'I feel so blessed.'"

Though McLachlan does not address the Cambodian situation directly in her songs, its impact can be felt. Critics imply that the garnered knowledge enriched her lyrics and music, even while both remained devoted to interpersonal relationships. Thigpen identified McLachlan's audience as "the desperately troubled," to whom she offers the suggestion "that the answers to life's emotional earthquakes can come through perseverance and compassion." Terry McBride, the president of Nettwerk Records, remarked, "There's more soul in her singing on this album. [This] record finally makes you believe that she means what she says."

Though still inspired to look outward, McLachlan insisted that her strengths as a singer and songwriter are nurtured in solitude. With Rainer Maria Rilke's self-searching philosophies at the core, in 1994 McLachlan was focused on how to reach the most of her artistic potential. With expressed gratitude toward her producer and sometime-collaborator, Pierre Marchand, and all the talking and thinking he required of her, she still remarked, "I find that to open up myself as much as I have to to get at what I need, I need to be by myself." Like the true Romantic she is, McLachlan conjured images of herself walking the moors of Nova Scotia, out in the country where "everything just seemed so huge and so much bigger than I'd ever known it to be before and I got really ... high about how overwhelmingly beautiful everything was."

Selected discography

Touch, Nettwerk, 1988.
Solace, Arista, 1991.
(Contributor) "Hold On," on *No Alternative,* Arista, 1993.
Fumbling Towards Ecstasy, Arista, 1994.

Sources

Billboard, January 8, 1994; March 19, 1994.
Cover, March 1994.
Melody Maker, June 13, 1992.
Rolling Stone, February 6, 1992; June 16, 1994.
Spin, March 1994.
Stereo Review, August 1989.
Time, March 21, 1994.

Additional information for this profile was obtained from Arista publicity materials, 1994.

—Diane Moroff

John McLaughlin

Guitarist

Photograph by J.P. Larcher, © Polygram, courtesy of Verve Records

Musician magazine, in a 1993 survey of "The 100 Great Guitarists of the 20th Century," referred to John McLaughlin as "the mystic credited with inventing real fusion." The guitarist himself—whose work has embraced jazz, rock, blues, Indian music, and flamenco, among other styles—has long disdained the label. "I'm not trying to make any kind of fusion—it just happens that way," he protested to *Guitar Player*. Yet McLaughlin's fearless hybridization of musical genres blazed a trail for other musicians and demonstrated a set of possibilities that spawned the eclectic jazz-rock movement that came to be known as "fusion."

McLaughlin has always been far too restless to dwell in any musical territory for long. From his early work with the Graham Bond Organization to his innovative excursions with jazz legend Miles Davis to his increasingly ambitious endeavors with the Mahavishnu Orchestra, Shakti, and his own trio as well as countless brief collaborations, McLaughlin has pursued his own musical development with an openly spiritual outlook. "My work in music is a work of the spirit," he proclaimed in a *Down Beat* interview. "It's a development of my spirit, and the development of myself as a human being."

That development began in Yorkshire, England, where he was born in 1942. Raised to a background of classical music, he studied the violin—as his mother had—as well as piano, but became interested in the guitar early in his adolescence. This was due in part to the influence of one of his brothers but largely to that of American blues, European jazz, and flamenco. Recordings by blues artists like Muddy Waters, Leadbelly, and Big Bill Broonzy, as well as jazz guitarist Django Reinhardt, were particularly galvanizing for the young musician. "When I first discovered guitar at age 11, it was a five-dollar acoustic nylon-string guitar," McLaughlin recalled in a *Guitar Player* interview. "I didn't know what acoustic or electric guitars were." He added that "The very first time I ever played the guitar I fell in love with it. I loved the sound, I loved the feeling."

As he got a bit older, he felt an increased desire to emulate the great jazz guitarists. Soon Reinhardt "was my hero," he told *Down Beat*. "Later I heard Tal Farlow and found what I consider a genius. Tal was a great source of inspiration for me." The great artists of bebop and post-bop jazz, too, made an indelible imprint on McLaughlin: Charles Mingus, Art Blakey, Miles Davis, and John Coltrane. The latter's spiritual odyssey *A Love Supreme* took him a long time to understand, he recalled, but years later he would translate the piece into a fiery guitar duet with Carlos Santana. It was drummer Tony Williams, however, whom he wanted to play with most of all.

145

> **For the Record...**
>
> Born January 4, 1942, in Yorkshire, England; mother was concert violinist.
>
> Worked as a guitar teacher, 1960s; joined group Tony Williams Lifetime, c. 1969; recorded with Miles Davis, 1969; released solo album *Extrapolation,* Polydor, 1969; formed Mahavishnu Orchestra and released its Columbia debut, 1972; formed Shakti and released its debut *Shakti With John McLaughlin,* 1976; recorded and performed as solo artist and guest performer, 1978—; recorded live and studio albums with Paco De Lucia and Al Di Meola, 1981-83; left Columbia and signed with Warner Bros., 1981; re-formed Mahavishnu Orchestra with new lineup, 1984; appeared in and performed on soundtrack of film *Round Midnight,* 1986; moved to Verve Records, c. 1987; formed John McLaughlin Trio, 1988.
>
> **Addresses:** *Record company*—Verve Records, Worldwide Plaza, 825 Eighth Ave., New York, NY 10019.

He began playing professionally in London in the early 1960s, hooking up with the Graham Bond Organization, a seminal outfit that included bassist Jack Bruce and drummer Ginger Baker, later the rhythm section of the influential psychedelic-blues trio Cream. McLaughlin also worked with Brian Auger's band Trinity and with Georgie Fame and the Blue Flames. He was still in England when he became interested in Eastern religion and music; the sitar master Ravi Shankar made a particularly strong impression on him. It was the beginning of a very long artistic and spiritual quest.

In the meantime, however, he was still searching for his niche as a musician. Working as a guitar teacher, he had a number of promising pupils, including future Yardbird and Led Zeppelin guitarist Jimmy Page. He shared a London apartment with bassist Dave Holland, and the two of them played experimentally with drummer Jack DeJohnette, who taped the session. When Holland hooked up with Miles Davis, he described his former roommate to Davis's drummer—Tony Williams—as a fantastic player. DeJohnette played the tape for Williams on a separate occasion; as a result, Williams invited McLaughlin to join his new band Lifetime.

It was early 1969 when the guitarist came to America to play in one idol's band; within two days he had met Miles Davis and found himself in the studio working on Davis's album *In a Silent Way.* He worked on a number of other albums with the legendary trumpeter-composer-bandleader, including *A Tribute to Jack Johnson, Live-Evil, Big Fun,* and the groundbreaking *Bitches Brew,* which saw Davis inaugurating the jazz-rock era almost singlehandedly. Davis titled one track "John McLaughlin"; the guitarist later told *Down Beat* this "was the biggest surprise to me. I mean, I saw it on the record. I was shocked, really shocked." He would return the compliment by placing a piece called "Miles Davis" on an album some ten years later. Davis also brought McLaughlin together with rock guitar trailblazer Jimi Hendrix for a jam session.

In a *Guitar Player* interview McLaughlin discussed Davis's profound influence upon him: "With Miles, for me, it was his simplicity, his directness, the authority of his music from a rhythmic, harmonic, and melodic point of view. His conceptualizations, from my point of view, were revolutionary. Everything I could see in Miles touched me."

Though Davis—who died in 1992—at times left composing and arranging to the many talented musicians in his fold, he displayed "the capacity and the ability to draw out of people things that even surprise the musicians themselves." McLaughlin found liberation in Davis's general, even cryptic directions: "He's amazing to work with, because he'd never say, 'I don't really want that'; he'd just say, 'play long' or 'play short'. Once he told me, 'Play like you don't know how to play guitar.' That's Miles, and you just go along with it."

Broke Musical Barriers With Mahavishnu

Though the guitarist had to refuse Davis's invitation to join his band because of his investment in Lifetime—which briefly featured Bruce on bass—he did later heed his recommendation to put his own band together. McLaughlin put out his first solo release, *Extrapolation,* in 1969. More solo efforts—notably 1971's *My Goals Beyond*—followed, but soon McLaughlin was driven to assemble a more ambitious group.

Having become a disciple of the guru Sri Chinmoy, he'd also become interested in fusing Eastern and Western musics. Working with keyboardist Jan Hammer, violinist Jerry Goodman, bassist Rick Laird, tabla player Alla Rakha and drummer Billy Cobham, he formed the Mahavishnu Orchestra. The band would do much to shape the fusion of the ensuing decade; McLaughlin's playing covered a huge stylistic territory. Indeed, wrote jazz scholar Joachim Berendt, "One is almost tempted to say that he plays all guitars simultaneously."

McLaughlin himself would adopt the name Mahavishnu; in 1973 he recorded an album with Santana and in the ensuing years made several more albums with the Orchestra, though with frequent personnel changes. According to *Down Beat*'s Lee Jeske, the group "reached a plateau for electric interplay and depth of feeling that has, to these ears, never been equaled."

Differences within the group caused friction, however, though McLaughlin revived Mahavishnu with different players some years later. "If you consider electric fusion music to be part of the jazz mainstream—not everyone does—then McLaughlin may be the most influential jazz figure since Coltrane," proclaimed *Rolling Stone* in 1976. "As far as guitar is concerned," Berendt opined around the same period, "McLaughlin certainly is *the* towering figure of this development."

Artistic Restlessness

By the mid-1970s he had grown restless again, however, and formed the more acoustically oriented Shakti, with violinist L. Shankar, tablaist Zakir Hussain, and two other Indian musicians. This project became his main focus until 1977, when, as he told *Guitar Player,* "I wanted to get back into some jazz and electric guitar." The solo albums *Johnny McLaughlin, Electric Guitarist* and *Electric Dreams,* with the One Truth Band, soon ranked among his most highly regarded works.

During the 1980s McLaughlin returned to the acoustic guitar. This led to a falling out with his record label Columbia and a move to Warner Brothers, which seemed to have more respect for his new direction. "One of the fundamental differences is that, with the acoustic guitar, the notes die out very quickly," he reflected in a colloquy with Jeske of *Down Beat*. "This is a more tragic sound, it's more poignant in a beautiful sense. So, that in itself compels the player to modify, in some far-reaching ways, what he'll play." McLaughlin added, "It reminds me of music I heard before I was born in this life," in a 1994 *Guitar Player* interview with Matt Resnicoff.

Struck by the impressive work of Spanish guitarist Paco De Lucia, McLaughlin sought him out; the two played some concerts with Larry Coryell, and performed and recorded with Al Di Meola. 1987 saw the release of an album by a new Mahavishnu Orchestra featuring McLaughlin's luthier Abraham Wechter on acoustic guitar. McLaughlin also wrote a concerto for guitar and orchestra and formed a trio with percussionist Trilok Gurtu and a changing roster of bassists including Kai Eckhardt and French sensation Dominique Di Piazza.

In 1990 McLaughlin's career was endangered by a freak accident: a television set moving on a mounting track sheared off the tip of his left index finger. Fortunately the finger was reassembled in surgery, but the guitarist couldn't play for two months and reported to *Musician* that he was "having nightmares, waking up in the middle of the night sweating." Soon, however, he was performing again. He released *Que Alegria* in 1992; recorded live in the studio, the album won a plaudit from *Down Beat*. "At 50, the inner fire is still burning," declared reviewer Bill Milkowski. "He's just cooking on a lower flame."

> "My work in music is a work of the spirit. It's a development of my spirit, and the development of myself as a human being."

The following year saw the appearance of his tribute to jazz pianist Bill Evans called *Time Remembered* in 1993. The Evans tribute involved a European guitar quartet; "I felt that if I transcribed it for a number of guitars, I could get this essential character, translated from the paino and the way he played, to the acoustic guitars," he noted in a *Down Beat* profile. Reviews mere mixed; some critics, like Howard Mandel of *Pulse!,* complained that McLaughlin "has stifled the momentum" of Evans's best work and made an album that "seems too still for jazz." *Entertainment Weekly's* David Hajdu, however, proclaimed "this guitar guru has finally found the God of the Details."

The guitarist didn't wait around for his review; he was already discussing forming an organ jazz trio and returning to the electric. He'd long since given up gurus and followed a more personal path, but as *Guitar Player's* James Rotondi observed, "McLaughlin's music continues to reflect his spirituality, passion for life, and great discipline."

Success at the critical or commercial level has always mattered less to the guitarist than the heroic process of creativity. "I'm an eternal learner," he insisted in a *Down Beat* profile. "I don't think I'll ever stop learning; it's a personal idiosyncrasy. I'm looking all the time for a way through music—searching, in a sense, for those different ways—harmonically, melodically, and rhythmically. For me the big joy of life is to play—that's the big joy—just to play music."

Selected discography

Solo albums

Extrapolation, Douglas Records, 1969.
Devotion, Douglas Records, 1971.
My Goals Beyond, Polydor, 1971.
Johnny McLaughlin, Electric Guitarist, Columbia, 1978.
The Best of John McLaughlin, Columbia, 1980.
Belo Horizonte, Warner Bros., 1981.
Music Spoken Here, Warner Bros., 1982.
Live at the Royal Festival Hall, JMT, 1989.
Mediterranean Concerto, Columbia, 1990.
Que Alegria, Verve, 1992.
Time Remembered: John McLaughlin Plays Bill Evans, Verve, 1993
Where Fortune Smiles, Pye Records.

With Tony Williams and Lifetime; on Polydor

Emergency!, 1969.
Turn It Over.
Lifetime.

With Miles Davis

In a Silent Way, 1969.
Bitches Brew (includes "John McLaughlin"), 1969.
A Tribute to Jack Johnson, 1970.
Live-Evil, 1971.
Big Fun, 1974.
Get Up With It, 1974.
Aura, 1984
You're Under Arrest, 1985.

With Devadip, Carlos Santana

Love, Devotion, Surrender (includes "A Love Supreme"), Columbia, 1973.

With the Mahavishnu Orchestra

The Inner Mounting Flame, Columbia, 1972.
Birds of Fire, Columbia, 1973.
Between Nothingness and Eternity, Columbia, 1973.
Apocalypse, Columbia, 1974.
Visions of the Emerald Beyond, Columbia, 1975.
Inner Worlds, Columbia, 1976.
Mahavishnu, Warner Bros., 1984.
Adventures in Radioland, Verve, 1987.

With Shakti; on Columbia

Shakti With John McLaughlin, 1976.
A Handful of Beauty, 1977.
Natural Elements, 1977.

With the One Truth Band

Electric Dreams (includes "Miles Davis"), Columbia, 1979.

With Paco De Lucia and Al Di Meola; on Columbia

Friday Night in San Francisco, 1981.
Passion, Grace & Fire, 1983.

Contributor

Carla Bley, *Escalator Over the Hill,* JCOA/ECM, 1971.
Graham Bond, *Solid Bond,* Warner Bros.
Jack Bruce, *Things We Like,* Atco.
Larry Coryell, *Spaces,* Vanguard, 1970.
Joe Farrell, *The Joe Farrell Quartet,* CTI.
Zakir Hussain, *Making Music,* ECM, 1987.
Round Midnight (soundtrack), Columbia, 1986.

Sources

Books

Berendt, Joachim, *The New Jazz Book,* translated by Morgenstern, et al., Lawrence Hill, 1975.
The Penguin Encyclopedia of Popular Music, Viking, 1989.

Periodicals

Down Beat, June 6, 1974; April 1982; March 1985; May 1991; December 1991; July 1992; December 1993; January 1994.
Entertainment Weekly, November 19, 1993.
Gramophone, December 1993.
Guitar Player, August 1978; July 1992; May 1994.
Musician, February 1993; August 1993.
Pulse!, March 1994.
Rolling Stone, June 3, 1976.

Additional information for this profile was provided by Verve Records publicity materials, 1993.

—Simon Glickman

Jim and Jesse McReynolds

Bluegrass duo

Jim and Jesse McReynolds and their group the Virginia Boys are a top-drawing bluegrass band with origins in Virginia's Clinch Mountains. The McReynolds brothers—who have been performing together since the early 1940s—are honored regulars on the Grand Ole Opry, where they play and sing an array of bluegrass, country, and even rockabilly tunes. As Irwin Stambler noted in the *Encyclopedia of Folk, Country, and Western Music,* Jim and Jesse "came to the foreground as one of the best Bluegrass troupes in the country" after the 1960s folk revival brought a surge of interest in stringband music. Since then the indefatigable entertainers have been a staple of bluegrass jamborees, Opry concerts, and folk festivals. In the *Country Music Encyclopedia,* Melvin Shestack contended that Jim and Jesse unquestionably rank "among the royalty of bluegrass performers."

The McReynolds brothers were born with musical blood in their veins. Their grandfather was one of the best-known traditional fiddlers in all of southern Virginia and their parents also played professionally. Both Jim

Photograph by Jon Sievert / MICHAEL OCHS ARCHIVES / Venice, CA

For the Record . . .

Jim McReynolds (born February 13, 1927, in Coeburn, VA; married; wife's name, Arreta), guitar, vocals; **Jesse McReynolds** (born July 9, 1929, in Coeburn, VA; married; wife's name, Darlene; children: Keith, Michael, Randy, Gwen), mandolin, vocals.

Bluegrass and country musicians and songwriters, 1940—. Made radio debut on WNVA, Norton, VA, as the McReynolds Brothers and the Cumberland Mountain Boys, 1947; signed with Kentucky Records, 1950; moved to Capitol Records, 1951; changed name to Jim and Jesse and the Virginia Boys; moved to Columbia label, 1960; had first Top Ten hit, "Diesel on My Tail," c. 1965; became regulars on the Grand Ole Opry, 1964; have made numerous live appearances in the United States and abroad, including tours of Japan.

Addresses: *Record company*—Rounder Records, One Camp St., Cambridge, MA 02140.

and Jesse started picking as young children, with Jim on mandolin and Jesse on guitar. Somehow neither boy could master his instrument at first, so they switched—Jesse took up mandolin and Jim began guitar. Soon they were masters, and Jesse in particular seemed never to stop practicing and experimenting with new licks.

Singing Brothers

The brothers formed their first band in the early 1940s, earning engagements at local establishments in the Clinch Mountain coal country. In 1947 they made their radio debut in Norton, Virginia, as the McReynolds Brothers and the Cumberland Mountain Boys. Their sound and picking style was influenced by Bill Monroe, Earl Scruggs, and other pioneers of bluegrass, but the major catalyst for their music was the "singing brothers" phenomenon that flourished in the South during mid-century.

In 1950 the brothers left the South and moved to Wichita, Kansas, where they worked under contract to radio station KFBI. They adapted their music to suit Midwestern tastes, adding accordion and steel guitar, and incorporating such flat-country standards as "Home on the Range" into their repertoire. After a year they returned east to Kentucky and Virginia and renamed their band the Virginia Trio. They cut several records during this period, first with Kentucky Records and then with the larger Capitol label.

The early Capitol recordings feature fine sidemen such as Hoke Jenkins on banjo and Curly Seckler on guitar, but are most notable for Jesse's mandolin playing. He had developed two new techniques for mandolin—crosspicking and split-string playing. The first, crosspicking, adapted Earl Scruggs's three-finger banjo licks to mandolin, using a straight pick instead of fingers. The second technique involved a complicated fingernail fretting that allowed the musician to introduce additional harmonies into his songs. According to Marilyn Kochman in *The Big Book of Bluegrass,* these innovations of Jesse's "tremendously expanded the capabilities of the mandolin by adding new dimensions to its sound."

Big Break

The band was quite prosperous by 1952, but history intervened. Jesse was drafted for military service in the Korean War. Shortly after his discharge two years later, the brothers earned a contract with radio station WWVA in Wheeling, West Virginia, where they played as Jim and Jesse and the Virginia Boys. WWVA had a strong signal, and sent its bluegrass music to an ever-growing audience throughout the South. This exposure led to the biggest break for the McReynolds brothers—a sponsorship by Martha White Flour, the company that made Flatt & Scruggs famous. The brothers and their group began appearing occasionally on the Grand Ole Opry. During this period the sidemen included Don McHan on guitar, Bobby Thompson on banjo and the talented Vassar Clements on fiddle.

Jim and Jesse and the Virginia Boys were poised to capitalize on the major revival of interest in bluegrass during the early to mid-1960s. They cut several quality albums with the Starday label, including *Country Express* and *Bluegrass Hall of Fame,* and were able to move to the Columbia label under its country subsidiary, Epic. Several of their best Epic albums are still available, most notably *Bluegrass Classics.* The group was also asked to perform at the prestigious Newport Folk Festival in 1963 and 1966. The brothers' greatest honor came in 1964, however, when they were invited to become regulars on the Grand Ole Opry, the summit of success for any country or bluegrass band.

Under the influence of their Opry stints, Jim and Jesse began to perform more in the country vein in the mid-1960s. They had their biggest hit with a song in this style, "Diesel on My Tail," which made it into the country Top Ten. The advent of summer bluegrass festivals in the early 1970s opened up new markets for their traditional work and they returned to classic bluegrass. Their later lineup included Keith McReynolds, one of Jesse's sons, on electric bass.

Returned to Their Classic Sound

In the Tradition, their 1988 release, featured a reunion with banjo wizard Allen Shelton, who had left the band more than 20 years before, to pursue a career as a pipefitter. The album also enlisted the artistry of Glen Duncan on fiddle, Roy Huskey on bass, and Charlie Collins on guitar. Critics were thrilled with the collaboration. *Victory Review* called the album "a clear and successful effort to recreate their classic sound," and *Bluegrass* magazine concluded that it was "such a rich experience that it is difficult for the reviewer to even begin to discuss it."

Jim and Jesse celebrated 25 years on the Grand Ole Opry in 1989 by recording *Music Among Friends,* an album of previously unreleased material. The brothers were joined on the album by a stellar cast of bluegrass and country artists including, Porter Waggoner, Emmylou Harris, Bill Monroe, and Ricky Scaggs.

In 1994, Bear Family Records released *Bluegrass and More,* a compilation of 136 recordings that the McReynolds made for Epic Records between 1960 and 1969. The five-disc CD set spans Jim and Jesse's entire career and covers the diversity of their early experimentation with mainstream country, vocals, and instrumentals as well as bluegrass and gospel. Included in the discography is "Berry Pickin' in the Country," their 1965 album of Chuck Berry classics, and their Top 20 hit, "Diesel on My Tail."

Although the group has undergone numerous personnel and recording label changes in its forty-plus-year existence, the bond between the McReynolds brothers appears as strong as ever. Jesse told Marilyn Kochman that he thinks the band has survived because he respectfully defers to his brother when the two disagree. "We compromise a lot with each other," he said. "When two people get together to do an arrangement, someone has to give somewhere. It's easier for one leader of a band to work at things than for two."

Jim and Jesse have had a profound influence on the younger generation of bluegrass musicians. They have been a vital link between the original bluegrass bands of Bill Monroe and Flatt & Scruggs and the current crop of newgrass innovators. According to Bill C. Malone in *Country Music U.S.A.,* Jim and Jesse have achieved fame as much for their beautiful vocals as for their pioneering instrumental work. Malone concludes: "Jim and Jesse brought a mellow, soft tone to bluegrass singing, and a receptivity to songs from other genres, that gave them an audience which extended well beyond the borders of their adopted musical field."

Selected discography

20 Great Songs by Jim and Jesse, Capitol.
Country Express, Starday.
Bluegrass Hall of Fame, Starday.
Bluegrass Special, Epic.
Bluegrass Classics, Epic.
Berry Pickin' in the Country, Epic.
Diesel on My Tail, Epic.
Jim and Jesse, Epic.
Bluegrass, Epic.
Old Country Church, Epic.
Country Music and Bluegrass at Newport, Vanguard.
Sacred Songs of the Virginia Trio, Double J Productions.
Country Express, Starday.
Homeland Harmony, Double J Productions.
Music Among Friends, Rounder.
Bluegrass and More (compilation), Bear Family, 1994.

Also recorded *All-Time Great Instrumentals, Saluting the Louvin Brothers, We Like Trains, Mandolin Workshop Hilltop, Jim and Jesse Today,* and *Y'All Come! Bluegrass Humor With Jim and Jesse and the Virginia Boys.*

Jesse McReynolds has also issued solo recordings, including *Jesse McReynolds: Me and My Fiddles,* Atteiram, and *Jesse's Guitar Pickin' Showcase,* Double J Productions.

Sources

Books

The Big Book of Bluegrass, edited by Marilyn Kochman, Morrow, 1984.
Illustrated Encyclopedia of Country Music, Harmony, 1977.
Malone, Bill C., *Country Music U.S.A.,* revised edition, University of Texas Press, 1985.
Shestack, Melvin, *The Country Music Encyclopedia,* Crowell, 1974.
Stambler, Irwin, and Grelun Landon, *The Encyclopedia of Folk, Country, and Western Music,* St. Martin's, 1969.

Periodicals

Billboard, February 20, 1988.
Bluegrass, February 1988.
Boston Globe, October 24, 1991.
Boston Herald, December 27, 1991.

Country Music, November/December 1992; March/April 1994.
Country Music Roundup, July 1991.
Victory Review, April 1988.

Additional information for this profile was obtained from Rounder Records publicity materials.

—*Anne Janette Johnson*

Meat Loaf

Singer

Photograph by Brian Smith/Outline, courtesy of MCA Records

Some folks say they dubbed Marvin Lee Aday "Meat Loaf" after he stepped on the foot of his high school football coach in 1961 in his home town of Dallas, Texas. Others say the big guy had already won the Meat Loaf moniker by the time he was in seventh grade and weighed over 240 pounds.

Perhaps the uncertainty stems from Meat's own hazy memory of his youth—for which he blames family circumstances. His mother died of cancer when Meat was only 15. Following the funeral, Meat Loaf's dad, an alcoholic, "flipped out" and came at his oversized offspring with a butcher knife. After this incident, Meat Loaf swapped Dallas for Los Angeles. Unlike the character Meat Loaf played in the 1980 movie *Roadie*—a roadie who hated to leave Texas—Meat never looked back.

By 1967 Meat had formed the L.A. band Meat Loaf Soul, later changed to Popcorn Blizzard. Despite opening for the likes of The Who, Iggy Pop, and the brothers Winter, two years later Meat was working as a parking lot attendant. On the job, he met an actor who encouraged him to try out for *Hair,* a musical that has provided many a talent with their first role in music showbiz. Meat landed the role of Ulysses S. Grant. This was the first of many "big" roles for the massive musician—for example, the 1972 casting of Meat as Buddha in a musical called *Rainbow.*

Thus it was as a musical actor, not a band vocalist, that Meat Loaf came to the attention of Jim Steinman, a man who would make Meat Loaf as popular as the dish he was named after. Steinman had written *More Than You Deserve,* a 1974 off-Broadway musical featuring Meat Loaf and had also worked extensively with New York theater producer Joseph Papp. In the next couple of years, Meat Loaf continued his Broadway work playing Eddie and Dr. Scott in *The Rocky Horror Picture Show,* later appearing in the cult film as well.

Went Mobile with *Bat*

Meat and Steinman hit it off and toured together with the National Lampoon Road Show in 1975. Joining up again a year later, the pair settled down in New York's Ansonia Hotel. There the duo began a year-long rehearsal of songs, some of which Steinman had written for the musical *Never Land,* a futuristic version of Peter Pan. Meat, surely an unlikely Pan, bellowed Steinman's grandiose lyrics on his first solo album, the 1977 phenomenon *Bat Out of Hell.* After various deals had fallen through, Todd Rundgren had produced the album for Epic.

For the Record . . .

Born Marvin Lee Aday, September 27, 1947, Dallas, TX.

Formed group Meat Loaf Soul (name later changed to Popcorn Blizzard), 1967; began collaboration with Jim Steinman on *Stoney and Meat Loaf,* Rare Earth, 1971; released debut solo album, *Bat Out of Hell,* 1977; rejoined Jim Steinman and released *Bat Out of Hell II: Back Into Hell,* 1993. Appeared in musicals on stage and screen, late 1970s—; film appearances include *The Rocky Horror Picture Show, Roadie,* and *Wayne's World.*

Addresses: *Record company*—MCA Records, 70 Universal City Plaza, Universal City, CA 91608.

To drum up interest in *Bat,* Meat toured the country with a seven-piece band and feisty Karla De Vito singing the female parts of what was essentially a teen opera. The song "Paradise by the Dashboard Light" typified *Bat*'s theme of teenage sexuality. America loved it; the bulging bard's album sat on the charts for over a year and a half, though it never broke into the Top Ten. And in the U.K. the album hit Number Nine and sold over two million copies during an eye-popping 395-week chart stay.

The only major U.S. city failing to fall under Meat Loaf's spell was Los Angeles—ironically the city where Meat began his rock and roll career after seeking refuge from his grief-crazed, cleaver-wielding pop. L.A.'s top radio stations declared the bulky balladeer wasn't right for their audiences. According to a 1978 article in *Rolling Stone,* that left Steinman "pissed off," for he'd written *Bat* as a righteous rock and roll attack on "L.A. music" poseurs like Rod Stewart, Fleetwood Mac, and the Eagles.

Meat Loaf Pinched

By the early nineties *Bat* had sold over 30 million copies world wide. But according to Steinman, since 1980 neither of its creators had seen one penny in royalties apparently due to legal squabbles. Meat lost his voice following the *Bat* tour, or at least claimed he'd lost it. He did manage to croak out a second album, also Steinman written, *Dead Ringer,* but this 1981 effort fell flat except for a couple of weeks at the top of the U.K. charts. The song from which the album took its name was a duet with Cher.

Impatient with the fame-troubled Meat, Steinman turned to other artists, drafting the lyrics and producing Bonnie Tyler's Number One *Total Eclipse of the Heart.* Meanwhile, Meat was sinking under the weight of his load. "Everyone wanted a little piece," a 1983 Billboard article quoted the artist. One might have thought there was enough Meat to go around, but apparently not and he retreated within himself, lubricating the path with a nine-month booze bender. Lawsuits sprang like mousetraps. Sued by his publisher, manager, and others in 22 separate suits totaling 85 million, Meat Loaf attempted to get out from under by declaring bankruptcy in 1983.

That same year the swollen songster's *Midnight at the Lost and Found* appeared without evoking much U.S. interest. The title seemed autobiographical, for Meat was down in the dumps. And it took four sessions a week of psychotherapy for a year to haul him back out. The mid-eighties were a doldrums for the Meat Loaf. The 1985 album Bad *Attitude* and 1986's *Blind Before I Stop*—both efforts without Steinman—fared worse than *Midnight.*

Bat II a Commercial Success

In 1988 Meat Loaf began a public Ultra Slim-Fast diet. Shortly after this, Steinman and Meat made up. Not that the weight loss drew Steinman; indeed, as the two geared up in 1991 to record *Bat Out of Hell II,* Steinman left trails of doughnuts around the studio in hopes of returning Meat Loaf to his former glory. Perhaps the composer was a little unsure just why the first *Bat* had done so well and didn't want to take chances. The weight loss didn't hurt Meat's film career—subsequent efforts included roles in *Wayne's World* and *Leap of Faith.*

MCA Music Entertainment Group signed up the pair but found themselves up against a decidedly unvisionary, "Are these guys kidding attitude?" according to a 1993 article in *Entertainment Weekly.* MCA embarked on an exhaustive marketing campaign of radio stations, record stores, and MTV for months before the record release. Despite negative reviews—one writer characterizing *Bat II* as 75 minutes of "operatic drivel"—the work paid off. The album contained such Steinman compositions as "Objects in the Rear View Mirror May Appear Closer Than They Are," an automotive ditty that lasted over ten minutes but lacked the sexual content of "Paradise By the Dashboard Lights."

New York Times critic Jon Pareles, reviewing a *Bat II* promotional concert, saw Meat as "the hulking everyman." Watching this self-proclaimed sex god mugging and singing to the pretty back-up singer suggested to Pareles the myth of Beauty and the Beast. Perhaps, concluded the critic, Meat gives his audience hope for themselves.

Apparently it gave them something, for Meat and Steinman had on their hands a comeback unique in the annals of rock history. As *Bat II* advertising boasted: "Number One in 20 countries ... Standing Room Only World-Wide Tour ... Madison Square Garden sold out in 90 minutes." Meat Loaf had dislodged another big one. Perhaps no other artist has so clearly demonstrated that success will come if you keep pushing.

Selected discography

Stoney and Meat Loaf, Rare Earth, 1971, reissued as *Meat Loaf (Featuring Stoney),* Prodigal/Motown, 1979.
Bat Out of Hell, (includes "Paradise By the Dashboard Lights"), Epic 1977.
Dead Ringer, Sony, 1981.
Midnight at the Lost and Found, Epic, 1983.
Bad Attitude, RCA, 1985.
Blind Before I Stop, Atlantic, 1986.
Bat Out of Hell II: Back Into Hell, (includes "Objects in the Mirror May Appear Larger Than They Are"), MCA 1993.

Sources

Books

Pareles, Jon, and Patricia Romanowski, *The Rolling Stone Encyclopedia of Rock & Roll,* Rolling Stone Press/Summit Books, 1983.
Rees, Dafydd, and Luke Crampton, *Rock Movers & Shakers,* Billboard Books, 1991.
Stambler, Irwin, *Encyclopedia of Pop Rock & Roll,* St. Martin's Press, 1989.

Periodicals

Billboard, August 27, 1983.
Entertainment Weekly, October 15, 1993.
New York Times, September 15, 1993; September 15, 1993.
People, December 20, 1993.
Rolling Stone, November 16, 1978; October 28, 1993.

—*Joseph M. Reiner*

Melanie

Singer, songwriter

Courtesy of Lonestar Records

Folk singer-songwriter Melanie recorded her first album in 1967 and attracted national attention as well as a loyal fan following two years later when she performed at Woodstock, the legendary rock festival. During the early 1970s, Melanie's gentle, acoustic sound on songs like "Lay Down," "Beautiful People," and "Brand New Key" was in sharp contrast to the hard-driving, heavy-metal rock that dominated the charts. Edwin Miller of *Seventeen* magazine observed that her "urgent ballads bind you to her with invisible threads of emotion."

Melanie was born Melanie Safka on February 3, 1947, in Queens, New York. Her mother was a blues singer at the local clubs who fostered a love of music in her daughter and entered her in area talent contests. "My mother always encouraged me," Melanie recalled to Miller. At age four, Melanie made her professional debut on a radio show called "Live Like a Millionaire," where she sang and played the ukelele.

When Melanie was a teenager, the family moved to southern New Jersey, where despite her mother's blues influence, she was drawn to the New York folk scene and the music of artists Pete Seeger and Woody Guthrie. At age 16, Melanie was hired to sing at a local club where, she told Miller, "I worked Monday nights. I would sing all the Peter, Paul and Mary songs, four and five hours, for $20." After graduating from high school, she enrolled at the New York Academy of Dramatic Arts, but continued to ply her musical trade in the coffee houses of Greenwich Village.

Though the young thespian enjoyed her drama studies, she found it extremely difficult to audition for acting jobs. "I was always simply too afraid to get up and say 'this is what I am,'" she confessed in *Seventeen*. "So I would sit there, reading the theatrical trade papers. Descriptions of the people wanted never [fit] me." She did manage to secure an acting role, but due to lack of funds, the play was never produced.

Melanie signed with a music publishing company and was assigned to producer Peter Schekeryk, whom she later married. In 1967 she landed a recording contract with Columbia Records. Her first single, "Beautiful People," became a moderate hit, but Melanie was dissatisfied with Columbia and switched to the Buddha label, where she recorded the album *Born to Be,* which contained 1969's smash hit "Look What They've Done to My Song, Ma."

That same year, Melanie was invited to play at the now-historic rock festival, Woodstock. Decades later, she reminisced about the event for *Rolling Stone:* "It was magical. I had never performed in front of so many

For the Record...

Born Melanie Safka, February 3, 1947, in Queens, NY; daughter of Fred (a retailer) and Polly (a singer) Safka; married Peter Schekeryk (a record producer) c. 1970; children: Leilah, Jeordie (daughter), Beau. *Education:* Attended the American Academy of Dramatic Arts and the Penland School of Crafts.

Sang in local clubs in the Long Branch, NJ, area beginning at age 16; signed recording contract with Columbia Records, 1967; performer at Woodstock music festival, 1969; took sabbatical from recording and performing, 1972-75; released critically acclaimed album, *Photograph,* 1975; released one more album, 1978, before retiring until 1993.

Awards: Selected top female vocalist of 1970 by *Billboard, Bravo, Cashbox,* and *Melody Maker;* Emmy Award (with composer Lee Holdridge), 1989, for lyrics to "The First Time I Loved Forever," theme song of television series *Beauty and the Beast.*

Addresses: *Office*—53 Baymont, Suite 5, Clearwater Beach, FL 34630. *Record company*—Lonestar Records, 519 Cleveland St., Suite 209, Clearwater Beach, FL 34615.

---

people in my life. I had my first out-of-body experience. I was terrified, I had to leave. I started across that bridge to the stage, and I just left my body.... I watched myself walk onto the stage, sit down and sing a couple of lines. And when I felt it was safe, I came back." Performing at Woodstock inspired Melanie to write and record her 1970 peace anthem "Lay Down"—subtitled "Candles in the Rain." She told *Rolling Stone:* "It started to rain right before I went on and the announcer said that if you lit candles, it would help to keep the rain away. By the time I finished my set, the whole hillside was a mass of little flickering lights."

Candle-lighting fans became a feature of Melanie's concerts, sometimes leading to trouble with authorities because of the potential fire hazard. She released *Candles in the Rain* in 1970. Six months later the album reached platinum status and earned her "top female vocalist of the year" awards from *Billboard, Melody Maker, Bravo,* and *Cashbox.*

In 1971 Melanie's tribute to roller skating, "Brand New Key," reached Number One on the pop charts, but critics were less than enthused with the cute, inane ditty. They were no more impressed with her 1972 follow-up, "The Nickel Song." Disillusioned by the unkind reviews, Melanie took a respite from music and focused her attentions on her family. She returned in 1975 on the Atlantic label with *Photograph,* an album that was, ironically, praised by the critics and virtually ignored by the public. In 1978, she released the album *Phonogenic, Not Just Another Pretty Face,* for Midsong International, before once again retiring from the music business.

Melanie eventually returned to the studio and recorded several albums throughout the 1980s. She sang her critically-panned "Brand New Key" in a television commercial for the Fisher-Price Toy Company. In 1989 she went on the road with the Woodstock Reunion Tour, which traveled through the United States and Europe. Melanie was also honored with an Emmy Award for penning the lyrics to "The First Time I Loved Forever," theme song of the award-winning television series *Beauty and the Beast.*

Though Melanie continued to release albums for the European market, it was nearly a decade before she recorded her next domestic album, *Freedom Knows My Name,* released in 1993. The recording was a family affair; produced by her husband, Peter Schekeryk, and recorded on his company label, Lonestar Records, the album features back-up vocals by all three of their children (who also tour with Melanie). Critics were divided on the album's merit, with *Entertainment Weekly* calling it a "tepid release, stuck in Woodstock-era reverie," and Philadelphia's *Daily Local News* concluding it was "full of vital, fresh tunes which hold up in the '90s."

Melanie's schedule remained full in 1994. She continued work on an unplugged album commemorating her 25 years as a recording artist, and had scheduled concerts throughout the United States and Europe. She was also slated to appear at "Bethany '94," a musical celebration of Woodstock's silver anniversary, to be held at the festival's original site. In spite of her strong ties with the past, Melanie has always had her sights set squarely on the future. "When people want to talk only about the good old days," she explained to *People,* "there's this horrible implication that you're nothing now. But I know I'm *better* than I used to be."

Selected discography

Melanie, Columbia, c. 1967.
Born to Be, Buddha, c. 1969.
Candles in the Rain, Buddha, 1970.
Leftover Wine, Buddha, 1970.

The Good Book, Buddha, 1971.
Gather Me, Neighborhood, 1971, reissued, C5, 1993.
Garden in the City, Buddha, c. 1972.
Four Sides of Melanie, Buddha, c. 1972.
Stoneground Words, Neighborhood, 1972.
Photograph, Atlantic, 1975.
Phonogenic, Not Just Another Pretty Face, Midsong International, 1978.
Freedom Knows My Name, Lonestar, 1993.

Sources

Daily Local News (Philadelphia), February 19, 1994.
Entertainment Weekly, January 14, 1994.
People, July 27, 1992.
Redbook, September 1972.
Rolling Stone, August 24, 1989.
Seventeen, June 1971.

—Elizabeth Wenning

Moby Grape

Rock band

"Columbia Records is devoting prime promotion time to the buildup of a new rock 'n' roll group from San Francisco called the Moby Grape," reported *Billboard* on June 6, 1967. "The campaign got under way last week with the unprecedented simultaneous release of five singles and one album." In retrospect the announcement reads like an optimistic forecast for the doomed Hindenburg zeppelin, because Columbia's full-scale hype contributed to the band's premature burnout.

After releasing a debut album that critics in the ensuing decades have come to regard as a classic, Moby Grape fizzled out and seemed destined to appear as a mere footnote to rock history. Yet critical respect and an enduring following among musicians and other fans kept their reputation alive, and the 1993 release of *Vintage,* a CD boxed set, promised to teach a new generation of listeners what all the hoopla was about.

"The Grape's sound was an ahead-of-its-time aural stew of blues and country and soul and rock and jazz and psychedelia dished out with a breathless ensemble approach that was almost proto-punk in its intensity and with high-lonesome neo-Everly Brothers vocals on top," wrote Steve Simels of *Stereo Review*. David Fricke, in the liner notes accompanying *Vintage,* deemed the group "the kind of do-it-all combo that comes along only once or twice in a rock & roll generation."

Yet if they were a band that "had it all," as Simels claimed, they were also a band that lost it all. The loss of the legal rights to the name Moby Grape and to their recordings—not to mention two members' affliction with severe mental problems—hampered most efforts at reconstruction; several reunions featuring various founding members under a variety of names have transpired over the years. Yet the spirit that animated the Grape's debut album still burned in its founders well into the 1990s.

Showed Promise Early On

The group formed in San Francisco in 1966. It consisted of guitarist Peter Lewis, the son of film star Loretta Young and alumnus of the band Peter and the Wolves; bassist Bob Mosley, formerly of San Diego; lead guitar veteran Jerry Miller and drummer Don Stevenson, refugees from Washington state who'd played with Mosley in their transplanted San Francisco group the Frantics; and Canadian-born guitarist Alexander "Skip" Spence, who'd played drums with the Jefferson Airplane, a band later to become one of the region's best-known musical exports.

For the Record...

Members include **Peter Lewis** (born July 15, 1945, in Los Angeles, CA), guitar and vocals; **Jerry Miller** (born July 10, 1943, in Tacoma, WA), guitar and vocals; **Bob Mosley** (born December 4, 1942, in Paradise Valley, CA; left band 1969 and rejoined in 1971), bass and vocals; **Alexander "Skip" Spence** (born April 18, 1946, in Windsor, Canada; left group 1968 and rejoined periodically), guitar and vocals; and **Don Stevenson** (born October 15, 1942, in Seattle, WA), drums and vocals.

Group formed in San Francisco, 1966; signed with Columbia Records and released debut, 1967; Spence diagnosed as schizophrenic and hospitalized after breakdown, 1968; Spence recorded solo album, *Oar*, 1969; Mosley left band to join Marine Corps, 1969; group broke up in 1969 and re-formed without Spence for *20 Granite Creek*, Reprise; lost rights to name and royalties, 1973; re-formed in various combinations and under various names for independent labels, including 1990 cassette release *The Melvilles*.

Addresses: *Record company*—Herman Records, P.O. Box 1947, Cave Junction, OR 97523.

While they were all talented players and songwriters, Spence radiated a special quality that seemed to lie behind his brilliant, offbeat compositions as well as his later disintegration. "Skippy was always 'high' on this other level," Lewis told Fricke. "His mind was always churning over with stuff. It was hard for him to sit and talk. He didn't deal in words, but in ideas. Yet he was an inspiration, always able to get people going on his trip." Lewis added that Spence "was the most unique songwriter I'd ever heard." He had a lot of competition in his own band, however, and with Mosley's ferocious, bluesy singing, Miller's stinging lead guitar, and the whole group's evanescent harmonies—not to mention good looks—Moby Grape seemed destined for superstardom.

Mosley came up with the name, which served as the punchline to a popular absurdist joke, "What's purple and swims in the ocean?" The grim resonances of *Moby Dick*, Herman Melville's novel about an obsessed sea captain's pursuit of the white whale that eventually sinks his ship, would not make themselves apparent until later. The quintet set up in a Sausalito, California, club called the Ark and began rehearsing on a regular work-week schedule. After a while, Fricke wrote, Moby Grape "went from being an extraordinary collision of strangers to the tightest, most talked-about band in San Francisco."

At a time when onstage diffidence, spacey, ponderous compositions, and an open contempt for "show business" were expected on the rock scene, they played carefully honed and energetic pop. As Simels of *Stereo Review* reflected years later, "the Grape differed from the rest of the Bay Area bands by playing mostly concise, singles-oriented rock-and-roll and openly aspiring to pop stardom, neither tendency exactly PC [politically correct]."

Disasters Followed Debut

Moby Grape's marathon rehearsals drew other local musicians, many of whom jammed with the group, and a growing number of music industry representatives. The band's obvious potential led to a bidding war won by Columbia Records. The agent of their signing—and, inadvertently, their near-destruction—was producer David Rubinson, who worked for the company. "I came out to San Francisco in December 1966, a month before [counterculture milestone] the Human Be-In," he told the authors of *Bill Graham Presents: My Life Inside Rock and Out*. "The best band out here then was Moby Grape. Bar *none*." The *Vintage* booklet cites Rubinson's hopes for the quintet: "When I first saw them play, I knew that this was a band that could go around the country, around the world, and really *kill*."

After signing Moby Grape in 1967, Rubinson brought them into the studio. He oversaw the album-making process carefully, focusing on potential singles at the expense of the members' more experimental side. Yet he helped capture the effervescence and invention of the group, and the result was, in Fricke's words, "that rarest of rock artifacts, the Perfect Debut Album." Simels insisted in 1978 that "no collection of American music, let alone rock-and-roll, is complete without it."

With songs like Mosley's barnburning "Mr. Blues," Lewis's melancholy "Sitting By the Window," and Spence's "Omaha," it reflected the talents of each player and formed a coherent document. Fricke dubbed the latter song "arguably Moby Grape's finest two-and-a-half minutes on record, the absolute distillation of everything that made them great, and should have made them famous." He added that the song "was the Beatles on speed, at once demonic, ravishing and irresistible."

Rubinson sold Columbia's promotional machine on the album only too well. The label released five singles at once, giving radio programmers too much to choose from and diluting the focus that usually characterizes an aggressive album promotion. A small furor erupted when Columbia discovered belatedly that Stevenson was sticking up his middle finger in the cover photo; subsequent airbrushing failed to suppress the controversy. Other disasters followed, most notably a release party at the Avalon Ballroom. Ten thousand purple orchids were dropped from the ceiling and had roughly the same effect as banana peels on the floor. Bottles of wine with "Moby Grape" labels sat unopened because someone forgot the corkscrews.

To top things off, Miller, Lewis, and Spence were arrested after the party for marijuana possession and for contributing to the delinquency of minors. Though Moby Grape retained some momentum, it was clear that things were happening too fast; they were expected to be superstars together without having come up together. As Stevenson remarked to Fricke, "It was like the bell that signalled us out of the gate was the death knell."

Failed to Wow

Moby Grape's jinxed beginning was soon followed by more trouble. *Wow,* released in 1968, featured one track—Spence's trippily nostalgic "Just Like Gene Autry: A Foxtrot"—that could only be played at 78 r.p.m. and a bonus album of lengthy improvisations called *Grape Jam.* It fared poorly. Skip Spence, meanwhile, had become seriously unbalanced and was briefly institutionalized; *Rolling Stone* translated Stevenson's phrase "psychological breakdown" as "a freakout." Spence left the group that year to record his solo opus *Oar,* which Mike Mettler of *Guitar Player* called "a textbook example of how to record the disintegration of a mind."

Moby Grape continued as a quartet; after an exceptional performance at a Philadelphia pop festival they knew they could survive as a band. They bought houses near one another in Boulder Creek, California, rehearsing on Stevenson's porch. Thus the four got to become friends more naturally, and wrote the material for *Moby Grape '69.* The album represented a partial recovery, but as Miller told Fricke, "the magic didn't happen."

The same was true, only more so, for *Truly Fine Citizen,* recorded without Mosley, who quit the group to join the Marine Corps. Lamented *Rolling Stone*'s Ben Gibson, a huge fan of the debut, "I couldn't believe my ears. I hadn't heard in months a more complacent, pathetic LP." The review ended by suggesting that perhaps the time had come for the band "to call it a day." And they did, breaking up just after its release.

The first Moby Grape "reunion" came with 1971's *20 Granite Creek,* which marked the return of Mosley and—for one instrumental track—Spence. It earned the approval of *Rolling Stone,* but wasn't a harbinger of great things to come: the group broke up again. Another reunion was planned but in 1974 the group found out that former manager Matthew Katz owned the rights to the name.

> "When I first saw them play, I knew that this was a band that could go around the country, around the world, and really kill."
> —David Rubinson

To add insult to injury, Katz assembled a group of unknowns that performed and even recorded as Moby Grape. The original members therefore performed under names like Maby Grope, Legendary Grape, and the Melvilles and released a cassette-only album in 1990 that Fricke considered "the closest thing to a real second album as the band has ever made." Miller's band continued to play, occasionally with Lewis and Stevenson, but Spence and Mosley suffered recurrences of their problems—both had been diagnosed as schizophrenic—and were, as *Guitar Player*'s Mettler explained, "at best regretfully described as 'itinerant.'"

Though the 1993 release of *Vintage* was described by Simels as "the rock reissue of the year," *Entertainment Weekly* reported that the boxed set would provide no royalties for the members since "the rights to their songs and even their name were signed away in a 1973 settlement without the band's knowledge," as a lawsuit filed on their behalf against Sony Music claimed. The article ended with Spence, who'd been under supervision in Northern California, hoping to "get Mosley and bring him in"; the bassist was reportedly living without shelter in San Diego. As Spence said in a 1968 *Jazz & Pop* interview before his breakdown, "All we have is each other, really—that's the nitty gritty basics. The rest of it goes, comes and goes—that's all we have, and that's the key."

The music, meanwhile, had finally achieved the recognition that had been forestalled the by the group's career woes. Celebrated musicians like Led Zeppelin singer Robert Plant and the Doobie Brothers had praised them publicly, and Michael Stipe, lead singer of alternative heroes-turned-superstars R.E.M. covered "Omaha" with the group the Golden Palominos.

Chrissie Hynde, whose group the Pretenders served up a mix of raw energy, pop smarts, and soul akin to the Grape's, told *Rolling Stone* in 1994 that she listened to their debut "a couple of hundred times in 1969, but when I heard it again [recently], it blew my mind. I realize[d] how very influenced I was by it. It's been in my subconscious the whole time." As Simels observed of the boxed set, "It's hard to imagine anybody hearing it without concluding that this was a very major band indeed. Not to mention a quintessentially American one."

Selected discography

On Columbia, unless otherwise noted

Moby Grape (includes "Hey Grandma," "Mr. Blues," "Sitting By the Window," "Indifference" and "Omaha"), 1967.
Wow (includes *Grape Jam* and "Just Like Gene Autry: A Foxtrot"), 1968.
Moby Grape '69, 1969.
Truly Fine Citizen, 1969.
20 Granite Creek, Reprise, 1971.
Live Grape, Escape, 1978.
Legendary Grape (cassette only), Herman Records, 1990.
Vintage: The Very Best of Moby Grape, Sony, 1993.

Solo and other recordings

Skip Spence, *Oar,* 1969.
Bob Mosley, *Bob Mosley,* Reprise, 1972.
Mosley and Jerry Miller, *Fine Wine* (released in Germany only), 1975.

Sources

Books

Graham, Bill, and Robert Greenfield, *Bill Graham Presents: My Life Inside Rock and Out,* Doubleday, 1992.
Rees, Dafydd, and Luke Campton, *Rock Movers and Shakers,* Billboard Books, 1991.
The Rolling Stone Illustrated Encyclopedia of Rock & Roll, Rolling Stone Press/Summit Books, 1983.

Periodicals

Billboard, June 17, 1967; October 26, 1968.
Entertainment Weekly, March 4, 1994.
Guitar Player, January 1994.
Jazz & Pop, May 1968.
L.A. Weekly, March 25, 1994.
People, June 21, 1993.
Rolling Stone, June 28, 1969; October 18, 1969; October 14, 1971; November 15, 1990; January 27, 1994.
Stereo Review, December 1972; April 1978; May 1993.

Additional information for this profile was provided by the liner notes to *Vintage,* written by David Fricke, 1993.

—*Simon Glickman*

Yves Montand

Singer, actor

Archive Photos

Yves Montand was Italian by birth, but he nonetheless came to represent the quintessential Frenchman: charming, politically outspoken, and possessing an air that was world-weary but at the same time lighthearted. Shifting effortlessly between the stage and screen throughout his career, he distinguished himself both as a singer and as an actor capable of playing a wide range of roles. In addition to his professional efforts, Montand drew much attention for his association with controversial political causes, as well as for his involvement with some of the world's most desirable women. So respected and popular was he in France that in the 1980s he was urged to run for public office. The London *Times* reported his response to that call: "[U.S. president Ronald] Reagan stood because he was a bad actor. Since I'm a good one, I won't."

Montand was taken to the south of France shortly after his birth, when his father, the owner of a broom factory, was threatened by the fascists then gaining power in Italy. Growing up in a poor suburb of Marseilles, Montand was a mediocre student, and his formal education was cut short when the family's financial troubles forced him to go to work full time at age 11.

He continued to work hard throughout his adolescence, finding relief from the burdens of everyday life in the local movie theater, which featured American comedies, musicals, and Westerns. In that theater, his dream to become a performer was born, and before he was 18 years old, he had made his debut at a local amateur night with an act that included imitations of Donald Duck and Maurice Chevalier. By 1939, he had graduated to the respectable Alhambra Theatre in Marseilles and an act with a Wild West theme.

World War II interrupted his career briefly, but by February, 1944, Montand had reached the ABC music hall in Paris, where his cowboy songs were again a success. Within a few months, he had become the lover of legendary French chanteuse Edith Piaf—as well as her protege. She convinced him to drop his cowboy image and provided him with a more romantic, poetic repertoire of songs, which he performed in his first one-man show at the Theatre de l'Etoile in October, 1945. French critics responded enthusiastically, proclaiming Montand to be a major new star.

Piaf continued to boost Montand's career, providing him with his first screen role in *Etoile sans lumiere* in 1946. That same year, he starred in *Les Portes de la nuit,* a musical that failed miserably at the box office but provided Montand with a song that remained his trademark throughout his career—Jacques Prevert's "Feuilles mortes" ("Autumn Leaves").

> **For the Record...**
>
> Born Yvo (some sources say Ivo) Livi, October 3, 1921, in Monsummano Alto, Italy; died November 9, 1991; changed name to Yves Montand c. 1930; son of Giovanni (a broom maker) and Giuseppina Livi; married Simone Signoret (an actress), December 22, 1951; children: Catherine Allegret (adopted stepdaughter), Valentin (son, with Carole Amiel).
>
> Singer and actor. Worked variously in a pasta factory, a metal factory, a beauty salon, and on the docks; performed as a singer, Marseilles, France, during the 1930s; debuted at ABC music hall, Paris, France, 1944; first one-man show at Theatre de l'Etoile, Paris, October, 1945; made film debut in *Etoile sans lumiere* ("Star Without Light"), 1946; appeared in 54 films, including *Le Salaire de la peur* ("The Wages of Fear"), 1953, *Let's Make Love*, 1960, *Sanctuary*, 1961, *My Geisha*, 1962, *Compartiment tueurs* ("The Sleeping Car Murders"), 1965, *Paris brule-ti-il?* ("Is Paris Burning?"), 1966, *La Guerre est finie* ("The War Is Over"), 1966, *Z*, 1969, *L'Aveu* ("The Confession"), 1970, *On a Clear Day You Can See Forever*, 1970, *Etat de siege* ("State of Siege"), 1973, *Cesar and Rosalie*, 1972, *Garcon!*, 1983, *Jean de Florette*, 1986, and *Manon des Sources* ("Manon of the Springs"), 1986.
>
> **Awards:** New York Film Critics Circle Award for best actor, 1966, for *The War Is Over*.

Upon his return to the Theatre de l'Etoile for another engagement in 1946, Montand was acknowledged as one of the most popular performers in France, but his career took a temporary nosedive shortly after that engagement, when Piaf broke her liaison with him. For many months he toured the provinces, uncertain of what his life held next. Then in August of 1949, he met the next woman who would further his success—actress Simone Signoret, then married to director Yves Allegret.

Signoret and Montand began a tempestuous affair that led to their marriage in 1951. The actress was, by Montand's own admission, much more culturally and politically aware than he, and he became her willing pupil, taking part in ban-the-bomb appeals and other leftist political activities. Their refusal to denounce the Communist Party (of which neither was a member) effectively barred them from entering the United States during the McCarthy era.

During 1950 and 1951, Montand made a musical tour of Europe and North Africa, then returned to the screen to play a radical driving through Central America with a truck full of nitroglycerine in the thriller *Salaire de la peur* (*The Wages of Fear*). That role established him as a serious actor, and he followed it with an acclaimed performance in a French adaptation of Arthur Miller's *The Crucible*, which also featured Signoret.

The couple then embarked on a tour of the Soviet bloc countries, but their support for the Communists had been cooled by the Soviet invasion of Hungary, and they expressed their disapproval to each Soviet leader they met. On returning to France, Montand enjoyed a six-month engagement at the Etoile in Paris and a record-breaking tour of the provinces. Shortly thereafter, he and Signoret were cordially invited to the United States.

After six sold-out weeks at the Henry Miller Theater in New York City, Montand and his wife travelled to Hollywood, where both were wooed by American movie makers. Montand agreed to star opposite Marilyn Monroe in the musical comedy *Let's Make Love*. The film itself generated far less excitement among the public than did the brief affair that occurred between the two leads.

After appearing in several more American films during the early 1960s, Montand embarked on a musical tour of Japan, England, France, and the United States, then took on another dramatic stage role in the French version of *A Thousand Clowns*. Several films followed, and it was not until 1968 that Montand once again assumed the role of singer. The occasion was a month-long engagement in Paris. The one-man show drew raves, with critics exclaiming that Montand did nothing but improve with age. Ironically, the performance prompted Montand to give up the concert stage for some thirteen years; he was concerned that the adulation he received would destroy his ability to look at himself critically.

The late 1960s and the 1970s ushered in the peak of Montand's film career. He starred in three classic political thrillers directed by Constantin Costa-Gavras, *Z*, *L'Aveu*, and *Etat de siege*, as well as numerous other dramas, comedies, and one musical, *On a Clear Day You Can See Forever*, in which he co-starred with Barbra Streisand. He interrupted his screen work only occasionally, to stage benefit concerts for political causes. But as the 1980s dawned, he revived his singing career once again, drawing huge and surprisingly young audiences in Paris, New York, Brazil, and Japan. In 1982, his one-week run at the Metropolitan

Opera House in New York made history as the first unaccompanied solo performance ever given there by a popular singer.

Montand was preparing for yet another concert tour in the mid-1980s when he was approached by film director Claude Berri, who offered him the role of the unethical French patriarch whose schemes prove to be his own undoing in the two-part saga *Jean de Florette* and *Manon des Sources*. Montand refused at first; he was unwilling to play an old man, and eager to get on with his tour. But he reconsidered, and finally accepted what is generally regarded as the finest movie role of his career. The two films were smash hits on both sides of the Atlantic, with Montand's performance considered at least as vital as that of co-star Gerard Depardieu.

Signoret died of cancer while Montand was at work on the films, and in the wake of her death, he drove himself at a more hectic pace than ever, promoting the films, continuing his political activism, and planning a television musical. He also became romantically involved with his secretary, Carole Amiel, and in 1988, she gave birth to his first child. He was 67 years old.

Montand slowed down briefly to enjoy his son's babyhood, but by the time the child had reached the age of three, he had decided to mount a new stage show. The show was in the planning stages, and Montand was filming a new movie with director Jean-Jacques Beineix when he suffered a fatal heart attack. According to *People* contributor Marjorie Rosen, as he was en route to the hospital where he died, Montand assured the ambulance crew: "I have lived well enough to have no regrets."

Selected discography

On a Clear Day You Can See Forever (soundtrack), 1970.
Montand d'hier a aujourd'hui (includes "Montand, from Yesterday to Today").

Sources

Los Angeles Times, November 10, 1991.
Maclean's, January 4, 1988; February 22, 1988.
New York Times, September 5, 1982; October 9, 1983; May 23, 1986; October 18, 1991; November 10, 1991; June 11, 1992.
New York Times Book Review, November 15, 1992.
People, May 16, 1988; August 15, 1988; November 25, 1991.
Times (London), November 11, 1991.
Variety, December 14, 1992.
Washington Post, September 5, 1982; November 10, 1991.

—*Joan Goldsworthy*

Bill Morrissey

Singer, songwriter, guitarist

Photograph by Tim Carter, courtesy of Rounder Records

Bill Morrissey is a gravel-voiced singer-songwriter who, over the course of six albums, has established a reputation as one of folk music's most literate and compelling voices. A native of New Hampshire, Morrissey skillfully mines the terrain of that northern clime to "capture the stark hardscrabble milieus of a subterranean New England culture—rootless drifters, despondent cabbies, beery, down-on-their-luck deckhands," as Kevin Ransom noted in *Rolling Stone*. This gift, referred to by Paul Evans in *Rolling Stone* as a talent to evoke "in dead-on detail life's quiet epiphanies and small cataclysms," has garnered Morrissey considerable critical acclaim and a growing public audience.

Born in Hartford, Connecticut, in 1951, Morrissey felt an affinity for songwriting at an early age. In an interview with Ted Drozdowski for the *Boston Phoenix,* Morrissey explained that "I used to make up pop song lyrics on my way home; when friends would come over in high school, I'd say, 'Hey, let's write a song.' They didn't believe that just anybody could write songs, so I pretty much had to figure it out by myself. It was a slow process." He persevered, however, for, as he noted in an interview with *Contemporary Musicians (CM),* "I always wanted to play music. I just never thought I'd be good enough to do it for a living. I was 17 when I dropped out of college and decided that I really wanted to write songs. I had no game plan, I just knew that this is what I had to do."

Paid His Dues

Armed with a few songs, a voice that *Stereo Review* called "a cross between an old, grizzled, black bluesman and a hip, friendly bullfrog," and a determination to crack the folk music circuit, Morrissey began playing bar and coffeehouse venues, where, by his own admission, he was a loquacious sort. "I knew I wasn't the greatest singer/writer/guitarist, but ... if I was funny, I knew they'd hire me back," he told interviewer Drodzowski. "I was a basket case before every show, because I didn't have a set routine. I'd talk 15 minutes, play a song, and go back to talking. Gradually, as I learned how to deal with an audience, I played more songs."

At the same time, Morrissey continued his exploration of America's rich and varied musical landscape: In discussing his musical influences with *CM,* Morrissey cited "anything, from the Beatles—they're a textbook in arranging and harmonies—to the Delta blues guys and country blues guys. Skip James, Robert Johnson, Mississippi John Hurt. My whole right-hand style is from John Hurt." He also cited such diverse musicians as

> **For the Record...**
>
> Born Bill Thomas Morrissey, November 25, 1951, in Hartford, CT; son of Joseph (an insurance executive) and Marion Morrissey; married second wife, Ellen Karas (a manager and producer of three of his albums, including *Friend of Mine*), 1993. *Education:* Attended Plymouth State College, Plymouth, NH, late 1960s.
>
> Performed throughout New England, 1970s; signed with Rounder Records and released self-titled debut album, 1984; has recorded six albums on that label.
>
> **Awards:** Boston Music Award for best folk recording, 1989, for *Standing Eight,* and 1992, for *Inside;* Grammy Award nomination for best traditional folk recording, 1993, for *Friend of Mine.*
>
> **Addresses:** *Management*—Sage Productions, 258 Harvard St., Suite 283, Brookline, MA 02146. *Record company*—Rounder Records, One Camp St., Cambridge, MA 02140.

Bob Dylan, Jimmy Reed, Merle Haggard, and Thelonious Monk as figures who had a significant impact on his approach to music.

After a number of years of working the mill bar and coffeehouse circuit of New England, Morrissey signed with Rounder Records and recorded his self-titled debut album in 1984. Accompanied only by his acoustic guitar, Morrissey rolled out a dozen songs rich in literary detail for his first recording. Clearly, Morrissey was a new talent worth watching. His second album, *North*, continued in the same vein, relating insightful, understated tales of ordinary folks struggling with internal demons and external circumstances that often seemed to spin out of control.

While his first two albums were warmly received, it was not until the release of his third album, *Standing Eight,* that Morrissey caught the attention of the national music press. *Standing Eight* featured fuller musical arrangements; an array of guests including Suzanne Vega, Shawn Colvin, Patty Larkin, and Johnny Cunningham; and top-notch material. The album was widely regarded as a tour de force. "In remarkably compressed portraits," wrote Martha Bustin in *Rolling Stone,* "Bill Morrissey melds the vaporish world of desire with the hard-edged world of daily life." Martin Keller, writing in *Request,* called *Standing Eight* "among the best records of 1989 and... full of the minutiae that often give way to deeper meanings and harder truths."

Literary Influences

By the time he released *Standing Eight,* Morrissey's songwriting abilities were garnering increased attention not only from the musical world but also from the literary arena. His lyrics were increasingly compared to the works of fictional luminaries such as Raymond Carver and Richard Ford. Indeed, Gary Fisketjon, who served as an editor for the late Carver, and writers Jay McInerney and Ford are among Morrissey's high-profile fans.

In an interview with *CM,* Morrissey discussed his literary influences and his tastes in fiction: "I think [as a teenager] I just read the usual stuff that you read in high school. A little later, though, I discovered the Beats, Kerouac and those folks. Kerouac was from a couple towns over, in Lowell, [Massachusetts], and so I used to hear him on the radio. Allen Ginsberg had a talk show and Jack would call in.

"The French Symbolist poets—Baudelaire and Rimbaud, people like that—really got my attention as well. But I always kept going back to very American stuff. Mark Twain was a big influence. He does it all. He's funny, he's serious. He's got a good edge. He was not a 'mellow' guy, especially in his later days.

"And then, as I got older, people like Robert Frost really hit me. I probably lived most of my life in New Hampshire, but Frost had a way of capturing the cadence of New Hampshire speech without making it sound like a parody or a Burl Ives record. He was rhythmically just incredible. And his poetry is also very sparse, which is a typical Yankee kind of thing, which is what I like."

Looking back, Morrissey has been surprised at the extent to which he has been influenced by fiction writers over other songwriters. "I used to hang out with this guy who taught at the University of New Hampshire who was a mentor of sorts. His name was Thomas Williams, and he won the National Book Award in 1975 [for *The Hair of Harold Roux*]. He died in 1990. We often went fishing and hunting together. A good many of his friends were also writers and so when they'd get together the talk would go from rainbow trout to Eudora Welty to rough grouse. So I just kept my mouth shut. There was a lot more I was going to learn than teach in that group. Tom always said, 'just say what you mean as economically as possible and get out,' and that's really what I try to do with my lyrics."

Asked about the comparisons by reviewers—growing increasingly more common with each new album he records—to Raymond Carver's fiction, the songwriter replies, "I'm not nuts about Carver's poetry, but I do like his fiction very much. Again, it's also very sparse. I think that is partly responsible for the comparisons. The other is subject matter. There's always a lot of divorces and drinking in his work."

In 1991, Rounder Records decided to release Morrissey's debut album on compact disc. Morrissey took advantage of the opportunity to re-record the album and add three additional tracks that he'd been performing back when the album was originally released. In the liner notes for the new CD, the songwriter noted, "I can't think of too many people who've gotten a chance to re-record their first album. It felt like a combination of getting to relive the innocence of my junior prom and returning to the scene of the crime to finish off the witness I'd only winged."

"When friends would come over in high school, I'd say, 'Hey, let's write a song.' They didn't believe that just anybody could write songs, so I pretty much had to figure it out by myself."

On the heels of that release came *Inside*, a work that was widely lauded as one of the finest folk releases of 1992. Reviewer Paul Evans called *Inside* "classic folk music, graced with an astonishingly subtle simplicity," in *Rolling Stone*. "It confirms Morrissey's place in that noble lineage that reaches back to Hank Williams and Woody Guthrie—the troubadour as truth teller, conveying wisdom with absolute economy and focused fire." Reviewer Lisa Shea of *People* weighed in as well, writing that the songs on *Inside* "are a terrific batch of tunes from one of the sharpest, most introspective songwriters in the business.... Morrissey is a unique talent. The truths he unearths aren't often pretty, but the way he tells them can take your breath away."

As with Morrissey's earlier albums, the lyrics on *Inside* received the most attention. His blue-collar vignettes are powerful ruminations on the complexity of the human experience. He feels for the troubled characters that roam across his lyric sheet, yet paints their portraits with an unsentimental eye. Often these characters are solitary figures, and Morrissey was asked by *CM* if he was particularly drawn to that theme. "I think so. I think when you travel for a living and you're always in somebody else's town, it's just something that I relate to, that I know, that I don't particularly like. It's a weird feeling. I remember in the early days what it was like to pull into some milltown bar where everybody knows everybody else, and you're performing there, and you're just sitting at the bar having a beer beforehand, and its like you're invisible. Everybody's chatting and laughing and having a good time, because they're all friends and know each other. And you're just the outsider. It's like you're the uninvited guest."

Morrissey avoids overtly political music as well. "The danger in writing those anthemic or real political songs is that it's easy to fall into the telling, not showing, mode of writing. It's easy to sound self-righteous. I would rather write about someone in a certain situation, write about an individual, than the cause. For instance, in a song like 'The Driver's Song' on *Standing Eight*, this guy's dumping toxic waste. But I don't want to come up with a rhyme for toxic waste. This guy is flesh and blood, and I want to know why he's doing this. Who is this person doing this? And what's his take on it?"

Grammy Nomination for Collaboration

After releasing *Inside*, Morrissey served as the producer on debut albums by Peter Keane and Ellis Paul, and then collaborated with singer-songwriter and fishing buddy Greg Brown on *Friend of Mine*, which was released in 1993. Brown first joined forces with Morrissey on the *Inside* album, contributing a soulful vocal performance on the haunting "Hang Me, Oh Hang Me," a traditional song given new life by the duo. The two musicians subsequently decided to record an album of songs originally penned by other artists. The result is a collection of easygoing covers of the works of such diverse songwriters as Chuck Berry, Hank Williams, Mick Jagger, and Keith Richards.

Once again, reviews were positive: *Request* called *Friend of Mine* "one of the most enjoyable releases of the year," while the *New England Folk Almanac* said that "this delightful anachronism of a record plays like a friendly front-porch pickin' session by two old fishin' buddies—who just happen to be absolute masters of the folk genre." *Dirty Linen* cautioned that portions of the album are "a tough go," but praised other songs on the album as "relaxing and wonderful." *Friend of Mine* eventually garnered a Grammy Award nomination for best traditional folk recording of 1993.

Morrissey's sixth album, *Night Train,* was released late in 1993. Returning to his own songs, Morrissey crafted an album that once again explored the many facets of the human experience. From lighthearted tunes such as "Letter From Heaven" to songs of physical and spiritual dislocation like "So Many Things," Morrissey muses on the spectrum of human emotions. "As evocative as black-and-white photographs, Bill Morrissey's songs freeze life's crucial moments with poignant clarity," wrote Bob Cannon in an *Entertainment Weekly* review. "Put simply, he is the best folk songwriter working today." And Kevin Ransom, writing in *Rolling Stone,* proclaimed "whether he's trolling the waters of history to find new truths in old songs or restocking the trad-music pond with his own incisive tunes, Morrissey is new folk's most distinctive voice—creaky and bruised, but standing tall."

Selected discography

Bill Morrissey, Rounder, 1985, re-recorded, 1991.
North, Rounder, 1986.
Standing Eight, Rounder, 1989.
Inside, Rounder, 1992.
(With Greg Brown) *Friend of Mine,* Rounder, 1993.
Night Train, Rounder, 1993.

Sources

Boston Phoenix, January 24, 1992.
Dirty Linen, August 1993.
Entertainment Weekly, September 24, 1993.
New England Folk Almanac, March 15, 1993.
New York Times, February 23, 1992.
People, June 8, 1992.
Performing Songwriter, March/April 1994.
Request, August 1993; January 1994.
Rolling Stone, August 23, 1990; February 20, 1992; November 11, 1993.
Stereo Review, May 1992.

Additional information for this profile was obtained from liner notes to the 1991 release of *Bill Morrissey,* and a November 30, 1993, interview with Bill Morrissey.

—*Kevin Hillstrom*

Nana Mouskouri

Singer

Photograph by Harry Langdon, courtesy of Princeton Entertainment

Mention the name Nana Mouskouri today in America, and someone is sure to ask, "Is that the woman with the glasses?" After over 30 years of European singing stardom, Nana Mouskouri is finally becoming known and recognized in the United States, and her trademark hairstyle and dark-rimmed glasses are becoming as familiar as her voice and sincerity. At an age when many singers retire, Mouskouri is still gaining new audiences and making new friends.

Nana Mouskouri first learned to sing from the movies. Her father was a movie projectionist, and when she was a child, her family lived behind the outdoor screen of their open-air theater. "So I grew up behind the big screen, listening to the music," she told the *Detroit Free Press*. "From the age of three or four, I heard the film music. Because I loved the music so much, I was inspired [to become a singer]." Her earliest influences were American popular singers. "I learned to sing in English from Judy Garland and Billie Holiday," she continued in the same interview.

As much as she loved pop, Mouskouri's earliest formal musical training was in classical music; she spent nine years studying classical singing at the Athens Conservatory. She continued to sing pop, jazz, and folk songs as well, much to her music professors' chagrin. They eventually told her to choose between pop and classical, for they did not believe anyone could sing both. In 1959 after winning the first Greek Song Festival, she opted for pop, and made her first record later that same year.

Mouskouri's early career coincided with an international interest in Greek popular music, due in part to the success of the movie *Never on Sunday,* the soundtrack of which contained several songs by the Greek composer Manos Hadjidakis. Hadjidakis wrote a number of songs for Mouskouri, including "White Rose of Athens," recorded in 1961, which became her first record to sell over one million copies.

In the early 1960s Mouskouri signed with the recording company Philips-Fontana France and moved to Paris. Her fame quickly spread throughout Europe. With her husband, guitarist George Petsilas, she formed the group the Athenians and began touring all over the world. "I became for Europe the first singer who both opened and closed an evening, alone with her musicians," she wrote in her autobiography. "I worked very hard and my popularity grew internationally."

She toured not only Europe, but other countries and continents, including Australia, New Zealand, Japan, Malaysia, Thailand, Mexico, and the United States; she appeared on television specials, and even had her own

> **For the Record . . .**
>
> Born Nana Mouskouri in Athens, Greece, October 10, 1936; married George Petsilas, 1961 (divorced 1975); children: Nicholas, Helen.
>
> Released first record, 1959; signed with the recording company Philips-Fontata France, 1961; recorded first English LP "A Girl From Greece Sings," 1962; formed the band Athenians, 1963; toured with Harry Belafonte 1964-66; appeared on BBC in *Nana and Guests,* 1967-69.
>
> **Awards:** First prize, Greek Song Festval, 1959 and 1960; first prize, Mediteranean Song Contest, Barcelona, 1960; received "Silver Lion" from Radio Luxembourg, 1961; gold record for "White Rose of Athens," 1961; gold and platinum records every year from 1968 to 1992; Academie Charles Cros Grand Prix du Disque, 1962; Academie du Disque, Institude of Musicolgie, 1963; silver medal from the "Schlagerfestspiele," 1964; Oscar Monte Carlo de la Chanson, 1968; Edison Award Statue, 1971; Golden Tulip Award from Holland, 1975; Golden Europa, 1978; Golden Ticket in Germany, 1980 and 1981; named chevalier des arts et des lettres, 1986.
>
> **Addresses:** *Office*—Princeton Entertainment, 20 Forest Blend Dr., Titusville, NJ 08560.

series in London. She received requests for royal command performances, and her concerts continually sold out. Her albums usually went platinum or gold. In 1975 she was awarded a wall of 100 gold and platinum records by Phonogram Philips Paris; by the early 1990s, she had received over 250 gold and platinum records. Her numerous awards include France's Grand Prix du Disque, the Golden Tulip Award in Holland, and the Golden Ticket Award in Germany for selling more than 100,000 seats in one year.

One of Mouskouri's popular appeals is the vast variety of songs she sings. "Music has so many faces, styles, different expressions," she told the *Detroit Free Press*. "When I started off, I was influenced by the classical singers and the Greek singers. But I also like rock and roll. I can go for [pop singer] Annie Lennox, [or the group] Dire Straits. I like jazz very much, and I love traditional music. I have sung traditional Greek songs, children's songs, German, English, Welsh, Irish, I have done Scottish folk songs."

She performs with equal ease the aria "Casta Diva" from Bellini's opera *Norma,* the spiritual "Amazing Grace," and Elvis Presley's "Love Me Tender." She tallied up more songs in her autobiography: "I have also sung songs of the Beatles, The Rolling Stones, Kris Kristofferson, James Taylor, Tom Paxton, Dolly Parton, Cat Stevens, Bette Midler, Serge Lama, Jacques Brel, Charles Aznavour, Edith Piaf, Marlene Dietrich, Neil Young, Neil Sedaka, John Denver, Judy Garland, Ella Fitzgerald, Nat 'King' Cole, Carole King, and Don McLean."

Mouskouri also sings most of her songs in their original language. Early in her career, she traveled extensively and found to no surprise that her fans preferred to hear their songs in their own language. She also wanted to talk to them, so she started learning languages. "I started to travel in the 1960s and I needed to explain my songs. I said to myself that if I want to be serious about this, I have to learn the languages," she told the *Washington Post*. "So I learned on stage. I would travel with a heavy bag of language books. Today it's so easy—I feel at home in Holland, Belgium ... in Italy." In any one concert, she might sing in any of a number of languages, including Spanish, French, and Hebrew as well as English and her native Greek. While on tour in Japan, she even sang a few songs in Japanese. The language seems to matter less than the meaning of the words.

"Success for me was always based on communicating with my audience, honesty and feelings," she wrote in her autobiography. "I always have expressed my feelings, my hopes my expectations, and the love I need to live. Sometimes I have also given words to my anger, my fear and my doubts." For Mouskouri, the most important aspect of a song is the meaning. "When I sing a song, I need to tell a story," she told the *Washington Free Press*. "I need to feel strongly about what I'm singing. If the song doesn't come from the heart, I can not sing it." Because songs combine music and poetry, the meaning can be unique. "The magic of a song is to belong to every one at the same time for different reasons," she continued in her autobiography. "To make you dream, and create your own reality in order to find your own truth and freedom in it."

In the early 1990s American fans finally began to appreciate and understand the magic of Nana Mouskouri. Although she started touring in the U.S. in the early 1960s, and has toured here more than ten times since then, she never spent enough time here to develop a large audience. With her release of the English-language album *Only Love* in 1993, however, she decided to change this.

With the support of her American label Polygram, she set off on a 34-city North American tour, selling out performances and garnering rave reviews. Although some have criticized her soft-pop material for being too syrupy, others care less about the type of songs she sings than about how she sings them. As music critic Paul Robicheau wrote in the *Boston Globe,* "When you possess a full, shimmering soprano like Mouskouri's, you could practically sing the phone book, and leave an audience in bliss." Finally Americans have begun to figure out what the Europeans have seemed to know all along.

Selected discography

Over and Over, Fontanel, 1969.
Turn on the Sun, Verve, 1971.
Passport, Mercury, 1976.
Vielles chansons de France, Verve, 1978.
Roses & Sunshine, Philips, 1979.
Nana (I), Verve, 1984.
Alone, Verve, 1986.
Libertad, Mercury, 1986.
Ma Vérité, Verve, 1986.
Why Worry, 1986.
Tierra Viva, Mercury, 1986.
Par Amour, Verve, 1987.
Je Chante Avec Toi Liberté, Verve, 1988.
The Magic of Nana Mouskouri, Verve, 1988.
Nana in English, Verve, 1988.
Nana (II), Verve, 1989.
The Classical Nana, Philips, 1990.
Oh Happy Day, Verve, 1991.
Only Love, Philips, 1991.
Falling in Love Again, Philips, 1993.
Nuestras Canciones, Polygram Latino, 1993.

Sources

Books

Gammond, Peter, *The Oxford Companion to Popular Music,* Oxford University Press, 1991.
The Guinness Encyclopedia of Popular Music, edited by Colin Larkin, Guinness Publishing, Ltd., 1992.
Hardy, Phil, and Dave Laing, *The Faber Companion to 20th-Century Popular Music,* Faber and Faber, 1990.
Mouskouri, Nana, *Nana Mouskouri,* 1993.

Periodicals

Boston Globe, May 5, 1993.
Detroit Free Press, May 7, 1993.
Variety, August 22, 1984; June 15, 1988.
Washington Post, September 15, 1991.

—Robin Armstrong

Alison Moyet

Singer, songwriter

Photograph by the Douglas Brothers, © 1994 Sony Music, courtesy of Columbia Records

Alison Moyet first gained attention as the powerful, blues-inflected voice of Yaz (know as Yazoo in Great Britain), the electro-pop duo that topped the British charts in the early 1980s. Since leaving Yaz in 1984 she has maintained a successful, if somewhat uneven, solo career as a singer-songwriter, in recent years returning to the rhythm and blues sound that she thrives on. Yaz—a collaboration between Moyet and Vince Clarke, now a member of Erasure—was distinguished from other synthesizer-based groups such as the Eurythmics, to whom they were often compared. Moyet's rich, emotive vocal style proved that synth-pop can have soul.

Moyet has been compared to female vocalists as diverse as Annie Lennox, Linda Thompson, Sade, Tina Turner, Dusty Springfield, Nona Hendryx, Marianne Faithful, and Janis Joplin, a favorite of Moyet's. Yet with her booming, soulful voice, her no-nonsense approach to the music business, and her frank if sometimes enigmatic lyrics about love, sex, and friendship, Moyet stands out as an original presence in the recording industry. She is also known for speaking her mind. Among other things, she has strong opinions about the role of women in popular music: "I like to cut out the *him* and *hers* in songs so both sexes can relate to it and I don't like the idea of songs portraying the female as submissive and always weak," she informed Colin Irwin in a *Melody Maker* interview.

An acclaimed pop star in Europe, in the United States Moyet has remained something of a dance-floor cult figure. Her United States audience is loyal, however, and when she toured the country after the release of her 1991 album *Hoodoo,* she played sold-out gigs, even though she had been off the club circuit for a number of years. Moyet, who has expressed more interest in having her music taken seriously than in selling a lot of records, views her relative obscurity in the United States as an opportunity to move past the Yaz years. In 1992 she told Julie Romandetta of the *Boston Herald,* "I never sold masses of records in America, therefore I'm a relatively new and unknown artist. Every piece of work I do is taken completely on its own merit, it doesn't come with a load of baggage."

Punk and Blues Roots

A thriving pub-rock scene in Moyet's hometown of Basildon, England, provided an outlet both for Moyet's love of music and her rebellious streak. She began playing in bands when she was 15 and left school at 16, later returning to study music. She performed in an all-female trio, the Vandals, which was influenced by X-Ray Spex; work with later bands the Vicars and then the

For the Record...

Born Genevieve Alison Moyet, June 18, 1961, in Basildon, Essex, England; known as "Alf"; married Malcolm Lee, c. 1983 (divorced, c. 1989); children: Joe, Alex (daughter). *Education:* Dropped out of school at age 16; returned to study music and music technology at two colleges; attended the College of Furniture.

Singer and songwriter. Began playing with bands in local pubs, c. 1976; played with the Vandals, the Vicars, and the Screaming Abdads before teaming up with Vince Clarke to form Yaz, 1982; recorded *Upstairs at Eric's,* 1982, and *You and Me Both* before disbanding, 1983; released debut solo ablum, *Alf,* 1984.

Awards: British Recording Industry awards for top British female artist, 1983, 1985, and 1987; Grammy Award nomination for best rock vocal performance, female, 1993, for "It Won't Be Long," from the album *Hoodoo.*

Addresses: *Record company*—Columbia Records, 550 Madison Ave., New York, NY 10022.

Screaming Abdads introduced Moyet to the rhythm and blues sound that has been a hallmark of her vocals ever since. In 1982, tired of the pub-rock circuit and also fed up with feeling like an outsider as the female singer in all-male bands, Moyet placed a classified ad in *Melody Maker,* a British music magazine. "Female singer looking for a rootsy blues band," she wrote in the ad. What she got instead was Vince Clarke.

Clarke had just left the techno-pop band Depeche Mode, which he had cofounded, and wanted a female singer to provide the vocals for a ballad he had written, "Only You." Despite their very different backgrounds, the two musicians sounded surprisingly good together, and so Yazoo was formed from the unlikely combination of synthesizer genius Clarke and blues belter Moyet. In the United States, they were known as Yaz, for legal reasons. "Only You" turned out to be a hit, one of four songs on the 1982 *Upstairs at Eric's* to make it into England's Top Ten.

Although their first album was wildly successful and brought Yaz an enthusiastic following, tensions between the duo were beginning to mount. By the following year, when Moyet and Clarke went into the studio to record their second album, *You and Me Both,* they no longer agreed on the sound they wanted. "We were having to compromise with each other too much," Moyet told Jon Young in *Musician.* "Vince liked lightweight pop and I wanted something with a bit more depth. That was okay on the first album, but after that we got stale." Relations became so strained between the two that they worked on the record during separate shifts. Moyet explained to Irwin that Clarke "was never there to listen to me sing. He was never there to say 'That's a good vocal' or 'That's not a good vocal.' And yet if he didn't like something I'd get rung up and made to come to the studio to do it again."

The perhaps inevitable clash between two willful artistic temperaments led to the breakup of the band once *You and Me Both* was completed. Moyet told Irwin that, in her opinion, there were only four good tracks on the whole album. The critics seemed to agree, and although the album sold fairly well, it did not enjoy the runaway success of *Upstairs at Eric's.*

Life After Yaz

Clarke went on to form the short-lived Assembly and then Erasure with singer Andy Bell, whom critics have noted sounds much like Moyet. Meanwhile, Moyet's attempts to establish a solo career ran into legal difficulties and for well over a year she found herself caught up in litigation concerning her recording contracts. In 1984 Moyet went back into the studio, this time with Tony Swain and Steve Jolley, veteran British producers who have had success with Bananarama and Spandau Ballet.

Her first solo venture, *Alf,* titled after Moyet's nickname, sold over a million and a half copies in Britain and hit the Top Ten in several European countries, New Zealand, and Japan. Three of its tracks, "Love Resurrection," "All Cried Out," and "Invisible," penned for her by Lamont Dozier, hit the Top Ten. Moyet was named top female vocalist at the 1985 British Record Industry Awards, the English version of the Grammys.

Yet *Alf,* dominated by the slick pop sound of Swain and Jolley's production, did not entirely satisfy either Moyet or the critics. Talking to Irwin, she dismissed her huge hit, "All Cried Out," as "a lightweight love song." A year after the release of *Alf,* she told *Billboard* she was looking for new producers to give her next album a different sound: "It will be something with a bit more energy; less glossy, with lots of color."

Moyet did not rush back into production. In the spring of 1985 she gave birth to her first child, Joe. That July she performed a duet with Paul Young at Live Aid, the benefit concert organized by Bob Geldof of the Boomtown Rats to raise money for famine relief in Africa. Her next album, the 1987 *Raindancing,* reflected Moyet's desire to take more responsibility for the songwriting, this time working with Jimmy Iovine, whose more understated production gave freer rein to Moyet's interpretations. *Raindancing* instantly hit England's Top Ten charts, although it did not fare any better in the United States than *Alf* had. The album earned Moyet another best female artist title at the British Record Industry Awards in 1988. Moyet still felt dissatisfied with her recordings, however. She was not enjoying her success, largely because she felt she was not in control of the music she was making. Chris Heim in the *Chicago Tribune* reported that Moyet "found producers treating her like just another instrument and hired hand."

Took Time to Reflect

Frustrated, Moyet took a four-year break from recording and spent the next several years struggling both with her personal life and her musical aspirations. During that time she divorced her husband, Malcolm Lee, had her second child, daughter Alex, and re-examined her career. She was not satisfied with selling millions of records. "I've never been the kind of person that lusted after fame or lusted after money," Moyet told Heim. She emerged from this period with a handful of songs that expressed the anguish and triumph she had been experiencing.

In 1991 she made her third record, the critically acclaimed *Hoodoo.* Discussing the album with Julie Romandetta in the *Boston Herald,* Moyet said, "I had a low period where I couldn't write or do anything and I was having a bit of a bad time in my personal life. Once I started examining what was happening to me, I was able to write again. Writing [*Hoodoo*] was a very cathartic experience." Although it was hailed by many critics as her finest album yet and garnered Moyet her first Grammy nomination, it was not a major commercial success in either Great Britain or the United States.

Nonetheless, Moyet possibly found that her career took a more satisfying direction than its earlier, headier stages. *Essex,* Moyet's 1994 release, continued to highlight the singer's very personal lyrics, giving fuller range to her voice than did her first two solo efforts. Emphasizing guitars over synthesizers, *Essex* found Moyet moving away from a strictly pop format.

If *Hoodoo* was a somewhat experimental venture, Moyet seemed to have taken away from it a clearer sense of what she wants out of her own music. And she seemed willing to forego the huge, adoring crowds of fans that Yaz inspired for a smaller, more seriously interested audience. After *Hoodoo* she told the *Chicago Tribune,* "To be honest I would much rather have an audience of 5 or maybe 10 percent of what I used to have, but people who understood what I was and where I could just be myself."

Selected discography

With Yaz

Upstairs at Eric's, Mute-Sire, 1982.
You and Me Both, Mute-Sire, 1983.

Solo albums; on Columbia

Alf, 1984.
Raindancing, 1987.
Hoodoo, 1991.
Essex, 1994.

Sources

Advocate, December 1993.
Billboard, November 2, 1985; February 19, 1994.
Boston Herald, March 4, 1992.
Chicago Tribune, March 6, 1992.
Detroit Free Press, June 10, 1994.
Melody Maker, September 25, 1982; September 29, 1984.
Metro Times (Detroit), June 8-14, 1994.
Musician, May 1985.
People, April 18, 1994.
Village Voice, November 8, 1983.

Additional information for this profile was obtained from Columbia Records press material, 1994.

—*Gina Hausknecht*

Red Norvo

Xylophonist, vibraphonist

"I play the vibraharp," declared Red Norvo in his 1968 interview with Whitney Balliett for the *New Yorker*. "Of course, I started on the xylophone and marimba in the mid-twenties, and up until then they were vaudeville instruments, clown instruments. They differ from one another chiefly in range.... The [xylophone's] bars, or what would be the keys of a piano, are made of rosewood. The vibraharp [a trade name for vibraphone] has the same keyboard, but it is lower in range than the marimba. It's an electronic instrument and its bars are made of aluminum. It's electronic because the resonator tubes that hang down underneath the bars, like an upside-down organ, have little paddle-shaped fans in them called pulsators that are driven by a small electric motor."

Virtually unaided, Red Norvo lifted the xylophone, and then the vibraharp, from the clown's role to one of jazz prominence. After trading his favorite pony and a summer's hard work for his first xylophone at about age 15, Norvo taught himself to play by ear, studying music rudiments as on-the-job training.

Musical Innovator

Through constant experimentation with a variety of mallets and techniques, Norvo conquered the physical limitations of the xylophone, transforming it into a melodic, expressive voice in jazz ensembles of all sizes. As virtuoso cornetist and writer Rex Stewart told *Down Beat* in 1968: "Red's contribution (over and above his being consistently one of the most gifted and communicative players on the vibraharp) lies in the fact that he singlehandedly made the xylophone sound a part of the lexicon of swing. Without question, he must be categorized as a charter member of that select group—the innovators—whom the profession considers immortals."

Norvo began playing professionally in Chicago at 17 as the entertaining leader of a marimba ensemble, the Collegians. Moving to the orchestra of Paul Ash, Kenneth Norville became Red Norvo, thanks to the leader's inability to remember the proper name. Later, as a solo vaudeville act, he added tap-dancing to his playing. At about the age of ten the youngster had been introduced to live jazz by listening to cornetist Bix Beiderbecke, saxophonist Frankie Trumbauer, and especially trumpeter Louis Armstrong on the visiting river boats in Beardstown on the Illinois River. And while he was influenced by the virtuosity of George Hamilton Green and a theater musician named Wentworth on xylophone, Norvo was irresistibly drawn toward jazz. He carried his Victrola and collection of the latest jazz records with him constantly.

> ## For the Record . . .
>
> Born Kenneth Norville, March 31, 1908, in Beardstown, IL; father was a railroad dispatcher, amateur pianist, and singer; mother's name, Estelle; married Mildred Bailey, 1930 (divorced, 1942); married Eve Rogers, 1946; children: Mark, Portia, Kevin.
>
> Began piano lessons, switched to xylophone, then marimba, and later vibraharp; began career in Chicago with marimba band, 1925; worked as a tap-dancing xylophonist in vaudeville; did radio staff work in Milwaukee, Kansas City, Detroit, Minneapolis, and with Victor Young in Chicago, 1927-29; released first records as leader, 1933; led small group at New York's Hickory House and Famous Door, 1934-35; expanded to 12 pieces with wife, Mildred Bailey, as vocalist, 1936-40; organized trio, 1949.
>
> **Awards:** Gold Award, *Esquire,* 1944-47.
>
> **Addresses:** *Office*—420 Alta Ave., Santa Monica, CA 90402.

Other constant companions were Norvo's innate good taste, his quest for innovation, and his infallible musical ear. In Chicago in 1929 he caught on with the popular orchestra of Paul Whiteman whose vocalist, Mildred Bailey, was to become one of jazz's most celebrated singers. Norvo and Bailey married in 1930, about the time the Whiteman troupe moved its base to New York. Very soon, Norvo began recording with Bailey and other Whiteman musicians, etching his first two sides as leader in 1933 with clarinetist Jimmy Dorsey, pianist Fulton McGrath, guitarist Dick McDonough, and bassist Artie Bernstein.

On these recordings Norvo demonstrated his formidable mallet technique, but it was not until November of that year that Norvo's unique jazz voice, both instrumentally and as a composer/arranger, was recorded. The tunes were Bix Beiderbecke's classic, "In A Mist," and Norvo's own "Dance of the Octopus."

In his *The Swing Era,* Gunther Schuller rates the former "the most moving and sympathetic performance of that work, including Beiderbecke's own," and the latter "clearly the most advanced composition of the early thirties." In addition to McDonough and Bernstein, Benny Goodman played bass clarinet on this session. Norvo quickly earned the attention and respect of New York's fertile music community. After leaving Whiteman in 1934, he recorded with the cream of the fraternity: trumpeter Bunny Berigan, clarinetist Artie Shaw, trombonist Jack Jenney, pianist Teddy Wilson, drummer Gene Krupa, saxophonist Chu Berry, guitarist Dave Barbour, cornetist Stew Fletcher, and bassist Pete Peterson, the latter three of whom played in Norvo's performing group on 52nd Street. Among this era's recordings, "Bughouse" and "Blues in E-Flat," done with Berigan and others, stand out as magnificent examples of Norvo's style.

Norvo the Leader

And it was in about 1935 that Norvo met soul mate Eddie Sauter, a Juilliard and Columbia University-trained mellophone and trumpet player, who became more noted for his inventive writing and arranging with Norvo, Goodman, and his own orchestra. Sauter helped shape the sound of the various groups that Norvo led, first an octet, later expanded to 12 pieces with Bailey as vocalist. This amalgam produced a brand of subtle swing that blended Bailey's unique voice with forward-looking instrumental timbres. Richard Gehman and Eddie Condon, writing for *Saturday Review,* claim this band "is now firmly entrenched in history as one of the finest of all time." In these and other small group contexts, the xylophonist recorded many memorable performances.

Norvo continued as a leader and pacesetter of various groups until 1944, one an all-star aggregation that included trumpeter/arranger Shorty Rogers, trombonist Eddie Bert, pianist/arranger Ralph Burns, and clarinetist Aaron Sachs. During the latter period Norvo switched to vibraharp. After forsaking leadership in 1945 to play with the Benny Goodman big band and sextet, Norvo rarely returned to the xylophone. During 1946 he switched to the exciting Woody Herman band and was also featured with that group's band-within-a-band, The Woodchoppers.

Home, Sweet Home

The Norvo/Bailey household in Forest Hills, New York, became a mid-thirties gathering place for musicians, and it was there that the Benny Goodman Trio was born. Norvo loves to tell the story of how Goodman and Wilson began jamming one night when Krupa was a guest and an idle set of drums happened to be available. Krupa sat in; the trio became a musical success and Goodman fixture, later evolving into the quartet with the addition of Lionel Hampton on vibes. Blues empress Bessie Smith, vocalist Lee Wiley, composer Alec Wilder, cornetist Red Nichols, pianist Fats Waller, and Berigan were among the regular guests.

Not all was sweet harmony in the household, however. "Mr. and Mrs. Swing," as they were titled by writer George Simon, engaged in some self-admitted monumental and destructive fights. A 1939 illness caused Bailey's temporary retirement, after which the couple rarely performed together. After 12 years of marriage, during which time Mildred sang for long stretches with Red's band, they divorced. Their relationship remained cordial until Mildred's death in 1951.

In 1947 Norvo moved to California with his second wife, Eve Rogers, the sister of Shorty Rogers, beginning a period of freelance playing in various settings. He returned east in 1949, fronting a sextet that included pianist Dick Hyman, clarinetist Tony Scott, and guitarist Mundell Lowe. This began a period of extensive travel for Norvo, during which he made his first overseas visit (1954), toured Europe with Benny Goodman (1959), and was featured globally with entrepreneur George Wein's groups. He continued switching between the coasts as well, appearing frequently in Las Vegas.

Norvo had long adjusted to performing with 60 percent hearing in one ear. When, in 1968, his "good" ear quit functioning temporarily and required surgery, he feared he would be forced to end his career. Eve died in 1972, and Norvo stayed away from music completely for two years. Returning in 1974, with the troublesome ear somewhat restored, Norvo began a nomadic existence in which he has billed himself as a solo act, rather than as the leader of a specific group, working with able local musicians and relying on his own formidable improvisational gifts.

High Water Marks

Always recognized for his ability to bridge varying musical styles while retaining his own voice, Norvo provided leadership in at least two memorable musical forays. The first was 1945's recording session by Red Norvo and His Selected Sextet. When approached by Comet records to organize a session, Norvo insisted upon freedom in choosing both the musicians and the material. He selected Dizzy Gillespie, trumpet; Charlie Parker, alto sax; Flip Phillips, tenor sax; Teddy Wilson, piano; Slam Stewart, bass; J.C. Heard or Specs Powell, drums. Parker and Gillespie represented the cutting edge of bebop, with Phillips leaning toward modernism; the others were identified with the swing era.

So skillfully did Norvo integrate these varying stylists that the four selections—"Hallelujah," "Get Happy," "Slam Slam Blues," and "Congo Blues"—remain as models of inventive transition. As Ira Gitler observed in his *Swing to Bop,* "It was a time when Dizzy and Bird were becoming more well known but were being put down by some critics. These recordings changed a lot of people's minds.... These recordings made logical to some people, who previously hadn't understood, the connection, the evolution of the music."

The second event was Norvo's formation in 1949 of the prototype trio featuring the obscure Tal Farlow on guitar and Charles Mingus, brought out of retirement from a job as letter carrier, on bass. Of this group, Schuller wrote: "Just as Art Tatum is remembered mostly for his Trio work, so too Norvo is today remembered for the outstanding trio he formed.... The Norvo Trio remains in memory as one of the finest small groups in jazz history."

In *The Big Bands,* George Simon summed up Norvo's jazz contributions: "He was great in those days [1936], he had been great before those days, and he is great today. Of all the musicians in jazz he has remained for me, through the years, the most satisfying of them all; in short, he remains my favorite of all jazz musicians."

Selected discography

Red Norvo All Star Sextet, Mercury, 1944.
Red Norvo and His Selected Sextet, Dial, 1945.
Music to Listen to Red Norvo By, Contemporary, 1957.
Red Plays the Blues, Contemporary, 1957.
Blues and Vanilla, Victor, 1958.
The Horn's Full, Victor, 1958.
Red Norvo With Strings, Fantasy.
The Red Norvo Trios, Fantasy.

Sources

Books

Balliett, Whitney, *American Musicians: 56 Portraits in Jazz,* Oxford University Press, 1986.
Chilton, John, *Who's Who of Jazz,* Time-Life, 1978.
Feather, Leonard, *The New Edition of the Encyclopedia of Jazz,* Bonanza Books, 1965.
Gitler, Ira, *Swing to Bop,* Oxford University Press, 1985.
Kinkle, Roger D., *The Complete Encyclopedia of Popular Music and Jazz 1900-1950,* Arlington House Publishers, 1974.
Rust, Brian, *Jazz Records 1897-1942,* Storyville Publications, 1982.
Schuller, Gunther, *The Swing Era: The Development of Jazz 1930-1945,* Oxford University Press, 1989.
Simon, George, *Best of the Music Makers,* Doubleday, 1979.
Simon, *The Big Bands, New Edition,* Macmillan, 1981.
Stewart, Rex, *Jazz Masters of the 30s,* Macmillan, 1971.

Periodicals

Detroit Free Press, November 2, 1958.
Detroit News, January 5, 1969.
Down Beat, September 7, 1967.
Saturday Review, February 8, 1958.
Mississippi Rag, April 1989.
New Yorker, December 28, 1968.
New York Times, April 22, 1977.

—Robert Dupuis

NRBQ

Rock band

"NRBQ's music suggests what might happen if Huck Finn and Bugs Bunny strapped on Stratocasters [electric guitars]," appraised Malcolm Jones, Jr., in *Newsweek*. Since the late 1960s, the New Rhythm and Blues Quartet—known to the world at large as NRBQ and to devotees as "the Q"—have played eclectic, playful, good-time music, becoming known in the process as one of rock's best live bands and working steadily despite a lack of impressive record sales.

Encompassing everything from 1950s rock to free jazz—*Rolling Stone*'s Michael Azerrad called them "spectacularly encyclopedic"—they have maintained one of the most loyal fan bases anywhere. "Pop music fans generally divide into two camps regarding NRBQ—those who consider them among the great bands of the last two decades, and those who have not yet heard them play," insisted Mark Rowland in the liner notes to the group's two-CD compilation *Peek-A-Boo*. "For more than 20 years NRBQ have been steadily converting audiences from the second camp into the first,

Photograph by Brian Smith, courtesy of Forward Records

For the Record . . .

Members include **Terry Adams,** keyboards and vocals; **Al Anderson** (bandmember 1971-94), guitar and vocals; **Tom Ardolino** (joined group 1974), drums; **Steve Ferguson** (left group 1971, returned briefly in 1972 and left again), guitar; **Frank Gadler** (left group 1971), vocals; **Joey Spampinato,** bass and vocals; **Johnny Spampinato** (joined group 1994), guitar; **Tom Staley** (left group 1974), drums. "Whole Wheat Horns" brass section has included **Donn Adams,** trombone; **Jim Hoke,** tenor saxophone; and **Keith Spring,** tenor saxophone.

Group formed in Miami, FL, 1968. Signed with Columbia and recorded self-titled debut album, 1969; recorded for various labels, 1972—; appeared on A&M Disney movie song tribute *Stay Awake,* 1988; performed tribute to Sun Ra, 1994.

Addresses: *Record company*—Forward, 10635 Santa Monica Blvd., Los Angeles, CA 90025. *Newsletter*—New Rhythm & Blues News, P.O. Box 311, Saugerties, NY 12477.

---

which is the only thing consistent throughout their otherwise confounding career."

It was a shock to fans when, in 1994, longtime guitarist Al Anderson left the Q; though his departure was the group's first break with tradition in many years, Anderson was replaced and the group vowed to go on. As Jones observed, "Bands like NRBQ live and breathe music onstage and off, and they're having much too much fun to dream of quitting."

Released Debut Album

The group was founded in the late 1960s by keyboardist Terry Adams, his trombonist brother Donn, and guitarist Steve Ferguson. NRBQ's earliest incarnation was floundering in Miami, Florida, when bassist Joey Spampinato and singer Frank Gadler of the band the Seven of Us arrived in town; the two newcomers joined Terry Adams, Ferguson, and drummer Tom Staley in a new incarnation of the Q, which was a quintet for several years. They signed with Columbia Records and released their self-titled debut album in 1969.

Though only Terry Adams and Joey Spampinato would stay with the band for the long haul, Ferguson left an indelible stamp. Indeed, the bassist remarked to Rowland in the *Peek-A-Boo* booklet, "He was one of the best guitar players I ever heard. It's a shame he didn't stay in the band longer, because he started writing songs that were really good and they never made it onto a record." The group recorded an album of rockabilly standards, *Boppin' the Blues,* with rock pioneer Carl Perkins.

Anderson, whose band the Wildweeds had seen a measure of success in the Northeast, replaced Ferguson in 1971. Webb Wilder of *Guitar Player* reported that Anderson considered his predecessor a heavy influence; he also mentioned James Burton, guitarist for early rock icon Elvis Presley, as an inspiration. Gadler left the Q in 1972, leaving the singing to the remaining members. Donn Adams appeared occasionally on recordings but was not a full-fledged member; drummer Staley departed in 1974 and was replaced by Tom Ardolino, who had never before played with a group. Even so, Terry Adams told Sally Eckhoff of the *Village Voice,* "We knew he was spiritually right for the band."

Ardolino told Dan Oulette of *Pulse!* that he heard the band for the first time in 1970 and two years later was called onstage by Terry Adams when Staley didn't appear for the group's encore. "I was afraid, but I went up there anyway," he recalled. "Playing with a real band for the first time was wild. At the end Al turned around and he couldn't believe it was me. He thought Staley was still onstage."

Off-Balance, Eclectic Approach

The *Village Voice*'s Eckhoff described the band's sound with its longtime lineup: "The Q sound, though achieved with a minimum of electronic gadgetry, can be about as complicated as pop gets. The use of each instrument fits into some iconoclastic tradition, and none of them match." Melding the modern jazz explorations of Thelonious Monk and Sun Ra (whose "Rocket Number 9" the band covered on its debut) with Anderson's sometimes countrified, sometimes bluesy leads, Joey Spampinato's love of pure-pop songcraft and Ardolino's versatile rhythmic approach, which Eckhoff declared "lands between New Orleans session man Zigaboo Modeliste and a bunch of cardboard boxes falling downstairs," the Q found balance in an off-balance dynamic. The group was often joined by the "Whole Wheat Horns," featuring Donn Adams. On top of this, a sense of surreal mischief and good-time nostalgia colored their lyrics.

NRBQ soon became known as one of the wildest and most enjoyable live acts on the rock scene. Unpredictability became the group's trademark, as *Village Voice* critic Jon Pareles explained: "At some point in their live set, NRBQ generally reaches into 'the Magic Box,' which contains song titles tossed in earlier by audience members. Whatever comes out, the band plays: [English rock legends the Rolling Stones' early single] 'Under My Thumb,' [the standard] 'The Shadow of Your Smile,' anything. They may not play it straight, but they play it, and that's something."

> NRBQ is known as one of the wildest and most enjoyable live acts on the rock scene. Unpredictability is the group's trademark.

This loyalty to the spontaneous, Pareles noted, "smacks of foolhardy bravado as well as craftsmanlike pride. We play popular music, they seem to be saying, and we play it all." As Terry Adams declared to Eckhoff, "I'm never happy unless something happens I didn't know was going to happen."

The band's trademark goofiness—an attribute not treasured equally by all fans—can be witnessed in NRBQ's song titles, such as Terry Adams's compositions "Wacky Tobacky" and "RC Cola and a Moon Pie"; through collaborations with wrestler "Captain" Lou Albano; and in the between-song performance art at their gigs. But even this lightheartedness seemed part of a serious commitment on the group's part to work on its own terms. The record industry, always enthusiastic at first, never knew what to do with the Q; as a result, the band shuffled from label to label.

Their 1970s album *At Yankee Stadium* received numerous plaudits, but it didn't keep them at Mercury for long. They moved from Red Rooster/Rounder to Bearsville to Virgin, eventually landing on Forward, the continuing artist subsidiary of the beloved reissue label Rhino. "There have always been other labels after us," Terry Adams told *Pulse!,* "but Rhino just seemed the rightest."

Despite not having had any mainstream hits themselves, NRBQ has recorded songs that are covered and admired by a number of other artists. British rocker Dave Edmunds fared well with his rendition of "Me and the Boys," and the Q has enjoyed the acclaim of respected rock songwriters like Elvis Costello, Bonnie Raitt, and the members of R.E.M. As Terry Adams remarked in *Down Beat,* the group's music "is made by people, not machines," unlike many of the records dominating the pop scene. NRBQ's esteem has led the individual members into some prestigious side projects: Joey Spampinato played with seminal rockers Chuck Berry and Keith Richards in the band Richards assembled for the film *Hail! Hail! Rock & Roll* and briefly filled in for the Stones' departing bassist Bill Wyman, joining celebrated guitarist Eric Clapton on tour as well; Anderson toured and wrote with singer Carlene Carter and composed for country star Hank Williams, Jr.; and Donn Adams has played with jazz artist Carla Bley and participated in producer Hal Willner's tribute album to Thelonious Monk. Willner invited the whole quartet to play on the album of songs from Walt Disney films he produced, and they obliged with a full-tilt version of "Whistle While You Work."

Exit Big Al

In 1994 NRBQ released *Message for the Mess Age,* a more political album than they had hitherto attempted. It was generally well received—*Musician* dubbed it their best since *At Yankee Stadium*—though *Spin's* Michael Corcoran used his review as an occasion to label them "the world's most overpraised bar band." The foursome also played a tribute concert to Sun Ra after the jazz innovator's death, employing his horn section for a mixture of their own standard repertoire and a number of Ra's compositions.

Anderson's rather abrupt exit, therefore, stunned their loyal following: "It is hard to imagine NRBQ without Big Al," *Guitar Player's* Wilder had mused some years earlier. "Say It Ain't So" read the headline over *Musician's* announcement of his split from the group. Joey Spampinato's brother Johnny, late of the Incredible Casuals, took Anderson's place; *BAM* reviewer Sean O'Neill declared that since "an essential, seminal element of a delicate balancing act had been removed," he feared at first that "the band would surely never be the same."

Anderson's departure gave too-free reign to Terry Adams's penchant for silliness, O'Neill reported of the early post-Al shows, "But guess what! It was still a helluva lot of fun." Johnny Spampinato, he noted, "sounded like he'd been studying the role for years. He had Big Al's squealy leads down pat, and NRBQ's trademark roadhouse sound remained intact."

The group clearly had no intention of slowing down, despite Anderson's departure. As Terry Adams told the *Village Voice,* "I've never had another job." In the words of *Newsweek's* Jones, "Bands like NRBQ live and breathe music onstage and off, and they're having too much fun to dream of quitting." Whether the mainstream music world ever came around to their offbeat view of things was as moot in the mid-1990s as it had been in the late 1960s.

Selected discography

NRBQ (includes "Rocket Number 9"), Columbia, 1969.
Boppin' the Blues, Columbia, 1969.
Scraps, Kama Sutra, 1972.
Workshop, Kama Sutra, 1973.
All Hopped Up, Red Rooster, 1977.
At Yankee Stadium, Mercury, 1978.
Kick Me Hard, Red Rooster, 1979.
"Me and the Boys," Red Rooster, 1980.
Tiddlywinks, Red Rooster, 1980.
Grooves in Orbit, Bearsville, 1983.
RC Cola and a Moon Pie, Red Rooster, 1983.
Tapdancin' Bats, Rounder, 1984.
God Bless Us All, Rounder, 1988.
Diggin' Uncle Q, Rounder, 1988.
Christmas Wish, Rounder, 1988.
Uncommon Denominators, Rounder, 1989.
Wild Weekend, Virgin, 1989.
Peek-A-Boo: The Best of NRBQ (includes "RC Cola and a Moon Pie" and "Wacky Tobacky"), Rhino, 1990.
Honest Dollar, Rykodisc, 1992.
Message for the Mess Age, Rhino/Forward, 1994.

With others

(With Skeeter Davis) *She Sings, They Play*, Red Rooster, 1985.
(With various artists) *Stay Awake: Music From Vintage Disney Films* (appear on "Whistle While You Work"), A&M, 1988.

Group members have also participated in various recordings for other artists.

Sources

BAM, May 20, 1994.
Billboard, October 14, 1989.
Down Beat, April 1989; November 1992; May 1994.
Guitar Player, July 1989; August 1989.
Musician, March 1994; May 1994.
Newsweek, April 25, 1994.
Pulse!, March 1994; May 1994.
Rolling Stone, April 12, 1984; February 24, 1994.
Spin, April 1994.
Village Voice, April 3, 1978; October 31, 1989.

Additional information was provided by printed materials accompanying *Peek-A-Boo*, 1990, and by Forward Records publicity materials, 1994.

—Simon Glickman

Laura Nyro

Singer, songwriter

Photograph by Richard Dunkley, © 1993 Sony Music

During Bronx-born Laura Nyro's 30-year career as a recording artist and songwriter, she has enjoyed public periods of recording and touring interspersed with frequent time out to enjoy her private life. Nyro has been hailed as one of the most visionary and powerful singers and songwriters of our time, inspiring and influencing both musicians and music lovers alike. To trace her career it is necessary to chart the evolution of soul, jazz, blues, and folk music during the last half of the twentieth century.

Nyro's songwriting began in her childhood and was perhaps encouraged by her musical Italian-Jewish parents—her father was a jazz trumpeter, and her mother would play recordings by Leontyne Price and classical compositions by Debussy and Persicetti while Nyro read poetry. At Manhattan's High School of Music and Art, Nyro's concentration was songwriting, and she sang at night with a neighborhood harmony street group in subway stations. In an interview with Columbia Records, Nyro recalled her teen years: "When I was sixteen years old and used to go out and sing ... the music was happening then: that's when John Coltrane was happening with jazz, when soul music and girl groups and everything was just really rich, and things were very open."

Launched Songwriting Career

By the time she was 17 she had already written what has been called her classic, "And When I Die," which was first performed by Peter, Paul and Mary, and later by Blood, Sweat and Tears. Other hits popularized by various singers and groups during the late 1960s and early 1970s included "Wedding Bell Blues," "Stoned Soul Picnic," "Blowin' Away," "Save the Country," and "Sweet Blindness," all for the Fifth Dimension; "Eli's Comin,"' for Three Dog Night; and "Stoney End" for Barbra Streisand. These songs have been acclaimed as "landmarks of an era." A biography from Columbia Records quoted *Stereo Review*'s description of them as "unexpected," with "a dazzling display of lyrical and musical innovation that gave [Nyro's] music a fresh feeling that set it apart." Nyro told *People* that "I just worked on my craft, and the next thing I knew, I would hear my work on the radio."

Other artists who have recorded Nyro's songs include Chet Atkins, Brian Auger and Julie Driscoll, Roy Ayers, Chris Connor, George Duke, "Mama" Cass Elliot, the Don Ellis Orchestra, Maynard Ferguson, the Four Tops, Aretha Franklin, Thelma Houston, Julie London, Carmen McRae, Melba Moore, Linda Ronstadt, Diana Ross and the Supremes, Mongo Santamaria, Frank Sinatra, and Junior Walker and the All-Stars. Her music

> **For the Record...**
>
> Born October 18, 1947, in Bronx, New York; father was a jazz trumpeter.
>
> Began career in 1964, writing songs for the Fifth Dimension, Blood, Sweat and Tears, Barbra Streisand, and Three Dog Night; first public performance at the hungry i coffeehouse, San Francisco, 1965; recorded first studio album for Verve/Folkways, 1967; toured the United States and recorded studio and live albums, 1967—; recorded for Columbia Records, 1967-94; first appeared at Carnegie Hall, 1970.
>
> **Addresses:** *Management*—William Morris Agency, Inc., 1350 Avenue of the Americas, New York, NY 10019.

has been performed by the Alvin Ailey dance company ("Cry") and the Canadian Ballet ("Emmie").

"San Francisco Sound"

Nyro's first public appearances were during a two-month stint in 1965 at the famous hungry i coffeehouse in San Francisco, where local radio stations described her singing as "the San Francisco sound." In 1966 Verve/Folkways released her first album, *More Than a New Discovery.* Other Verve/Folkways artists during that time included the Blues Project, Tim Hardin, Richie Havens, Janis Ian, and Dave Van Ronk. Nyro joined Columbia Records in 1967, and *Eli and the Thirteenth Confession* was brought out in 1968. Columbia Records reported that *Eli* was hailed by Jon Landau in *Rolling Stone* as the work of "an original and brilliant young talent" and by Pete Johnson of the *Los Angeles Times* as "one of the most stunning creations of recent pop music."

In the late 1960s Nyro began appearing throughout the United States at music festivals, including the 1967 Monterey Pop Festival. In 1970 Dave Dexter, Jr., of *Billboard* described how Nyro performed her "Monterey act" to "an overflow, almost hysterically demonstrative crowd in Royce Hall on the spacious UCLA campus." She "reigned as Queen of the Campus," Dexter commented, adding that Nyro was also "perhaps Queen of California."

At the Berkeley Community Theater, Nyro again performed to a standing room only audience. Ralph Gleason of *Rolling Stone* observed, "One of the most impressive things about Laura Nyro's concert is her extraordinary contact with her audience. They are deep into her songs, they pick up on the opening piano chords and applaud. While she sings, they writhe in their seats and call out requests when she pauses." David Nathan of *Billboard* praised her as one of the "most compelling performers" of the late 1960s and early 1970s.

Appeared at Carnegie Hall

During 1970, Nyro also made her first major appearance in New York City with two sold-out performances at Carnegie Hall. In describing the concert, Nancy Erlich of *Billboard* reported, "In a voice as gentle as a razor, Miss Nyro communicated her very personal vision of the world through her distinctive compositions." Vince Aletti of *Rolling Stone* believed that the high point of the concert was the songs from her albums, with Nyro's version of "Spanish Harlem" the piece that "received the heaviest response."

Nyro's recordings over the next few years were impressive. In 1969 *New York Tendaberry* was released to more critical acclaim, followed by *Christmas and the Beads of Sweat* in 1970. Alec Dubro of *Rolling Stone* commented on *Christmas* and *Tendaberry,* pointing out that they "form a chapter in her book, just as her first Verve album and *Eli* did. She has moved out of the small cult status. Her position now is the result of her own work rather than any capture of the public's fickle fancy." *Gonna Take a Miracle,* with backup provided by Patti LaBelle, was released in 1971 by Columbia, which acquired and reissued *More Than a New Discovery* as *The First Songs* in 1973. After taking time out for her personal life, Nyro released *Smile* in 1976.

Nancy Erlich of *Billboard* noted that upon Nyro's 1976 return to Carnegie Hall, the performer was "in different form." The reviewer stated, "The image of the eccentric stage personality and the songwriter of constant inspiration but erratic control is wiped out completely." The new Nyro, described Erlich, "held the stage with grace and dignity. The show was paced and rehearsed to fine detail and flowed like a continuous thought." David McGee of *Rolling Stone* remarked that the concert "brought back meaning to that misused, overused word, magic."

Nyro's four-month tour following the release of *Smile* resulted in a live album in 1977, *Season of Light/Laura Nyro in Concert.* She then turned producer for her subsequent album, *Nested,* in 1978. The singer explained to Columbia Records that the tour following the release of *Nested* "was very special. I'd sing my new songs and just drift into the old Curtis Mayfield and the

Impressions songs I sang as a kid. I was pregnant at the time and I felt super healthy—I sang up until a few weeks before I had the baby."

> "When I was sixteen years old and used to go out and sing ... the music was happening then: that's when John Coltrane was happening with jazz, when soul music and girl groups and everything was just really rich, and things were very open."

Tim Windbrandt of the *Soho News,* according to Columbia Records, remarked that her "show was almost understated in its simplicity. Miss Nyro wore a red, strapless dress and performed without any backup musicians at all. What the performance lacked in texture, it made up for in intimacy. It was almost like having Laura in one's own living room. The baby figured into the between-song patter: 'We're both really happy to be here,' [Nyro] announced."

For the next six years, Nyro took time off to raise her son. In 1984 she broke her silence with the release of *Mother's Spiritual,* described by Columbia as "a major work of 14 original new songs. The lyrics of *Mother's Spiritual* were presented on the walls of the Chicago Peace Museum as a feminist vision ... they still stand as a statement of Laura's unwavering principles."

By 1988, however, Nyro was back on the tour circuit, playing 35 concerts in major cities around the United States. David Nathan of *Billboard* described her concert at the Mayfair Theater in Santa Monica: "Nyro's appeal lies as much in occasional on-stage glimpses of her off-stage persona as it does in her pointed, image-provoking material; her easy camaraderie with both musicians and audience and a wry humor are very endearing. But it was Nyro's poetic imagery coupled with her distinctive vocal delivery that made her show simply spellbinding."

Laura Live at the Bottom Line was released on the Cypress/A&M label in 1989. She explained to reporters that she wasn't ready for another studio recording because of a strong urge to "be singing and to be a musician again, but in a soulful way." *Laura Live* introduced eight original songs and included some of her classics as well as "street-corner songs of her youth."

Songs Address Sociopolitical Issues

In 1993 Nyro recorded her first studio album in nine years, *Walk the Dog and Light the Light,* after working on it with Gary Katz for a year and a half. A *Rolling Stone* reviewer called the album "irresistible" and a writer for *People* magazine described it as "seductive." Nyro herself said the album is about compassion and healing. Her new songs showed concern for many contemporary sociopolitical issues; for example, she wrote the Native American protest song "Broken Rainbow" for the 1985 Academy Award-winning documentary of the same name, and an animal-rights song, "Lite a Flame."

Nyro's feminist concerns emerge with "A Woman of the World," a song, Nyro said, about "healing, asking more joy for yourself ... [and] harmony." "'The Descent of Luna Rose,'" the singer explained, "is about women's monthly cycles of renewal laced with a sense of humor." Another song, "Louise's Church," was dedicated to the sculptor Louise Nevelson "and other artists of inspiration," including the ancient Greek poet Sappho, singer Billie Holiday, and painter Frida Kahlo.

Nyro described "Art of Love" as a "holiday song and a peace song." She used international voices to sound her message of peace: a Tibetan monk and an Iraqi woman mingle with voices from Israel, Africa, America, and Italy. These voices represent the voice of people with a "Peace on Earth" vision of life—"just decent people," Nyro elaborated, "the man on the street, the child from the school down the block." Nyro's "To a Child" was rerecorded for *Walk the Dog,* and Jim Bessman in *Billboard* observed that it "reflects Nyro's devotion to raising her son, who is now a teenager."

Nyro described her career in the early 1990s to Bessman: "I have complete freedom as a songwriter, which is a very good feeling.... I can take a 'Mother Earth' approach to its children, write about the environment, about peace. I look at my music as 'soul talk,' a healing using the language of love, and I think there's more of that kind of feeling in it now."

When Nyro's contract with Columbia Records expired in 1994, she told *Contemporary Musicians* in a telephone interview that she felt this was the appropriate time for her to review her options and search for alternatives "that fit me a little better." Nyro explained that she was interested in continuing to make music in situations that were "less corporate, less competitive, and less capitalistic."

Selected discography

On Columbia Records, except where noted

More Than a New Discovery, Verve/Folkways, 1966, reissued as *The First Songs,* 1972.
Eli and the Thirteenth Confession, 1968.
New York Tendaberry, 1969.
Christmas and the Beads of Sweat, 1970.
(With Patti LaBelle) *Gonna Take a Miracle,* 1971.
Smile, 1975.
Season of Lights, 1977.
Nested, 1978.
Mother's Spiritual, 1984.
Laura Live at the Bottom Line, Cypress/A&M, 1989.
Walk the Dog and Light the Light, 1993.

Sources

Books

Pareles, Jon, and Patricia Romanowski, editors, *The Rolling Stone Encyclopedia of Rock and Roll,* Summit Books, 1983.

Periodicals

Billboard, June 14, 1969; December 13, 1969; February 21, 1970; July 4, 1970; March 13, 1971; May 8, 1971; April 17, 1976; October 1, 1988; October 21, 1989; August 26, 1993.
BMI Music World, July 1968; October 1969; November 1969.
Down Beat, July 24, 1969; April 2, 1970; April 15, 1971.
Life, January 30, 1970.
Melody Maker, January 30, 1971; February 13, 1971; May 15, 1971; January 8, 1972; March 18, 1972; November 9, 1974; February 7, 1976; April 17, 1976; October 24, 1987.
People, August 30, 1993.
Rolling Stone, January 21, 1970; April 16, 1970; February 18, 1971; April 8, 1976; May 6, 1976; June 3, 1976; October 14, 1993.
Variety, March 25, 1970; August 24, 1988.
Village Voice, April 10, 1984; December 5, 1989.

Additional information for this profile was obtained from Columbia Records and from phone interviews with Nyro in May-June, 1994.

—Mary Katherine Wainwright

Alan Parsons

Producer, engineer

Photograph by Dennis Keeley, courtesy of Arista Records

The history of nearly every successful rock music professional can be traced back to that proverbial first big break—and the multi-platinum career of Alan Parsons is no exception. Unlike most, however, Parsons's golden opportunity had nothing to do with endless performances at dingy clubs nor recording contracts won or lost: it came when he landed a job as an assistant recording engineer at Abbey Road Studios in 1967. "I played lead guitar with a blues band during the blues boom of the late '60s," Parsons told *Keyboard* magazine. "I was just another guitar player trying to sound like Eric Clapton. But at the same time I was trying to get a job at Abbey Road. Eventually, Abbey Road became more important than trying to be a struggling musician."

Under producer George Martin's tutelage he worked with the Beatles on their albums *Let it Be* and *Abbey Road*. The recording and production techniques he learned from Martin and the Beatles would serve as the foundation for his later endeavors. "I was just an assistant who made tea and pushed buttons," Parsons later explained. "But I did get to watch how he [Martin] works."

After the Beatles went their separate ways, Parsons continued to engineer at Abbey Road, working with solo Beatle Paul McCartney on his albums *Wild Life* and *Red Rose Speedway*. In 1973, he had the opportunity to engineer Pink Floyd's *Dark Side of the Moon,* for which he received a Grammy Award nomination. Parsons's work with Pink Floyd was a major landmark in his career, as it gave him the confidence he needed to become a producer in his own right. Following *Dark Side of the Moon,* he went on to produce albums for the Hollies, Al Stewart, Cockney Rebel, Pilot, and Olivia Newton-John, among others.

Started the Alan Parsons Project

It was during this period that Parsons met future Project collaborator Eric Woolfson. Woolfson was working as a songwriter and producer at the time, but was so impressed with Parsons's talents that he quickly signed on as his manager. After a few years of moderate success as a production team, the two decided to put together their own record based on the writings of Edgar Allan Poe, an idea Woolfson had been toying with for some time.

With Woolfson as lyricist collaborating with Parsons on the music, engineering, and production, the Alan Parsons Project's *Tales of Mystery and Imagination* was unveiled to the world in 1976 after nearly two years of effort. A major achievement—especially for a debut

For the Record...

Born in 1949 in England.

Recording engineer and producer, 1967—; with Eric Woolfson, formed the Alan Parsons Project, mid-1970s; released debut album, *Tales of Mystery and Imagination,* 1976; signed with Arista Records, 1977; produced documentary *London Calling,* MTV; collaborated with Woolfson and Brian Brolly on *Freudiana* (stage production), 1989; recorded first solo album, *Try Anything Once,* 1993.

Addresses: *Home*—Sussex, England. *Record company*—Arista Records, 6 West 57th St., New York, NY 10019.

offering—*Tales of Mystery and Imagination* included the core of all future Project releases: a wide range of lead vocalists (including Woolfson); guitar- and keyboard-based songs with long, lushly orchestrated instrumental passages; a pervasive central theme; and, of course, immaculate production. It remains one of Parsons's favorites.

"To me, *Tales of Mystery* represents everything that was right about what the Project was meant to be," Parsons told *Keyboard.* "It took risks. It was experimental. It had some good songs. It had a good choice of vocalists and musicians. Everything about it was right. It did well, and it paved the way for the future."

The Alan Parsons Project was soon after contracted to Arista and, with the release of *I Robot* in 1977, began a decade of surprising chart success—surprising for a band which never played live and whose principal members hardly appeared on the albums. The Project scored eight Top 40 singles—including "Games People Play," "Don't Answer Me," "Time," and "Eye in the Sky"—and seven Top 40 albums, as well as several Grammy nominations.

Felt Manipulated by Record Company

Unfortunately, this success was not without its negative side: Parsons and Woolfson began to feel that record company pressures were robbing them of artistic control. "We were manipulated into making music that was too commercial for what the Project originally set out to do," Parsons told *Keyboard.* "It was not meant to be a commercial band. It was meant to be a band that went in its own direction, not into a safe area as defined by the media or a record company, which is where we were in fact led."

Added Woolfson: "We felt very much in tune with Arista when we started out with them in the days of *I Robot.* But I can't pretend that we're traveling along the same road these days. They don't know how to promote quality product like us outside of hit singles, and that's a problem for them and us. These sorts of problems will always exist between artists and record companies." Indeed, disagreements between the Project and Arista resulted in several bitter contract disputes during the early and mid-1980s.

Despite the unexpected prosperity, Parsons continued to widen his musical breadth throughout the 1980s—both with the Project and on outside production jobs—while still managing to hang on to much of his original vision. The Project continued to feature a plethora of vocalists, including such notables as Terry Sylvester and Allan Clarke of the Hollies, Colin Blunstone of the Zombies, and Gary Brooker of Procul Harum. Each vocalist was carefully chosen according to his or her suitability for the material.

"I think artists have a problem when they make an album that has the same vocal sound throughout," Parsons said in *Billboard.* "It's hard for any listener to spend 40 minutes in the company of a single voice. That's why compilation albums do so well: you get variety." "Not having a fixed personality does mean listeners don't immediately know 'this is the Alan Parsons Project,'" Woolfson added. "But quality itself is a valuable market commodity."

Their commitment to quality was undoubtedly responsible for much of the Project's success, and a large part of this hinged on Parsons's skill with the latest recording technology. His unrelenting efforts to achieve the perfect sound even forced him to try his hand at building his own equipment. When recording *Tales of Mystery and Imagination,* Parsons and Woolfson constructed a unique musical machine. Woolfson explained in *Keyboard:* "When we did *Tales of Mystery and Imagination,* there was no such thing as a sampling keyboard, but even then we wanted to take a lot of sounds that we had developed and turn them into full keyboard things. So we built an instrument called the Projectron, which was based on tape loops, more or less along the lines of the Mellotron. It was enormously complicated. Not being too technical, I have no idea how it actually worked. Equipment has since come along that can do in moments what it took us days, weeks, or months to do on the Projectron. But we were at least able to build up some sounds of our own."

Longed for the Studio

Unlike some, however, Parsons doesn't believe that technology is the ultimate destination of recorded music. His aim of achieving the best possible sound drives him to do whatever is necessary for a particular song, whether it be the spontaneity of a rock band playing live in the studio, the studied expertise of a symphony orchestra and full choir, or the computerized overtones of a synthesizer. Parsons believes that focusing too much on the recording technology can produce a sterile result. "I think that great records come from great moments—not great equipment," he told *EQ*.

The release of *Gaudi* in 1987 concluded the Project's contractual obligations to Arista, and Parsons and Woolfson began to explore other artistic outlets. Among other things, Parsons directed the documentary *London Calling* for MTV; built a home studio he dubbed Parsonics; moved to the United States; decided he didn't like it much and moved back to England; and lectured and wrote extensively on sound and recording techniques.

Woolfson became interested in musical theater, and collaborated with Parsons and Andrew Lloyd Weber associate Brian Brolly in creating the stage show *Freudiana*, which *Variety* described as "a highly theatrical evocation of the phobias and psychic archetypes identified with the godfather of psychoanalysis." The well-received show ran in Vienna for more than a year.

Following *Freudiana*, Woolfson decided to further his interest in theatrical productions. Parsons, on the other hand, longed for the studio. In 1993, he recorded *Try Anything Once* at Parsonics as a "solo" album, which, in spite of past problems, was released by Arista. *Try Anything Once* contained all the trademark Parsons touches: long orchestral passages; melodic, elaborately arranged songs; and, naturally, a wide range of vocalists. As before, Parsons considered himself to be the musical analog of a film director. Like a director who doesn't write the script or appear in the film, Parsons (for the most part) didn't write the material or appear on the album, but was largely responsible for the artistic impact of the finished product.

Parsons has enjoyed "getting his hands dirty" once in a while, playing an occasional guitar or keyboard and contributing an odd vocal here and there. "Hitchcock liked to appear in his movies in a small cameo," Woolfson explained in *db*. "Alan likes to do the same thing on his records, he always likes to do a little something."

Not the Singer

Try Anything Once did nothing to injure Parsons's reputation as a creator of new sounds and novel production techniques—although the bottom line was, as always, making a good record. "I'm not really the best judge of whether we are innovative or not," he explained in *Melody Maker*. "If I was to make the next album based around dustbin lids, then you could say it's innovative. There are certain areas in contemporary pop which have been accepted and which people enjoy listening to and that's all we're trying to do. We're trying to entertain people, give them what they want to hear. If, on the way, we can give them something that they haven't heard before and they like it, that's fine."

Unfortunately, even after all this time Parsons still finds himself misunderstood by press and fans alike. "To this day, there are people who find it hard to accept that I'm not the singer," he noted. "They'll say to me, 'You've got a really diverse style. How do you manage to sing in all those different voices?'"

Parsons's recipe for the future calls for generous helpings of current trends and technologies blended with an undiminished sense of the importance of quality in sound and music. "The last thing I want to do is to grow old gracefully," he told *Keyboard*. "I like to feel that we're right in there competing with everybody else. It would be a disaster to fall into a middle market and become adult contemporary, when we should really be album-oriented. I would hate to be on the same program with Frank Sinatra and that type. I want to be thought of as someone whose music could be played on a current kids' radio station at any time."

Selected discography

(With Eric Woolfson) *Freudiana* (soundtrack), EMI, 1990.
Try Anything Once, Arista, 1993.

With the Alan Parsons Project

Tales of Mystery and Imagination, PolyGram, 1976, remastered with new performances, 1987.
I Robot, Arista, 1977.
Pyramid, Arista, 1978.
Eve, Arista, 1979.
The Turn of a Friendly Card (includes "Games People Play" and "Time"), Arista, 1980.
Eye in the Sky (includes title track), Arista, 1982.
The Best of the Alan Parsons Project, Arista, 1983.
Ammonia Avenue (includes "Don't Answer Me"), Arista, 1984.

Vulture Culture, Arista, 1984.
Stereotomy, Arista, 1985.
Gaudi, Arista, 1987.
The Best of the Alan Parsons Project Volume 2, Arista, 1988.
Instrumental Works, Arista, 1988.
Anthology, Arista, 1991.

Sources

Billboard, March 15, 1986; November 13, 1993.
db, May/June 1986.
EQ, January 1994.
Keyboard, August 1986.
Melody Maker, July 10, 1976; July 30, 1977; July 15, 1978.
Stereo Review, October 1978.
Variety, January 7, 1991.

—Alan Glenn

Pearl Jam

Rock band

"Pearl Jam is much more than a popular band to the many who look to their emotion-driven music for comfort, solidarity, and a sense of connectedness," noted *Guitar Player*'s Mike Mettler. A remarkable 1990s success story, the band is also part of the fierce Seattle rock scene that stunned the music industry by turning soulful, cathartic themes, punk attitude, and metal guitar into multi-platinum sales. Though at first thrown for a loop by their success, Pearl Jam—fronted by charismatic lead vocalist Eddie Vedder—followed their multi-platinum debut album with a strong and popular sophomore release, making their huge appeal even harder to write off as a mere trend.

Much of the credit for Pearl Jam's sudden and solid connection with its devoted, youthful audience must go to Vedder, whose "vocalized anguish seems to strike the raw and hurting nerve of a young generation raised on divorce and dysfunction," according to a *People* magazine writer. The singer's own troubled past informs his lyrics—rife with images of violence and loneliness—and his singing balances rage, despair,

Photograph by Lance Mercer, © 1993 Sony Music, courtesy of Epic Records

> **For the Record . . .**
>
> Members include **Dave Abbruzzese** (born c. 1968 in Texas), drums; **Jeff Ament** (born c. 1963 in Montana), bass; **Stone Gossard** (born c. 1966), guitar; **Dave Krusen,** drums (left band 1991); **Mike McCready** (born c. 1965), guitar; **Eddie Vedder** (born Edward Louis Seversen III in Evanston, IL, c. 1965; married Beth Liebling [a writer], 1994), vocals.
>
> Recording and performing artists, 1991—. Band formed in Seattle, WA; signed with Epic and released debut album *Ten,* 1991; contributed to Bob Dylan Tribute concert and album, 1992; appeared on Victoria Williams tribute album *Sweet Relief,* 1993; collaborated with group Cypress Hill on song for soundtrack to film *Judgment Night,* 1993.
>
> **Awards:** Platinum records for *Ten,* 1992, and *Vs.*, 1993; favorite new artist, pop/rock and favorite new artist heavy metal/hard rock, 1993 American Music Awards; best video of the year, best group video and best metal/hard rock video for "Jeremy" (director: Mark Pellington), MTV Video Music Awards, 1993; *Rolling Stone* artists of the year, 1994.
>
> **Addresses:** *Record company*—Epic Associated, Sony Music Entertainment Inc., 550 Madison Ave., New York, NY 10022; 2100 Colorado Ave., Santa Monica, CA 90404. *Fan club*—Pearl Jam Ten Club, P.O. Box 4570, Seattle, WA 98104.

yearning, and hope in a way that has struck a chord with listeners since the release of Pearl Jam's Epic debut *Ten* in 1991. "I mean, my upbringing was like a hurricane, and music was the tree I held onto," Vedder explained to *Melody Maker*. "That's how important it was, and is. It's everything." The vocalist had more difficulty than his bandmates dealing with the demands of sudden fame and seemed taken aback by the realization of his own impact: "The fact that so many people relate to these songs is kind of depressing," he told *Details*. A *Rolling Stone* review called Vedder both "a heroic figure" and "a big force without bulls—; he bellows doubt."

Formed From Ashes of Mother Love Bone

Pearl Jam was started by guitarist Stone Gossard and bassist Jeff Ament. The two had played together in the Seattle outfit Green River (along with two founders of the influential band Mudhoney) and helped to develop the "grunge" rock sound that would later be celebrated and scrutinized by the very industry pundits who originally ignored the bands developing the trend. It was with the glam-metal group Mother Love Bone, however, that Gossard and Ament fully expected to hit the big time; fronted by flamboyant singer Andy Wood, the group was signed and had recorded an album when Wood died of a heroin overdose in 1990.

Though devastated by Wood's death, Ament and Gossard vowed to struggle on. Seeing no point in trying to replace the inimitable Wood, they decided to put together a new project. Gossard—lacking the "ego" to move from rhythm to lead guitar, as Devon Jackson of *Details* expressed it—enlisted Mike McCready, a guitarist who had played in such unheralded Seattle bands as Shadow and Love Chile. While long an idolizer of rock trailblazer Jimi Hendrix, McCready's playing had recently been energized by the work of blues guitar greats like Muddy Waters and Stevie Ray Vaughn. Describing Waters's performance in the concert documentary *The Last Waltz* to *Guitar Player*'s Mettler, McCready declared, "I couldn't believe the raw, emotional power he generated; it was just what I was looking for as a player. The blues is all about intense, cathartic feelings and finding that special place where you can channel all your stress into something else." Gossard's compositions, which *Guitar Player* noted were often predicated on unusual guitar tunings, provided a perfect springboard for what Mettler called McCready's "raw, Hendrix-inspired lead work."

Vedder Brought Passion, Work Ethic

Brought together, the two guitar players "just clicked," McCready declared. All that remained, McCready recalled to Mettler, was "to find Eddie and a drummer." It's understandable that Vedder seemed in retrospect the only person to front Pearl Jam (which was originally named Mookie Blaylock, after a hard-working pro basketball player admired by the hoop-obsessed musicians). Drummer Jack Irons, formerly of alternative-rock sensations the Red Hot Chili Peppers, declined the drummer spot but recommended that Gossard and company send a tape of instrumentals to Vedder, an Evanston, Illinois native who was living in San Diego. Vedder loved the tape, wrote lyrics to three of the tunes and sang them over the music, made his own photocopied art for it, titled the whole package "Mamasan," and sent it back to Seattle. Ament listened to it and promptly phoned Gossard, according to a *Rolling Stone* profile. "Stone," he reportedly insisted, "you better get over here."

Vedder told his new bandmates that he wanted to rehearse as soon as he arrived in Seattle. With Dave Krusen on drums, the group spent a week writing and rehearsing and then played their first show. They took the name Pearl Jam, allegedly after a mysterious preserve made by Vedder's great-grandmother. Their debut album—which they produced along with Rick Parashar, who also worked with the band Blind Melon—was called *Ten* after Mookie Blaylock's jersey number. "We were green when we made *Ten*," McCready revealed to *Guitar Player*. "Aside from Jeff and Stone, nobody else had really done a record before."

> "The fact that so many people relate to these songs is kind of depressing."
> —Eddie Vedder

A writer for *Details* noted that the recording contained "everything you'd expect of a Seattle band: roaring guitars, rough edges, no frills or flash. And plenty of musical hooks." *Music Express* declared, "There's absolutely nothing new about Pearl Jam," although it judged Vedder's voice and the group's hard-hitting sound "irresistible." Critical admiration, however, was not required to make the band a sensation. They appeared as the backing musicians for the character played by Matt Dillon in Cameron Crowe's motion picture *Singles* (filmed before *Ten* but released after the album had begun rocketing up the charts). Gossard and McCready also joined members of fellow Seattle rockers Soundgarden for a one-off album—called *Temple of the Dog*—dedicated to Wood. Vedder put in an appearance on the song "Hunger Strike." That album, too, became a hit after Pearl Jam began to chart.

The initial single from *Ten,* the furious rocker "Alive," became a major hit, thanks in part to a video that showed a raucous live performance. It was the mainstream music audience's first exposure to Vedder, whose anguished yet resilient presence became an overnight sensation. The singer later revealed to *Rolling Stone* that "Alive"—despite having been adopted as a survival anthem by critics and fans alike—was a far darker and more despairing tale than anyone seemed to realize. (He later described it as the story of a mother's sexual attraction to her son, based on his resemblance to his dead father.)

The song "Evenflow" also fared well, and the band's appearance on *MTV Unplugged* broadened its audience considerably. But it was the first "concept video" for a Pearl Jam song—something the group had initially vowed not to do—that took them over the top. "Jeremy," a tragic story of a misunderstood boy who kills himself before his classmates, became the group's biggest hit thanks in large part to a dramatic video by Mark Pellington that won three trophies at the MTV Video Awards. The group resisted Epic's efforts to make a video for the emotional "Black," believing it would compromise the song's personal meaning. Even so, *Ten* became a multi-platinum sensation, and Pearl Jam was suddenly one of the biggest bands in the music world. Among other honors, they took home trophies at the 1993 American Music Awards for favorite new artist in both the pop/rock and heavy metal/hard rock categories.

The band toured the world, making converts everywhere they went. *Melody Maker* reported that at a concert in Oslo, Norway, the fans "kn[ew] all the words. It takes something less than seconds for Pearl Jam, in a live context, to astonish." *Ten* continued to rise up the charts, though it didn't get to the top position. Nonetheless, Pearl Jam had arrived.

Vedder was a bona fide rock hero in the grand tradition, a development reinforced by his singing in front of the reunited 1960s band The Doors—in place of the band's late and legendary vocalist Jim Morrison—on the occasion of their induction into the Rock and Roll Hall of Fame and his participation in the 1992 anniversary tribute to visionary singer/songwriter Bob Dylan. The band would rub shoulders with other rock idols: they opened for Rolling Stones guitarist Keith Richards at a New Year's Eve concert and joined rock survivor Neil Young onstage at the MTV Video Music Awards for a raucous version of Young's "Rockin' in the Free World." They joined Young for a tour, and shared a European bill with Irish superstars U2. The group also participated in a number of benefit albums, including the *Sweet Relief* tribute to singer/songwriter Victoria Williams.

Dealt With Fame, Pressure for Follow-Up

By the time the group finished recording its second album, the sense of anticipation in the rock world was palpable. Vedder, having emerged as a rock hero, served as tabloid fodder for months; speculation abounded that he had become an alcoholic, and one briefly circulated rumor had him dead of a heroin overdose. (In 1994, bandmate Abbruzzese commented wryly in *Rolling Stone,* "Eddie died three times last year.") At one point Vedder phoned underground musician and writer Henry Rollins—a fiercely independent and self-reliant figure—for advice. "My take on the whole thing was, here's an honest guy in a very weird situation," Rollins recalled to *Rolling Stone*. "I said, 'Eddie, usually people as big as you are are real schmucks. Because they pulled every string to make that happen. But you haven't. You put the shit out there, and people went "Thank you, that's what I've been waiting to hear."'" Rollins said he advised the singer to "drink your carrot juice, breathe deep, have fun, and don't do what you don't want to." Despite his struggle with the limelight, however, Vedder had thrown himself into the band's new batch of songs.

Between the release of *Ten* and the completion of the follow-up, of course, there had been a few changes in the cultural landscape. Most notably, "grunge" was a term bandied about by magazine publishers, talk-show pundits, and fashion designers, and the term "the next Seattle" had been hurled at every burgeoning local music scene. Vedder himself had become an unwilling spokesperson for youthful angst, not to mention the subject of considerable theorizing on the pages of teen magazine *Sassy*.

Sophomore Release a Smash Success

Pearl Jam's second album, originally titled *Five Against One* but changed to *Vs.* after its initial pressing, hit retail outlets in the fall of 1993. It sold 950,000 copies in its first week, reported *Variety,* and went quintuple-platinum in three months. By that time, *Ten* was officially a sextuple-platinum recording. Produced by the band with alternative-rock scion Brendan O'Brien and recorded at a remote, posh studio in northern California, the record displayed an expanded musical palette, most evident in Abbruzzese's diverse rhythms and a greater range of guitar tones. "It's tempting," wrote James Rotondi of *Guitar Player,* "to suggest the term *grunge-funk*." Cameron Crowe ventured in *Rolling Stone* that the album "is the band's turf-statement, a personal declaration of the importance of music over idolatry." The songs cover the spectrum from the scorching "Leash" and "W.M.A.," among other songs raging against oppression and violence to softer, more introspective compositions like "Daughter" and "Elderly Woman Behind the Counter in a Small Town."

Vs. suggested to many critics that the band had matured considerably. "The songs are less anthemic but every bit as gripping," Rotondi mused, "ripe with meaning that gradually unfolds upon deeper listening." *Rolling Stone* gave the album four and one-half stars and heaped special praise on Vedder's "smart singing" and "the muscular roil of Dave Abbruzzese's percussion," concluding that "there's always enough going on beneath the surface to remind us that magic in this band's music builds from the bottom up."

Richard Cromelin of the *Los Angeles Times,* more a fan of Vedder's style and power than the band's music, dubbed the sophomore effort "a palpably stronger album" than Pearl Jam's debut, adding that by its close the band "have reaffirmed that rock album can be a grueling, blood-and-guts experience that leaves a listener bruised, muddy—and ultimately elevated." *USA Today,* meanwhile, called *Vs.* "crunching a melodic, raw and graceful, mystical and visceral."

Yet despite all of their success, Pearl Jam has not forgotten about their fans. A writer for *Billboard* noted that the band has gladly accepted the "challenge of balancing their enormous success with delivering what they think loyal fans deserve: access and reasonably priced music." Some of the ways Pearl Jam has tried to achieve this goal include notifying fan club members of upcoming shows and giving them first dibs on tickets, refusing to sell limited-view tickets, and keeping ticket prices (before service charges) at $18. The band has taken particular exception to the concept of service charges; in May of 1994 they filed a brief with the U.S. Department of Justice charging Ticketmaster, a national ticket distributer, with forming a monopoly.

Pearl Jam is staunchly opposed to the service charge—ranging from three to six dollars—that Ticketmaster tacks onto the price of concert tickets that are bought by phone. (The band would accept a service charge of $1.80.) The argument intensified when Pearl Jam claimed that Ticketmaster had used its influence to keep promoters from booking the band's 1994 summer tour. Ticketmaster denies the allegations, but the Justice Department is proceeding with an investigation of "possible anti-competitive practice in the ticket distribution industry," according to the *Detroit News*.

In their *Rolling Stone* interview with Crowe—an old friend from Seattle—the band reflected on the ramifications of large-scale success. Gossard addressed claims that fame deprives musicians of their edge: "To me, the problem with getting too big is not, innately, you get too big and all of a sudden you stop playing good music. The problem is, when you get too big, you stop doing the things you used to do. Just being big doesn't mean you can't go in your basement and write a good song."

Abbruzzese, meanwhile, good-humoredly noted, "when I was younger and I heard about a band selling a million records, I thought the band would get together and jump up and down for at least a *minute,* and just go, 'Wow, I can't believe it.' But it doesn't happen that way [in this band]. Me, I flip out. I jump up and down by myself." Ultimately, it's the balance between painful introspection and jumping up and down that summarizes Pearl Jam's artistic philosophy. As Ament expressed it to *Spin*, "Eddie's lyrics take you to an open window, and just when you've got one foot out on the ledge, it's our job to bring you back in to celebrate."

Selected discography

On Epic

Ten (includes "Alive," "Evenflow," "Jeremy" and "Black"), 1991.
Alive (EP), 1991.
Vs. (includes "Leash," "W.M.A.," "Daughter" and "Elderly Woman Behind the Counter in a Small Town"), 1993.

With other artists

Mother Love Bone, *Mother Love Bone* (includes Gossard and Ament), Stardog/Mercury, 1992.
Temple of the Dog (includes Gossard, Ament and McCready on all tracks; Vedder appears on "Hunger Strike"), A&M, 1991.
Bob Dylan Thirtieth-Anniversary Tribute (Vedder and McCready appear on "Masters of War"), Columbia, 1993.
Various, *Sweet Relief: A Tribute to Victoria Williams* (band appears on "Crazy Mary"), Thirsty Ear/Chaos, 1993.
Brad (featuring Stone Gossard), *Shame*, Epic, 1993.
Various, *Judgment Night* soundtrack (bands appears with Cypress Hill on "Real Thing"), Epic Soundtrax/Immortal, 1993.
Various, *Stone Free: A Tribute to Jimi Hendrix* (includes McCready, Ament and others as M.A.C.C. on "Hey Baby/New Rising Sun"), Warner Bros., 1993.

Sources

Billboard, September 11, 1993; October 16, 1993; April 23, 1994.
Circus, March 31, 1992.
Details, August 1992.
Detroit News, June 10, 1993.
Entertainment Weekly, January 31, 1992; July 31, 1992; September 25, 1992; January 8, 1993; April 9, 1993.
FMQB, June 12, 1992.
Guitar Player, February 1992; December 1992; December 1993; January 1994.
Los Angeles Times, October 17, 1993; May 1, 1994.
Melody Maker, February 22, 1992.
Music Express, January 1993.
Musician, July 1992; April 1993.
New Yorker, April 20, 1992.
People, January 25, 1993; December 6, 1993; December 27, 1993; June 27, 1994.
Pollstar, September 23, 1991.
Pulse!, August 1993.
Reflex, June 1992.
Rolling Stone, July 9, 1992; February 4, 1993; February 18, 1993; March 18, 1993; April 1, 1993; June 10, 1993; July 8, 1993; September 2, 1993; October 28, 1993; November 11, 1993; December 9, 1993; December 23, 1993; January 27, 1994; May 5, 1994.
San Diego Union Tribune, October 14, 1993.
Seattle Times, December 8, 1993.
Spin, September 1991; June, 1992; November 1992; December 1992; January 1993; April 1993; September 1993; June 1994.
Time, October 25, 1993.
USA Today, October 15, 1993.
Variety, November 4, 1993.

Additional information was provided by Epic promotional materials, 1991 and 1993.

—*Simon Glickman*

Sam Phillips

Singer, songwriter, guitarist

Photograph by Melodie McDaniel, courtesy of Virgin Records

Although she began her pop music career in the 1980s, Sam Phillips would find herself at home in any decade or style. She draws from such early twentieth-century poets as Thomas Merton, William Butler Yeats, Pablo Neruda, and Rainer Maria Rilke, but also from later, musical poets—Randy Newman, Bruce Cockburn, Joni Mitchell, and John Lennon. Though she infuses her music with a 1960s psychedelia, she is also rooted in the pop of earlier generation, adoring "melodic music, first and foremost," she explained in a Virgin Records press release—old jazz, composer George Gershwin, and vocalist Nat King Cole reign among her favorites. She produces deeply spiritual albums, yet she retains a very sharp sense of wit and irony.

Phillips's music, which Craig Tomashoff of *People* described as "too hip for radio," has struggled to find a wide audience. Yet early in her career, Phillips became a favorite of music critics, who seemed to like the combination of "dark lyrics and light sounds," in the words of *Rolling Stone*'s Patti O'Brien, and her voice, which *Interview*'s Dimitri Ehrlich likened to a "soprano bagpipe."

Thom Jurek of the Detroit *Metro Times* ventured an explanation of her critical success: "Phillips makes the kind of pop records that most musicians only dream of. She consistently writes intelligent words; combines them with delightful, often stunning melodies; and delivers them in an unusual, yet attractive voice—with unexpected surprises popping out of the mix at every turn." Ron Givens of *Stereo Review* put it succinctly: "Sam Phillips is always wondrous to hear."

Career Began in Christian Music

Phillips was born in East Hollywood, California, in 1962, the second of William and Peggy Phillips's three children. Though named Leslie, she was called by her nickname, Sam. She grew up in suburban Glendale, California, in what she described to *Musician*'s Mark Rowland as a "standard dysfunctional house."

She first entered the music world through dance and turned to writing and playing in her early teens as she watched her parents' marriage disintegrate and end in divorce. "Basically, I was crying into the piano," she confessed to Jeff Giles in *Newsweek.* "One of the first songs I wrote was called 'Walls of Silence,' about the fact that my father would go days, weeks, even months without speaking." She learned to play her brother's guitar and began exploring music outside the Top 20, finding such artists as singer-songwriters Randy Newman and Bruce Cockburn. Her non-musical interests

For the Record...

Born Leslie Phillips, June 28, 1962, in East Hollywood, CA; daughter of William (an accountant) and Peggy (a medical secretary) Smith; married T-Bone Burnett (a musician and producer); has two stepchildren.

Signed with gospel label Word/Myrrh records, c. 1980; recorded and toured as Leslie Phillips, 1980-87; signed with Virgin Records, c. 1987; changed professional name to Sam Phillips; released first secular album, *The Indescribable Wow,* 1988.

Addresses: *Record company*—Virgin Records, 338 North Foothill Rd., Beverly Hills, CA 90210.

---

led her even further from the Top 20. She studied philosophy and religion—primarily fundamentalism—and found herself drawn to the counterculture Christian movement of southern California.

Undoubtedly, the splintering of her family contributed to this attraction. "Because of that pain, I've always been interested in metamorphosis, and when that can happen to a human being, emotionally and spiritually," Phillips revealed to Rowland. "I've always loved that theme throughout literature. I think that's what attracted me to Christianity the most." She also found the church attractive because of her music. "I thought I would find an audience there that would want to listen to songs about spiritual things," she explained to David Wild in *Rolling Stone.*

At 18 years old, Phillips signed a contract with A&M's gospel label, Word/Myrrh Records, and performing as Leslie Phillips, she became a Christian music star. A 1985 press release, reprinted in *Harper's,* described her image: "If ever there was a Queen of Christian Rock, she's it. She's 22, blond, hazel-eyed, lovely, and single, and her hair and clothing are up-to-date, California youth style." Her albums sold well, up to 200,000 a piece, and she toured the country, performing in churches, coffeehouses, and festivals.

Her last album as Leslie, 1987's *The Turning,* was produced by T-Bone Burnett, a musician as well as producer who had worked with such rock luminaries as Bob Dylan, Roy Orbison, Elvis Costello, and Los Lobos. Their collaboration impressed critics outside Christian music. Jimmy Guterman asserted in *Rolling Stone* that *The Turning* "is far more generous of spirit than most secular-gospel records nowadays, mostly because Phillips is such an adept writer." *High Fidelity*'s Jeff Nesin found the album "spare and compelling," and Wild called it "an ethereal beauty."

Switched to Secular Music

After she released *The Turning,* Phillips left the Christian music scene, a world in which she had become increasingly uncomfortable. As she recalled in *Billboard,* she "wanted to explore spirituality, not dispense God propaganda." She elaborated in a Virgin press release: "I was naive enough to think I could talk about spiritual issues in my songs within the church. I wanted to ask questions, push the boundaries, and they wanted me to say that I'd found all the answers.... I just don't think life is that simple. True spirituality is much bigger than that."

Burnett introduced her to people at Virgin Records, and she had signed with them by 1988. The move to secular music meant a hit to her income, but as she insisted in *Musician,* "It wasn't a career decision to quit gospel music, it was a soul decision—and a turn-of-the-stomach decision." With this metamorphosis, Phillips decided to change her professional name as well, and redubbed herself Sam Phillips. She had no idea she was taking the name of the legendary Sam Phillips who founded Memphis's Sun Records, and who is credited with the discovery of Elvis Presley. Some things about Phillips did not change. Burnett remained her producer, and critics continued to love her music. Wild applauded *The Indescribable Wow,* her first release as Sam Phillips, calling it "an exquisitely crafted, introspectively romantic pop gem," and Nesin considered it one of the best albums of 1988.

Some critics noticed the influence of 1960s pop music, especially the Beatles, in her use of harpsichord, electric sitar, organ, and reverse tape. In Nesin's words, the album was "chock-full of dazzlingly arranged and executed pop songs redolent of the 1960s—not just in instrumentation ... but in a willingness to experiment, to push farther, that just hasn't been heard much since those hybrid, halcyon days."

Despite her move into the secular world, Phillips's work retained a spiritual edge. In her later material, the lyrics dwelt, Jurek noted, "on questions rather than answers." David Okamoto of *CD Review* also observed that, "Phillips no longer evangelizes, but she still celebrates her faith via secular signposts that everyone can follow."

Opting for one of the more out-of-the-ordinary routes of promotion, Phillips followed the release of *The Inde-*

scribable Wow with a tour of the country, bowling with radio program directors. She also married Burnett, and they began working on her next album. With *Cruel Inventions,* released in 1991, Phillips and Burnett took the experimentation up a notch. Musically, Rowland noticed "increasingly elaborate and unpredictably textured arrangements."

Josef Woodard of *Rolling Stone* found the album more complex than *The Indescribable Wow.* He noted "alien guitar sounds," "savory string arrangements," and "unusual percussion." Woodard wrote, "conventional ingredients are transformed into something stranger, more evocative, to suit Phillips's cryptic lyrics." The underlying the lyrical and musical experimentation on the album was Phillips's increasingly characteristic wit and pop flair—qualities that led *Rolling Stone* to insist that Phillips helped "prove that it actually is possible to find beautiful, articulate pop in the nineties," and to rate the album "one of the years most arresting treasures."

Songs Featured in Film

Before she released her next album, Phillips discovered fans in important places. While working on his film *Ruby in Paradise,* director Victor Nunez heard "Raised on Promises," a cut from *Cruel Inventions,* on his car radio. He loved the song enough to drive immediately to a record store and buy the album. Eventually that song, and "Holding on to the Earth" from *The Indescribable Wow,* were added to the film, which became the Grand Prize winner at the 1993 Sundance Film Festival.

With her next release, Phillips sought a less complex album. "I think the experimenting wore us out a little bit in the past," she explained to Rowland. "These songs are a little simpler and maybe easier to figure out." In the resulting album, 1994's *Martinis and Bikinis,* Phillips's penchant for 1960s pop and unusual instrumentation was still evident. In addition to the harpsichord, sitars, and reverse tape, Phillips included a string quartet, treble guitars, and a mandolin. She also included an overt nod to John Lennon, covering his song "Gimme Some Truth."

Once again the album was a critical success, with Okamoto proclaiming it "the first pop masterpiece of this young year." Giving the album four stars, *Rolling Stone's* Kara Manning delighted in Phillips exploration of "not only the poetry of words, but the poetry inherent in stunning production techniques." Above all, critics were fascinated with Phillips's ability to balance the exuberance of pop music and a love of melody with a probing and unflinching quest for virtue and truth.

"Phillips has developed a singular voice, coopting the stylistic quirks of pop innocence in a heady search for modern maturity," *Musician's* Chris Willman averred. "Druggy with youth and punch-sober with experience, this album feels a little like getting to have your cake and eat it too. The effect is delicious, and uneasy."

Throughout her secular career, commercial success had eluded Phillips, and critics hoped *Martinis and Bikinis* would be her breakthrough album. Finding a niche for delicious and uneasy music on popular radio was not easy. "I'm not soft enough to be considered 'easy listening' or hard or weird enough to be considered 'alternative,'" she complained to the *Merto Times'* Jurek. "And in a way that's understandable, because I can't describe what my music is either." Phillips was also hindered by her aversion to adopting an image in a field where image can be everything.

Phillips remarked that she is not interested in the glaring stereotypes the industry markets in the name of image. Furthermore, after a career as the "Queen of Christian Rock," she had reasons to avoid image. "I'm leery, I've been through that once already," she told Jurek. Yet her lack of celebrity didn't particularly bother Phillips—she'd been there before as well. "Celebrity is really uninteresting, and it's tiring," she revealed to Woodard. "The work is the thing," she emphasized, "the great thing."

White conjectured that it will be the impact of her work, not any manufactured image, that will last. "Generations onward, when others reflect on the hollows of our faithless age, the work of Phillips, like that of the poets she holds dear, will show that many still sought to improvise virtue after much common evidence of it had evaporated."

Selected discography

Dancing with Danger, Word/Myrrh, 1985.
The Turning, Word/Myrrh, 1987.
The Indescribable Wow, Virgin, 1988.
Cruel Inventions, Virgin, 1991.
Martinis and Bikinis, Virgin, 1994.

Sources

Billboard, January 22, 1994; March 5, 1994; July 9, 1994.
Boston Globe, April 19, 1989.
CD Review, April 1994.
Chicago Tribune, June 27, 1991.
Guitar Player, June 1994.
Harper's, May 1985.

High Fidelity, February 1989.
Interview, June 1991.
Metro Times (Detroit), March 23, 1994; May 18, 1994.
Musician, August 1991; July 1992; March 1994.
Newsweek, April 4, 1994.
People, October 21, 1991.
Pulse!, November 1993.
Rolling Stone, June 18, 1987; August 24, 1988; November 17, 1988; May 18, 1989; October 17, 1991; August 8, 1991; December 12, 1991; March 24, 1994.
Stereo Review, August 1991.

Additional information for this profile was obtained from Virgin Records publicity materials.

—*Megan Rubiner Zinn*

Chris Rea

Singer, songwriter

Chris Rea is hardly a household name in the United States, but this unassuming singer has been a constant figure on the European music scene for more than a decade. He is sometimes referred to as the "British Bruce Springsteen" because of the gruff, raspy quality of his voice and the themes that run through his music; like Springsteen, Rea often writes about the search for meaningful values in a world gone awry. Coincidentally, both Springsteen and Rea are of Irish-Italian extraction. Rea cites the music of Joe Walsh as his inspiration for becoming a guitar player. He began playing in his twenties, and in 1975 he formed the band Magdelene, later to be called the Beautiful Losers. The group, which included future Whitesnake member David Cloverdale, won *Melody Maker* magazine's "Best New Band" award that year.

In 1976 Rea signed as a solo artist with Magnet Records. He got off to a flying start with the single "Fool If You Think It's Over," which charted in both the United Kingdom and the United States and earned him a Grammy nomination for best new artist. Unfortunately for Rea, he was making the right music at the wrong time. Soon after his initial burst of popularity, punk swept over England, overshadowing every other style of music. Rea slipped into a period of relative obscurity. He wrote some fine albums, such as *Shamrock Diaries* and *Do You Like Tennis,* but sales of these were far too small to satisfy record company executives.

During this period, Rea became quite disillusioned with the machinations of the recording industry. "I was very close to completely stopping music and opening an Italian restaurant," he told Kent Zimmerman of the *Gavin Report.* "I was sick to death of it. I didn't want to be a rock star. I just wanted to enjoy the music, which is what I started out doing.... Everyone wanted me to be the next Elton John or George Michael-type superstar. That's not where I come from. I come from the school of Joe Walsh, Bonnie Raitt, Ry Cooder, Lowell George."

Rea's label was as disenchanted with him as he was with them. When he delivered the demo tapes for the album *Watersign,* the company skipped over the usual remixing process and released the tapes untouched, apparently aiming to fulfill his contract and release him. The unexpected happened, however: *Watersign* became a respectable hit, selling half a million copies and producing a top single, "I Can Hear Your Heart Beat." Rea began touring heavily to bolster the album's success, and built up a loyal following in Germany and France as well as the United Kingdom.

Rea's greatest recognition in the United States came with his 1990 recording, *The Road to Hell.* Zimmerman stated that "Out of ... ten-plus years of recording

> **For the Record ...**
>
> Born in Middlesbrough, England, 1951; married. Played with band Magdalene, later called the Beautiful Losers, 1970s; signed as solo artist with Magnet Records, 1976; released debut album, *Whatever Happened to Benny Santini*, 1978.
>
> **Addresses:** *Record company*—EastWest Records, 75 Rockefeller Plaza, New York, NY 10019.

music, *Road to Hell* stands out as his masterwork.... There's a feel of environmental politics threading its way, conceptually, through most of the songs.... Mixed in with the doomy lyrics and instrumentation are a few choice love songs."

Rea conceived of the album while trapped in an all-too-typical traffic jam in the south of England. The isolation of the thousands of commuters in their cars struck him forcefully, and within days he had written several songs concerning the ills of modern life. The music behind the lyrics has an ominous, eerie quality. "That's deliberate," Rea explained. "I'm trying to bring a bit of Alfred Hitchcock into the music.... A lot of folks do think that we're on the edge of some terrible, impending disaster."

Rea had another success in America in 1994 with *Espresso Logic,* which showcased "a number of genres, from crunching blues, to Beatlesque pop, to fluent jazz," according to Steve White in the Lowell, Massachusetts *Sun.* The album consists of tracks previously included on European releases, one of which was also called *Espresso Logic;* the other was titled *God's Great Banana Skin.*

The U.S. album, however, included a duet by Rea with Elton John titled "If You Were Me." Reviewers commented on Rea's fluid slide guitar and praised his throaty yet polished vocals. In addition, Lee Barrish, writing for Cleveland's *Scene,* observed, "The elements of woe (thoughts of mortality and death) that coursed their way through the last three albums have finally been laid to rest." A *Network Forty* reviewer remarked that the release "is a bold milestone" in Rea's career and also noted that Rea's relative obscurity in the United States despite his immense popularity in Europe does not affect him: "He has always stood for quality music with intelligence, not just commercial appeal."

Selected discography

On Magnet

Whatever Happened to Benny Santini (includes "Fool If You Think It's Over"), 1978.
Deltics, 1979.
Do You Like Tennis, 1980.
Chris Rea, 1982.
Watersign, 1983.
Shamrock Diaries, 1985.
Wired to the Moon, 1985.
On the Beach, 1986.
Dancing with Strangers, 1987.

Other

The Road to Hell, Geffen, 1989.
Auberge, 1991.
God's Great Banana Skin, 1992.
Espresso Logic (contains material from earlier European releases *God's Great Banana Skin* and *Espresso Logic*), EastWest, 1994.

Sources

Billboard, March 19, 1994.
Gavin Report, March 30, 1990.
Morning Call, April 2, 1994.
Network Forty, March 1994.
Northern Iowan, March 18, 1994.
Scene (Cleveland, OH), March 10, 1994.
Sun (Lowell, MA), March 24, 1994.

Additional information for this profile was obtained from EastWest Records publicity material.

—*Joan Goldsworthy*

Joshua Redman

Saxophonist

Photograph by Tom Tavee, © 1993 Warner Bros. Records

In the spring of 1991 Joshua Redman was finishing up an undergraduate degree at Harvard University and jamming informally with friends in the Boston area. Two years later he was performing alongside fellow saxophonists Illinois Jacquet and U.S. President Bill Clinton on the White House lawn. Rarely has a jazz musician gone from obscurity to international stardom in such a brief span of time. By age 24 Redman had appeared onstage and on recordings with some of the greatest names in jazz, made two critically acclaimed albums under his own name, and toured nationally with the Lincoln Center Jazz Orchestra. With his stunning instrumental technique, intellectual prowess, and handsome appearance, Redman was by the spring of 1994 one of the most talked-about people in music.

Much like an earlier jazz *wunderkind,* Wynton Marsalis, who by the age of 19 was playing with Art Blakey's Jazz Messengers, Redman has received a great deal of attention because of his youth. Bassist Charlie Haden, for example, who appeared on Redman's second solo album, *Wish,* described the saxophonist to *Down Beat*'s Zan Stewart as "very mature and very deep—way ahead for his age." Yet Redman himself has seemed largely unimpressed with the hype. "I'm *not* a great jazz musician," he insisted to *New York*'s Stephen J. Dubner. "I'm a *beginner.* I've been playing this music seriously for *two years.*" And, as he told James T. Jones IV of *USA Today,* "Youth is not going to sell the music now. People are looking for substance."

It is that quest for "substance" in his own work that has prompted Redman to work extensively with veteran musicians. On *Wish,* for example, he was joined by guitarist Pat Metheny and drummer Billy Higgins in addition to Haden. "It was a music lesson," he told *Down Beat*'s Pat Cole. "It was a chance to learn from three of my idols." When he signed his recording contract with Warner Bros., he insisted that he be allowed to work as a sideman as well as a leader. "That's going to be an ongoing part of my career," he told Cole. "It's very, very important for me to continue to play with master musicians."

Redman's musical education began at an early age. He was born in Berkeley, California, and was raised by his mother, Renee Shedroff, an artists' model, dancer, and librarian with an Orthodox Jewish background. Shedroff observed her son's musical interests almost immediately; she related to Stewart of *Down Beat,* "Even as a baby, I noticed he would perk up to any kind of musical sound. I'd take Joshua to gamelan [percussion orchestra] concerts, and he'd come home and line up pots and pans and dishes in sequence according to tone." When her son was only five, Shedroff enrolled Redman in music classes at Berkeley's Center for

> **For the Record...**
>
> Born February 1, 1969, in Berkeley, CA; son of Dewey Redman (a jazz saxophonist) and Renee Shedroff (an artists' model, dancer, and librarian). *Education:* Graduated *summa cum laude* from Harvard University, 1991.
>
> Enrolled in music classes at Berkeley's Center for World Music at age five; after experimenting with recorder, guitar, and piano, began playing tenor saxophone at age 10; member of a jazz band at Berkeley High School, 1983-86; performed with Harvard University's jazz band and participated in informal jam sessions in the Boston area, 1986-91; moved to Brooklyn and began performing and recording with such jazz artists as drummers Elvin Jones and Jack DeJohnette, bassist Charlie Haden, and guitarist Pat Metheny; signed with Warner Bros., 1992, and released debut album, *Joshua Redman,* 1993; performed on the White House lawn with President Bill Clinton, 1993; performed extensively with his own quartet and toured with the Lincoln Center Jazz Orchestra, 1994.
>
> **Awards:** First place award, Thelonius Monk International Jazz Saxophone Competition, 1991; named "Best New Artist" by *Jazz Times,* 1992, and "Hot Jazz Artist of 1993" by *Rolling Stone* and "#1 Tenor Saxophonist (Talent Deserving of Wider Recognition)" by a *Down Beat* critics' poll, both 1993.
>
> **Addresses:** *Record company*—Warner Bros., 75 Rockefeller Plaza, New York, NY, 91505.

World Music and later encouraged his experimentations on recorder, piano, and guitar.

Shedroff also influenced Redman through her extensive record collection, which included discs by saxophonists John Coltrane and Cannonball Adderly, as well as Joshua's father, Dewey Redman, a well-respected and influential artist who played with fellow saxophonist Ornette Coleman for many years. During his youth, Joshua saw his father only once a year; nevertheless, as Redman pointed out to Herb Boyd of Detroit's *Metro Times,* "He still had a huge influence on my life. I've listened to his records quite a bit over the years."

Even though Joshua later achieved the kind of commercial and critical success that had largely eluded his father, the younger Redman maintained cordial ties with his father. As he commented to *New York* writer Dubner, "I have a good relationship with my dad—it's just not a father-son relationship. It's more of a buddy relationship, a mentor-student relationship."

Redman began performing on the tenor saxophone when he was ten. As he told *People*'s David Grogan, he was drawn to the sound of the instrument, "so commanding, yet at the same time so compassionate." He quickly became a proficient player and, after entering Berkeley High School in 1983, joined the school's big band. Yet he also made the important decision that academics would take precedence over music. As he told *Down Beat* contributor Stewart, "I wanted to make sure that even if I ended up in music, I would never be forced to do something that runs counter to my artistic instincts in order to put food on the table." Redman's hard work paid off; he was valedictorian of his class and was accepted to Harvard on a full scholarship.

While at Harvard, Redman spent time with musicians at Boston's Berklee School of Music and participated in a few informal jam sessions, yet his focus remained mainly on his education. He graduated *summa cum laude* in 1991 and was accepted to Yale University's law school. The young saxophonist, however, decided to move to New York City and explore the music scene there before continuing his studies.

Redman's performing career shifted into high gear after he won first prize at the Thelonius Monk International Jazz Saxophone Competition, judged by such jazz luminaries as Benny Carter, Jackie McLean, and Branford Marsalis. Soon he was receiving offers to perform and record with some of the most important figures in jazz. In 1992 Warner Bros. Records' Matt Pierson, who had been profoundly moved by Redman's performance at the competition, signed the saxophonist to a major contract.

Gary Giddins of the *Village Voice* called Redman's self-titled first album for Warner Bros. "one of the most impressive debut albums I've ever heard" and praised the conviction of the saxophonist's performances as well as the sense of balance and architecture in his solos. The second album, *Wish,* was equally well received; Jim Fusilli of the *Wall Street Journal* called it "jazz with a small combo at its best" and commented that Redman "displays a style that is respectful of the tradition but not overly bound by it." *Wish* featured an intriguing blend of repertory, including Ornette Coleman's quirky blues "Turnaround," several pieces by Redman himself, and a touching version of Eric Clapton's "Tears in Heaven," performed as a duet with Pat Metheny. A phenomenal commercial success, the album placed near the top of the jazz charts and within a week of its release became the most-played jazz album on radio stations nationwide, according to the Gavin Report.

Early 1994 saw Redman continuing to build an international reputation. He performed extensively with his own quartet, which featured the brilliant young bassist Christian McBride. On tour with the Lincoln Center Jazz Orchestra, he re-created Paul Gonsalves's famous 1956 solo on Duke Ellington's "Diminuendo and Crescendo in Blue," though with an interpretation all his own. What the future holds for the young musician is uncertain, but there are undoubtedly many more peaks for Joshua Redman to climb.

Selected discography

Joshua Redman, Warner Bros., 1993.
Wish, Warner Bros., 1993.

Contributor to Dewey Redman, *Choices,* enja, 1992; John Hicks, *Friends Old and New,* RCA, 1992; Bob Thiele Collective, *Louis Satchmo,* Red Baron, 1992; Danny Gatton and Bobby Watson, *New York Stories,* Blue Note, 1992; Elvin Jones, *Youngblood,* enja, 1992; Kenny Drew, Jr., *A Look Inside,* Antilles, 1993; Eric Felten and Jimmy Knepper, *T-Bop,* Soul Note, 1993.

Sources

Billboard, July 3, 1993.
Down Beat, June 1993; December 1993; February 1994.
Metro Times, October 13, 1993.
New York, January 24, 1994.
New York Post, June 21, 1993.
New York Times, June 24, 1993.
People, May 10, 1993.
Time, November 22, 1993.
USA Today, November 22, 1993.
Vibe, November 1993.
Village Voice, April 13, 1993.
Wall Street Journal, November 15, 1993.

Additional information for this profile was obtained from Warner Bros. Records, Inc., 1993.

—*Jeffrey Taylor*

Restless Heart

Country band

Photograph by Ron Keith, courtesy of RCA Records

Restless Heart is yet another band riding the present wave of country music popularity and diversity. The group's soft country-rock sound harkens back to the Eagles and America, finding fans among the country and rock crowds. According to Chris Heim in the *Chicago Tribune,* Restless Heart "sits squarely in the middle of the country music mainstream. The band's sound, a smooth, mid-tempo pop-country blend with tight, Eagles-like harmonies, is a relatively safe distance from either the radical traditionalists or hip country rockers. And with its striking commercial success, the group can no longer be viewed as interlopers."

Though many crossover artists tend to be viewed with suspicion, the members of Restless Heart have been able to place hits on the pop charts without alienating their core group—the younger generation of country fans. Guitarist Greg Jennings told *Who's Who in New Country Music* that the band appeals to "a new age of country listeners—people who grew up listening to both country and rock music in the sixties and seventies." Jennings added: "It's this sort of hybrid listener that our music particularly appeals to, because it's got country harmonies but a sort of rock edge to it."

When Restless Heart formed in Nashville, most of its members came from other parts of the country. Original lead singer Larry Stewart was the son of a gospel musician, born and raised in Paducah, Kentucky. Both Dave Innis and Greg Jennings were from Oklahoma. They moved to Nashville more or less by chance and wound up working as session musicians in the recording industry there. Stewart was also employed in Nashville as a vocalist and a producer, but he met Innis at Belmont College, where both were business majors. Jennings, Innis, and Stewart began to jam together and help each other find work in the Nashville studios.

A Warm Reception From RCA Records

Jennings was close friends with Tim DuBois, a professor at Vanderbilt University who also wrote songs. In 1983 DuBois decided to put together a band to record the music he had written. He recruited Jennings and Innis, who recommended Stewart for vocals. The group was rounded out by the addition of John Dittrich on drums and Paul Gregg on bass. The initial outlook for the group was not terribly rosy. DuBois invested his entire life savings—some $40,000—into making the recordings, and the young musicians had yet to arrive at a philosophy or a style that they thought would work.

Innis is quoted on those days in *Who's Who in Country Music.* "We didn't have a record deal and Tim was paying us out of his savings account," he said. "We

For the Record...

Members include **John Dittrich,** drums, vocals; **Paul Gregg,** vocals, bass; **Dave Innis,** (left band, 1992), keyboards; **Greg Jennings,** vocals, guitar; and **Larry Stewart** (left band to pursue solo career, 1991), vocals. Backup musicians include **Chris Hicks,** guitar, saxophone; and **Dwain Rowe,** keyboards.

Group formed in Nashville, TN, 1983; signed with RCA Records, 1984, and released debut album, *Restless Heart,* 1985; albums have yielded more than six Number One country singles, including "The Bluest Eyes in Texas," "I'll Still Be Loving You," and "Big Dreams in a Small Town"; have made numerous live appearances in the United States, Canada, and Europe.

Awards: Vocal Group of the Year Award, Academy of Country Music, 1990.

Addresses: *Record company*—RCA Records, 1 Music Center N., Nashville, TN 37203.

---

decided that instead of doing something that we thought we could get a deal on, let's do something we believe in. Let's have fun and make the kind of music we want to make, so if we get a deal we can really hold our heads high and be proud and continue to play the songs for years to come."

Restless Heart emerged from the studio in 1984 with a demo tape that reflected their West Coast country-rock roots. They took the tape to RCA Records and were offered a contract on the spot. In the *Akron Beacon Journal,* Stewart recalled that the executives at RCA told him: "Don't change a thing. We've been looking for a band like you for years."

Produced First Number One Single

A debut album, *Restless Heart,* was released in 1985, and the group's first single, "Let the Heartache Ride," rose to Number 23 on the country charts. In 1986 the band put out its second album, *Wheels,* which produced their first Number One hit, "That Rock Won't Roll." Another single from the album, "I'll Still Be Loving You," made it to Number One on the country charts and became the group's first crossover hit, climbing into the Top Ten on the Adult/Contemporary charts—a feat unequaled by any other band in nearly five years. *Wheels* won the Gold Record Award in 1988.

Subsequent Restless Heart albums sold well, with more than a half dozen singles in the country Top Ten. The group's hits include "Fast Movin' Train," "The Bluest Eyes in Texas," "Big Dreams in a Small Town," and "Dancy's Dreams." In the spring of 1990, the Academy of Country Music named Restless Heart vocal group of the year.

The band's success was even more remarkable in light of the press it received. Most critics scorned Restless Heart's music, calling it "faceless" and "fabricated," the product of a cadre of mediocre studio musicians. Critics notwithstanding, the public responded to Restless Heart—especially those listeners who preferred acoustic rock to hard-core country. The group's sound may be derivative, but the songs are fresh and moving, and the vocals exceptional. As Andrew Vaughan noted in *Who's Who in New Country Music,* "Restless Heart have proved that soft country need not mean boring country."

Lead Singer Left the Band

In December of 1991 vocalist Larry Stewart announced that he was leaving the group to pursue a solo career. "We had finished our last concert date of the year," Dittrich recalled in *The Tennessean.* "Larry called a band meeting ... and announces his resignation. Our jaws dropped." Though the parting was an amicable one, the band was at a loss without their enormously popular lead singer. The critics, who had never been kind, predicted doom for the group. The remaining members auditioned several vocalists before deciding to split the singing duties among themselves. "There was music deep inside of us that needed to come out," Gregg revealed to *Country Spectacular,* and jokingly added, "Now we each get to star in our own video."

Despite the critics dire predictions, audiences across the country responded enthusiastically to the newly pared-down band. Though the *Abilene Reporter-News* noted that "a few of the songs ... longed for [Stewart's] voice in front of the group's dynamic harmony," they concluded that "the show rolled along just fine without him."

Restless Heart's sixth album, *Big Iron Horses,* which includes "Mending Fences," "When She Cries," "Born in a High Wind," and "As Far As I Can Tell," was released in October of 1992, and the band set out on a promotional tour that was cut short before the year's end. It was announced in December that keyboardist Innis, whose battle with alcoholism had been adversely affecting his performance, was no longer with Restless Heart. To fill the gap, the remaining trio enlisted the aid of keyboardist Dwain Rowe and guitarist and saxophone player Chris Hicks.

The success of *Big Iron Horses,* selling over 500,000 copies, carried the band through 1993. By the end of the year, Restless Heart was back in the studio working on their next release, 1994's *Matters of the Heart,* which David Hiltbrand described in *People* as "a sweet suite of pop-heavy country." Drummer Dittrich, pondering the changes Restless Heart has seen since its inception, articulated the band's feelings: "I think we've taken a giant step as far as getting down on record who Restless Heart really is as a band. And I think you're going to see and hear a lot more of that from us in the future."

Selected discography

Restless Heart, RCA, 1985.
Wheels, RCA, 1987.
Big Dreams in a Small Town, RCA, 1988.
Fast Movin' Train, RCA, 1990.
(Contributor) *Home for the Holidays,* RCA, 1990.
Big Iron Horse, RCA, 1992.
Matters of the Heart, RCA, 1994.

Sources

Books

Vaughan, Andrew, *Who's Who in New Country Music,* St. Martin's, 1989.

Periodicals

Abilene Reporter-News, April 28, 1992.
Akron Beacon Journal, March 25, 1990.
Billboard, April 24, 1993.
Chicago Tribune, March 9, 1990; March 11, 1990.
Country Music, May/June 1992.
Country Spectacular, 1993.
Entertainment Weekly, November 20, 1992; June 3, 1994.
People, June 13, 1994.
Salt Lake Tribune, July 4, 1992.
The Tennessean, January 30, 1993.
Wichita Eagle, October 26, 1990.

—Anne Janette Johnson

Jonathan Richman

Singer, songwriter

Photograph by Hank Meals, courtesy of Rounder Records

Jonathan Richman picked up a guitar at age 15 and let out, in what Derek Richardson of *Pulse!* called "a permanent head-cold voice," a brood of adolescent laments that later became the signature of his art-punk band, the Modern Lovers. Young and angst-ridden when he actually wrote some of his first songs (including "Pablo Picasso," "Roadrunner," and "Girlfriend"), Richman was barely 20 when they were finally recorded. He has since recorded over 17 albums, spanning a stylistic musical gamut that includes surf-rock, country-western, insect love songs, and Egyptian reggae recorded with a frequently changing crew of musicians that have comprised the Modern Lovers over the years.

Influenced most heavily by the Velvet Underground, particularly their ability to improvise music and lyrics on stage, Richman began playing publicly in Boston's Harvard Square at the age of 16. According to his artist profile from Rounder Records, by the age of 17 he had caused "many people to leave coffee shops ... quickly ... with their hands over their ears." When he turned 18 Richman moved to New York City and wound up sleeping on the couch of the Velvet Underground's personal manager for two weeks until he was finally settled in what he called "New York's legendary (and rat infested) Hotel Albert." He lived in New York for nine months, working as a busboy and a foot-messenger, trying to find a place to sing his songs in public.

Richman became so frustrated with desire to perform that one afternoon he climbed onto the roof of the Hotel Albert, where he began strumming his unplugged electric guitar and yelling his song lyrics loudly at the pedestrians passing below. His delight at having attracted a large crowd on the sidewalk turned to disappointment when he discovered the people were not lingering to hear his great lyrics, but rather waiting to see if he would jump.

Formed the Modern Lovers

Richman moved back to Boston in the summer of 1970. Wanting to put a band together, he contacted his friend and former neighbor John Felice, who was 15 years old at the time. They then recruited drummer David Robinson (who eventually became the drummer for the Cars). Robinson's cousin Rolfe Anderson also joined in as the Modern Lovers' first bass player. According to Richman, the first meeting with Robinson was rather serendipitous. Looking to advertise for a drummer and a bass player, Richman went to a record store where Robinson worked. Robinson recognized Richman from his solo performances on the Cambridge Commons and said something like, "If you ever put a band

> **For the Record . . .**
>
> Born in 1951 in Boston, MA; married; wife's name, Gail; children: A son and a daughter.
>
> Began playing guitar c. 1966; moved to New York City c. 1969; started band the Modern Lovers, 1970; band signed with Warner Bros., 1972, and broke up, 1973; first album released on Beserkely Records, 1976; went solo for several years playing in coffee houses and for kids in elementary schools, mid-1970s; toured Europe singing disco hit "Egyptian Reggae," 1976; continued to record as soloist and with back-up bands, 1976—; signed with Rounder Records, 1987.
>
> **Addresses:** *Record company*—Rounder Records, One Camp Street, Cambridge, MA 02140.

together, I want to be the drummer." Richman, having just then begun to write "WANTED, DRUMMER," on an index card, replied, "Now's your chance!"

The Modern Lovers played their first show at Simmon's College in Boston in September of 1970 as an opening act for a band formed by Andy Paley (who later produced both *Rock'n Romance* and *It's Time for Jonathan Richman and the Modern Lovers*). Within six months, Rolfe was replaced by Ernie Brooks, John Felice left the band, and Jerry Harrison joined. In the spring of 1972, Harrison engineered a record-industry first by coercing Warner Bros. and A&M to split the cost of flying the entire band to California. The resulting recordings by John Cale and Alan Manson comprised *The Modern Lovers,* which was bought and released by Berserkely in 1976.

Many of Richman's cult classics like "Pablo Picasso," "Roadrunner," and "Girlfriend," were recorded on this first album, which Dave Winans of the Jacksonville *Jam Entertainment News* called "the darkest music of Jonathan's career, showcasing both his disdain for the hippie fashions of the time and the musical influence of the Velvet Underground." Although Winans later added that the lyrics also reveal the young songwriter's unpretentious humor, the release is not one of Richman's personal favorites. "People who wonder why I'm not that proud of the *Modern Lovers* album should know that on a good night we did 'Roadrunner' ten times better than you ever heard it recorded. We got kind of a dark Rolling Stones vibe in our rhythm sometimes." The difference between their live performances and their recordings became a well-known characteristic of Richman and the Modern Lovers; like the Velvet Underground, Richman is known for his improvisation on stage and his ability to constantly recycle material in long, verbal monologues that were difficult to duplicate in the recording studio. Often Richman and his producers attempted to replicate this impromptu performance style by recording in garages and using sound instruments.

Richman's love of improvisation and his idiosyncratic performance personality began to undermine his ability to keep a band together; Richman's playing became more spontaneous—changing keys, adding verses—as he slowly convinced himself that this was the best way to communicate with his audience. Of the band, Richman stated: "We didn't always like each other when we played. We were just this side o' twenty and out to explore the world.... But boy, could we hang out at your local college-age rock-star and Jimmy Page-Keith Richards imitator bar. I was even snottier than the other three so I'd be disgusted at how fake everyone was. But not disgusted enough to stay home. So like I said, we didn't always like each other. But we were not musicians, we were a band."

Began Solo Career

In the fall of 1973, Warner Bros. heard a rumor that the Modern Lovers were going to break up, and they sent producer Kim Fowley to record some material from the band. These tracks later became the bootleg *Original Modern Lovers*; by the time it was released, Richman had already decided to quit. He was tired of the band's loud, electric sound, and at the age of 23 embarked on a new trend of writing "happy songs." He played his acoustic guitar in solo concerts at hospitals and elementary schools, convinced that "high volume was not a necessity but a hindrance to communication and intimacy."

According to *Spin,* Richman's albums grew more and more childish. Richman began writing children's songs (with lyrics such as "the wheels on the bus go round and round," and "I'm a little airplane, wheee, wheee"), although he maintains that the songs were still of more or less adult subject matter and not aimed directly at children. "Do you know why I made up some of my funny songs?," Richman responded in the *Spin* interview. "Because I went through children's folk songs and I didn't think they were good enough. I just write them like I'm talking to anyone else." Jim Sullivan of the *Boston Globe* stated that Richman "spends more time upon minutiae than any of his contemporaries. That is, he is the only song-writer in the world who has written an ode to a chewing gum wrapper—and has made you feel for the damned thing."

In 1976, Berserkely released both *The Modern Lovers* and *Jonathan Richman and the Modern Lovers*. Late that year, Richman hooked up with yet another set of musicians to record *Rock 'n' Roll with the Modern Lovers,* an acoustic album containing the single "Egyptian Reggae," which became a smash disco hit in Europe in 1978. In the late seventies and early eighties, Richman experimented with performing by himself in small clubs, and the press speculated that he had retired, hinting that Richman's solo venture was due more to his problems working with other musicians than to any lack of songwriting inspiration.

"Take it from me, it's better that I'm a solo act," said Richman referring to an incident that occurred at the Bottom Line Club in New York with Modern Lovers drummer from that period, Michael Guardabasico. Guardabasico had just set up his drum set and finished a sound check when Richman asked him to put the whole thing away and simply use a dumbek (a small hand drum) during the performance. Richman admits to being completely stubborn and completely changeable at the same time, a combination often fascinating for audiences, but trying for his accompanying musicians.

In 1982, Richman recorded *Jonathan Sings* with back-up vocalists the Rock'n Robins (Ellie Marshall and Beth Harrington) and *Rock'n Romance* in 1984, two albums that marked his self-described coming of age process. Over the next ten years, Richman released nine more albums, including a country-western album recorded with the Skeletons, and *Jonathan, Te Vas A Emocionar!,* recorded completely in Spanish. In 1987, he signed with Rounder Records and began working with producer Brennan Totten on *Modern Lovers '88* and *Jonathan Richman*. Totten also played guitar as a Modern Lover on tour with Richman and helped Richman record a song commemorating the animated figure Gumby for Walt Disney Records.

Music Highlights Life's Details

Although his later albums are decidedly more mature than his burst of children's songs in the 1970s, Richman maintains his Peter Pan persona and his emphasis on the spontaneity of sound in his music. *Having a Party with Jonathan Richman* and *I, Jonathan* are decidedly party albums that rehash some old fifties doo-wop songs, recycling a few of his earlier recordings, and remaining within his style of post-modern wit and lyricism. "Richman rattles through a record in a couple of weeks," said Richardson in *Pulse!,* "and he does his best, without overdubs, to impact the party ambience and twangy sounds of the cheapest kind."

On his 1993 release, *I, Jonathan,* Richman's 17-year-old son (with the help of a friend) played drums on many of the tracks. "I don't know how to play what's fashionable now," Richman told the *Houston Press*. Yet both of these albums contain New-Age jargon and a recurring regionalism that fans found in old songs like "Government Center." He also sings about the 12-step program's "Higher Power," as well as the Dunkin Donuts in Mattapan.

> *"Do you know why I made up some of my funny songs? Because I went through children's folk songs and I didn't think they were good enough."*

Denny Dyroff of the *Boston Globe* described this element of Richman as "exhaulting the ordinary," while still maintaining loopy humor; these albums also contain song titles such as "I Was Dancing in the Lesbian Bar," and "You Can't Talk to the Dude." "He can turn words and witty rhymes the way [professional baseball players] Alan Trammell and Lou Whitaker turned the double-play in their prime," wrote *Boston Phoenix* columnist Fran Fried, "flawlessly, smoothly, and before you realize what's happened." In "The Girl Stands Up to Me Now," on *Having a Party With Jonathan Richman,* he sings: "Now when she says no/ comes out smooth as silk/ she don't act like no bad breakfast cereal/ waitin' to wilt in the milk."

Writing for *Pulse!,* Richardson described Richman's old and new work as establishing a balance between "cozy reflections on emotional resonances from the past and specific details from real-life experiences in the here-and-now." Richman admits to not knowing "whether I'm gonna talk about the future or the past minute to minute." The musician lives with his wife, Gail, and his two children in the Sierra Nevada Mountains, taking a lot of time off to camp in the desert and jump on his trampoline in his backyard. The landscapes that he still writes about in his songs, however, are the cities of his youth: Boston and New York.

On *I, Jonathan,* Richman plays tribute to his past, and specifically to the band that inspired him as a teenager to pick up a guitar and eventually move to New York City, the Velvet Underground. In a tribute to them, he sings: "They were wild like the USA/ A mystery band in a New York way/ Rock & Roll, but not like the rest/ And to me, America at its best/ How in the world were they making that sound?/ The Velvet Underground." Perhaps 24 years and 17 albums later, Richman has finally figured it out.

Selected discography

(Contributor) *Beserkely Chartbusters,* Beserkely, 1975.
The Modern Lovers, Beserkely, 1976.
Jonathan Richman and the Modern Lovers, Beserkely, 1976.
Original Modern Lovers (bootleg with Warner Bros. tracks; recorded, 1973), c. 1976.
Rock 'n' Roll With the Modern Lovers, Beserkley, c. 1977.
Back in Your Life, 1979.
Jonathan Sings, 1982.
Rock'n Romance, TTN, 1984.
It's Time for Jonathan Richman and the Modern Lovers, Upside Records, 1985.
Modern Lovers '88, Rounder, 1988.
Having a Party With Jonathan Richman, Rounder, 1991.
I, Jonathan, Rounder, 1993.
Jonathan, Te Vas A Emocionar!, Rounder 1993.
Beserkely Years: Best of Jonathan Richman and the Modern Lovers, Rhino.
Modern Lovers Live, Rhino.
Jonathan Richman, Rounder.
(With the Skeletons) *Jonathan Goes Country,* Rounder.

Sources

Billboard, January 9, 1993; February 5, 1994.
Boston Globe, June 28, 1990; October 9, 1992.
Boston Phoenix, November 1, 1991.
Details, September 1993.
Houston Press, January 21, 1993.
Jam Entertainment News, April 30, 1993.
Los Angeles Times, January 15, 1993.
Orlando Sentinel, October 30, 1992.
Pulse!, April 1993.
Spin, February 1993.

Additional information for this profile was obtained from Rounder Records press materials.

—*Sarah Messer*

Max Roach

Drummer, composer

MICHAEL OCHS ARCHIVES / Venice, CA

An individual of multidimensional vision, drummer Max Roach has constantly expanded his creative horizons while stressing the sociopolitical and historical roots of his art. Over the last five decades, Roach has been idolized by drummers as one of the premier originators of modern jazz. Rising to prominence in the bands of Dizzy Gillespie and Charlie Parker during the mid-1940s, Roach emerged as a powerful force in defining the conception and rhythmic foundations of what became known as bebop, or modern jazz—titles Roach refuses to recognize in reference to an African-American art form he believes was prejudiciously named by those outside the musical community. In the university classroom and on the concert stage, Roach has devoted his life to musical exploration and the struggle against cultural discrimination among all people of African descent.

Born in Newland, North Carolina, on January 10, 1924, Maxwell Roach moved with his family to the Bedford-Stuyvesant section of Brooklyn at age four. Roach's mother, a gospel singer, took him to church where he received his first musical instruction on trumpet and piano. When he was eight, Roach studied keyboard harmony with his aunt and within a year played piano in the summer Bible school of the Concord Baptist Church. Outside of church, Roach's interest in music was heightened by the sounds of his Brooklyn neighborhood. "You could walk down the street; you heard people singing, you heard people playing," he recalled in *Swing to Bop*. "The community was just fraught with music."

Introduced to the drums in high school, Roach joined the school marching band. From radio shows and recordings he heard the drumming of Jo Jones and "Big" Sid Catlett who, as Roach told Don Gold in *Down Beat,* became his "main source of inspiration." Along with high school friends trumpeter Leonard Hawkins and saxophonist Cecil Payne, Roach watched the latest jazz bands at the Apollo Theater in Harlem. While playing in Brooklyn rehearsal bands, he read stock arrangements from the band books of Count Basie and Jimmie Lunceford. During weekends spent at Coney Island he performed in the Darktown Follies, sometimes accompanying up to 18 different acts in one day.

Jam Sessions: The Jazz Classroom

Local jam sessions became the main outlet for the development of Roach's rhythmic ideas. At these fiercely competitive exchanges, his drum technique began to deviate from the standard swing patterns of the period. While still a minor, Roach often wore a penciled mustache to attend after-hours jam sessions at Harlem

> **For the Record . . .**
>
> Born Maxwell Roach, January 10, 1924, in Newland, NC; married Anne Marie "Abbey" Lincoln (a singer), 1962 (divorced). *Education:* B.A. in music composition, Manhattan School of Music, c. 1955.
>
> Played in jam sessions throughout Harlem, 1942; joined Dizzy Gillespie and recorded first session with Coleman Hawkins, 1944; played with the Paker-Gillespie quintet, 1946-53; formed quintet with trumpeter Clifford Brown, then with trumpeter Booker Little, 1954-61; worked with wife, vocalist Abbey Lincoln, c. 1960s; University of Massachusetts at Amherst, teacher, beginning 1971; formed M'Boom percussion section, 1972; Bluemoon Records, record producer, beginning in 1980s; artistic director, Jazz Institute.
>
> **Awards:** Composer/Reader's Digest Commisioning Program grant, 1988; MacArthur fellowship recipient.
>
> **Addresses:** *Management*—Brad Simon Organization, 122 East 57th St., New York, NY 10022.

nightclubs like Monroe's Uptown House on 138th Street and Minton's Playhouse located next to the Hotel Cecil on 118th Street.

When most of the experienced jazz drummers left New York to serve in the armed services during World War II, Roach's musical reputation and his ability to read music allowed him to find employment in some of the finest bands of the period. At age 16 he played three nights at the Paramount Theater with Duke Ellington's Orchestra, filling for the ailing Sonny Greer. "I had no rehearsal," he explained in *Jazz Masters of the Forties*. "The stage came up and I was sitting on Sonny's drums all about me. I followed Duke—his conducting was so hip while he played the piano."

After graduating from high school with full honors in 1942, Roach set out to study bebop at jam sessions around the city. In the evenings, following his regular jobs at white clubs, Roach traveled uptown to play at Monroe's and Minton's. At these late-night dates he established a name as one of the most formidable of the "up-and-coming" modern jazzmen.

In 1944, Gillespie and bassist Oscar Pettiford hired him to play with their group at the Onyx Club on 52nd Street. Upon first hearing Roach at the Onyx Club, drummer Stan Levey recalled to *Down Beat*, "I was petrified. Max was a radically new experience for me. He was completely different in his technique and musical approach."

First Recording

During the same year, Roach made his recording debut with veteran swing saxophonist Coleman Hawkins on the Apollo label. One of the first big-name musicians to hire Roach, Hawkins nurtured the talents of a number of young modern jazzmen. In *Song of the Hawk*, Roach stated that "when the movement was in its infancy Coleman was the guy who encouraged many of us. He always made me feel like something." A few months following the session with Hawkins, Roach went on the road with saxophonist Benny Carter's band.

Returning to New York in the spring of 1945, Roach joined the legendary Dizzy Gillespie-Charlie Parker quintet at the Three Deuces on 52nd Street. After Dizzy left the group, 19-year-old Miles Davis took over the trumpet chair. Davis related in his autobiography *Miles* that "everybody was talking about Max becoming the next Kenny Clarke, who was considered bebop's top drummer. Max and I were roommates and went everywhere together. All I wanted to do was play with Bird [Parker] and Max and make some good music." Early in 1945 Roach and Davis, along with Gillespie on piano and trumpet, backed Parker on the recording *Charlie and His Reeboppers,* producing the classic numbers "Billie's Bounce," "Now's the Time," "Thriving on a Riff," and "Ko Ko."

Stint With Charlie Parker

Working with Parker's quintet between 1946 and 1953 allowed Roach artistic freedom to create new rhythmic patterns to accompany the complex arrangements and often breakneck tempos of modernist jazz. "Everything was on the edge with Bird," he told Suzanne McElfresh in *Down Beat*; "you never knew what he was going to do musically, but it always worked out." To compensate for the polyrhythmic texture of bebop, Roach abandoned the steady four-four bass pedal and repetitive ride cymbal patterns of earlier jazz drummers. Through the variation of rhythm he developed what has been called "melodic" drumming—an approach which freed the instrumentalist from his traditional role as time-keeping accompanist.

Aside from taking part in Davis's groundbreaking recording *Birth of the Cool* in 1949, Roach played on pianist Bud Powell's legendary Latin-influenced "Uno

Poco Loco," which appeared on the Blue Note label in 1951. Around this time Roach also earned a bachelor's degree in music theory from the Manhattan School of Music.

In 1954, Roach and trumpeter Clifford Brown formed a quintet featuring saxophonist Harold Land and pianist Richie Powell. Their recordings for Mercury's Emarcy label received acclaim from musicians and critics. Upon the departure of Land in 1955, Roach and Brown recruited the talents of saxophonist Walter "Sonny" Rollins. The horns of Brown and Rollins, along with Roach's inventively propulsive drumming, proved a brilliant combination. The group's success, however, was short-lived—Brown and Powell died in a auto accident in 1956.

During this same period, Roach met rhythm and blues singer Ann Marie "Abbey" Lincoln. Through Roach's encouragement, Lincoln began to record with jazz accompanists. "When he came to see me he was just wonderful to be around, handsome, sophisticated," related Lincoln in *Down Beat*; "he gave me sanctuary." Married in 1962, Roach and Lincoln formed a musical association which would last over ten years.

Music and Militancy

Roach entered the decade of the 1960s committed to the struggle against racial subjugation. Together Lincoln and Roach became outspoken critics of white society. In 1961, Roach explained in *Down Beat* that he would "never again play anything" that did not "have social significance." Devoted to expanding the horizons of African-American music, Roach fused jazz with elements of Negro spirituals to create a voice of artistic expression and social protest.

As drummer-bandleader, Roach wrote and arranged choral and orchestral works, the first of which appeared on the album *It's Time* in 1962. His work *Percussion BitterSweet* remains a testament of the times, blending political passions with the vocals of Lincoln and the first-rate musicianship of Clifford Jordan, Julian Priester, and Booker Little.

In 1971, Roach began teaching at the University of Massachusetts at Amherst, where he helped establish a jazz major. A year later, he founded the M'Boom, an all-percussion ten-man ensemble featuring over a hundred different Third World instruments, including vibes, steel pans, marimbas, and chimes. For over 20 years M'Boom has been active playing concerts and making appearances on recordings such as 1992's *To the Max!* In keeping with current musical trends, Roach collaborated with MTV's rap-music host Fab Five Freddie in recording the program *From Bebop to Hip-hop*. Always attentive to new musical ideas, Roach views rap as a creative form based upon the African art of the spoken word. "I hear the Charlie Parkers in these young people," explained Roach in the *Metro Times*. "They've figured out a way to improvise on a subject the way we improvised on thematic material."

That Roach continues to embrace new musical ideas exemplifies his vast creative vision and his incessant need to interpret the world around him. At the close of the twentieth century, Roach's musical career will serve as a time line with which to trace the creative legacy of modern African-American music. Drummer, educator, and composer, as well as political activist, Roach has brought new direction and meaning to the art of jazz drumming.

Selected discography

(With Clifford Brown) *At Basin Street,* Mercury, 1956.
It's Time, Impulse, 1962.
(With Parker) *Bird: The Complete Charlie Parker On Verve,* Verve, 1989.
(With Dizzy Gillespie) *Max & Dizzy: Paris 1989,* A&M, 1989.
To the Max!, Bluemoon, 1992.
(With Miles Davis) *Birth of the Cool,* Capitol.
Bright Moments, Soul Note.
Drums Unlimited, Atlantic.
Percussion BitterSweet, Impulse.
Percussion Ensemble, Mercury.
Quartet, Fantasy.
(With Charlie Parker) *The Very Best of Bird,* Warner Bros.
We Insist! Freedom Now, Candid.

Sources

Books

Davis, Miles, with Quincy Troupe, *Miles: The Autobiography,* Simon & Schuster, 1989.
Gillespie, Dizzy, *To Be, or Not to Bop,* Doubleday, 1979.
Gitler, Ira, *Jazz Masters of the Forties,* Collier Books, 1966.
Gitler, *Swing to Bop: An Oral History of the Transition of Jazz in the 1940s,* Oxford University Press, 1985.
Taylor, Arthur, *Notes and Tones: Musician-to-Musician Interviews,* Da Capo Press, 1993.

Periodicals

Black Perspective in Music, 1990.
Detroit Free Press, December 6, 1991.

Down Beat, March 21, 1968; July 24, 1969; March 16, 1972; November 1978; September 1989; November 1990; February 1992; May 1993; November 1993.
Metro Times (Detroit), December 4, 1991.
Musician, January 1994.
Pulse!, September 1992; November 1992.

—*John Cohassey*

Otis Rush

Guitarist, singer

A stinging guitar vibrato and gospel-like voice are the definitive trademarks of bluesman Otis Rush. One of the founders of the Westside Chicago blues sound in the 1950s, Rush fused deep Mississippi blues with modern urban styles to produce a formidable guitar combined with vocals capable of agonized high falsetto shouts. During the blues revival of the 1960s, Rush emerged as a mentor for musicians from Mike Bloomfield to Eric Clapton. For three decades, Rush has continued to record and tour, bringing audiences throughout the world his fierce brand of electric blues.

Born one of seven children in Philadelphia, Mississippi, on August 29, 1934, Rush was raised on a farm by his father O. C. Rush and mother Julia Boyd. While he occasionally sang in the church choir, Rush remained drawn to the country blues sounds of Tommy McClennan and Lightnin' Hopkins. Although he began to pick up the guitar at age eight, Rush recalled in the liner notes to *Chicago/The Blues Today* that "as a kid I just liked the looks of guitars, but I didn't play." Instead, Rush began to teach himself harmonica.

Photograph by Masaki Rush, courtesy of Rick Bates

> **For the Record . . .**
>
> Born April 29, 1934, in Philadelphia, MI; son of O. C. Rush (a farmer) and Julia Boyd.
>
> Played first job, under name "Little Otis," 1954; first hit record on Cobra label, 1956; signed with Chess Records, 1959; recorded for Vanguard label and toured Europe with American Folk Blues Festival, 1966; played concerts throughout America, 1969-72 and 1980s; toured Japan and recorded live album for Delmark label, 1975; released album *Ain't Enough Comin' In,* 1994.
>
> **Addresses:** *Agent*—Rick Bates, 714 Brookside Ln., Sierra Madre, CA 91024.

In the winter of 1948 Rush went to Chicago, where he stayed at the home of his sister. Working in the Chicago stockyards, he continued to play harmonica. Finally, inspired by the live performances of Muddy Waters and Jimmy Rogers, he began to study the guitar in 1953. Within a year, Rush fronted a band under the name of "Little Otis," playing his first job with Arkansas-born guitarist Bob Woodfolk. Introduced to the guitar playing of T-Bone Walker and B. B. King, Rush incorporated modern phrasing and rhythmic ideas into his deep Mississippi sound. "I can remember when Otis was playing just like Muddy Waters," explained Luther Tucker in *Blues Guitarists.* "T-Bone Walker was pretty hot at that time and he gave Otis some ideas. He kept the Muddy Waters feel but added little more modern chord progressions."

The Birth of the West Side Sound

In the mid-1950s, Rush's maturing style caught the attention of bassist Willie Dixon. As Dixon explained in his autobiography *I Am the Blues,* "I found Otis Rush down on 47th Street and I knew he was good but Leonard Chess thought he sounded too close to Muddy Waters." Consequently, Dixon signed Rush with Eli Tascano's newly established Cobra label in 1956. At Tascano's Westside studio, Rush's guitar was brought to the forefront of the band. Accentuated by a driving horn section, his solos exhibited a drive and volume unknown to earlier Chicago bluesmen.

Cobra's Westside blues guitarists like Rush and Buddy Guy drew upon the influences of jazz, rhythm and blues, and the horn-based ensemble of B. B. King to produce a modern urban sound. Written and engineered by Dixon, Rush's first Cobra recording, "I Can't Quit You," became the label's only national hit. From its tormented vocal introduction, "I Can't Quit You" was an eerie slow blues, augmented with brilliantly phrased guitar fills. Rush's next single was "My Love Will Never Die," a powerful minor-key slow blues which set the trend for Rush's unique West Side sound. Two more excellent examples of this style were the blues masterpieces "Double Trouble" and "All Your Love (I Miss Loving)," which later became a guitar standard for young bluesman Eric Clapton. "'All Your Love,'" wrote blues historian and critic Paul Oliver in his *Blues Records,* "shows Rush in top form, harboring insane pockets of energy released into an atmosphere of tense expectation." Incorporating Latin and straight shuffle rhythms, the song features odd, minor-inflected chord breaks and searing single note passages unsurpassed in the modern electric blues idiom.

At this period in Rush's career, his back-up musicians often included guitarists Dave and Louis Meyers, drummer Odie Payne, and Dixon on acoustic bass. In 1958, Rush hired Arkansas-born Willie D. Warren who played electric bass on the bottom three strings of his guitar. The addition of Warren brought further attention to Rush's band, for it marked the introduction of the electric bass into blues music. In an interview with *Contemporary Musicians,* Warren emphasized the importance of this event: "There wasn't any electric basses back then. There was only upright bass fiddles like Willie Dixon played. After joining Otis I met Little Walter, Magic Sam, and Buddy Guy. They wanted me to teach their bass players what I was doing." Thus, Rush's band earned a reputation as a first-rate ensemble which helped set the trend for the development of modern electric blues.

After Tascano's death and the departure of Warren in 1959, Dixon brought Rush to Chess Records. That same year, Rush recorded "So Many Roads So Many Trains," an excellent single reminiscent of his finest Cobra material. Following this session, however, Rush experienced numerous setbacks. Without commercial success on the Chess label, he signed with Duke which resulted in the release of one single, "Homework," in 1962. Active primarily in the local Chicago club scene, Rush performed at occasional out-of-town shows with such artists as T-Bone Walker and Little Richard.

The Great Blues Revival

In 1966, Rush appeared on Vanguard's *Chicago: The Blues Today,* the first recorded blues anthology directed toward a young white folk/rock audience. Participating in that year's American Folk Blues Festival, he played concert dates throughout Europe—the exposure brought him a devout following among musicians in both England and America. Between 1969 and 1972, Rush played before large crowds of enthusiastic listeners at the annual Ann Arbor Blues Festival.

While Rush's songs were being covered—and often directly imitated—by bands from Paul Butterfield to Led Zeppelin, he struggled to eke out a living in small Chicago clubs. Plagued by inadequate back-up bands, he failed to produce an album equal in quality to his earlier work. His 1971 release *Mourning in the Morning,* though it contained moments of brilliance from Rush, suffered from over-production and poorly selected material. In 1975, after years of personal and career problems, Rush's spirits were lifted when his band was greeted at Tokyo's Haneda Airport by thousands of fans who covered the runway with flowers. "I never saw so many flowers before in my life," commented Rush in *Down Beat.* "They had our baggage covered in flowers, the car we were in was full of flowers, at the gate people were standing around me with flowers."

Unfortunately for Rush, his successful Japanese tour represented only a brief moment in a career marked by setbacks and financial problems. Disillusioned, he quit performing for two years in the early 1980s. But when the blues experienced a second revival during the middle of the decade, Rush found a new audience among young musicians, including Texas guitarist Stevie Ray Vaughn who paid tribute to him by naming his band Double Trouble after Rush's 1958 Cobra recording.

King of the "Singing String"

Despite his quiet and congenial disposition offstage, Rush remains a powerful performer. Employing a left-handed upside-down guitar technique, Rush bends notes that are reminiscent of slide guitar tones and inflections. "I practiced to get that sound without using a slide," explained Rush in *Blues Guitar.* "I'm still trying to develop it." By imitating the slide sounds of Robert Nighthawk and Earl Hooker, he developed a lyrical string vibrato, colored by full chords inspired by the recordings of jazz guitarist Kenny Burrel.

Despite many years of hardships, Rush has remained optimistic that he will attain rightful recognition for his work. His 1994 release *Ain't Enough Comin' In* featured the production team that brought recent commercial success to friend and Chicago blues guitarist Buddy Guy. Critical of many second-generation bluesmen, Muddy Waters often commended Rush for possessing a "deeper" blues sound than most of his contemporaries. A true exponent of the deep-blues tradition, Rush remains a guitar legend, one of the last living giants of Chicago blues.

Selected discography

(With others) *Chicago/Blues Today!,* Vanguard, 1966.
(With others) *American Folk Blues Festival, 66',* L&R, 1966.
Mourning in the Morning, Atlantic, 1969.
So Many Roads, Delmark, 1975.
Cold Day in Hell, Delmark, 1975.
Lost Blues, Alligator, 1977.
Live in Europe, Isabel, 1977.
Ain't Enough Comin' In, Mercury, 1994.
Albert King/Otis Rush: Door to Door, Chess.
(With others) *The Best of Duke-Peacock Blues,* MC.
The Classic Recordings, Charly R&B.
Cobra Alternates, P-Vine.
(With others) *The Cobra Records Story,* Capricorn.
Groaning the Blues: Cobra Sides 56-58, Flyright.
Otis Rush 1956-1958, Paula.
Otis Rush and Magic Sam—The Other Takes, 1956-58, Flyright.
Right Place, Wrong Time, Hightone.
Screamin' and Crying, Evidence.
This One's a Good 'Un, Blue Horizon/Polydor.
Tops, Blindpig.

Sources

Books

The Blackwell Guide to Blues Records, edited by Paul Oliver, Basil Blackwell, 1989.
Blues Guitarists: Collected From the Pages of Guitar Player Magazine, Guitar Player Productions, 1975.
Blues Guitar: The Men Who Made the Music, From the Pages of Guitar Magazine, edited by Jas Obrecht, Miller Freeman Books, 1993.
Cohn, Lawrence, *Nothing But the Blues: The Music and the Musicians,* Abbeville Press, 1993.
Dixon, Willie, with Don Snowden, *The Willie Dixon Story,* Da Capo, 1989.
Palmer, Robert, *Deep Blues,* Viking, 1981.
Rowe, Mike, *Chicago Blues: The City and the Music,* Da Capo, 1975.

Periodicals

Down Beat, April 7, 1977.
Guitar Player, November 1993.

Additional information for this profile obtained from liner notes by Samuel Charters to *Chicago/The Blues Today!,* Vanguard, 1966.

—John Cohassey

Boz Scaggs

Singer, songwriter

Photograph by Dennis Keely, courtesy of Virgin Records

Although Boz Scaggs is perhaps best known for his innovative white soul music during the 1970s, this versatile musician has recorded many other styles of music as well, ranging from rhythm and blues and folk to slick urban pop and disco. Born in Ohio, Scaggs moved with his family to Plano, Texas (a suburb of Dallas), when he was quite young. His interest in music was sparked by his childhood friendship with Steve Miller, with whom he attended St. Mark's Preparatory School in Dallas. Miller, who would grow up to front the highly successful Steve Miller Band, taught Scaggs the rudiments of guitar playing and encouraged him to sing.

In the early 1960s the two friends formed the Marksmen Combo and gained performance experience by playing local venues. A few years later, the pair headed north to attend the University of Wisconsin in Madison, drawn to the area in part because of its proximity to Chicago's thriving blues culture. In Madison they met another developing musician, Ben Sidran, and performed with him as the Ardells.

Scaggs left the University of Wisconsin without graduating and returned to Texas alone. He formed a new group, the Wigs, and flew to England with them, confident that they would make their mark on the British music scene. Success never materialized for the Wigs, however, and they disbanded within a few months. Scaggs traveled through Europe on his own, supporting himself by singing on plazas and street corners. The continent appealed to him, and by the mid-1960s he had established a home base in Stockholm, Sweden, where he became affiliated with Karusell Records, the company that released his first album. *Boz,* a collection of folk songs, was a substantial success in Europe, although it remains relatively obscure in the United States.

Just as he was settling down for a long stay in Europe, Scaggs received an urgent postcard from Miller, who had migrated from Madison to San Francisco and formed one of the area's first "psychedelic" rock groups. The Steve Miller Blues Band, as it was then known, was the first such group to be offered a contract with a major record label, and Miller wanted his old partner to share in his success. Scaggs agreed, but stayed with the group just long enough to record two albums: *Children of the Future* and *Sailor,* regarded by some as the best albums ever made by the Miller band. After those projects were completed, Scaggs's restless nature drove him to strike out on his own once more.

His solo debut in the United States, entitled *Boz Scaggs,* was produced by *Rolling Stone* editor Jann Wenner

> **For the Record . . .**
>
> Born William Royce Scaggs, June 8, 1944, in Ohio; father was in sales; married Carmella Storniola, 1972 (divorced 1980); children: two sons.
>
> Member of bands the Marksmen Combo, the Ardells, and the Wigs, early 1960s, and of the Steve Miller Blues Band, late 1960s; solo performer, mid-1960s and 1970—; founder and owner of the Blue Light Cafe in San Francisco.
>
> **Addresses:** *Residence*—San Francisco, CA. *Record company*—Columbia Records, 51 West 52nd St., New York, NY 10019.

and featured some powerful guitar work by Duane Allman, an unknown at the time. *Rolling Stone* contributor Michael Goldberg called it a "classic [that] instantly established Scaggs as a gifted songwriter and musician." *High Fidelity* reviewer Steven X. Rea also commented enthusiastically on the album, classifying it as "a milestone ... full of bluesy rock aggressiveness and spooky ballads." But despite reviewers' high opinions of the album, it was not a great commercial success. Scaggs's audience was still limited to the San Francisco Bay area and a small but intensely loyal following scattered about the rest of the country.

During the next few years Scaggs worked hard to win more listeners. He refined his rough-edged blues style into a smoother, less rootsy sound. The transformation can be heard on the albums *Boz Scaggs and Band, My Time,* and *Slow Dancer.* In 1976, Scaggs finally achieved the success he'd so long desired when his album *Silk Degrees* sold over five million copies and produced the Number One single "Lowdown."

Rea described *Silk Degrees* as "a precise, passionate synthesis of rock, soul, and disco that was the epitome of blue-eyed soul." Goldberg noted that the album also "cemented Boz's uptown image. Scaggs had traded in his blue jeans and funky shirts for a designer wardrobe and a blow-dried look that made him a sex symbol the world over." The singer followed his breakthrough album with two more that sold millions of copies: *Down Two Then Left* and *Middle Man.* In 1980 alone, he had four Top 20 singles, and his concerts were sellouts across the nation.

Legions of Scaggs fans were stunned when, at the peak of his success, the singer announced plans to take an indefinite hiatus from the music business. Personal difficulties, including a divorce and bitter child-custody battle, figured in his decision. Scaggs also admitted to feeling lost in the image that had taken him to superstardom and overwhelmed by the pressures that celebrity had thrust upon him. "Fortune and fame aren't what they appear to be," he told *Rolling Stone.* "The demands that are created by a career on that level were more than I wanted to continue at that time. I wanted to step outside it."

At the time, Scaggs expected his break to last for a year or so, but in fact it stretched to nearly eight years, during which time he played only occasionally at jam sessions in bars, or in benefit concerts for the inmates of San Quentin Prison.

Scaggs began work on a comeback album in the spring of 1985. He put nearly three years of painstaking effort into the project, only to be told by top executives at Columbia Records that it would have to be almost completely redone. The final product, 1988's *Other Roads,* was a mixture of his trademark ballads (including "Heart of Mine," which became a minor hit), danceable music, and a harder-edged sound than he had produced in years. Scaggs confided to Goldberg that despite initial conflicts with Columbia over the changes, "I enjoy listening to this album more than any other album I've ever made." Despite his satisfaction, the album floundered. It would be another six years before the public again heard from Scaggs.

After devoting most of the 1980s to operations at his San Francisco restaurant, the Blue Light Cafe, Scaggs was lured back to the studio by Virgin records, which felt the time was right for a Scaggs comeback. The singer agreed. "I just wanted to get away from the music side of the business," he told Melinda Newman of *Billboard.* "I didn't realize it would be such a long break."

Some Change was released in April 1994. Penned entirely by Scaggs, who also handled keyboard and guitar duties, the album was hailed as a dazzling display of the singer's versatility. The songs range from the cajun/country, "Fly Like a Bird" and the bluesy title track to the "Lowdown"-like "I'll Be the One." Though *Some Change* was less slick than previous Scaggs albums, Paul Evans of *Rolling Stone* noted "the insinuating ballads that slowly build into lush set pieces, vocals that simmer and then soar," and concluded that *Some Change* brings Boz Scaggs back, "lit by the fire at the heart of cool." Though he seldom performed concerts, even at the pinnacle of his success, Scaggs told *Billboard* that he wasn't opposed to touring to promote *Some Change.* "If there is a demand for me to perform.... I want to play," he asserted.

Selected discography

Boz, Polydor, 1965 (originally released in Europe by Karusell).
Boz Scaggs, Atlantic, 1969.
Moments, Columbia, 1971.
Boz Scaggs and Band, Columbia, 1971.
My Time, Columbia, 1972.
Slow Dancer, Columbia, 1974.
Silk Degrees, Columbia, 1976.
Down Two Then Left, Columbia, 1977.
Middleman, Columbia, 1980.
Hits, Columbia, 1980.
Other Roads, Columbia, 1988.
Some Change, Virgin, 1994.

Sources

Billboard, February 26, 1994.
Harper's, May 1989.
High Fidelity, June 1980; August 1988.
Pulse!, June 1992.
Request, May 1994.
Rolling Stone, June 16, 1988; July 14, 1988; March 19, 1992; May 5, 1994; May 19, 1994.
Stereo Review, August 1980.

—*Joan Goldsworthy*

The Scorpions

Rock band

In 1970 the working-class town of Hannover, Germany, was decidedly not a bastion of rock and roll music. But Klaus Meine and brothers Rudolf and Michael Schenker changed the way the world perceived Hannover—and even the rest of Germany. As originators of the hard rock band the Scorpions, the trio created Top Ten hits and generated worldwide attention through both their musical talent and controversial album covers. By 1994, with 15 albums to their credit, the band was deemed "the greatest German rock export" by a writer for *RIP* magazine.

Singer Meine first performed in a band called the Mushrooms. His budding musical career was interrupted, however, by a stint in the German Army. Upon his return to civilian life at age 23, he met a 16-year-old guitarist named Michael Schenker who, four years earlier, had started playing guitar for a young German band (nearly becoming an alcoholic in the process). Meine approached Schenker's father, a violin teacher and retired construction engineer, about starting a rock band. Meine was forced to prove his responsibility and seriousness before the elder Schenker relented and allowed Michael to join the band.

Shortly after Meine and Schenker formed the band, named Copernicus, Michael got an offer from his brother Rudolf to join a band called the Scorpions. Although Rudolf was the Scorpions original singer, he extended the invitation to Meine after seeing his work with Copernicus. On December 31, 1970, rhythm guitarist Rudolf Schenker, lead guitarist Michael Schenker, and singer Meine kicked off what would become an international rock and roll force for decades.

Rough Beginnings in Germany

"It was really difficult for us in the early 1970s," Rudolf Schenker told *Billboard* magazine. "We were outsiders, and we got no support from the media. Nobody really believed that a German band could begin to compete in the rock n' roll idiom with American and British groups. 'Who needs a German band singing in English?' they asked." But the group's determination never wavered. They struggled playing the clubs, driving their own truck and moving their own equipment (Meine made his living as a window dresser). After more than a year of hard work, they released their first album, *Lonesome Crow*, on the German label Metronome Records. The Scorpions recorded the LP in producer Conny Plank's studio in Hamburg. The Chicago label Billingsgate later released *Lonesome Crow*, selling 25,000 copies before the band ever made it to the United States.

> **For the Record...**
>
> Original members include **Klaus Meine** (born in Hannover, Germany), vocals; **Rudolf Schenker** (born in Hannover, Germany), rhythm guitar; **Michael Schenker** (born in Hannover, Germany) lead guitar; **Francis Buchholz**, bass guitar; **Jurgen Rosenthal**, drums.
>
> Later members include **Ulrich Roth** (band member 1973-1978), lead guitar; **Rudy Lenners** (band member 1974-1977), drums; **Herman Rarebell** (joined band, 1977), drums; **Matthias Jabs** (joined band, 1979), lead guitar; **Ralph Rieckermann** (born Lubeck, Germany; joined band, 1993), bass guitar.
>
> Band formed in Hannover, Germany, in 1970. Released first album, *Lonesome Crow,* on Metronome Records in 1972; signed with RCA Records and released five albums through various member changes from 1974 to 1978; signed with Mercury/PolyGram Records for first internationally recognized album, *Lovedrive,* 1979; released eight more LPs and one live concert video from 1980 to 1993 with Mercury/PolyGram.
>
> **Addresses:** *Record company*—Mercury/PolyGram Records, 825 Eighth Avenue, New York, NY 10019.

In 1972 the band went on to a 136-date tour of Europe, opening for various major acts. In April of 1973, Michael Schenker left the band to join the English hard rock group UFO, whom the Scorpions had supported on the tour. After Michael's departure, the Scorpions broke up, but the separation was not permanent. Rudolf Schenker and Meine re-formed the band later that year with guitarist Ulrich Roth, bassist Francis Buchholz, and drummer Jurgen Rosenthal. The reconfigured group signed with RCA Records and released *Fly to the Rainbow* in 1974. Once they had released this second effort, Rosenthal left the Scorpions, and Rudy Lenners stepped in on the drums.

Despite their steady growth, the Scorpions continued to manage themselves—from booking concerts to dealing with the record company—because personal management of artists in Germany was illegal. In 1975 the band released *In Trance* on RCA Records. This marked the first LP produced by fellow German Dieter Dierks and the beginning of a 15-year association. Realizing that it was time to try their luck outside of their homeland, the Scorpions made their concert debut in England by opening at the Cavern in Liverpool. The group subsequently toured Britain, France, and Belgium. *In Trance* became a best-selling album in Japan, so the band headed for the Far East. By the time *Virgin Killer* was released the following year, the Scorpions had reached headline status in Europe and Japan. Within a week of its debut, the album had already gone gold in Japan. *Virgin Killer* also started the Scorpions' trend of controversial album covers; RCA Records rejected their first cover design.

Group Gained International Exposure

When the Scorpions hit the road in 1977, critics lauded them as Germany's top rock band. At the conclusion of their extensive tour of Britain, drummer Rudy Lenners left the band because of heart trouble. Yet during the band's tour of England, they had met fellow countryman and drummer Herman Rarebell in a London speakeasy. So when Lenners left the band, Rarebell stepped in as his replacement.

Once Rarebell took over the drums, the Scorpions recorded and released *Taken By Force*. Although they were winning more and more fans with their German-based brand rock and roll, the group still had to disprove the misconception that the only successful German bands were practitioners of electronic pop-rock. "When I was living in England, when everybody saw that the Scorpions were German, they would say, 'Oh, it's Kraftwerk or Tangerine Dream or Can, again.' And, we don't do that type of stuff," Rarebell told *Melody Maker*. "We do something completely else. What we do is very English, because we are oriented more towards English and American bands. Most German bands orient themselves on classical music and space music. We don't do that because we feel in our hearts we are rockers."

In 1978 the Scorpions played a sold-out, five-day tour of Japan. Deciding that the time had come for a live recording, the band released excerpts from their two performances at Tokyo's Sun Plaza on *The Tokyo Tapes*. Later that year, lead guitarist Ulrich Roth quit the band to pursue a solo career in progressive rock. The remaining members of the Scorpions auditioned 170 guitarists in London to find a replacement for Roth. Eventually they decided on Matthias Jabs, a guitarist from Hannover who was playing in a band called Fargo.

With their new guitarist in place and a new record contract with Mercury/PolyGram Records in the United States, the Scorpions started work on their 1979 *Lovedrive* LP. The band continued to have trouble keeping a steady guitarist. Michael Schenker contributed half of the guitar solos on the record after he left

UFO to rejoin the Scorpions. Jabs left the band, but stayed on permanent stand-by during the Scorpions' tour. Because of personal reasons, Schenker again quit the group. Finally, Jabs returned as the group's lead guitarist.

The Scorpions made their concert debut in the United States opening for hard rocker Ted Nugent at the World Series of Rock in the Cleveland Municipal Stadium in Ohio. Following that performance, *Lovedrive* entered the U.S. charts and stayed for 30 weeks.

1980s Brought Victory and Tragedy

Hoping to build on their worldwide following, the Scorpions didn't waste any time returning to the studio; they released *Animal Magnetism* in March of 1980. Featuring the hit single "Make It Real," *Animal Magnetism* became the Scorpions' first U.S. gold album. Once again their album's cover design—this one depicting a woman kneeling in front of a man's clothed legs and a Doberman thrusting out its tongue—incited controversy. Deliberations concerning the cover aside, the Scorpions launched an extensive tour of the United States, Britain, and continental Europe the following year.

Misfortune struck the German group when Meine developed nodes and a polyp on his vocal cords, making it impossible for him to sing. The Scorpions were forced to cancel tour dates and put their ninth album on hold. "I wanted to quit so that the band could carry on with another singer," Meine told *Billboard*. "But all the guys said, 'No way. You do everything you can to get your voice back, and we'll wait until you are ready.'"

Two operations and six months of vocal training later, Meine had restored his singing voice. In 1982 the Scorpions released *Blackout*. The discussion-generating cover featured a Gottfried Helnwein painting of a lobotomy patient with bent forks clawing out his eyes. The album became the group's first Top Ten and platinum album in the United States and reached gold status in many other countries throughout the world. The band embarked on a seven-month world tour, played 150 concerts, and entertained a total of 1.5 million people. They wrapped up their tour in 1983 as co-headliners for the world's biggest rock festival, the US Festival, where they played to 300,000 fans in southern California.

The group's tenth album, *Love at First Sting,* hit the stores the following year with yet another battle concerning its cover. The original design featured fashion photographer Helmut Newton's photograph of a leather-clad man embracing a mostly nude woman with a scorpion tattoo on her thigh. When some retail stores refused to carry the album with its existent packaging, PolyGram Records marketed an optional cover. The second design—also photographed by Newton—was a black-and-white shot of the band that was meant as the record's inner sleeve. The Scorpions, however, defended the original cover: "We think it's a little piece of art," Meine told *Musician.* "The leather, the guy, he can stand for 'Rock You Like A Hurricane'; the girl, she's sophisticated looking, she could stand for the ballad 'Still Loving You.'"

"Rock You Like A Hurricane," the first single from the album, hit the *Billboard* Top 40 and lasted on the chart for seven weeks with a peak at the 15th spot. The second single, "Still Loving You," broke first in France and then continued to spread throughout Europe and the United States. "I'm Leaving You" made the third single and video. *Love at First Sting* thus became the runaway success that elevated the Scorpions to international superstar status.

> *"There's so much competition out there—so much good music—that you have to continually prove to the world that you still belong there."*
> —Klaus Meine

The band's success inspired the release of a live album and a one-hour video movie about the tour titled *Worldwide Live.* They took part in a record-breaking rock festival in Brazil called Rock in Rio, where they played for 350,000 people. Jabs had a Gibson guitar custom made for the event in the shape of Brazil. After their performance, Jabs presented the guitar to the concert promoter to express the band's collective gratitude for the opportunity to play the show. The German rockers went on to play behind the Iron Curtain in Budapest in 1987, thus becoming one of the first Western bands to venture into the Eastern Bloc. They also performed in the Monsters of Rock open-air concert in Europe.

Savage Amusement, the Scorpions' final album produced by Dieter Dierks, entered the *Billboard* Top Ten in the third week of its release in 1988. The band's tour included a performance in Leningrad, Russia, making them the first major hard rock band to play in the former Soviet Union. Supported by the Russian hard rock band Gorky Park, the Scorpions played ten concerts to

15,000 people each night. They returned to the United States to play the Monsters of Rock festival with fellow rockers Van Halen. Eighteen years after their inception, the Scorpions agreed that they should release a greatest hits album. The *Best Of Rockers N' Ballads* included both popular hits and personal favorites of each band member. (In fact, the album's tentative name was *The Best of Scorpions' Favorites*.)

The Scorpions continued to break international, geographical, and political boundaries. They band returned to the Soviet Union in 1989 to play in the Moscow Music Peace Festival at Lenin Stadium. They performed in front of 100,000 people, and the experience provided the inspiration for their megahit single on the *Crazy World* album—"Winds of Change."

"Winds of Change" Ushered in 1990s

Recorded in Los Angeles with producer Keith Olsen, *Crazy World* sold nearly seven million copies worldwide. The Scorpions launched the album with the single "Tease Me, Please Me," but it was "Winds of Change" that took *Crazy World* to megaplatinum status. During the Persian Gulf War, troops adopted "Winds of Change" as an anthem; the song also served as an inspiring soundtrack to the destruction of the Berlin Wall and the repressive Communist policies it embodied.

The single reached Number One in 13 countries, including Israel and Chile, and won the ASCAP Award as one of the most performed songs of 1992. Russian leader Mikhail Gorbachev was honored with an acoustic performance of the song at the Kremlin. Soon after the Berlin Wall fell, the Scorpions played to more than 350,000 fans in the Roger Waters's production of Pink Floyd's *The Wall—Live in Berlin '90*. And at the Artists for Freedom, Equality and Humanity peace rally in 1992, the band once again performed an acoustic version of "Winds of Change." By 1994, *Crazy World* stood as the best-selling rock album ever in Germany.

This level of success led the Scorpions full force into their second decade, but personnel changes struck again in 1992. Bassist Francis Buchholz parted ways with the band after an 18-year association. With Buchholz's departure, "our whole world was turned upside down," Rarebell recalled in the band's biography. "Instead of having a never-ending party on [the] heels of *Crazy World*'s success, we had to deal with the anger, aggression and uncertainty of the changes in OUR world. It was a real emotional and creative challenge."

Although the members of the Scorpions tried to convince Buchholz to stay with the band, they realized that his goals for the groups's musical direction differed from their own. Another German band, Bonfire, recommended Ralph Rieckermann to fill the void on bass guitar. Without any further auditions, the Scorpions had a new member and, by 1993, their next album, *Face the Heat*. Produced by Bruce Fairbairn, *Face the Heat* launched the band into another stage of musical variety. Beginning with the first single, "Alien Nation," the band took a sonic trip through various influences ranging from punk metal to jazz and blues. The ballad side of the band still existed, as evidenced by "Under the Same Sun."

Despite their longevity in the rock world, the Scorpions have vowed not to be satisfied with their past accomplishments. "There's so much competition out there— so much good music—that you have to continually prove to the world that you still belong there," Meine told *Billboard*. "This is still a band of today, not a nostalgic trip. We still have a lot to achieve."

Selected discography

Lonesome Crow, Metronome, 1972.
Fly to the Rainbow, RCA, 1974.
In Trance, RCA, 1975.
Virgin Killer, RCA, 1976.
Taken by Force, RCA, 1977.
Tokyo Tapes, RCA, 1978.
Lovedrive, Mercury/PolyGram, 1979.
Animal Magnetism (includes "Make It Real"), Mercury/PolyGram, 1980.
Blackout, Mercury/PolyGram, 1982.
Love at First Sting (includes "Rock You Like a Hurricane," "Still Loving You," and "I'm Leaving You"), Mercury/PolyGram, 1984.
Worldwide Live, Mercury/PolyGram, 1985.
Savage Amusement, Mercury/PolyGram, 1988.
Best of Rockers N' Ballads, Mercury/PolyGram, 1989.
Crazy World (includes "Tease Me, Please Me" and "Winds of Change"), Mercury/PolyGram, 1990.
Face the Heat (includes "Alien Nation" and "Under the Same Sun"), Mercury/PolyGram, 1993.

Sources

Album Network, September 10, 1993; September 17, 1993.
Billboard, May 5, 1984; December 1, 1990; November 16, 1991; February 29, 1992; October 9, 1993.
Circus, August 31, 1985; October 31, 1985; November 30, 1985; January 31, 1986; August 31, 1988.
Foundations, September 13, 1993.

Hit Parader, February 1985; March 1985; September 1985; December 1985; January 1986; September 1986; November 1986; December 1986.

Hit Parader Annual, fall 1986.

Hit Parader's Heavy Metal Awards, spring 1986.

Los Angeles Times, July 11, 1982; April 26, 1984.

Melody Maker, April 14, 1979; May 19, 1979; April 12, 1980; November 8, 1980; May 8, 1982.

Metal Edge, November 1985.

Music Connection, May 30, 1988.

Musician, September 1984.

RIP, June 1994.

Screamer, December 1989; March 1990; January 1991; April 1991.

Additional information for this profile was obtained from Mercury/PolyGram Records press material, 1993.

—*Sonya Shelton*

Sepultura

Heavy metal band

Rage. Frustration. Violence. These factors surrounded members of the thrash band Sepultura as they struggled to survive in their hometown of Belo Horizonte, Brazil. Living in a Third World country surrounded by poverty and aggression, Max Cavalera and his younger brother Igor were inspired to start their own band after acquiring bootleg copies of recordings by Venom, Metallica, and Voivod.

Originally, the brothers had no intention of launching a music career. They simply wanted something to do to entertain themselves. "I was into real aggressive and extreme things," Max Cavalera explained to *Screamer* magazine. "That's why I decided to make this kind of music. I saw that it fit in with what I was doing. All my violent life was the same as what I was listening to." With Max singing and playing rhythm guitar and Igor planted firmly behind the drum kit, they quickly enlisted lead guitarist Jairo T. and bassist Paulo Jr. to complete Sepultura's original line-up.

Taking their lead from their name—"sepultura" means "grave" in Portuguese—the group wrote songs relat-

Photograph by Gary Monroe, © 1993 Sony Music, courtesy of Roadrunner/Epic Records

> **For the Record...**
>
> Members include **Igor Cavalera**, drums; **Max Cavalera**, vocals, rhythm guitar; **Jairo T.** (left group, 1986), lead guitar; **Paulo Jr.**, bass guitar. Later members include **Andreas Kisser** (joined group, 1986), lead guitar.
>
> Band formed in Belo Horizonte, Brazil, c. 1983; released *Bestial Devastation,* 1984; signed with Roadrunner Records and released first international album, *Beneath the Remains,* 1989; released video, *Under Siege (Live in Barcelona),* 1991.
>
> **Addresses:** *Record company*—Roadrunner Records, 550 Madison Avenue, New York, NY 10022-3297.

ed to death, outrage, and destruction. They performed anywhere they could in Belo Horizonte and eventually recorded a few primitive demos. In 1984, they released their first EP, *Bestial Devastation,* on Cogumelo Records, a tiny Brazilian label.

Two years later, Sepultura increased their following in Brazil with their first full-length album, titled *Morbid Visions.* The members of the band gained underground attention in both the United States and Europe by sending cassettes to hundreds of fan magazines around the world. The heaviness and aggression in the band's music earned them the endorsement of the underground press, and the word about Sepultura began to spread. In 1986, Jairo T. decided to leave the band, and Andreas Kisser stepped in as Sepultura's new lead guitarist. With the new lineup in place, the band went back into the studio to record *Schizophrenia.*

Made International Debut

More critical acclaim by the music press and an increasing fan base through word of mouth prompted independent U.S. Roadrunner Records to sign the band. Though Sepultura had difficulty communicating in English and the band's members continued to live in Brazil, Roadrunner released *Beneath the Remains,* the group's first international album, in 1989. Recorded in Brazil and mixed in Florida, *Beneath the Remains* sold more than 200,000 copies in the United States and Europe combined.

The band ventured out of Brazil to tour clubs in the United States and Europe for the very first time. Not only did Sepultura spread their music throughout the continents, they brought with them stories of a Brazil that went beyond the travelogues. "I think we are the most realistic persons in the country," Max Cavalera said in *Screamer.* "We are the people that don't talk about the beautiful beaches and the beautiful view, like a postcard. We talk about the reality that we see, just living there and how we felt."

Building a following worldwide, Sepultura returned to their home country in January of 1991 to open for Guns n' Roses, Megadeth, and David Lee Roth at Rio de Janeiro's second Rock in Rio festival. The band performed to a live audience of several hundred thousand people while an estimated 540 million others watched on the television screen.

They returned to Florida to record their second effort with Roadrunner, *Arise,* which they released later that year. With this album, which sold over one million copies worldwide, Sepultura got their first taste of stardom as they were featured on covers of music magazines around the world. The four boys from Brazil subsequently kicked off their "New Titans on the Bloc" tour across the United States with fellow thrashers Sacred Reich and Napalm Death. They then headed abroad, performing in Israel, Portugal, Italy, Britain, Australia, Japan, New Zealand, Spain, and Greece. The band played four shows in Russia to 60,000 people, two shows in Indonesia to an audience of 70,000, and of course, Brazil where they performed in front of 40,000 fans in their homeland.

New Heights of International Success

Arise sent Sepultura to an entirely new level of success in the world of music, but they vowed they would continue their musical integrity against the pull of commercialism. "We've done it because this kind of music is important to us," Max Cavalera told *Melody Maker.* "The craziness here is unreal; the craziness where we come from is very real. It's a violent place; there's a lot of crime, a lot of violence. So, for us, no matter what happens, there'll always be a truth to our music. Punk and metal have always spoken the truth to us. Coming from that place, we find real truth in hard things."

In 1992, Sepultura finished nearly two solid years of touring, opening for Ozzy Osbourne, Ministry, and Helmet in American arenas. They documented one of their live performances with a home video concert of a show in Spain. *Under Siege (Live in Barcelona)* sold over 75,000 copies worldwide. The band finished their tour and traveled to South Wales where they recorded their 1993 release, *Chaos A.D.,* with producer Andy Wallace. Roadrunner Records signed a distribution partnership with Epic/Sony Records, increasing Sepultura's market across the world.

Chaos Spawned Musical Changes

Steering away from previous themes of death, Sepultura used *Chaos A.D.* to reflect the strife in Brazil as a metaphor for the decay of the modern world. "I always liked the word 'chaos,'" Max Cavalera said in *Kerrang!* magazine. "There's been chaos over the last 2,000 years, and it seems to get worse every day. So, we named our album after that situation."

Because their road crew resided in Arizona, along with Max's wife/band manager, Gloria Cavalera, Sepultura decided the time had come to move to the United States in 1991. Before their sixth release made it out to the stores, the band relocated to Phoenix, Arizona, where Gloria and Max celebrated the birth of their son, Zyon Graziano Cavalera, in January of 1992. The first sound heard on *Chaos A.D.* is Zyon's heartbeat, recorded in utero.

"People ask me, 'Did you move because it was dangerous (in Brazil)?'" Max said in *Request*. "That was not really the reason, but somehow it is involved. I mean, I don't really wanna raise my kid there right now, because the situation there is pretty bad. And even my mother and sister are in Phoenix now. But I don't know, maybe in the future we'll go back there 'cause I think it would be cool to return to Brazil."

With their move to the United States, Sepultura charted new musical territory as well. When the Brazilian government tried to move a tribe of Brazilian Indians out of the rain forest, the tribe committed mass suicide rather than leave their home. This tragedy inspired Sepultura's song "Kaiowas," which the band recorded in a castle to achieve just the right sound. They also incorporated Brazilian instruments like the tamburin and cuica. "Kaiowas" was the first of several songs to reflect the band's rising social sense. In a later recording, "Manifest," Sepultura gave a haunting spoken-word recitation of a hideous massacre at a South American penitentiary.

As Sepultura's music continued to grow, their recognition rose even higher, but their roots in self-entertainment still rang true. "It would be cool if Sepultura got as big as possible," said Max Cavalera in the *Los Angeles Times,* "but with all the integrity that belongs to the band. If we don't get big, at least the integrity will still be around."

Selected discography

Bestial Devastation, Cogumelo, 1984.
Morbid Visions, Cogumelo, 1986.
Schizophrenia, Cogumelo, 1987.
Beneath the Remains, Roadrunner, 1989.
Arise, Roadrunner, 1991.
Chaos A.D., Epic/Roadrunner, 1993.

Sources

Billboard, November 6, 1993.
Los Angeles Times, December 22, 1993
Melody Maker, November 25, 1989; December 16, 1989; April 13, 1991; July 6, 1991; July 20, 1991
New York Times, December 5, 1992.
Pulse!, September 1993.
Request, December 1993.
RIP Magazine, May 1993.
Screamer Magazine, December 1990.

Additional information for this profile was obtained from Epic Records press material, 1993.

—Sonya Shelton

Terrance Simien

Accordionist, singer

Photograph by Brian Ashley White, courtesy of Black Top Records

"Where we come from, if people don't dance it's an insult!," said Terrance Simien in *Billboard*. "The real deal is: We a lot of times get people in the crowd who are kinda shy and really wanna dance. We kinda *force* things so the ones that should dance will come up." Simien accomplishes this by interspersing frantically fluttering hand gestures with riffs from his diatonic button accordion equipped with an extra-long bellows that he allows to hang and shake as he bounds about the stage playing it behind his back and between his legs.

Zydeco has always been high energy music, but Simien's frenetic presence sets him apart from his contemporaries. According to Rick Mason in the *St. Paul Pioneer Press-Dispatch,* even when Simien was virtually unknown in Louisiana, his performance at the New Orleans Jazz and Heritage Festival generated sparks in the crowd. With "his face painted in a vivid rainbow of colors" and his "long hair flying in every direction, Simien tore up the place with a sweaty, explosive performance," Mason remarked.

The word zydeco is a modification of *les haricots,* or snap beans, as popularized by the traditional Cajun song "The Snap Beans Aren't Salty." According to Timothy White in *Billboard,* zydeco grafts Acadian folk songs on to the Afro-Caribbean rhythms brought to Louisiana by French-speaking slaves and free men of color after the Haitian Revolution at the end of the eighteenth century. German immigrants introduced the accordion to the fiddle-focused Cajun instrumentals in the 1870s, and the washboard or "frottoir," played with spoons or bottle openers, gave zydeco its unique percussive drive.

Homage to Clifton Chenier

Clifton Chenier did much to popularize the music in the 1950s; in the *St. Petersburg Times,* Simien credited him with opening new vistas for zydeco. Chenier expanded the slower, mostly acoustical sound of traditional zydeco by adding drums and electrical instruments, infusing it with a strong rhythm and blues feeling. Indeed, today's zydeco bands often carry strong guitarists capable of delivering hard-edged blues.

Simien noted in the *St. Paul Pioneer Press-Dispatch* that the music continues to evolve: "We grew up listening to different kinds of music—rock and roll, soul, reggae, pop, and stuff like that. So I incorporate some of that stuff with our zydeco music, just by writing songs that might have been influenced by maybe a Bob Dylan, a Mick Jagger, or something like that."

> **For the Record...**
>
> Born September 3, 1965, in Mallet, LA.
>
> Formed the first incarnation of the Mallet Playboys, 1981; group played at World's Fair in New Orleans, 1984; band showcased at Lone Star Cafe, New York City, 1985; appeared in film and on soundtrack of *The Big Easy,* 1987; toured North Africa, 1988; released debut album with the Mallet Playboys, *Zydeco on the Bayou,* 1990; group appeared on *Lonesome Pine Specials,* PBS, 1992; band signed with Black Top/ Rounder Records, 1993.
>
> **Addresses:** *Record company*—Black Top Records, P.O. Box 56691, New Orleans, LA 70156.

Born in Mallet, Louisiana, on September 3, 1965, Simien spent three years studying jazz and classical trumpet at Lawtell Elementary and grew up watching his mother sing in the choir of St. Ann's Catholic Church. Like many people of his generation, Simien initially didn't care much for zydeco. As he said in the *St. Petersburg Times:* "There was a time, mostly in the 1970s, when zydeco was almost extinct. It was confined to the older generation. Younger people thought it wasn't cool to go to the zydeco dances. I was into soul music and rock and roll."

Fell in Love With Zydeco

But that changed when he stopped going to the record hops at the church hall because he thought they were too juvenile and uptight. At 13, he started sneaking into local clubs like Slim's Y-Ki-Ki in Opelousas. In the *St. Paul Pioneer Press-Dispatch,* Simien recalled that he "fell in love with the music 'cause it was something that I could really dance to and didn't have to dress a certain way or dance a certain way. It was laid-back stuff, man, something I could really relate to."

Soon Simien was a regular listener to the weekly *Lou Collins' Black Zydeco Special* out of Eunice, teaching himself the music of Fernest Arceneaux, the Sam Brothers, and Clifton Chenier on a $250 Hohner single-row diatonic accordion he had received for his fifteenth birthday. Unlike other zydeco performers such as Buckwheat Zydeco and Clifton Chenier, who play the bulkier piano version, Simien has stuck with the cruder button accordion. Although it limits virtuoso technique, Simien's instrument of choice rocks harder and lets him move around more, according to Eric Snider in the *St. Petersburg Times.* In 1982 Simien started the initial and short-lived incarnation of the Mallet Playboys, because as he explained in *Billboard,* it "was an older clan that didn't want to learn more than five songs."

Noticed at World's Fair

Simien was more careful with his band selection from then on, holding auditions to assemble a younger group comprised of his longtime rubboard player Earl Sally, bassist Popp Esprite, Troy Gaspard on drums, and Mark Simar on guitar. Simien had been splitting his time between working with his father as a bricklayer and playing at local clubs. At the 1984 World's Fair in New Orleans, however, he was noticed by a woman who booked him for several dates in the Washington, D.C., area. Soon the band was touring all over the United States.

In 1985 Simien performed at New York's Lone Star Cafe. He related in *The New Folk Music* that "all kinds of musicians showed up to hear us. Keith Richards and Ron Wood got on stage and played. Paul Simon came down to hear us, Mick Jagger, Bob Dylan." Simon heard about Simien from Dickie Landry, a Cajun saxophonist, composer, and producer who had spent a couple of decades in the New York music scene. Simon considered the band for his *Graceland* album, but ultimately settled on the more traditional Rockin' Dopsie.

Nevertheless, their meeting was fortuitous because Simon produced a 12-hour recording session for the band. As Simien recounted in the *St. Petersburg Times:* "Paul gave us the tapes and said, 'This is a present, do what you want to do with it.'" Simon even sang background vocals on the song "You Used to Call Me," which was released as a regional single on the small Grand Point label. And as Rick Mason commented in the *St. Paul Pioneer Press-Dispatch:* "The single nonetheless became part of the band's promotional package, helping the Playboys secure gigs for its increasingly hectic international schedule."

Film, TV, Tours Kept Band Busy

Dickie Landry also got Simien an audition with director Jim McBride and Dennis Quaid for a cameo during a club scene in the 1987 movie *The Big Easy.* Hired on the spot, Simien ended up co-writing one of the two songs on the soundtrack. The year 1987 also marked the band's first European tour, which included the prestigious Bern Jazz Festival in Switzerland, where they opened for Fats Domino and Sarah Vaughan. In

1990 Simien and the Mallet Playboys released their first album, *Zydeco on the Bayou,* on Restless and performed on a national Chevrolet commercial. The band tours constantly and has opened for Los Lobos and Robert Palmer.

In 1992 the Mallet Playboys taped a television show for PBS's *Lonesome Pine Specials* and began recording their second project, *There's Room for Us All.* This album is indicative of Simien's eclectic musical vision. From adding a talkbox to zydeco oldies and turning Boozoo Chavis's classic "Dog Hill" into an extended party mix, to experimenting with reggae and soul—for years Simien has covered Peter Tosh—Simien continued to expand zydeco.

The album also boasted the presence of guests like bassist/producer Daryl Johnson, pianist Art Neville, and the Meters. As Simien commented in *Billboard,* "The album's title says it best: There's a lot of musicians on this record that came from different bands and different backgrounds, and there are a lot of different people in this world that we gotta learn to love and accept." For Simien there is even room for the audience, whom he often welcomes on stage, giving them tambourines, cowbells, and washboards, inviting them to join him as he carries on.

Selected discography

With the Mallet Playboys

Zydeco on the Bayou, Restless Records, 1990.
There's Room for Us All, Black Top/Rounder Records, 1993.

Sources

Books

Harris, Craig, *The New Folk Music,* White Cliffs Media Company, 1991.

Periodicals

Billboard, July 31, 1993.
Black Top Records Biography, 1994.
Kalamazoo Gazette (Michigan), November 4, 1990.
Montgomery Journal and Advertiser (Alabama), April 13, 1990.
Philadelphia Inquirer, November 7, 1990.
Rolling Stone, April 21, 1994.
St. Paul Pioneer Press-Dispatch, July 6, 1990.
St. Petersburg Times, August 19, 1988.
Times-Picayune (New Orleans), September 30, 1988.

—John Morrow

Donna Summer

Singer, songwriter

Courtesy of Mercury Records

Pop vocalist Donna Summer's first U.S. release was, arguably, her most famous recording. The 17-minute disco anthem "Love to Love You Baby," replete with orgasmic moaning sounds, began Summer's undisputed reign as Disco Queen during the 1970s. In the last few years of that decade, she had numerous hit songs and albums both in pop and rhythm and blues. When disco finally faded from the musical scene, Summer became a born-again Christian, revealing a religious side to her music. Although no longer a dominating pop music force, Summer continued to make bankable albums during the 1980s, and her willingness to adapt to currently popular musical styles has suggested that she will continue to generate hits for the remainder of her musical career.

Born Donna Adrian Gaines, Summer grew up in Dorchester, Massachusetts, a working class city adjoining Boston. Her father was a butcher, her mother a school teacher. As a child she sang in Boston-area church choirs but by high school her tastes had grown more secular. She piled up hundreds of truancy slips, skipping school in order to sing with a local rock band. Two months before high school graduation, Summer dropped out. In 1967, at age 18, she debuted at Boston's Psychedelic Supermarket.

The following year found her abroad in the German production of *Hair*. Europe would be her home for the next eight years. After a year and a half of *Hair*, Summer moved to Austria, becoming a regular with the Vienna Folk Opera. The Opera offered productions of *Porgy and Bess* and *Showboat* during her tenure.

It was in Austria, in 1971, that she married local actor Helmut Sommer. Although their marriage would dissolve in 1976 under the pressure of Summer's disco success, she continued to use the anglicized version of his last name.

Back in Germany in 1973, performing in a production of *Godspell* and working as a session singer in Munich's Musicland studios, Summer met producer Giorgio Moroder. Moroder was to be called Summer's "Svengali" due to his influence on her career. On the Oasis label, owned by Moroder and partner Pete Bellotte, Summer made a couple of European hits that were never released in the United States.

Queen of Disco

1975 saw the end of Summer's relative obscurity, and "Love to Love You Baby" was the reason why: 17 minutes of romantic lyrics, disco beat, and feigned

> **For the Record...**
>
> Born Donna Adrian Gaines (also cited variously as Donna Gaines and LaDonna Gaines), December 31, 1948, in Dorchester, MA; married Helmut Sommer (an actor), 1971, (divorced, 1976); married Bruce Sudano (a musician), c. 1981; children: (second marriage) Brook Lyn (daughter).
>
> Debuted as vocalist at Psychedelic Supermarket, Boston, MA, 1967; toured Europe with German production of *Hair,* 1968-69; joined Vienna Folk Opera, 1969-73; Musicland Studio, Munich, Germany, session singer, 1973; signed with Oasis Records (Germany), 1973-75; signed with Casablanca, 1975; had role in film *Thank God It's Friday,* 1979; released from contract and signed with Geffen Records, 1980.
>
> **Selected awards:** Grammy Award for best female rhythm and blues vocal performance, 1978, for "Last Dance"; best female rock vocal performance, 1979, for "Hot Stuff"; best inspirational performance, 1983, for "He's a Rebel"; and best inspirational performance, 1984, for "Forgive Me"; numerous gold and platinum albums and singles.
>
> **Addresses:** *Record company*—Mercury Records, 825 Eighth Avenue New York, NY 10019.

orgasm delivered while lying down on the studio floor with the lights dimmed. *Spin* magazine said of this song that it "launched the extended dance mix as we know it—the zygote of house and industrial ... and invented the 12-inch." Casablanca records received the U.S. license and became Summer's record company upon her return to the United States. The song was an immediate disco hit and within months found its way up both the pop and rhythm and blues charts, hitting Numbers Two and Three, respectively.

Summer released an album named for the hit single in 1976. *Love to Love You Baby* nearly made the U.S. Top Ten and reached Number 16 in the United Kingdom. She and her producers were determined not to be merely a flash in the pan. In June of that year, the Summer-Moroder-Bellotte team released *A Love Trilogy* and also managed to squeeze in *The Four Seasons of Love* by December.

The first of her albums with a title that did not contain the word "love," the 1977 release *I Remember Yesterday* generated the singer's second gold single "I Feel Love." The song, a synthesizer pop hit, extended Summer's stylistic range, according to *The Rolling Stone Encyclopedia of Rock and Roll*. In 1978, Summer contributed most of the lyrics to the disco/fairy tale concept album *Once Upon a Time,* which she claimed was mostly autobiographical. The Cinderella-toned lyrics talked of girls who "live in a land of dreams unreal / Hiding from reality ... trapped within their world." Later in 1978, on *Live and More,* Donna covered Jimmy Webb's "MacArthur Park" for an unpredictable massive hit—her first appearance in slot Number One on the pop charts.

Summer's Golden Days

As the 1970s ended, it seemed Summer could do no wrong. Between 1978 and 1980 she earned eight Top Ten hits. She even became a film star, portraying an aspiring singer in 1979's *Thank God It's Friday*. While one critic suggested audiences would thank god when this movie was over, the film's Number Three hit song "Last Dance" won an Oscar and two Grammys—one for Summer and one for writer Paul Jabara.

Bad Girls, a 1979 number one double album, was Donna's last recording for Casablanca. Four songs from this album reached the Top Ten, many sitting there for weeks, variously occupying the Number One and Two positions. But according to *The Encyclopedia of Pop Rock & Soul* Summer was depressed by her struggle with Casablanca to go beyond disco. She claimed that she'd been "stuck doing something that had been choking me to death for three years." She began including religious songs in her performances, a return to her church roots and a reflection of a desire for inner peace.

This soul weariness took formal expression in a lawsuit against manager Joyce Bogart and husband Neil Bogart's Casablanca Records to the tune of $10 million. When the legal dust settled, Summer was released from her contract and signed with Warner Brothers' newly formed Geffen label.

Born Again in the 1980s

The Wanderer was Donna's first album for Geffen. The title track reached Number Three by 1981; the song addressed the singer's recent born-again Christianity. The religious thread in her music continued for the next few years but did not cost her much popular appeal, perhaps because the disco fever had already lifted. "He's a Rebel," from her 1983 Mercury release, *She Works Hard for the Money,* won a Grammy for best inspirational performance—a trick Summer would repeat the following year with the cut "Forgive Me" off *Cats Without Claws*.

A further abdication of Summer's reign as Disco Queen occurred when the singer allegedly remarked that AIDS was a form of divine ruling on homosexuality. Gay club enthusiasts who had embraced her and helped make her a star were angry. Despite Summer's denial of making the AIDS remark, the rift never healed. On the home front, the beginning of the 1980s saw her marriage to Bruce Sudano, lead singer of Brooklyn Dreams. They named their daughter Brook Lyn.

Donna continued to work steadily throughout the eighties, although six years were to pass after "She Works Hard for Her Money" before she penetrated the Top Ten again. "This Time I Know It's for Real," off 1989's *Another Place Another Time,* reached Number Seven. By this time Summer had moved into other areas of self-expression. Her neo-Primitive paintings and lithographs proved popular; in June 1990, a Beverly Hills gallery sold 75 such works for up to $38,000 apiece.

Summer has never stopped producing or changing. In a *Billboard* interview, she discussed her latest transformation—into a country music singer. Together with musician/husband Sudano, she has penned several country songs, including the hit "Starting Over" with Dolly Parton. Questioned by the interviewer regarding these many transformations, as well as the personal and professional ups and downs of her life, Summer responded with a painting metaphor. Think of a painting, she said, which is left in the sun. The painting fades but "also takes on new colors. And instead of the colors being as vivid as they once were, they change into different and perhaps richer colors." One cannot help but sense that Summer's rainbow of colors will continue to grow richer for many years.

Selected discography

Love to Love You Baby, Oasis, 1975.
A Love Trilogy, Casablanca, 1976.
Four Seasons of Love (EP), Casablanca, 1976.
I Remember Yesterday, Casablanca, 1977.
Once Upon a Time, Casablanca, 1977.
Live and More (includes "MacArthur Park"), Casablanca, 1978.
Bad Girls, Casablanca, 1979.
The Wanderer, Geffen, 1980.
Donna Summer, Geffen, 1982.
She Works Hard for the Money, Mercury, 1983.
Cats Without Claws, Geffen, 1984.
The Summer Collection, Mercury, 1985.
All Systems Go, Geffen, 1987.
Another Place and Time, Atlantic, 1989.
Mistaken Identity, Atlantic, 1991.
The Donna Summer Anthology (includes "Carry On"), Mercury, 1993.

Sources

Books

Pareles, Jon, and Patricia Romanowski, *The Rolling Stone Encyclopedia of Rock & Roll,* Rolling Stone Press/Summit Books, 1983.
Rees, Dafydd, and Luke Crampton, *Rock Movers & Shakers,* Billboard Books, 1991.
Stambler, Irwin, *Encyclopedia of Pop Rock & Roll,* St. Martin's Press, 1989.

Periodicals

Billboard, September 25, 1993.
Jet, September 18, 1989; October 16, 1991.
New York Times, May 14, 1989.
People, October 14, 1991.
Rolling Stone, March 23, 1978.
Spin, November 1993.
Stereo Review, September 1989; January 1992.
Variety, April 2, 1980.
Village Voice, May 28, 1979.

—Joseph M. Reiner

Sweethearts of the Rodeo

Country duo

Courtesy of Sugar Hill Records

Sweethearts of the Rodeo took country music by storm in 1986 with their harmony-infused blend of bluegrass, folk, and traditional country. The fresh, contemporary sound helped to pave the way for other artists who rode in on the new wave of country music. For three years sisters Janis Gill and Kristine Arnold dominated the charts. They were nominated for Duo of the Year by the Country Music Association and their songs were featured in the 1987 movie *Nadine*. The second Sweethearts of the Rodeo album sold well, but not as well as the first, and the third, not as well as the second. Their fourth album, according to Arnold, "was dead when it came out."

When the sisters found themselves shunned by radio and ignored by their record company, Columbia, they seriously considered calling it quits. Instead, Sweethearts of the Rodeo signed on with independent label Sugar Hill Records and released *Rodeo Waltz,* a back-to-basics album that had the critics taking a second look.

Janis and Kristine Oliver grew up in Manhattan Beach, California, and credit their older brothers' record collection—which included Sonny Terry, John Lee Hooker, Doc Watson, and Bill Monroe—as their musical influence. "I was just beginning to learn how to play guitar, and listening to those records really had an effect on me," Gill recalled to *Country Guitar*. It wasn't long before Kristine began to accompany her sister on vocals, and by high school they'd formed a folksy bluegrass band.

Billing themselves as Sweethearts of the Rodeo, after the classic Byrds album, the sisters spent years on the California club circuit. The influence of such artists as Bob Dylan, the Beatles, and the Eagles became intertwined with the Sweetheart's traditional, down-home melodies to produce a perfect harmony of country and rock. The sisters were also renowned for their stagewear—outlandish homemade outfits with little regard for fashion. They were well received by local audiences, but the big time continued to elude them.

Both women married in the early 1980s. Janis wed Vince Gill, a struggling country singer at the time, who by the early 1990s had become one of country's most popular artists. Kristine married musician Leonard Arnold. Both couples started families, and Sweethearts of the Rodeo disbanded in order to meet the demands of parenthood. They moved apart in 1983—the Arnolds moved to Austin, Texas, and the Gills settled in Nashville, Tennessee.

The sisters reunited in 1985 when the Arnolds moved to Nashville at Janis's request. "[Janis] called me ... and

> **For the Record . . .**
>
> **Janis Gill** (born Janice Oliver in California; married Vince Gill [a singer], April 12, 1979; children: Jenny); **Kristine Arnold** (born Kristine Oliver in California; married Leonard Arnold [a singer and manager], c. 1982; children: two daughters).
>
> Duo formed in California, c. 1975, and played at local clubs; moved to Nashville, TN, c. 1985; signed with CBS Records, 1986, and released debut album, *Sweethearts of the Rodeo*, 1987.
>
> **Addresses:** *Record company*—Sugar Hill Records, P.O. Box 55300, Durham, NC 27717-5300.

said 'can you move? There's no female duo here. The timing is perfect for us,'" Kristine told *The Tennessean*. That same year, the twosome won the Wrangler Country Showdown talent contest and signed a contract with Columbia Records. Their 1986 self-titled debut album was a runaway hit, with five singles—including "Since I Found You" and "Midnight Girl/Sunset Town"—reaching the Top Ten.

The duo's earthy music and harmony-laced vocals were praised by fans and critics alike. In *Who's Who in New Country Music,* Andrew Vaughan noted that the sisters' "cascading harmonies and tight country rock instrumentation swept hard and clear across country airwaves quickly putting [them] at the head of the Nashville newcomer league."

Sweethearts of the Rodeo headlined in concerts across the country and were nominated for Duo of the Year by the Country Music Association. In 1987 they provided the soundtrack for the movie *Nadine,* which starred Jeff Bridges and Kim Bassinger. The suddenness of their popularity and the unprecedented demands on their time put the sisters in an awkward position. The little time they had to spend with their husbands and children was time that their record company felt could be more profitably spent.

Over the next two years the sisters juggled their home lives and careers. Their second album, *One Time One Night,* was warmly received by both critics and fans, but their third album, *Buffalo Zone,* was given little publicity by the record company. Columbia virtually ignored Sweethearts of the Rodeo's fourth album, *Sisters,* which was their last recording on that label. "Radio wasn't playing us anymore," Arnold told Robert K. Oermann in *The Tennessean*. "The record company wasn't giving us the priority. We got frustrated and thought maybe we ought to quit."

Both women admitted to "some tearful conversations" while deciding what to do next. "Finally," Gill told Oermann, "we thought, 'gee, are we gonna quit because radio is through with us and turn our backs on nearly 30 years of singing together?'" They didn't. Instead, Sweethearts of the Rodeo signed on with Sugar Hill Records, home to many of new country's more innovative bands as well as established artists, including Doc Watson, Leon Redbone, Chris Hillman, and Ricky Scaggs.

Rodeo Waltz, the duo's 1993 "comeback" album, was recorded live in one week (vocals in two days) on a budget of $10,000—considerably less than the $100,000 Capital had allowed. The 12 songs offer charming acoustic renderings of old and new country, from Johnny Cash's rockabilly "Get Rhythm" to the haunting strains of Robbie Robertson's "Broken Arrow." The sisters drew from a well of talented tunesmiths for the album, including Hank Locklin, the Delmore Brothers, Gordon Lightfoot, and Jesse Winchester.

Critics were lavish in their praise of *Rodeo Waltz.* "The Sweethearts," noted Geoffrey Himes of *Country Music,* "sing with a kind of old-timey purity and power ... never displayed in all their years on a big label." *Musician* magazine's Holly Gleason lauded the duo's return to their roots, referring to the new songs as "the turpentine that strips the radio sheen off Sweethearts of the Rodeo."

Despite the accolades, this time around Gill and Arnold are determined to find a balance between their music and family life. Rather than arenas and amphitheaters, their 1994 schedule included a number of small-venue performances at folk and bluegrass festivals. Sweethearts of the Rodeo have another Sugar Hill release planned for late 1994 and though they hope that *Rodeo Waltz* receives adequate air time, the sisters are more than comfortable with their less-than-hectic careers. As Gill told Gordon Ely in Virginia's *Richmond Times-Dispatch:* "The trade-off in smaller sales is worth the freedom and peace we've found now, a thousand times over."

Selected discography

Sweethearts of the Rodeo, CBS, 1986.
One Time One Night, CBS, 1988.
Buffalo Zone, CBS, 1990.
Sisters, CBS, 1992.
Rodeo Waltz, Sugar Hill, 1993.

Sources

Books

Vaughan, Andrew, *Who's Who in New Country Music*, St. Martin's, 1989.

Periodicals

Billboard, August 21, 1993.
Country America, October 1990; March 1991.
Country Guitar, April 1994.
Country Music, January/February 1994.
Country Standard Time, March/April 1994.
Music City News, 1994.
Musician, 1994.
New Country Music, April 1994.
Patriot News, 1994.
Pulse!, February 1994.
Richmond Times-Dispatch, 1994.
The Tennessean, January 29, 1994.
USA Today, 1994.

—*Anne Janette Johnson*

Tangerine Dream

New Age band

The terms "New Age" and "Space Music" have been aptly applied to the ethereal improvisational electronic work of Tangerine Dream. This German band's influences include early electronic groups like Kraftwerk and modern experimental composers like Steve Reich. Tangerine Dream has never earned mass appeal but has maintained a steady following both in the United States and abroad. More people have been exposed to the band's unique sounds than many realize, for the abstract instrumental nature of the work of Tangerine Dream lends itself to movie soundtracks; their music graces dozens of popular motion pictures.

From time to time, the sturdily built, blond-mustached band leader Edgar Froese has complained in his thick German accent of the New Age label critics attach to the band. This apparent calumny has dogged the band almost since its inception in 1967. Tangerine Dream prefers to view its clouds of loosely structured synthesized sounds as belonging to the avant-garde experimental tradition.

Courtesy of Miramar® Recordings

For the Record...

Members include **Edgar Froese** (born June 6, 1944, in Germany), keyboards, synthesizer, guitar; **Conrad Schnitzler** (born in Germany; left band, 1971), flute and other instruments; and **Klaus Schulze** (born in Germany; left band, 1971), synthesizer, keyboards. Later members include **Peter Baumann** (bandmember, 1972-75), keyboards, synthesizer, flute; **Chris Franke** (bandmember, 1971-88), keyboards, synthesizer; **Paul Haslinger** (joined band, 1985), keyboards, synthesizer; **Michael Hoenig** (joined band, 1975), keyboards; **Johannes Schmelling** (joined band, c. 1978), keyboard, synthesizer; **Steve Schroyder** (joined band, 1971), organ; and **Ralf Wadephal** (joined band, c. 1988), keyboards.

Group formed in Germany, 1967; recorded debut album, *Electronic Meditation,* 1970; toured England, 1975.

Addresses: *Record company*—Miramar, 200 Second Ave. W., Seattle, WA 98119.

As a youth, Froese trained as a classical musician but found it stifling; in the early sixties he began playing guitar in various German rock bands. A friend of Salvador Dali, Froese provided music for some of the famous artist's openings. Froese pointed out in *Down Beat* that then as now, German youth has tried to compete with Anglo rock and roll. However, young Germans have lacked the experience of growing up in the culture that first bred rock, and Froese felt this doomed them to mediocrity. He knew he had to turn to other sources for inspiration, sources more suited to his past. He found it in "people like Xenakis and our own countryman Karlheinz Stockhausen."

Tangerine Dream's first album, 1970's *Electronic Meditation,* featured Froese on a very fuzz-boxed guitar, with fellow Germans Klaus Schulze playing free style drums and Conrad Schniztler dipping into processed cello arcs and electronics. No actual synthesizers were used on the band's debut effort, released under the now-defunct Ohr label.

By the time the band's second album, *Alpha Centauri,* came out the following year, Schulze and Schniztler had departed the group and were replaced by organist Steve Schroyder and synth-man Christophe Franke. Franke, also classically trained, would remain with Dream for 17 years, the most permanent fixture in the band besides Froese.

Eine Kleine Space Music

While turning from rock and roll as inspiration in the early seventies, Froese admits the band did not turn away from what inspired rock musicians of the time: psychedelics. The search was on for "cosmic" sounds, perhaps mirroring the exploratory nature of hallucinogen consumption. Joining Dream's fleet of space explorers were groups like Synergy, Kraftwerk, Popol Vuh, the Cosmic Couriers, and Jean-Michel Jarre.

By 1972, Peter Baumann joined Franke as the third member of the ensemble. All three musicians played the same equipment: synthesizers and keyboards. Vanished from the band's landscape were the familiar signs of rock: drums, singers, and guitars. Their music, too, drifted without the usual signposts—no chord changes, solos, or catchy melodies.

In 1974 Tangerine Dream gained some press notoriety when, during a gig at Rheims Cathedral in France, 6,000 fans tried to jam the 2,000-parishioner-capacity church. No doubt the crush of human bodies tempered the stony acoustics that made the venue desirable. In the same year, the band's album *Phaedra,* as well as *Rubycon* the following year, finally broke the band onto the charts. The two albums, released on the then-avant garde Virgin label, found their way near the U.K. Top Ten.

In a profile of the band for *Down Beat,* a Tangerine Dream band member admitted to Ted Greenwald that the music of the early seventies came close to fitting the New Age label. But Greenwald found no label that would fit the Dream's more complex brew of later years. He noted of *Phaedra:* "Envelope generators shaped not just individual note events, but entire phrases. Clock pulses drove sequenced rhythms and articulated improvised chords ... the resulting pitches, timbres and rhythms collided and melted into one another, washing over static harmonic centers that ebbed and flowed in tides of undifferentiated sounds."

Tangerine Dream left for England in 1975, touring cathedrals across the country. The tour, which featured Michael Hoenig in place of Baumann, sold out, in part because of the popularity of Froese's first solo album, *Aqua,* which had appeared the year before. The band leader's solo career was prolific—he recorded five more albums before the end of 1979 alone, including 1976's *Electronic Dreams* and 1979's *Stunt Man.* Most of the members of Tangerine Dream would issue solo albums during their time with the band. Musical influences on the band now included Terry Riley and later Steve Reich—from whom Froese said the band adopted the use of "minimalist structures."

Earthly Ambitions

Despite a sold-out U.S. cross-country tour in 1976, the American public's awareness of Tangerine Dream has never been great. Indeed, the band's name is most often noticed during the running of movie soundtrack credits. The band's film work has ranged from William Friedkin's 1977 intense thriller *Sorcerer* to the light-hearted *Risky Business* starring the young Tom Cruise, and the 1987 vampire film *Near Dark*. In addition, dozens of other filmakers have sought out the open-ended sound of Tangerine Dream's instrumentals.

By the late seventies, the band had moved away from its improvisatory roots. The 1976 album *Stratosfear,* for example, was mostly composed, as were subsequent efforts. Composing their music allowed the band to return to more melodic rhythmic structures—not accidentally making their music more accessible. This pattern culminated in the addition of drummer Klaus Krieger and vocalist Steve Jollife for 1978's *Cyclone*. Only a couple of years later, Froese would call *Cyclone,* which sounded like the work of an art-rock band, "a mistake, a very heavy mistake." The album hurt the band's reputation as a committed experimental group yet earned little recompense in increased mass appeal. Tangerine Dream was quick to correct course.

Unlike many electronic groups, the band has always maintained its ability to perform live. However, in a performance style suggestive of the primacy of hardware in their work, Tangerine Dream appeared on stage behind a screen of black gauze in their 1981 concert tour. This translucent curtain gently reflected the soft-hued lights and blurred the band members' silhouettes—already half-hidden in wells of synthesizers—the musicians appearing as ghostly, mystical creatures.

Computer Age

In 1988, 17-year band veteran Franke departed to become a full-time electronic music hardware developer. The work of this era, reported Dream keyboardist Paul Haslinger, was approximately 70 percent composed and 30 percent improvised. The band used all three major computers of the time: Apple, Atari, and PC's. Software varied continuously and the band developed a reputation for buying each new electronic gizmo as soon as it came out.

Changing their equipment every few months kept the band members' interest up but also had its pitfalls. The band reported spending $150,000 on two cutting-edge computer music systems, only to scrap them 18 months later for $20,000 after finding them useless. Of course, such tales are standard lore in the computer electronics world. However, in a 1988 *Keyboard* magazine interview, Haslinger admitted to sometimes being shamed by the excellent work turned out by young people on low budget equipment.

The band's dependence on complex equipment has led to a growing interdependency upon music software and hardware manufacturers. The band meets regularly with industry reps to learn about new products and receive training on what they already own. Indeed, the industry is even sort of a fourth band member, for Tangerine Dream uses factory-supplied sounds in their sampling work.

Wandering through a maze of sounds, software, and machines, each member of Tangerine Dream pursues the elusive, ethereal, and new. And when they find it? "Thank god for the memory button," responded Haslinger. Over a quarter of a century past its inception, Tangerine Dream has continued to push the right buttons, earning almost annual Grammy nominations for their albums in the early 1990s, including *Canyon Dreams, Rockoon,* and *220 VOLT Live*—although the band has yet to capture this award.

Selected discography

Electronic Meditation, Ohr/Relativity, 1970.
Alpha Centauri, Ohr, 1971, reissued, Polydor, 1975.
Zeit, Ohr, 1972, reissued, Virgin, 1976.
Atem, Ohr, 1972, reissued, Virgin, 1976.
Phaedra, Virgin, 1974.
Rubycon, Virgin, 1975.
Stratosfear, Virgin, 1976.
Cyclone, Virgin, 1978.
Tamgram, Virgin, 1980.
White Eagle, Virgin, 1982.
Le Parc, Jive Electro, 1986.
Livemiles, Jive Electro, 1988.
Canyon Dreams, Miramar, 1991.
Rockoon, Miramar, 1992.
(With Jerome Froese) *220 VOLT Live,* Miramar, 1993.
Hyperborea, Virgin.
Logos, Virgin.
Tangerine Dream Live, Virgin.
Turn of the Tides, Miramar.

Solo albums by Froese

Aqua, Blue Plate, 1974.
Electronic Dreams, Blue Plate, 1976.
Stunt Man, Blue Plate, 1979.

Sources

Books

Heatly, Michael, *The Ultimate Encyclopedia of Rock,* HarperCollins, 1993.

Pareles, Jon, and Patricia Romanowski, *The Rolling Stone Encyclopedia of Rock & Roll,* Rolling Stone Press/Summit Books, 1983.

Periodicals

Billboard, April 30, 1977.
Down Beat, March 1981; December 1981.
Entertainment Weekly, May 13, 1994.
Keyboard, November 1988.

Additional information for this profile was obtained from Miramar press releases, 1994.

—*Joseph M. Reiner*

Aaron Tippin

Singer, songwriter, guitarist

Photograph by Peter Nash, courtesy of Starstruck Entertainment

"I've been in love with country music since I was a young teenager," exclaimed country singer and songwriter Aaron Tippin. "And I saw it have to live in the ditch for so many years. Now I see today how popular it is ... some of the greatest country songs I've ever heard being written and sung." Tippin's personal enthusiasm for country music is reflected by the many loyal fans who hear in his twangy voice and raw, hard-hitting lyrics a return to country's hillbilly roots.

Tippin was born in Pensacola, Florida, but grew up in the farmland outside Greenville, South Carolina. While he began playing guitar when he was ten, young Tippin was satisfied to confine his singing to performing with his Baptist church choir. Intent upon following his father's lead and becoming a commercial jet pilot, he worked on nearby farms and in his father's air-taxi business to earn money for the flying lessons that would earn Tippin his pilot's license by the time he was 15.

In the midst of building a career as a corporate pilot, Tippin renewed his interest in country music. Wooed by the heartrending lyrics of Hank Williams, Sr., and the songs of Jimmie Rodgers, Hank Thompson, and Lefty Frizzell, Tippin began playing rhythm guitar in local bluegrass and country groups. Music remained a hobby until his dreams of becoming a jet pilot were grounded by the energy crisis of the early 1970s. Tippin began to think seriously about trading in his pilot's license for a one-way ticket to Nashville.

Once his mind was made up, Tippin refocused the enormous energy he had once devoted to flying on his music. For several years, he worked strenuous day jobs, interspersing them with nights spent playing the Southern honky-tonk circuit. Encouragement came when a gospel tune he wrote came to the attention of a publisher who advised Tippin to move to Nashville, home to the Gospel music publishing industry. In 1985, he finally made it to Music City by way of a television talent show. Once Tippin had arrived, he was determined to stay on.

Determined to Succeed

Opportunities for an unknown vocalist proved scarce, so Tippin decided to pursue a job where he could learn about the music business. "Figured I'll do something easy, I'll be a songwriter," he told the *Chicago Tribune*'s Hugh Hart. He quickly discovered that there was more to writing hit songs than a short session with the typewriter. "The only thing in my favor was, I was smart enough to see that I didn't know nothing," he confessed. "I remember the times I'd be ready to pack up and go home," Tippin told the *Modesto Bee*'s Linda

For the Record...

Born July 3, 1958, in Pensacola, FL; son of Willis Emory (a pilot) and Mary Tippin; divorced; children: Charla.

Country-western singer and songwriter. Worked variously as a farm hand, welder, corporate pilot, truck driver, and heavy equipment operator; staff songwriter, Acuff-Rose, Nashville, TN, c. 1985; signed with RCA, 1990.

Addresses: *Record company*—RCA Records, One Music Circle North, Nashville, TN 37203. *Agent*—Jessie Schmidt, Starstruck Entertainment, P.O. Box 121996, Nashville, TN 37212-1996. *Fan club*—Aaron Tippin International Fan Club, P.O. Box 121709, Nashville, TN 37212.

Cearley, "but I'd think about the people in my hometown who said 'You ought to go to Nashville' and I'd stay for another day.... I'd think there are a lot of people who believe in me so I have to believe in myself."

Tippin's determination paid off. The many hours alone with his guitar in a songwriter's cubicle eventually earned him recognition as a songwriter. His gospel tune, "Tell Everyone You Know," was picked up by the Kingsmen. Several of Tippin's songs went on to be recorded by popular country artists: "Something With a Ring to It" was recorded by coauthor Mark Collie, and "Whole Lot of Love on the Line" by veteran country performer Charley Pride. "We've quit writing songs like 'Okie from Muskogee' and 'The Fightin' Side of Me'—songs of just being proud," said Tippin. "I guess that's why I try to bring it back." His personal beliefs inspire many of his lyrics. "I think that standing there in the middle of the storm—knowing that it's going to be over and that you stayed until it was—has a lot of value to it," he flatly stated. "Being a feather in the wind is not much of a way for a person to live."

Bridged Gap Between Old and New Country

After several years as a songsmith, Tippin decided to save some production costs by doing his own vocals on a demo-tape he was preparing for RCA. He recalled the record company's response for Hart: "They came back and said, 'We really like these songs, and, hey, who's that hillbilly singin' 'em?'" RCA found in Tippin a sound that linked the old and new in country music: they signed the songwriter on in 1990. With a blue yodel reminiscent of the late great Jimmie Rodgers, Tippin's music runs the gamut between red-neck battle-cries and soul-searching ballads, carrying a moral resoluteness echoing country music's not-too-distant past. "Ironically, Tippin's sound probably would have stood no chance in modern Nashville before Randy Travis led the roots movement [in the mid-1980s]," noted Jack Hurst in the *Chicago Tribune.* Tippin agreed. "They would have laughed me out of here five years ago," Hurst quoted him as saying.

In addition to his emotionally engaging lyrics, much of Tippin's appeal comes from his energetic stage performance. His body-builder physique has screaming female fans leaping to their feet. "You might call him a 'warm-up,'" recalled *Union City Daily Messenger's* Glenda H. Caudle. "But then you'd be severely understating what Tippin managed to do. Because he left the audience not just warm. By the time he finished, they were hot enough to temper steel." "There's sure nothing subtle about Aaron Tippin's music," Bob Allen commented in his review of Tippin's 1993 *Call of the Wild* in *Country Music.* "It's unadulterated twang and good-natured, iron-pumping musical aggression *in extremis.* Most people tend to either love it a lot or hate it, because 'The Tipper' doesn't pull punches or hedge his bets."

Lyrics Celebrate Working-Class Values

Tippin's 1990 single "You've Got to Stand for Something (Or You'll Fall for Anything)" coincided with the U.S. intervention in Iraq, and many listeners found in the singer's personal anthem a national battle cry. The song's popularity gained Tippin an invitation from comedian Bob Hope to entertain American troops in Saudi Arabia. "I got to take the message to them about how we felt," he told Caudle. "That was an honor."

Many of Tippin's lyrics celebrate the dignity of the American worker. "Working Man's Ph.D." has become a rallying cry for the blue-collar worker since its release on *Call of the Wild,* and the song speaks to its author's pride in his years performing hard, physical labor. "It's not that I put down education," Tippin explained. But, he told *Country Song Roundup's* Jennifer Fusco-Giacobbe, "For some reason or another, in our society, we've decided if you weren't a brain surgeon or an astronaut, that you didn't have much worth. That's sad, because no matter what you do in this world, no matter how small it may seem, as long as you do it the absolute best you can, then I think folks should be proud of what they do."

"I used to think that being a singer/songwriter was a whole lot tougher than just being a singer," Tippin noted of his craft. "But I've found out that even though writing is more work, it's a whole lot easier when you're getting ready to put an album together." He sees each completed album as a stage in his musical development. 1991's *You've Got to Stand for Something* showcased his unique vocal style and songwriting abilities.

A year later, *Read Between the Lines* generated a string of hit singles on its way to going platinum, proving that his musical instincts were on target. His next album, *Call of the Wild*, takes its lead from the humorous single "Ain't Nothing Wrong With the Radio" in showcasing Tippin's lighter side. "I think *Call of the Wild* is my dawning," said Tippin. "It shows I've passed the storm." Although his music continues to attract attention, Tippin remains pragmatic about his career. "You've got to get it out of your head that this is all for you and get it in [your head] that this is for the betterment of country music," he told Caudle, "and if you can carry it a few miles and a few years down the road to a higher plateau, then you're doing your job."

Selected discography

You've Got to Stand for Something, RCA, 1991.
Read Between the Lines (includes "There Ain't Nothin' Wrong With the Radio," "I Wouldn't Have It Any Other Way," and "My Blue Angel"), RCA, 1992.
Call of the Wild (includes "Working Man's Ph.D."), RCA, 1993.

Sources

Chicago Tribune, January 6, 1991; June 17, 1992.
Country Music, September 1991; November 1993.
Country Song Roundup, September 1993; January 1994.
Modesto Bee, December 11, 1992.
Union City Daily Messenger (Tennessee), April 27, 1992.
USA Today, January 22, 1991; September 9, 1991.

Additional information for this profile was obtained from RCA press materials, 1994.

—*Pamela Shelton*

Tony! Toni! Toné!

Rhythm and blues trio

The three members of the smash R&B band Tony! Toni! Toné! grew up in Oakland, California, when that city was a hotbed of funk and soul innovation. As a result, they bring to their own records a dedication to the old-style melodic groove that stands out in the polished, machine-driven, hip-hop era. Playing their own instruments and singing harmonies modeled on their favorite soul artists' finest singles, the Tonys please both fans and critics and have managed to extend their audience beyond even their impressive R&B following. Though walking the line between continuing in an honored tradition and purveying unabashed nostalgia has been a tricky task, the group came into its own enough to claim the mantle—used as the title of their 1993 album—*Sons of Soul*.

Brothers Dwayne and Raphael Wiggins are actually sons of the blues; their father played guitar in a blues band, and Raphael first played in front of an audience as the group's bassist at the age of seven. Dwayne told *Request* that his father "was the one who got me started on the guitar. He was down with us being musicians, but he was also down with being a man and being responsible for yourself. You gotta go out there and work. He was always a working man." Like his brother, Dwayne began playing in nightclubs at a very young age. "We got to play," he recalled, "and then when the break time came, they had to take us out the back." Their cousin Tim Christian Riley had a similar musical upbringing—he continued to play drums in church even after achieving fame as one of the Tonys—and the three played music together growing up.

Riley described this atmosphere of constant jamming in *Rolling Stone:* "Like in the neighborhood, there was always competitions. I mean, it would be like school talent shows, and you'd come home from school, and there would be like five or six drummers in their houses playing. Everyone just played, and you had to stay on top of it." The three attended Castlemont High School and sang in its esteemed Castleers Choir, which performed in Hawaii and Jamaica.

Named for "Fly" Character

Even before the trio decided to form a band—which they intended to do "from day zero," Raphael claimed in *People*—they came up with the name they would eventually use. "When we went out," Dwayne recollected in *Rolling Stone,* "we liked to go shopping at vintage-clothing stores, buy old suits and big shoes, and it was more a character thing. We invented this character, Tony Toni Toné." Riley elaborated in *People* that a "guy on TV named Tony who used to dress real fly, and a friend of ours always had to be looking

---

For the Record...

Members include **Timothy Christian Riley** (born c. 1965, in Oakland, CA), drums, keyboards, and vocals; **Dwayne Wiggins** (born c. 1962, in Oakland, CA), guitar, bass, and vocals; **Raphael Wiggins** (born c. 1966, in Oakland, CA), bass, keyboards, and vocals.

Trio formed in mid-1980s and released debut album, *Who?*, Wing/Mercury, 1988; contributed to soundtracks for films *Boyz N the Hood* and *House Party 2*, both 1991, and *Poetic Justice*, 1993.

Awards: Gold record for *Who?*; platinum record for *The Revival*, 1990.

Addresses: *Record company*—Wing/Mercury, 825 Eighth Avenue, New York, NY 10019; 11150 Santa Monica Blvd., Suite 1100, Los Angeles, CA 90025.

---

perfect—his hair looking good and everything—so we gave him Tony as a nickname and started having fun with it. If somebody else came into the house who looked better than he did, we'd say, 'That's a *Tony* Tony.' When we had our first gig, we were like, 'We don't have a name.' So we just invented it on the spot."

Before they had a first gig together, though, the trio spent years on the Oakland music scene, which had been dominated by such influential figures as "East Bay Grease" pioneers Tower of Power, singer-songwriter and multi-instrumentalist Sly Stone, and bassist Larry Graham, who played with Stone's band and later led his own successful outfit. Dwayne claimed in the *Request* interview that he met Graham "back when he had this 1970 Cadillac with big-ass side pipes on it." The Wiggins brothers and Riley played with a number of different acts before joining up to back singer-percussionist and former Prince acolyte Sheila E. on tour. Afterward they began work on their own project.

The group eventually signed with Mercury Records, having made a strong impression on label president Ed Eckstine. Five songs from the Tonys' 1988 debut album *Who?*—among them "Little Walter," "Baby Doll" and "For the Love of You"—became hits, and the album went gold. Produced by Denzil Foster and Thomas McElroy, who would later develop and produce the smash vocal quartet En Vogue, the album immediately established the Tonys as contenders on the tough and volatile R&B scene.

Self-Produced Platinum Sophomore Album

Tony! Toni! Toné! produced their follow-up, 1990's *The Revival*, themselves. Gerry Brown, who engineered the group's second and third albums, told *Musician* that "Eckstine gave the Tonys about $3000 to go into the studio. They came up with 'Feels Good' and 'The Blues.' That gave Ed an indication that they could get some stuff done." Eckstine was right. *The Revival* reached and exceeded platinum status; "Feels Good" made it to the pop Top Ten and the number one R&B position, while "The Blues," "It Never Rains in Southern California," and "Whatever You Want" were also R&B Top Ten hits.

As to producing, Raphel opined in *Request* that it was "harder to think about than to actually do. Thinking about completing a project from A to Z is probably worse than just to go ahead with it." Dwayne, meanwhile, said in an interview with Michael Goldberg of *Musician* that "we still don't known how to produce," while Riley confided, "We were forced. That's the bottom line. We're just musicians. But someone had to do it." *Vibe*'s Elysa Gardner felt that the album, "following on the heels of a charming but unspectacular debut," showed that the trio "had the stuff that separates those artists who synthesize their influences in fresh, exciting ways from those who merely wear them on their sleeves."

In addition to their own albums, Dwayne, Raphel, and Riley also contributed the song "Me and You" to the platinum soundtrack of John Singleton's hit 1991 film *Boyz N the Hood*, the title song to 1991's *House Party 2*, the comedy sequel starring rappers Kid 'n Play, and "Waiting on You" to Singleton's second film, *Poetic Justice*. By 1993, however, the Tonys were concentrating primarily on their new album. They wanted to emphasize the warm, spontaneous feel of their favorite soul albums. "Guys would sit down with a guitar, drums and a keyboard and come up with somethin'," Dwayne reminded Goldberg, speaking of the legendary sounds produced for the Motown and Stax soul labels. "But today when most people write, it's like a computer get-down. We just went back to home with our thing. That's where the flavor came from and that's what the whole title is about, *Sons of Soul*. Like a tribute to the old flavor."

Though it was begun in California, much of *Sons of Soul* was written and recorded in Trinidad. "There were a couple of times when I think the record company really wanted to put what we had out," Dwayne recalled, "but we ourselves didn't feel like the album was done." Intending merely to polish what they'd begun in the United States, the group ended up starting a number of new songs in the tropical spot, while immersing themselves in Caribbean musical styles.

Critically Acclaimed *Sons of Soul*

"We'd heard dancehall, but we didn't really know anything about it before going there," Dwayne explained in *Request*. "We would go to these block parties"—nighttime dance-fests in blockaded parking lots powered by massive loudspeakers—"and you could hear them from almost a mile away. You'd just park on the street and walk to the party along with four or five thousand other people, all partying with these giant speakers all over the place. And this happened just about every weekend." The trio would record well into the night, go out and immerse themselves in the nightlife until the wee hours, and then return to the studio to work some more. The track "Dance Hall" even features a "ragamuffin" rap from Trinidadian MC General Grant. All in all, the Tonys recorded nearly 40 songs for *Sons of Soul*. Dwayne told *Billboard* that narrowing them down wasn't terribly hard: "The love songs, the lovemaking songs set the pace for the album. We kept our audience in mind in deciding what would make the final selection."

The album's first single, "If I Had No Loot," was an immediate smash, and the ballad "Anniversary" looked to follow in its footsteps. But Bill Forman of *Request* referred to "Tell Me Mama" as the recording's "most brilliant track," calling it "the greatest hit the Jackson 5 never recorded, an instant classic with an airtight groove and the kind of hooks you'll still be humming long after you've lasered the CD into dust." A *GQ* reviewer felt that "the musicianly details justify the album's title," while an *Entertainment Weekly* writer declared, "It's fresh, funky, fierce, and it *feels good.*" Jonathan Bernstein of *Spin* was one of the few detractors, criticizing the Tonys for "sequeling previous hits" and for what he called "the oafish 'Ex-Girlfriend,' whose smooth refrain suffixes the title's tune with the words '... is a ho.' Talk about breaking the mood."

In any event, the Tonys had clearly established themselves as fixtures on the R&B scene. "Conscious of history, the Tonyies have made themselves a band of the here and now," wrote Christopher John Farley of *Time*. "We're not trying to be 'retro,'" Dwayne insisted in *Billboard*, "we're just being the bridge between old R&B and hip-hop. We're just using the music we grew up listening to, the music we always enjoyed as the basis for what we're doing now." Like those enduring records, he noted in the *Musician* interview, "Our production philosophy is 'Less is more.' Put it like that. It's all about making it fun, man. Having fun and taking chances."

Selected discography

Who? (includes "Little Walter," "Baby Doll," and "For the Love of You"), Wing/Mercury, 1988.
The Revival (includes "Feels Good," "The Blues," "It Never Rains in Southern California," and "Whatever You Want"), Wing/Mercury, 1990.
Sons of Soul (includes "Dance Hall," "If I Had No Loot," "Anniversary," "Tell Me Mama," and "Ex-Girlfriend"), Wing/Mercury, 1993.

With other artists

"Me and You," *Boyz N the Hood* (soundtrack), Sony, 1991.
"House Party II (I Don't Know What You Come to Do)," *House Party 2* (soundtrack), MCA, 1991.
"Waiting on You," *Poetic Justice* (soundtrack), New Deal, 1993.

Sources

Billboard, May 29, 1993.
Entertainment Weekly, June 25, 1993.
GQ, August 1993.
Guitar Player, June 1994.
Musician, November 1993.
People, July 5, 1993; November 22, 1993.
Request, October 1993.
Rolling Stone, September 30, 1993.
Source, September 1993.
Spin, August 1993.
Time, July 26, 1993.
Vibe, September 1993; October 1993.

Additional information for this profile was provided by Wing/Mercury promotional materials, 1993.

—*Simon Glickman*

Sophie Tucker

Singer, performer

Sophie Tucker was loud, lavish, brash, brassy, sexy, sassy, and just a little bit naughty. With limitless energy, she traveled constantly for many years, giving several shows a night. She picked songs she knew her audiences would love, both tear-jerking ballads and comic "hot" songs—she laughed uproariously, and wept copiously on stage as in life. Known as "The Last of the Red Hot Mamas," she thoroughly enjoyed her slightly risque reputation.

Tucker always boasted that she was born on the road, not between theaters, but between countries. Her parents, Russian Jews, fled their country in the late nineteenth century for the better life America had to offer. The family lived first in Boston, and then when Tucker was eight, moved to Hartford, Connecticut, to open the restaurant where she was to get her first taste of show business. Because the restaurant offered good food at low prices, it was often filled with the entertainers playing the local vaudeville house. Tucker, an energetic extrovert even as a child, picked up their songs quickly, and found she could also pick up some spare change when she sang them for the diners. She soon realized that singing for the customers was easier than cooking for them, and decided go into show business herself.

All throughout her school years, Tucker helped in the restaurant—cooking, cleaning, and serving. She would rise early before school to prepare food, and work after school washing dishes until very late. She witnessed her mother working even harder, and she wanted to create an easier life for herself and her mother. Soon after finishing high school, Sophie Tucker married Louis Tuck. It quickly became evident that while Louis Tuck was a good man, he was not a hard worker, and was not going to give his wife the life she wanted. After the birth of their first child, Albert, he left them. Tucker continued working for the restaurant until she had a small savings of her own, and then, leaving Albert in the loving care of her sister and mother, left Hartford for the lights of Broadway.

Performed in Vaudeville

Breaking into show business is hard work, but Sophie Tucker, as she began calling herself, was used to that. For months, she tramped around the city of New York trying to get someone to give her a chance. When money became low, she ended up singing for her supper at small cafes. Eventually, she was able to get a job singing at a beer hall. Perseverance led to a performance at an amateur hour, which led to an agent, which led to vaudeville. By 1906, Tucker was traveling the New England Vaudeville circuit.

> **For the Record...**
>
> Born Sophie Kalish, January 13, 1884, in Russia; died February 9, 1966, in New York. Married Louis Tuck (d. 1914), 1900; son Albert Tuck, b. 1901; married Frank Westphal, 1914, divorced 1917; married Al Lackey 1930, divorced 1933.
>
> Debuted at the Village Cafe, New York City, 1906; began singing in Vaudeville, 1906. Sang in Ziegfeld Follies, Atlantic City, 1909; toured with Frank Westphal, 1914-1916; toured with The Kings of Syncopation, 1916-1919; sang in the Winter Garden Theater, 1919; toured England, 1922 and 1925; command performance for King and Queen of England, 1934. Musicals include: *Mary Mary*, 1911; *Louisiana Lou*, 1912; *Hello Alexander*, 1919; *Follow a Star*, 1930; *Leave It to Me*, 1938. Movies include: *Honky Tonk*, 1929; *Gay Love*, 1934; *Broadway Melody of 1938*, 1937; *Thoroughbreds Don't Cry*, 1937; *Follow the Boys*, 1944; *Sensations of 1945*, 1944; *Atlantic City*, 1944.
>
> **Awards:** Election to the Friars Club, 1950; Gold Seal Commendation from the Mayor of San Francisco, 1953; Citation of Merit from the Mayor of New York City, 1953; Gold Heart Award, London Variety Club, 1959.

Because Tucker was somewhat hefty, and was not considered to be one of the beauties of her day, her manager and producers had her sing in black face as a comic singer. One day, after several years performing in black face, her trunks were not delivered in time for a performance, and she was forced to sing in every day clothes and no make up. The audience still loved her, so she dropped the black face altogether.

She began adding Yiddish songs to her act, new comic songs, and even sentimental songs and blues. Risque songs were always popular. Variety was one key to her success. "I would start off with a lively rag, then would come a ballad, followed by a comedy song, and a novelty number," she wrote in her autobiography, *Some of These Days*. "And finally, the hot song. In this way, I left the stage with the audience laughing their heads off. For encores, I always had popular songs, new ones." By continually adding new songs and new costumes, she kept her act fresh. "Playing two months or more in one city meant new songs all the time," she continued. "If people paid their dimes to see and hear Sophie Tucker, they didn't want to hear the same songs over and over or see the same clothes." Her costumes were as lavish as possible. One of her last costumes consisted of a 24-carat-gold cloth gown, a white mink coat, and a diamond headdress. She boasted that each new act cost $50,000—$25,000 each for the new songs and the gowns.

Command Performance

By the second decade of the twentieth century, Sophie Tucker was a headliner, receiving top billing everywhere she played. She earned the highest salaries, and played the best theaters. She even played a command performance for the King and Queen of England in 1934.

While her style and attitude remained constant, her act changed through the years. For several years, Tucker's second husband, Frank Westphal, accompanied her on piano, but their act and marriage broke apart, because she earned more money and received more attention than he did. She then traveled with a small combo, the Five Kings of Syncopation. When that act broke up, she hired pianist Ted Shapiro, who stayed with her for over 40 years. She also worked with the songwriter Jack Yellen, whom she kept on salary and commission; he wrote many songs just for her. From his song "The Last of the Red Hot Mamas" she took her most famous nickname.

Vaudeville Died

After two decades in show business, vaudeville, the business Tucker knew best, began to die, done in by the movies—especially talkies—and the depression of the 1930s. Tucker began singing in revues, such as "Gay Paree" and musicals, such as "Leave it to Me." She made a few movies, including "Broadway Melody of 1938," and sang on radio, but none of these fit her style well, and she had trouble finding the right venue, until she turned to nightclubs. Once she started singing in clubs, she was back on top. The intimate atmosphere and the immediate communication between artist and audience was just right for her type of show. She could say whatever she wanted to the audience, and sing their favorite songs.

While Tucker demanded, and received, top salaries, she did it as much for others as herself. With her very first paycheck, she began sending money home to help support her family. In 1910, as soon as her increasing income became large enough, she bought her parents a new home, and provided enough money for them to retire. When she began earning more money than both she and her family needed, she gave to charities, a practice she maintained all of her life.

Through the years, her efforts supported many different groups including the Jewish Theatrical Guild, the Negro Actors guild, the Catholic Actors Guild, the Will Rogers Memorial Hospital, the Motion Picture Relief Fund, and Save the Children Foundation.

In 1945, with the publication of her autobiography, she set up the Sophie Tucker Foundation. All of the profits for her book went into the fund, as well as all of the revenues from her Golden Jubilee album, *Sophie Tucker—50 Glorious Years,* which came out in 1953. In 1955, in addition to its other donations, the Sophie Tucker Foundation endowed a chair in theater arts at Brandeis University. The *New York Times* reported, shortly after her death, that during the six decades of her career, she donated more than four million dollars to charity. Tucker also liked to sing benefits. She sang without fee at innumerable orphanages and prisons, and was famous for performing for charity at the drop of a hat. "Benefits? I've never refused one," she once said, as quoted in *Sophie: The Sophie Tucker Story.*

Whether she was singing to royalty in England, or prisoners in California, spending her money on sequined gowns worth thousands, or the Jewish Actors Temple, everything Sophie Tucker did was on a grand scale—she was larger than life. "She was a giant," her agent Able L. Lastfogel told the *New York Times* after she died. "She was unique. She was a star who stayed important, through her lifetime. Her work and effort and her willingness to help those who needed help will be remembered in years to come."

Selected discography

Sophie Tucker—50 Glorious Years, Mercury, 1953.
Miff Mole's Molers, Jazz Makers, 1971.
Follow a Star, Academy Sound and Vision, 1985.
Is Everybody Happy, Halcyon, 1986.
Sophie Tucker: Jazz Age Hot Mama, Take Two Records, 1992.

Sources

Books

Freedland, Michael, *Sophie: The Sophie Tucker Story,* Woburn Press, 1978.
Hardy, Phil, and Dave Laing, *The Faber Companion to 20th-Century Popular Music,* Faber and Faber, 1990.
The New Grove Dictionary of American Music, edited by Wiley H. Hitchcock and Stanley Sadie, Macmillan Publishing, Ltd.
Simon, George, *Best of the Music Makers,* Doubleday, 1979.
Tucker, Sophie, *Some of These Days; The Autobiography of Sophie Tucker,* Doubleday, 1945.

Periodicals

Life, February 18, 1966.
Newsweek, October 5, 1953; February 21, 1966.
New York Times, February 10, 1966.
New York Times Magazine, September 27, 1953.

—*Robin Armstrong*

U2

Rock band

Photograph by Anton Corbijn, courtesy of Island Records

In 1984, U2 lead singer Bono told Jim Miller in *Newsweek,* "The message, if there is a message in our music, is the hope that it communicates." Nearly ten years later, after being called everything from "pompous and self-righteous social crusaders" to "sincere and involved political activists," U2 decided it was time to step out of the identities the world had superimposed on them. Bono Vox, who by this time had become simply Bono, told Robert Hilburn of the *Los Angeles Times,* "We felt we were being made a cartoon of 'the good guys of rock and so forth' so we decided to make some cartoons of our own and send them out as disinformation." The band wanted to make sure that there was no one identity that could be forced on them. So who are they really? Four young men from Ireland who became megastar rock gods with a reported $60-million-plus, six-record deal with PolyGram's Island Records.

U2 started off humbly enough as a Dublin, Ireland, schoolboy band formed in response to an ad placed on the Mount Temple High School notice board by Larry Mullen, Jr. in 1976. Of the several students that came to his house to audition for the rock band, Mullen noted that, although some could play, technical merit wasn't the decisive factor. Mullen told Jay Cocks of *Time* that the original band consisted of one fellow who "meant to play the guitar, but he couldn't play very well, so he started to sing. He couldn't do that either. But, he was such a charismatic character that he was in the band as soon as he arrived."

That fellow was Paul Hewson, who later adopted the name Bono Vox (Latin for "good voice," which Hewson appropriated from a billboard advertisement for a hearing aid retailer). David "The Edge" Evans, a guitarist who *could* play, Adam Clayton, a bassist who "just looked great and used all the right words, like gig," Larry Mullen, Jr. on drums, and second guitarist Dick (Dik) Evans, The Edge's older brother, made up the rest of the band.

Originally Known as Feedback

U2 began their musical odyssey as Feedback. After playing mainly cover tunes for a few shows in small local venues, Dik Evans left the band to form the Virgin Prunes, and the band changed its name to the Hype. Clayton, acting as band manager, sought advice from all the music industry sources he knew, including Steve Rapid, a singer for the local band the Radiators, who suggested that they change their name. Clayton wanted something ambiguous; Rapid suggested U2 because there was a U2 spy plane, a U2 submarine, a U2 battery made by Eveready, as well as the obvious

> **For the Record . . .**
>
> Members include **Bono** (originally Bono Vox; born Paul Hewson, May 10, 1960), vocals; **Adam Clayton** (born March 13, 1960), bass; **The Edge** (born David Evans, August 8, 1961), guitar; **Dick Evans** (left band, 1976), guitar; and **Larry Mullen, Jr.** (born October 31, 1961), drums.
>
> Group formed in Dublin, Ireland. 1976; began as Feedback, then toured locally as the Hype, playing mainly cover tunes; changed name to U2, 1977; won talent competition, signed with CBS Ireland, and released first EP, *U2:3,* 1978; signed with Island Records, U.K., 1980; released debut album, *Boy,* 1980; Bono and Clayton participated in Band Aid recording, 1984; appeared in Live Aid, 1985.
>
> **Selected awards:** British Record Industry Award for best international group, 1988 and 1989; Grammy awards for best rock performance by a duo or group with vocals, and album of the year, both 1988, both for *Joshua Tree;* Grammy awards for best rock performance by a duo or group with vocal, for "Desire," and best performance music video, for "Where The Streets Have No Name," both 1989; Grammy Award for producer of the year, 1991, for *Achtung Baby;* Grammy Award for best alternative album, 1993, for *Zooropa;* MTV Music Video Award for viewer's choice, 1987, for "With or Without You," for best video from film, 1989, for "When Love Comes To Town" (with B. B. King), and for best group video and best special effects in a video, 1992, for "Even Better Than the Real Thing."
>
> **Addresses:** *Publicist*—The Wasserman Group Inc., 6500 Wilshire Blvd., Suite 500, Los Angeles, CA 90048. *Record company*—Island, 14 East 4th St., New York, NY 10012.

"you, too" and "you two." The remaining members were skeptical at first but eventually accepted it.

In March of 1978, U2 entered a talent competition sponsored by Guinness at the Limerick Civic Week. They won £500 and the opportunity to audition for CBS Ireland, after which they secured supporting spots on tours with the Stranglers and the Greedy Bastards. In September, they recorded additional demos at Dublin's Windmill Lane Studios with Chas de Whalley, which subsequently lead to their signing by CBS Ireland. After building a considerable following in Ireland, they released their first EP, *U2:3,* which featured the tracks "Out Of Control," "Stories," and "Boy-Girl." It was available only in Ireland, where it topped the charts. It was in December of the next year that U2 played their first U.K. dates—to a cool reception. They were even mis-billed as "V2" at the Hope & Anchor pub in London, where a mere nine people showed up to see them perform.

Although they played to sold-out shows in their homeland, U2 had yet to conquer the U.K. charts. In February of 1980, "Another Day" hit Number One in Ireland and the band took another try at playing the United Kingdom. This time around the reception was better and talent recruiter Bill Stewart signed them to U.K.'s Island Records (although they remained on CBS in Ireland). In May, their debut Island single, "11 o'clock Tick Tock," was released but it failed to break into the U.K. charts. The band embarked on another U.K. tour and appeared at the Dalmount Festival in Dublin with the Police and Squeeze.

Their debut album, *Boy,* was preceded by the singles "A Day Without Me" and "I Will Follow," both of which failed to chart in either the U.K. or the U.S. However, in conjunction with the release of *Boy,* U2 was given the opportunity to embark on their first U.S. campaign: a three-week club tour of the East Coast. When they returned to the U.K. in December, they supported Talking Heads on a U.K. tour.

First Break Into Charts

In 1981 U2 embarked on their first major U.S. tour, pushing *Boy* onto the U.S. charts. In July, U2 finally broke into the U.K. charts at Number 35 with "Fire," which was then followed by *Boy,* belatedly breaking in at Number 52. By the end of the year, after an 18-date U.K. tour and the release of the album *October,* U2 readied themselves for a new series of U.S. dates. By mid-1982, after playing to an Irish audience for the first time in over a year and to sold-out crowds in the United Kingdom, U2 retired to the studio to record new music. It was that October, during a concert in Belfast, that they introduced "Sunday, Bloody Sunday" to their fans. That song carried a message of peace in Northern Ireland that would later become the focal point of the band, seemingly fusing their lyrics and politics.

In February of 1983, the band that had played to only nine people in a London pub just four years earlier, opened a sold-out, 27-date U.K. tour with the single "New Year's Day." The song topped the U.K. charts at Number Ten, and their album *War* reached Number 12 in the U.S. By March, their album took the Number One spot on the U.K. charts. It looked as though U2 had finally arrived. The band spent the next few months touring arenas in the U.S., including participating in the three-day US Festival in San Bernardino, California. In November, as a bid to meet the growing demand for new work, U2 released *Under a Blood Red Sky,* their first live album. It became the most successful live album of the time, but it didn't end the circulation of bootleg U2 recordings, which was rampant.

Their next studio album, 1984's *The Unforgettable Fire,* reached Number One in the United Kingdom. Later that year, the band's humanitarian side resurfaced when they participated in the Band Aid recording of "Do They Know It's Christmas?" for Ethiopian famine relief, with Bono contributing a lead vocal and Clayton playing bass. 1985 found the band headlining at Madison Square Garden; *Rolling Stone* touted them as "The Band of the Eighties."

Once again giving in to their charitable tendencies, U2 performed at Live Aid in July, and in November, Bono appeared in the Little Steven-organized Artists Against Apartheid single and video "Sun City." U2 also released a U.S. EP, *Wide Awake in America.* In 1986 they resumed their world touring, which included performing on Amnesty International's 25th anniversary tour with artists like Peter Gabriel and Sting. Also lending a hand at home, U2 helped to raise funds for the unemployed in Ireland by playing Self Aid with other Irish rock acts.

Although it seemed that U2 were the social crusaders of their generation, Bono assured *Time's* Cocks that he "would hate to think everybody was into U2 for 'deep' and 'meaningful' reasons. We're a noisy rock n' roll band. If we got on stage, and instead of going 'Yeow!' the audience all went 'Ummmm' or started saying the rosary, it would be awful." Regardless of how Bono saw it, the band's social consciousness is one of the main reasons, according to Christopher Connelly of *Rolling Stone,* U2 "has become one of the handful of artists in rock (and) roll history ... that people are eager to identify themselves with."

Finally Won Critical Acclaim

In 1987 U2 embarked on a 110-date world tour. Their new album, *The Joshua Tree,* entered the U.K. charts at Number One and went platinum in 48 hours, making it, at the time, the fastest-selling album in U.K. history. In mid-April, *The Joshua Tree* reached the top of the U.S. charts where it remained for nine weeks. Shortly thereafter, the band appeared on the cover of *Time* with the headline: "U2: Rock's Hottest Ticket" and everyone seemed to want a piece of them. The Edge released a soundtrack for the political kidnapping film *Captive.* Favorably reviewed, the soundtrack will always be remembered for featuring the album debut of yet another Irish act, Sinead O'Connor, who sings "Heroine (Theme from Captive)." In November, Eamon Dunphy's book *Unforgettable Fire: The Story of U2* was released. It became a bestseller in the U.K. although the band retracted their support of the volume after they could not get parts of the text changed that they maintained were inaccurate. They received the MTV viewer's choice award for the video of "With or Without You," and in December, contributed "Christmas (Baby Please Come Home)" to noted producer Jimmy Iovine's charity album *Special Christmas.*

"I would hate to think everybody was into U2 for 'deep' and 'meaningful' reasons. If we got on stage, and instead of going 'Yeow!' the audience all went 'Ummmm' or started saying the rosary, it would be awful."
—Bono

In 1988 U2 received the award for best international group at the British Record Industry Awards, which was followed by their first Grammy awards—for best rock performance by a group and album of the year for *The Joshua Tree.* That same year, the Iovine-produced double album *Rattle and Hum,* featuring live recordings from the previous two years as well as studio tracks, was released and topped the charts in both the U.S. and the U.K. U2 also released the live documentary film *Rattle and Hum,* directed by Philip Joanou. As if these achievements hadn't raised their profile high enough, the band also appeared on the live television show *Smile Jamaica* for Jamaican Hurricane relief, where they were joined onstage by Keith Richards and Ziggy Marley.

The year 1989 brought the group the British Record Industry Award for best international group for the second year in a row. Grammy awards for best rock performance for "Desire," best performance music video for "Where The Streets Have No Name," and an MTV Music Video award for their collaboration with B.B. King on "When Love Comes to Town," followed. The rest of the year, the band spent working tirelessly, touring Australia, New Zealand, Japan, and then finally returning home to Dublin, where the tour culminated with a New Year's Eve show that was broadcast live on the radio. The BBC and RTE, which collaborated to transmit the show throughout Europe and the former U.S.S.R., estimated the listening audience at more than 500 million.

Although they had not released an album since 1988, U2 discovered new diversions in 1990. In February, the Royal Shakespeare Company produced *A Clockwork Orange 2004,* which featured music by The Edge. In June, drummer Mullen wrote the official Eire World Cup Soccer team's song. But as always, busy as they were, U2 found time for good works. This time they contributed to an anthology of Cole Porter songs that was released as *Red Hot + Blue* and benefitted AIDS education. They also traveled to Berlin to film a video featured in a TV special airing on International AIDS Day.

In November of 1991, U2's next, long-awaited album finally surfaced—but without the media blitz that seemed to accompany all the other year-end major releases. The band had decided that the album would sell itself to their fans just fine without all the fanfare. They were proven right, as initial shipments of *Achtung Baby* totalled upwards of 1.4 million units. They were also the first major act to request that their CD be distributed in the shrink-wrapped jewel box only, or the non-disposable DigiTrak (longbox size) packaging, which folds into a jewel box-sized case.

Zoo TV and Beyond

In February of the next year, U2 began their "Zoo TV" tour. They took the radio transmission concept inaugurated on New Year's Eve '89 one step further by incorporating a satellite dish into the show. A short European tour followed, during which a contest winner had the show beamed live by satellite to his home in Nottinghamshire from Stockholm, courtesy of MTV. The tour concluded with a Greenpeace concert in Manchester to protest a second nuclear processing plant being opened at Sellafield in Cumbria.

In spite of (but not in breach of) a court injunction preventing a protest at the plant, U2 participated in a "by sea on the beach" protest with Greenpeace, during which they delivered barrels of contaminated sand from the beaches of England, Ireland, Scotland, and Wales back to the plant. In August, they went back on the tour circuit, taking "Zoo TV" to the stadiums of the U.S. with their outside broadcast tour. When the tour ended in mid-November in Mexico City, U2 had played to an estimated 2.5 million people.

During a break in the "Zoo TV" tour, U2 took the time to record an EP. That EP eventually became the ten-song *Zooropa* album, winner of the 1993 Grammy Award for alternative album of the year. For the first time in his career, The Edge took on producing duties with Flood and Brian Eno; he also performed a lead vocal on the album's first single, "Numb." On May 9th the "Zoo TV" tour, which had since mutated into the "Zooropa '93" tour, started an ambitious schedule of visiting 18 countries in four months. Closing the trip back in Dublin on August 28th, the boys were glad that they were finally home.

When asked what they're all about, Bassist Adam Clayton explained it best in an interview with Robert Hilburn of the *Los Angeles Times* when he said, "I feel we made a decision then [going into the 90's] that if we are going to be the righteous men of rock n' roll, we are going to be very miserable. I think we realized that issues are more complicated than we once thought, and we don't want to be continually earnest about what we do. We are not a religious cult...we are not a political theory. We are a rock n' roll band."

Selected discography

U2:3 (EP; includes "Out of Control," "Stories," and "Boy-Girl"), CBS Ireland, 1979.
Boy (includes "A Day Without Me" and "I Will Follow"), Island, 1980.
October (includes "Fire" and "Gloria"), Island, 1981.
War (includes "New Year's Day" and "Two Hearts Beat as One"), Island, 1983.
Under A Blood Red Sky (live album), Island, 1983.
Unforgettable Fire (includes "Pride [In the Name of Love]"), Island, 1984.
Wide Awake in America (EP; includes live version of "Bad," "Three Sunrises," and "Love Comes Tumbling"), Island, 1985.
Joshua Tree (includes "With or Without You," "I Still Haven't Found What I'm Looking For," and "Where the Streets Have No Name"), Island, 1987.
Rattle and Hum (includes "Desire," "Angel of Harlem," "When Love Comes to Town," and "All I Want Is You"), Island, 1988.
Achtung Baby (includes "The Fly," "Mysterious Ways," "One," "Even Better Than the Real Thing," and "Wild Horses"), Island, 1991.
Zooropa (includes "Numb" and "Lemon"), Island, 1993.

Sources

Books

Dickey, Lorraine, *The Ultimate Encyclopedia of Rock,* Carlton Books, 1993.

Dolgins, Adam, *Rock Names,* Citadel Press, 1993.

Rees, Dafydd, and Luke Crampton, *Rock Movers & Shakers,* Billboard Books, 1991.

Robbins, Ira A., *Trouser Press Record Guide,* fourth edition, Collier Books, 1991.

Periodicals

Billboard, November 16, 1991.

Hollywood Reporter, March 2, 1994.

Los Angeles Times, March 1, 1992; March 22, 1992; June 4, 1993; September 12, 1993.

Maclean's, November 2, 1987.

Melody Maker, May 30, 1992; December 5, 1992.

Musician, March 1992; September 1992.

Newsweek, December 31, 1984.

People, April 1, 1985.

Rolling Stone, October 11, 1984; March 14, 1985; May 7, 1987; September 8, 1988.

Spin, August 1993.

Time, April 27, 1987.

Village Voice, December 10, 1991; December 22, 1992.

Additional information for this profile was obtained from the Wasserman Group, Island Records, and MTV, all 1994.

—*Charlie Katagiri*

Dave Van Ronk

Singer, songwriter, guitarist

"The cult of art is strangling us," said Dave Van Ronk in *Melody Maker.* "Jazz musicians, blues musicians, folk musicians, we're all being strangled by it. Somebody comes along and says: Ah, someone here is an *artiste.* Poor so-and-so. They don't know what an *artiste* is. Neither does the critic: We're skilled workers." Perhaps Van Ronk's long association with the sometimes artsy Greenwich Village music scene has made him a little defensive about the sorts of music he has come to make his own. Or perhaps his accomplished finger-picking guitar and evocative voice have allowed him to think of himself as a musician, capable of expressing himself in many genres, not simply as a jazz, blues, or folk singer burdened by their attendant mystiques.

Dave Van Ronk is a professional folk singer in the tradition of Odetta, Josh White, Cynthia Gooding, Oscar Brand and Pete Seeger. Born in Brooklyn, New York, in 1936, Van Ronk was introduced to music by his grandfather, a pianist with a fondness for Scott Joplin and John Philip Sousa. Van Ronk's own musical prefer-

Photograph by Manny Greenhill, courtesy of Folklore Productions

> **For the Record . . .**
>
> Born June 30, 1936, in Brooklyn, NY; married; wife's name, Terri.
>
> Worked as a merchant marine; performed with Odetta, 1957; recorded debut album for Folkways, 1959; played set of jazz and jug band music at the Newport Jazz Festival, 1964; featured performer at the New York Folk Festival at Carnegie Hall, 1965; recorded jug band version of *Peter and the Wolf*; released album of original compositions, *Going Back to Brooklyn*, 1985.
>
> **Addresses:** *Management*—Folklore Productions, Inc., 1671 Appian Way, Santa Monica, CA 90401.

ences leaned toward the jazz of the 1920s and the blues. "My first influences were Jelly Roll Morton, Leadbelly, Bessie Smith—all your standard old-time greats," he told the *International Herald Tribune*.

Following the completion of high school, Van Ronk began spending more time in Manhattan, sharing cheap apartments in the Bowery and then in Greenwich Village, where he continues to live today. He tried to make his living playing tenor banjo in the Brute Force Jazz Band, where he discovered rhythm was not his strong suit. "They sat me next to the drummer," he said. "I couldn't keep time. Drummers hated me."

Picking the Country Blues

In the late 1950s Van Ronk found himself increasingly attracted to the urban blues, dismissing the folk music revival of the time as "corny," he told *Melody Maker*. As he told Ralph Rush in *Sing Out!*, "I was one of the worst music snobs that ever came down the pike. I didn't get interested in folk music as such until I was convinced that country blues was folk music." It was Van Ronk's desire to learn finger-picking, a three-fingered guitar style that uses the thumb to play the bass line and the other fingers the melody, that finally brought him to Washington Square, where he met Tom Paley and Barry Kornfeld as well as Reverend Gary Davis. He was soon performing solo at private parties and coffee houses, but had trouble making a living.

It was not until he had spent some time as a merchant marine that he returned to the Village to make music again. Encouraged to play professionally by renowned folk singer Odetta, Van Ronk took his unique style combining jazz, blues, and folk on the road. By the early 1960s he was firmly entrenched in the burgeoning folk revival. There he turned down the chance to perform as a member of what was to become Peter, Paul and Mary. "Albert Grossman and Milt Okun had an idea to put together a trio," he related in *The New Folk Music*. "Albert handled Mary Travers and Peter Yarrow as solo performers and they needed a third. They wanted someone that could carry a tune, sing harmony, and be reasonably strong as an instrumentalist. Peter wasn't that facile on the guitar and Mary didn't play at all. They encouraged me, but I didn't want to do it."

Van Ronk was an early friend of Bob Dylan, sometimes allowing Dylan to stay at his apartment. But they grew apart sometime after Dylan's second album and were not reunited until 1974 at a benefit for Chilean political prisoners. Van Ronk claimed in *The New Folk Music* that Dylan's phenomenal success had a damaging impact on the folk song movement. "It pretty much put a stop to the folksong revival. Before Bobby, everybody was singing folksongs. Afterwards everyone was doing their own stuff."

Jug Band Influences

Van Ronk has been a longtime proponent of jug band music, which consists of homemade instruments like washtubs and saws in conjunction with jiving hands and stomping feet. In the late 1950s he recorded a jug band album with Sam Charters, and his festival appearances have often featured jug band influences. In 1964, he recorded another album with Sam Charters and the Ragtime Jug Stompers.

Eventually Van Ronk was to make a jug band version of *Peter and the Wolf*, Prokofiev's children's classic. Van Ronk commented in the *Boston Herald*, "It was an old idea, a running joke of the jug bands of the early 1960s. We would sit around and imagine jug band versions of Beethoven's 'Ninth' or Tchaikovsky's '1812 Overture.'" The original version was intended to introduce children to the instruments of the symphony orchestra. In Van Ronk's version, however, the tale's characters are represented by the folk and jug band instruments—guitars, mandolins, penny whistles, kazoos, jaw harps, banjos, and a washtub bass—of the Uncle Mouse and Kazoo-o-phonic Jug Band.

Daniel Gewertz of the *Boston Herald* highlighted the originality of Van Ronk's narration, featuring "his familiar wheezing, grumbling voice, which is the opposite of the smooth, sweet voices of many children's recordings." Van Ronk explained, "I suspect that kids get bored with straight treacle and molasses. When I was a kid, my favorite singer was Louis Armstrong."

Throughout his career Van Ronk has kept on the move, singing all types of songs in numerous places. Though he is often considered an interpreter of well-known songs, such as "Candyman," Van Ronk also recorded his own compositions on the well-received 1985 album *Going Back to Brooklyn,* which reveals his ribald wit. In 1990 he recorded a collection of 13 pop songs from the 1930s and 1940s called *Hummin' to Myself.*

He has served as a mentor to the most recent wave of New York folk singer/songwriters, such as Christine Lavin, his former guitar student, and continues to teach guitar in the Village, where he also writes occasional articles on music. He performed in an off-Broadway production of the Bertolt Brecht/Kurt Weill opera *Mahagonny* and has collaborated on an album of Brecht songs in German and English with English folk singer Frankie Armstrong entitled *Let No One Deceive You: Songs of Bertolt Brecht.* According to the *Boston Globe*'s Patricia Smith, "What Van Ronk does is strip wonderful songs down to their bare bones so you can hear what made them wonderful songs in the first place."

His musicianship has allowed him to be adaptable without seeming a chameleon. He puts his own stamp on what he plays and sings. As Van Ronk related in the *Evening Gazette,* "You can use an ugly voice to sing a pretty song and make it a lot more interesting. It creates tome tensions there. It's the kind of thing that Kurt Weill and Bertolt Brecht used to do—get the prettiest melody they could and set it to the nastiest lyrics they could find."

Selected discography

Ballads, Blues and a Spiritual, Folkways, 1959.
Black Mountain Blues, Folkways, 1959.
Dave Van Ronk, Folksinger, Prestige, 1963.
Dave Van Ronk's Ragtime Jug Stompers, Mercury, 1964.
In the Tradition, Prestige, 1964.
No Dirty Names, Verve, 1967.
Dave Van Ronk and the Hudson Dusters, Verve, 1968.
Going Back to Brooklyn, Reckless, 1985.
Just Van Ronk, Mercury.
Inside Dave Van Ronk, Prestige.
Dave Van Ronk, Fantasy.
Van Ronk, Polydor.
Songs for Aging Children, Chess/Cadet.
Sunday Street, Philo.
Somebody Else, Not Me, Philo.
Your Basic Dave Van Ronk Album, Kicking Mule.
Dave Van Ronk in Rome, Folkstudio.
Let No One Deceive You: Songs of Bertolt Brecht, Aural Tradition.
Peter and the Wolf, Alacazam.
Hummin' to Myself, Gazell.
A Chrespomathy, Gazell.

Sources

Books

Harris, Craig, *The New Folk Music,* White Cliffs Media Company, 1991.

Periodicals

Austin American-Statesman, January 20, 1986.
Boston Globe, January 6, 1992.
Boston Herald, July 24, 1990.
Chronicle, January 31, 1991.
Evening Gazette (Worcester, MA), March 9, 1989.
Face Magazine, June 5, 1991.
International Herald Tribune, April 20, 1983.
Melody Maker, March 21, 1981.
Musician, July 1985.
New York Newsday, October 21, 1990.
Rolling Stone, July 9, 1992.
Sing Out!, September 1979.

—*John Morrow*

Bobby Vinton

Singer

Equipped with an angelic voice and singing sincere songs about undying love, Bobby Vinton had a string of hits when he burst onto the pop scene in 1962 with "Roses Are Red." He generated 30 Top 40 songs in the 1960s and 1970s, and 24 of his albums made the *Billboard* Top 200. Vinton's romantic love songs had particular appeal to young fans, but later in his career he was able to adjust his style to appeal to adult audiences. He had remarkable staying power for a teen idol, continuing to record songs that registered on the charts for well over a decade.

Growing up in the same home town that produced Perry Como, Vinton showed an early musical interest in the Big Band sound that sprang from his father's work as a bandleader in the Pittsburgh area. As a child Vinton played clarinet, then the trumpet in a band he formed in high school. He first began singing at the urging of other members of his high school group, but his primary musical interest at the time was in band direction. While attending Duquesne University, Vinton further pursued bandleading, forming a combo that played at college functions and dances in the Pittsburgh area.

During service in the army Vinton continued playing trumpet in a military band. As soon as he was out of uniform he got together another band that was later selected to perform on a variety show for NBC. Dick Lawrence, a popular disc jockey in Pittsburgh, was impressed by Vinton's voice and made some demo tapes of the singer's work. Eventually, the tapes made their way to CBS Records, and Vinton was offered a contract with the company's Epic label in 1960. Vinton was managed in his early career by Allen Klein, who later took the helm for the Beatles and Rolling Stones.

Vinton had an uneventful start with Epic, recording two albums of band music that generated minimal interest. Seeing no future in the young performer, Epic was about to let him go when Vinton noticed that his contract allowed him to record two more songs. When he told Epic that he wanted to sing the songs, the company was skeptical at first, but finally gave him the okay. Vinton surprised everyone by recording four Number One hits from 1962 to 1964.

After topping the charts with "Roses Are Red" in 1962, he reached the top position again in 1963 with his version of "Blue Velvet," which had been recorded by the Clovers in 1955, and "There! I Said It Again." In 1964 he topped the Hit Parade with "Mr. Lonely," a song he co-wrote with Gene Allen that became his personal favorite. As a result of his success, Vinton said goodbye to his band and remained a solo act.

For the Record...

Born Stanley Robert Vinton, April 16, 1941, in Canonsburg, PA; son of Stanley (a bandleader) and Dorothy (maiden name, Studinsky) Vinton; married Dolly Dobbin, December 17, 1962; children: Robert, Kristin, Christopher, Jennifer, Rebecca. *Education:* Attended Duquesne University, 1950s.

Pop singer. Played trumpet and sang vocals for band formed in high school, 1950s; created band in college to perform at school affairs, late 1950s; signed recording contract with Epic Records, 1960; toured with Bobby Vee, 1960-61; recorded first albums as bandleader, *Dancing at the Hop* and *Bobby Vinton Plays for L'il Darlin's,* 1961; released first single as solo vocalist, "Roses Are Red," 1962; had four Number One hits in a row ("Roses Are Red," "Blue Velvet," "There! I've Said It Again," and "Mr. Lonely"), 1962-65; recorded 30 Top 40 songs, 1962-75; signed contract with ABC Records, 1972; hosted television program *The Bobby Vinton Show,* 1975-78; performed as headline act in Las Vegas, oldies shows, and other concerts, 1980s. *Military service:* U.S. Army, late 1950s.

Addresses: c/o Rexford Productions, 9255 Sunset Blvd., Suite 706, Los Angeles, CA 90069.

Young fans made up the core of Vinton's audience, and they eagerly bought up his recordings of heartrending love ballads. Timing was part of the formula for Vinton's popularity, since pop music was in a lull in the early 1960s. The doo-wop music of the 1950s had run its course, the Beatles' "British invasion" had yet to occur, and fresh new idols for music fans were in short supply. When the Beatles and other English bands arrived in the United States in the mid-1960s, however, they generally undercut the popularity of gentle crooners like Bobby Vinton.

Nevertheless, Vinton continued to stay on the charts with songs such as "Please Love Me Forever" in 1967 and "I Love How You Love Me," which made Number One in 1969. Although he was still listed in many Top 20 polls for favorite male vocalists at the end of the 1960s, by 1971 his career had leveled off, and he had become a regular on the hotel and nightclub circuit. He bounced back in 1972 with covers of old songs such as "Sealed With a Kiss," which had been a hit for Brian Hyland in 1962.

Epic began to regard Vinton as a fading star, and the singer ended his 13-year pact with the company to sign a new contract with ABC Records. Much to Epic's dismay, Vinton brought ABC a gold record in 1974 with the Top Ten single "My Melody of Love," which included some lines in Polish. His popularity again bolstered, Vinton got his own syndicated television series, "The Bobby Vinton Show," which remained on the air from 1975 to 1978.

No longer a teen idol but retaining the loyalty of former teen fans who had grown up, Vinton became known as "The Polish Prince" due to the musical homage he paid regularly to his family's heritage. Vinton stayed active performing in Las Vegas, oldies concerts, and other venues during the 1980s. While other stars who were his peers during his early days as a pop sensation had long faded from the scene, he managed to stay active and retain a loyal following right into his 40s.

Selected discography

Singles

"Roses Are Red," Epic, 1962.
"Blue Velvet," Epic, 1963.
"There! I've Said It Again," Epic, 1963.
"Mr. Lonely," Epic, 1965.
"I Love How You Love Me," Epic, 1968.
"No Arms Can Ever Hold You," Epic, 1970.
"I'll Make You My Baby," Epic, 1971.
"Sealed With a Kiss," Epic, 1972.
"But I Do," Epic, 1973.
"My Melody of Love," ABC, 1974.

Albums

Roses Are Red, Epic, 1962.
Bobby Vinton Sings the Big Ones, Epic, 1962.
Blue Velvet, Epic, 1963.
Bobby Vinton's Greatest Hits, Epic, 1964.
Bobby Vinton Sings for Lonely Nights, Epic, 1965.
Please Love Me Forever, Epic, 1967.
Bobby Vinton's All-Time Greatest Hits, Epic, 1972.
Melodies of Love, ABC, 1974.

Sources

Vinton, Bobby, with Robert F. Burger, *Bobby Vinton: The Polish Prince,* M. Evans, 1978.

—Ed Decker

Violent Femmes

Rock band

Photograph by Francis Ford, courtesy of Borman Entertainment

Songs of adolescent sexual frustration have riddled the airwaves since the inception of rock and roll. Rarely, however, does a band combine teenage longings with the seemingly discordant theme of religious awakening in such a collision of musical genres as the Violent Femmes. The Femmes have been preaching this formidable combination of sounds and images with their unique brand of neo-punk, hardcore acoustic music since their formation in Milwaukee, Wisconsin, in the early 1980s.

The band's unusual album content sets them apart from the crowd and forces listeners to reassess the dividing lines between rock, punk, folk, jazz, and country and western. *Musician* contributor David Fricke hailed the band as "a fresh wind of post-punk originality rooted in rockabilly simplicity. [Their] songs vibrate with an almost psychotic tension underlined by the Femmes' naked acoustic force.... The fatal charms of the Violent Femmes are a secret Milwaukee shouldn't keep to itself."

Lead vocalist and songwriter Gordon Gano grew up playing violin and guitar while writing tunes that alternately seethed with religious imagery and poignantly repressed sexual desire. Gano, the son of an American Baptist minister, presents a split vision of the world that expresses an almost psychotic self-depravation. It was during his senior year in high school that Gano met future bandmate Brian Ritchie when they both performed at the same variety show. Ritchie, who played guitar and bass, later attended another of Gano's performances and asked him to open for his Irish folk duo. Gano, in turn, asked Ritchie to join him at a high school assembly where they belted out the pleading "Gimme The Car," a teenage supplication for the wanton use of dad's coveted vehicle. As Ritchie recalled in *Musician,* "It erupted into a near-riot. It was fantastic!"

Opportune Gig Sparked First Album

In 1981 jazz-trained percussionist Victor DeLorenzo joined Gano and Ritchie and the Violent Femmes were officially formed—their name gleaned from an early 1970s grade-school insult. They rapidly became a Milwaukee mainstay, performing at coffeehouses and nightclubs across the city. Their ascension came one night in 1981, when members of the popular rock band the Pretenders noticed the Femmes performing outside of that evenings' concert venue and asked the trio to open the show. While most bands recall such stories with nostalgic repose, however, the Femmes maintain that their so-called breakthrough was just a matter of time. They told *Melody Maker:* "It's been passed

> **For the Record...**
>
> Members include **Gordon Gano** (born June 7, 1963), lead vocals and guitar; **Brian Ritchie** (born November 21, 1960), bass; **Victor DeLorenzo** (born October 25, 1954; left band, 1993), percussion; **Guy Hoffman** (born May 20, 1954; joined band, 1993), percussion.
>
> Group formed in Milwaukee, WI, 1981; signed with Slash Records, 1982; released debut album, *Violent Femmes*, 1983; terminated contract with Slash Records, 1993; released *New Times* (produced by Gano and Ritchie), Elecktra, 1994.
>
> **Addresses:** *Record company*—Elektra Records, 75 Rockefeller Plaza, New York, NY 10019. *Management*—Borman Entertainment, 9220 Sunset Blvd., Suite 320, Los Angeles, CA 90069.

around the press to the point where it's like Chrissie Hynde [lead singer for the Pretenders] 'discovered' the Violent Femmes, when all she did was give us one gig. Which was great, it was the first time we ever played to 2,000 people. [But] we'd have gotten here without that."

A contract with Slash Records followed in 1982. In 1983 the band made its debut with *Violent Femmes,* a trendsetting album fraught with raw sexual frustration and teenage fears. A writer for *Billboard* deemed the album "a seminal document of hormonal angst and black humor." Cuts from *Violent Femmes* such as "Blister in the Sun," "Add It Up," and "Kiss Off"—fueled by lyrics like "Why can't I get just one screw/ Believe me I know what to do/ But something won't let me make love to you" ("Add It Up") and "You can all just kiss off into the air/ Behind my back I can see them stare/ They'll hurt me bad/ But I won't mind/ They'll hurt me bad/ They do it all the time" ("Kiss Off")—quickly gained cult status around the world.

The album's minimalist arrangements were for the most part created with just acoustic guitar, acoustic bass, snare drum, and the "tranceaphone," DeLorenzo's invention of a tin bucket suspended over a tom. Gano's youthful, whining vocals emphasized loneliness, anger, and tension, which caused many reviewers to label the album as a "teenage record." Gano disagreed. "One thing I've often thought of certain songs, is that, rather than saying that they're the result of teen or adolescent (thinking), they're often not being expressed from the most mature of viewpoints, which to a greater or lesser degree people carry with them all their lives," he commented in the St. Louis *Riverfront Times.*

Steady Output Marked the Decade

The Femmes' follow-up album, 1984's *Hallowed Ground,* took a new, more introspective direction with an emphasis on religious imagery and a strong gospel tone. Many of the tracks focus on biblical themes, such as "It's Gonna Rain," an upbeat version of the Noah's Ark story, and "Jesus Walking on the Water," a straightforward tale of spiritual awakening. These songs are contrasted with unsettling tunes like "Country Death Song," a psychotic confessional of a man who throws his daughter down the well and then hangs himself, and the sexually explicit "Black Girls."

The album's atypical content led reviewers and fans to question the motives and musical direction of the band. DeLorenzo, however, explained the groups's stylistic choices in a 1986 interview with *Musician:* "Those songs are part of Gordon's make-up, and the idea of this band is to indulge ourselves musically and also to remain real people in doing so."

Hallowed Ground was also the group's first album to feature The Horns of Dilemma, an aggregation of woodwind, brass, and string instruments which supplement the Femmes' basic acoustic unit. The Horns of Dilemma would later mutate into different musicians and/or instruments, depending upon the requirements of a certain album or a particular live show. "We've had people come up and play comb with wax paper, a tabla player played with us in Boston," said Gano in *Melody Maker.* "We've had oboe, sackbut, toy piano, Melodica, banjo—just about any instrument that you can think of."

The release of *The Blind Leading the Naked*—produced by Jerry Harrison of the Talking Heads (also a Milwaukee native)—in 1986 marked a turning point for the Violent Femmes. *Blind* is comprised of a diverse group of songs and styles—from the 33-second political outcry "Old Mother Reagan" to the cover of T. Rex's "Children of the Revolution"—that chronicle the band's musical growth. *Blind* also featured the widest range of instruments yet to appear on a Femmes album, including a greatly expanded Horns of Dilemma, and boasts vocals by all three band members. Ritchie summed up the Femmes' four-year evolution in *Musician:* "We imposed a stylistic approach upon all the songs on the first album. Then we imposed a philosophy on the second album. On the third album we threw all our previous ideas out the window and decided to do each song as an individual song, the best we could do it."

A two-year separation followed the release of *Blind*, with the bandmembers pursuing their own interests. Gano formed the rock-gospel band Mercy Seat and released a self-titled album in 1988, while Ritchie recorded three solo albums: *The Blend* (1987), *Sonic Temple and the Court of Babylon* (1989), and *I See a Noise* (1990). DeLorenzo's sole effort, *Peter Corey Sent Me* (1991), included his talents on guitar and keyboard on one track.

The Femmes' next two albums, *3* (1988) and *Why Do Birds Sing?* (1991), both represented a return to their earlier, characteristic style. The rebirth of the Femmes led *Rolling Stone* reviewer David Browne to praise their efforts: "Gordon Gano seems like the creepy kid next door who'll go off the deep end any minute, and the more he acts that way, the better the Violent Femmes are." *Why Do Birds Sing?* includes a skewed cover of Culture Club's 1983 hit "Do You Really Want To Hurt Me"—a song Gano performs like the vocal equivalent of the film *Psycho*'s sexually repressed Norman Bates—contrasted with songs such as the lyrical "Hey Nonny Nonny," based on a sixteenth-century shepherd's poem. The band also supplemented their album tours with appearances at the Earth Day festivities in 1992 and 1993.

Changes Hit Band

In 1993 the band's contract with Slash Records ended with the release of the compilation album *Add It Up (1981-1993)*. Citing their incompatibility with Slash, Gano told the Phoenix *New Times* that "they kept asking us if we could sound like R.E.M." Still, *Add It Up* is more than just a greatest hits collection. It is a testament to the Femmes 12-year musical odyssey and includes unreleased songs, demos, and live tracks—not to mention the humorous answering machine message left by Gano explaining that he had become locked inside his own house and hence would be late for the very first Femmes recording session.

Drummer DeLorenzo left the band in 1993 and was replaced by Guy Hoffman, a founding member of another Milwaukee band, the BoDeans, and a member of the new-wave band The Oil Tasters. DeLorenzo's apparently amicable departure signaled the end of an era for the band, but the future of the Femmes seemed intact as Ritchie told the *Milwaukee Journal* that "Guy understands where we're coming from. He knows the history of the band without having been a member."

In 1994 the regrouped Femmes released *New Times*—produced by Gano and Ritchie—on the Elektra label. A *Billboard* contributor noted that this seventh album "should please both the diehard fans of Violent Femmes' first album as well as those devotees who relish the band's growth and the continued maturation of Gano's songwriting." Gano revealed to *Billboard* that the change in labels is like "going from a minor-league contract to a major-league contract.... We have a level of respect artistically that we've never had before." The first single from *New Times* was "Breakin' Up," an angst-ridden commentary on relationships that nearly was included on the band's first album. Other selections include "Mirror Mirror (I See a Damsel)" that borrows a polka sound and the rocking "Don't Start Me on the Liquor."

With every album, the Violent Femmes have attempted to simultaneously confront the dichotomies of life and expand the definition of rock and roll. Although their combination of purity and depravity may be controversial, Gano explained his antithetical approach in *Melody Maker:* "Heidegger said that a faith that doesn't perpetually keep itself open to the possibility of unfaith isn't even faith. I respond to that, but I feel that Violent Femmes songs do more good than bad when you hear them. But perhaps I'm totally wrong ... I could really be what some people already think of me—a borderline mentally ill person who's adding to the troubles but deludes himself he's doing some good."

Selected discography

Violent Femmes (includes "Blister in the Sun," "Add It Up," and "Kiss Off"), Slash, 1982.
Hallowed Ground (includes "It's Gonna Rain," "Jesus Walking on the Water," "Country Death Song," and "Black Girls"), Slash, 1984.
The Blind Leading the Naked (includes "Old Mother Reagan" and "Children of the Revolution"), Slash, 1986.
3, Slash, 1988.
Debacle: The First Decade, Liberation Records, 1990.
Why Do Birds Sing? (includes "Do You Really Want To Hurt Me" and "Hey Nonny Nonny"), Slash, 1991.
Add It Up (1981-1993), Slash, 1993.
New Times (includes "Breaking Up"), Elektra, 1994.

Solo albums; Gordon Gano

The Mercy Seat, Slash, 1987.

Solo albums; Brian Ritchie

The Blend, SST, 1987.
Sonic Temple and the Court of Babylon, SST, 1989.
I See a Noise, Dali-Chameleon, 1990.

Solo albums; Victor DeLorenzo

Peter Corey Sent Me, Dali-Chameleon, 1991.

Sources

Billboard, April 9, 1994.
Melody Maker, March 10, 1984; September 28, 1991.
Milwaukee Journal, September 23, 1993.
Musician, December 1982; May 1986.
New Times (Phoenix), November 17, 1993.
Riverfront Times (St. Louis), November 16, 1993.
Rolling Stone, February 23, 1989.

Additional information for this profile was provided by Elektra Entertainment publicity materials, 1994.

—Debra Power

Tom Waits

Singer, songwriter, actor

Photograph by Hermann & Clärchen Braus, © PolyGram 1993, courtesy of Island Records

Tom Waits, the poet of the downtrodden, entertains listeners with his graveyard-growl voice, sophisticated lyrics and melodies, and haunting junkyard orchestration. Since his recording debut in 1973, Waits has cut over 15 albums, including *Swordfishtrombones, Frank's Wild Years,* and *Bone Machine.* A respected actor with more than 15 film credits, he has also become a successful playwright with his stage adaptation of *Frank's Wild Years* and his collaboration on the musical *The Black Rider.*

From the very beginning, Waits has been an original. Born to a middle-class family in Whittier, California, in 1949, Thomas Alan Waits made his entrance into the world in the back seat of a Yellow cab. Though both of his parents were schoolteachers, Waits considered high school a joke and dropped out to join the work force. "I listened to records and got into trouble," he told the *Minneapolis Star.* "Ya see, I was a bit of an insubordinate ... in academic situations. I wanted to own a gas station."

Mark Richard in *Spin,* however, related that Waits's father was in a mariachi band and taught him to play guitar on "low-end Mexican specials that cost $9 and lasted two weeks, bending so that the strings were three inches off the neck, and you had to play the things with welding gloves." Richard also noted that the elder Waits had been a radio technician in World War II and would help his son build Heathkit radios; he used the wireless sets to pick up Wolfman Jack and evangelist Brother Springer from Oklahoma City.

Discovered Beat Poets

As a teenager Waits wasn't swept up into his generation's culture of flower power, free love, peace, drugs, and Woodstock. "I was a misfit," Waits told *Newsweek.* "I didn't have any Jimi Hendrix posters up on my wall. I didn't even have a black light." What made him tick was writing songs, playing an old guitar and piano, working the 6:00 p.m. to 4:00 a.m. shift at the pizza parlor, and listening to Ray Charles, George Gershwin, Frank Sinatra, and the blues as he cruised the open road.

But Waits also read a lot, and he discovered the works of Beat author Jack Kerouac. The Beat Generation was a name given to a group of American writers—including Kerouac, Allen Ginsberg, and William S. Burroughs—who through their poetry, novels, and jazz poetry albums rejected the middle-class values and commercialism of the 1950s. Kerouac's 1957 book *On the Road* is considered the masterpiece of the Beat Generation, and to this day it remains Waits's favorite book.

For the Record...

Born Thomas Alan Waits, December 7, 1949, in Whittier (one source says Pomona), CA; son of Jesse Frank Waits and Alma (Johnson) McMurray (both schoolteachers); married Kathleen Patricia Brennan (a script editor and playwright), August 10, 1980; children: Kellesimone Wylder (daughter), Casey Xavier (son), one other child.

Began performing professionally in nightclubs in Hollywood and Los Angeles, CA, late 1960s; received first record contract with Asylum, 1972; released debut album, *Closing Time*, 1973; made acting debut in *Paradise Alley*, 1978; composed film scores, beginning in 1980; coproduced and starred in the musical play *Frank's Wild Years*, 1986; collaborated on the musical play *The Black Rider*, 1993.

Awards: Academy Award nomination for best original score, 1983, for *One From the Heart*; *Rolling Stone* Magazine Music Award—Critics' Picks for Best Songwriter, 1985; Grammy Award for best alternative album, 1992, for *Bone Machine*; awarded guitar by Club Tenco, Italy.

Addresses: *Office*—c/o Ellen Smith, 11 Eucalyptus Lane, San Rafael, CA 94901. *Record company*—Island Records, 400 Lafayette St., New York, NY 10003.

By his late teens, Waits was being drawn to the underbelly of Los Angeles. The lonely, burnt-out characters of the night and snatches of their conversations took root in his mind and became the source for his songs, as did much of his experience from these days of inhabiting fleabag motels, composing in greasy spoons and seedy bars, and hitching rides with truck drivers from gig to gig.

In the late 1960s Waits became a doorman at a small club. "I listened to all kinds of music there," he told *Rolling Stone*, "from rock to jazz to folk to anything else that happened to walk in. One night I saw a local guy onstage playing his own material. I don't know why but at that moment I knew what I wanted to do: live or die on the strength of my *own* music."

By the time Tom Waits was "discovered" in 1969 at the Troubadour in West Hollywood, California, he already had a cult following. Herb Cohen, manager for such artists as Frank Zappa and Linda Ronstadt, signed him on, and three years later Waits was picked up by Asylum Records and cut his first album. *Closing Time* won him an immediate audience and made fans out of contemporaries like Elton John, Joni Mitchell, Keith Richards, and Bonnie Raitt. Under the Asylum label, Waits put out eight albums between 1973 and 1981. Several of Waits's songs from that period were made famous by other artists, including "Ol' 55," sung by the Eagles, Bette Midler's rendition of "Shiver Me Timbers," and Bruce Springsteen's "Jersey Girl."

Film Career Took Off

Waits used his stage persona—the thin, bent figure in a wrinkled secondhand suit, holding a cigarette butt in one hand and snapping his fingers with the other, while delivering whiskey-voiced scat into the spotlight microphone—to develop his skills as an actor. Waits began with a bit part in *Paradise Alley* with Sylvester Stallone in 1978 and subsequently acted in more than 15 films, including roles in Francis Copolla's *The Outsiders*, *Rumble Fish*, *Ironweed*, and *The Cotton Club*.

Perhaps his finest work was in the 1986 film *Down by the Law*, directed by Jim Jarmusch. Waits also produced and starred in *Big Time* in 1988, a tale of a drifter who dreams of a successful music career. He has also written film scores, including *On the Nickle*, 1980; *One From the Heart*, 1983; *Streetwise*, 1985; and Jarmusch's *Night on Earth*, 1993.

Waits's music has continued to gain recognition. In the 1980s Waits himself produced the albums *Swordfishtrombones*, *Rain Dogs*, and *Frank's Wild Years*, all released by Island Records. In his later music, such as the 1992 Grammy Award-winning album *Bone Machine*, Waits departed from his earlier tradition of sung jazz to search for raw sound with all the fluff stripped away. "To me," Waits explained in the *New York Times*, "everything is really music—words are music, every sound is music, it all depends on how it's organized."

The *New York Times* compared *Bone Machine* to the three earlier albums: "The dominant image over those three albums, both in lyrics and in the organ-grinder tilt of the music, was the carnival." This album is "what the carnival fairgrounds might look like after the carnival has left town.... Instead of Waits's former snake-pit orchestra of swamp guitar, honking saxophone, wheezing accordion and pump organ, the songs here are constructed on a percussive skeleton of bangs and twonks." Waits recorded *Bone Machine* in a shed with musicians, friends, and his wife, Kathleen Brennan, banging on metal and wood with sticks.

Collaborated on Stage Productions

While his music has become more surreal, Waits's characters have taken on more substance. His earlier work was typically filled with a stream of forgotten drunks, prostitutes, tired waitresses, and two-bit hustlers with dreams of making it big. But the story of Frank, a character who first appeared in *Swordfishtrombones*, was developed into *Frank's Wild Years*, a stage musical by Waits and his wife that premiered in 1986 at Chicago's Steppenwolf Theater. The musical presents the saga of Frank O'Brien, a down-and-out accordion player on a hallucinatory journey through his life as he sits freezing to death on a park bench. The record of the same name was released the following year.

In 1993, Waits collaborated with Robert Willson and William Burroughs, the Beat godfather, on a dark and satirical avant-garde version of Carl Maria von Weber's 1821 folk opera *Der Freischütz*. *The Black Rider* is based, like Weber's work, on a fable about a desperate man who makes a deal with the devil in order to win the right to marry his beloved. "The rich dizzying tunes," noted a reviewer in *Rolling Stone*, "incorporate graveyard fright noises, bizarre piano sounds and creepy sci-fi whistles into traditional, orchestrated 'Fiddler on the Roof'-style melodies." *Spin*'s Richard related that the show was a hit in Europe and New York.

Waits, the self-titled "sound scavenger," was married in 1980 and has three children. His work has grown steadily stronger, more ambitious, and more commercially successful. Characterizing his unique creativity, a writer in the *New York Times* commented that Waits "honors the emotional lives of his humble characters. His lyrics ... express what might be described as a primal sentimentality. His heart bleeds for characters who cry out their needs and dreams in songs that sound like reassembled fragments of tunes learned as a child."

Selected compositions

On the Nickle, 1980.
One From the Heart (film score), 1983.
Streetwise (film score), 1985.
Night on Earth (film score), 1993.
(With wife, Kathleen Brennan) *Frank's Wild Years* (musical), first produced at the Steppenwolf Theatre, Chicago, IL, 1986.
(With Robert Willson and William S. Burroughs) *The Black Rider* (musical), 1993.

Selected discography

On Elektra/Asylum

Closing Time, 1973, reissued, 1993.
The Heart of Saturday Night, 1974.
Nighthawks at the Diner, 1975.
Foreign Affairs, 1977.
Small Change, 1977.
Blue Valentine, 1978.
Heart Attack and Vine, 1980.
Asylum Years, 1984.
Anthology, 1985.

On CBS

One From the Heart, 1982.

On Island

Swordfishtrombones, 1983.
Rain Dogs, 1985.
Frank's Wild Years, 1987.
Big Time, 1988.
Bone Machine, 1992.
(With William S. Burroughs) *Black Rider,* 1993.

Sources

Books

Humphries, Patrick, *Small Change: A Life of Tom Waits*, St. Martin's Press, 1989.

Periodicals

Audio, February 1984; December 1987.
Down Beat, March 1986.
High Fidelity, December 1985.
Interview, October 1988.
Minneapolis Star, December 22, 1975.
National Observer, January 5, 1976.
New Statesman, October 1985.
Newsweek, April 23, 1976.
New York Times, September 27, 1992; November 14, 1993; November 22, 1993; December 5, 1993.
People, October 21, 1985; September 28, 1987.
Playboy, March 1988.
Rolling Stone, January 27, 1977; October 1988; October 29, 1992; March 3, 1994.
Spin, June 1994.
Stereo Review, September 1987.

—Iva Sipal

Jimmy Webb

Singer, songwriter

Courtesy of Lorimar Records

For almost 30 years, Jimmy Webb has been a master of the art of writing love songs. Few composers' songs have burst on the scene with the impact Webb's creations made in the years from 1966 to 1969. "By the Time I Get to Phoenix," "Wichita Lineman," and "MacArthur Park" spearheaded a string of hits so enduring that the Webb catalogue ranks second in total airplay only to the songs of John Lennon and Paul McCartney of the Beatles. More important than that commercial success, however, Jimmy Webb stands tall among the handful of writers who have significantly expanded the vocabulary of contemporary popular song.

Jimmy Layne Webb was born on August 15, 1946, in Elk City, Oklahoma. His father, Robert Lee Webb, was a Baptist minister, and young Jimmy learned piano and organ to accompany the choir in the elder Webb's rural churches in southwestern Oklahoma and west Texas. Later discussing his 1990 composition "Elvis and Me," Webb explained in *Song Talk* how he had come to discover to the music of the King of Rock, Elvis Presley: "When I was a kid growing up I wasn't allowed to listen to Elvis. My father always controlled the radio very empirically and it was always either country music or white gospel music, quartet music. And we weren't allowed to touch that dial because if we did we would get smacked."

Part of the reason for Webb's strict adherence to certain music types was religious, and part was simply his own taste. Still, after hearing Presley's music, he found himself bitten by the music bug. He began slipping his own arrangement variations into the Sunday services, much to the displeasure of the straight-laced church elders. Or, he would organize clandestine combos at school to play the music that was forbidden at home. Webb also began writing songs of his own. Hearing something in a stolen moment listening to the radio, he would try to write a follow-up to it.

Webb's family moved to southern California in 1964, and Jimmy entered San Benardino Valley College. When his mother died and the family returned to Oklahoma the following year, he elected to remain in California. Though a music major at the college, Webb was hearing his own music; it wasn't long before he decided to see how far his songs would take him in Los Angeles.

"Up, up and Away"

Webb's first job was transcribing other people's music for a small music publisher on Melrose Avenue in Hollywood. But within a year he had secured a contract with Jobete Music, the publishing arm of increasingly

> **For the Record . . .**
>
> Born Jimmy Layne Webb, August 15, 1946, in Elk City, OK; married Patsy Sullivan c. 1972; children: five sons. *Education:* Attended San Bernardino Valley College.
>
> Singer, songwriter, composer, arranger, and producer. Signed briefly to Motown Records' Jobete Publishing, 1965; signed a publishing contract with Johnny Rivers, 1966, and penned hits "Up, up and Away" and "By the Time I Get to Phoenix"; created production and publishing company, Canopy; released first album, *Words and Music,* on Reprise, 1970; composed scores for film and television projects and produced and arranged numerous albums for other artists.
>
> **Selected awards:** Grammy awards for song of the year for "Up, up and Away," and record of the year, both 1967, and for country song of the year, 1985, for "The Highwayman"; several Grammy Award nominations; Country Music Association award for single of the year, 1985, for "The Highwayman"; elected to National Academy of Songwriters (NAS) Hall of Fame; received NAS Lifetime Achievement Award.
>
> **Addresses:** *Record company*—Elektra, 75 Rockefeller Plaza, New York, NY 10019.

westward-looking Motown Records. The result of this brief liaison was Webb's first royalty check—for a song on a Supremes Christmas album—and his first hit tune, "Honey Come Back," which Glenn Campbell would re-release in 1970.

Webb's big break came in meeting Johnny Rivers the following year. Rivers, as shrewd a music businessman as he was a successful recording artist, signed Webb to a publishing deal and put one of Jimmy's new songs, "By the Time I Get to Phoenix," on his late 1966 album, *Changes.* Rivers also enlisted Webb's help in finding material for a group on Rivers's own Soul City Records called the Fifth Dimension.

Webb subsequently penned "Up, up and Away," the title track of the debut Fifth Dimension album. Released as a single in May of 1967, it leaped into the Top Ten and battled the Doors' "Light My Fire" for chart supremacy throughout that summer. Glen Campbell, meanwhile, had covered Webb's "By the Time I Get to Phoenix," which, though only reaching Number 26, became an immediate pop standard.

At the 1967 Grammy Award ceremonies "Up, Up and Away" was named record of the year and song of the year. Altogether, "Up, Up and Away" and "By the Time I Get to Phoenix" collected a staggering eight Grammys. Such acclaim was unprecedented for a rookie songwriter, but it also presented what would be the central dilemma in Webb's career. Only 21, his melodic sophistication and orchestral sensibility was embraced by an older, more traditional pop audience. While his peers were dropping out and going underground, their parents were swaying to the melodies of Jimmy Webb. He was a man out of sync. But so explosive was his momentum, that it overwhelmed any other considerations.

The year 1968 was a blur of continuing success for Webb songs. The Fifth Dimension hit the Top 40 with both "Paper Cup" and "Carpet Man." Glen Campbell came back with the million-selling "Wichita Lineman," which *Creem* magazine once called "one of the most perfect pop records ever made." Also in 1968, Brooklyn Bridge, the group led by former Crests vocalist Johnny Maestro, scored a gold record for "The Worst That Could Happen."

Produced Immensely Popular Songs

Webb soon formed his own production and publishing company, Canopy, and his first project was an unlikely album pairing with Irish actor Richard Harris, then coming off a starring role in the film version of *Camelot.* Among the tracks cut was an extended piece with multiple movements that the group Association had originally commissioned Webb to compose. When asked to edit it for Top 40 airplay, Jimmy refused. Such was Webb's commercial clout that radio stations played all seven minutes and twenty-one seconds of "MacArthur Park." It reached Number Two on the singles chart, while the album, *A Tramp Shining,* stayed on the charts for almost a year. Before the year was out, a second Harris-Webb album, *The Yard Went on Forever,* was also on the charts.

"MacArthur Park," "Wichita Lineman," and "By the Time I Get to Phoenix" all won 1968 Grammys. Glen Campbell started 1969 with a gold record with Webb's "Galveston," considered one of the most effective antiwar songs ever written, and hit later in the year with another Webb composition, "Where's the Playground Susie." "Didn't We" was included on the first Richard Harris album and became a standard despite only rising to Number 63. Perhaps more interestingly, two Webb songs became hits for the second time. Isaac Hayes's soul interpretation of "By the Time I Get to Phoenix" and Waylon Jennings's Grammy-winning country version of "MacArthur Park" showed how deeply Webb's songs influence many facets of the music world.

Even as the popularity of his material was cresting in 1969, Webb was withdrawing from his instant empire. The title of a semiautobiographical Broadway musical he was working on around this time, *His Own Dark City*, seemed to indicate that the emotional displacement of his success was weighing heavily. He contributed music to the films *How Sweet It Is* and *Tell Them Willie Boy Is Here* in 1969, but no new Webb songs were blazing up the charts.

Personal Freedom

Words and Music, Webb's debut album as the performer of his own songs, was released in late 1970. The songwriter "had exhausted one avenue of musical expression," wrote Jon Landau in *Rolling Stone*, "and he has now shifted into a context that allows him more personal freedom. It's unlikely that he will achieve comparable popularity in his new surroundings, but his music has never sounded better than it does on *Words and Music*." Landau singled out the track "P. F. Sloan," calling it a "masterpiece" that "could not be improved upon."

Unfortunately, Landau's comment about Webb's commercial success proved prescient. "P. F. Sloan" set the tone for Webb's career as a performer; he was critically lauded, frequently covered, but not nearly as successful as he was as a songsmith. The numbers, however, told only part of the story. Though a singer of modest gifts, each of his albums as a performer became noted for their inventive, satisfying music and memorable lyrics.

Rolling Stone called Webb's 1971 album *And So: On* "another impressive step in the conspiracy to recover his identity from the housewives of America and rightfully install him at the forefront of contemporary composers/performers." Upon the release of *Letters* in 1972, Peter Reilly of *Stereo Review* wrote, "Jimmy Webb is the most important pop music figure to emerge since Bob Dylan." Similar praise met the release of 1974's *Land's End*, 1977's *El Mirage*, and 1982's *Angel Heart*.

Webb's albums may not have been chart climbers, but they did not go completely unnoticed. Having become known as a "singer's songwriter," Webb saw the best crooners in the business plunder his albums for the many gems they contained. Judy Collins, Joe Cocker, Art Garfunkel, Linda Ronstadt, Cher, Lowell George, Joan Baez, and Amy Grant are just a few of the artists who have made Webb material a staple of their repertoires.

Webb still had his share of commercial hits. "All I Know," for example, remains Garfunkel's only Top Ten solo hit. Waylon Jennings, Johnny Cash, Kris Kristofferson, and Willie Nelson topped the charts in 1985 with "The Highwayman," earning Webb yet another Grammy for best country song of the year and a Country Music Association citation for single of the year. In addition, "MacArthur Park" continued to earn notice when the Four Tops recorded it in 1970 and Donna Summer's disco rendition of the tune stayed at Number One for almost a month in the fall of 1978.

Contemporary Admiration

Webb moved to New York City in the mid-1980s to try his hand at Broadway musicals, prompting collaborations with Peter Stone on *Love Me, Love My Dog* and with science fiction writer Ray Bradbury on *Dandelion Wine*. In 1986 CBS Records issued an album of the Webb cantata *The Animals' Christmas*, featuring Garfunkel, Amy Grant, and the London Symphony Orchestra. Webb continued contributing music to films—including *Doc, The Last Unicorn, The Hanoi Hilton*, and *Fern Gulley: The Last Rain Forest*—and wrote scores for television projects headed by such stars as Olivia Newton-John, Ringo Starr, and Steven Spielberg.

Linda Ronstadt, who has consistently championed Webb's songwriting, coaxed him back into the recording studio for the 1993 release of *Suspending Disbelief*. Coproduced by Ronstadt and George Massenburg, it was referred to by *Time* as "an important record of an American tale teller, our best raveler of the blind spots of the heart."

Given his 1960s mega-success as a songwriter and the enduring appeal of his songs for both singers and pop music fans, it seems safe to say that Jimmy Webb's position in pop music history is secure. In fact, his stature is sure to increase as future song connoisseurs discover the depth of inspiration that lies beneath the surface sheen of Webb's chart hits and pop standards.

Selected discography

Words and Music, Reprise, 1970.
And So: On, Reprise, 1971.
Letters, Reprise, 1972.
Land's End, Asylum, 1974.
El Mirage, Atlantic 1977.

Angel Heart, Columbia, 1982.
The Animals' Christmas, Columbia, 1986.
Suspending Disbelief, Elektra, 1993.

Sources

Billboard, October 2, 1993.
Creem, October 1972; November 1974.
Newsweek, December 23, 1968; June 13, 1977.
New Yorker, January 9, 1971.
New York Times, September 29, 1993.
Rolling Stone, March 4, 1971; September 2, 1971; October 14, 1993; April 21, 1994.
SongTalk, winter 1989; spring 1994.
Stereo Review, November 1972
Time, May 24, 1968; October 18, 1993.

Additional material for this profile was obtained from Columbia Records publicity materials, 1982, and Elektra Records publicity materials, 1993.

—Ben Edmonds

Kurt Weill

Composer

An intriguing figure in twentieth-century music, Kurt Weill was a unique composer who virtually closed the gap between "serious" and "light" music. He began his musical career composing complex modernist music that was appreciated by an esoteric elite, then shifted to creating music for the general public. Weill composed works ranging from symphonic music and opera to tangos, jazz songs, and pop hits for the theater, radio, and films. By combining different forms of music within his operatic scores, Weill, as John Rockwell wrote in the *New York Times,* "sought simultaneously to sustain the operatic tradition and to communicate with a contemporary audience through popular musical idioms."

Weill received early exposure to music from his father, Albert, who was a Jewish cantor and composer, and his mother, Emma, who studied the piano. He received lessons as a youth from Albert Bing, and by the time he was 17 he was already helping to support the family with money earned as an accompanist. After enrolling in the Berlin Hochschule in 1918 to receive training from

AP/Wide World Photos

For the Record...

Born Kurt Julian Weill, March 2, 1900, in Desau, Germany; emigrated to United States, 1936, naturalized citizen, 1943; died April 3, 1950, in New York, NY; son of Albert (a cantor and composer) and Emma (maiden name, Ackermann) Weill; married Lotte Lenya Blamauer, January 28, 1926. *Education:* Took piano lessons as a child with Albert Bing; studied composition under Krasselt and Engelbert Humperdinck at Berlin Hochschule, Germany, 1918; studied music theory and harmony under Ferruccio Busoni, 1921-24.

Composer of symphonic music, opera, songs, arias, and popular hits for theater, radio, and films. Coach at the Desau Theater, 1919; became director of the Ludenscheid Opera House, 1920; wrote first opera, *The Protagonist,* 1926; began long-term collaboration with Bertolt Brecht, late 1920s; wrote songs for *The Three Penny Opera,* late 1920s; became a leading spokesman of modernist movement in art and culture; went to Paris due to Nazi condemnation of his work, early 1930s; composed score for ballet *The Seven Deadly Sins* in Paris, 1933; moved to London, mid-1930s; wrote music for *Johnny Johnson,* a play produced by the Group Theater, 1936; was given a contract with a Hollywood studio; wrote songs for *Knickerbocker Holiday,* 1938, *Lady in the Dark,* 1941, *Street Scene,* 1947, and other theatrical works; collaborated on musicals with Maxwell Anderson, Ira Gershwin, Ogden Nash, and S. J. Perleman, 1930s-1940s.

noted proponents of nineteenth-century Romanticism Krasselt and Engelbert Humperdinck, Weill tired of formal teaching and left the school after only a year. He held a few musical directorship positions, then realized that he needed more training and returned to Berlin to study under the great Italian pianist and musical theorist Ferruccio Busoni. His compositions of abstract, disharmonic pieces from this time reflect the influence of Busoni's musical ideas.

Became Adept at Satire

Weill's musical perspective broadened with the widespread popularity of his music for *Die Zaubernacht,* a children's ballet performed in 1922. Pleasing a wider audience appealed to him, and he began to feel disdain for the practice of writing highly technical compositions accessible only to a small minority of listeners. He became especially interested in American jazz. His second opera, *The Royal Palace,* featured experimentation with various jazz forms, and he incorporated even more jazz into *The Czar Has Himself Photographed,* which was very popular with German audiences. Some German critics, however, felt that this work was a sellout of his talent to accommodate the tastes of the masses.

While working on the *Czar* score, Weill became acquainted with Bertolt Brecht, an avant-garde German poet and dramatist. In the late 1920s they began working on a modern version of John Gay's eighteenth-century play *The Beggar's Opera,* which had satirized society as well as the then-fashionable Italian opera. Reflecting Brecht's radical views, the resulting *Threepenny Opera* satirized virtually all aspects of modern culture and incorporated musical styles ranging from blues songs to tangos. The featured role of a prostitute named Jenny was played by Lotte Lenya Blamauer, whom Weill had married in 1926.

The opera at first found no backers among German producers, but when it was finally staged in 1928, it became the rage of Europe. Within a year after its first staging, the opera was performed more than 4,200 times in the major capitals of Europe. Although *The Threepenny Opera* was a failure with critics in its American debut in 1933, a 1954 revival ran for six years and became one of the most successful musicals ever staged in the United States. Weill's best-known song from the production was "Mack the Knife," which in 48 recorded versions sold over ten million copies. The song reached Number One on the Hit Parade in the United States in 1955. Collaborating with Brecht convinced Weill that he was through with traditional opera, and that musical theater was the one medium that allowed him to satisfy all his musical interests.

Labeled a Communist

Weill and Brecht followed *The Threepenny Opera* with *The Rise and Fall of the City of Mahagonny,* an even more scathing attack on society, that was presented as a full musical play in 1930. The story centers on three ex-convicts who establish an anti-utopian town in Alabama dedicated to serving man's basest instincts. Weill used a number of popular musical forms, including jazz, in his score, and his "Alabamy Song" from the show became a popular hit in Germany. Public reaction to the show, however, was mixed—while some loved it, others found it extremely distasteful and even threw stinkbombs on the stage in protest.

After the 1933 staging in Leipzig of *Der Silbersee,* which featured a song that was clearly an attack on

Hitler and Nazism, Weill was labeled a communist, and his works were banned in Germany. Personal condemnation and the increasing persecution of Jews made it imperative for the composer to leave the country, and he fled to France. In Paris he wrote the score for the highly successful ballet *The Seven Deadly Sins,* a collaboration with Brecht choreographed by George Balanchine. The theme of the ballet, which focused on the split personality of its heroine, somewhat echoed Weill's dilemma of the time. During this period he wanted both to please his audiences and to be guided by his own creativity, regardless of his music's acceptance by the public.

> *"I have never acknowledged the difference between 'serious' and 'light' music. There is only good music and bad music."*

Discussing Weill's score for the ballet, Edward Rothstein wrote in the *New Republic,* "Weill seems to anticipate precisely the debate over his attitudes and career that accompanied his move to America; it is a prescient chronicle of his consistent ambivalence about his work—an ambivalence that unites rather than divides his work." This "unity" is demonstrated by the daring score of the ballet that ventures from circus-like music and cabaret songs to popular dances.

After spending time in London, Weill was asked by Austrian theatrical director Max Reinhardt to go with him to the United States. Reinhardt wanted Weill to create music for his production of *The Eternal Road,* which was intended to be a history of the Jewish people. Once he had arrived in 1935, Weill settled into a new career in New York and wrote a number of popular scores for the theater.

His music for the 1936 play *Johnny Johnson,* written by Paul Green for the Group Theatre, received favorable reviews. News of his success reached Hollywood, and he was given a contract to produce music for films. Among his projects for motion pictures was the musical accompaniment for Fritz Lang's *You and Me,* released in 1938. He returned to Broadway that year to write music for Maxwell Anderson's *Knickerbocker Holiday,* and, even though the play was a failure, Weill's music was lauded. Weill was also commissioned to compose the score for the Ballet Theatre's *The Judgment of Paris,* which opened in 1940.

Weill continued to embrace American projects eagerly, setting Walt Whitman's poetry to music and writing a score for a railway pageant at the 1939 World's Fair in New York City. In his new country Weill sought a closer relationship to the audience through a gentler form of satire. As Rothstein wrote, "Weill found a distinctly American way to be popular: he continued to use parody of popular song styles and mannerisms, as he had in his German period, this time not to mock his listeners, but to imply a 'sophisticated' perspective—a sort of snobbish populism, clubbishly kidding the audience about Broadway itself."

As a result of this new collusion with his audience, Weill's Broadway works lost the sharp edge of his German collaborations. For example, *Lady in the Dark* lightly mocks the growing practice of psychiatry, and *One Touch of Venus* presents a barber who wants to improve his social standing by bringing the ancient Greek goddess Venus to life, only to find that she feels threatened by life in the modern-day suburbs. Rather than court controversy, Weill's Broadway projects address nonthreatening subjects to which his audiences could readily relate.

Echoes of Handel and Bach

Weill's background in complex composition gave him a style unique among musical theater composers. His scores deliver echoes of Handel choruses and Bach chorales, as well as idioms of grand opera, hymns, marches, music-hall numbers, and even Tin Pan Alley ditties. He could write a serious fugue as well as a song that made fun of a fugue. Most interesting of all was his ability to create songs that capture both high and low culture. As Lloyd Schwartz wrote in the *Atlantic,* "One of Weill's best jokes is the way his songs mix the elegant and the tawdry, the serious and the trivial, the cynical and the sentimental."

Although some critics lamented that Weill sentimentalized his music after moving to the United States, and that he had lost the daring of his German period when he had consistently challenged audiences rather than pleased them, Weill was less interested in creating music for posterity than in using everything he knew to reach people. He also refused to set any one form of music above another. "I have never acknowledged the difference between 'serious' and 'light' music," Weill was quoted as saying in the *New Republic.* "There is only good music and bad music."

No other composer has so successfully blurred the boundaries between opera and musical theater, as evidenced by Weill's later scores for *Lost in the Stars* and Elmer Rice's *Street Scene.* Achieving great success as a composer of operas that defied all the traditions of the genre in Europe, he then moved on to set new standards for musical theater in the United States. When Weill died in 1950, Olin Downes wrote in the *New York Times* that the composer "stands as a sovereign example of the forces that merge in the American 'melting pot' toward a national expression, and the forces of this period which are working to create new forms of operative expression in our theatre."

Selected compositions

Fantasy, Passacaglia, and Hymn, 1923.
The Protagonist (opera), 1926.
(With Bertolt Brecht) *The Threepenny Opera,* 1928.
(With Brecht) *The Rise and Fall of the City of Mahagonny* (opera), 1930.
(With Brecht) *Happy End* (opera), 1929.
(With Brecht) *The Seven Deadly Sins* (ballet), 1933.
Knickerbocker Holiday (musical), 1938.
Lady in the Dark, (musical), 1940.
The Judgment of Paris (ballet), 1940.
One Touch of Venus (musical), 1943.
Street Scene (opera), 1946.
Lost in the Stars (opera), 1949.

Sources

Books

Jarman, Douglas, *Kurt Weill, An Illustrated Biography,* Indiana University Press, 1982.
International Dictionary of Opera, St. James Press, 1993.
Schonberg, Harold C., *The Lives of the Great Composers,* revised edition, Norton, 1981.
Taylor, Ronald, *Kurt Weill,* Northeastern University Press, 1992.

Periodicals

Atlantic, December 1989; November 1992..
Herald Tribune, April 9, 1950.
New Republic, November 23, 1987.
New Statesman & Society, June 22, 1990.
New Yorker, October 19, 1987.
New York Times, April 9, 1950; January 5, 1993; May 30, 1993; December 17, 1993.

—Ed Decker

Kelly Willis

Singer

Photograph by Kurt Markus, courtesy of MCA Nashville

Country music's critical darling of the early 1990s, Kelly Willis took the tough, edgy, country rock of Austin, Texas, and brought it to the center of the country industry in Nashville. Willis, a striking young woman, virtually alone among country vocalists, has made inroads into the world of high fashion. But she kept the camera lens secondary to her singing, and purposefully continued to work out a distinct and personal musical vision—combining rockabilly toughness with country heartache.

Boldly inviting comparisons between herself and the legendary country-pop singer Patsy Cline, she has in fact received several that were not unfavorable. As her singing matured, the biggest challenge before her was to somehow make a connection with the mainstream country fans who could take her to the top of the charts.

Army Brat

Willis was born in Lawton, Oklahoma, in 1968, but as a young child she lived in several different places. Her father, a U.S. army colonel, divorced her mother when Willis was nine years old. Her mother had played the piano and acted in musicals, and in her absence Willis began to sing to herself very frequently. In an interview with *Rolling Stone*'s Karen Schoemer she recalled her father's reaction: "Well, that means you're happy," he said. "But actually," Willis continued, "I think ... it's more to help you if you're not happy. That's what it was for me."

She spent most of her teen years in the Washington suburb of Annandale, Virginia, and remembers driving and singing along with a tape that had Patsy Cline's music on one side and blues-rock cult favorites NRBQ on the other. She talked her way into the job of lead vocalist with her boyfriend's rockabilly band, which was soon rechristened Kelly and the Fireballs. When the band moved to the musically overflowing city of Austin, Texas, in 1987, Willis went along. Her "very strict" father, she told Rob Tannenbaum of *Rolling Stone,* did not approve.

In Austin, Willis encountered a great variety of musical influences. The city, located squarely in the middle of country music's Texan heartland, had a music scene in the late 1980s that mixed the country heritage with an experimental spirit that admitted rockabilly, blues, and even the brittle gloom of alternative rock. Willis, who by 1990 was fronting a band called Radio Ranch, absorbed these influences and rose to the top of Austin's intensely competitive live-music hierarchy. She was only 21 years old.

> **For the Record . . .**
>
> Born October 1, 1968, in Lawton, OK; daughter of a U.S. Army colonel; grew up in Annandale, VA.
>
> Progressive country vocalist; lead vocalist, Kelly and the Fireballs, c. 1986; lead vocalist, successful Austin, Texas band Radio Ranch, 1988-90; signed with MCA Records and released *Well Travelled Love,* 1990.
>
> **Awards:** Nominee for best new female vocalist, Academy of Country Music, 1994.
>
> **Addresses:** *Record label*—MCA Records, 1514 South St., Nashville, TN 37212. *Management*—Mark Rothbaum & Associates, Inc., 36 Mill Plain Rd., #406, Danbury, CT 06811.

Word of Willis's talents reached country music's power brokers in several stages. She made a strong impression with a performance at Austin's South by Southwest music festival, an annual spring meeting of great importance in Texas music industry circles. The Texan folk singer-songwriter Nanci Griffith, at the time well placed with MCA Nashville executives as a result of having written several hit songs for other country artists, brought Willis to their attention. Finally, MCA president Tony Brown, who had already championed innovative country newcomers Steve Earle and Lyle Lovett, called Willis to Nashville. After a showcase at the Bluebird Cafe, one of the Nashville nightspots most frequented by music industry figures, she was signed to MCA.

Attracted Attention With Passionate Voice

Willis's first album, 1990's *Well Travelled Love,* immediately vaulted into several critics' year-end, best-of-the-season lists. Her voice, full-throated and passionate, attracted the most attention. Jan Hoffman wrote in the *Village Voice* that as a singer, Willis had "the smooth confidence of a power-lifter oiled for competition."

The album featured her bandmates from Austin and included several compositions by her drummer, Mas Palermo, with whom Willis was said to be romantically involved at the time. Other songs were written by Steve Earle ("Hole in My Heart"), whose compositional combination of belligerence and longing proved ideally suited to Willis's own style, and by John Hiatt ("Drive South"), another artist who has fallen into the ferment-filled crack between country and rock.

Bob Millard's review of the album in *Country Music* noted that "Willis manages ... to capture on record all the vitality of Austin's young country scene." The wiry energy of many of the album's songs betrayed a strong rock influence. And while Willis's promotional literature tended to stress her rather tenuous connections with Patsy Cline (she and Willis were "fellow Virginians"), a different 1950s vocalist showed up in the cover iconography of Willis's album—the teenaged rockabilly star Janis Martin.

Martin's "Bang Bang" became the title track of Willis's second album, released in 1992. *Bang Bang* featured mostly Nashville studio musicians in place of the Austin players, but otherwise remained similar to the singer's debut outing. The album contained another Steve Earle piece and a scorching cover of Texas rocker Joe Ely's "Settle for Love." But once more most of the songs were by Palermo and Willis's other Texas associates. Willis had always chosen songs primarily by turning to her circle of musical associates. "I've always been part of a band when I made a record, and I'm used to the band technique of making music," she explained in her press biography.

Sought Mainstream Acceptance

Willis's first two albums generated considerable word-of-mouth praise in the industry and were moderately successful sellers. Her reputation extended beyond the field of country, as she opened on tour for alternative rock bands such as the Del Lords and the Silos, and placed two songs on the soundtrack of the hit film *Thelma and Louise.* She also landed a part in actor Tim Robbins's political satire *Bob Roberts.*

But wide exposure on country radio had for the most part eluded her, and with her third album, simply titled *Kelly Willis,* set for release in 1993, she and Tony Brown set out to reconcile her rock-inflected hard edges with the requirements of mainstream appeal. "Trying to find [songs] that are mainstream, but keep that edge and are *real* Kelly Willis, is hard," Brown told *Billboard.* "But after two years of looking, she found every one of them." Veteran rock producer Don Was came on board as a result of a chance meeting with Brown in Los Angeles, but he wisely refrained from tampering much with Willis's basic style, choosing instead to expand the album's instrumental palette in subtle ways.

Willis gained some radio exposure with "Whatever Way the Wind Blows," composed by the offbeat rock singer Marshall Crenshaw, and with a remake of the Kendalls' lusty "Heaven's Just a Sin Away." The critics were as friendly as ever, with Karen Schoemer writing in *Rolling Stone* that Willis, "like Loretta Lynn or Patsy Cline, can spear your heart with the slightest catch, quaver or sigh." But neither single reached top chart levels. Still, Willis's appeal continued to build. Whenever Willis could be showcased visually, she attracted new fans. Her videos received considerable play on country cable television, and she was the subject of fashion spreads in *Vogue, Interview,* and *Mademoiselle* magazines. "Kelly Willis has a face that you could look at a thousand times and never quite memorize," Schoemer wrote. As she continued to play her progressive brand of country music, Willis neared the goal of making her music as fascinating as her appearance.

Selected discography

Well Travelled Love, MCA, 1990.
Bang Bang, MCA, 1991.
Kelly Willis, MCA, 1993.

Sources

Books

All Music Guide, Miller-Freeman, 1992.

Periodicals

Billboard, July 24, 1993.
Country Music, September/October 1990; May/June 1991; September/October 1993.
Rolling Stone, September 6, 1990; August 19, 1993; September 2, 1993.
Village Voice, August 7, 1990.

Additional information for this profile was obtained from press materials furnished by Mark Rothbaum & Associates, Inc.

—*James M. Manheim*

Cassandra Wilson

Singer, composer

Photograph © 1993 by Chris Callas, courtesy of Blue Note Records

One of the most prominent jazz vocalists of the late twentieth century, Cassandra Wilson has a contralto voice that has been variously described as rich, smoky, and deep and hazy. Her repertoire is diverse; it includes jazz standards, Mississippi reggae, blues, and pieces that edge into pop, although Wilson brings a jazz singer's sensibility and phrasing to everything she does. Wilson's recording career began with Steve Coleman as part of the M-Base collective and progressed to the production of several solo albums of which she wrote, co-wrote, or arranged about half herself. Her most popular albums, *Blue Skies,* a collection of jazz standards, and *Blue Light 'Til Dawn,* a mix of blues, jazz, and folk, departed from her usual metaphysical lyrics.

Wilson's childhood entry into music was influenced by her father, jazz guitarist and bassist Herman B. Fowlkes. She studied classical piano from age six or seven to her early teens. Taught basic guitar chords by her father at 11 or 12, Wilson began writing her own songs. Over the next five years she wrote approximately 20 folk-type tunes, inspired by Joni Mitchell, Joan Baez, and Judy Collins. It was while attending Milsaps College in the mid-1970s that Wilson got her first gig singing and playing guitar at a nearby folk club every Tuesday. And although the response to her performances gave her confidence in her singing, she also received some valuable criticism. "I used to have this nyaa-a-a-a-h vibrato," she told Kevin Whitehead in a *Down Beat* interview. "The club owner told me nobody could make it with a voice like that. I got rid of it, but there is a trace of it left; you can hear it."

Moved to New Orleans

After graduating with a degree in mass communications from Jackson State, Wilson moved to New Orleans, where she began sitting in with Earl Turbinton and Ellis Marsalis. In 1982 she arrived in New York and soon found her way into the M-Base jazz collective, a group of avant-garde musicians mixing jazz improvisation with precise composition and the rhythms of hip-hop, rap, and funk.

Saxophonist Steve Coleman, whom Wilson met in 1983, played a significant role in Wilson's career at the time. "He was the first one that really encouraged me to write my own material, to do original music, and to just spot a direction of my own," Wilson explained in her *Down Beat* interview. At the time a bebopper, Wilson was attracted to the music of Charlie Parker and the singing of Betty Carter; Coleman introduced her to the singing of Abbey Lincoln, who became an important influence on her development. Coleman also gave Wilson her

> **For the Record...**
>
> Born Cassandra Marie Fowlkes, in 1955, in Jackson, MS; daughter of Herman B. Fowlkes (a jazz guitarist, bassist, and schoolteacher), and Mary Fowlkes (a schoolteacher); married Anthony Wilson, 1981 (divorced, 1983). *Education:* Attended Milsaps College; received degree in mass communications from Jackson State.
>
> First professional gig at a folk club near Milsaps College, mid-1970s; joined Blue John, a rock band from Arkansas; moved to New Orleans and began sitting in with Earl Turbinton and Ellis Marsalis, 1981; moved to New York and joined what would become the M-Base collective, 1982; made several albums with Steve Coleman, mid-1980s; recorded with Jim DeAngelis and Tony Signs and Henry Threadgill's New Air, 1980s; recorded first solo album, 1986; recorded seven more solo albums, mostly avant-garde jazz, although one was a collection of standards and one a mix of blues, folk, and jazz, late 1980s and early 1990s.
>
> **Addresses:** *Home*—New York, NY. *Publicity*—Shore Fire Media, 193 Joralemon St., Brooklyn, NY 11202. *Record company*—Blue Note, 810 Seventh Ave., 4th Floor, New York, NY 10019.

first recording opportunity on his 1985 release, *Motherland Pulse.* Whitehead described her recording debut in *Down Beat:* "You could already hear her well-developed ear, a taste for unlikely intervals, and a refreshing refusal to wow us to death."

Explored Diverse Musical Genres

Over the next several years Wilson continued to collaborate with Coleman; she also recorded with Henry Threadgill's New Air and with Jim DeAngelis and Tony Signs. Her first solo album, *Point of View,* was released by JMT in 1986, having taken only two days to record and mix. She did most of the producing for *Days Aweigh,* taking only four days but finishing with a more polished album than her previous release. The songs on these two albums do not represent the usual jazz singer's repertoire. A mix of funk, fusion, and reggae, the music combines with lyrics that border on metaphysical. Praised for their ambitious scope, these early albums have also been criticized as too ethereal.

In 1988 Wilson showcased her talents in a different venue, a collection of standards. *Blue Skies,* with the traditional trio of piano, bass, and drums to support Wilson's vocals, includes material from Rodgers and Hammerstein, Irving Berlin, and Johnny Mercer. "The readings never get too deep," described Brian Cullman in *Vogue,* "but her phrasing is consistently thoughtful and original." Her treatment of such songs as "I've Grown Accustomed to His Face," "Sweet Lorraine," "Shall We Dance," and "I Didn't Know What Time It Was," led many to compare her to Betty Carter. Jazz fans seemed to appreciate Wilson's skills as a dramatist; this album outsold her previous recordings by almost ten to one.

In *Dance to the Drums Again,* released by DIW/Columbia in 1993, Wilson turned away from the winning formula of *Blue Skies.* She returned to ethereal lyrics, but leaned toward a black pop format. Jean-Paul Bourelly co-wrote most of the tracks, incorporating guitar and even some synthetic strings and a drum machine. An African choral influence can be heard in places. According to a 1993 *Essence* profile, "Her highly metaphysical lyrics, she says, are inspired by her dreams as well as by African religions and mythology, which she has studied extensively."

Blue Light Highlighted Vocal Stylings

First-time producer Craig Street worked with Wilson on her next album, *Blue Light 'Til Dawn.* Originally planned as a collection of Southern soul music, the album evolved into an earthy mix of Delta blues, African harmonies, and folk/pop tracks. Themes of restlessness and unrequited love tie the disparate styles and genres together. The tracks are also all given the same reductionist treatment by Street, using blues and classical guitars, African and Brazilian percussion, and a little bass. With no keyboard and few horns, the pieces feature percussion as an important foil for Wilson's floating and soaring improvisation. Her voice is in the forefront on this album, which includes material by the Stylistics, Van Morrison, Joni Mitchell, and Delta blues legend Robert Johnson.

Wilson next cut two songs with Robbie Robertson for the film *Jimmy Hollywood* and was expected to begin work on her next album in the spring of 1994. Meanwhile, the cross-generational appeal of *Blue Light 'Til Dawn,* the uniformly strong reviews it received, and its unusual mix of genres was moving Wilson into the mainstream. According to Tate, "*Blue Light 'Til Dawn* is the kind of album that gets called timeless on the way to becoming a classic. It stirs up misty visions of jazz antiquity in thoroughly modern ways, eschewing the use of tradition as a crutch and embracing black music's past as a place where emancipation begins rather than ends."

Selected discography

Point of View, JMT, 1986.
Days Aweigh, JMT, 1987.
Blue Skies, JMT, 1988.
She Who Weeps, JMT, 1991.
Dance to the Drums Again, DIW/Columbia, 1992.
Blue Light 'Til Dawn, Blue Note, 1993.
Live, 1993.
Jump World, JMT.

With others

(With Steve Coleman) *Motherland Pulse*, JMT, 1985.
(With Coleman) *World Expansion*, JMT.
(With Coleman) *On the Edge of Tomorrow*, JMT.
(With New Air) *Air Show No. 1*, Black Saint.
(With Jim DeAngelis and Tony Signs) *Straight From the Top*, Statiras.

Sources

Billboard, February 12, 1994.
Down Beat, February 1988; January 1989; December 1993.
Essence, February 1993.
Los Angeles Times, December 28, 1993.
Musician, May 1994.
Pulse!, June 1993.
Vogue, February 1989.

Additional information for this profile was provided by Shore Fire Media.

—*Susan Windisch Brown*

The Winans

Gospel group

Years ago, the Winans family would gather on important holidays for gospel concerts at Detroit's Zion Congregational Church of God in Christ. According to Richard Harrington in the *Washington Post,* at the end of the these concerts, the kids would give each other imaginary Grammys. Eventually the ten children grew up and split into separate performing groups: the Winans, consisting of Michael, Ronald, and twins Carvin and Marvin; Benjamin and Priscilla, who perform as BeBe and CeCe; Debbie and Angie, billed as the Sisters; and Daniel Winans, the only solo artist in the family.

Eventually they started winning Grammys for real. The Winans alone have received four, in addition to Stellar, Dove, and *Soul Train* music awards. Even the elder Winans, Mom and Pop, received a Grammy nomination after they received a recording contract from Sparrow stemming from a guest appearance on the televised Grammy Awards program with the family in 1989. Though they have often sung together in church, 1992 marked the first time that the family ever toured as a

Photograph by Ameen Howrani, © 1992 Warner Bros. Records

> **For the Record...**
>
> Members include **Carvin** and **Marvin Winans** (twins; born 1958), **Michael Winans** (born 1959), and **Ronald Winans** (born 1955); all born in Detroit, MI.
>
> Sang in the Zion Congregational Church of God in Christ; appeared in a high school talent show, 1973; changed name from Testimonial Singers to the Winans, 1975; released debut album, *Long Time Coming,* 1983; began working with producer Quincy Jones, 1984; toured with all Winans family members, 1992.
>
> **Awards:** Grammy awards for best soul gospel performance for *Tomorrow,* 1985, *Let My People Go,* 1986, and (with Anita Baker) *Ain't No Need to Worry,* 1987; Grammy Award for best gospel performance for *The Winans Live at Carnegie Hall,* 1988; recepients of Stellar, Dove, and *Soul Train* music awards.
>
> **Addresses:** *Record company*—Qwest Records, 3800 Bonham Blvd., Suite 503, Los Angeles, CA, 90068.

unit, as 12 performers, three buses, two trucks, and 40 people combined for the "Winans' One Family World Tour." On stage each group does its own songs. They also work in various combinations, occasionally with the entire family together, reported Larry Kelp in the *Oakland Tribune.*

A Family Tradition

Touring comes naturally for the Winans brothers and sisters. Their parents, Delores and David, met while singing in the Lemon Gospel Chorus, a choir that traveled around the country. Delores played piano for the chorus, and David sang in the classic quartet format. His group, the Nobelaires, was very much in the tradition of the Dixie Hummingbirds, the Mighty Clouds of Joy, and the Soul Stirrers, from whose ranks emerged Sam Cooke, a friend of David's who later abandoned gospel and became one of the first great soul stars, Harrington noted in the *Washington Post.*

The day before their wedding in 1953, David Winans was laid off his job on the Dodge assembly line. According to Marvin Winans in the *Oakland Tribune:* "We were by all economic standards considered poor. We grew up on the west side of Detroit in the Parkside projects they've just now finished rebuilding from the '67 riots. We went through Volunteers of America, the food projects."

Both parents worked, sometimes two or three jobs, but the family and the church were most important in their lives. The Winans children were reared in the strict Pentecostal teachings of the Detroit church founded by their great-grandfather and pastored by their father. As Pop Winans remarked in the *Washington Post,* "We were oriented to gospel music and we taught our children nothing but the ways of the Lord, I never let them go to shows or even to the theater; I never let them get involved with any other activity *but* church."

The Children Carry It On

In the *Washington Post,* Carvin Winans remembered a house full of music: "Everybody was always singing—we always had a piano. We'd walk through the house humming and harmonizing. It was *all* we did." But it was not until 1973, while their parents were on vacation, that the Winans children realized their singing had appeal outside of the church. Ronald convinced CeCe, BeBe, and Michael to perform in a high school talent show. In the *Philadelphia Inquirer,* he took credit for their success. They rehearsed for hours, coordinating their voices and their moves. The high school audience was thrilled and gave the group a standing ovation.

Though they would be the first group to get a contract, the four brothers who became the Winans briefly had quit singing as adolescents. They abandoned singing, explained Carvin in the *Washington Post,* "because all those years our parents made us sing. But when something is put in you, you find yourself coming back to it when you get older." When they were a few years older they formed the Testimonial Singers and started taking music more seriously.

In 1975 four of the older brothers—Ronald, Michael, and the twins, Carvin and Marvin—formed the Winans. As they began to perform around the Motor City area, demand for their distinctive gospel style increased and soon they came to the attention of Grammy-winning gospel artist Andrae Crouch. The Winans' first single, on the gospel label Light, was titled "The Question Is" and received heavy airplay and rave reviews, according to their Qwest Records biography. They recorded *Long Time Comin'* in 1983, and in 1985 they released *Tomorrow,* for which they were to receive the first of four Grammy awards.

The group began an extensive round of touring, bringing the intensity of their live show to audiences across the country. Quincy Jones, the legendary producer and impresario, heard the Winans and began working with the group and their manager, Barry Hankerson, in 1984. Their 1986 debut on Jones' Qwest Records, *Let*

My People Go, would win a Grammy Award for best soul gospel performance. Meanwhile, their collaborations with Michael McDonald on "Love Has No Color" and Anita Baker on "Ain't No Need to Worry" (another Grammy winner) reached out to pop and urban contemporary audiences. Their powerful stage presence was captured live on the 1988 release *The Winans Live at Carnegie Hall,* which garnered them their fourth Grammy Award in as many years.

Crossing Over

The Winans have continued to team up with secular musicians such as Stevie Wonder, Kenny G, and Ricky Scaggs. Their 1990 album, *Return,* featured Teddy Riley, producer of new jack swing music, and in 1993 the release *All Out* reaffirmed their position on the cutting edge of contemporary gospel with its throbbing hip-hop rhythms. The group received increasing criticism, however, as their crossover success continued, and the music became more upbeat in tempo.

John Clayton, a West Philadelphia collector of gospel music, maintained in the *Philadelphia Inquirer,* "You can't have it both ways. How can you sing worldly music, have people slow dancing to your songs and still say you are gospel? There has to be a line drawn." But according to Carvin Winans in the *Washington Post,* "The music our parents made us sing, we never liked those songs. We wanted to write music that would be pleasing to our ears and maybe to other young people too. I really cannot stand quartet music."

Likewise, when asked in the *Oakland Tribune* if their music had changed since the early years, Marvin responded: "To us it hasn't. It's just kept evolving with time. We never were traditionalists. Even now I don't carry any tradition, but I carry a message. Our message as a gospel group, the thing that's kept our family together is the strong belief in the Lord that was put there and shown to us by our mom and dad's belief and commitment to the gospel of the Lord Jesus Christ."

The Winans believe that by reaching out to today's youth with music they can understand and make their own, they are spreading the gospel. And they've always pleased their most important critics. As Pop Winans related in the *Washington Post,* "Some people were caught up in the old hymns, the slow beats. But when you hear [contemporary gospel] and analyze the lyrics, you can't frown on it because they're talking about Jesus, about the Lord, about the love of God.... It's not how fast the song is sung, it's the lyrics and what they say."

And the people are listening to what the Winans say, whether on the radio or on one of their many television appearances. Marvin Winans has even been pastoring and developing a Detroit congregation called Perfecting Church, as well as hosting a weeknight radio show. The other brothers are equally busy starring in musical theater productions or working with youth choirs. Whatever they are doing, the Winans keep on singing, and more and more people seem to be hearing their word.

Selected discography

Long Time Comin', 1983, reissued, CGI, 1993.
Tomorrow, 1985, reissued, CGI, 1993.
Let My People Go, Qwest Records, 1986.
Decisions, Qwest Records, 1988.
The Winans Live at Carnegie Hall, 1988.
Return, Qwest Records, 1990.
All Out, Qwest Records, 1993.
Introducing the Winans (reissue), CGI, 1993.
Tomorrow and More (reissue), CGI, 1993.
Yesterday and Today (reissue), CGI, 1993.

Sources

Billboard, November 2, 1985; September 12, 1987; September 19, 1987; September 18, 1993.
Detroit Free Press, April 17, 1992.
Detroit News, April 13, 1990.
Ebony, April 1994.
Miami Herald, April 26, 1992.
Oakland Tribune, May 3, 1992.
Philadelphia Inquirer, July 15, 1990.
Rejoice!, October 1991.
Vibe, September 1993.
Washington Post, April 5, 1992.

Additional information for this profile was obtained from Qwest Records publicity material.

—*John Morrow*

Cumulative Indexes

Cumulative Subject Index

Volume numbers appear in **bold**.

A cappella
   Bulgarian State Female Vocal Choir **10**
   Nylons, The **6**
   Take 6 **6**

Accordion
   Buckwheat Zydeco **6**
   Chenier, Clifton **6**
   Queen Ida **9**
   Richard, Zachary **9**
   Rockin' Dopsie **10**
   Simien, Terrance **12**
   Sonnier, Jo-El **10**
   Yankovic, "Weird Al" **7**

Banjo
   Clark, Roy **1**
   Crowe, J.D. **5**
   Eldridge, Ben
     See Seldom Scene, The
   Fleck, Bela **8**
     Also see New Grass Revival, The
   Hartford, John **1**
   Johnson, Courtney
     See New Grass Revival, The
   Scruggs, Earl **3**
   Seeger, Pete **4**
     Also see Weavers, The
   Skaggs, Ricky **5**
   Stanley, Ralph **5**
   Watson, Doc **2**

Bass
   Bruce, Jack
     See Cream
   Clarke, Stanley **3**
   Collins, Bootsy **8**
   Dixon, Willie **10**
   Entwistle, John
     See Who, The
   Fender, Leo **10**
   Haden, Charlie **12**
   Hill, Dusty
     See ZZ Top
   Hillman, Chris
     See Byrds, The
       Also see Desert Rose Band, The
   Johnston, Bruce
     See Beach Boys, The
   Jones, John Paul
     See Led Zeppelin
   Lake, Greg
     See Emerson, Lake & Palmer/Powell
   McCartney, Paul **4**
     Also see Beatles, The

McVie, John
   See Fleetwood Mac
Meisner, Randy
   See Eagles, The
Mingus, Charles **9**
Porter, Tiran
   See Doobie Brothers, The
Rutherford, Mike
   See Genesis
Schmit, Timothy B.
   See Eagles, The
Simmons, Gene
   See Kiss
Sting **2**
Sweet, Matthew **9**
Vicious, Sid
   See Sex Pistols, The
     Also see Siouxsie and the Banshees
Waters, Roger
   See Pink Floyd
Weymouth, Tina
   See Talking Heads
Wyman, Bill
   See Rolling Stones, The

Big Band/Swing
   Andrews Sisters, The **9**
   Arnaz, Desi **8**
   Bailey, Pearl **5**
   Basie, Count **2**
   Bennett, Tony **2**
   Berrigan, Bunny **2**
   Blakey, Art **11**
   Calloway, Cab **6**
   Carter, Benny **3**
   Clooney, Rosemary **9**
   Dorsey, Jimmy
     See Dorsey Brothers, The
   Dorsey, Tommy
     See Dorsey Brothers, The
   Dorsey Brothers, The **8**
   Eckstine, Billy **1**
   Eldridge, Roy **9**
   Ellington, Duke **2**
   Ferguson, Maynard **7**
   Fitzgerald, Ella **1**
   Fountain, Pete **7**
   Getz, Stan **12**
   Gillespie, Dizzy **6**
   Goodman, Benny **4**
   Herman, Woody **12**
   Hines, Earl "Fatha" **12**
   James, Harry **11**
   Jones, Spike **5**

Jordan, Louis **11**
Lee, Peggy **8**
Miller, Glenn **6**
Norvo, Red **12**
Parker, Charlie **5**
Roomful of Blues **7**
Severinsen, Doc **1**
Shaw, Artie **8**
Sinatra, Frank **1**
Teagarden, Jack **10**
Torme, Mel **4**
Vaughan, Sarah **2**

Bluegrass
   Auldridge, Mike **4**
   Country Gentlemen, The **7**
   Crowe, J.D. **5**
   Flatt, Lester **3**
   Fleck, Bela **8**
     Also see New Grass Revival, The
   Gill, Vince **7**
   Hartford, John **1**
   Krauss, Alison **10**
   Louvin Brothers, The **12**
   Martin, Jimmy **5**
     Also see Osborne Brothers, The
   McReynolds, Jim and Jesse **12**
   Monroe, Bill **1**
   New Grass Revival, The **4**
   O'Connor, Mark **1**
   Osborne Brothers, The **8**
   Parsons, Gram **7**
     Also see Byrds, The
   Scruggs, Earl **3**
   Seldom Scene, The **4**
   Skaggs, Ricky **5**
   Stanley, Ralph **5**
   Stuart, Marty **9**
   Watson, Doc **2**

Blues
   Bailey, Pearl **5**
   Berry, Chuck **1**
   Bland, Bobby "Blue" **12**
   Blood, Sweat and Tears **7**
   Blues Brothers, The **3**
   Brown, Clarence "Gatemouth" **11**
   Charles, Ray **1**
   Clapton, Eric **11**
     Earlier sketch in CM **1**
     Also see Cream
     Also see Yardbirds, The
   Collins, Albert **4**
   Cray, Robert **8**
   Diddley, Bo **3**

Dixon, Willie 10
Dr. John 7
Dupree, Champion Jack 12
Earl, Ronnie 5
    Also see Roomful of Blues
Fabulous Thunderbirds, The 1
Guy, Buddy 4
Handy, W. C. 7
Hawkins, Screamin' Jay 8
Healey, Jeff 4
Holiday, Billie 6
Hooker, John Lee 1
House, Son 11
Howlin' Wolf 6
James, Elmore 8
James, Etta 6
Johnson, Robert 6
Joplin, Janis 3
King, Albert 2
King, B.B. 1
Leadbelly 6
Led Zeppelin 1
Little Feat 4
Lockwood, Robert, Jr. 10
Mayall, John 7
Patton, Charley 11
Plant, Robert 2
    Also see Led Zeppelin
Professor Longhair 6
Raitt, Bonnie 3
Redding, Otis 5
Rich, Charlie 3
Robertson, Robbie 2
Robillard, Duke 2
Roomful of Blues 7
Rush, Otis 12
Smith, Bessie 3
Snow, Phoebe 4
Taj Mahal 6
Taylor, Koko 10
Vaughan, Stevie Ray 1
Waits, Tom 1
Walker, T-Bone 5
Wallace, Sippie 6
Washington, Dinah 5
Waters, Ethel 11
Waters, Muddy 4
Williams, Joe 11
Williamson, Sonny Boy 9
Winter, Johnny 5
ZZ Top 2

Cajun/Zydeco
Brown, Clarence "Gatemouth" 11
Buckwheat Zydeco 6
Chenier, Clifton 6
Doucet, Michael 8
Queen Ida 9
Richard, Zachary 9
Rockin' Dopsie 10
Simien, Terrance 12
Sonnier, Jo-El 10

Cello
Casals, Pablo 9

Gray, Walter
    See Kronos Quartet
Harrell, Lynn 3
Jeanrenaud, Joan Dutcher
    See Kronos Quartet
Ma, Yo-Yo 2

Children's Music
Chapin, Tom 11
Harley, Bill 7
Lehrer, Tom 7
Nagler, Eric 8
Penner, Fred 10
Raffi 8
Rosenshontz 9
Sharon, Lois & Bram 6

Christian Music
Grant, Amy 7
King's X 7
Patti, Sandi 7
Petra 3
Smith, Michael W. 11
Stryper 2
Waters, Ethel 11

Clarinet
Adams, John 8
Braxton, Anthony 12
Dorsey, Jimmy
    See Dorsey Brothers, The
Fountain, Pete 7
Goodman, Benny 4
Herman, Woody 12
Shaw, Artie 8

Classical
Anderson, Marian 8
Arrau, Claudio 1
Bernstein, Leonard 2
Boyd, Liona 7
Bream, Julian 9
Bronfman, Yefim 6
Canadian Brass, The 4
Casals, Pablo 9
Chang, Sarah 7
Clayderman, Richard 1
Copland, Aaron 2
Davis, Chip 4
Fiedler, Arthur 6
Galway, James 3
Gingold, Josef 6
Gould, Glenn 9
Hampson, Thomas 12
Harrell, Lynn 3
Hendricks, Barbara 10
Hinderas, Natalie 12
Horne, Marilyn 9
Horowitz, Vladimir 1
Jarrett, Keith 1
Kennedy, Nigel 8
Kissin, Evgeny 6
Kronos Quartet 5
Levine, James 8
Liberace 9
Ma, Yo-Yo 2

Marsalis, Wynton 6
Masur, Kurt 11
Mehta, Zubin 11
Menuhin, Yehudi 11
Midori 7
Ott, David 2
Parkening, Christopher 7
Perahia, Murray 10
Perlman, Itzhak 2
Phillips, Harvey 3
Rampal, Jean-Pierre 6
Rubinstein, Arthur 11
Salerno-Sonnenberg, Nadja 3
Schuman, William 10
Schickele, Peter 5
Segovia, Andres 6
Shankar, Ravi 9
Stern, Isaac 7
Takemitsu, Toru 6
Upshaw, Dawn 9
von Karajan, Herbert 1
Weill, Kurt 12
Wilson, Ransom 5
Yamashita, Kazuhito 4
Zukerman, Pinchas 4

Composers
Adams, John 8
Allen, Geri 10
Alpert, Herb 11
Anka, Paul 2
Atkins, Chet 5
Bacharach, Burt 1
Benson, George 9
Berlin, Irving 8
Bernstein, Leonard 2
Bley, Carla 8
Braxton, Anthony 12
Brubeck, Dave 8
Burrell, Kenny 11
Byrne, David 8
    Also see Talking Heads
Cage, John 8
Cale, John 9
Casals, Pablo 9
Clarke, Stanley 3
Coleman, Ornette 5
Cooder, Ry 2
Cooney, Rory 6
Copland, Aaron 2
Crouch, Andraé 9
Davis, Chip 4
Davis, Miles 1
de Grassi, Alex 6
Dorsey, Thomas A. 11
Elfman, Danny 9
Ellington, Duke 2
Eno, Brian 8
Enya 6
Gillespie, Dizzy 6
Glass, Philip 1
Gould, Glenn 9
Grusin, Dave 7
Guaraldi, Vince 3
Hamlisch, Marvin 1
Hancock, Herbie 8

Handy, W. C. 7
Hartke, Stephen 5
Hunter, Alberta 7
Jarre, Jean-Michel 2
Jarrett, Keith 1
Jones, Quincy 2
Joplin, Scott 10
Jordan, Stanley 1
Kitaro 1
Lee, Peggy 8
Lincoln, Abbey 9
Lloyd Webber, Andrew 6
Mancini, Henry 1
Marsalis, Branford 10
Masekela, Hugh 7
Menken, Alan 10
Metheny, Pat 2
Mingus, Charles 9
Monk, Meredith 1
Monk, Thelonious 6
Morton, Jelly Roll 7
Nascimento, Milton 6
Newman, Randy 4
Ott, David 2
Parker, Charlie 5
Peterson, Oscar 11
Ponty, Jean-Luc 8
Porter, Cole 10
Reich, Steve 8
Reinhardt, Django 7
Ritenour, Lee 7
Roach, Max 12
Rollins, Sonny 7
Satriani, Joe 4
Schickele, Peter 5
Schuman, William 10
Shankar, Ravi 9
Shaw, Artie 8
Shorter, Wayne 5
Solal, Martial 4
Sondheim, Stephen 8
Sousa, John Philip 10
Story, Liz 2
Summers, Andy 3
Sun Ra 5
Takemitsu, Toru 6
Talbot, John Michael 6
Taylor, Cecil 9
Threadgill, Henry 9
Tyner, McCoy 7
Washington, Grover, Jr. 5
Weill, Kurt 12
Williams, John 9
Wilson, Cassandra 12
Winston, George
Winter, Paul 10
Worrell, Bernie 11
Yanni 11
Zimmerman, Udo 5

Conductors
Bacharach, Burt 1
Bernstein, Leonard 2
Casals, Pablo 9
Copland, Aaron 2
Domingo, Placido 1

Fiedler, Arthur 6
Jarrett, Keith 1
Levine, James 8
Mancini, Henry 1
Marriner, Neville 7
Masur, Kurt 11
Mehta, Zubin 11
Menuhin, Yehudi 11
Rampal, Jean-Pierre 6
Schickele, Peter 5
von Karajan, Herbert 1
Williams, John 9
Zukerman, Pinchas 4

Contemporary Dance Music
Abdul, Paula 3
B-52's, The 4
Bee Gees, The 3
Brown, Bobby 4
Brown, James 2
Cherry, Neneh 4
Clinton, George 7
Deee-lite 9
De La Soul 7
Depeche Mode 5
Earth, Wind and Fire 12
English Beat, The 9
En Vogue 10
Erasure 11
Eurythmics 6
Exposé 4
Fox, Samantha 3
Gang of Four 8
Hammer, M.C. 5
Harry, Deborah 4
Ice-T 7
Idol, Billy 3
Jackson, Janet 3
Jackson, Michael 1
James, Rick 2
Jones, Grace 9
Madonna 4
New Order 11
Pet Shop Boys 5
Prince 1
Queen Latifah 6
Rodgers, Nile 8
Salt-N-Pepa 6
Simmons, Russell 7
Summer, Donna 12
Technotronic 5
Village People, The 7
Was (Not Was) 6
Young M.C. 4

Contemporary Instrumental/New Age
Ackerman, Will 3
Clinton, George 7
Collins, Bootsy 8
Davis, Chip 4
de Grassi, Alex 6
Enya 6
Hedges, Michael 3
Jarre, Jean-Michel 2
Kitaro 1
Kronos Quartet 5

Story, Liz 2
Summers, Andy 3
Tangerine Dream 12
Winston, George 9
Winter, Paul 10
Yanni 11

Cornet
Cherry, Don 10
Handy, W. C. 7

Country
Acuff, Roy 2
Alabama 1
Anderson, John 5
Arnold, Eddy 10
Asleep at the Wheel 5
Atkins, Chet 5
Auldridge, Mike 4
Autry, Gene 12
Black, Clint 5
Bogguss, Suzy 11
Brooks, Garth 8
Brooks & Dunn 12
Brown, Clarence "Gatemouth" 11
Buffett, Jimmy 4
Byrds, The 8
Campbell, Glen 2
Carpenter, Mary-Chapin 6
Carter, Carlene 8
Carter Family, The 3
Cash, Johnny 1
Cash, June Carter 6
Cash, Rosanne 2
Clark, Roy 1
Cline, Patsy 5
Coe, David Allan 4
Cooder, Ry 2
Cowboy Junkies, The 4
Crowe, J. D. 5
Crowell, Rodney 8
Cyrus, Billy Ray 11
Daniels, Charlie 6
Denver, John 1
Desert Rose Band, The 4
Diamond Rio 11
Dickens, Little Jimmy 7
Diffie, Joe 10
Dylan, Bob 3
Flatt, Lester 3
Ford, Tennessee Ernie 3
Frizzell, Lefty 10
Gayle, Crystal 1
Gill, Vince 7
Gilley, Mickey 7
Gilmore, Jimmie Dale 11
Greenwood, Lee 12
Griffith, Nanci 3
Haggard, Merle 2
Hall, Tom T. 4
Harris, Emmylou 4
Hartford, John 1
Hay, George D. 3
Hiatt, John 8
Highway 101 4
Jackson, Alan 7

Jennings, Waylon 4
Jones, George 4
Judd, Wynonna
   See Wynonna
Judds, The 2
Kentucky Headhunters, The 5
Kristofferson, Kris 4
Lang, K. D. 4
Lawrence, Tracy 11
LeDoux, Chris 12
Lee, Brenda 5
Little Feat 4
Louvin Brothers, The 12
Loveless, Patty 5
Lovett, Lyle 5
Lynn, Loretta 2
Lynne, Shelby 5
Mandrell, Barbara 4
Mattea, Kathy 5
McEntire, Reba 11
Miller, Roger 4
Milsap, Ronnie 2
Monroe, Bill 1
Morgan, Lorrie 10
Murphey, Michael Martin 9
Murray, Anne 4
Nelson, Willie 11
   Earlier sketch in CM 1
Newton-John, Olivia 8
Nitty Gritty Dirt Band, The 6
Oak Ridge Boys, The 7
O'Connor, Mark 1
Oslin, K. T. 3
Owens, Buck 2
Parsons, Gram 7
   Also see Byrds, The
Parton, Dolly 2
Pearl, Minnie 3
Price, Ray 11
Pride, Charley 4
Rabbitt, Eddie 5
Raitt, Bonnie 3
Reeves, Jim 10
Restless Heart 12
Rich, Charlie 3
Robbins, Marty 9
Rodgers, Jimmie 3
Rogers, Kenny 1
Rogers, Roy 9
Scruggs, Earl 3
Seals, Dan 9
Skaggs, Ricky 5
Sonnier, Jo-El 10
Statler Brothers, The 8
Stevens, Ray 7
Stone, Doug 10
Strait, George 5
Stuart, Marty 9
Sweethearts of the Rodeo 12
Texas Tornados, The 8
Tillis, Mel 7
Tillis, Pam 8
Tippin, Aaron 12
Travis, Randy 9
Tritt, Travis 7
Tubb, Ernest 4
Tucker, Tanya 3
Twitty, Conway 6
Van Shelton, Ricky 5
Watson, Doc 2
Wells, Kitty 6
West, Dottie 8
Whitley, Keith 7
Williams, Don 4
Williams, Hank, Jr. 1
Williams, Hank, Sr. 4
Willis, Kelly 12
Wills, Bob 6
Wynette, Tammy 2
Wynonna 11
   Also see Judds, The
Yearwood, Trisha 10
Yoakam, Dwight 1
Young, Faron 7

Dobro
   Auldridge, Mike 4
      Also see Country Gentlemen, The
      Also see Seldom Scene, The
   Burch, Curtis
      See New Grass Revival, The
   Knopfler, Mark 3

Drums
   See Percussion

Dulcimer
   Ritchie, Jean 4

Fiddle
   See Violin

Film Scores
   Anka, Paul 2
   Bacharach, Burt 1
   Berlin, Irving 8
   Bernstein, Leonard 2
   Byrne, David 8
      Also see Talking Heads
   Cafferty, John
      See Beaver Brown Band, The
   Cahn, Sammy 11
   Cliff, Jimmy 8
   Copland, Aaron 2
   Crouch, Andraé 9
   Dolby, Thomas 10
   Donovan 9
   Eddy, Duane 9
   Elfman, Danny 9
   Ellington, Duke 2
   Ferguson, Maynard 7
   Gershwin, George and Ira 11
   Gould, Glenn 9
   Grusin, Dave 7
   Guaraldi, Vince 3
   Hamlisch, Marvin 1
   Hancock, Herbie 8
   Harrison, George 2
   Hayes, Isaac 10
   Hedges, Michael 3
   Jones, Quincy 2
   Knopfler, Mark 3

Lennon, John 9
   Also see Beatles, The
Mancini, Henry 1
Marsalis, Branford 10
Mayfield, Curtis 8
McCartney, Paul 4
   Also see Beatles, The
Menken, Alan 10
Metheny, Pat 2
Nascimento, Milton 6
Nilsson 10
Peterson, Oscar 11
Porter, Cole 10
Richie, Lionel 2
Robertson, Robbie 2
Rollins, Sonny 7
Sager, Carole Bayer 5
Schickele, Peter 5
Shankar, Ravi 9
Taj Mahal 6
Waits, Tom 12
   Earlier sketch in CM 1
Weill, Kurt 12
Williams, John 9
Williams, Paul 5
Willner, Hal 10
Young, Neil 2

Flute
   Anderson, Ian
      See Jethro Tull
   Galway, James 3
   Rampal, Jean-Pierre 6
   Wilson, Ransom 5

Folk/Traditional
   Arnaz, Desi 8
   Baez, Joan 1
   Belafonte, Harry 8
   Blades, Ruben 2
   Brady, Paul 8
   Bragg, Billy 7
   Bulgarian State Female Vocal Choir 10
   Byrds, The 8
   Carter Family, The 3
   Chapin, Harry 6
   Chapman, Tracy 4
   Cherry, Don 10
   Chieftains, The 7
   Childs, Toni 2
   Clegg, Johnny 8
   Cockburn, Bruce 8
   Cohen, Leonard 3
   Collins, Judy 4
   Colvin, Shawn 11
   Crosby, David 3
      Also see Byrds, The
   Cruz, Celia 10
   de Lucia, Paco 1
   Donovan 9
   Dr. John 7
   Dylan, Bob 3
   Elliot, Cass 5
   Enya 6

Estefan, Gloria 2
Feliciano, José 10
Galway, James 3
Gilmore, Jimmie Dale 11
Gipsy Kings, The 8
Griffith, Nanci 3
Guthrie, Arlo 6
Guthrie, Woodie 2
Harding, John Wesley 6
Hartford, John 1
Havens, Richie 11
Iglesias, Julio 2
Indigo Girls 3
Ives, Burl 12
Kingston Trio, The 9
Kuti, Fela 7
Ladysmith Black Mambazo 1
Larkin, Patty 9
Lavin, Christine 6
Leadbelly 6
Lightfoot, Gordon 3
Los Lobos 2
Makeba, Miriam 8
Masekela, Hugh 7
McLean, Don 7
Melanie 12
Mitchell, Joni 2
Morrison, Van 3
Morrissey, Bill 12
Nascimento, Milton 6
N'Dour, Youssou 6
Near, Holly 1
Ochs, Phil 7
O'Connor, Sinead 3
Odetta 7
Parsons, Gram 7
    Also see Byrds, The
Paxton, Tom 5
Peter, Paul & Mary 4
Pogues, The 6
Prine, John 7
Redpath, Jean 1
Ritchie, Jean, 4
Rodgers, Jimmie 3
Sainte-Marie, Buffy 11
Santana, Carlos 1
Seeger, Pete 4
    Also see Weavers, The
Shankar, Ravi 9
Simon, Paul 1
Snow, Pheobe 4
Sweet Honey in the Rock 1
Taj Mahal 6
Thompson, Richard 7
Tikaram, Tanita 9
Van Ronk, Dave 12
Vega, Suzanne 3
Wainwright III, Loudon 11
Watson, Doc 2
Weavers, The 8

French Horn
    Ohanian, David
        See Canadian Brass, The

Funk
    Brown, James 2
    Clinton, George 7
    Collins, Bootsy 8
    Fishbone 7
    Gang of Four 8
    Jackson, Janet 3
    Khan, Chaka 9
    Mayfield, Curtis 8
    Parker, Maceo 7
    Prince 1
    Red Hot Chili Peppers, The 7
    Stone, Sly 8
    Toussaint, Allen 11
    Worrell, Bernie 11

Fusion
    Anderson, Ray 7
    Beck, Jeff 4
        Also see Yardbirds, The
    Clarke, Stanley 3
    Coleman, Ornette 5
    Corea, Chick 6
    Davis, Miles 1
    Fishbone 7
    Hancock, Herbie 8
    McLaughlin, John 12
    Metheny, Pat 2
    O'Connor, Mark 1
    Ponty, Jean-Luc 8
    Reid, Vernon 2
    Ritenour, Lee 7
    Shorter, Wayne 5
    Summers, Andy 3
    Washington, Grover, Jr. 5

Gospel
    Anderson, Marian 8
    Brown, James 2
    Carter Family, The 3
    Charles, Ray 1
    Cleveland, James 1
    Cooke, Sam 1
        Also see Soul Stirrers, The
    Crouch, Andraé 9
    Dorsey, Thomas A. 11
    Five Blind Boys of Alabama 12
    Ford, Tennessee Ernie 3
    Franklin, Aretha 2
    Green, Al 9
    Houston, Cissy 6
    Jackson, Mahalia 8
    Knight, Gladys 1
    Little Richard 1
    Louvin Brothers, The 12
    Oak Ridge Boys, The 7
    Pickett, Wilson 10
    Presley, Elvis 1
    Redding, Otis 5
    Robbins, Marty 9
    Smith, Michael W. 11
    Soul Stirrers, The 11
    Staples, Pops 11
    Take 6 6

Waters, Ethel 11
Watson, Doc 2
Williams, Deniece 1
Winans, The 12
Womack, Bobby 5

Guitar
    Ackerman, Will 3
    Allman, Duane
        See Allman Brothers, The
    Atkins, Chet 5
    Autry, Gene 12
    Baxter, Jeff
        See Doobie Brothers, The
    Beck, Jeff 4
        Also see Yardbirds, The
    Belew, Adrian 5
    Benson, George 9
    Berry, Chuck 1
    Bettencourt, Nuno
        See Extreme
    Betts, Dicky
        See Allman Brothers, The
    Boyd, Liona 7
    Bream, Julian 9
    Buck, Peter
        See R.E.M.
    Buckingham, Lindsey 8
        Also see Fleetwood Mac
    Burrell, Kenny 11
    Campbell, Glen 2
    Christian, Charlie 11
    Clapton, Eric 11
        Earlier sketch in CM 1
        Also see Cream
        Also see Yardbirds, The
    Clark, Roy 1
    Cockburn, Bruce 8
    Collins, Albert 4
    Cooder, Ry 2
    Cray, Robert 8
    Cropper, Steve 12
    Daniels, Charlie 6
    de Grassi, Alex 6
    de Lucia, Paco 1
    Dickens, Little Jimmy 7
    Diddley, Bo 3
    Di Meola, Al 12
    Earl, Ronnie 5
        Also see Roomful of Blues
    Eddy, Duane 9
    Edge, The
        See U2
    Feliciano, José 10
    Fender, Leo 10
    Flatt, Lester 3
    Ford, Lita 9
    Frampton, Peter 3
    Frehley, Ace
        See Kiss
    Fripp, Robert 9
    Garcia, Jerry 4
    George, Lowell
        See Little Feat

Gibbons, Billy
    See ZZ Top
Gilmour, David
    See Pink Floyd
Gill, Vince 7
Green, Peter
    See Fleetwood Mac
Guy, Buddy 4
Haley, Bill 6
Harrison, George 2
Hatfield, Juliana 12
    Also see Lemonheads, The
Havens, Richie 11
Healey, Jeff 4
Hedges, Michael 3
Hendrix, Jimi 2
Hillman, Chris
    See Byrds, The
    Also see Desert Rose Band, The
Hitchcock, Robyn 9
Holly, Buddy 1
Hooker, John Lee 1
Howlin' Wolf 6
Iommi, Tony
    See Black Sabbath
Ives, Burl 12
James, Elmore 8
Jardine, Al
    See Beach Boys, The
Johnson, Robert 6
Jones, Brian
    See Rolling Stones, The
Jordan, Stanley 1
Kantner, Paul
    See Jefferson Airplane
King, Albert 2
King, B. B. 1
Klugh, Earl 10
Knopfler, Mark 3
Larkin, Patty 9
Leadbelly 6
Lennon, John 9
    Also see Beatles, The
Lindley, David 2
Lockwood, Robert, Jr. 10
Marr, Johnny
    See Smiths, The
May, Brian
    See Queen
Mayfield, Curtis 8
McGuinn, Roger
    See Byrds, The
McLachlan, Sarah 12
McLaughlin, John 12
McReynolds, Jim
    See McReynolds, Jim and Jesse
Metheny, Pat 2
Montgomery, Wes 3
Morrissey, Bill 12
Nugent, Ted 2
Owens, Buck 2
Page, Jimmy 4
    Also see Led Zeppelin
    Also see Yardbirds, The
Parkening, Christopher 7
Patton, Charley 11

Perkins, Carl 9
Perry, Joe
    See Aerosmith
Petty, Tom 9
Phillips, Sam 12
Prince 1
Raitt, Bonnie 3
Ray, Amy
    See Indigo Girls
Reid, Vernon 2
    Also see Living Colour
Reinhardt, Django 7
Richards, Keith 11
    Also see Rolling Stones, The
Richman, Jonathan 12
Ritenour, Lee 7
Robbins, Marty 9
Robertson, Robbie 2
Robillard, Duke 2
Rodgers, Nile 8
Rush, Otis 12
Santana, Carlos 1
Saliers, Emily
    See Indigo Girls
Satriani, Joe 4
Scofield, John 7
Segovia, Andres 6
Skaggs, Ricky 5
Slash
    See Guns n' Roses
Springsteen, Bruce 6
Stewart, Dave
    See Eurythmics
Stills, Stephen 5
Stuart, Marty 9
Summers, Andy 3
Taylor, Mick
    See Rolling Stones, The
Thompson, Richard 7
Tippin, Aaron 12
Townshend, Pete 1
Tubb, Ernest 4
Vai, Steve 5
Van Halen, Edward
    See Van Halen
Van Ronk, Dave 12
Vaughan, Jimmie
    See Fabulous Thunderbirds, The
Vaughan, Stevie Ray 1
Waits, Tom 12
    Earlier sketch in CM 1
Walker, T-Bone 5
Walsh, Joe 5
    Also see Eagles, The
Watson, Doc 2
Weir, Bob
    See Grateful Dead, The
Wilson, Nancy
    See Heart
Winston, George 9
Winter, Johnny 5
Yamashita, Kazuhito 4
Yarrow, Peter
    See Peter, Paul & Mary
Young, Angus
    See AC/DC

Young, Malcolm
    See AC/DC
Young, Neil 2
Zappa, Frank 1

Harmonica

Dylan, Bob 3
Guthrie, Woodie 2
Lewis, Huey 9
Waters, Muddy 4
Williamson, Sonny Boy 9
Wilson, Kim
    See Fabulous Thunderbirds, The

Heavy Metal

AC/DC 4
Aerosmith 3
Alice in Chains 10
Anthrax 11
Black Sabbath 9
Danzig 7
Deep Purple 11
Def Leppard 3
Faith No More 7
Fishbone 7
Ford, Lita 9
Guns n' Roses 2
Iron Maiden 10
Judas Priest 10
King's X 7
L7 12
Led Zeppelin 1
Megadeth 9
Metallica 7
Mötley Crüe 1
Motörhead 10
Nugent, Ted 2
Osbourne, Ozzy 3
Petra 3
Queensryche 8
Reid, Vernon 2
    Also see Living Colour
Roth, David Lee 1
    Also see Van Halen
Sepultura 12
Slayer 10
Soundgarden 6
Spinal Tap 8
Stryper 2
Whitesnake 5

Humor

Coasters, The 5
Jones, Spike 5
Lehrer, Tom 7
Pearl, Minnie 3
Russell, Mark 6
Schickele, Peter 5
Spinal Tap 8
Stevens, Ray 7
Yankovic, "Weird Al" 7

Inventors

Fender, Leo 10
Paul, Les 2

Scholz, Tom
   See Boston
Teagarden, Jack 10

Jazz
Allen, Geri 10
Anderson, Ray 7
Armstrong, Louis 4
Bailey, Pearl 5
Baker, Anita 9
Basie, Count 2
Belle, Regina 6
Benson, George 9
Berigan, Bunny 2
Blakey, Art 11
Bley, Carla 8
Blood, Sweat and Tears 7
Braxton, Anthony 12
Brubeck, Dave 8
Burrell, Kenny 11
Burton, Gary 10
Calloway, Cab 6
Canadian Brass, The 4
Carter, Benny 3
Carter, Betty 6
Charles, Ray 1
Cherry, Don 10
Christian, Charlie 11
Clarke, Stanley 3
Clooney, Rosemary 9
Cole, Nat King 3
Coleman, Ornette 5
Coltrane, John 4
Connick, Harry, Jr. 4
Corea, Chick 6
Davis, Miles 1
DeJohnette, Jack 7
Di Meola, Al 12
Eckstine, Billy 1
Eldridge, Roy 9
Ellington, Duke 2
Ferguson, Maynard 7
Fitzgerald, Ella 1
Fleck, Bela 8
   Also see New Grass Revival, The
Fountain, Pete 7
Galway, James 3
Getz, Stan 12
Gillespie, Dizzy 6
Goodman, Benny 4
Gordon, Dexter 10
Grappelli, Stephane 10
Guaraldi, Vince 3
Haden, Charlie 12
Hampton, Lionel 6
Hancock, Herbie 8
Hawkins, Coleman 11
Hedges, Michael 3
Herman, Woody 12
Hines, Earl "Fatha" 12
Hirt, Al 5
Holiday, Billie 6
Horn, Shirley 7
Horne, Lena 11
Hunter, Alberta 7
James, Harry 11
Jarreau, Al 1
Jarrett, Keith 1
Jones, Elvin
Jones, Quincy 2
Jordan, Stanley 1
Kennedy, Nigel 8
Kirk, Rahsaan Roland 6
Kitt, Eartha 9
Klugh, Earl 10
Kronos Quartet 5
Laine, Cleo 10
Lee, Peggy 8
Lincoln, Abbey 9
Mancini, Henry 1
Manhattan Transfer, The 8
Marsalis, Branford 10
Marsalis, Wynton 6
Masekela, Hugh 7
McFerrin, Bobby 3
McLaughlin, John 12
McRae, Carmen 9
Metheny, Pat 2
Mingus, Charles 9
Monk, Thelonious 6
Montgomery, Wes 3
Morgan, Frank 9
Morton, Jelly Roll 7
Nascimento, Milton 6
Norvo, Red 12
Parker, Charlie 5
Parker, Maceo 7
Paul, Les 2
Peterson, Oscar 11
Ponty, Jean-Luc 8
Professor Longhair 6
Rampal, Jean-Pierre 6
Redman, Joshua 12
Reid, Vernon 2
   Also see Living Colour
Reinhardt, Django 7
Roach, Max 12
Roberts, Marcus 6
Robillard, Duke 2
Rollins, Sonny 7
Sanborn, David 1
Santana, Carlos 1
Schuur, Diane 6
Scofield, John 7
Severinsen, Doc 1
Shaw, Artie 8
Shorter, Wayne 5
Simone, Nina 11
Solal, Martial 4
Summers, Andy 3
Sun Ra 5
Take 6 6
Taylor, Cecil 9
Teagarden, Jack 10
Threadgill, Henry 9
Torme, Mel 4
Tucker, Sophie 12
Turtle Island String Quartet 9
Tyner, McCoy 7
Vaughan, Sarah 2
Walker, T-Bone 5
Washington, Dinah 5
Washington, Grover, Jr. 5
Williams, Joe 11
Wilson, Cassandra 12
Winter, Paul 10

Keyboards, Electric
Corea, Chick 6
Davis, Chip 4
Dolby, Thomas 10
Emerson, Keith
   See Emerson, Lake & Palmer/Powell
Eno, Brian 8
Hancock, Herbie 8
Jackson, Joe 4
Jarre, Jean-Michel 2
Jones, Booker T. 8
Kitaro 1
Manzarek, Ray
   See Doors, The
McDonald, Michael
   See Doobie Brothers, The
McVie, Christine
   See Fleetwood Mac
Pierson, Kate
   See B-52's, The
Sun Ra 5
Waller, Fats 7
Wilson, Brian
   See Beach Boys, The
Winwood, Steve 2
Wonder, Stevie 2
Worrell, Bernie 11
Yanni 11

Liturgical Music
Cooney, Rory 6
Talbot, John Michael 6

Mandolin
Bush, Sam
   See New Grass Revival, The
Duffey, John
   See Seldom Scene, The
Hartford, John 1
Lindley, David 2
McReynolds, Jesse
   See McReynolds, Jim and Jesse
Monroe, Bill 1
Rosas, Cesar
   See Los Lobos
Skaggs, Ricky 5
Stuart, Marty 9

Musicals
Allen, Debbie 8
Allen, Peter 11
Andrews, Julie 4
Andrews Sisters, The 9
Bacharach, Burt 1
Bailey, Pearl 5
Baker, Josephine 10
Berlin, Irving 8
Buckley, Betty 1
Burnett, Carol 6
Carter, Nell 7
Channing, Carol 6

Chevalier, Maurice 6
Crawford, Michael 4
Crosby, Bing 6
Curry, Tim 3
Davis, Sammy, Jr. 4
Garland, Judy 6
Gershwin, George and Ira 11
Hamlisch, Marvin 1
Horne, Lena 11
Jolson, Al 10
Laine, Cleo 10
Lloyd Webber, Andrew 6
LuPone, Patti 8
Masekela, Hugh 7
Menken, Alan 10
Moore, Melba 7
Patinkin, Mandy 3
Peters, Bernadette 7
Porter, Cole 10
Robeson, Paul 8
Rodgers, Richard 9
Sager, Carole Bayer 5
Sondheim, Stephen 8
Waters, Ethel 11
Weill, Kurt 12

Opera

Adams, John 8
Anderson, Marian 8
Bartoli, Cecilia 12
Battle, Kathleen 6
Callas, Maria 11
Carreras, José 8
Caruso, Enrico 10
Cotrubas, Ileana 1
Domingo, Placido 1
Gershwin, George and Ira 11
Hampson, Thomas 12
Hendricks, Barbara 10
Horne, Marilyn 9
Norman, Jessye 7
Pavarotti, Luciano 1
Price, Leontyne 6
Sills, Beverly 5
Te Kanawa, Kiri 2
Upshaw, Dawn 9
von Karajan, Herbert 1
Weill, Kurt 12
Zimmerman, Udo 5

Percussion

Baker, Ginger
  See Cream
Blakey, Art 11
Bonham, John
  See Led Zeppelin
Burton, Gary 10
Collins, Phil 2
  Also see Genesis
DeJohnette, Jack 7
Densmore, John
  See Doors, The
Dunbar, Aynsley
  See Jefferson Starship
  Also See Whitesnake

Fleetwood, Mick
  See Fleetwood Mac
Hampton, Lionel 6
Hart, Mickey
  See Grateful Dead, The
Henley, Don 3
Jones, Elvin
Jones, Kenny
  See Who, The
Jones, Spike 5
Kreutzman, Bill
  See Grateful Dead, The
Mason, Nick
  See Pink Floyd
Moon, Keith
  See Who, The
N'Dour, Youssou 6
Palmer, Carl
  See Emerson, Lake & Palmer/Powell
Peart, Neil
  See Rush
Powell, Cozy
  See Emerson, Lake & Palmer/Powell
Roach, Max 12
Sheila E. 3
Starr, Ringo 10
  Also see Beatles, The
Watts, Charlie
  See Rolling Stones, The

Piano

Allen, Gerri 10
Amos, Tori 12
Arrau, Claudio 1
Bacharach, Burt 1
Basie, Count 2
Berlin, Irving 8
Bley, Carla 8
Bronfman, Yefim 6
Brubeck, Dave 8
Bush, Kate 4
Charles, Ray 1
Clayderman, Richard 1
Cleveland, James 1
Cole, Nat King 3
Collins, Judy 4
Collins, Phil 2
  Also see Genesis
Connick, Harry, Jr. 4
Crouch, Andraé 9
DeJohnette, Jack 7
Domino, Fats 2
Dr. John 7
Dupree, Champion Jack 12
Ellington, Duke 2
Feinstein, Michael 6
Flack, Roberta 5
Frey, Glenn 3
Glass, Philip 1
Gould, Glenn 9
Grusin, Dave 7
Guaraldi, Vince 3
Hamlisch, Marvin 1
Hancock, Herbie 8
Hinderas, Natalie 12
Hines, Earl "Fatha" 12

Horn, Shirley 7
Hornsby, Bruce 3
Horowitz, Vladimir 1
Jackson, Joe 4
Jarrett, Keith 1
Joel, Billy 12
  Earlier sketch in CM 2
John, Elton 3
Joplin, Scott 10
Kissin, Evgeny 6
Levine, James 8
Lewis, Jerry Lee 2
Liberace 9
Little Richard 1
Manilow, Barry 2
McDonald, Michael
  See Doobie Brothers, The
McRae, Carmen 9
McVie, Christine
  See Fleetwood Mac
Milsap, Ronnie 2
Mingus, Charles 9
Monk, Thelonious 6
Morton, Jelly Roll 7
Newman, Randy 4
Perahia, Murray 10
Peterson, Oscar 11
Professor Longhair 6
Rich, Charlie 3
Roberts, Marcus 6
Rubinstein, Arthur 11
Russell, Mark 6
Schickele, Peter 5
Sedaka, Neil 4
Solal, Martial 4
Story, Liz 2
Taylor, Cecil 9
Tyner, McCoy 7
Waits, Tom 12
  Earlier sketch in 1
Waller, Fats 7
Wilson, Cassandra 12
Winston, George 9
Winwood, Steve 2
Wonder, Stevie 2
Wright, Rick
  See Pink Floyd

Piccolo

Galway, James 3

Pop

Abba 12
Abdul, Paula 3
Adams, Bryan 2
Alpert, Herb 11
Amos, Tori 12
Andrews Sisters, The 9
Armatrading, Joan 4
Arnold, Eddy 10
Astley, Rick 5
Atkins, Chet 5
Avalon, Frankie 5
B-52's, The 4
Bacharach, Burt 1

Bailey, Pearl 5
Basia 5
Beach Boys, The 1
Beatles, The 2
Beaver Brown Band, The 3
Bee Gees, The 3
Bennett, Tony 2
Benson, George 9
Benton, Brook 7
Blood, Sweat and Tears 7
BoDeans, The 3
Bolton, Michael 4
Boston 11
Bowie, David 1
Bragg, Billy 7
Branigan, Laura 2
Brickell, Edie 3
Brooks, Garth 8
Brown, Bobby 4
Browne, Jackson 3
Bryson, Peabo 11
Buckingham, Lindsey 8
   Also see Fleetwood Mac
Buffett, Jimmy 4
Campbell, Glen 2
Carey, Mariah 6
Carlisle, Belinda 8
Carnes, Kim 4
Chapin, Harry 6
Chapman, Tracy 4
Charles, Ray 1
Checker, Chubby 7
Cher 1
Cherry, Neneh 4
Chicago 3
Chilton, Alex 10
Clapton, Eric 11
   Earlier sketch in CM 1
   Also see Cream
   Also see Yardbirds, The
Clayderman, Richard 1
Clooney, Rosemary 9
Coasters, The 5
Cocker, Joe 4
Cocteau Twins, The 12
Cole, Lloyd 9
Cole, Natalie 1
Cole, Nat King 3
Collins, Judy 4
Collins, Phil 2
Colvin, Shawn 11
Connick, Harry, Jr. 4
Cooke, Sam 1
   Also see Soul Stirrers, The
Costello, Elvis 12
   Earlier sketch in CM 2
Crenshaw, Marshall 5
Croce, Jim 3
Crosby, David 3
   Also see Byrds, The
Crowded House 12
Daltrey, Roger 3
   Also see Who, The
D'Arby, Terence Trent 3
Darin, Bobby 4
Dave Clark Five, The 12

Davies, Ray 5
Davis, Sammy, Jr. 4
Dayne, Taylor 4
Denver, John 1
Depeche Mode 5
Diamond, Neil 1
Dion, Céline 12
Dion 4
Donovan 9
Doobie Brothers, The 3
Doors, The 4
Duran Duran 4
Dylan, Bob 3
Eagles, The 3
Earth, Wind and Fire 12
Easton, Sheena 2
Edmonds, Kenneth "Babyface" 12
Electric Light Orchestra 7
Elfman, Danny 9
Elliot, Cass 5
En Vogue 10
Estefan, Gloria 2
Eurythmics 6
Everly Brothers, The 2
Exposé 4
Fabian 5
Feliciano, José 10
Ferguson, Maynard 7
Ferry, Bryan 1
Fiedler, Arthur 6
Fisher, Eddie 12
Fitzgerald, Ella 1
Flack, Roberta 5
Fleetwood Mac 5
Fogelberg, Dan 4
Four Tops, The 11
Fox, Samantha 3
Frampton, Peter 3
Francis, Connie 10
Franklin, Aretha 2
Frey, Glenn 3
   Also see Eagles, The
Garfunkel, Art 4
Gaye, Marvin 4
Gayle, Crystal 1
Geldof, Bob 9
Genesis 4
Gershwin, George and Ira 11
Gibson, Debbie 1
Gift, Roland 3
Goodman, Benny 4
Gordy, Berry, Jr. 6
Grant, Amy 7
Grebenshikov, Boris 3
Green, Al 9
Guthrie, Arlo 6
Hall & Oates 6
Hammer, M.C. 5
Hancock, Herbie 8
Harding, John Wesley 6
Harrison, George 2
   Also see Beatles, The
Harry, Deborah 4
Healey, Jeff 4
Henley, Don 3
   Also see Eagles, The

Herman's Hermits 5
Hitchcock, Robyn 9
Holland-Dozier-Holland 5
Horne, Lena 11
Hornsby, Bruce 3
Houston, Whitney 8
Ian, Janis 5
Idol, Billy 3
Iglesias, Julio 2
Indigo Girls 3
Ingram, James 11
Isaak, Chris 6
Isley Brothers, The 8
Jackson, Janet 3
Jackson, Joe 4
Jackson, Michael 1
Jacksons, The 7
Jam, Jimmy, and Terry Lewis 11
James 12
James, Harry 11
James, Rick 2
Jarreau, Al 1
Jefferson Airplane 5
Joel, Billy 12
   Earlier sketch in CM 2
John, Elton 3
Johansen, David 7
Jolson, Al 10
Jones, Quincy 2
Jones, Rickie Lee 4
Jones, Tom 11
Joplin, Janis 3
Khan, Chaka 9
King, Ben E. 7
King, Carole 6
Kiss 5
Kitt, Eartha 9
Knight, Gladys 1
Knopfler, Mark 3
Kraftwerk 9
Kristofferson, Kris 4
LaBelle, Patti 8
Lauper, Cyndi 11
Lee, Brenda 5
Lennon, John 9
   Also see Beatles, The
Lennon, Julian 2
Lewis, Huey 9
Liberace 9
Lightfoot, Gordon 3
Loggins, Kenny 3
Lovett, Lyle 5
Lowe, Nick 6
Lynne, Jeff 5
MacColl, Kirsty 12
Madonna 4
Mancini, Henry 1
Manhattan Transfer, The 8
Manilow, Barry 2
Marley, Bob 3
Marley, Ziggy 3
Marsalis, Branford 10
Martin, Dean 1
Martin, George 6
Marx, Richard 3
Mathis, Johnny 2

Cumulative Subject Index • **297**

McCartney, Paul 4
   Also see Beatles, The
McFerrin, Bobby 3
McLachlan, Sarah 12
McLean, Don 7
Medley, Bill 3
Melanie 12
Michael, George 9
Midler, Bette 8
Miller, Mitch 11
Miller, Roger 4
Milli Vanilli 4
Mitchell, Joni 2
Monkees, The 7
Montand, Yves 12
Morrison, Jim 3
Morrison, Van 3
Morrissey 10
Mouskouri, Nana 12
Moyet, Alison 12
Murray, Anne 4
Myles, Alannah 4
Neville, Aaron 5
   Also see Neville Brothers, The
Neville Brothers, The 4
New Kids on the Block 3
Newman, Randy 4
Newton, Wayne 2
Newton-John, Olivia 8
Nicks, Stevie 2
Nilsson 10
Nitty Gritty Dirt Band 6
Nyro, Laura 12
Oak Ridge Boys, The 7
Ocasek, Ric 5
Ocean, Billy 4
O'Connor, Sinead 3
Osmond, Donny 3
Page, Jimmy 4
   Also see Led Zeppelin
   Also see Yardbirds, The
Page, Patti 11
Parsons, Alan 12
Parton, Dolly 2
Pendergrass, Teddy 3
Penn, Michael 4
Pet Shop Boys 5
Peter, Paul & Mary 4
Phillips, Sam 12
Piaf, Edith 8
Plant, Robert 2
   Also see Led Zeppelin
Pointer Sisters, The 9
Porter, Cole 10
Presley, Elvis 1
Prince 1
Queen 6
Rabbitt, Eddie 5
Raitt, Bonnie 3
Rea, Chris 12
Redding, Otis 5
Reddy, Helen 9
Reeves, Martha 4
R.E.M. 5
Richie, Lionel 2
Robbins, Marty 9

Robinson, Smokey 1
Rogers, Kenny 1
Rolling Stones 3
Ronstadt, Linda 2
Ross, Diana 1
Roth, David Lee 1
   Also see Van Halen
Ruffin, David 6
Sade 2
Sager, Carole Bayer 5
Sainte-Marie, Buffy 11
Sanborn, David 1
Seals & Crofts 3
Seals, Dan 9
Sedaka, Neil 4
Sheila E. 3
Shirelles, The 11
Siberry, Jane 6
Simon, Carly 4
Simon, Paul 1
Sinatra, Frank 1
Smiths, The 3
Snow, Pheobe 4
Spector, Phil 4
Springfield, Rick 9
Springsteen, Bruce 6
Squeeze 5
Stansfield, Lisa 9
Starr, Ringo 10
Steely Dan 5
Stevens, Cat 3
Stewart, Rod 2
Stills, Stephen 5
Sting 2
Streisand, Barbra 2
Summer, Donna 12
Supremes, The 6
Sweet, Matthew 9
Talking Heads 1
Taylor, James 2
Tears for Fears 6
Temptations, The 3
10,000 Maniacs 3
They Might Be Giants 7
Three Dog Night 5
Tiffany 4
Tikaram, Tanita 9
Timbuk 3 3
Tony! Toni! Toné! 12
Torme, Mel 4
Townshend, Pete 1
   Also see Who, The
Turner, Tina 1
Valli, Frankie 10
Vandross, Luther 2
Vega, Suzanne 3
Vinton, Bobby 12
Walsh, Joe 5
Warnes, Jennifer 3
Warwick, Dionne 2
Was (Not Was) 6
Washington, Dinah 5
Watley, Jody 9
Webb, Jimmy 12
Who, The 3

Williams, Andy 2
Williams, Deniece 1
Williams, Joe 11
Williams, Lucinda 10
Williams, Paul 5
Williams, Vanessa 10
Wilson, Jackie 3
Wilson Phillips 5
Winwood, Steve 2
Womack, Bobby 5
Wonder, Stevie 2
"Weird Al" Yankovic 7
XTC 10
Young M.C. 4
Young, Neil 2

Producers
Ackerman, Will 3
Alpert, Herb 11
Baker, Anita 9
Bogaert, Jo
   See Technotronic
Browne, Jackson 3
Cale, John 9
Clarke, Stanley 3
Clinton, George 7
Collins, Phil 2
Costello, Elvis 2
Cropper, Steve 12
Crowell, Rodney 8
Dixon, Willie 10
Dolby, Thomas 10
Dozier, Lamont
   See Holland-Dozier-Holland
Edmonds, Kenneth "Babyface" 12
Eno, Brian 8
Ertegun, Ahmet 10
Fripp, Robert 9
Grusin, Dave 7
Holland, Brian
   See Holland-Dozier-Holland
Holland, Eddie
   See Holland-Dozier-Holland
Jam, Jimmy, and Terry Lewis 11
Jones, Booker T. 8
Jones, Quincy 2
Jourgensen, Al
   See Ministry
Lanois, Daniel 8
Lynne, Jeff 5
Marley, Rita 10
Martin, George 6
Mayfield, Curtis 8
Miller, Mitch 11
Parsons, Alan 12
Prince 1
Robertson, Robbie 2
Rodgers, Nile 8
Rubin, Rick 9
Rundgren, Todd 11
Simmons, Russell 7
Skaggs, Ricky 5
Spector, Phil 4
Toussaint, Allen 11
Vandross, Luther 2

Willner, Hal 10
Wilson, Brian
    See Beach Boys, The

Promoters
Clark, Dick 2
Geldof, Bob 9
Graham, Bill 10
Hay, George D. 3
Simmons, Russell 7

Ragtime
Joplin, Scott 10

Rap
Basehead 11
Beastie Boys, The 8
Biz Markie 10
Campbell, Luther 10
Cherry, Neneh 4
Cypress Hill 11
De La Soul 7
Digital Underground 9
DJ Jazzy Jeff and the Fresh Prince 5
EPMD 10
Eric B. and Rakim 9
Geto Boys, The 11
Hammer, M.C. 5
Heavy D 10
Ice Cube 10
Ice-T 7
Kane, Big Daddy 7
Kid 'n Play 5
Kool Moe Dee 9
Kris Kross 11
KRS-One 8
L.L. Cool J. 5
MC Lyte 8
MC Serch 10
Naughty by Nature 11
N.W.A. 6
P.M. Dawn 11
Public Enemy 4
Queen Latifah 6
Rubin, Rick 9
Run-D.M.C. 4
Salt-N-Pepa 6
Shanté 10
Simmons, Russell 7
Tone-L c 3
A Tribe Called Quest 8
Vanilla Ice 6
Young M.C. 4
Yo Yo 9

Record Company Executives
Ackerman, Will 3
Alpert, Herb 11
Busby, Jheryl 9
Davis, Chip 4
Ertegun, Ahmet 10
Geffen, David 8
Gordy, Berry, Jr. 6
Hammond, John 6
Harley, Bill 7
Jam, Jimmy, and Terry Lewis 11

Marley, Rita 10
Martin, George 6
Mayfield, Curtis 8
Miller, Mitch 11
Mingus, Charles 9
Near, Holly 1
Penner, Fred 10
Phillips, Sam 5
Robinson, Smokey 1
Rubin, Rick 9
Simmons, Russell 7
Spector, Phil 4

Reggae
Black Uhuru 12
Cliff, Jimmy 8
Marley, Bob 3
Marley, Rita 10
Marley, Ziggy 3
Tosh, Peter 3
UB40 4
Wailer, Bunny 11

Rhythm and Blues/Soul
Abdul, Paula 3
Baker, Anita 9
Basehead 11
Belle, Regina 6
Berry, Chuck 1
Bland, Bobby "Blue" 12
Blues Brothers, The 3
Bolton, Michael 4
Brown, James 2
Bryson, Peabo 11
Busby, Jheryl 9
Carey, Mariah 6
Charles, Ray 1
Cole, Natalie 1
Cooke, Sam 1
    Also see Soul Stirrers, The
Cropper, Steve 12
D'Arby, Terence Trent 3
Diddley, Bo 3
Domino, Fats 2
Dr. John 7
Earth, Wind and Fire 12
Edmonds, Kenneth "Babyface" 12
En Vogue 10
Fabulous Thunderbirds, The 1
Four Tops, The 11
Fox, Samantha 3
Franklin, Aretha 2
Gaye, Marvin 4
Gordy, Berry, Jr. 6
Green, Al 9
Hall & Oates 6
Hayes, Isaac 10
Holland-Dozier-Holland 5
Ingram, James 11
Isley Brothers, The 8
Jackson, Freddie 3
Jackson, Janet 3
Jackson, Michael 1
Jacksons, The 7
Jam, Jimmy, and Terry Lewis 11
James, Etta 6

Jones, Booker T. 8
Jones, Grace 9
Jones, Quincy 2
Jordan, Louis 11
Khan, Chaka 9
King, Ben E. 7
Knight, Gladys 1
LaBelle, Patti 8
Los Lobos 2
Mayfield, Curtis 8
Medley, Bill 3
Milli Vanilli 4
Moore, Melba 7
Morrison, Van 3
Neville, Aaron 5
    Also see Neville Brothers, The
Neville Brothers, The 4
Ocean, Billy 4
Pendergrass, Teddy 3
Pickett, Wilson 10
Pointer Sisters, The 9
Prince 1
Redding, Otis 5
Reeves, Martha 4
Richie, Lionel 2
Robinson, Smokey 1
Ross, Diana 6
    Also see Supremes, The
Ruffin, David 6
    Also see Temptations, The
Sam and Dave 8
Scaggs, Boz 12
Shirelles, The 11
Stansfield, Lisa 9
Staples, Pops 11
Stone, Sly 8
Stewart, Rod 2
Supremes, The 6
    Also see Ross, Diana
Temptations, The 3
Tony! Toni! Toné! 12
Toussaint, Allen 11
Turner, Tina 1
Vandross, Luther 2
Watley, Jody 9
Was (Not Was) 6
Williams, Deniece 1
Williams, Vanessa 10
Wilson, Jackie 3
Winans, The 12
Womack, Bobby 5
Wonder, Stevie 2

Rock
AC/DC 4
Adams, Bryan 2
Aerosmith 3
Alice in Chains 10
Allman Brothers, The 6
Anthrax 11
Band, The 9
Basehead 11
Beach Boys, The 1
Beastie Boys, The 8
Beatles, The 2
Beaver Brown Band, The 3

Beck, Jeff 4
  Also see Yardbirds, The
Belew, Adrian 5
Benatar, Pat 8
Berry, Chuck 1
Black Crowes, The 7
Black Sabbath 9
Blood, Sweat and Tears 7
BoDeans, The 3
Bon Jovi 10
Boston 11
Bowie, David 1
Bragg, Billy 7
Brickell, Edie 3
Browne, Jackson 3
Buckingham, Lindsey 8
  Also see Fleetwood Mac
Buzzcocks, The 9
Byrds, The 8
Byrne, David 8
  Also see Talking Heads
Cale, John 9
Captain Beefheart 10
Cave, Nick 10
Cheap Trick 12
Cher 1
Chicago 3
Clapton, Eric 11
  Earlier sketch in CM 1
  Also see Cream
  Also see Yardbirds, The
Clash, The 4
Clemons, Clarence 7
Clinton, George 7
Coasters, The 5
Cocker, Joe 4
Collins, Phil 2
Cooder, Ry 2
Cooke, Sam 1
  Also see Soul Stirrers, The
Cooper, Alice 8
Costello, Elvis 12
  Earlier sketch in CM 2
Cougar, John(ny)
  See Mellencamp, John "Cougar"
Cracker 12
Cream 9
Crenshaw, Marshall 5
Crosby, David 3
  Also see Byrds, The
Crowded House 12
Cure, The 3
Curry, Tim 3
Daltrey, Roger 3
  Also see Who, The
Daniels, Charlie 6
Danzig 7
D'Arby, Terence Trent 3
Dave Clark Five, The 12
Davies, Ray 5
Deep Purple 11
Def Leppard 3
Depeche Mode 5
Diddley, Bo 3
Dinosaur Jr. 10
Doobie Brothers, The 3

Doors, The 4
Duran Duran 4
Dylan, Bob 3
Eagles, The 3
Eddy, Duane 9
Electric Light Orchestra 7
Elliot, Cass 5
Emerson, Lake & Palmer/Powell 5
English Beat, The 9
Eno, Brian 8
Etheridge, Melissa 4
Eurythmics 6
Extreme 10
Faith No More 7
Fall, The 12
Ferry, Bryan 1
fIREHOSE 11
Fishbone 7
Fleetwood Mac 5
Fogelberg, Dan 4
Fogerty, John 2
Ford, Lita 9
Fox, Samantha 3
Frampton, Peter 3
Frey, Glenn 3
  Also see Eagles, The
Gabriel, Peter 2
Gang of Four 8
Garcia, Jerry 4
Genesis 4
Gift, Roland 3
Graham, Bill 10
Grateful Dead 5
Grebenshikov, Boris 3
Guns n' Roses 2
Hall & Oates 6
Harrison, George 2
  Also see Beatles, The
Harry, Deborah 4
Harvey, Polly Jean 11
Hatfield, Juliana 12
  Also see Lemonheads, The
Healey, Jeff 4
Hendrix, Jimi 2
Henley, Don 3
  Also see Eagles, The
Hiatt, John 8
Holland-Dozier-Holland 5
Idol, Billy 3
INXS 2
Iron Maiden 10
Isaak, Chris 6
Jackson, Joe 4
Jagger, Mick 7
  Also see Rolling Stones, The
Jane's Addiction 6
Jefferson Airplane 5
Jesus and Mary Chain, The 10
Jethro Tull 8
Jett, Joan 3
Joel, Billy 12
  Earlier sketch in CM 2
Johansen, David 7
John, Elton 3
Joplin, Janis 3
Judas Priest 10

Kennedy, Nigel 8
Kiss 5
Knopfler, Mark 3
Kravitz, Lenny 5
L7 12
Led Zeppelin 1
Lemonheads, The 12
Lennon, John 9
  Also see Beatles, The
Lennon, Julian 2
Lindley, Dave 2
Little Feat 4
Living Colour 7
Loggins, Kenny 3
Los Lobos 2
Lydon, John 9
  Also see Sex Pistols, The
Lynne, Jeff 5
Lynyrd Skynyrd 9
Martin, George 6
Marx, Richard 3
MC5, The 9
McCartney, Paul 4
  Also see Beatles, The
McKee, Maria 11
McMurtry, James 10
Meat Loaf 12
Megadeth 9
Mellencamp, John "Cougar" 2
Metallica 7
Midnight Oil 11
Miller, Steve 2
Ministry 10
Moby Grape 12
Morrison, Jim 3
  Also see Doors, The
Morrison, Van 3
Mötley Crüe 1
Motörhead 10
Mould, Bob 10
Myles, Alannah 4
NRBQ 12
Nelson, Rick 2
Newman, Randy 4
Nicks, Stevie 2
Nirvana 8
Nugent, Ted 2
Ocasek, Ric 5
O'Connor, Sinead 3
Ono, Yoko 11
Orbison, Roy 2
Osbourne, Ozzy 3
Page, Jimmy 4
  Also see Led Zeppelin
  Also see Yardbirds, The
Palmer, Robert 2
Parker, Graham 10
Parker, Maceo 7
Parsons, Alan 12
Parsons, Gram 7
  Also see Byrds, The
Pearl Jam 12
Petty, Tom 9
Perkins, Carl 9
Phillips, Sam 5
Pink Floyd 2

Plant, Robert 2
    Also see Led Zeppelin
Pogues, The 6
Poison 11
Pop, Iggy 1
Presley, Elvis 1
Pretenders, The 8
Primus 11
Prince 1
Prine, John 7
Queen 6
Queensryche 8
Raitt, Bonnie 3
Ramones, The 9
Red Hot Chili Peppers, The 7
Reed, Lou 1
    Also see Velvet Underground, The
Reid, Vernon 2
    Also see Living Colour
R.E.M. 5
Replacements, The 7
Richards, Keith 11
    Also see Rolling Stones, The
Richman, Jonathan 12
Robertson, Robbie 2
Rolling Stones, The 3
Rollins, Henry 11
Roth, David Lee 1
    Also see Van Halen
Rubin, Rick 9
Rundgren, Todd 11
Rush 8
Ryder, Mitch 11
Satriani, Joe 4
Scaggs, Boz 12
Scorpions, The 12
Sepultura 12
Sex Pistols, The 5
Shannon, Del 10
Shocked, Michelle 4
Simon, Carly 4
Simon, Paul 1
Siouxsie and the Banshees 8
Slayer 10
Smith, Patti 1
Smiths, The 3
Sonic Youth 9
Soul Asylum 10
Soundgarden 6
Spector, Phil 4
Spinal Tap 8
Springsteen, Bruce 6
Squeeze 5
Starr, Ringo 10
Steely Dan 5
Stevens, Cat 3
Stewart, Rod 2
Stills, Stephen 5
Sting 2
Stone, Sly 8
Stray Cats, The 11
Stryper 2
Sugarcubes, The 10
Summers, Andy 3
T. Rex 11

Tears for Fears 6
10,000 Maniacs 3
Texas Tornados, The 8
They Might Be Giants 7
Thompson, Richard 7
Three Dog Night 5
Timbuk 3 3
Townshend, Pete 1
    Also see Who, The
Turner, Tina 1
U2 12
    Earlier sketch in CM 2
Vai, Steve 5
Valli, Frankie 10
Van Halen 8
Vaughan, Stevie Ray 1
Velvet Underground, The 7
Violent Femmes 12
Waits, Tom 12
    Earlier sketch in CM 1
Walsh, Joe 5
    Also see Eagles, The
Whitesnake 5
Who, The 3
Winter, Johnny 5
Winwood, Steve 2
X 11
Yardbirds, The 10
Yes 8
Young, Neil 2
Zappa, Frank 1
Zevon, Warren 9
ZZ Top 2

Rock and Roll Pioneers
Berry, Chuck 1
Clark, Dick 2
Darin, Bobby 4
Didley, Bo 3
Dion 4
Domino, Fats 2
Eddy, Duane 9
Everly Brothers, The 2
Francis, Connie 10
Haley, Bill 6
Hawkins, Screamin' Jay 8
Holly, Buddy 1
James, Etta 6
Jordan, Louis 11
Lewis, Jerry Lee 2
Little Richard 1
Nelson, Rick 2
Orbison, Roy 2
Paul, Les 2
Perkins, Carl 9
Phillips, Sam 5
Presley, Elvis 1
Professor Longhair 6
Sedaka, Neil 4
Shannon, Del 10
Shirelles, The 11
Spector, Phil 4
Twitty, Conway 6
Valli, Frankie 10
Wilson, Jackie 3

Saxophone
Braxton, Anthony 12
Carter, Benny 3
Clemons, Clarence 7
Coleman, Ornette 5
Coltrane, John 4
Dorsey, Jimmy
    See Dorsey Brothers, The
Getz, Stan 12
Gordon, Dexter 10
Hawkins, Coleman 11
Herman, Woody 12
Kirk, Rahsaan Roland 6
Marsalis, Branford 10
Morgan, Frank 9
Parker, Charlie 5
Parker, Maceo 7
Redman, Joshua 12
Rollins, Sonny 7
Sanborn, David 1
Shorter, Wayne 5
Threadgill, Henry 9
Washington, Grover, Jr. 5
Winter, Paul 10

Songwriters
Acuff, Roy 2
Adams, Bryan 2
Allen, Peter 11
Alpert, Herb 11
Amos, Tori 12
Anderson, Ian
    See Jethro Tull
Anderson, John 5
Anka, Paul 2
Armatrading, Joan 4
Atkins, Chet 5
Autry, Gene 12
Bacharach, Burt 1
Baez, Joan 1
Baker, Anita 9
Balin, Marty
    See Jefferson Airplane
Barrett, (Roger) Syd
    See Pink Floyd
Basie, Count 2
Becker, Walter
    See Steely Dan
Belew, Adrian 5
Benton, Brook 7
Berlin, Irving 8
Berry, Chuck 1
Black, Clint 5
Blades, Ruben 2
Bono
    See U2
Brady, Paul 8
Bragg, Billy 7
Brickell, Edie 3
Brooks, Garth 8
Brown, Bobby 4
Brown, James 2
Browne, Jackson 3
Buck, Peter 5
    See R.E.M.

Buck, Robert
  See 10,000 Maniacs
Buckingham, Lindsey 8
  Also see Fleetwood Mac
Buffett, Jimmy 4
Bush, Kate 4
Byrne, David 8
  Also see Talking Heads
Cahn, Sammy 11
Cale, John 9
Calloway, Cab 6
Captain Beefheart 10
Carpenter, Mary-Chapin 6
Carter, Carlene 8
Cash, Johnny 1
Cash, Rosanne 2
Cetera, Peter
  See Chicago
Chapin, Harry 6
Chapman, Tracy 4
Charles, Ray 1
Childs, Toni 2
Chilton, Alex 10
Clapton, Eric 11
  Earlier sketch in CM 1
  Also see Cream
  Also see Yardbirds, The
Cleveland, James 1
Clinton, George 7
Cockburn, Bruce 8
Cohen, Leonard 3
Cole, Lloyd 9
Cole, Nat King 3
Collins, Albert 4
Collins, Judy 4
Collins, Phil 2
Cooder, Ry 2
Cooke, Sam 1
  Also see Soul Stirrers, The
Cooper, Alice 8
Costello, Elvis 12
  Earlier sketch in CM 2
Crenshaw, Marshall 5
Croce, Jim 3
Crofts, Dash
  See Seals & Crofts
Cropper, Steve 12
Crosby, David 3
  Also see Byrds, The
Crowe, J. D. 5
Crowell, Rodney 8
Daniels, Charlie 6
Davies, Ray 5
Denver, John 1
Diamond, Neil 1
Diddley, Bo 3
Difford, Chris
  See Squeeze
Dion 4
Dixon, Willie 10
Domino, Fats 2
Donovan 9
Dorsey, Thomas A. 11
Doucet, Michael 8

Dozier, Lamont
  See Holland-Dozier-Holland
Dylan, Bob 3
Edge, The
  See U2
Edmonds, Kenneth "Babyface" 12
Elfman, Danny 9
Ellington, Duke 2
Emerson, Keith
  See Emerson, Lake & Palmer/Powell
Ertegun, Ahmet 10
Etheridge, Melissa 4
Everly, Don
  See Everly Brothers, The
Everly, Phil
  See Everly Brothers, The
Fagen, Don
  See Steely Dan
Ferry, Bryan 1
Flack, Roberta 5
Flatt, Lester 3
Fogelberg, Dan 4
Fogerty, John 2
Frampton, Peter 3
Frey, Glenn 3
  Also see Eagles, The
Fripp, Robert 9
Frizzell, Lefty 10
Gabriel, Peter 2
Garcia, Jerry 4
Gaye, Marvin 4
Geldof, Bob 9
George, Lowell
  See Little Feat
Gershwin, George and Ira 11
Gibb, Barry
  See Bee Gees, The
Gibb, Maurice
  See Bee Gees, The
Gibb, Robin
  See Bee Gees, The
Gibbons, Billy
  See ZZ Top
Gibson, Debbie 1
Gift, Roland 3
Gill, Vince 7
Gilley, Mickey 7
Gilmour, David
  See Pink Floyd
Goodman, Benny 4
Gordy, Berry, Jr. 6
Grant, Amy 7
Green, Al 9
Greenwood, Lee 12
Griffith, Nanci 3
Guthrie, Arlo 6
Guthrie, Woodie 2
Guy, Buddy 4
Haggard, Merle 2
Hall, Daryl
  See Hall & Oates
Hall, Tom T. 4
Hamlisch, Marvin 1
Hammer, M.C. 5

Hammerstein, Oscar
  See Rodgers, Richard
Harding, John Wesley 6
Harley, Bill 7
Harris, Emmylou 4
Harrison, George 2
  Also see Beatles, The
Harry, Deborah 4
Hart, Lorenz
  See Rodgers, Richard
Hartford, John 1
Hatfield, Juliana 12
  Also see Lemonheads, The
Hawkins, Screamin' Jay 8
Hayes, Isaac 10
Healey, Jeff 4
Hedges, Michael 3
Hendrix, Jimi 2
Henley, Don 3
  Also see Eagles, The
Hiatt, John 8
Hidalgo, David
  See Los Lobos
Hillman, Chris
  See Byrds, The
  Also see Desert Rose Band, The
Hitchcock, Robyn 9
Holland, Brian
  See Holland-Dozier-Holland
Holland, Eddie
  See Holland-Dozier-Holland
Holly, Buddy 1
Hornsby, Bruce 3
Hutchence, Michael
  See INXS
Hynde, Chrissie
  See Pretenders, The
Ian, Janis 5
Ice Cube 10
Ice-T 7
Idol, Billy 3
Isaak, Chris 6
Jackson, Alan 7
Jackson, Joe 4
Jackson, Michael 1
Jagger, Mick 7
  Also see Rolling Stones, The
Jam, Jimmy, and Terry Lewis 11
James, Rick 2
Jarreau, Al 1
Jennings, Waylon 4
Jett, Joan 3
Joel, Billy 12
  Earlier sketch in CM 2
Johansen, David 7
John, Elton 3
Jones, Brian
  See Rolling Stones, The
Jones, George 4
Jones, Mick
  See Clash, The
Jones, Quincy 2
Jones, Rickie Lee 4
Joplin, Janis 3

Judd, Naomi
  See Judds, The
Kane, Big Daddy 7
Kantner, Paul
  See Jefferson Airplane
Khan, Chaka 9
King, Albert 2
King, B. B. 1
King, Ben E. 7
King, Carole 6
Knopfler, Mark 3
Kravitz, Lenny 5
Kristofferson, Kris 4
Lake, Greg
  See Emerson, Lake & Palmer/Powell
Lang, K. D. 4
Larkin, Patty 9
Lavin, Christine 6
LeDoux, Chris 12
Lee, Peggy 8
Lehrer, Tom 7
Lennon, John 9
  Also see Beatles, The
Lennon, Julian 2
Lewis, Huey 9
Lightfoot, Gordon 3
Little Richard 1
Llanas, Sammy
  See BoDeans, The
L.L. Cool J 5
Loggins, Kenny 3
Loveless, Patty 5
Lovett, Lyle 5
Lowe, Nick 6
Lydon, John 9
  Also see Sex Pistols, The
Lynn, Loretta 2
Lynne, Jeff 5
Lynne, Shelby 5
MacColl, Kirsty 12
MacDonald, Barbara
  See Timbuk 3
MacDonald, Pat
  See Timbuk 3
Madonna 4
Manilow, Barry 2
Manzarek, Ray
  See Doors, The
Marley, Bob 3
Marley, Ziggy 3
Marx, Richard 3
Mattea, Kathy 5
May, Brian
  See Queen
Mayfield, Curtis 8
McCartney, Paul 4
  Also see Beatles, The
McDonald, Michael
  See Doobie Brothers, The
McGuinn, Roger
  See Byrds, The
McLachlan, Sarah 12
McLean, Don 7
McMurtry, James 10

McVie, Christine
  See Fleetwood Mac
Medley, Bill 3
Melanie 12
Mellencamp, John "Cougar" 2
Merchant, Natalie
  See 10,000 Maniacs
Mercury, Freddie
  See Queen
Michael, George 9
Miller, Roger 4
Miller, Steve 2
Milsap, Ronnie 2
Mitchell, Joni 2
Morrison, Jim 3
Morrison, Van 3
Morrissey, Bill 12
Morrissey 10
Morton, Jelly Roll 7
Mould, Bob 10
Moyet, Alison 12
Nascimento, Milton 6
Near, Holly 1
Nelson, Rick 2
Nelson, Willie 11
  Earlier sketch in CM 1
Nesmith, Mike
  See Monkees, The
Neville, Art
  See Neville Brothers, The
Newman, Randy 4
Newmann, Kurt
  See BoDeans, The
Nicks, Stevie 2
Nilsson 10
Nugent, Ted 2
Nyro, Laura 12
Oates, John
  See Hall & Oates
Ocasek, Ric 5
Ocean, Billy 4
Ochs, Phil 7
O'Connor, Sinead 3
Odetta 7
Orbison, Roy 2
Osbourne, Ozzy 3
Oslin, K. T. 3
Owens, Buck 2
Page, Jimmy 4
  Also see Led Zeppelin
  Also see Yardbirds, The
Palmer, Robert 2
Parker, Graham 10
Parsons, Gram 7
  Also see Byrds, The
Parton, Dolly 2
Paul, Les 2
Paxton, Tom 5
Penn, Michael 4
Perez, Louie
  See Los Lobos
Perkins, Carl 9
Perry, Joe
  See Aerosmith

Petty, Tom 9
Phillips, Sam 12
Pickett, Wilson 10
Pierson, Kate
  See B-52's, The
Plant, Robert 2
  Also see Led Zeppelin
Pop, Iggy 1
Porter, Cole 10
Prince 1
Prine, John 7
Professor Longhair 6
Rabbitt, Eddie 5
Raitt, Bonnie 3
Ray, Amy
  See Indigo Girls
Rea, Chris 12
Redding, Otis 5
Reddy, Helen 9
Reed, Lou 1
  Also see Velvet Underground, The
Reid, Vernon 2
  Also see Living Colour
Rich, Charlie 3
Richards, Keith 11
  Also see Rolling Stones, The
Richie, Lionel 2
Richman, Jonathan 12
Ritchie, Jean 4
Robbins, Marty 9
Robertson, Robbie 2
Robillard, Duke 2
Robinson, Smokey 1
Rodgers, Jimmie 3
Rodgers, Richard 9
Roth, David Lee 1
  Also see Van Halen
Russell, Mark 6
Rutherford, Mike
  See Genesis
Sade 2
Sager, Carole Bayer 5
Saliers, Emily
  See Indigo Girls
Satriani, Joe 4
Scaggs, Boz 12
Schneider, Fred III
  See B-52's, The
Scruggs, Earl 3
Seals, Dan 9
Seals, Jim
  See Seals & Crofts
Sedaka, Neil 4
Seeger, Pete 4
  Also see Weavers, The
Shannon, Del 10
Sheila E. 3
Shocked, Michelle 4
Siberry, Jane 6
Simmons, Gene
  See Kiss
Simmons, Patrick
  See Doobie Brothers, The
Simon, Carly 4

Simon, Paul 1
Skaggs, Ricky 5
Slick, Grace
  See Jefferson Airplane
Smith, Patti 1
Smith, Robert
  See Cure, The
    Also see Siouxsie and the Banshees
Sondheim, Stephen 8
Spector, Phil 4
Springsteen, Bruce 6
Stanley, Paul
  See Kiss
Stanley, Ralph 5
Starr, Ringo 10
  Also see Beatles, The
Stevens, Cat 3
Stevens, Ray 7
Stewart, Dave
  See Eurythmics
Stewart, Rod 2
Stills, Stephen 5
Sting 2
Stipe, Michael
  See R.E.M.
Strait, George 5
Streisand, Barbra 2
Strickland, Keith
  See B-52's, The
Strummer, Joe
  See Clash, The
Stuart, Marty 9
Summer, Donna 12
Summers, Andy 3
Sweet, Matthew 9
Taj Mahal 6
Taylor, James 2
Taylor, Koko 10
Thompson, Richard 7
Tikaram, Tanita 9
Tilbrook, Glenn
  See Squeeze
Tillis, Mel 7
Tillis, Pam 8
Timmins, Margo
  See Cowboy Junkies, The
Timmins, Michael
  See Cowboy Junkies, The
Tippin, Aaron 12
Tone-L c 3
Torme, Mel 4
Tosh, Peter 3
Toussaint, Allen 11
Townshend, Pete 1
  Also see Who, The
Travis, Randy 9
Tritt, Travis 7
Tubb, Ernest 4
Twitty, Conway 6
Tyler, Steve
  See Aerosmith
Vai, Steve 5
  Also see Whitesnake
Vandross, Luther 2

Van Halen, Edward
  See Van Halen
Van Ronk, Dave 12
Van Shelton, Ricky 5
Vedder, Eddie
  See Pearl Jam
Vega, Suzanne 3
Bono
  See U2
Waits, Tom 12
  Earlier sketch in CM 1
Walker, T-Bone 5
Waller, Fats 7
Walsh, Joe 5
  Also see Eagles, The
Waters, Muddy 4
Waters, Roger
  See Pink Floyd
Webb, Jimmy 12
Weill, Kurt 12
Weir, Bob
  See Grateful Dead, The
Welch, Bob
  See Grateful Dead, The
West, Dottie 8
Whitley, Keith 7
Williams, Deniece 1
Williams, Don 4
Williams, Hank, Jr. 1
Williams, Hank, Sr. 4
Williams, Lucinda 10
Williams, Paul 5
Wills, Bob 6
Wilson, Brian
  See Beach Boys, The
Wilson, Cindy
  See B-52's, The
Wilson, Ricky
  See B-52's, The
Winter, Johnny 5
Winwood, Steve 2
Womack, Bobby 5
Wonder, Stevie 2
Wynette, Tammy 2
Yoakam, Dwight 1
Young, Angus
  See AC/DC
Young, Neil 2
Zappa, Frank 1
Zevon, Warren 9

Trombone
Anderson, Ray 7
Dorsey, Tommy
  See Dorsey Brothers, The
Miller, Glenn 6
Teagarden, Jack 10
Watts, Eugene
  See Canadian Brass, The

Trumpet
Alpert, Herb 11
Armstrong, Louis 4
Berigan, Bunny 2

Cherry, Don 10
Coleman, Ornette 5
Davis, Miles 1
Eldridge, Roy 9
Ferguson, Maynard 7
Gillespie, Dizzy 6
Hirt, Al 5
James, Harry 11
Jones, Quincy 2
Loughnane, Lee 3
Marsalis, Wynton 6
Masekela, Hugh 7
Mills, Fred
  See Canadian Brass, The
Romm, Ronald
  See Canadian Brass, The
Severinsen, Doc 1

Tuba
Daellenbach, Charles
  See Canadian Brass, The
Phillips, Harvey 3

Vibraphone
Burton, Gary 10
Hampton, Lionel 6
Norvo, Red 12

Viola
Dutt, Hank
  See Kronos Quartet
Jones, Michael
  See Kronos Quartet
Killian, Tim
  See Kronos Quartet
Menuhin, Yehudi 11
Zukerman, Pinchas 4

Violin
Acuff, Roy 2
Anderson, Laurie 1
Bush, Sam
  See New Grass Revival, The
Chang, Sarah 7
Coleman, Ornette 5
Daniels, Charlie 6
Doucet, Michael 8
Gingold, Josef 6
Grappelli, Stephane 10
Gray, Ella
  See Kronos Quartet
Harrington, David
  See Kronos Quartet
Hartford, John 1
Hidalgo, David
  See Los Lobos
Kennedy, Nigel 8
Krauss, Alison 10
Lewis, Roy
  See Kronos Quartet
Marriner, Neville 7
Menuhin, Yehudi 11
Midori 7
O'Connor, Mark 1

Perlman, Itzhak **2**
Ponty, Jean-Luc **8**
Salerno-Sonnenberg, Nadja **3**
Shallenberger, James
  See Kronos Quartet
Sherba, John
  See Kronos Quartet
Skaggs, Ricky **5**
Stern, Isaac **7**
Wills, Bob **6**
Zukerman, Pinchas **4**

Cumulative Musicians Index

Volume numbers appear in **bold**.

Abba **12**
Abbruzzese, Dave
  See Pearl Jam
Abdul, Paula **3**
Abrahams, Mick
  See Jethro Tull
Abrantes, Fernando
  See Kraftwerk
AC/DC **4**
Ackerman, Will **3**
Acuff, Roy **2**
Adams, Bryan **2**
Adams, Donn
  See NRBQ
Adams, John **8**
Adams, Terry
  See NRBQ
Adcock, Eddie
  See Country Gentleman, The
Adler, Steven
  See Guns n' Roses
Aerosmith **3**
Alabama **1**
Albuquerque, Michael de
  See de Albuquerque, Michael
Alexander, Tim
  See Asleep at the Wheel
Alexander, Tim "Herb"
  See Primus
Alice in Chains **10**
Allen, Duane
  See Oak Ridge Boys, The
Allen, Peter **11**
Allen, Rick
  See Def Leppard
Ali
  See A Tribe Called Quest
Allcock, Martin
  See Jethro Tull
Allen, Dave
  See Gang of Four
Allen, Debbie **8**
Allen, Geri **10**
Allen, Red
  See Osborne Brothers, The
Allman Brothers, The **6**
Allman, Duane
  See Allman Brothers, The
Allman, Gregg
  See Allman Brothers, The
Allsup, Michael Rand
  See Three Dog Night
Alpert, Herb **11**
Alston, Shirley
  See Shirelles, The

Alvin, Dave
  See X
Ament, Jeff
  See Pearl Jam
Amos, Tori **12**
Anderson, Al
  See NRBQ
Anderson, Ian
  See Jethro Tull
Anderson, John **5**
Anderson, Jon
  See Yes
Anderson, Laurie **1**
Anderson, Marian **8**
Anderson, Ray **7**
Anderson, Signe
  See Jefferson Airplane
Andersson, Benny
  See Abba
Andrews, Barry
  See XTC
Andrews, Julie **4**
Andrews, Laverne
  See Andrews Sisters, The
Andrews, Maxene
  See Andrews Sisters, The
Andrews, Patty
  See Andrews Sisters, The
Andrews Sisters, The **9**
Anger, Darol
  See Turtle Island String Quartet
Anka, Paul **2**
Anthony, Michael
  See Van Halen
Anthrax **11**
Anton, Alan
  See Cowboy Junkies, The
Antunes, Michael
  See Beaver Brown Band, The
Appice, Vinnie
  See Black Sabbath
Araya, Tom
  See Slayer
Ardolino, Tom
  See NRBQ
Armatrading, Joan **4**
Armstrong, Louis **4**
Arnaz, Desi **8**
Arnold, Eddy **10**
Arnold, Kristine
  See Sweethearts of the Rodeo
Arrau, Claudio **1**
Asleep at the Wheel **5**
Astley, Rick **5**
Astro
  See UB40

Atkins, Chet **5**
Atkinson, Sweet Pea
  See Was (Not Was)
Augustyniak, Jerry
  See 10,000 Maniacs
Auldridge, Mike **4**
  Also see Country Gentlemen, The
  Also see Seldom Scene, The
Autry, Gene **12**
Avalon, Frankie **5**
Avery, Eric
  See Jane's Addiction
Aykroyd, Dan
  See Blues Brothers, The
B-52's, The **4**
Babyface
  See Edmonds, Kenneth "Babyface"
Bacharach, Burt **1**
Badger, Pat
  See Extreme
Baez, Joan **1**
Bailey, Pearl **5**
Bailey, Phil
  See Earth, Wind and Fire
Baker, Anita **9**
Baker, Ginger
  See Cream
Baker, Josephine **10**
Balakrishnan, David
  See Turtle Island String Quartet
Baldursson, Sigtryggur
  See Sugarcubes, The
Baldwin, Donny
  See Starship
Baliardo, Diego
  See Gipsy Kings, The
Baliardo, Paco
  See Gipsy Kings, The
Baliardo, Tonino
  See Gipsy Kings, The
Balin, Marty
  See Jefferson Airplane
Ballard, Florence
  See Supremes, The
Balsley, Phil
  See Statler Brothers, The
Band, The **9**
Banks, Peter
  See Yes
Banks, Tony
  See Genesis
Barbata, John
  See Jefferson Starship
Barber, Keith
  See Soul Stirrers, The

307

Bargeron, Dave
    See Blood, Sweat and Tears
Barker, Paul
    See Ministry
Barlow, Barriemore
    See Jethro Tull
Barlow, Lou
    See Dinosaur Jr.
Barnwell, Ysaye Maria
    See Sweet Honey in the Rock
Barr, Ralph
    See Nitty Gritty Dirt Band, The
Barre, Martin
    See Jethro Tull
Barrere, Paul
    See Little Feat
Barrett, (Roger) Syd
    See Pink Floyd
Bartoli, Cecilia 12
Barton, Lou Ann
    See Fabulous Thunderbirds, The
Bartos, Karl
    See Kraftwerk
Basehead 11
Basher, Mick
    See X
Basia 5
Basie, Count 2
Battin, Skip
    See Byrds, The
Battle, Kathleen 6
Baumann, Peter
    See Tangerine Dream
Bautista, Roland
    See Earth, Wind and Fire
Baxter, Jeff
    See Doobie Brothers, The
Bayer Sager, Carole
    See Sager, Carole Bayer
Baynton-Power, David
    See James
Beach Boys, The 1
Beale, Michael
    See Earth, Wind and Fire
Beastie Boys, The 8
Beard, Frank
    See ZZ Top
Beatles, The 2
    Also see Harrison, George
Beaver Brown Band, The 3
Beck, Jeff 4
    Also see Yardbirds, The
Becker, Walter
    See Steely Dan
Bee Gees, The 3
Beers, Garry Gary
    See INXS
Behler, Chuck
    See Megadeth
Belafonte, Harry 8
Belew, Adrian 5
Belfield, Dennis
    See Three Dog Night
Bell, Andy
    See Erasure
Bell, Derek
    See Chieftains, The
Belladonna, Joey
    See Anthrax
Belle, Regina 6
Bello, Frank
    See Anthrax
Belushi, John
    See Blues Brothers, The
Benante, Charlie
    See Anthrax
Benatar, Pat 8
Bennett, Tony 2
Benson, George 9
Benson, Ray
    See Asleep at the Wheel
Benson, Renaldo "Obie"
    See Four Tops, The
Bentley, John
    See Squeeze
Benton, Brook 7
Bentyne, Cheryl
    See Manhattan Transfer, The
Berigan, Bunny 2
Berlin, Irving 8
Berlin, Steve
    See Los Lobos
Bernstein, Leonard 2
Berry, Bill
    See R.E.M.
Berry, Chuck 1
Berry, Robert
    See Emerson, Lake & Palmer/Powell
Best, Pete
    See Beatles, The
Bettencourt, Nuno
    See Extreme
Betts, Dicky
    See Allman Brothers, The
Bevan, Bev
    See Black Sabbath
    Also see Electric Light Orchestra
Big Mike
    See Geto Boys, The
Big Money Odis
    See Digital Underground
Bingham, John
    See Fishbone
Binks, Les
    See Judas Priest
Bird
    See Parker, Charlie
Birdsong, Cindy
    See Supremes, The
Birchfield, Benny
    See Osborne Brothers, The
Biscuits, Chuck
    See Danzig
Biz Markie 10
Björk
    See Gudmundsdottir, Björk
Black, Clint 5
Black Crowes, The 7
Black Sabbath 9
Black Uhuru 12
Blackmore, Ritchie
    See Deep Purple
Blades, Ruben 2
Blakey, Art 11
Bland, Bobby "Blue" 12
Bley, Carla 8
Blood, Sweat and Tears 7
Blues, Elwood
    See Blues Brothers, The
Blues, "Joliet" Jake
    See Blues Brothers, The
Blues Brothers, The 3
BoDeans, The 3
Bogaert, Jo
    See Technotronic
Bogguss, Suzy 11
Bolade, Nitanju
    See Sweet Honey in the Rock
Bolan, Marc
    See T. Rex
Bolton, Michael 4
Bon Jovi 10
Bon Jovi, Jon
    See Bon Jovi
Bonebrake, D. J.
    See X
Bonham, John
    See Led Zeppelin
Bono
    See U2
Bonsall, Joe
    See Oak Ridge Boys, The
Booth, Tim
    See James
Bordin, Mike
    See Faith No More
Bostaph, Paul
    See Slayer
Boston 11
Bottum, Roddy
    See Faith No More
Bouchikhi, Chico
    See Gipsy Kings, The
Bowen, Jimmy
    See Country Gentlemen, The
Bowens, Sir Harry
    See Was (Not Was)
Bowie, David 1
Boyd, Liona 7
Brady, Paul 8
Bragg, Billy 7
Bramah, Martin
    See Fall, The
Branigan, Laura 2
Brantley, Junior
    See Roomful of Blues
B-Real
    See Cypress Hill
Braxton, Anthony 12
Bream, Julian 9
Brickell, Edie 3
Bright, Ronnie
    See Coasters, The
Briley, Alex
    See Village People, The

Brix
　See Fall, The
Brooks, Garth 8
Bronfman, Yefim 6
Brooks, Leon Eric "Kix"
　See Brooks & Dunn
Brooks & Dunn 12
Brown, Bobby 4
Brown, Clarence "Gatemouth" 11
Brown, James 2
Brown, Jimmy
　See UB40
Browne, Jackson 3
　　Also see Nitty Gritty Dirt Band, The
Brubeck, Dave 8
Bruce, Jack
　See Cream
Bruford, Bill
　See Yes
Bruster, Thomas
　See Soul Stirrers, The
Bryant, Elbridge
　See Temptations, The
Bryan, David
　See Bon Jovi
Bryson, Bill
　See Desert Rose Band, The
Bryson, Peabo 11
Buchholz, Francis
　See Scorpions, The
Buck, Mike
　See Fabulous Thunderbirds, The
Buck, Peter
　See R.E.M.
Buck, Robert
　See 10,000 Maniacs
Buckingham, Lindsey 8
　　Also see Fleetwood Mac
Buckley, Betty 1
Buckwheat Zydeco 6
Budgie
　See Siouxsie and the Banshees
Buffett, Jimmy 4
Bulgarian State Female Vocal Choir, The 10
Bulgarian State Radio and Television Female Vocal Choir, The
　See Bulgarian State Female Vocal Choir, The
Bumpus, Cornelius
　See Doobie Brothers, The
Bunker, Clive
　See Jethro Tull
Burch, Curtis
　See New Grass Revival, The
Burnett, Carol 6
Burnette, Billy
　See Fleetwood Mac
Burnham, Hugo
　See Gang of Four
Burns, Bob
　See Lynyrd Skynyrd
Burns, Karl
　See Fall, The
Burr, Clive
　See Iron Maiden

Burrell, Kenny 11
Burton, Cliff
　See Metallica
Burton, Gary 10
Busby, Jheryl 9
Bush, Dave
　See Fall, The
Bush, John
　See Anthrax
Bush, Kate 4
Bush, Sam
　See New Grass Revival, The
Bushwick Bill
　See Geto Boys, The
Butler, Terry "Geezer"
　See Black Sabbath
Buzzcocks, The 9
Byrds, The 8
Byrne, David 8
　　Also see Talking Heads
Cafferty, John
　See Beaver Brown Band, The
Cage, John 8
Cahn, Sammy 11
Cale, John 9
　　Also see Velvet Underground, The
Calhoun, Will
　See Living Colour
Callas, Maria 11
Calloway Cab 6
Cameron, Matt
　See Soundgarden
Campbell, Ali
　See UB40
Campbell, Glen 2
Campbell, Luther 10
Campbell, Phil
　See Motörhead
Campbell, Robin
　See UB40
Canadian Brass, The 4
Cantrell, Jerry
　See Alice in Chains
Captain Beefheart 10
Carey, Mariah 6
Carlisle, Belinda 8
Carlos, Bun E.
　See Cheap Trick
Carlos, Don
　See Black Uhuru
Carlson, Paulette
　See Highway 101
Carnes, Kim 4
Carpenter, Bob
　See Nitty Gritty Dirt Band, The
Carpenter, Mary-Chapin 6
Carr, Eric
　See Kiss
Carrack, Paul
　See Squeeze
Carreras, José 8
Carroll, Earl "Speedo"
　See Coasters, The
Carruthers, John
　See Siouxsie and the Banshees

Carter, Anita
　See Carter Family, The
Carter, A. P.
　See Carter Family, The
Carter, Benny 3
Carter, Betty 6
Carter, Carlene 8
Carter, Jimmy
　See Five Blind Boys of Alabama
Carter Family, The 3
Carter, Helen
　See Carter Family, The
Carter, Janette
　See Carter Family, The
Carter, Joe
　See Carter Family, The
Carter, June 6
　　Also see Carter Family, The
Carter, Maybell
　See Carter Family, The
Carter, Nell 7
Carter, Sara
　See Carter Family, The
Caruso, Enrico 10
Casady, Jack
　See Jefferson Airplane
Casals, Pablo 9
Cash, Johnny 1
Cash, Rosanne 2
Cates, Ronny
　See Petra
Cavalera, Igor
　See Sepultura
Cavalera, Max
　See Sepultura
Cave, Nick 10
Cavoukian, Raffi
　See Raffi
Cease, Jeff
　See Black Crowes, The
Cervenka, Exene
　See X
Cetera, Peter
　See Chicago
Chambers, Martin
　See Pretenders, The
Chambers, Terry
　See XTC
Chang, Sarah 7
Channing, Carol 6
Chapin, Harry 6
Chapin, Tom 11
Chapman, Tony
　See Rolling Stones, The
Chapman, Tracy 4
Chaquico, Craig
　See Jefferson Starship
Charles, Ray 1
Chea, Alvin "Vinnie"
　See Take 6
Cheap Trick 12
Checker, Chubby 7
Cheeks, Julius
　See Soul Stirrers, The
Chenier, Clifton 6

Cher 1
Cherone, Gary
    See Extreme
Cherry, Don 10
Cherry, Neneh 4
Chevalier, Maurice 6
Chevron, Phillip
    See Pogues, The
Chicago 3
Chieftains, The 7
Childs, Toni 2
Chilton, Alex 10
Chimes, Terry
    See Clash, The
Chopmaster J
    See Digital Underground
Christ, John
    See Danzig
Christian, Charlie 11
Christina, Fran
    See Fabulous Thunderbirds, The
    Also see Roomful of Blues
Chuck D
    See Public Enemy
Church, Kevin
    See Country Gentlemen, The
Clapton, Eric 11
    Earlier sketch in CM 1
    Also see Cream
    Also see Yardbirds, The
Clark, Dave
    See Dave Clark Five, The
Clark, Dick 2
Clark, Gene
    See Byrds, The
Clark, Roy 1
Clark, Steve
    See Def Leppard
Clarke, "Fast" Eddie
    See Motörhead
Clarke, Michael
    See Byrds, The
Clarke, Stanley 3
Clarke, Vince
    See Depeche Mode
    Also see Erasure
Clash, The 4
Clayderman, Richard 1
Claypool, Les
    See Primus
Clayton, Adam
    See U2
Clayton, Sam
    See Little Feat
Clayton-Thomas, David
    See Blood, Sweat and Tears
Cleaves, Jessica
    See Earth, Wind and Fire
Clegg, Johnny 8
Clemons, Clarence 7
Cleveland, James 1
Cliff, Jimmy 8
Cline, Patsy 5
Clinton, George 7
Clooney, Rosemary 9

Coasters, The 5
Cobain, Kurt
    See Nirvana
Cockburn, Bruce 8
Cocker, Joe 4
Cocteau Twins, The 12
Coe, David Allan 4
Cohen, Jeremy
    See Turtle Island String Quartet
Cohen, Leonard 3
Cohen, Porky
    See Roomful of Blues
Cole, Lloyd 9
Cole, Nat King 3
Cole, Natalie 1
Coleman, Ornette 5
Collin, Phil
    See Def Leppard
Collins, Albert 4
Collins, Allen
    See Lynyrd Skynyrd
Collins, Bootsy 8
Collins, Judy 4
Collins, Phil 2
    Also see Genesis
Collins, William
    See Collins, Bootsy
Colomby, Bobby
    See Blood, Sweat and Tears
Colt, Johnny
    See Black Crowes, The
Coltrane, John 4
Colvin, Shawn 11
Conneff, Kevin
    See Chieftains, The
Connick, Harry, Jr. 4
Cooder, Ry 2
Cook, Jeff
    See Alabama
Cook, Paul
    See Sex Pistols, The
Cooke, Sam 1
    Also see Soul Stirrers, The
Cooney, Rory 6
Cooper, Alice 8
Copland, Aaron 2
Copley, Al
    See Roomful of Blues
Corea, Chick 6
Cornell, Chris
    See Soundgarden
Cornick, Glenn
    See Jethro Tull
Costello, Elvis 12
    Earlier sketch in CM 2
Cotoia, Robert
    See Beaver Brown Band, The
Cotrubas, Ileana 1
Cougar, John(ny)
    See Mellencamp, John "Cougar"
Country Gentlemen, The 7
Coverdale, David
    See Whitesnake 5
Cowan, John
    See New Grass Revival, The

Cowboy Junkies, The 4
Cox, Andy
    See English Beat, The
Cracker 12
Crain, S. R.
    See Soul Stirrers, The
Crawford, Ed
    See fIREHOSE
Crawford, Michael 4
Cray, Robert 8
Creach, Papa John
    See Jefferson Starship
Cream 9
Crenshaw, Marshall 5
Criss, Peter
    See Kiss
Croce, Jim 3
Crofts, Dash
    See Seals & Crofts
Cropper, Steve 12
Crosby, Bing 6
Crosby, David 3
    Also see Byrds, The
Crouch, Andraé 9
Crowded House 12
Crowe, J. D. 5
Crowell, Rodney 8
Cruz, Celia 10
Cure, The 3
Curless, Ann
    See Exposé
Currie, Steve
    See T. Rex
Curry, Tim 3
Cypress Hill 11
Cyrus, Billy Ray 11
D'Angelo, Greg
    See Anthrax
DJ Domination
    See Geto Boys, The
D.J. Minutemix
    See P.M. Dawn
DJ Muggs
    See Cypress Hill
DJ Ready Red
    See Geto Boys, The
Dacus, Donnie
    See Chicago
Dacus, Johnny
    See Osborne Brothers, The
Daddy Mack
    See Kris Kross
Daellenbach, Charles
    See Canadian Brass, The
Daisley, Bob
    See Black Sabbath
Dall, Bobby
    See Poison
Dalton, Nic
    See Lemonheads, The
Daltrey, Roger 3
    Also see Who, The
Dando, Evan
    See Lemonheads, The
Daniels, Charlie 6

Daniels, Jack
  See Highway 101
Danko, Rick
  See Band, The
Danzig 7
Danzig, Glenn
  See Danzig
D'Arby, Terence Trent 3
Darin, Bobby 4
Darling, Eric
  See Weavers, The
Dave Clark Five, The 12
Davidson, Lenny
  See Dave Clark Five, The
Davies, Ray 5
Davies, Saul
  See James
Davis, Chip 4
Davis, Michael
  See MC5, The
Davis, Miles 1
Davis, Sammy, Jr. 4
Dayne, Taylor 4
DeLorenzo, Victor
  See Violent Femmes
Deacon, John
  See Queen
de Albuquerque, Michael
  See Electric Light Orchestra
Dee, Mikkey
  See Motörhead
Deee-lite 9
Deep Purple 11
Def Leppard 3
DeGarmo, Chris
  See Queensryche
de Grassi, Alex 6
DeJohnette, Jack 7
De La Soul 7
Deily, Ben
  See Lemonheads, The
Delp, Brad
  See Boston
de Lucia, Paco 1
Dempsey, Michael
  See Cure, The
Dennis, Garth
  See Black Uhuru
Densmore, John
  See Doors, The
Dent, Cedric
  See Take 6
Denton, Sandy
  See Salt-N-Pepa
Denver, John 1
De Oliveria, Laudir
  See Chicago
Depeche Mode 5
Derosier, Michael
  See Heart
Desert Rose Band, The 4
DeVille, C. C.
  See Poison
Devoto, Howard
  See Buzzcocks, The
DeWitt, Lew C.
  See Statler Brothers, The
de Young, Joyce
  See Andrews Sisters, The
Di Meola, Al 12
Diagram, Andy
  See James
Diamond, Mike
  See Beastie Boys, The
Diamond, Neil 1
Diamond Rio 11
Di'anno, Paul
  See Iron Maiden
Dickens, Little Jimmy 7
Dickinson, Paul Bruce
  See Iron Maiden
Diddley, Bo 3
Diffie, Joe 10
Difford, Chris
  See Squeeze
Diggle, Steve
  See Buzzcocks, The
Digital Underground 9
DiMucci, Dion
  See Dion
Dinosaur Jr. 10
Dio, Ronnie James
  See Black Sabbath
Dion 4
Dion, Céline 12
Dittrich, John
  See Restless Heart
Dixon, Willie 10
DJ Fuse
  See Digital Underground
DJ Jazzy Jeff and the Fresh Prince 5
DJ Terminator X
  See Public Enemy
Doe, John
  See X
Dolby, Thomas 10
Dolenz, Micky
  See Monkees, The
Domingo, Placido 1
Domino, Fats 2
Donovan 9
Doobie Brothers, The 3
Doors, The 4
Dorsey, Jimmy
  See Dorsey Brothers, The
Dorsey, Thomas A. 11
Dorsey, Tommy
  See Dorsey Brothers, The
Dorsey Brothers, The 8
Doucet, Michael 8
Douglas, Jerry
  See Country Gentlemen, The
Dowd, Christopher
  See Fishbone
Downes, Geoff
  See Yes
Downing, K. K.
  See Judas Priest
Dozier, Lamont
  See Holland-Dozier-Holland
Drayton, Leslie
  See Earth, Wind and Fire
Dr. Dre
  See N.W.A.
Dreja, Chris
  See Yardbirds, The
Drew, Dennis
  See 10,000 Maniacs
Dr. John 7
Dryden, Spencer
  See Jefferson Airplane
Duffey, John
  See Country Gentlemen, The
  Also see Seldom Scene, The
Dunbar, Aynsley
  See Jefferson Starship
  Also see Whitesnake
Duncan, Steve
  See Desert Rose Band, The
Dunlap, Slim
  See Replacements, The
Dunn, Holly 7
Dunn, Larry
  See Earth, Wind and Fire
Dunn, Ronnie
  See Brooks & Dunn
Dupree, Champion Jack 12
Duran Duran 4
Dutt, Hank
  See Kronos Quartet
Dylan, Bob 3
E., Sheila
  See Sheila E.
Eagles, The 3
Earl, Ronnie 5
  Also see Roomful of Blues
Earth, Wind and Fire 12
Easton, Sheena 2
Eazy-E
  See N.W.A.
Eckstine, Billy 1
Eddy, Duane 9
Edge, The
  See U2
Edmonds, Kenneth "Babyface" 12
Edwards, Dennis
  See Temptations, The
Edwards, Mike
  See Electric Light Orchestra
Eldon, Thór
  See Sugarcubes, The
Eldridge, Ben
  See Seldom Scene, The
Eldridge, Roy 9
Electric Light Orchestra 7
Elfman, Danny 9
Elias, Manny
  See Tears for Fears
Ellefson, Dave
  See Megadeth
Ellington, Duke 2
Elliot, Cass 5
Elliot, Joe
  See Def Leppard
Ellis, Terry
  See En Vogue

ELO
    See Electric Light Orchestra
Ely, John
    See Asleep at the Wheel
Emerson, Bill
    See Country Gentlemen, The
Emerson, Keith
    See Emerson, Lake & Palmer/Powell
Emerson, Lake & Palmer/Powell 5
English Beat, The 9
Eno, Brian 8
Enos, Bob
    See Roomful of Blues
Entwistle, John
    See Who, The
En Vogue 10
Enya 6
EPMD 10
Erasure 11
Eric B.
    See Eric B. and Rakim
Eric B. and Rakim 9
Ertegun, Ahmet 10
Estefan, Gloria 2
Estrada, Roy
    See Little Feat
Etheridge, Melissa 4
Eurythmics 6
Evan, John
    See Jethro Tull
Evans, Dick
    See U2
Evans, Mark
    See AC/DC
Everly, Don
    See Everly Brothers, The
Everly, Phil
    See Everly Brothers, The
Everly Brothers, The 2
Everman, Jason
    See Soundgarden
Exkano, Paul
    See Five Blind Boys of Alabama
Exposé 4
Extreme 10
Fabian 5
Fabulous Thunderbirds, The 1
Fadden, Jimmie
    See Nitty Gritty Dirt Band, The
Fagan, Don
    See Steely Dan
Faith No More 7
Fakir, Abdul "Duke"
    See Four Tops, The
Falconer, Earl
    See UB40
Fall, The 12
Fallon, David
    See Chieftains, The
Farley, J. J.
    See Soul Stirrers, The
Farndon, Pete
    See Pretenders, The
Farrell, Perry
    See Jane's Addiction

Farriss, Andrew
    See INXS
Farriss, Jon
    See INXS
Farriss, Tim
    See INXS
Fay, Martin
    See Chieftains, The
Fearnley, James
    See Pogues, The
Feinstein, Michael 6
Fela
    See Kuti, Fela
Felder, Don
    See Eagles, The
Feliciano, José 10
Fender, Freddy
    See Texas Tornados, The
Fender, Leo 10
Ferguson, Keith
    See Fabulous Thunderbirds, The
Ferguson, Maynard 7
Ferguson, Steve
    See NRBQ
Ferry, Bryan 1
Fiedler, Arthur 6
Fielder, Jim
    See Blood, Sweat and Tears
Fields, Johnny
    See Five Blind Boys of Alabama
Finch, Jennifer
    See L7
Finer, Jem
    See Pogues, The
Finn, Micky
    See T. Rex
Finn, Neil
    See Crowded House
Finn, Tim
    See Crowded House
fIREHOSE 11
Fishbone 7
Fisher, Eddie 12
Fisher, Jerry
    See Blood, Sweat and Tears
Fisher, John "Norwood"
    See Fishbone
Fisher, Phillip "Fish"
    See Fishbone
Fisher, Roger
    See Heart
Fitzgerald, Ella 1
Five Blind Boys of Alabama 12
Flack, Roberta 5
Flansburgh, John
    See They Might Be Giants
Flatt, Lester 3
Flavor Flav
    See Public Enemy
Flea
    See Red Hot Chili Peppers, The
Fleck, Bela 8
    Also see New Grass Revival, The
Fleetwood Mac 5
Fleetwood, Mick
    See Fleetwood Mac

Flemons, Wade
    See Earth, Wind and Fire
Fletcher, Andy
    See Depeche Mode
Flür, Wolfgang
    See Kraftwerk
Flynn, Pat
    See New Grass Revival, The
Fogelberg, Dan 4
Fogerty, John 2
Ford, Lita 9
Ford, Mark
    See Black Crowes, The
Ford, Tennessee Ernie 3
Fortune, Jimmy
    See Statler Brothers, The
Fossen, Steve
    See Heart
Foster, Malcolm
    See Pretenders, The
Foster, Paul
    See Soul Stirrers, The
Fountain, Clarence
    See Five Blind Boys of Alabama
Fountain, Pete 7
Four Tops, The 11
Fox, Lucas
    See Motörhead
Fox, Oz
    See Stryper
Fox, Samantha 3
Frampton, Peter 3
Francis, Connie 10
Francis, Mike
    See Asleep at the Wheel
Franke, Chris
    See Tangerine Dream
Franklin, Aretha 2
Franklin, Larry
    See Asleep at the Wheel
Franklin, Melvin
    See Temptations, The
Frantz, Chris
    See Talking Heads
Fraser, Elizabeth
    See Cocteau Twins, The
Frehley, Ace
    See Kiss
Freiberg, David
    See Jefferson Starship
Frey, Glenn 3
    Also see Eagles, The
Friedman, Marty
    See Megadeth
Friel, Tony
    See Fall, The
Fripp, Robert 9
Frizzell, Lefty 10
Froese, Edgar
    See Tangerine Dream
Frusciante, John
    See Red Hot Chili Peppers, The
Fältskog, Agnetha
    See Abba
Gabriel, Peter 2
    Also see Genesis

Gadler, Frank
　See NRBQ
Gahan, Dave
　See Depeche Mode
Gaines, Steve
　See Lynyrd Skynyrd
Gaines, Timothy
　See Stryper
Gale, Melvyn
　See Electric Light Orchestra
Gallup, Simon
　See Cure, The
Galway, James 3
Gambill, Roger
　See Kingston Trio, The
Gang of Four 8
Gano, Gordon
　See Violent Femmes
Garcia, Jerry 4
　Also see Grateful Dead, The
Gardner, Carl
　See Coasters, The
Gardner, Suzi
　See L7
Garfunkel, Art 4
Garland, Judy 6
Garrett, Peter
　See Midnight Oil
Garvey, Steve
　See Buzzcocks, The
Gaskill, Jerry
　See King's X
Gaudreau, Jimmy
　See Country Gentlemen, The
Gaye, Marvin 4
Gayle, Crystal 1
Geary, Paul
　See Extreme
Geffen, David 8
Geldof, Bob 9
Genesis 4
Gentry, Teddy
　See Alabama
George, Lowell
　See Little Feat
Gershwin, George
　See Gershwin, George and Ira
Gershwin, George and Ira 11
Gershwin, Ira
　See Gershwin, George and Ira
Geto Boys, The 11
Getz, Stan 12
Gibb, Barry
　See Bee Gees, The
Gibb, Maurice
　See Bee Gees, The
Gibb, Robin
　See Bee Gees, The
Gibbons, Billy
　See ZZ Top
Gibson, Debbie 1
Gibson, Wilf
　See Electric Light Orchestra
Gifford, Peter
　See Midnight Oil
Gift, Roland 3

Gilbert, Gillian
　See New Order
Gilbert, Ronnie
　See Weavers, The
Gilkyson, Tony
　See X
Gill, Andy
　See Gang of Four
Gill, Janis
　See Sweethearts of the Rodeo
Gill, Pete
　See Motörhead
Gill, Vince 7
Gillan, Ian
　See Deep Purple
Gillespie, Dizzy 6
Gilley, Mickey 7
Gillian, Ian
　See Black Sabbath
Gilmore, Jimmie Dale 11
Gilmour, David
　See Pink Floyd
Gingold, Josef 6
Gioia
　See Exposé
Gipsy Kings, The 8
Glass, Philip 1
Glasscock, John
　See Jethro Tull
Glennie, Jim
　See James
Glover, Corey
　See Living Colour
Glover, Roger
　See Deep Purple
Godchaux, Donna
　See Grateful Dead, The
Godchaux, Keith
　See Grateful Dead, The
Golden, William Lee
　See Oak Ridge Boys, The
Gooden, Ramone PeeWee
　See Digital Underground
Goodman, Benny 4
Gordon, Dexter 10
Gordon, Kim
　See Sonic Youth
Gordy, Berry, Jr. 6
Gore, Martin
　See Depeche Mode
Gorman, Steve
　See Black Crowes, The
Gossard, Stone
　See Pearl Jam
Gott, Larry
　See James
Goudreau, Barry
　See Boston
Gould, Billy
　See Faith No More
Gould, Glenn 9
Gradney, Ken
　See Little Feat
Graham, Bill 10
Graham, Johnny
　See Earth, Wind and Fire

Gramolini, Gary
　See Beaver Brown Band, The
Grant, Amy 7
Grant, Lloyd
　See Metallica
Grappelli, Stephane 10
Grateful Dead, The 5
Gray, Ella
　See Kronos Quartet
Gray, Tom
　See Country Gentlemen, The
　Also see Seldom Scene, The
Gray, Walter
　See Kronos Quartet
Grebenshikov, Boris 3
Green, Al 9
Green, Karl Anthony
　See Herman's Hermits
Green, Peter
　See Fleetwood Mac
Green, Susaye
　See Supremes, The
Green, Willie
　See Neville Brothers, The
Greenspoon, Jimmy
　See Three Dog Night
Greenwood, Lee 12
Gregg, Paul
　See Restless Heart
Gregory, Dave
　See XTC
Griffin, Bob
　See BoDeans, The
Griffith, Nanci 3
Grohl, Dave
　See Nirvana
Groucutt, Kelly
　See Electric Light Orchestra
Grove, George
　See Kingston Trio, The
Grusin, Dave 7
Guaraldi, Vince 3
Guard, Dave
　See Kingston Trio, The
Gudmundsdottir, Björk
　See Sugarcubes, The
Guerin, John
　See Byrds, The
Guest, Christopher
　See Tufnel, Nigel
Guns n' Roses 2
Gunther, Cornell
　See Coasters, The
Gustafson, Steve
　See 10,000 Maniacs
Guthrie, Arlo 6
Guthrie, Robin
　See Cocteau Twins, The
Guthrie, Woodie 2
Guy, Billy
　See Coasters, The
Guy, Buddy 4
Hackett, Steve
　See Genesis
Haden, Charlie 12

Hagar, Sammy
  See Van Halen
Haggard, Merle 2
Haley, Bill 6
Halford, Rob
  See Judas Priest
Hall & Oates 6
Hall, Daryl
  See Hall & Oates
Hall, Randall
  See Lynyrd Skynyrd
Hall, Tom T. 4
Hall, Tony
  See Neville Brothers, The
Hamilton, Frank
  See Weavers, The
Hamilton, Tom
  See Aerosmith
Hamlisch, Marvin 1
Hammer, M.C. 5
Hammerstein, Oscar
  See Rodgers, Richard
Hammett, Kirk
  See Metallica
Hammond, John 6
Hammond-Hammond, Jeffrey
  See Jethro Tull
Hampson, Sharon
  See Sharon, Lois & Bram
Hampson, Thomas 12
Hampton, Lionel 6
Hancock, Herbie 8
Handy, W. C. 7
Hanley, Steve
  See Fall, The
Hanna, Jeff
  See Nitty Gritty Dirt Band, The
Hanneman, Jeff
  See Slayer
Harding, John Wesley 6
Harley, Bill 7
Harrell, Lynn 3
Harrington, David
  See Kronos Quartet
Harris, Addie "Micki"
  See Shirelles, The
Harris, Damon Otis
  See Temptations, The
Harris, Emmylou 4
Harris, Evelyn
  See Sweet Honey in the Rock
Harris, R. H.
  See Soul Stirrers, The
Harris, Steve
  See Iron Maiden
Harrison, George 2
  Also see Beatles, The
Harrison, Jerry
  See Talking Heads
Harry, Deborah 4
Hart, Lorenz
  See Rodgers, Richard
Hart, Mark
  See Crowded House
Hart, Mickey
  See Grateful Dead, The

Hartford, John 1
Hartke, Stephen 5
Hartman, Bob
  See Petra
Hartman, John
  See Doobie Brothers, The
Harvey, Polly Jean 11
Hashian
  See Boston
Haslinger, Paul
  See Tangerine Dream
Hassan, Norman
  See UB40
Hatfield, Juliana 12
  Also see Lemonheads, The
Hauser, Tim
  See Manhattan Transfer, The
Havens, Richie 11
Hawkins, Coleman 11
Hawkins, Screamin' Jay 8
Hay, George D. 3
Hayes, Isaac 10
Haynes, Warren
  See Allman Brothers, The
Hays, Lee
  See Weavers, The
Hayward, Richard
  See Little Feat
Headon, Topper
  See Clash, The
Healey, Jeff 4
Heart 1
Heavy D 10
Hedges, Michael 3
Heggie, Will
  See Cocteau Twins, The
Hellerman, Fred
  See Weavers, The
Helm, Levon
  See Band, The
  Also see Nitty Gritty Dirt Band, The
Hendricks, Barbara 10
Hendrix, Jimi 2
Henley, Don 3
  Also see Eagles, The
Herman, Woody 12
Herman's Hermits 5
Herndon, Mark
  See Alabama
Herron, Cindy
  See En Vogue
Hester, Paul
  See Crowded House
Hetfield, James
  See Metallica
Hewson, Paul
  See U2
Hiatt, John 8
Hickman, Johnny
  See Cracker
Hicks, Chris
  See Restless Heart
Hidalgo, David
  See Los Lobos
Highway 101 4

Hijbert, Fritz
  See Kraftwerk
Hill, Dusty
  See ZZ Top
Hill, Ian
  See Judas Priest
Hillman, Bones
  See Midnight Oil
Hillman, Chris
  See Byrds, The
  Also see Desert Rose Band, The
Hinderas, Natalie 12
Hines, Earl "Fatha" 12
Hirst, Rob
  See Midnight Oil
Hirt, Al 5
Hitchcock, Robyn 9
Hodo, David
  See Village People, The
Hoenig, Michael
  See Tangerine Dream
Hoffman, Guy
  See BoDeans, The
  Also see Violent Femmes
Hoke, Jim
  See NRBQ
Holiday, Billie 6
Holland, Brian
  See Holland-Dozier-Holland
Holland, Dave
  See Judas Priest
Holland, Eddie
  See Holland-Dozier-Holland
Holland, Julian "Jools"
  See Squeeze
Holland-Dozier-Holland 5
Holly, Buddy 1
Honeyman-Scott, James
  See Pretenders, The
Hook, Peter
  See New Order
Hooker, John Lee 1
Hopwood, Keith
  See Herman's Hermits
Horn, Shirley 7
Horn, Trevor
  See Yes
Horne, Lena 11
Horne, Marilyn 9
Hornsby, Bruce 3
Horovitz, Adam
  See Beastie Boys, The
Horowitz, Vladimir 1
Hossack, Michael
  See Doobie Brothers, The
House, Son 11
Houston, Cissy 6
Houston, Whitney 8
Howe, Steve
  See Yes
Howlin' Wolf 6
Hubbard, Preston
  See Fabulous Thunderbirds, The
  Also see Roomful of Blues
Hudson, Garth
  See Band, The

Huffman, Doug
  See Boston
Hughes, Bruce
  See Cracker
Hughes, Glenn
  See Black Sabbath
Hughes, Glenn
  See Village People, The
Hughes, Leon
  See Coasters, The
Hunt, Darryl
  See Pogues, The
Hunter, Alberta 7
Hunter, Mark
  See James
Hunter, Shepherd "Ben"
  See Soundgarden
Hurley, George
  See fIREHOSE
Hutchence, Michael
  See INXS
Huth, Todd
  See Primus
Huxley, Rick
  See Dave Clark Five, The
Hütter, Ralf
  See Kraftwerk
Hutton, Danny
  See Three Dog Night
Hyman, Jerry
  See Blood, Sweat and Tears
Hynde, Chrissie
  See Pretenders, The
Ian, Janis 5
Ian, Scott
  See Anthrax
Ibbotson, Jimmy
  See Nitty Gritty Dirt Band, The
Ice Cube 10
  Also see N.W.A
Ice-T 7
Idol, Billy 3
Iglesias, Julio 2
Indigo Girls 3
Inez, Mike
  See Alice in Chains
Ingram, James 11
Innis, Dave
  See Restless Heart
INXS 2
Iommi, Tony
  See Black Sabbath
Iron Maiden 10
Irons, Jack
  See Red Hot Chili Peppers, The
Isaak, Chris 6
Isley, Ernie
  See Isley Brothers, The
Isley, Marvin
  See Isley Brothers, The
Isley, O'Kelly, Jr.
  See Isley Brothers, The
Isley, Ronald
  See Isley Brothers, The
Isley, Rudolph
  See Isley Brothers, The

Isley Brothers, The 8
Ives, Burl 12
Ivey, Michael
  See Basehead
Jabs, Matthias
  See Scorpions, The
Jackson 5, The
  See Jacksons, The
Jackson, Alan 7
Jackson, Eddie
  See Queensryche
Jackson, Freddie 3
Jackson, Jackie
  See Jacksons, The
Jackson, Janet 3
Jackson, Jermaine
  See Jacksons, The
Jackson, Joe 4
Jackson, Karen
  See Supremes, The
Jackson, Mahalia 8
Jackson, Marlon
  See Jacksons, The
Jackson, Michael 1
  Also see Jacksons, The
Jackson, Randy
  See Jacksons, The
Jackson, Tito
  See Jacksons, The
Jacksons, The 7
Jacox, Martin
  See Soul Stirrers, The
Jagger, Mick 7
  Also see Rolling Stones, The
Jairo T.
  See Sepultura
Jam, Jimmy
  See Jam, Jimmy, and Terry Lewis
Jam, Jimmy, and Terry Lewis 11
Jam Master Jay
  See Run-D.M.C.
James 12
James, Andrew "Bear"
  See Midnight Oil
James, Cheryl
  See Salt-N-Pepa
James, Doug
  See Roomful of Blues
James, Elmore 8
James, Etta 6
James, Harry 11
James, Rick 2
Jane's Addiction 6
Jardine, Al
  See Beach Boys, The
Jarobi
  See A Tribe Called Quest
Jarre, Jean-Michel 2
Jarreau, Al 1
Jarrett, Keith 1
Jasper, Chris
  See Isley Brothers, The
Jay, Miles
  See Village People, The
Jeanrenaud, Joan Dutcher
  See Kronos Quartet

Jefferson Airplane 5
Jefferson Starship
  See Jefferson Airplane
Jennings, Greg
  See Restless Heart
Jennings, Waylon 4
Jessie, Young
  See Coasters, The
Jesus and Mary Chain, The 10
Jethro Tull 8
Jett, Joan 3
Jimenez, Flaco
  See Texas Tornados, The
Jobson, Edwin
  See Jethro Tull
Joel, Billy 12
  Earlier sketch in CM 2
Johansen, David 7
Johanson, Jai Johanny
  See Allman Brothers, The
John, Elton 3
Johnson, Brian
  See AC/DC
Johnson, Courtney
  See New Grass Revival, The
Johnson, Daryl
  See Neville Brothers, The
Johnson, Gene
  See Diamond Rio
Johnson, Mike
  See Dinosaur Jr.
Johnson, Ralph
  See Earth, Wind and Fire
Johnson, Robert 6
Johnson, Shirley Childres
  See Sweet Honey in the Rock
Johnston, Bruce
  See Beach Boys, The
Johnston, Tom
  See Doobie Brothers, The
Jolson, Al 10
Jones, Booker T. 8
Jones, Busta
  See Gang of Four
Jones, Brian
  See Rolling Stones, The
Jones, Davy
  See Monkees, The
Jones, Elvin 9
Jones, George 4
Jones, Grace 9
Jones, John Paul
  See Led Zeppelin
Jones, Kendall
  See Fishbone
Jones, Kenny
  See Who, The
Jones, Maxine
  See En Vogue
Jones, Michael
  See Kronos Quartet
Jones, Mick
  See Clash, The
Jones, Quincy 2
Jones, Rickie Lee 4

Jones, Sandra "Puma"
　See Black Uhuru
Jones, Spike 5
Jones, Steve
　See Sex Pistols, The
Jones, Tom 11
Jones, Will "Dub"
　See Coasters, The
Joplin, Janis 3
Joplin, Scott 10
Jordan, Louis 11
Jordan, Stanley 1
Jorgensor, John
　See Desert Rose Band, The
Jourgensen, Al
　See Ministry
Joyce, Mike
　See Buzzcocks, The
　Also see Smiths, The
Judas Priest 10
Judd, Naomi
　See Judds, The
Judd, Wynonna
　See Judds, The
　Also see Wynonna
Judds, The 2
Jukebox
　See Geto Boys, The
Jungle DJ "Towa" Towa
　See Deee-lite
Jurado, Jeanette
　See Exposé
Kahlil, Aisha
　See Sweet Honey in the Rock
Kakoulli, Harry
　See Squeeze
Kalligan, Dick
　See Blood, Sweat and Tears
Kaminski, Mik
　See Electric Light Orchestra
Kanawa, Kiri Te
　See Te Kanawa, Kiri
Kane, Big Daddy 7
Kanter, Paul
　See Jefferson Airplane
Karajan, Herbert von
　See von Karajan, Herbert
Kath, Terry
　See Chicago
Katz, Steve
　See Blood, Sweat and Tears
Kaukonen, Jorma
　See Jefferson Airplane
Kaye, Tony
　See Yes
Kay Gee
　See Naughty by Nature
Keane, Sean
　See Chieftains, The
Kelly, Kevin
　See Byrds, The
Kendricks, Eddie
　See Temptations, The
Kennedy, Nigel 8
Kenner, Doris
　See Shirelles, The

Kentucky Headhunters, The 5
Khan, Chaka 9
Kibble, Mark
　See Take 6
Kibby, Walter
　See Fishbone
Kid 'n Play 5
Kiedis, Anthony
　See Red Hot Chili Peppers, The
Killian, Tim
　See Kronos Quartet
King, Albert 2
King, B. B. 1
King, Ben E. 7
King, Bob
　See Soul Stirrers, The
King, Carole 6
King, Ed
　See Lynyrd Skynyrd
King, Jon
　See Gang of Four
King, Kerry
　See Slayer
King Ad-Rock
　See Horovitz, Adam
Kingston Trio, The 9
King's X 7
Kinney, Sean
　See Alice in Chains
Kirk, Rahsaan Roland 6
Kirwan, Danny
　See Fleetwood Mac
Kiss 5
Kisser, Andreas
　See Sepultura
Kissin, Evgeny 6
Kitaro 1
Kitt, Eartha 9
Klein, Jon
　See Siouxsie and the Banshees
Klugh, Earl 10
Knight, Gladys 1
Knight, Jon
　See New Kids on the Block
Knight, Jordan
　See New Kids on the Block
Knopfler, Mark 3
Knudsen, Keith
　See Doobie Brothers, The
Konto, Skip
　See Three Dog Night
Kool Moe Dee 9
Kooper, Al
　See Blood, Sweat and Tears
Kotzen, Richie
　See Poison
Kraftwerk 9
Kramer, Joey
　See Aerosmith
Kramer, Wayne
　See MC5, The
Krause, Bernie
　See Weavers, The
Krauss, Alison 10
Kravitz, Lenny 5

Kreutzman, Bill
　See Grateful Dead, The
Krieger, Robert
　See Doors, The
Kris Kross 11
Kristofferson, Kris 4
Kronos Quartet 5
KRS-One 8
Krusen, Dave
　See Pearl Jam
Kulick, Bruce
　See Kiss
Kunkel, Bruce
　See Nitty Gritty Dirt Band, The
Kuti, Fela 7
L7 12
LaBelle, Patti 8
Lady Miss Kier
　See Deee-lite
Ladysmith Black Mambazo 1
Laine, Cleo 10
Lake, Greg
　See Emerson, Lake & Palmer/Powell
LaLonde, Larry "Ler"
　See Primus
Lamm, Robert
　See Chicago
Lane, Jay
　See Primus
Lang, K. D. 4
Lanois, Daniel 8
Larkin, Patty 9
Lataille, Rich
　See Roomful of Blues
Lauper, Cyndi 11
Laurence, Lynda
　See Supremes, The
Lavin, Christine 6
Lavis, Gilson
　See Squeeze
Lawrence, Tracy 11
Lawry, John
　See Petra
Laws, Roland
　See Earth, Wind and Fire
Lawson, Doyle
　See Country Gentlemen, The
Leadbelly 6
Leadon, Bernie
　See Eagles, The
　Also see Nitty Gritty Dirt Band, The
Leavell, Chuck
　See Allman Brothers, The
LeBon, Simon
　See Duran Duran
Leckenby, Derek "Lek"
　See Herman's Hermits
Ledbetter, Huddie
　See Leadbelly
LeDoux, Chris 12
Led Zeppelin 1
Lee, Beverly
　See Shirelles, The
Lee, Brenda 5
Lee, Geddy
　See Rush

Lee, Peggy 8
Lee, Sara
　See Gang of Four
Lee, Tommy
　See Mötley Crüe
Leese, Howard
　See Heart
Lehrer, Tom 7
Lemmy
　See Motörhead
Lemonheads, The 12
Le Mystère des Voix Bulgares
　See Bulgarian State Female Vocal Choir, The
Lenners, Rudy
　See Scorpions, The
Lennon, John 9
　Also see Beatles, The
Lennon, Julian 2
Lennox, Annie
　See Eurythmics
Leonard, Glenn
　See Temptations, The
Lesh, Phil
　See Grateful Dead, The
Levene, Keith
　See Clash, The
Levine, James 8
Levy, Ron
　See Roomful of Blues
Lewis, Huey 9
Lewis, Jerry Lee 2
Lewis, Otis
　See Fabulous Thunderbirds, The
Lewis, Peter
　See Moby Grape
Lewis, Roy
　See Kronos Quartet
Lewis, Samuel K.
　See Five Blind Boys of Alabama
Lewis, Terry
　See Jam, Jimmy, and Terry Lewis
Liberace 9
Lifeson, Alex
　See Rush
Lightfoot, Gordon 3
Lilienstein, Lois
　See Sharon, Lois & Bram
Lilker, Dan
　See Anthrax
Lincoln, Abbey 9
Lindley, David 2
Linnell, John
　See They Might Be Giants
Lipsius, Fred
　See Blood, Sweat and Tears
Little, Keith
　See Country Gentlemen, The
Little Feat 4
Little Richard 1
Living Colour 7
Llanas, Sammy
　See BoDeans, The
L.L. Cool J. 5
Lloyd Webber, Andrew 6
Lockwood, Robert, Jr. 10

Loggins, Kenny 3
Lombardo, Dave
　See Slayer
Lord, Jon
　See Deep Purple
Los Lobos 2
Los Reyes
　See Gipsy Kings, The
Loughnane, Lee
　See Chicago
Louvin, Charlie
　See Louvin Brothers, The
Louvin, Ira
　See Louvin Brothers, The
Louvin Brothers, The 12
Love, Mike
　See Beach Boys, The
Loveless, Patty 5
Lovering, David
　See Cracker
Lovett, Lyle 5
Lowe, Chris
　See Pet Shop Boys
Lowe, Nick 6
Lowery, David
　See Cracker
Lozano, Conrad
　See Los Lobos
Lucia, Paco de
　See de Lucia, Paco
Luke
　See Campbell, Luther
Lupo, Pat
　See Beaver Brown Band, The
LuPone, Patti 8
Lydon, John 9
　Also see Sex Pistols, The
Lyngstad, Anni-Frid
　See Abba
Lynn, Loretta 2
Lynne, Jeff 5
　Also see Electric Light Orchestra
Lynne, Shelby 5
Lynyrd Skynyrd 9
Ma, Yo-Yo 2
MacColl, Kirsty 12
MacGowan, Shane
　See Pogues, The
Mack Daddy
　See Kris Kross
Madonna 4
Magoogan, Wesley
　See English Beat, The
Maher, John
　See Buzzcocks, The
Makeba, Miriam 8
Malone, Tom
　See Blood, Sweat and Tears
Mancini, Henry 1
Mandrell, Barbara 4
Maness, J. D.
　See Desert Rose Band, The
Manhattan Transfer, The 8
Manilow, Barry 2
Manuel, Richard
　See Band, The

Manzarek, Ray
　See Doors, The
Marie, Buffy Sainte
　See Sainte-Marie, Buffy
Marini, Lou, Jr.
　See Blood, Sweat and Tears
Marley, Bob 3
Marley, Rita 10
Marley, Ziggy 3
Marr, Johnny
　See Smiths, The
Marriner, Neville
Mars, Chris
　See Replacements, The
Mars, Mick
　See Mötley Crüe
Marsalis, Branford 10
Marsalis, Wynton 6
Martin, Barbara
　See Supremes, The
Martin, Christopher
　See Kid 'n Play
Martin, Dean 1
Martin, George 6
Martin, Greg
　See Kentucky Headhunters, The
Martin, Jim
　See Faith No More
Martin, Jimmy 5
　Also See Osborne Brothers, The
Martin, Tony
　See Black Sabbath
Marx, Richard 3
Mascis, J
　See Dinosaur Jr.
Masdea, Jim
　See Boston
Masekela, Hugh 7
Maseo, Baby Huey
　See De La Soul
Mason, Nick
　See Pink Floyd
Masse, Laurel
　See Manhattan Transfer, The
Masur, Kurt 11
Mathis, Johnny 2
Matlock, Glen
　See Sex Pistols, The
Mattea, Kathy 5
May, Brian
　See Queen
Mayall, John 7
Mayfield, Curtis 8
Mazibuko, Abednigo
　See Ladysmith Black Mambazo
Mazibuko, Albert
　See Ladysmith Black Mambazo
MC5, The 9
MCA
　See Yauch, Adam
McBrain, Nicko
　See Iron Maiden
McCarrick, Martin
　See Siouxsie and the Banshees
McCartney, Paul 4
　Also see Beatles, The

McCarty, Jim
  See Yardbirds, The
MC Clever
  See Digital Underground
McCracken, Chet
  See Doobie Brothers, The
McCready, Mike
  See Pearl Jam
McDaniels, Darryl "D"
  See Run-D.M.C.
McDonald, Barbara Kooyman
  See Timbuk 3
McDonald, Michael
  See Doobie Brothers, The
McDonald, Pat
  See Timbuk 3
McDorman, Joe
  See Statler Brothers, The
McDowell, Hugh
  See Electric Light Orchestra
McEntire, Reba 11
MC Eric
  See Technotronic
McEuen, John
  See Nitty Gritty Dirt Band, The
McFee, John
  See Doobie Brothers, The
McFerrin, Bobby 3
McGeoch, John
  See Siouxsie and the Banshees
McGuinn, Jim
  See McGuinn, Roger
McGuinn, Roger
  See Byrds, The
McIntosh, Robbie
  See Pretenders, The
McIntyre, Joe
  See New Kids on the Block
McKagan, Duff
  See Guns n' Roses
McKay, Al
  See Earth, Wind and Fire
McKay, John
  See Siouxsie and the Banshees
McKean, Michael
  See St. Hubbins, David
McKee, Maria 11
McKernarn, Ron "Pigpen"
  See Grateful Dead, The
McKnight, Claude V. III
  See Take 6
McLachlan, Sarah 12
McLaughlin, John 12
McLean, Don 7
McLeod, Rory
  See Roomful of Blues
MC Lyte 8
McMeel, Mickey
  See Three Dog Night
McMurtry, James 10
McRae, Carmen 9
MC Serch 10
McReynolds, Jesse
  See McReynolds, Jim and Jesse
McReynolds, Jim
  See McReynolds, Jim and Jesse

McReynolds, Jim and Jesse 12
McShane, Ronnie
  See Chieftains, The
McVie, Christine
  See Fleetwood Mac
McVie, John
  See Fleetwood Mac
Mdletshe, Geophrey
  See Ladysmith Black Mambazo
Meat Loaf 12
Medley, Bill 3
Medlock, James
  See Soul Stirrers, The
Megadeth 9
Mehta, Zubin 11
Meine, Klaus
  See Scorpions, The
Meisner, Randy
  See Eagles, The
Melanie 12
Melax, Einar
  See Sugarcubes, The
Mellencamp, John "Cougar" 2
Menken, Alan 10
Menuhin, Yehudi 11
Menza, Nick
  See Megadeth
Merchant, Natalie
  See 10,000 Maniacs
Mercier, Peadar
  See Chieftains, The
Mercury, Freddie
  See Queen
Metallica 7
Methembu, Russel
  See Ladysmith Black Mambazo
Metheny, Pat 2
Meyers, Augie
  See Texas Tornados, The
Michael, George 9
Michaels, Bret
  See Poison
Midler, Bette 8
Midnight Oil 11
Midori 7
Mike D
  See Diamond, Mike
Miles, Richard
  See Soul Stirrers, The
Miller, Glenn 6
Miller, Jerry
  See Moby Grape
Miller, Mitch 11
Miller, Rice
  See Williamson, Sonny Boy
Miller, Roger 4
Miller, Steve 2
Milli Vanilli 4
Mills, Fred
  See Canadian Brass, The
Milsap, Ronnie 2
Mingus, Charles 9
Ministry 10
Miss Kier Kirby
  See Lady Miss Kier

Mitchell, John
  See Asleep at the Wheel
Mitchell, Joni 2
Mizell, Jay
  See Run-D.M.C.
Moby Grape 12
Moginie, Jim
  See Midnight Oil
Molloy, Matt
  See Chieftains, The
Moloney, Paddy
  See Chieftains, The
Money B
  See Digital Underground
Monk, Meredith 1
Monk, Thelonious 6
Monkees, The 7
Monroe, Bill 1
Montand, Yves 12
Montgomery, Wes 3
Moon, Keith
  See Who, The
Moore, Alan
  See Judas Priest
Moore, Angelo
  See Fishbone
Moore, Melba 7
Moore, Sam
  See Sam and Dave
Moore, Thurston
  See Sonic Youth
Moraz, Patrick
  See Yes
Morgan, Frank 9
Morgan, Lorrie 10
Morley, Pat
  See Soul Asylum
Morris, Kenny
  See Siouxsie and the Banshees
Morris, Stephen
  See New Order
Morrison, Bram
  See Sharon, Lois & Bram
Morrison, Jim 3
  Also see Doors, The
Morrison, Sterling
  See Velvet Underground, The
Morrison, Van 3
Morrissey 10
  Also see Smiths, The
Morrissey, Bill 12
Morrissey, Steven Patrick
  See Morrissey
Morton, Everett
  See English Beat, The
Morton, Jelly Roll 7
Morvan, Fab
  See Milli Vanilli
Mosely, Chuck
  See Faith No More
Moser, Scott "Cactus"
  See Highway 101
Mosley, Bob
  See Moby Grape
Mouskouri, Nana 12
Moyet, Alison 12

Mullen, Larry, Jr.
　See U2
Mötley Crüe **1**
Motörhead **10**
Motta, Danny
　See Roomful of Blues
Mould, Bob **10**
Moulding, Colin
　See XTC
Mueller, Karl
　See Soul Asylum
Mullen, Larry
　See U2
Murph
　See Dinosaur Jr.
Murphy, Dan
　See Soul Asylum
Murphey, Michael Martin **9**
Murray, Anne **4**
Murray, Dave
　See Iron Maiden
Mustaine, Dave
　See Megadeth
　　Also see Metallica
Mwelase, Jabulane
　See Ladysmith Black Mambazo
Mydland, Brent
　See Grateful Dead, The
Myles, Alannah **4**
Nagler, Eric **8**
Nascimento, Milton **6**
Naughty by Nature **11**
Navarro, David
　See Jane's Addiction
N'Dour, Youssou **6**
Near, Holly **1**
Neel, Johnny
　See Allman Brothers, The
Negron, Chuck
　See Three Dog Night
Neil, Vince
　See Mötley Crüe
Nelson, Errol
　See Black Uhuru
Nelson, Rick **2**
Nelson, Willie **11**
　Earlier sketch in CM **1**
Nesmith, Mike
　See Monkees, The
Neville, Aaron **5**
　Also see Neville Brothers, The
Neville, Art
　See Neville Brothers, The
Neville Brothers, The **4**
Neville, Charles
　See Neville Brothers, The
Neville, Cyril
　See Neville Brothers, The
New Grass Revival, The **4**
New Kids on the Block **3**
Newman, Randy **4**
Newmann, Kurt
　See BoDeans, The
New Order **11**
New Rhythm and Blues Quartet
　See NRBQ

Newton, Wayne **2**
Newton-John, Olivia **8**
Nicholls, Geoff
　See Black Sabbath
Nicks, Stevie **2**
　Also see Fleetwood Mac
Nico
　See Velvet Underground, The
Nielsen, Rick
　See Cheap Trick
Nilsson **10**
Nilsson, Harry
　See Nilsson
Nirvana **8**
Nitty Gritty Dirt Band, The **6**
Noone, Peter
　See Herman's Hermits
Norica, Sugar Ray
　See Roomful of Blues
Norman, Jessye **7**
Norman, Jimmy
　See Coasters, The
Norvo, Red **12**
Novoselic, Chris
　See Nirvana
NRBQ **12**
Nugent, Ted **2**
Nunn, Bobby
　See Coasters, The
N.W.A. **6**
Nyro, Laura **12**
Oak Ridge Boys, The **7**
Oakley, Berry
　See Allman Brothers, The
Oates, John
　See Hall & Oates
Ocasek, Ric **5**
Ocean, Billy **4**
Oceans, Lucky
　See Asleep at the Wheel
Ochs, Phil **7**
O'Connell, Chris
　See Asleep at the Wheel
O'Connor, Mark **1**
O'Connor, Sinead **3**
Odetta **7**
O'Donnell, Roger
　See Cure, The
Ohanian, David
　See Canadian Brass, The
Olafsson, Bragi
　See Sugarcubes, The
Olander, Jimmy
　See Diamond Rio
Olson, Jeff
　See Village People, The
Ono, Yoko **11**
Orbison, Roy **2**
O'Riordan, Cait
　See Pogues, The
Örn, Einar
　See Sugarcubes, The
Örnolfsdottir, Margret
　See Sugarcubes, The
Orzabal, Roland
　See Tears for Fears

Osborne, Bob
　See Osborne Brothers, The
Osborne, Sonny
　See Osborne Brothers, The
Osborne Brothers, The **8**
Osbourne, Ozzy **3**
　Also see Black Sabbath
Oslin, K. T. **3**
Osmond, Donny **3**
Ott, David **2**
Outler, Jimmy
　See Soul Stirrers, The
Owen, Randy
　See Alabama
Owens, Buck **2**
Owens, Ricky
　See Temptations, The
Page, Jimmy **4**
　Also see Led Zeppelin
　Also see Yardbirds, The
Page, Patti **11**
Paice, Ian
　See Deep Purple
Palmer, Carl
　See Emerson, Lake & Palmer/Powell
Palmer, David
　See Jethro Tull
Palmer, Robert **2**
Pankow, James
　See Chicago
Parazaider, Walter
　See Chicago
Parkening, Christopher **7**
Parker, Charlie **5**
Parker, Graham **10**
Parker, Kris
　See KRS-One
Parker, Maceo **7**
Parsons, Alan **12**
Parsons, Gene
　See Byrds, The
Parsons, Gram **7**
　Also see Byrds, The
Parsons, Tony
　See Iron Maiden
Parton, Dolly **2**
Partridge, Andy
　See XTC
Pasemaster, Mase
　See De La Soul
Patinkin, Mandy **3**
Patti, Sandi **7**
Patton, Charley **11**
Patton, Mike
　See Faith No More
Paul, Alan
　See Manhattan Transfer, The
Paul, Les **2**
Paulo, Jr.
　See Sepultura
Pavarotti, Luciano **1**
Paxton, Tom **5**
Payne, Bill
　See Little Feat
Payne, Scherrie
　See Supremes, The

Payton, Denis
  See Dave Clark Five, The
Payton, Lawrence
  See Four Tops, The
Pearl, Minnie 3
Pearl Jam 12
Peart, Neil
  See Rush
Pedersen, Herb
  See Desert Rose Band, The
Peduzzi, Larry
  See Roomful of Blues
Pegg, Dave
  See Jethro Tull
Pendergrass, Teddy 3
Pengilly, Kirk
  See INXS
Penn, Michael 4
Penner, Fred 10
Perahia, Murray 10
Peretz, Jesse
  See Lemonheads, The
Perez, Louie
  See Los Lobos
Perkins, Carl 9
Perkins, John
  See XTC
Perkins, Percell
  See Five Blind Boys of Alabama
Perkins, Steve
  See Jane's Addiction
Perlman, Itzhak 2
Perry, Doane
  See Jethro Tull
Perry, Joe
  See Aerosmith
Pet Shop Boys 5
Peter, Paul & Mary 4
Peters, Bernadette 7
Peterson, Oscar 11
Petersson, Tom
  See Cheap Trick
Petra 3
Petty, Tom 9
Phantom, Slim Jim
  See Stray Cats, The
Phelps, Doug
  See Kentucky Headhunters, The
Phelps, Ricky Lee
  See Kentucky Headhunters, The
Phife
  See A Tribe Called Quest
Phil, Gary
  See Boston
Philips, Anthony
  See Genesis
Phillips, Chynna
  See Wilson Phillips
Phillips, Harvey 3
Phillips, Sam 5
Phillips, Sam 12
Phillips, Simon
  See Judas Priest
Phungula, Inos
  See Ladysmith Black Mambazo

Piaf, Edith 8
Piccolo, Greg
  See Roomful of Blues
Pickett, Wilson 10
Pierson, Kate
  See B-52's, The
Pilatus, Rob
  See Milli Vanilli
Pink Floyd 2
Pinnick, Doug
  See King's X
Pirner, Dave
  See Soul Asylum
Pirroni, Marco
  See Siouxsie and the Banshees
Plakas, Dee
  See L7
Plant, Robert 2
  Also see Led Zeppelin
P.M. Dawn 11
Pogues, The 6
Poindexter, Buster
  See Johansen, David
Pointer, Anita
  See Pointer Sisters, The
Pointer, Bonnie
  See Pointer Sisters, The
Pointer, June
  See Pointer Sisters, The
Pointer, Ruth
  See Pointer Sisters, The
Pointer Sisters, The 9
Poison 11
Poland, Chris
  See Megadeth
Ponty, Jean-Luc 8
Pop, Iggy 1
Porter, Cole 10
Porter, Tiran
  See Doobie Brothers, The
Posdnuos
  See De La Soul
Potts, Sean
  See Chieftains, The
Powell, Billy
  See Lynyrd Skynyrd
Powell, Cozy
  See Emerson, Lake & Palmer/Powell
Prater, Dave
  See Sam and Dave
Presley, Elvis 1
Pretenders, The 8
Price, Leontyne 6
Price, Louis
  See Temptations, The
Price, Ray 11
Price, Rick
  See Electric Light Orchestra
Pride, Charley 4
Primettes, The
  See Supremes, The
Primus 11
Prince 1
Prince Be
  See P.M. Dawn

Prine, John 7
Professor Longhair 6
Prout, Brian
  See Diamond Rio
Public Enemy 4
Pyle, Artemis
  See Lynyrd Skynyrd
Q-Tip
  See A Tribe Called Quest
Queen 6
Queen Ida 9
Queen Latifah 6
Queensryche 8
Querfurth, Carl
  See Roomful of Blues
Rabbitt, Eddie 5
Rabin, Trevor
  See Yes
Raffi 8
Raheem
  See Geto Boys, The
Raitt, Bonnie 3
Rakim
  See Eric B. and Rakim
Ramone, C. J.
  See Ramones, The
Ramone, Dee Dee
  See Ramones, The
Ramone, Joey
  See Ramones, The
Ramone, Johnny
  See Ramones, The
Ramone, Marky
  See Ramones, The
Ramone, Ritchie
  See Ramones, The
Ramone, Tommy
  See Ramones, The
Ramones, The 9
Rampal, Jean-Pierre 6
Ranaldo, Lee
  See Sonic Youth
Ranken, Andrew
  See Pogues, The
Ranking Roger
  See English Beat, The
Rarebell, Herman
  See Scorpions, The
Ray, Amy
  See Indigo Girls
Raymonde, Simon
  See Cocteau Twins, The
Rea, Chris 12
Reagon, Bernice Johnson
  See Sweet Honey in the Rock
Redding, Otis 5
Reddy, Helen 9
Red Hot Chili Peppers, The 7
Redman, Joshua 12
Redpath, Jean 1
Reed, Lou 1
  Also see Velvet Underground, The
Reeves, Jim 10
Reeves, Martha 4
Reich, Steve 8

Reid, Christopher
 See Kid 'n Play
Reid, Delroy "Junior"
 See Black Uhuru
Reid, Don
 See Statler Brothers, The
Reid, Harold
 See Statler Brothers, The
Reid, Janet
 See Black Uhuru
Reid, Jim
 See Jesus and Mary Chain, The
Reid, Vernon 2
 Also see Living Colour
Reid, William
 See Jesus and Mary Chain, The
Reinhardt, Django 7
Relf, Keith
 See Yardbirds, The
R.E.M. 5
Ren, M.C.
 See N.W.A.
Reno, Ronnie
 See Osborne Brothers, The
Replacements, The 7
Restless Heart 12
Reyes, Andre
 See Gipsy Kings, The
Reyes, Canut
 See Gipsy Kings, The
Reyes, Nicolas
 See Gipsy Kings, The
Reynolds, Nick
 See Kingston Trio, The
Reynolds, Sheldon
 See Earth, Wind and Fire
Rhodes, Nick
 See Duran Duran
Rich, Charlie 3
Richard, Keith
 See Richards, Keith
Richard, Zachary 9
Richards, Keith 11
 Also see Rolling Stones, The
Richie, Lionel 2
Richman, Jonathan 12
Rieckermann, Ralph
 See Scorpions, The
Rieflin, William
 See Ministry
Riley, Timothy Christian
 See Tony! Toni! Toné!
Ritchie, Brian
 See Violent Femmes
Ritchie, Jean 4
Ritenour, Lee 7
Roach, Max 12
Robbins, Marty 9
Roberts, Marcus 6
Robertson, Brian
 See Motörhead
Robertson, Robbie 2
 Also see Band, The
Robeson, Paul 8
Robillard, Duke 2

Also see Roomful of Blues
Robinson, Chris
 See Black Crowes, The
Robinson, Dawn
 See En Vogue
Robinson, R. B.
 See Soul Stirrers, The
Robinson, Rich
 See Black Crowes, The
Robinson, Smokey 1
Rockenfield, Scott
 See Queensryche
Rocker, Lee
 See Stray Cats, The
Rockett, Rikki
 See Poison
Rockin' Dopsie 10
Rodgers, Jimmie 3
Rodgers, Nile 8
Rodgers, Richard 9
Roe, Marty
 See Diamond Rio
Roeder, Klaus
 See Kraftwerk
Rogers, Kenny 1
Rogers, Roy 9
Rogers, Willie
 See Soul Stirrers, The
Rolling Stones, The 3
Rollins, Henry 11
Rollins, Sonny 7
Romm, Ronald
 See Canadian Brass, The
Ronstadt, Linda 2
Roomful of Blues 7
Roper, De De
 See Salt-N-Pepa
Rosas, Cesar
 See Los Lobos
Rose, Axl
 See Guns n' Roses
Rose, Michael
 See Black Uhuru
Rosen, Gary
 See Rosenshontz
Rosenshontz 9
Rosenthal, Jurgen
 See Scorpions, The
Rosenthal, Phil
 See Seldom Scene, The
Ross, Diana 1
 Also see Supremes, The
Rossi, John
 See Roomful of Blues
Rossington, Gary
 See Lynyrd Skynyrd
Roth, David Lee 1
 Also see Van Halen
Roth, Ulrich
 See Scorpions, The
Rotsey, Martin
 See Midnight Oil
Rotten, Johnny
 See Lydon, John
 Also see Sex Pistols, The

Rourke, Andy
 See Smiths, The
Rowe, Dwain
 See Restless Heart
Rubin, Rick 9
Rubinstein, Arthur 11
Rudd, Phillip
 See AC/DC
Ruffin, David 6
 Also see Temptations, The
Rundgren, Todd 11
Run-D.M.C. 4
Rush 8
Rush, Otis 12
Russell, Mark 6
Rutherford, Mike
 See Genesis
Rutsey, John
 See Rush
Ryan, David
 See Lemonheads, The
Ryan, Mick
 See Dave Clark Five, The
Ryder, Mitch 11
Ryland, Jack
 See Three Dog Night
Sabo, Dave
 See Bon Jovi
Sade 2
Sager, Carole Bayer
Sahm, Doug
 See Texas Tornados, The
Sainte-Marie, Buffy 11
St. Hubbins, David
 See Spinal Tap
St. John, Mark
 See Kiss
St. Marie, Buffy
 See Sainte-Marie, Buffy
Salerno-Sonnenberg, Nadja 3
Saliers, Emily
 See Indigo Girls
Salt-N-Pepa 6
Sam and Dave 8
Sambora, Richie
 See Bon Jovi
Sampson, Doug
 See Iron Maiden
Samuelson, Gar
 See Megadeth
Samwell-Smith, Paul
 See Yardbirds, The
Sanborn, David 1
Sanders, Steve
 See Oak Ridge Boys, The
Sanger, David
 See Asleep at the Wheel
Santana, Carlos 1
Saraceno, Blues
 See Poison
Satriani, Joe 4
Savage, Rick
 See Def Leppard
Saxa
 See English Beat, The

Cumulative Musicians Index • 321

Saxon, Stan
  See Dave Clark Five, The
Scaccia, Mike
  See Ministry
Scaggs, Boz 12
Scanlon, Craig
  See Fall, The
Scarface
  See Geto Boys, The
Schenker, Michael
  See Scorpions, The
Schenker, Rudolf
  See Scorpions, The
Schermie, Joe
  See Three Dog Night
Schickele, Peter 5
Schlitt, John
  See Petra
Schmelling, Johannes
  See Tangerine Dream
Schmit, Timothy B.
  See Eagles, The
Schmoovy Schmoove
  See Digital Underground
Schneider, Florian
  See Kraftwerk
Schneider, Fred III
  See B-52's, The
Schnitzler, Conrad
  See Tangerine Dream
Scholz, Tom
  See Boston
Schroyder, Steve
  See Tangerine Dream
Schulze, Klaus
  See Tangerine Dream
Schuman, William 10
Schuur, Diane 6
Scofield, John 7
Scorpions, The 12
Scott, Bon (Ronald Belford)
  See AC/DC
Scott, George
  See Five Blind Boys of Alabama
Scott, Sherry
  See Earth, Wind and Fire
Scruggs, Earl 3
Seals, Dan 9
Seals, Jim
  See Seals & Crofts
Seals & Crofts 3
Sears, Pete
  See Jefferson Starship
Sedaka, Neil 4
Seeger, Pete 4
  Also see Weavers, The
Segovia, Andres 6
Seldom Scene, The 4
Sen Dog
  See Cypress Hill
Sepultura 12
Seraphine, Daniel
  See Chicago
Sermon, Erick
  See EPMD

Setzer, Brian
  See Stray Cats, The
Severin, Steven
  See Siouxsie and the Banshees
Severinsen, Doc 1
Sex Pistols, The 5
Seymour, Neil
  See Crowded House
Shabalala, Ben
  See Ladysmith Black Mambazo
Shabalala, Headman
  See Ladysmith Black Mambazo
Shabalala, Jockey
  See Ladysmith Black Mambazo
Shabalala, Joseph
  See Ladysmith Black Mambazo
Shallenberger, James
  See Kronos Quartet
Shane, Bob
  See Kingston Trio, The
Shankar, Ravi 9
Shannon, Del 10
Shanté 10
Shanté, Roxanne
  See Shanté
Sharon, Lois & Bram 6
Shaw, Artie 8
Shearer, Harry
  See Smalls, Derek
Sheehan, Fran
  See Boston
Sheila E. 3
Shelley, Peter
  See Buzzcocks, The
Shelley, Steve
  See Sonic Youth
Sherba, John
  See Kronos Quartet
Sherman, Jack
  See Red Hot Chili Peppers, The
Shirelles, The 11
Shock G
  See Digital Underground
Shocked, Michelle 4
Shogren, Dave
  See Doobie Brothers, The
Shontz, Bill
  See Rosenshontz
Shorter, Wayne 5
Siberry, Jane 6
Siegal, Janis
  See Manhattan Transfer, The
Sikes, C. David
  See Boston
Sills, Beverly 5
Silva, Kenny Jo
  See Beaver Brown Band, The
Simien, Terrance 12
Simmons, Gene
  See Kiss
Simmons, Joe "Run"
  See Run-D.M.C.
Simmons, Patrick
  See Doobie Brothers, The
Simmons, Russell 7

Simon, Carly 4
Simon, Paul 1
Simone, Nina 11
Simonon, Paul
  See Clash, The
Simpson, Derrick "Duckie"
  See Black Uhuru
Simpson, Ray
  See Village People, The
Sinatra, Frank 1
Singer, Eric
  See Black Sabbath
Sioux, Siouxsie
  See Siouxsie and the Banshees
Siouxsie and the Banshees 8
Sir Rap-A-Lot
  See Geto Boys, The
Sixx, Nikki
  See Mötley Crüe
Skaggs, Ricky 5
  Also see Country Gentlemen, The
Skillings, Muzz
  See Living Colour
Slash
  See Guns n' Roses
Slayer 10
Sledd, Dale
  See Osborne Brothers, The
Slick, Grace
  See Jefferson Airplane
Slovak, Hillel
  See Red Hot Chili Peppers, The
Smalls, Derek
  See Spinal Tap
Smith, Adrian
  See Iron Maiden
Smith, Bessie 3
Smith, Chad
  See Red Hot Chili Peppers, The
Smith, Curt
  See Tears for Fears
Smith, Fred
  See MC5, The
Smith, Garth
  See Buzzcocks, The
Smith, Mark E.
  See Fall, The
Smith, Michael W. 11
Smith, Mike
  See Dave Clark Five, The
Smith, Parrish
  See EPMD
Smith, Patti 1
Smith, Robert
  See Cure, The
  Also see Siouxsie and the Banshees
Smith, Smitty
  See Three Dog Night
Smith, Willard
  See DJ Jazzy Jeff and the Fresh Prince
Smiths, The 3
Sneed, Floyd Chester
  See Three Dog Night
Snow, Don
  See Squeeze

Snow, Phoebe 4
Solal, Martial 4
Soloff, Lew
    See Blood, Sweat and Tears
Sondheim, Stephen 8
Sonic Youth 9
Sonnenberg, Nadja Salerno
    See Salerno-Sonnenberg, Nadja
Sonnier, Jo-El 10
Sosa, Mercedes 3
Soul Asylum 10
Soul Stirrers, The 11
Soundgarden 6
Sousa, John Philip 10
Spampinato, Joey
    See NRBQ
Spampinato, Johnny
    See NRBQ
Sparks, Donita
    See L7
Spector, Phil 4
Spence, Alexander "Skip"
    See Jefferson Airplane
        Also see Moby Grape
Spence, Skip
    See Spence, Alexander "Skip"
Spencer, Jeremy
    See Fleetwood Mac
Spencer, Jim
    See Dave Clark Five, The
Spinal Tap 8
Spitz, Dan
    See Anthrax
Spitz, Dave
    See Black Sabbath
Spring, Keith
    See NRBQ
Springfield, Rick 9
Springsteen, Bruce 6
Squeeze 5
Squire, Chris
    See Yes
Stacey, Peter "Spider"
    See Pogues, The
Staley, Layne
    See Alice in Chains
Staley, Tom
    See NRBQ
Stanley, Ian
    See Tears for Fears
Stanley, Paul
    See Kiss
Stanley, Ralph 5
Stansfield, Lisa 9
Staples, Pops 11
Starling, John
    See Seldom Scene, The
Starr, Mike
    See Alice in Chains
Starr, Ringo 10
    Also see Beatles, The
Starship
    See Jefferson Airplane
Statler Brothers, The 8
Steele, David
    See English Beat, The

Steely Dan 5
Sterban, Richard
    See Oak Ridge Boys, The
Stern, Isaac 7
Stevens, Cat 3
Stevens, Ray 7
Stevenson, Don
    See Moby Grape
Stewart, Dave
    See Eurythmics
Stewart, Ian
    See Rolling Stones, The
Stewart, John
    See Kingston Trio, The
Stewart, Larry
    See Restless Heart
Stewart, Rod 2
Stills, Stephen 5
Sting 2
Stinson, Bob
    See Replacements, The
Stinson, Tommy
    See Replacements, The
Stipe, Michael
    See R.E.M.
Stoltz, Brian
    See Neville Brothers, The
Stone, Curtis
    See Highway 101
Stone, Doug 10
Stone, Sly 8
Stookey, Paul
    See Peter, Paul & Mary
Story, Liz 2
Stradlin, Izzy
    See Guns n' Roses
Strait, George 5
Stratton, Dennis
    See Iron Maiden
Stray Cats, The 11
Street, Richard
    See Temptations, The
Streisand, Barbra 2
Strickland, Keith
    See B-52's, The
Strummer, Joe
    See Clash, The
Stryper 2
Stuart, Marty 9
Stubbs, Levi
    See Four Tops, The
Such, Alec Jon
    See Bon Jovi
Sugarcubes, The 10
Summer, Donna 12
Summer, Mark
    See Turtle Island String Quartet
Summers, Andy 3
Sumner, Bernard
    See New Order
Sun Ra 5
Super DJ Dmitry
    See Deee-lite
Supremes, The 6
Sutcliffe, Stu
    See Beatles, The

Sweet Honey in the Rock 1
Sweet, Matthew 9
Sweet, Michael
    See Stryper
Sweet, Robert
    See Stryper
Sweethearts of the Rodeo 12
Sykes, John
    See Whitesnake
Tabor, Ty
    See King's X
Taj Mahal 6
Take 6 6
Takemitsu, Toru 6
Talbot, John Michael 6
Talking Heads 1
Tandy, Richard
    See Electric Light Orchestra
Tangerine Dream 12
Tate, Geoff
    See Queensryche
Taylor, Andy
    See Duran Duran
Taylor, Cecil 9
Taylor, Dick
    See Rolling Stones, The
Taylor, Earl
    See Country Gentlemen, The
Taylor, James 2
Taylor, John
    See Duran Duran
Taylor, Johnnie
    See Soul Stirrers, The
Taylor, Koko 10
Taylor, Leroy
    See Soul Stirrers, The
Taylor, Mick
    See Rolling Stones, The
Taylor, Philip "Philthy Animal"
    See Motörhead
Taylor, Roger
    See Duran Duran
Taylor, Roger (Meadows)
    See Queen
Teagarden, Jack 10
Tears for Fears 6
Technotronic 5
Te Kanawa, Kiri 2
Temptations, The 3
Tennant, Neil
    See Pet Shop Boys
10,000 Maniacs 3
Terminator X
    See Public Enemy
Terrell, Jean
    See Supremes, The
Texas Tornados, The 8
Thayil, Kim
    See Soundgarden
They Might Be Giants 7
Thomas, Alex
    See Earth, Wind and Fire
Thomas, David
    See Take 6
Thomas, David Clayton
    See Clayton-Thomas, David

Thomas, Mickey
　See Jefferson Starship
Thomas, Olice
　See Five Blind Boys of Alabama
Thompson, Dennis
　See MC5, The
Thompson, Les
　See Nitty Gritty Dirt Band, The
Thompson, Porl
　See Cure, The
Thompson, Richard 7
Threadgill, Henry 9
Three Dog Night 5
Tiffany 4
Tikaram, Tanita 9
Tilbrook, Glenn
　See Squeeze
Tillis, Mel 7
Tillis, Pam 8
Timbuk 3 3
Timmins, Margo
　See Cowboy Junkies, The
Timmins, Michael
　See Cowboy Junkies, The
Timmins, Peter
　See Cowboy Junkies, The
Tippin, Aaron 12
Tipton, Glenn
　See Judas Priest
Tolhurst, Laurence
　See Cure, The
Toller, Dan
　See Allman Brothers, The
Tone-L c 3
Tony K
　See Roomful of Blues
Tony! Toni! Toné! 12
Took, Steve Peregrine
　See T. Rex
Topham, Anthony "Top"
　See Yardbirds, The
Tork, Peter
　See Monkees, The
Torme, Mel 4
Torres, Hector "Tico"
　See Bon Jovi
Tosh, Peter 3
Toussaint, Allen 11
Townes, Jeffery
　See DJ Jazzy Jeff and the Fresh Prince
Townshend, Pete 1
　Also see Who, The
Travers, Brian
　See UB40
Travers, Mary
　See Peter, Paul & Mary
Travis, Randy 9
Treach
　See Naughty by Nature
T. Rex 11
A Tribe Called Quest 8
Tritt, Travis 7
Trucks, Butch
　See Allman Brothers, The
Trugoy the Dove
　See De La Soul

Truman, Dan
　See Diamond Rio
Tubb, Ernest 4
Tubridy, Michael
　See Chieftans, The
Tucker, Moe
　See Velvet Underground, The
Tucker, Sophie 12
Tucker, Tanya 3
Tufnel, Nigel
　See Spinal Tap
Turbin, Neil
　See Anthrax
Turner, Joe Lynn
　See Deep Purple
Turner, Tina 1
Turtle Island String Quartet 9
Twitty, Conway 6
2Pac
　See Digital Underground
Tyler, Steve
　See Aerosmith
Tyner, McCoy 7
Tyner, Rob
　See MC5, The
Tyson, Ron
　See Temptations, The
U2 12
　Earlier sketch in CM 2
UB40 4
Ulrich, Lars
　See Metallica
Ulvaeus, Björn
　See Abba
Upshaw, Dawn 9
Vachon, Chris
　See Roomful of Blues
Vai, Steve 5
　Also see Whitesnake
Valli, Frankie 10
Vandenburg, Adrian
　See Whitesnake
Vandross, Luther 2
Van Halen 8
Van Halen, Alex
　See Van Halen
Van Halen, Edward
　See Van Halen
Vanilla Ice 6
Van Ronk, Dave 12
Van Shelton, Ricky 5
Van Vliet, Don
　See Captain Beefheart
Van Zant, Johnny
　See Lynyrd Skynyrd
Van Zant, Ronnie
　See Lynyrd Skynyrd
Vaughan, Jimmie
　See Fabulous Thunderbirds, The
Vaughan, Sarah 2
Vaughan, Stevie Ray 1
Vedder, Eddie
　See Pearl Jam
Vega, Suzanne 3
Velvet Underground, The 7

Vettese, Peter-John
　See Jethro Tull
Vicious, Sid
　See Sex Pistols, The
　Also see Siouxsie and the Banshees
Village People, The 7
Vincent, Vinnie
　See Kiss
Vinnie
　See Naughty by Nature
Vinton, Bobby 12
Violent Femmes 12
Virtue, Michael
　See UB40
Vito, Rick
　See Fleetwood Mac
Volz, Greg
　See Petra
Von, Eerie
　See Danzig
von Karajan, Herbert 1
Vox, Bono
　See Bono
Wadenius, George
　See Blood, Sweat and Tears
Wadephal, Ralf
　See Tangerine Dream
Wagoner, Faidest
　See Soul Stirrers, The
Wahlberg, Donnie
　See New Kids on the Block
Wailer, Bunny 11
Wainwright III, Loudon 11
Waits, Tom 12
　Earlier sketch in CM 1
Wakeling, David
　See English Beat, The
Wakeman, Rick
　See Yes
Walker, Colin
　See Electric Light Orchestra
Walker, Ebo
　See New Grass Revival, The
Walker, T-Bone 5
Wallace, Sippie 6
Waller, Charlie
　See Country Gentlemen, The
Waller, Fats 7
Wallinger, Karl 11
Wallis, Larry
　See Motörhead
Walls, Chris
　See Dave Clark Five, The
Walls, Greg
　See Anthrax
Walsh, Joe 5
　Also see Eagles, The
Ward, Bill
　See Black Sabbath
Warnes, Jennifer 3
Warren, George W.
　See Five Blind Boys of Alabama
Warren, Mervyn
　See Take 6
Warwick, Dionne 2

Was, David
　See Was (Not Was)
Was, Don
　See Was (Not Was)
Was (Not Was) 6
Washington, Chester
　See Earth, Wind and Fire
Washington, Dinah 5
Washington, Grover, Jr. 5
Waters, Ethel 11
Waters, Muddy 4
Waters, Roger
　See Pink Floyd
Watley, Jody 9
Watson, Doc 2
Watt, Mike
　See fIREHOSE
Watts, Charlie
　See Rolling Stones, The
Watts, Eugene
　See Canadian Brass, The
Weaver, Louie
　See Petra
Weavers, The 8
Webb, Jimmy 12
Webber, Andrew Lloyd
　See Lloyd Webber, Andrew
Weill, Kurt 12
Weir, Bob
　See Grateful Dead, The
Welch, Bob
　See Fleetwood Mac
Wells, Cory
　See Three Dog Night
Wells, Kitty 6
Welnick, Vince
　See Grateful Dead, The
West, Dottie 8
Westerberg, Paul
　See Replacements, The
Weymouth, Tina
　See Talking Heads
Whelan, Gavan
　See James
White, Alan
　See Yes
White, Barry 6
White, Clarence
　See Byrds, The
White, Freddie
　See Earth, Wind and Fire
White, Maurice
　See Earth, Wind and Fire
White, Verdine
　See Earth, Wind and Fire
Whitehead, Donald
　See Earth, Wind and Fire
Whitesnake 5
Whitford, Brad
　See Aerosmith
Whitley, Keith 7
Whitwam, Barry
　See Herman's Hermits
Who, The 3
Wiggins, Dwayne
　See Tony! Toni! Toné!

Wiggins, Raphael
　See Tony! Toni! Toné!
Wilder, Alan
　See Depeche Mode
Wilkeson, Leon
　See Lynyrd Skynyrd
Wilkinson, Keith
　See Squeeze
Williams, Andy 2
Williams, Boris
　See Cure, The
Williams, Cliff
　See AC/DC
Williams, Dana
　See Diamond Rio
Williams, Deniece 1
Williams, Don 4
Williams, Hank, Jr. 1
Williams, Hank, Sr. 4
Williams, Joe 11
Williams, John 9
Williams, Lamar
　See Allman Brothers, The
Williams, Lucinda 10
Williams, Otis
　See Temptations, The
Williams, Paul
　See Temptations, The
Williams, Paul 5
Williams, Phillard
　See Earth, Wind and Fire
Williams, Vanessa 10
Williamson, Sonny Boy 9
Willie D.
　See Geto Boys, The
Willis, Kelly 12
Willis, Larry
　See Blood, Sweat and Tears
Willis, Pete
　See Def Leppard
Willis, Victor
　See Village People, The
Willner, Hal 10
Wills, Bob 6
Wilson, Anne
　See Heart
Wilson, Brian
　See Beach Boys, The
Wilson, Carl
　See Beach Boys, The
Wilson, Carnie
　See Wilson Phillips
Wilson, Cassandra 12
Wilson, Cindy
　See B-52's, The
Wilson, Dennis
　See Beach Boys, The
Wilson, Jackie 3
Wilson, Kim
　See Fabulous Thunderbirds, The
Wilson, Mary
　See Supremes, The
Wilson, Nancy
　See Heart
Wilson, Ransom 5

Wilson, Ricky
　See B-52's, The
Wilson, Wendy
　See Wilson Phillips
Wilson Phillips 5
Wilton, Michael
　See Queensryche
Wimpfheimer, Jimmy
　See Roomful of Blues
Winans, Carvin
　See Winans, The
Winans, Marvin
　See Winans, The
Winans, Michael
　See Winans, The
Winans, Ronald
　See Winans, The
Winans, The 12
Winfield, Chuck
　See Blood, Sweat and Tears
Winston, George 9
Winter, Johnny 5
Winter, Paul 10
Winwood, Steve 2
Wolstencraft, Simon
　See Fall, The
Womack, Bobby 5
Wonder, Stevie 2
Wood, Danny
　See New Kids on the Block
Wood, Ron
　See Rolling Stones, The
Wood, Roy
　See Electric Light Orchestra
Woods, Terry
　See Pogues, The
Woodson, Ollie
　See Temptations, The
Woody, Allen
　See Allman Brothers, The
Woolfolk, Andrew
　See Earth, Wind and Fire
Worrell, Bernie 11
Wreede, Katrina
　See Turtle Island String Quartet
Wright, David "Blockhead"
　See English Beat, The
Wright, Norman
　See Country Gentlemen, The
Wright, Rick
　See Pink Floyd
Wright, Simon
　See AC/DC
Wurzel
　See Motörhead
Wyman, Bill
　See Rolling Stones, The
Wynette, Tammy 2
Wynonna 11
　Also see Judds, The
X 11
XTC 10
Ya Kid K
　See Technotronic
Yamamoto, Hiro
　See Soundgarden

Cumulative Musicians Index · 325

Yamashita, Kazuhito 4
Yankovic, "Weird Al" 7
Yanni 11
Yardbirds, The 10
Yarrow, Peter
  See Peter, Paul & Mary
Yates, Bill
  See Country Gentlemen, The
Yauch, Adam
  See Beastie Boys, The
Yearwood, Trisha 10
Yella
  See N.W.A.
Yes 8
Yoakam, Dwight 1
York, John
  See Byrds, The
Young, Angus
  See AC/DC
Young, Faron 7
Young, Fred
  See Kentucky Headhunters, The
Young, Grant
  See Soul Asylum
Young, Jeff
  See Megadeth
Young, Malcolm
  See AC/DC
Young M.C. 4
Young, Neil 2
Young, Richard
  See Kentucky Headhunters, The
Yo Yo 9
Yule, Doug
  See Velvet Underground, The
Zander, Robin
  See Cheap Trick
Zappa, Frank 1
Zevon, Warren 9
Zimmerman, Udo 5
Zoom, Billy
  See X
Zukerman, Pinchas 4
ZZ Top 2